Praise for *The Allies Strike Back, 1941–1943*

A Military History Book Club Main Selection
An Amazon Best Book of the Month (History)

"Holland puts the case for Allied technological and military skills as a vital factor in turning the war's tide, and makes us eager for the third and final part of what now ranks as a towering work of historical research and writing." —*BBC History Magazine*

"Detailed, well-researched, and comprehensive ... Holland makes a strong case ... [He] shifts smoothly between high-level strategy and tactical battlefield events, producing a good refresher to the large strategic picture for those who are deeply read in WWII history and an excellent introduction to the war in Western Europe for the general reader." —*Publishers Weekly*

"An illuminating read from a skilled historian ... Holland delivers a detailed, opinionated account of fighting in North Africa, the Atlantic submarine campaign, and the air war while acknowledging (and often describing) the far larger war in Russia ... Expert, anecdote-filled, thoroughly entertaining." —*Kirkus Reviews*

"A well-researched, lively account." —*Choice*

"Holland's two greatest qualities, his engaging writing style and his ability to weave multiple threads into a convincing whole, are on display once more in this accessible and authoritative history ... Holland, a successful fiction author as well, keeps his reader gripped with an engrossing tale, which both educates and entertains. In Holland's own words this is 'a truly epic and astonishing story' and the same could be said for his book." —*History of War* (UK)

"Holland shoots down the myth of German invincibility ... All the great turning points of 1941–43 are here. A triumph." —*Sunday Express* (UK)

The Allies Strike Back
1941–1943

The Allies Strike Back

1941–1943

The War in the West

Volume Two

James Holland

Grove Press
New York

First Published in Great Britain in 2017 by Bantam Press,
an imprint of Transworld Publishers

Published simultaneously in Canada
Printed in the United States of America

First Grove Atlantic hardcover edition: October 2017
First Grove Atlantic paperback edition: October 2018

Library of Congress Cataloging-in-Publication data is available for this title.

ISBN 978-0-8021-2857-7
eISBN 978-0-8021-9014-7

Grove Press
an imprint of Grove Atlantic
154 West 14th Street
New York, NY 10011

Distributed by Publishers Group West

groveatlantic.com

18 19 20 21   10 9 8 7 6 5 4 3 2 1

For Ned

Contents

Part III: The Allies Strike Back

Part IV: Crushing the Wolfpacks

List of Maps and Diagrams

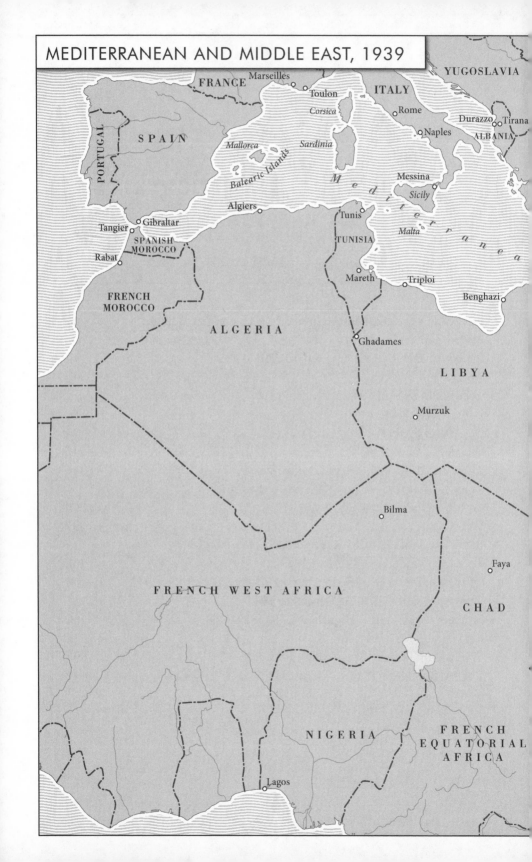

MEDITERRANEAN AND MIDDLE EAST, 1939

FRANCE
Marseilles
Toulon
Corsica
ITALY
Rome
YUGOSLAVIA
Durazzo
Tirana
ALBANIA
Naples
PORTUGAL
SPAIN
Mallorca
Sardinia
Balearic Islands
Messina
Mediterranea
Sicily
Algiers
Tunis
Malta
Tangier
Gibraltar
SPANISH
MOROCCO
TUNISIA
Rabat
Mareth
Triploi
FRENCH
MOROCCO
Benghazi
ALGERIA
Ghadames
LIBYA
Murzuk
Bilma
Faya
FRENCH WEST AFRICA
CHAD
NIGERIA
FRENCH
EQUATORIAL
AFRICA
Lagos

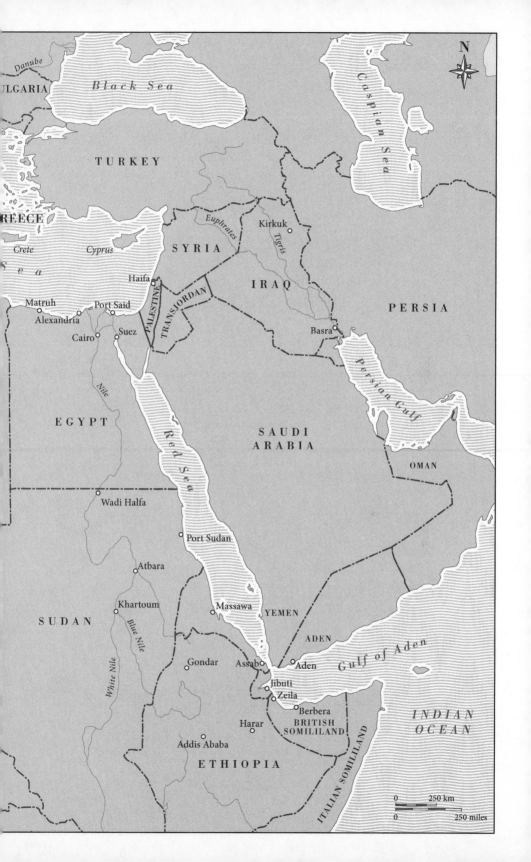

GERMANY AT THE BEGINNING OF 1942

N

NORWAY

Oslo

SWEDEN

North Sea

DENMARK

Berlin

Dublin

IRELAND

GREAT BRITAIN

HOLLAND

GERMAN REICH

Prot. Bohem & Mora

London

BELGIUM

LUX.

Vienna

ATLANTIC OCEAN

Paris

FRANCE

Berne

SWITZERLAND

CROATIA

PORTUGAL

Madrid

SPAIN

ITALY

Corsica

Rome

Balearic Islands

Sardinia

Gibraltar (GB)

M e d i t e r r a n e a n

Algiers

Sicily

Tunis

Malta (GB)

FRENCH MOROCCO

ALGERIA (France)

TUNISIA (France)

KEY

- ▨ German Reich
- ▨ annexed territories and allies of German Reich
- ▨ territories occupied by Germans and allies
- ▨ Allies
- ▨ colonies, etc.
- ▨ Allied-occupied territories
- ▨ neutral and non-combatant countries
- - - - fighting fronts early Sept. 1941

FINLAND

Helsinki

Stockholm

Leningrad

Gulf of Finland

ESTONIA

Baltic Sea

LATVIA

LITHUANIA

Moscow

East Prussia

Białystock

overnment
eneral

Warsaw

Kiev

SOVIET
UNION

Lvov

SLOVAKIA

Budapest

HUNGARY

ROMANIA

Crimea

Belgrade

Bucharest

SERBIA

MONTENEGRO

BULGARIA

Black Sea

ALBANIA

Sofia

Ankara

GREECE

TURKEY

IRAN

Athens

SYRIA
(France)

Crete

Cyprus
(GB)

IRAQ

Sea

0   250 km

0   250 miles

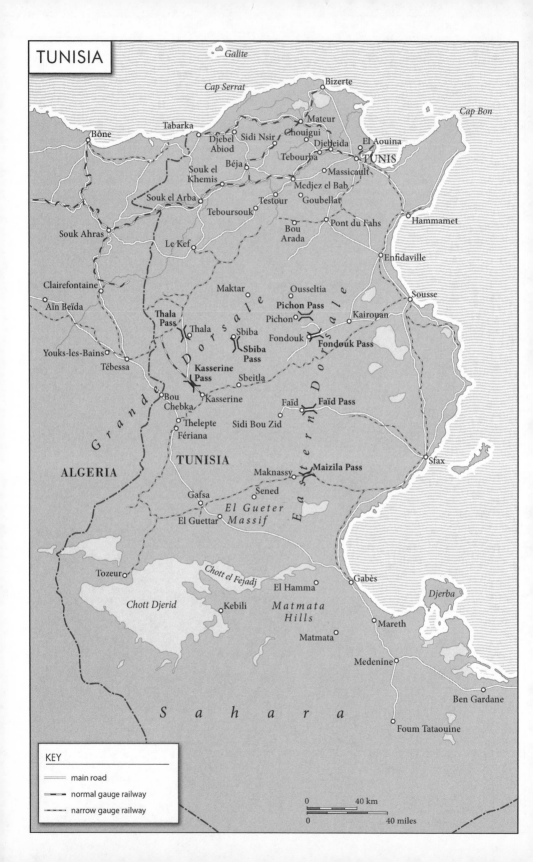

TUNISIA

Galite

Cap Serrat

Bizerte

Cap Bon

Bône

Tabarka

Mateur

Djebel
Abiod

Sidi Nsir

Chouigui

Djebeida

El Aouina

Béja

Tebourba

TUNIS

Souk el
Khemis

Massicault

Souk el Arba

Testour

Medjez el Bab

Goubellat

Teboursouk

Bou
Arada

Pont du Fahs

Hammamet

Souk Ahras

Le Kef

Clairefontaine

Enfidaville

Aïn Beïda

Maktar

Ousseltia

Sousse

**Thala
Pass**

Thala

Sbiba

Pichon Pass

Pichon

Kairouan

Youks-les-Bains

*G
r
a
n
d
e*

Sbiba

Fondouk

**Sbiba
Pass**

Fondouk Pass

Tébessa

*D
o
r
s
a
l
e*

**Kasserine
Pass**

Sbeitla

Bou
Chebka

Kasserine

Faïd

Faïd Pass

Thelepte

Sidi Bou Zid

*E
a
s
t
e
r
n*

Fériana

TUNISIA

Maizila Pass

Maknassy

Sfax

ALGERIA

Gafsa

Sened

*D
o
r
s
a
l
e*

El Guettar

*El Gueter
Massif*

Tozeur

Chott el Fejadj

Gabès

El Hamma

Djerba

Chott Djerid

Kebili

*Matmata
Hills*

Mareth

Matmata

Medenine

Ben Gardane

S a h a r a

Foum Tataouine

KEY

········· main road

━━━━ normal gauge railway

─·─·─ narrow gauge railway

0   40 km

0   40 miles

LUFTWAFFE DAY- AND NIGHT-FIGHTER AIRFIELDS AND AIR DEFENCE

North Sea

SWEDEN

DENMARK

GREAT BRITAIN

FRANCE

SWITZERLAND

ITALY

SLOVAKIA

HUNGARY

PROTECTORATE OF BOHEMIA & MORAVIA

German Bight

Holland and the Ruhr

Central Germany

South Germany

BERLIN CENTRE

XII

West

PARIS

Husum III/JG1
Stade Staff/NJG3
Parchim II/NJG5
2
Jever
Leeuwarden IV/NJG1
Vechta II/NJG3
Wunstorf I/NJG3
Lüneburg IV/NJG3
Stendal I/NJG5
Döberitz Staff/NJG5
4
Jüterbog 11/NJG4
Bergen 1/JG1
Schiphol 4/JG1
Twente III/NJG1
Deelen 10/JG1
1
Zeist
Woensdrecht 6/JG1
Venlo I/NJG1
St Trond II/NJG1
Wevelghem III/JG26
München 11/JG1
Gladbach I/JG1
(w/o 13. Staffel)
Düsseldorf 11/JG1
Haamstade 5/JG1
Brandis I/NJG4
Fürth
Fl. Sch. 4
Regensburg
op. Messerschmitt
Ingolstadt 3 NF Sch. 1
Shiessheim Staff I/NJG1
(w/o 3. Staffel)
Neubiberg II/2 Fl Sch 2
Lechfeld II NF Sch. 1
(w/o 6. Staffel)
Memmingen I/2 NF Sch. 2
Echterdingen III/NF Sch. 1
3 NF Sch. 1
Merz Staff/NJG4
IV/NJG4
(w/o 12. Staffel)
St-Dizier II/NJG4
3
Chantilly
Wizernes Staff/JG26
2
St-Pol I/JG26
Abbeville II/JG26
Monchy en Breton 11/JG26 (est)
Caen Triqueville I/JG2
Beaumont le Roger Staff/JG2
3
Carpiquet 10/JG2
3
Brest 8/JG2
Vannes III/JG2

200 km
200 miles
0

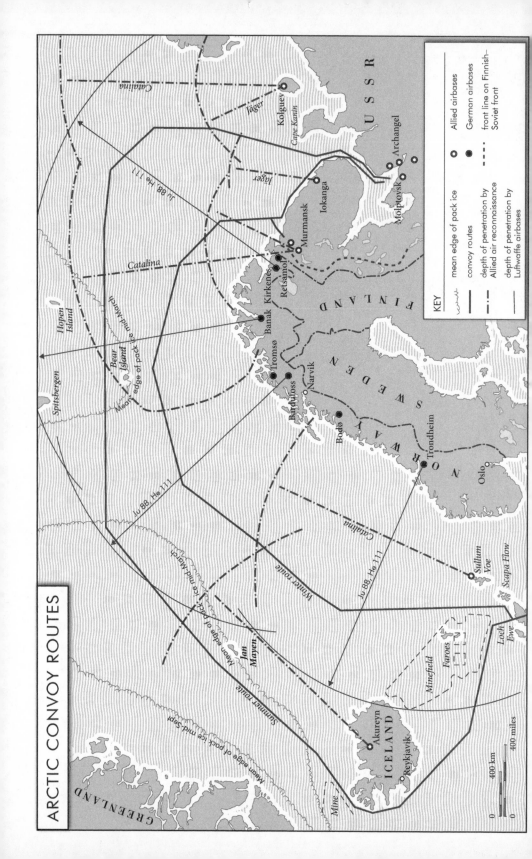

ARCTIC CONVOY ROUTES

KEY

∼∼∼ mean edge of pack ice	○ Allied airbases
── convoy routes	● German airbases
─·─·─ depth of penetration by Allied air reconnaissance	┊┊┊ front line on Finnish–Soviet front
── depth of penetration by Luftwaffe airbases	

GREENLAND

ICELAND
Akureyri
Reykjavik

Mean edge of pack ice mid-Sept

Summer route

Jan Mayen

Mean edge of pack ice mid-March

Mine

Faroes
Minefield

Loch Ewe

Sullum Voe
Scapa Flow

Ju 88, He 111

Catalina

Winter route

Ju 88, He 111

Spitsbergen

Hopen Island

Bear Island

Mean edge of pack ice mid-March

Ju 88, He 111

Catalina

Jäger

Kolguev
Cape Kanin

Jäger

U S S R

Archangel
Molotovsk
Iokanga
Murmansk

Banak
Kirkenes
Retsamol
Tromsø
Bardufoss
Narvik
Bodø
Trondheim
Oslo

NORWAY

SWEDEN

FINLAND

400 km
400 miles
0
0

PRINCIPAL ATLANTIC CONVOY ROUTES, 1941–1943

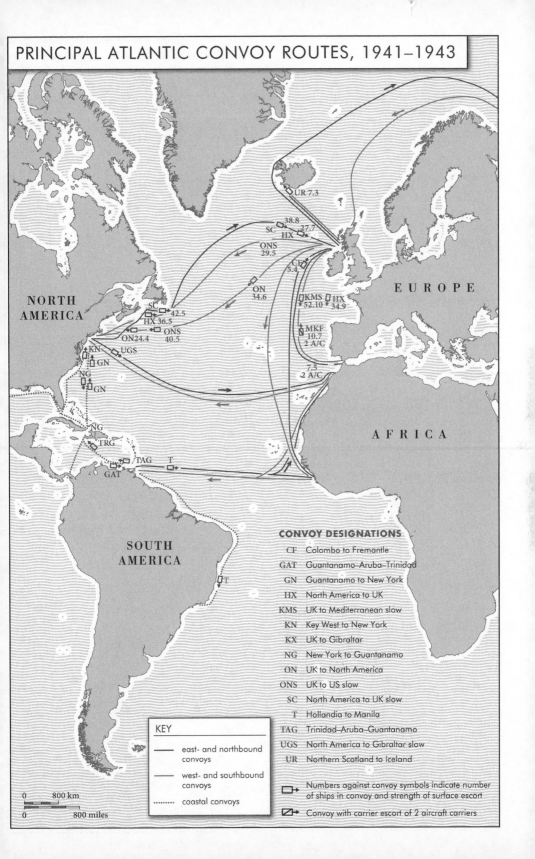

NORTH AMERICA

EUROPE

AFRICA

SOUTH AMERICA

UR 7.3

SC 38.8
HX 27.7

ONS 29.5

CF 5.4

ON 34.6

KMS 52.10
HX 34.9

MKF 10.7 2 A/C

7.5 2 A/C

SC 42.5
HX 36.5
ON 24.4
ONS 40.5

KN
GN
UGS
NG
GN

NG
TRG
TAG
GAT
T

T

CONVOY DESIGNATIONS

CF   Colombo to Fremantle
GAT   Guantanamo–Aruba–Trinidad
GN   Guantanamo to New York
HX   North America to UK
KMS   UK to Mediterranean slow
KN   Key West to New York
KX   UK to Gibraltar
NG   New York to Guantanamo
ON   UK to North America
ONS   UK to US slow
SC   North America to UK slow
T   Hollandia to Manila
TAG   Trinidad–Aruba–Guantanamo
UGS   North America to Gibraltar slow
UR   Northern Scotland to Iceland

KEY

——— east- and northbound convoys

——— west- and southbound convoys

········· coastal convoys

0   800 km
0   800 miles

◻→ Numbers against convoy symbols indicate number of ships in convoy and strength of surface escort

◩→ Convoy with carrier escort of 2 aircraft carriers

ASDIC and Hedgehog

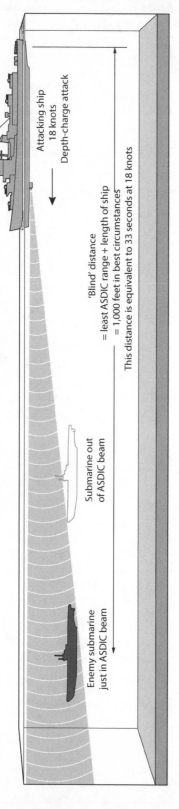

Attacking ship
18 knots
Depth-charge attack

'Blind' distance
= least ASDIC range + length of ship
= 1,000 feet in best circumstances
This distance is equivalent to 33 seconds at 18 knots

Submarine out
of ASDIC beam

Enemy submarine
just in ASDIC beam

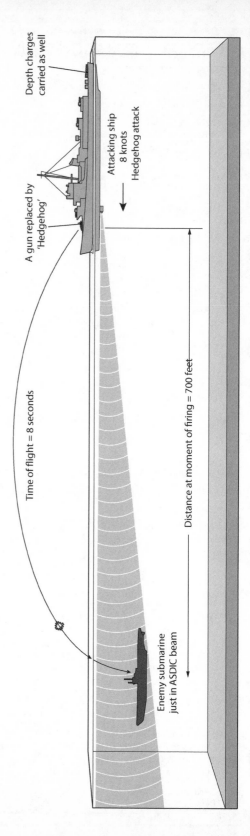

Depth charges
carried as well

A gun replaced by
'Hedgehog'

Attacking ship
8 knots
Hedgehog attack

Time of flight = 8 seconds

Distance at moment of firing = 700 feet

Enemy submarine
just in ASDIC beam

Types of Merchant Vessels

An average ship type as below has a:	Length of	When loaded floats in	Speed loaded of	Tonnage of	Loading capacity of
Passenger Liner	657.6 ft	34 ft 1.5 in	19 knots	17,350 gross	658,960 cub. ft 517 passengers
Cargo Liner	516.3 ft	29 ft 7 in	17 knots	12,320 gross	750,839 cub. ft 12 passengers
Oil Tanker	462.8 ft	27 ft 0 in	11 knots	8,012 gross	12,000 tons oil
Tramp	414 ft	25 ft 3.5 in	11 knots	4,719 gross	585,420 cub. ft
Ore Carrier	387.1 ft	24 ft 4 in	10 knots	5,787 gross	161,380 cub. ft
Cross-Channel Ship	353 ft	15 ft 1 in	17.5 knots	4,320 gross	725,755 cub. ft 1,000 passengers
Tug (salvage)	198.3 ft	17 ft 11 in	17 knots (without tow)	793 gross	No loading capacity: carries tyre and salvage pumps
Coaster	197 ft	8 ft 6 in	9 knots	200 gross	62,480 cub. ft
Trawler	134.6 ft	11 ft 9 in	11 knots	130 gross	400,000 lb fish

U-Boat Type VIIC

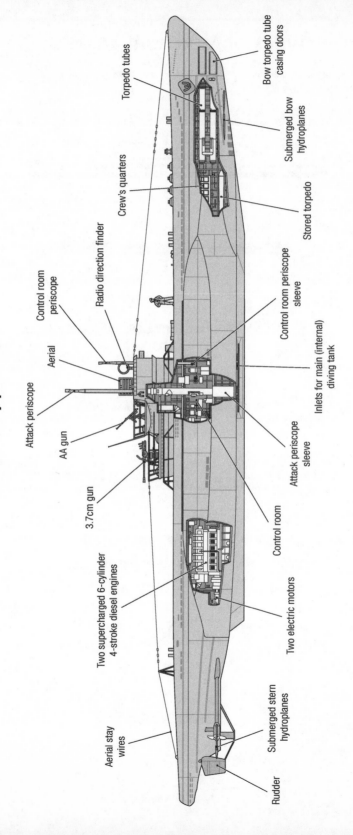

Attack periscope

Control room periscope

Aerial

Radio direction finder

AA gun

Crew's quarters

3.7cm gun

Torpedo tubes

Bow torpedo tube casing doors

Submerged bow hydroplanes

Stored torpedo

Control room periscope sleeve

Inlets for main (internal) diving tank

Attack periscope sleeve

Control room

Two supercharged 6-cylinder 4-stroke diesel engines

Two electric motors

Aerial stay wires

Submerged stern hydroplanes

Rudder

LIST OF PRINCIPAL CHARACTERS FEATURED

(Ranks at June 1943)

General Sir Harold Alexander
– *British*
Commander of 1st Division in
France, last man to leave Dunkirk,
later commander Southern Division,
then British Forces in Burma, before
becoming C-in-C Middle East in
August 1942. Appointed
commander, 18th Army Group, in
February 1943.

Generalleutnant Hermann Balck
– *German*
General of Mobile Forces in the
OKH, then commanding
11. Panzerdivision from May 1942.
Promoted to lieutenant-general in
January 1943 and given command
of Gross-Deutschland Division in
April 1943.

**Flight Lieutenant Cyril 'Bam'
Bamberger** – *British*
NCO fighter pilot in 610 and 41
Squadrons during the Battle of
Britain, he was later commissioned
and flew with 261 Squadron on
Malta and then 93 Squadron in
Tunisia.

Obersturmführer Klaus Barbie
– *German*
Head of Section IV,
Sicherheitsdienst, Lyons.

Lieutenant Jean-Mathieu Boris
– *French*
Officer in the Free French Army.

Pfc Henry 'Dee' Bowles – *American*
Served in 18th Infantry Regiment,
1st Infantry Division, in North
Africa.

Pfc Tom Bowles – *American*
Served in 18th Infantry Regiment,
1st Infantry Division, in North
Africa.

Air Commodore Sydney Bufton
– *British*
Commander 10 and 76 Squadrons,
RAF Bomber Command, then
became station commander at
RAF Pocklington before becoming
Deputy Director of Bomber
Operations at the Air Ministry.

Major Stanley Christopherson
– *British*
A squadron commander in the
Nottingham Sherwood Rangers
Yeomanry.

Count Galeazzo Ciano – *Italian*
Son-in-law of Mussolini and Italian
Foreign Secretary.

Lieutenant-General Mark Clark
– *American*
Appointed Deputy Chief of Staff,
US Army Ground Forces in January
1942 and then went to England as
Eisenhower's deputy and Chief of
Combined Planning for Operation
TORCH. He was Deputy
Commander-in-Chief, Allied Land
Forces in North Africa, then given
command of US Fifth Army.

Sergent-chef Pierre Clostermann
– *French*
Fighter pilot flying with 341 'Alsace'
Squadron, RAF Fighter Command.

Jock Colville – *British*
One of the secretaries to the Prime
Minister, first Neville Chamberlain
and then Winston Churchill.

Gwladys Cox – *British*
Civilian living in London.

**Admiral Sir Andrew Browne
Cunningham** – *British*
Commander of the Mediterranean
Fleet until 1942, then posted to
Washington.

Lieutenant Dale R. Deniston
– *American*
Fighter pilot in North Africa and the
Middle East with the 57th Fighter
Group.

Admiral Karl Dönitz – *German*
Commander of the Kriegsmarine's
U-boat fleet.

Squadron Leader Billy Drake
– *British*
Commander of 112 Squadron in the
RAF's Desert Air Force.

Lieutenant Douglas Fairbanks, Jr
– *American*
Officer serving on USS *Wasp* and
USS *Wichita*.

Capitaine Henri Frenay – *French*
Leader of the Combat resistance
group.

Général Charles de Gaulle – *French*
Army officer then leader of the Free
French.

Wing Commander Guy Gibson
– *British*
Bomber pilot and commander of 106
Squadron.

Andrée Griotteray – *French*
French civilian and member of the
Resistance.

Ted Hardy – *Australian*
Sapper in the 2/3rd Field Company,
9th Australian Division, serving in
North Africa and the Middle East.

Major Hajo Herrmann – *German*
Flew Heinkel 111s in Poland and
Norway with KG4 before becoming
a *Staffel* commander and switching
to Ju88s. He later served in the
Mediterranean before transferring
to Norway to command III/KG30.

Harry Hopkins – *American*
President Roosevelt's closest friend
and advisor, and unofficial emissary
to Winston Churchill.

Henry Kaiser – *American*
Construction tycoon and director of
Todd California Shipyards.

Major-General John Kennedy
– *British*
Director of Military Operations
(DMO) at the War Office.

Feldmarschall Albert Kesselring
– *German*
Commanded Luftflotte I in Poland,
then Luftflotte II in France and
during the Battle of Britain. Later
transferred to the Mediterranean.
Later appointed Commander-in-
Chief South in the Mediterranean.

Leutnant Heinz Knoke – *German*
Fighter pilot, serving initially in
Russia and then in Norway and the
Western Front, first with JG52 and
then with JG1.

Bill Knudsen – *American*
Chairman of General Motors, then
Chairman of the Office of
Production Management, and later,
in 1942, Director of Production at the
Office of the Under-Secretary of War.

Hauptmann Helmut Lent
– *German*
Luftwaffe night-fighter ace, who
served in Norway then in Holland
with NJGI and later NJGII.

Corinne Luchaire – *French*
French film star and daughter of
Vichyist Jean Luchaire, and married
to a Frenchman serving with the
Luftwaffe.

Major Hans von Luck – *German*
Served with Rommel during the
invasion of France and then
throughout most of the North
African campaign.

**Brigadier-General Lyman
Lemnitzer** – *American*
Assigned to Eisenhower's staff in
June 1942, and helped work on plans
for Operation TORCH.

Oliver Lyttelton – *British*
Appointed Controller of Non-
Ferrous Metals at the outbreak of
war, and in 1940 became President
of the Board of Trade, then later
joined the War Cabinet as Minister
of State, Middle East. He returned to
the UK in 1942 as Minister of
Production.

Commander Donald Macintyre
– *British*
Served as a convoy escort commander
on destroyers, first on HMS
Hesperus, then on HMS *Walker*.

Colonello Publio Magini – *Italian*
Pilot and staff officer in the Regia
Aeronautica.

Major Helmut Mahlke – *German*
Stuka pilot serving in France then
the Balkans and Mediterranean.

Corporal Mangal Singh – *Indian*
Signaller in C Section, 1 Company,
4th Indian Division.

Luigi Marchese – *Italian*
Soldier in 2 Regimento
Paracadutisti, Folgore Division.

General George C. Marshall
– *American*
Chief of Staff of the United States
Army.

Sergeant Albert Martin - *British*
Rifleman with 2nd Battalion, the
Rifle Brigade.

Walter Mazzacuto – *Italian*
Sailor in Regia Marina, serving first
on the battleship *Vittorio Veneto*
and then on escort destroyers in the
Mediterranean.

Feldmarschall Erhard Milch
– *German*
State Secretary for Aviation and
Deputy Head of the Luftwaffe.

Lieutenant Farley Mowat
– *Canadian*
Infantry officer in the Hastings and
Prince Edward Regiment.

Pilot Officer Ken Neill – *New
Zealander*
Fighter pilot with 225 Squadron.

Don Nelson – *American*
Head of the War Production Board.

Flight Lieutenant Jean Offenberg
– *Belgian*
Fighter pilot who flew with the 4ᵉ
Escadrille, 2ᵉ Groupe, 2ᵉ Régiment
Aéronautique I of the Belgian Air
Force, then later joined 145 and 609
Squadrons, RAF.

Lieutenant Dick Pearce – *Canadian*
Lieutenant in the Royal Canadian Navy.

**Air Chief Marshal Sir Charles
Portal** – *British*
Commander-in-Chief of Bomber
Command from April 1940, then
became Chief of the Air Staff in
October the same year.

Lieutenant Jens-Anton Poulsson
– *Norwegian*
Register and member of Linge
Company, attached to SOE.

Ernie Pyle – *American*
Journalist and war correspondent
for Scripps Howard Newspapers.

Feldmarschall Erwin Rommel
– *German*
Commanded 7. Panzerdivision in
France in 1940, then took command
of the Deutsches Panzerkorps in
North Africa in February 1942, and
later became commander of the
Italo-German Panzerarmee Afrika.
Promoted to Feldmarschall in July
1942.

Leutnant Günther Sack – *German*
Anti-aircraft gunnery officer in the
Luftwaffe.

Giuseppe Santaniello – *Italian*
Soldier in 48th Artillery Regiment,
Bari Division.

Sergeant Ralph B. Schaps
– *American*
Soldier in the 34th 'Red Bull'
Division.

Generalmajor Adolf von Schell
– *German*
General Plenipotentiary of Motor
Vehicles within the Defence
Economy and Armaments
Office.

Hans Schlange-Schöningen
– *German*
First World War veteran and former
politician, during the war he
continued his family duties as owner
of a large estate in Pomerania.

Gunnar Sønsteby – *Norwegian*
Fought in the Norwegian Army in
1940, then joined the Resistance
movement. He later joined the
British SOE and went to Britain for
saboteur training, and became chief
of operations in the Norwegian
Resistance.

**Lieutenant-General Sir Edward
Spears** – *British*
Member of Parliament and
Chairman of the Anglo-French
Committee, and then Churchill's
Personal Representative to the
French Prime Minister. Later
became the PM's Personal
Representative to the Free French.

Reichsminister Albert Speer
– *German*
Hitler's Chief Architect, and from
November 1942 Minister of
Armaments and War Production.

**Oberstleutnant Johannes 'Macky'
Steinhoff** – *German*
Fighter pilot and commander with
JG2 and JG52.

Henry L. Stimson – *American*
US Secretary of State for War.

Arthur 'A. G.' Street – *British*
Wiltshire farmer, writer and
broadcaster for the Ministry of
Information.

**Gruppenführer Reinhard 'Teddy'
Suhren** – *German*
First Watch Officer on *U-48*, then
took command of *U-564*, before
leaving the service in October 1942
to become an instructor.

**Air Chief Marshal Sir Arthur
Tedder** – *British*
Director of Research at the Ministry
of Aircraft Production, then posted
to the Middle East to become Air
Officer Commanding. Later, in
February 1943, he became C-in-C
Mediterranean Air Command.

Generalleutnant Georg Thomas
– *German*
Head of the Defence Economy and
Armaments Office and chief
economic advisor to the Army from
1939 to 1942.

Korvettenkapitän Erich Topp
– *German*
First Watch Officer on *U-46* and then commander of *U-57* and *U-552*.

Captain Hedley Verity – *British*
Company commander in the 1st Green Howards.

Paul Vigouroux – *French*
Served in Morocco at the beginning of the war, but when demobilized joined the Légion volontaires français (LVF) in the summer of 1941 and fought on the Eastern Front. After being wounded, returned to France and edited the anti-Semitic journal *Au Pilori*.

General Walter Warlimont
– *German*
Served as Senior Operations Staff Officer to the Oberkommando der Wehrmacht (OKW).

Lieutenant-Commander Vere Wight-Boycott – *British*
First Lieutenant on destroyer HMS *Delight*, and served in the Norwegian campaign until taking command of his own destroyer, HMS *Roxborough* and then HMS *Ilex*, carrying out convoy escort work in the Atlantic and Mediterranean.

Note on the Text

I AM VERY CONSCIOUS that the narrative in this book is repeatedly switching from one perspective to another: from British to German, and from French to Italian and then to American and even Belgian and Norwegian. In an effort to help distinguish who is who, I have written ranks in the language of the respective nationality. Thus it is Captain Macintyre, but Capitaine Frenay, and Major-General Kennedy, but Generalmajor Rommel. The aim is not to be pretentious but rather just to help with the flow of the narrative.

I have applied this rule somewhat inconsistently to military units too. As a rough rule of thumb, any unit of corps or above in size has been similarly written in the vernacular, but there are also a few other examples of using German words, especially. Luftwaffe squadrons are *Staffeln*, because actually a German *Staffel* was not quite the same as a British squadron. German paratroopers and mountain troops are written as *Fallschirmjäger* and *Gebirgsjäger* – which will certainly help lessen any confusion by the time I reach Volume III and D-Day, for example, where there were German, American, Polish, Canadian and French airborne troops all operating, and in the case of Americans, Poles and Germans, often with similar sounding surnames.

I should also explain how some military units were written. A corps is numbered in Roman numerals and a military operation in upper case. Luftwaffe *Gruppen* were written in Roman numerals, but *Staffeln* in Arabic numbering. There were three *Staffeln* per *Gruppe*, so 5/JG2, for example, would be in II/JG2, but 7/JG2 would be in III/JG2.

Introduction

JUNE 1941 WAS a momentous month in world history. At its start, Nazi
Germany was at war with Britain and her Dominions, but all her other
enemies had been subdued in what had been an astonishing run of
victories: first Poland in September 1939, then Denmark and Norway in
April the following year. Then the Low Countries and even mighty
France had been crushed. France had been overrun in just six weeks; a
generation earlier, French troops had resisted every German assault for
four years, but in May 1940 the outcome had been effectively decided in
a matter of days. Britain, that island nation hanging off the edge of
continental Europe, had managed to hold out, but there were not many
people around the world who questioned Germany's supremacy or who
doubted that Britain would eventually be subdued too. In the meantime,
first Yugoslavia and then Greece had also been overrun with clinical and
ruthless efficiency, and then, in May 1941, so too had Crete, the largest
island in the Aegean. The British had been forced into their third large-
scale evacuation of the war – another humiliating defeat.

So it was that by the start of June 1941 only Britain remained, holding
out against this seemingly unstoppable military machine. In Germany,
and on newsreels around the world, it was pictures of columns of
panzers and swastikas rising over the Parthenon in Athens that
dominated. America, it was clear, had the potential to produce large
amounts of arms, but potential was one thing and reality was another;
certainly not a huge volume of war materiel was yet emerging from US
factories, for all the British insistence that it soon would. Britain's failure

on land suggested that here was a global power that was past its prime; trouble had been brewing throughout much of its Empire in the 1930s and its democracy and so-called liberal values were looking rather limp in the face of the dictators. Liberalism, the Nazis were shouting from the rooftops, meant weakness. As the British forces on Crete tramped south through the mountains and escaped on their ships, it seemed to much of the world that the Nazis were right. Nationalism and militarism appeared to be the dominant forces in the Western world in this second summer of war. On the face of it, this was understandable enough. The notion that Germany was an unstoppable military machine in those first years of war is something that still holds sway to this day.

War is understood to be fought on three levels: the strategic, which is the high-level aims and goals; the tactical, which is the coal-face of war – that is, the actual fighting; and the operational: the means by which the other levels connect, or in other words the supply of war, the logistics – a nation's ability to produce tanks or aircraft and deliver them to the front line. Such a construct is, to some extent, a slightly artificial way of looking at conflict, and yet those three levels do none the less encapsulate what is involved in war.

Perhaps a simpler way of looking at it is like this: at the top are the war leaders – such as Hitler, Churchill, Roosevelt or Mussolini – and their commanders. They have their overall aims for their countries. At the bottom is the man in his tank or plane, or the infantryman with his rifle or machine gun. Watch any movie or read any book on the subject and the chances are the focus will be on these people – after all, what's interesting about factories or nuts and bolts?

That's all very well, but it has meant that an entire part of the story has been, to all intents and purposes, left out. Nearly every narrative history of the Second World War has focused almost entirely on these two levels, the strategic and the tactical. There is lots about Churchill, Stalin, Roosevelt and the senior commanders, whether it be Montgomery's lack of tact, Patton's bravado or German and Soviet ruthlessness. There has also been a lot written about the man in the fox-hole or bunker or bomber, from moving last letters home to oral testimonies, memoirs and diaries.

If the supply of war is mentioned, it is almost as an aside or after-thought, and often much of what is said about this aspect is based on assumed knowledge rather than genuine research. The Tiger was the best tank of the war, for example; or the German MG42 was the pre-eminent small-arms weapon. Were they, though? Says who? On what basis are these assumptions being made? And once challenged, fascinating and often revelatory answers start to emerge – answers that begin to alter long-held views of the war.

This is the second of a three-volume history of the Second World War in the West. The first ends on the eve of Operation BARBAROSSA, the German invasion of the Soviet Union in June 1941, and central to the thesis put forward in that book was reinserting the operational level into the narrative. Far from being dull, however, that aspect is as rich in human drama as the other levels, and involves the overcoming of seemingly overwhelming odds, personality clashes, political beliefs, ineptitude, breathtaking skill and vision and even courage. The supply of war is not just about logistics and statistics, and, interestingly, was something that was understood much more clearly at the time. Look at contemporary German or British newsreels, for example, and there is every bit as much about factories and production as there is about the fighting on the front line. Britain, especially, made it clear that she was fighting an industrial war, bolstered by advances in science and technology and by galvanizing the country to produce more food, more planes, more tanks – more everything. Germany, too, made sure that on radio or on the screen, her mechanized might was at the forefront.

This rebalancing of the narrative also helps provide greater clarity about the major combatants in the war and reveals a startlingly different picture to the familiar story of those opening years of the conflict. Britain began the war with a very small army, not because of the Government's appeasement policy up to and beyond the Munich Crisis of the autumn of 1938, but because it made no real sense to have a large one. Britain's ally was France, which had a vast reserve army that could be mobilized in a trice. The United Kingdom was a democracy and throughout much of the 1930s the population would not have put up with conscription, a prerequisite for a large army. Finally, because the UK was geographically a comparatively small country island, housing, training and moving a large army was no easy matter – and expensive. On the other hand, the Royal Navy was the world's biggest, as was Britain's merchant fleet, and her global trading empire was also the largest the world had ever known. Britain's access to the world's resources was unparalleled. Great emphasis had also been laid on air power, which was growing all the time. Even after the fall of France in June 1940, the Government agreed to cap the British Army at fifty-five divisions; Germany had invaded France and the Low Countries with 135. When the new, enlarged Army was called upon to fight, it would do so using technology and mechanization as far as possible; those men at the coal-face of the fighting would be kept to a bare minimum. The thinking was that the larger the army, the greater the casualties. If machinery and technology could be used instead, and save lives, then so much the better. The last war, in 1914–18, had shown the British that large armies were inherently inefficient.

Britain had resisted the urge to sue for terms with Germany in May and early June 1940, as France was collapsing and the tiny British Expeditionary Force (BEF) was beginning its evacuation from Dunkirk. The British – and this included senior commanders and politicians – had been utterly shocked by the easy defeat of France, her greatest ally. Panic had gripped Britain's leaders, but the new Prime Minister, Winston Churchill, had persuaded his War Cabinet and then the wider nation to fight on. He had realized there could be neither compromise nor trust with Hitler and that, actually, Britain had much in her favour: the English Channel, the Royal Navy, the RAF, the world's first-ever fully co-ordinated air defence system and, at the time the Luftwaffe launched its all-out attack on the RAF on 13 August, nearly 2 million troops on the ground. Once the initial invasion crisis had passed there was an increased belief that eventually Nazi Germany could be defeated. In a long and attritional war, Britain believed it would surely win because its access to resources – oil, food, steel and so on – was so much better than that of Germany.

The British strategy was therefore a simple one: to fight on and to use shipping, global clout and the world's resources slowly but surely to claw back, grinding down Germany through economic blockade, increased bombing and a steady tightening of the economic noose, which was what they had done in the First World War. Key to this was going to be the harnessing of her fellow democracy in the West, the United States. British investment in the fledgling American armaments industry was a key part of this strategy; the US could not be expected to mass-produce tanks, aircraft and weapons immediately, but Britain was confident of holding out until such time as these fruits could come to bear. It was an entirely reasonable and pragmatic approach.

And the truth was, by the beginning of June 1941, Britain was making ground, not least in the Atlantic, which, as far as she was concerned, was the most important theatre of them all. If Britain's supply lines were severed, then the country – and the free world – really would be in trouble, but by May 1941 the Royal Navy, with the help of the small but growing Royal Canadian Navy and the RAF, had definitely got the upper hand. The Kriegsmarine's (German Navy's) surface fleet had been largely destroyed or neutralized, while the U-boat force had not proved large enough to make a really serious impact. Furthermore, a German Enigma coding machine as well as a book of codes had been captured without the German High Command knowing. Increasingly, British cryptanalysts were beginning to break coded German traffic.

On land, Britain had been able to harness troops and supplies from the Empire and defeat the Italian threat in Egypt, the Suez Canal, the Middle East and East Africa. The intervention of German forces into the Mediterranean had tipped the balance partially back in favour of the Axis, and British forces, defeated in Greece and on Crete, had been driven back across Libya and into Egypt. None of this territory threatened the sovereignty of Britain, however. Only the battle raging in the Atlantic could possibly bring that about and, by June 1941, that was a fight that was most definitely being won: by stronger naval forces and by increasingly superior technology too. What's more, across the far side of the Atlantic, American factories were whirring into life, its armed forces growing, and public opinion starting to shift with a newly re-elected President who was determined Nazi Germany should be defeated.

Thus, by the middle of 1941 there was no reason for Britain to be especially downhearted, despite the defeats in Greece and Crete. Or put it another way: those first years of war had not been entirely one-way traffic for Germany by any stretch of the imagination.

Germany was the largest country in Europe and in 1939 had, along with France, the largest army and the biggest air force in the world. The truly significant battle of those early years of the war was that against France and it was the shock defeat of this leading nation that was so remarkable, especially considering France had bigger, better tanks and more of them, more artillery pieces, and that, generally, it is easier to defend than attack. Victories against Poland, Denmark, Norway, the Low Countries, Yugoslavia and Greece were impressive but, militarily, these nations were significantly inferior and Germany had been allowed to defeat them in turn. What the world saw were dive-bombing Stukas, columns of tanks and armoured cars, and confident, ruthless young men. The speed of operation and emphatic nature of these victories ensured that Germany gained an unparalleled reputation for military fire-power, force and fury.

Certainly, the French had few answers to this onslaught, despite having many advantages. They were highly industrialized and mechan-ized, were the most productive nation in Europe in terms of agriculture – there had been no rationing in France before the armistice – and their Army was both vast and well equipped. Their Navy was stronger than that of Germany, their Air Force not appreciably smaller than the Luftwaffe, and they had useful overseas possessions that brought with them both resources and a source of manpower – something denied to Nazi Germany.

Unfortunately, they were politically fractious, which made successive Prime Ministers impotent and unable to galvanize the large number of disparate coalition partners, which had a knock-on effect for the military. The generals, most of whom were ageing, out of touch and lacking political direction, had been desperately trying to avoid any kind of conflict on French soil. Memories of the First World War, and especially Verdun, the most violent battle ever fought in terms of numbers of casualties, were still very fresh. Despite ill-conceived joint plans with the British to take the war to Scandinavia, it was once again northern France that bore the brunt of the German attack when it came.

The trouble was, the French commanders had assumed this new war would be fought rather like the last; they assumed it would be long, attritional and largely static. Consequently, the French armed forces were trained for defence of a fixed position and not for a mobile war or move-ment at pace. They had the best tanks, the most guns and millions of men, but they had overlooked the importance of swift communications. There were not enough radios and, once refugees started to clog the roads and Stukas were dive-bombing and breaking telephone lines, differing units were unable to speak to each other with the kind of speed that was needed in order to co-ordinate an effective defence. Nor were the men trained to think on their feet. As a result, the German spear-head, in their lightly armed panzers but with large numbers of radios, ran rings around them. When the crust of the French defence was broken, few of the *poilus*, as their soldiers were known, knew what to do. Far too many put up their hands in surrender before barely firing a shot. There was to be no '*On ne passe pas*' – they shall not pass – this time around, and no mass slaughter of Frenchmen. France had fallen, an armistice with the Germans was signed, but at least a generation of young men had been saved. Or so they thought at the time.

There could be no doubting the stunning and overwhelming speed of the German victory against France, but it was, none the less, as much about French failings as it was about German brilliance. Had the line at Sedan or at Dinant held, as it so easily could have done, or had the French responded to reconnaissance reports and heavily bombed the Ardennes as the bulk of German armour was gridlocked trying to get through, things might have been very different. It was not to be, however.

The stunning German victories achieved thus far had, however, hidden some rather serious cracks. Germany had traditionally practised rapid wars of manoeuvre, known as *Bewegungskrieg*, in which they brought to bear overwhelming superiority at the point of attack – or *Schwerpunkt*. The idea was to knock their enemy off balance with this lightning-quick thrust, then equally swiftly envelop their foe in an encirclement and annihilate them. This was known as the *Kesselschlacht*, or 'cauldron battle', and was something Prussian armies and more recently German armies always practised because they were all too well aware that they were not suited to a long, drawn-out conflict of attrition.

This was because of Germany's geographical position in the heart of Europe and its inherent lack of natural resources. No country in the world had all the resources needed for war-making, but while Britain and France could easily import what they lacked, this was not the case for Germany. Largely landlocked, it had a narrow border on to the North Sea and a slightly larger coastline facing into the Baltic, a sea of many islands and narrow channels. This meant that in terms of access to the world's oceans, the principal means of getting goods to and from a country, Germany could be very easily blockaded – which was precisely what Britain had been doing since the start of the war.

The truth was, Germany was very under-mechanized, despite the photographs and film footage of columns of panzers. At the outbreak of the war, it had been one of the least automotive of all the world's leading powers. In May 1940, only sixteen of the 135 divisions employed had been motorized at all – the vast majority of German troops moved around on their own two feet or by using horses and carts. This meant all aspects of society were under-mechanized too, including agriculture. The German agricultural system was inefficient, there were not enough tractors or other modern farm machinery and most farms were small. As a result, Germany did not have enough food to feed its people sufficiently. Nor did it have enough oil, or iron ore, or copper or bauxite, or a host of other resources that were essential for sustained armed conflict.

These shortages were nothing new, which was why Germany had traditionally favoured short, sharp wars in which overwhelming and emphatic victory was the swift result. Sometimes it worked, such as against Austria in 1866 and France in 1870, and sometimes it did not – France in 1914, for example. The point was this: whenever Germany had to fight a long and drawn-out war, the odds were dramatically stacked against it.

This was why, by June 1941, Germany's future hung by a string. Crushing France had been a spectacular achievement and back home in Germany most people thought the war had been won. Hitler himself believed the fight had been all but won and so too did most of his senior commanders. With France defeated and the British Expeditionary Force overwhelmed too, surely there was only one course left for Great Britain: to come to the peace table and sue for terms.

Hitler and his generals, however, were looking at the situation through the narrow prism of their own world-view – one in which land power was everything. Britain, as an island nation, and with tentacles that reached around the globe as a direct result of sea-power, looked at things from a different perspective. The Royal Navy, for example, was not called the 'Senior Service' for nothing. By contrast, the Kriegsmarine was most definitely the junior service in the minds of Hitler and most Germans.

When Britain showed no sign of talking terms and instead not only fought on but soundly defeated the mighty Luftwaffe, this threw Hitler's plans into complete disarray. His intention had always been to turn east, because there, in the farmlands of Ukraine and the steppes beyond, lay the food he required and resources he needed. Britain and other powers used the world's sea-lanes, but Nazi Germany would use railways and maybe, one day, highways and even oil pipelines. That was some way off in the future, however, and his strategy had been to neutralize the threat from the West, build up his forces once more, and then, when he was ready, strike into the Soviet Union.

The trouble was, Britain was still there, not neutralized at all, her

Army growing once more and her factories producing more tanks and aircraft than those in Germany. France and the Low Countries should have been providing the extra capacity needed, but Germany had already asset-stripped those countries. By the end of 1940, France, the most motorized European nation, had just 8 per cent of the vehicles it had had at the start of the year because the Germans had taken most of them. This meant France's workforce was no longer as efficient and, because reserves of resources had been swallowed by Germany, factories could no longer function at pre-surrender levels.

To make matters worse for Germany, hovering in the background was the USA, which had begun the war both isolationist and with an insignificant Army and even smaller Air Force. Nearly two years on, however, with President Roosevelt newly elected for an historic third term and quite openly hostile to Germany, there was no doubting that America posed a potentially enormous – and war-changing – threat. By the summer of 1941, US factories were slowly but surely starting to crank into gear – and producing arms that were being shipped across the Atlantic to Britain. There was not a senior German alive who did not understand that fighting a war on two fronts, as they had been forced to do in the First World War, was potentially fatal – and yet that was precisely what Hitler had been forced to do with Britain still in the war and with the United States now hovering in the wings.

America was not an official ally of Britain, but had quite clearly pinned her colours to the mast. The United States was the leading oil producer in the world, had a massive workforce, an economy that was growing, and the space and technology to out-produce any other country on the planet. In contrast, Germany's primary ally, Italy, had proved considerably more of a hindrance than a help. It had even fewer natural resources than Germany, was effectively locked into the Mediterranean, its armed forces were outmoded and ill-trained, and whether it be against the British in Egypt, Libya and East Africa, or against the Greeks in the Balkans, its armies had suffered one ignominious defeat after another. Mussolini, the Fascist dictator, had promised to fight a parallel war in the Mediterranean sphere that would be separate from that of Germany. And that had been what Hitler had wanted: for Italy to fight her own battles, but above all to protect Germany's southern flank. The last thing Hitler needed was to fight a war on three fronts; two were bad enough.

Yet Italian failures had forced the Führer to send precious forces and resources to Mussolini's rescue, in Libya and then the Balkans. What's more, this diversion to the south came on top of the Luftwaffe's failure in the Battle of Britain. This strategic disaster ensured there could be no possibility of invading England in the near future, and proved that their invasion plans had come a cropper at the first hurdle. At the same time, British and American factories were building ever more planes, guns and tanks, while the German booty from conquest was rapidly running out, along with the food, oil and resources needed to successfully defeat Britain's burgeoning Air Force, Army and ever-powerful Navy. And waiting in the wings was the United States.

Hitler's grand strategy had been simple enough: destroy Poland, then, once France and Britain had declared war, destroy them too. With Britain and France subdued, the threat from the United States would be significantly tempered; after all, there would be no springboard from which American forces could, should they ever try it, break into Nazi-held continental Europe. With his western flank therefore secure, he could take his time to build up strength and prepare for the clash that was both materially and ideologically the most important to him: with the Soviet Union. Two birds would be killed with one stone: Communism would be crushed and the USSR morphed into the German Reich.

Yet by the end of 1940, this strategy was already beginning to unravel. Defeating France had been only half the job and this was a war in which only complete victory would do. Britain remained, blockading Germany, drawing troops into the Mediterranean, bombing German cities (albeit not very effectively) and, by May 1941, crushing the Kriegsmarine's surface fleet as an effective fighting force. Despite horror stories of Allied convoys being mauled by U-boats, some 85 per cent of them were getting through unscathed and Germany was not coming close to throttling Britain's supply lines. The war at sea is often told as a separate story and nearly always plays second fiddle to what was happening on land. That, however, is to view this aspect of war in much the same way as the German leadership did at the time. It was a mistake to do so then, and it remains so now. To defeat Britain, Germany had to win the Battle of the Atlantic. In June 1941, they were still falling some way short of that goal.

Thus, despite the continued German successes in the Balkans and Mediterranean, Britain's stubborn refusal to play ball had ensured that Hitler had turned his thoughts eastwards much earlier than he had originally planned. This change of strategy had been unavoidable. Now, he planned to invade the Soviet Union in the summer of 1941 in yet another lightning strike. After all, it had worked against one of the most sophisticated nations in the world, so how hard could it be against a Red Army full of inferior *Untermenschen*? German forces would strike hard and fast and obliterate the Red Army in a matter of weeks. With victory in the east, Germany would then turn back west and deal with Britain once and for all.

That was the plan, but it was another massively high-risk gamble, because it meant Germany would be forced to fight on two fronts – something that even Hitler recognized was not a good idea; it was a lesson from history none of his senior commanders wanted to risk again. Nor could they expect Britain to sit back quietly and watch as Hitler's armies rolled east. Already, British intervention in the Mediterranean and Italian shortcomings had forced Hitler – in his mind at any rate – to intervene in the Balkans, and in Greece and Crete too. These campaigns, although they had been victorious, not only put back plans for the attack in the east by a month, they also deprived German forces of men, materiel and, perhaps most importantly of all, air transports; some 250 had been lost over Crete alone, a large number that could not be replaced in time.

Operation BARBAROSSA was due to be the largest clash of arms the world had ever witnessed and, once again, German victory depended entirely on speed of manoeuvre and the ability of the forces assembled to smash the Red Army completely. Quite simply, nothing less would do.

This, then, was the situation in the war in June 1941, and it was where the first volume left off. This second book covers the crucial middle years of the War in the West and, like the first, is a narrative history, told in the round and as objectively as possible. It is not a complete history, however, and I have quite deliberately focused on the main protagonists: Germany and Italy on the Axis side, and Britain and the United States on the Allied. France, both the pro-Axis Vichy and the Free French, gets its share, and I am also including Norway, the Netherlands and other nations caught between occupation and gradually growing resistance. There is not, however, the space to cover the Eastern European countries, nor to give the War in the East the detailed attention it deserves. This is the War in the West.

Through the narrative run the individual tales of just some of those who lived through – and died during – these tumultuous years, many of whose stories follow on from the first book in this planned trilogy. I have tried to provide a broad sweep – different nationalities and creeds, men, women, old and young, factory workers, politicians, civilians, business-men, sailors, soldiers and airmen, war leaders and humble privates. They are a tiny cross-section of this conflict that affected the lives of every man, woman and child of every combatant nation, but, I hope, they are broadly representative of the millions upon millions involved.

It was, and remains, a truly epic and astonishing story.

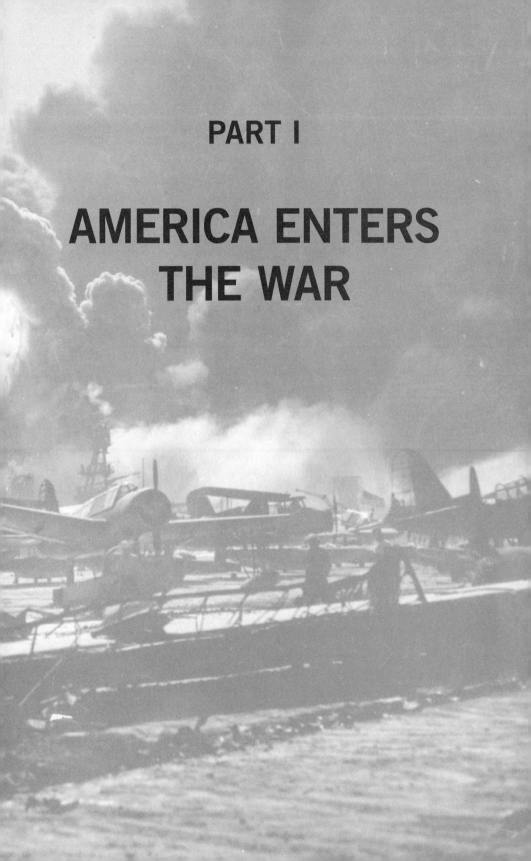

PART I

AMERICA ENTERS THE WAR

CHAPTER 1

The Largest Clash of Arms

OBERST HERMANN BALCK was one of the deep-thinking, progressive and vastly experienced fighting Army officers that had played such a crucial part in Germany's string of land victories so far in this second European war in a generation. Forty-seven years old in June 1941, he had soldiering in his blood: his great-grandfather had fought under Wellington in the King's German Legion in the Peninsular War; his grandfather had fought with the British Army too, with the Argyll and Sutherland Highlanders, while his father was a general under the Kaiser and had won a *Pour le mérite*, or the 'Blue Max' as it was known, the highest award a soldier could get, and was regarded as one of the finest tactical writers in the Imperial Army. From a very early age it was understood that young Hermann would also become a soldier, something he accepted without question; in fact, from the age of ten, he would ride most days with his father, who would talk to him about history and great leaders and battles, but also about a sense of responsibility for the men that he would one day command. 'What I observed and heard during these exercises,' he wrote, 'made a deep impression on me.' Like his father before him, he became an ardent student of history and warfare but a highly cultured man too.

By 1913, he was officially in the Army as a *Fahnenjunker*, that is, an officer cadet, in a *Jäger* – infantry – regiment, and was among the first wave of troops to advance into France as part of the Schlieffen Plan, crossing the River Meuse at Sedan. Over the next four years he served on the Western Front, the Eastern Front, the Italian Front and in the Balkans, and even spent several weeks commanding a company of men behind Russian lines. Wounded seven times, he was awarded the Iron Cross First Class and had been nominated for a Blue Max like his father when the war finally ended before the citation could be rubber-stamped.

Repeatedly, Balck had proved himself as a highly effective combat commander, and although he was one of the comparatively few officers to remain in the Army following the end of the last war, time and again he turned down the chance to join the General Staff, the accepted route for career advancement, in favour of remaining an officer in the line. By 1940, he was commanding 1. Rifle Regiment under General Heinz Guderian, the practical architect of the attack in the West. It was Balck who had led the first troops across the River Meuse at Sedan, where he had seen action in 1914, and it was Balck who had given an inspiring speech to his men at the end of that crucial day, 13 May 1940, spurring them to take a critical hill overlooking the town in the fading light.

Later promoted to command of a panzer (tank) regiment, he had been at the spearhead during the German invasion of Greece, had once again led from the front and by June 1941 had been given command of the Panzerbrigade 2 in the elite 1. Panzerdivision. Even by June 1941, panzer divisions were comparatively few in number; the vast majority of German divisions were not mechanized in any way and were dependent on using the feet of their soldiers and horse and wagon. This meant that panzer divisions really were the elite, and tended to have some of the most motivated and well-trained troops of the Wehrmacht.

There was no real equivalent to a panzer division in any other army in the world. The British, because they were entirely mechanized, believed the fighting units of an armoured division should consist almost entirely of tanks. The French, before they surrendered the previous June, had taken a similar approach. For the vehicle-starved Germans, however, the panzer division was a formation in which all three arms – infantry, armour and artillery – would be motorized and could work together. What bound these arms together was radio – every part of the formation had radios, whether motorcycles, armoured cars, half-tracks, lorried infantry or the panzers themselves. This meant they could move forward with speed, each part mutually supporting the other. The theory was that these spearhead divisions, with the Luftwaffe providing close air support, would bulldoze their way forward, with the foot-slogging infantry divisions and field artillery mopping up behind and adding weight to the advance.

So far in the war, no other army they had come up against had been able to bring this combination to bear with the same level of speed of manoeuvre and ability to keep in close communication. The Nazis had been great advocates of radio from the moment Hitler took power in 1933; radios became smaller and cheaper so that by the outbreak of war in September 1939 there were more radio sets per household in Germany than in any other country in the world, including the technologically advanced United States. This meant Germany was in the strange position of being one of the least automotive societies in the Western world, but leaders in communications and radios.

Only France had had an army comparable in size to that of Germany, but although it had bigger and better tanks and double the number of guns, it had neglected radio communication, and this proved to be a fatal flaw. It didn't really matter that the much larger part of the German Army was under-mechanized and, more often than not, not especially well trained. The hard yards – the decisive breakthrough – had been achieved already by the panzer spearhead: a fast-moving combined assault of furious fire-power.

There were now twenty panzer divisions in the Germany Army, and seventeen available for Operation BARBAROSSA, as well as a further seven motorized divisions and four Waffen-SS divisions, which were well equipped and fully motorized, but whose training was not quite up to those of the panzer units of the Oberkommando des Heeres (OKH – or Supreme Command of the German Army); this was because their commanders were primarily Nazis and SS men rather than long-serving Army officers. Theodor Eicke, for example, the commander of the Waffen-SS Totenkopf Division, had served in the last war as a private and formed the division from concentration camp guards at Dachau. It was hardly surprising they were a little rough around the edges.

In other words, it was the Wehrmacht panzer divisions that were very much the *corps d'élite*. There had been just ten of them for the attack in the west the previous year, so there was now double that number in the OKH. However, the number of panzer battalions in each division had been reduced from four to three. This meant that while Germany had launched the attack on the West with 35 panzer battalions, for BARBAROSSA the number was now 49, an increase of just 30 per cent.

There was no doubt that Germany had amassed a mighty army for this clash. In all, the German Army that crossed the border of the Soviet Union on 22 June stood at just over 3 million men, 500,000 horses, 600,000 vehicles and some 3,350 armoured vehicles, including tanks, armoured cars and half-tracks. On paper, certainly, this was an enormous force, yet so it needed to be if it was going to encircle and annihilate the Red Army in quick order and within 500 miles – the effective range within which they could operate with the kind of speed and weight of force needed before everything began grinding to a halt.

Yet as with the panzer divisions, once this force was broken down a bit, it no longer appeared so very impressive. Back in May 1940, Germany had invaded France and the Low Countries with 91 divisions in the initial waves along a border that spanned some 600 miles, but, in reality, they had a striking operational distance of less than 150 miles. By June 1941, the German Army had swollen to 208 divisions, but only 121 were directly involved in BARBAROSSA, and of those 64 in all were either mechanized or 'First Wave' – that is, fully trained and fit – infantry divisions. That was still, obviously, a lot; but, in contrast with a year earlier, the front they were now about to attack was over 1,300 miles in length. And while the overall size of the Army had increased by 52 divisions, 49 of those were now tied down maintaining their conquests in the West.

In other words, the German Army was invading a country more than ten times the size of France and the Low Countries with a force that was only slightly larger than that of a year earlier.

Over-confidence and hubris was once more clouding sound military judgement. During the previous summer, woeful intelligence combined with over-confidence had led to the Luftwaffe seriously underestimating the strength of the RAF, a very dangerous policy by an attacking force. In the summer of 1940, the Luftwaffe had paid a terrible price for their hubris. Hitler had to hope history was not about to repeat itself.

Hermann Balck, however, felt Germany now had little other choice but to attempt such an ambitious assault. Time, he believed, was running against them. Russia was an old enemy and ideologically opposed to Germany too. Right now, in June 1941, Balck felt the Russians were militarily inferior. In the later 1930s, much of the Red Army's leadership had been arrested and executed: three out of five marshals, including the enlightened Marshal Mikhail Tukhachevsky, had been shot, along with three out of five army commanders, fifty out of fifty-seven corps commanders and 154 out of 186 divisional commanders. The details were not known outside the Soviet Union, but the culling of so many senior commanders was. Recovery from this purge of the Red Army leadership was taking time, as Hitler was well aware. The poor performance of the Red Army in Finland had demonstrated that all too clearly.

None the less, Soviet military power was not standing still, and Balck wondered what the situation would be when Russia had grown and Germany had suffered some terrible harvest failure? 'Then Russia will pursue its political goals against us with all means,' he noted in his journal. 'In other words, it will attack us together with England and America. The tight encirclement that we have destroyed will be replaced by a more dangerous wide one.'

Balck was revealing the insecurity that was shared by so many Germans: that their geographical position at the heart of Europe meant they were always threatened on all sides. For Balck, Germany had so far simply unpicked what, on paper, should have been an impregnable alliance of states that surrounded them – and justifiably too. The Soviet Union did not seem to him to be a threat at that moment, but it would be, and before too long. And lurking in the west was 'England' – rarely did Germans refer to the United Kingdom as 'Britain' – her factories building ever-more aircraft and armaments, and, across the Atlantic, the United States, which had already made clear to which mast it was tying its colours. 'For us,' Balck concluded, 'the only course of action must be to attack Russia as soon as possible, to destroy it, to gain control of the Baltic States, the Ukraine, and the Caucasus, and then to turn our attention calmly to the Anglo-Americans.'

In this neat summary, Balck was reflecting Hitler's own strategy and the view that had been promulgated by the Nazi machine: that for Germany, this was a fight for national survival, and a pre-emptive strike to neutralize a potential serious threat. The difference between Hitler's view and Balck's, however, was that woven into this war of national necessity and survival were the Führer's own warped ideologies of racial and political supremacy. The Russians, in Hitler's view, were down-trodden Slavs – they were *Untermenschen*, a large mass of ill-educated, illiterate and inferior people who would, after a hard initial blow, quickly collapse and with them their corrupt Bolshevik leadership. 'The upcoming campaign,' Hitler told General Alfred Jodl, the Chief of Staff of the Oberkommando der Wehrmacht (OKW), 'is more than a mere contest of arms. It will be a struggle between two world-views.'

In fact, unlike with the earlier campaigns, both the OKW and OKH, working alongside the SS, had been preparing for this coming clash since the previous summer when Hitler had first begun to realize that he would have to turn east before he could deliver any kind of killer blow to Britain. Right from the outset, they had been told to prepare for an ideological war as well as a military campaign. This included earmarking territory for *Lebensraum* – living space – and primarily for growing food. The so-called 'Hunger Plan', developed by the OKW, acknowledged that some 20–30 million Soviet citizens would probably starve to death as a consequence of channelling desperately needed food into the mouths of Germans instead. Since it was a war of survival, however, this regrettable plan was none the less accepted as a necessity. The second part of the ideological war was to get rid of the Soviet leadership and intelligentsia.

Detailed planning had begun on 3 March 1941 when Hitler gave General Jodl his comments on a draft administrative directive for the Soviet Union. The entire area had to be dissolved into new German states, he told Jodl. 'The socialist idea,' he wrote, 'alone can form the domestic basis for the creation of new states and governments. The Jewish-Bolshevik intelligentsia, as the oppressor in the past, must be liquidated.' This 'liquidation' was to be carried out by Reichsführer Heinrich Himmler's SS, operating independently of the Wehrmacht and on their own responsibility.

None the less, the Wehrmacht High Command was entirely complicit. On 17 March, General Franz von Halder, the Chief of Staff of the OKH, had had a conference with the Führer in which Hitler again reiterated the need to exterminate the Soviet leadership and intelligentsia. 'The controlling machinery of the Russian Empire,' recorded Halder, 'must be smashed.' Force, he added, was to be used 'in its most brutal form.' Halder, a career staff officer and the chief planner – in many ways architect – of the early campaigns, had never been a Nazi and in the autumn of 1939 had even been part of a plot to assassinate Hitler. His nerve had failed him then, and now he made no attempt to question what the Führer was saying. Just ten days later, on 27 March, Halder's immediate superior, Feldmarschall Walther von Brauchitsch, spoke to senior Army commanders at the OKH Headquarters at Zossen, to the south-east of Berlin. 'The troops have to realize,' he told them, 'that this struggle is being waged by one race against another, and proceed with the necessary harshness.' The Wehrmacht top brass, at any rate, appeared to have swallowed Hitler's ideological claptrap hook, line and sinker.

From the outset, when Germany had invaded Poland in September 1939, it had been clear that nothing less than complete victory – that is, the annihilation of their enemies – would ultimately win them the war. What was equally clear as their massed armies prepared for BARBAROSSA was that this battle was going to be conducted with immense violence and brutality unprecedented so far in this war. Hitler had repeatedly gambled the future not only of his armies, but also the entire German people. Never was this more the case than now, on the eve of the largest clash of arms the world had ever seen. If the Germans failed in this latest enterprise, then they could expect little mercy in turn. The consequences of failure would be almost too terrible for the German people to bear.

Few were thinking of such visions of apocalypse, however, and certainly not Oberst Hermann Balck. No army had proved able to stop the Wehrmacht so far. Could a nation that had defeated the sophisticated modern armies of France and Britain really be halted by a mass of backward Soviet peasants? The Red Army had, after all, been given a bloody nose by the Finns just over a year earlier. The Finns! That hardly said much for Soviet military prowess. 'At the present time,' noted Balck, 'we are so superior to the Russians that they cannot seriously compete with us.'

On the eve of BARBAROSSA, German confidence was high.

CHAPTER 2

Manoeuvring

ON SUNDAY, 22 JUNE at 3.30 a.m., German summertime, BARBAROSSA was finally launched. Guns opened up as some 3,600,000 men, more than 3,500 panzers and 2,700 aircraft began streaming across the Soviet border of former Poland along a 1,200-mile front. To the far north, two Finnish armies were also on the move, joining forces with Germany against an enemy that had invaded their country back in 1939; this was their chance for revenge. Now they were heading across Karelia towards Leningrad and supported by 97,000 German mountain troops from Norway. Prior to this massive movement of armies, 800 'Brandenburgers' – special forces disguised as Russians – had crossed into Soviet territory and blown up power stations, cut telegraph wires and other communications, so that at the moment BARBAROSSA began, telephone lines up to 30 miles inside the border had been severed. Soviet security in the border area had proved extraordinarily lax; this augured well for the Germans.

Much to his frustration, however, and despite his proven track record, Oberst Balck was not part of this first wave of German panzer units in the attack on the Soviet Union. To his chagrin, he was called to Berlin where he was to help the beleaguered General Adolf von Schell, the General Plenipotentiary of Motor Vehicles at the OKW, and General Friedrich Fromm, who commanded the *Ersatzheer*, or Reserve Army, which co-ordinated all personnel from training to replacements sent to the front.

In many ways, however, attempting to streamline military motor production was a greater challenge than fighting the Red Army. Ever since 1938, General von Schell had been valiantly trying to make German motor production more efficient and to make the Army increasingly mechanized. The trouble was that right up to the war and beyond, the German motor industry was both small and disparate, made up of numerous independent companies. Compared with Britain, France – which had been Europe's leading motor-vehicle producer before the war – or especially the United States, Germany had been, and remained, way behind.

This could not be rectified overnight, particularly in a country so short of resources such as oil and even steel; there were simply too many competing areas, such as ships and aircraft. Nor were there enough factories, or garages, or enough spare parts. Lots of small companies making lots of different models was inherently inefficient and meant large-scale mass production was impossible. Yet Hitler wanted his armies to be increasingly mechanized. It had been von Schell's task to make possible the impossible. It had been a Herculean one, and he had achieved a great deal, all things considered, but the string of victories had, in many ways, only added to the problems. Part of the booty of war had been vast numbers of captured vehicles, but these were all different too and rarely came with spares. Von Schell had just managed to partially streamline vehicle production in Germany only to be saddled with a whole load more different types.

Repeatedly, he had been told how important it was that the Army have as many vehicles as possible for BARBAROSSA, yet further compounding the challenge had been the campaigns in the Balkans, Greece and North Africa, all of which had been conducted over difficult terrain with few and very poor roads. It was also clear that the wear and tear on vehicles in the Soviet Union was going to be considerable, as it was a country with few properly metalled roads.

Balck arrived in Berlin a few days after BARBAROSSA had begun, only to learn that his young son, a platoon commander, had already been killed in the fighting. Reeling from this blow, he was relieved to have so much work on his hands to take his mind off his family's loss. The task ahead of him was truly daunting, however, because as matters stood there was not a hope of making the Wehrmacht more mechanized – not with the inevitable strain that would be placed on vehicles operating somewhere as vast and underdeveloped as the Soviet Union, and while

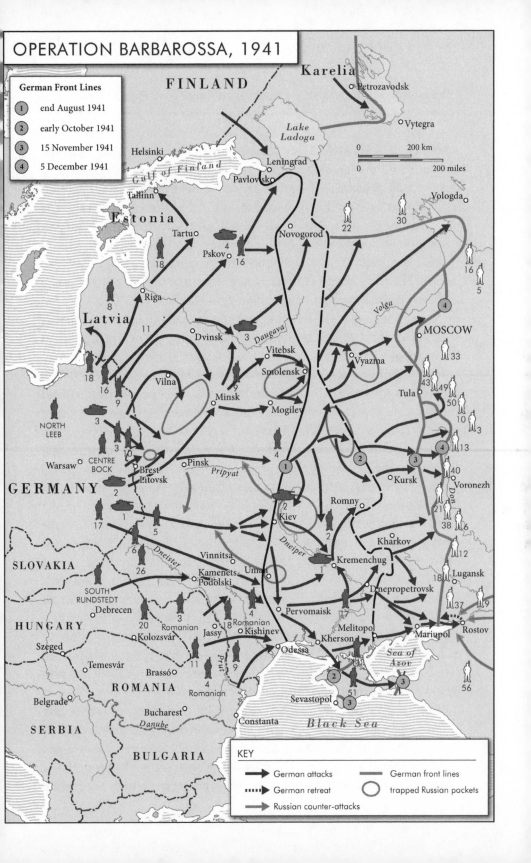

OPERATION BARBAROSSA, 1941

German Front Lines

① end August 1941
② early October 1941
③ 15 November 1941
④ 5 December 1941

FINLAND

Karelia

Petrozavodsk

Vytegra

Lake Ladoga

Helsinki

Gulf of Finland

Leningrad

Pavlovsko

Vologda

Tallinn

Estonia

Tartu

Pskov

16

Novogorod

22

30

18

4

16

5

Riga

Dvinsk

Daugava

Vitebsk

Volga

MOSCOW

4

33

Latvia

8

11

3

Smolensk

Vyazma

43 49

Tula

50

10 3

Vilna

Minsk

Mogilev

13

18

16

9

3

Kursk

40

Voronezh

NORTH LEEB

3

10

4

1

2

3

Romny

21

38 6

Warsaw

CENTRE BOCK

Brest Litovsk

Pinsk

Pripyat

Kiev

2

Kharkov

12

GERMANY

2

17

1

5

Dnieper

Kremenchug

18 Lugansk

SLOVAKIA

6

Dneister

Vinnitsa

Dnepropetrovsk

37 9

Kamenets-Podolski

Uman

SOUTH RUNDSTEDT

Debrecen

3

4

17

Pervomaisk

Melitopol

Mariupol

Rostov

HUNGARY

20

Romanian

18

Kishinev

Kherson

Szeged

Jassy

Romanian

Odessa

2

Sea of Azov

3

Temesvár

11

9

51

3

56

Brassó

4

ROMANIA

Romanian

Sevastopol

3

Belgrade

Bucharest

Constanta

Black Sea

Danube

SERBIA

BULGARIA

KEY

→ German attacks   — German front lines

┈▶ German retreat   ◯ trapped Russian pockets

→ Russian counter-attacks

0 _____ 200 km

0 _____ 200 miles

vehicle production was still stuttering. Somehow, some way, he was to try to conserve or find up to 100,000 vehicles. It was a lot to expect.

Although BARBAROSSA had an ideological dimension that had been absent from the early campaigns, it was none the less based on the age-old German principles of war. It was to be *Bewegungskrieg* on a grand scale – that is, heavily front-loaded, with the aim of smashing and annihilating the Red Army swiftly in a gargantuan *Kesselschlacht*, or encirclement, as close as possible to the western edge of the Soviet Empire in order to keep supply lines and distances generally as short as possible. In other words, the plan was, in essence, the same plan Prussian and then German armies had used for centuries.

To begin with, BARBAROSSA appeared to be going spectacularly well for the Germans, helped by Stalin's curious refusal to accept any warning signs of an imminent attack. The Soviet leader had been in denial about the build-up of troops near the border in former Poland, as well as intensive German road and airfield building, repeated infringements of their air space, and the mass of intelligence that all seemed to point in one direction; BARBAROSSA had been the world's worst-kept secret. Despite these indications, however, it was less tactical surprise that caught out the Red Army than overwhelming force at the *Schwerpunkt* – the point of attack. Sweeping across a 500-mile front, all three Army Groups gouged huge chunks out of the Soviet Union in the first fortnight alone. In the north, Feldmarschall Wilhelm Ritter von Leeb's Army Group North overran the Baltic States; in the centre, Generaloberst Fedor von Bock used the panzers of Army Group Centre to charge across Poland and envelop a massive pocket around Białystok; in the south, Feldmarschall Gerd von Rundstedt faced stiff resistance, but Army Group South still made huge strides. By 13 July, as the 'frontier battles' phase ended, the Germans had advanced between 300 and 600 kilometres and had killed, wounded or captured 589,537 – that is, some 44,000 Red Army troops per day, or the equivalent of three divisions. They had also destroyed 6,857 Soviet aircraft, mostly on the ground.

After giving himself a brief resumé of the situation, on 3 July Halder wrote in his diary, 'It is thus probably no overstatement to say that the Russian Campaign has been won in the space of two weeks.' There then came a caveat: 'The sheer geographical vastness of the country and the stubbornness of the resistance, which is carried on with all means, will claim our efforts for many more weeks to come.'

By the end of July, German advances were such that their drive looked as unstoppable as it had done in Poland, Norway, France and the Balkans. Guderian had taken Smolensk and now his forces were pushing south-wards, while General Hermann Hoth's to the north looked like they would encircle three Soviet armies. Further to the north, German forces were sweeping towards Leningrad. Victory appeared to be within their grasp. It was not, however – not by any means; rather, Red Army forces were starting to coalesce and even counter-attack. And it was at this moment that the German wheels, literally, began to come off the campaign.

General Walter Warlimont and his Section L of the Operations Staff at the OKW had moved to the field headquarters near Rastenburg in East Prussia, which was called HQ Area 2 but known as the 'Wolf's Lair'. It was a mixture of wooden huts and gaily painted underground concrete catacombs surrounded by high barbed wire, with an old and now appro-priated country inn at its centre. Warlimont, who felt quite claustrophobic in his underground double room, soon moved into the inn, which became an unofficial Officers' Mess. From HQ Area 2, Warlimont was able to follow the growing frustrations of both Halder and the OKH General Staff and his own team at Section L as Hitler once again began inter-fering with the day-to-day conduct of operations. For men such as Halder and Warlimont, hugely experienced in staff work and fully conscious of the enormous task facing the Wehrmacht, it was painfully frustrating to witness the Führer's glaringly poor, self-taught generalship and incapacity to accept well-tested military principles.

Hitler had already insisted on 19 July that Leningrad in the north and the Ukraine to the south were the priorities and that Army Group Centre was to hand over its two panzer groups once the huge pocket around Smolensk had been crushed. Moscow, he ordered, would be bombed by the Luftwaffe, as though that were enough to bring the Soviet capital to its knees, and even though the Air Force's track record when operating unilaterally was hardly one to inspire much confidence.

Then four days later the Führer issued a supplementary order, which demanded even further objectives in the south and insisted that the Luftwaffe then turn to support the drive of the Finnish armies. 'This,' he declared, 'will also reduce the temptation for England to intervene in the fighting along the Arctic coast.' How on earth Hitler thought Britain would quickly send a task force to the Arctic is not clear, but there were obviously far more important targets for the Luftwaffe. As it was, Moscow was never bombed by anything close to a massed raid.

A further directive appeared on 30 July, with yet another amendment on 12 August, as Hitler obsessed about his flanks and worried about the slowing pace in the south. The trouble was, just as had been feared by the logisticians, the Germans had reached the limits of their lines of supply. The speed of advance had taken a terrible toll on German mechanization. Günther Sack, for example, a young anti-aircraft gunner and now attached to 9th Division with von Kleist in Army Group South, suffered a puncture on their gun carriage, which held them up. On 15 July, their truck broke down with a seized engine. By the time they had a replacement, the rest of their battery was way ahead. Then the trailer broke again and had to spend several days in the divisional workshop that had hastily been set up. Not until 26 July did they finally catch up. Sack's experience was a common one.

Meanwhile, the Panzergruppen of Generals Guderian and Hoth had smashed Smolensk only by another furious drive that pushed their men and machines to the limits of their capabilities. When that ran out of steam, they were forced to dig in and fight off a string of furious counter-attacks. This was where BARBAROSSA differed from earlier campaigns. The Red Army appeared to have collapsed – but it had not entirely. The German way of war was to knock the enemy off balance, then drive home the killer punch. The Soviet Army had been knocked spectacularly off balance, but was already beginning to get back on its feet again as a further 5 million men were called up. No fewer than seventeen armies were thrown into the counter-attacks opposite Army Group Centre; at this time, Britain barely had one.

Hans von Luck was now a reluctant staff officer with 7. Panzerdivision HQ, part of Army Group Centre. 'We very soon had to accustom our-selves,' he wrote, 'to her almost inexhaustible masses of land forces, tanks, and artillery.' The Soviet Union was not France. It had enormous geo-graphical reach with no English Channel or Atlantic Ocean limiting any retreat, vast amounts of manpower and, unlike the Western democracies, it was a totalitarian state whose leaders had not a single humanitarian care for the lives of their men.

In Britain, the reaction to the German invasion of the Soviet Union was mixed. On the one hand, it was good to know that any further plans for an invasion of Britain must have been shelved for the foreseeable future and that the USSR was now bearing the brunt of Hitler's military ambitions. On the other hand, the prospect of a German victory was terrifying to say the least; British war leaders were every bit as aware as those of Germany that the Soviet Union was a giant expanse containing critical resources of food, fuel, manpower and industrial potential.

British mistrust of Communism and the new Russian order had ensured they had missed the diplomatic boat back in the months leading up to the outbreak of war. There could be no more political reticence, however. *Realpolitik* needed to trump political sensitiveness. 'My enemy's enemy is my friend' was a mantra that had to be acknowledged and acted upon swiftly; the fact that the British king's relatives had been murdered by the Soviets, or that the Prime Minister had been among the most eager of British politicians to try to quell Bolshevism, or that the totalitarian control of the Communist state was uncomfortably similar to the totalitarian control of the Nazis, had to be put to one side. Yes, ridding the world of Hitler and the Nazis was Britain's strategic end-goal, but they had to ensure the safety of their own sovereignty first.

Three weeks after BARBAROSSA was launched, on 12 July 1941 an agreement was signed between Britain and the USSR to provide 'help and support of any kind in the present war against Nazi Germany.' There was most definitely a certain degree of gritted teeth from both parties as they signed the agreement, but what the Kremlin was asking for in the short term was supplies: tanks, aircraft, trucks, uniforms – anything, frankly, that might help the Red Army. Britain, of course, had innumerable demands herself for such war materiel, but it was a question of priorities. Right now, in the second week of July, Soviet prospects did not look good; they needed help and urgently. In any case, it was far better to send tanks and aircraft – which were, after all, only machines – for Red Army troops to be killed and wounded in rather than British. The British strategy of 'steel not flesh' could be applied to sending aid to the Soviet Union too. Even so, getting these supplies there would not only place an extra burden on the already overstretched Navy and Merchant Navy, it would inevitably cost British lives too – just not as many lives as would be lost if the Soviet Union was defeated.

The United States, meanwhile, was taking this approach a step further by sending aid not only to Britain but now also to the Soviet Union; far better that British *and* Soviet servicemen face the fire than Americans.

At any rate, it was clear to Roosevelt that the US, like Britain, must hurry to the USSR's aid pretty darn quickly, and so he sent his friend and most trusted confidant, Harry Hopkins, first to confer with the British once more and then to fly on to Moscow.

It was a frenetic few weeks for the US President's special envoy. Although Hopkins was only fifty years old, illness had plagued him for years and travel never did much for his precarious health – especially not long-distance travel in a succession of American heavy bombers and flying boats – but he none the less had reached Britain and then London safely, renewed his growing friendship with Churchill, attended a War Cabinet meeting – the first foreigner ever to do so – and arranged for Churchill, Roosevelt and the Chiefs of Staff to meet at Placentia Bay in Newfoundland on 9 August.

While he was in London, Hopkins also met Ivan Maisky, the Soviet Ambassador. During their conversations it became clear to both men that a visit to Moscow would be of enormous benefit. By meeting Stalin, Hopkins could see for himself exactly what Soviet intentions were and precisely what they most needed and hoped for from the United States. Stalin would also be able to draw reassurance from seeing the President's special envoy in person.

On Sunday evening, 27 July, Hopkins made a broadcast on the BBC from Chequers. 'I did not come from America alone,' he told his listeners. 'I came in a bomber plane, and with me were twenty other bombers made in America.' He also made it clear that Roosevelt was as one with Churchill in his determination 'to break the ruthless power of that sinful psychopath in Berlin.' Afterwards, Churchill and Hopkins talked together in the garden; it was around ten o'clock but still light, and the PM spoke of the importance of Russia now being in the fight and the aid Britain planned to send. Hopkins asked if he could repeat this to Stalin.

'Tell him,' Churchill said, 'that Britain has but one ambition today, but one desire – to crush Hitler. Tell him that he can depend upon us.'

Hopkins flew to the Soviet Union the next day. It was an exhausting trip for him, but a success. Once again, his unerring ability to charm people with whom, on one level, he had very little in common won him renewed admiration. In two lengthy meetings with Stalin he was able to discern a sense of the Soviet leader's determination to keep fighting and to convey the earnestness of America's willingness to help. Hopkins had been careful not to patronize. Equally, he had been impressed by Stalin's list of requirements. The fact that aluminium was high on his list, for example, suggested the Soviet leader was expecting a long war, not imminent defeat. These were potentially fraught – even surreal – circumstances between two ideologically and politically diverse men. A deft touch of diplomacy was needed from both parties. Both provided it.

Hopkins flew back to Britain in time to join the Prime Minister and the British Chiefs of Staff for the trip across the Atlantic on the battleship HMS *Prince of Wales*. What a tasty target this giant ship would have been for any skulking U-boat – yet thanks to decrypted German Enigma traffic, known as 'Ultra', to high-frequency direction finding – HF/DF, or 'Huff-Duff' – and to the 40-knot speed of the ship, it was about as safe a means of travel as any in the summer of 1941. At any rate, they reached Placentia Bay untroubled and made their rendezvous with the Americans on the morning of Saturday, 9 August.

For Churchill this was a big moment. He had been striving to draw ever-closer co-operation from the United States since his time at the Admiralty and was equally eager to forge a sense of common purpose and even friendship. 'He is excited as a schoolboy on the last day of the term,' noted Churchill's secretary Jock Colville before the PM left. Certainly he was in his element on board the *Prince of Wales* – he was the nation's war leader crossing the Atlantic battleground on a mighty warship, sailors and senior commanders all around him. He found it thrilling.

There was a dinner and discussions on the USS *Augusta*, then, the following day, a church service and lunch on the *Prince of Wales*. Finally, on Monday 11th, by which time Lord Beaverbrook, the Minister of Production and close confidant of the Prime Minister, had joined them, Churchill and Roosevelt had a more intimate, less formal lunch. Much of the discussion was about the growing aggression of Japan, but it was also reaffirmed that if the US entered the war then together with Britain they would focus on the defeat of Nazi Germany before Imperial Japan. US naval participation in the Battle of the Atlantic was also confirmed again, and it was agreed there would be a three-way conference between Britain, the US and the Soviet Union in September, while a pledge of aims, which became known as the Atlantic Charter, was also drawn up and signed.

In it, Churchill and Roosevelt declared to the world eight common principles. They sought 'no aggrandisement, territorial or other'. They also respected the rights of all peoples 'to choose the form of government under which they will live'. The sixth point dealt directly with Germany: 'after the final destruction of Nazi tyranny, they hope to see established a peace which will afford to all nations the means of dwelling in safety within their own boundaries, and which will afford assurance that all the men in all the lands may live out their lives in freedom from fear and want.' It was heady, utopian stuff, and back in Britain caused some embarrassment for Churchill; India, for example, had been on the cusp of independence before the war, but there were many there who believed they were not being given the chance to choose their own government. The Atlantic Charter hardly endorsed empire.

None the less, the charter was significant and placed the war firmly on a moral footing in the eyes of Britain and the United States. This alone set the current conflict apart from those that had come before.

Just as importantly, Roosevelt and Churchill had finally had the chance to meet one another properly and, while neither forgot that theirs was a professional relationship, they liked one another and got on well. Roosevelt was a head of state, Churchill was a chief minister – and there was a difference – but both were global military-politico leaders speaking the same language and with the same essential aims. The importance of this meeting in Placentia Bay has often been played down. It should not be.

While much of the Luftwaffe had been sent east, the burgeoning night-fighter force was continuing to do its best to combat the almost nightly RAF raids over occupied Europe. The night-fighters had been formed into XII. Fliegerkorps under Josef Kammhuber, who had been promoted to general the previous summer and made Inspector-General of Night-Fighters.

In July, Helmut Lent, only twenty-three but already a veteran of Poland, Norway and the Battle of Britain, was given command of 4/NJG1 based at Leeuwarden in Holland. With twenty-seven victories to its name, it was, by some distance, the most successful night-fighter unit and already contained several aces, including the aristocratic Leutnant Egmont Prinz zur Lippe-Weissenfeld. Its reputation, however, rested not only on its young aces, but also on the part it was playing in developing night-fighter tactics. As in Britain, the Germans had been trying to harness new technology to interception techniques.

By the time Lent took over 4/NJG1, Kammhuber had developed a defensive line in which a system of controlled sectors, equipped with radar and searchlights, were linked to a night-fighter unit. Each sector was known as a *Himmelbett* zone of about 20 miles by 15 and included a Freya and later two Würzburg radar sets, a 'master' radar-guided searchlight, a number of manually controlled searchlights, and had two night-fighters attached – one primary and one back-up. As an enemy bomber crossed into the range of the Würzburg, one radar set tracked it while the other followed the movement of the night-fighter patrolling that particular zone, or box. The zone's controller then radioed interception vectors to the night-fighter and, once the attacker was close, his target was lit up by searchlights.

What was setting 4/NJG1 apart, however, was the determination of its pilots to be guided to their targets without the use of searchlights, which they considered unsatisfactory because of the glare and because of the evasive moves a trapped bomber would then make. They felt it was far better to trust one's instruments and prowl up to a target without the enemy crew realizing. *Dunkle Nachtjagd* – dark night hunting, as it was known – of course, took huge skill.

Lent's new command, he told his parents, was 'fit and cheerful and safe in God's hands', and after familiarizing himself with a new Dornier 215 night-fighter, he wasted no time in getting flying. Within a week of joining his new *Staffel* he had shot down three enemy aircraft – no small achievement. 'Last night my eighth kill went down,' he wrote to them, 'that is my fifteenth victory. I'm enormously pleased that I've been able to get off to such a good start in my new staffel.'

Back in the United States, the US Army was now preparing for war, and certainly the Atlantic Conference was a further step towards full involvement in the conflict. Stalin had kept pushing Hopkins, and Churchill continued to exert pressure, but while the Americans studiously refused to be drawn into any kind of discussion on the matter, it didn't take a genius to see that it was increasingly a question of when, not if. In any case, to all intents and purposes, their Navy was already at war with Germany.

Certainly the US Army was now preparing for combat and growing in size too. The old pre-war atmosphere of easy laissez-faire had gone, replaced with a new sense of purpose and a determination at the very top to revolutionize the Army into an efficient, modern fighting machine. It was beginning to look different too.

Ever since the last war, the US Army had equipped its men with the standard round-rimmed Tommy helmet, as used by the British. A completely new design was now coming into service, however, known as the M1. This fitted comfortably over the head and covered much of the back of the neck and ears, but its liner was both more comfortable than the old helmet and a closer fit. It was 'cleared for procurement' on 7 May 1941 and it was recommended that 'the item be given priority as essential.' It would take time for the changeover to be completed, but in keeping with the rapid rearmament programmes now under way, a variety of civilian firms would be involved in its manufacture, including, for example, the McCord Radiator Company of Detroit, who within a year would be producing no fewer than 400,000 M1 helmets per month.

New uniforms were entering service as well. The US Army had issued its men with a wool 'OD' – olive drab – service coat, which was similar to the field tunics worn by many nationalities; it was, in essence, a tunic with big pockets and brass buttons that came halfway down the thigh. By early 1940, however, General George C. Marshall, the Army Chief of Staff, felt it was time for a new look – one that reflected the largely civilian and modern army he hoped it would become, and one that provided both comfort and easy movement. A number of civilian windbreakers were examined, but none quite hit the mark, so Major-General J. K. Parsons, commanding the 5th Division, was given the task of overseeing the design, trials and eventual procurement of a new field jacket. 'In deciding upon the garment to be recommended,' he wrote to the Adjutant-General, 'the needs of the Infantry soldier were given primary consideration. It was therefore decided that a suitable jacket to meet his needs must not only be warm and comfortable, but must be light in weight and have the minimum in bulkiness.' This was much the same brief given the designers of the British Battledress, but in its consideration of comfort for the ordinary soldier, quite radical.

A design was drawn up and produced. Although it was olive drab in colour, it did look very like a civilian windcheater, with a centre zip-and-button combination, generous under the arms and coming down to just below the waist. General Parsons tested the jacket extensively using 400 of his men as guinea pigs. Any adjustments – such as taking the flaps off the side pockets – were due to the advice of the majority of these soldiers.

The Quartermaster General's office still sent the design to *Esquire* magazine, who advised further on cloth and, inevitably, the look of the thing, which prompted a rather terse reply from General Parsons. 'Esquire may be an authority on what a well dressed gentleman should wear,' he wrote, 'but a study of its comments and the design of the garment it submitted as a substitute shows plainly that it does not understand the purpose of the garment and is ignorant of the needs of the soldier in the field.' Someone else from behind a desk then suggested it was too short and in cold weather might cause kidney trouble. 'All I can say,' replied Parsons, 'is most men have kidney trouble when in the presence of the enemy and it is fear not the length of the garment that causes it.'

The new M1941 field jacket, known, perhaps justifiably, as the 'Parsons Jacket', was duly adopted. Made of water-resistant cotton and lined with warm but lightweight wool, there was no other military jacket in the world that looked so casual or modern, nor one that had been designed and adopted with such thorough testing by those who would subsequently be wearing it in combat. As the US Army prepared for war, it was demonstrating a highly pragmatic but forward-thinking outlook – and, crucially, one that was not constrained by its military past.

Having snappy new uniforms in the pipeline was all well and good, but the men in this rapidly expanding Army had to be trained, and with suitable principles of doctrine at both the tactical and operational level. In Washington, GHQ had been renamed Army Ground Forces (AGF), and one of the up-and-coming officers in the US Army, Lieutenant-Colonel Mark Clark, had been promoted two jumps – and over a number of men who had been his senior – to Brigadier-General and Chief of Staff to General Leslie McNair, Chief of Staff at US General Headquarters. After long years in the 1930s barely progressing at all, the tall, 45-year-old Clark was suddenly going places.

McNair had asked Clark to prepare a series of large-scale military manoeuvres so that Army Ground Forces could test the soundness of their logistical doctrine and the men could live, sleep and operate as close to combat conditions as possible. The Louisiana Maneuvers that August were the fruits of Clark's efforts and those of McNair's staff at AGF, and marked the first time infantry, artillery and armour were placed on an exercise with air forces too, and in which the medical, signals and other support services were tested together. They were, in effect, a massive war game, in which the Second and Third Armies were pitted against one another.

Among those taking part were Tom and Henry 'Dee' Bowles, identical twins from Russellville, Alabama. They had just suffered a terrible blow, because in July they had received telegrams telling them their father was critically ill. At the time they had been carrying out amphibious training, not least because part of the AGF plans were amphibious invasions of Dakar and the Azores. Put ashore, they hitchhiked back to Russellville. 'Daddy died on 31 July,' said Henry. He had been just fifty-four. Both their parents had now gone.

They had returned in time for the manoeuvres, however, which, if anything, opened their eyes to how ill-prepared the US Army was for war. They were still wearing their old uniforms and wide-brimmed felt hats, and, although they had been issued with the new M1 Garand rifle, they noticed that many of those in the National Guard divisions were still using wooden rifles. Nor did they see any tanks, but, instead, trucks with logs sticking out the front in an effort to simulate armour. 'You'd have planes flying over,' said Henry, 'dropping paper bags full of flour instead of bombs.'

Another taking part was Sergeant Ralph B. Schaps, from Lastrup, Minnesota. Schaps was twenty years old and, although he had younger brothers and a sister, was, like the Bowles twins, effectively on his own in the world – his mother had died in 1937 and his father had been badly burned in a garage fire back in 1930 and had been in a nursing home ever since. While his siblings had been looked after by uncles and aunts, Ralph had largely managed to fend for himself, attending the Mechanics Arts High School in St Paul, from where he had graduated in 1939. While there, he had also joined the Minnesota National Guard, largely because it had meant being paid $24 every three months for just one three-hour training session per month and a two-week annual summer camp. It seemed like a fair deal. After graduating he had gone to work for his uncle in a garage in Austin, Minnesota, and so transferred to the National Guard there, which was Company H of the 2nd Battalion, 135th Regiment, 34th 'Red Bull' Division. Schaps had assumed that he would simply continue in the same vein – working in the garage and attending his monthly training sessions – but on 10 February 1941 his regiment had been activated and placed into the US Army for one year of training and service. Anyone who didn't want to go full-time could leave with no questions asked, but Schaps had decided to stay. Placed in the 1st Platoon, Heavy Weapons Company, he was posted with the regiment to Camp Claiborne, Louisiana, where he was put through the non-commissioned officers course. Now an NCO with stripes on his sleeves, he had joined the Training Cadre. It was his job to help lick the new recruits into shape.

Everyone in the regiment took part in the manoeuvres, however. Also still kitted out in the old army leggings and Montana peak hats, Schaps and his fellow Minnesotans did not much like the swamps of Louisiana, with their bugs and mosquitoes, and they were resentful, too, that they were still using antiquated kit. 'There was a lot of griping and bitching among the troops,' noted Schaps. None the less, he thought the man-oeuvres did them a lot of good. 'We learned how to live and get along in the field, and that it was necessary to depend on and trust one another. We learned to get along with one another and work as a team.'

While invaluable lessons were being learned by the Army in Louisiana, the Air Forces were also expanding and preparing for war. On 21 June 1941, the Air Corps had been redesignated Army Air Forces (AAF), with General 'Hap' Arnold as chief, and with 'Tooey' Spaatz, now a Brigadier-General, as the first Chief of the Air Staff as well as continuing his role as Chief of Plans in what was now called the Air War Plans Division (AWPD). Although still part of the US Army, rather than an entirely independent service, the Air Forces did now have their own staff. None the less, this lack of complete autonomy threatened to come to the fore almost immediately, because on 9 July Roosevelt asked the Army and Navy to prepare a new revised estimation of requirements needed to defeat America's potential enemies – that is, Imperial Japan and Germany. When Spaatz realized the Army were planning to submit air plans them-selves, he asked Arnold to intervene, aware that the Army would view air requirements in terms of close tactical support for the ground forces.

Much to Spaatz's relief, the Army War Plans Division accepted the argument that the Air War Plans Division should draw up their own appreciation of requirements. The result, prepared in just one week in early August, became the key document in the Army Air Forces' prepar-ations for war, outlining as it did their strategy for the use of air power as worked out by pre-war study and by observation during the Battle of Britain. The AWPD/1, as it became known, ranged well beyond what the

Plans Division had been asked to provide. Key to this strategic vision was to wage a sustained strategic air offensive against Germany and Japan. As far as Germany was concerned, AWPD/1 outlined a sustained strategic air offensive in which industrial, civil and communications targets were identified. In fact, quite specific targets were included, such as power stations, aircraft factories, oil and other war production facilities. They also anticipated supporting a land invasion of occupied Europe. Another assumption was that bombing needed to be accurate and that the only way to do that was by attacking in daylight hours. This was a pre-war view and one that Spaatz had been determined to stick with following his experiences in Britain the previous summer. High-altitude, massed formations, heavy armour and armament, speed, and the sophistication of the pioneering and closely guarded Norden bomb-sight, which could measure an aircraft's ground speed and direction as well as flight conditions, were seen as key elements that would ensure success. To achieve these ambitious goals, AWPD/1 called for the precise figures of 2,164,916 men and 63,467 aircraft, of which 4,300 were to be allocated for Britain.

At the time of AWPD/1, there were just 150,000 men in the Army Air Forces, so there was still a long way to go, but around the United States more and more men were undergoing flying training. The Air Forces *were* expanding, but there were simply not enough facilities or airfields to train the numbers needed for such a sudden increase, so some civilian flying schools were roped in to help. It was as part of these Government-backed civilian training schemes, for example, that Dale R. Deniston managed to get through Civilian Pilot Training. From Akron, Ohio, where his father worked for the Goodyear rubber company, Deniston had grown up obsessed with aviation. Goodyear had built two airships at Akron and as a boy he had followed their construction avidly, joining thousands of others to watch the test flights. Then, when he was still only eleven years old, a friend of his parents took him in a flight over Niagara Falls. It had been unbelievably thrilling. Another year, he managed to save up enough money for a trip on a Ford tri-motor, but while those flights were very rare treats, he still enjoyed spending as much time as he could at the Akron airfield, watching planes. When he grew up, he knew what he wanted to be: a pilot in the US Army Air Corps.

In 1939, Deniston entered Kent State University, and it was while there that he was given the chance to learn to fly. Having got through his civilian pilot training, he then applied for US Army Aviation Cadet Training. With his degree, and after a rigorous medical screening, he was accepted. In February 1941, he was told he was in – part of Class 42-C – and sent to Fort Hayes, Columbus, Ohio, to be sworn in and then posted to begin flying training. 'Oh happy day!' he noted. 'I was on my way, hoping to make my dream come true.' From Fort Hayes, he was put on a train to Los Angeles, California, and from there to Oxnard for Primary Flight Training. Within four days of his arrival, he was flying a Stearman biplane trainer and loving every moment. That he was training for war barely crossed his mind. He was flying. That was all that mattered.

A number of his fellow cadets were thrown out as the course progressed – a fate that had very nearly befallen another trainee pilot, Francis 'Gabby' Gabreski. The son of first-generation Polish immigrants, from Oil City, Pennsylvania, Gabreski had similarly developed a passion for flying at an early age. At Notre Dame University, where he had just managed to scrape himself in, he had begun private flying lessons, but discovered to his dismay that he lacked any kind of natural aptitude. After about six hours' instruction, he ran out of money, but then the Army Air Corps recruiting team showed up on campus. By this time the war in Europe had begun and Gabreski, whose mother still spoke only Polish, was more keenly aware than most that Poland had been invaded and destroyed. He applied to join and was accepted.

He arrived at Parks Air College in East St Louis, Illinois, in July 1940, but two months later was still struggling to master flying. He was just too heavy-handed, and after a particularly dismal flying lesson in which he singularly failed to perform an adequate 'lazy eight' manoeuvre, his instructor told him flatly that if he continued training he would probably kill himself and take someone with him. He was putting Gabreski up for an elimination flight.

This would be his final chance to prove himself. The night before, Gabreski took himself off to a Catholic church and prayed hard. And as he did so, a feeling of confidence swept over him.

The next day he went up for his elimination flight and performed lazy eights, loops and slow rolls without too much problem. He even brought the plane down perfectly when his instructor unexpectedly cut the power on him. 'I think you just need a little bit more time to catch up with the other students,' his examiner told him. And a change of flying instructor. Gabreski had been given a second chance.

In March 1941 he graduated, and with around two hundred hours' flying under his belt. This was more than either RAF or Luftwaffe pilots would expect to have before going operational. Gabreski knew he wasn't the best pilot that ever lived, but he had got through and with his wings on his chest he had been posted to Hawaii and, even better as far as he was concerned, to a fighter unit, the 45th Fighter Squadron.

On Hawaii, Gabreski finally got to grips with flying as he notched up another thirty hours or more a month and was able to draw on the experience of his fellow pilots. 'The training brings about experience,' he wrote, 'and once you get the experience, you have that final edge – professionalism. I pushed myself to the maximum every time I took an airplane off the ground. I wanted to make that airplane become a part of me.'

The rapidly growing US Army Air Forces had a huge advantage: a vast area of land in which to train in ideal weather conditions and without the threat of interruption by enemy attack. So, too, did the RAF, now that the Empire Training Scheme was fully under way in Canada and Rhodesia; having colonies and dominions around the world was proving very useful in this continuing war.

The same could not be said, however, for either the Luftwaffe or the Regia Aeronautica. The longer the war continued, the harder it was going to be for them to grow their air forces to the scale needed, just in terms of pilots and aircrew, let alone the manufacture of aircraft. It was another reason why German strategy had been to carry out short, sharp, decisive campaigns.

Reichsmarschall Hermann Göring, the world's only six-star general and Commander-in-Chief of the Luftwaffe as well as President of Prussia, had been against BARBAROSSA. The Luftwaffe was the one arm of the Wehrmacht that had had no break to regroup and regain strength since the launch of the Western campaign on 10 May 1940 – when it had suffered catastrophic losses of some 353 aircraft, by some margin its worst single day since the war had begun. There had been no such catastrophe on the opening day of the campaign in the East, but the Luftwaffe was also conducting operations in North Africa and the Mediterranean, and against Britain from northern France and Norway. It was horribly stretched.

Göring had implored the Führer to reconsider. 'The sacrifices made so far by the Luftwaffe in its attacks on England would be in vain,' he told him. 'The British aircraft industry would have time to recover; Germany would renounce certain sure victories (Suez, Gibraltar), and with them the possibility of reaching an agreement with England and, thereby, of guiding Russia's armament activity into another channel.' Hitler had replied, 'You will be able to continue operations against England in six weeks.'

Göring's arguments would have been more valid had the Blitz shown much sign of affecting British war industry, but he was right in principle. However, by the eve of BARBAROSSA he had acquiesced to the will of the Führer. 'The rest of us,' he told the Luftwaffe's operational chief, Feldmarschall Erhard Milch, 'we lesser mortals, can only march behind him with complete faith in his ability. Then we cannot go wrong.'

But they could. They could go very badly wrong.

CHAPTER 3

Summer '41

B Y THE SUMMER of 1941, the German war machine was horribly overstretched and no part of that machine represented this over-reach of commitment better than the Luftwaffe. Two pilots now flying over the Eastern Front were Hauptmann Johannes 'Macky' Steinhoff and Major Helmut Mahlke. Both had joined the Luftwaffe before the war and seen combat over Poland, then in the western campaigns and the Battle of Britain. Mahlke had served in the Balkans, Greece and over Malta too.

Leutnant Heinz Knoke, still only twenty, had also been flying as part of BARBAROSSA, but on 2 July he had been posted to the Western Front, where he began carrying out shipping patrols for the Kriegsmarine. 'If only we had a free hand in the West,' he had written the day the offensive in the East had begun, 'we could inflict a shattering defeat on the Bolshevist hordes despite the Red Army. That would save Western Civilization.'

A fighter pilot who had been operating in France ever since the Battle for France was Oberleutnant Siegfried Bethke. He'd been flying operationally now for over thirteen months; relentless operational service was another feature of the pressure on the Luftwaffe. In June he had been given leave to marry his girlfriend, Hedi, with whom he was deeply in love. Getting married, however, had worried him and he had written a number of pages in the journal Hedi had given him back in September 1939, agonizing over whether it was the right thing to do in wartime. The future seemed so uncertain: his own and that of

Germany. Was it fair to Hedi? But he had walked down the aisle and by the beginning of July, his brief honeymoon over, he was back in Brest, ostensibly to provide cover for the *Scharnhorst* and *Gneisenau* undergoing repairs there. Not only were those capital ships drawing off workmen from Dönitz's U-boat force, they were demanding fighter defence as well.

By 24 July, the *Scharnhorst* had been moved to La Pallice, but more than a hundred British bombers and escorts came over to bomb the *Gneisenau*, which was reportedly hit six times. Bethke was in the thick of the action. One of his men shot down a Spitfire, while he attacked a British bomber until it burst into flames but continued to fly. 'The gruppe had 12–15 kills,' he scribbled. 'On the other hand, we also had five losses, Schleicher and Schumann from my staffel, as well as Reins, Richey and Fock – all by the tail-gunners of Wellingtons. Very tough! A hot day – take-off, land, take-off, land – take off, with the enemy in view!' In fact, they had shot down ten British aircraft. He confessed that his own nerves were, by now, quite shot. It was hardly surprising after such a sustained period of continual front-line action. What's more, now that he was married he felt he had more to live for.

There were still Luftwaffe Condors flying over the Atlantic under control of the U-Boat Command, the Befehlshaber der U-Boote, or BdU, and there were further Luftwaffe aircraft working in conjunction with the Kriegsmarine in the Mediterranean. One of the pilots crossing this curious dividing line between Navy and Air Force was Hans-Hellmuth Kirchner. Formerly a sailor on the *Scharnhorst*, he had been chosen for his pilot training and had duly gained his wings and been deployed to Greece in early May. Although flying in support of the Kriegsmarine, he was now, none the less, part of the Luftwaffe: Göring had always insisted that any aircraft were his. Flying seaplanes as part of Aufklärungsfliegerstaffel 1/126 – aircraft reconnaissance squadron – he had supported naval and air operations during the battle for Crete in May and was now flying convoy escorts and anti-submarine patrols; British submarines operating from Alexandria and Malta were causing havoc. Since General Erwin Rommel's efforts in North Africa had to be supported entirely by trans-Mediterranean shipping, his was an important role.

Flying the Dutch-built Fokker T.VIII, one of only a handful ever built, and based at the port of Skaramagkas in Athens, he and his comrades would typically stop over in Crete, then continue to Libya. Crete was not an easy staging post, because Suda Bay was filled with wrecks while Maleme airfield was still strewn with a hundred and more broken aircraft from the bitter fighting there. 'The wrecks inhibited our take-off and landing quite a bit,' Kirchner noted, 'but they were removed, bit by bit.' Nor was it safe to wander about on the island – Cretan partisans had already made it treacherous even to try.

Admittedly, the numbers of Luftwaffe units on Sicily and in North Africa were now far fewer than they had been. One bomber pilot who had recently left the Mediterranean was Major Hajo Herrmann, who had seen as much action as almost anyone in the Luftwaffe since the start of the war: Poland, Norway, France, the Battle of Britain, the tiny British island of Malta in the Mediterranean, Yugoslavia, Greece. Back in April, Herrmann had flown a raid on Piraeus harbour and in hitting a British ammunition ship had almost single-handedly destroyed the port. Before the war, he had also flown in Spain with the German Condor Legion.

British bomber crews were expected to fly two tours – one of thirty ops and then, after a break, a further tour of twenty. Then they were never expected to fly operationally again. It had taken almost four times that number without any break at all before Herrmann was finally posted off ops altogether, to take up a staff post as an operations officer at IX. Fliegerkorps, first in Holland and then, by July, near Paris. And although he was no longer risking life and limb on a daily basis, he was still being worked extremely hard. By night he was expected to be in the Operations Room and keeping a watch on the weather, and by day he was dealing with any number of problems that needed solving. He had been on night duty when a teleprinter message arrived announcing the launch of BARBAROSSA. 'Our Russian campaign seemed to me to be a daring enterprise,' he wrote, 'but fully justified.'

Feldmarschall Erhard Milch, Göring's number two, would not have agreed with him, however. Not only had he been against the invasion of the Soviet Union, he had been utterly horrified by the prospect. When informed that Russia would be beaten before winter, Milch had replied, 'Whoever said that must be mad.' As if to prove the point, he wasted no time in insisting on ordering the manufacture of new woollen underwear, fur boots and sheepskins for a million Luftwaffe personnel. He was the only senior commander to do so.

Milch was very aware that the strength of the Luftwaffe by the summer and autumn of 1941 now flattered to deceive. Germany had begun the war with the finest air force in the world, and that had worked spectacularly well for the short, sharp wars for which it had been designed, and where they could dominate air space over the battleground and bludgeon their enemies who had inferior air forces. The Luftwaffe – and especially its strafing Messerschmitts and screaming Stukas – was the dominating symbol of these rapid conquests: in Norway, in France and the Low Countries and most certainly in the Balkans.

The Luftwaffe had been designed and built up with precisely these kinds of campaigns in mind and primarily to provide close air support for the ground forces. It was, in effect, a tactical air force, and this was one of the reasons why two of its key players, General Hans Jeschonnek, the Chief of Staff, and General Ernst Udet, the Chief of Procurement, had been such advocates of dive-bombing, which was far more suited to this role than it was to independent strategic bombing operations. Indeed, it was whenever the Luftwaffe had tried to play a strategic role that it had come rather unstuck. It was all very well destroying vast numbers of Soviet aircraft on the ground, as they had done, spectacularly well, in the opening days of the Russian campaign, but they had been unable to strike effectively at either Moscow or the Soviet aircraft industry. When Harry Hopkins had been in Moscow there had been an air raid, but it had been remarkably undramatic and the damage had been slight. Since Russia had very few anti-aircraft defences at this time, a golden opportunity to strike hard and without much impunity had gone begging.

Moreover, as Göring had pointed out, in terms of Britain's ability to continue waging the war, the Blitz would count for absolutely nothing if the Luftwaffe was unable to return to the offensive very soon. As it was, the bombing of London had achieved little in strategic terms, but a sustained attack on Britain's port facilities, especially along the west coast, might well have had a more obvious effect; at any rate, if properly executed, it could have delayed Britain's capacity to go on the offensive.

However, by the summer of 1941, the Luftwaffe was in crisis, which would have surprised many Greeks or Yugoslavs, or even Russians in the opening days of BARBAROSSA; but it was true, none the less. Production had not kept pace with demands. New aircraft projects were in meltdown. And it was not big enough to fight the kind of maximum-effort war that was being demanded of it on multiple fronts. The German way of war was about concentration of force, but the Luftwaffe was now split up and spread to the four winds, and that provided ever-more logistical headaches. Fuel, parts, tools, ammunition and other equipment, as well as men and machines, had to be sent to these far-flung places. The biggest fear for the German leadership had been fighting a war on two fronts – Hitler had even made this point in his own written mantra, *Mein Kampf* – but Germany was now fighting on three fronts: in the East, in the Mediterranean and North Africa, and in the Atlantic. And, unlike the Kriegsmarine and Army, the Luftwaffe was needed in all three.

President Roosevelt's announcement that the United States would produce 50,000 aircraft had shocked the Luftwaffe leadership. Not only was there no chance of them matching those levels any time soon, but their existing aircraft were not up to the job, as the Battle of Britain had proved. The Junkers 88, on which so much time, money, effort and hopes had been pinned, had ended up not much better than the pre-war twin-engine bombers. The Me110 had been hammered in air-to-air combat, and the Me109, brilliant though it was in many ways, was not a forgiving aircraft to fly – such were the torque and wing-loading, many new pilots struggled to master it. After being in action for so long, the Luftwaffe had, as was utterly inevitable, suffered terrible attritional casualties; the numbers of men like Macky Steinhoff and Siegfried Bethke who had managed to keep flying were rapidly decreasing. This meant more and more new pilots were entering service; for a significant number of these greenhorns, the Me109 proved lethal – which was, of course, a waste of both pilots and machines.

In fact, by the middle of 1941, most of the front-line aircraft were models that had been developed and entered service prior to 1936, when the brilliant Chief of Staff, General Walther Wever, had been killed and Ernst Udet had joined the Luftwaffe General Staff. An old friend of Göring's, Udet was a Great War fighter ace and a brilliant pilot; he was also a bon viveur, cartoonist and good-time boy. None of these characteristics qualified him to be head of Luftwaffe procurement, however, and in the cut-throat and Machiavellian world of Nazi politics Udet was massively out of his depth. Since he had taken over procurement, matters had gone badly awry, and the Ju88 and Heinkel 177 heavy bomber were just two casualties.

The problem was that developing new aircraft properly took time. There was the design and construction, then proper test-flying, the building of machine tools, and then full production. Under Udet, certain projects had snowballed – such as the Ju88 – which then meant other projects came under even greater pressure in terms of development time. Such was the urgency to get new aircraft flying and in production, he had allowed corners to be cut and the aircraft manufacturers to run rings around him. These were fatal mistakes.

A classic example of this was the Messerschmitt 210. This was supposed to be nothing more than an upgraded version of the Me110 'Zerstörer', but with a few aerodynamic tweaks and the adoption of the more powerful Daimler-Benz 603 engine. Udet had expected these changes to be made without interrupting the production of the Me110 but, without telling him, Professor Willi Messerschmitt had designed an entirely new aircraft. Göring had a large number of shares in Messerschmitt AG, and Professor Messerschmitt himself was both a good party man and personally liked by Hitler, which meant such arrogance was tolerated. None the less, because no one dared change the production schedule, the first batch of Me210s was delivered at the end of 1940 before proper trials had been completed. Production of further variants began, but because corners had been cut, its lethal tendency to spin at the slightest provocation had never been properly rectified.

The first thousand Me210s had been due in the spring of 1941, but only a handful had been delivered by then and these were proving death-traps. So much had been pinned on this one aircraft, but, like the four-engine Heinkel 177 bomber, it was simply not fit for purpose. The money wasted, the materials thrown down the drain and the loss of valuable production time were disastrous. It meant that the Luftwaffe in the middle of 1941 was, to all intents and purposes, the same Luftwaffe that had begun the war. The only real ray of hope was the new Focke-Wulf 190 fighter plane, but even that was having problems with its BMW engine.

Feldmarschall Milch, who was the ideal person to oversee procurement but who had been kept in the dark on such matters at Göring's behest, only discovered the extent of the rot in May, when the Reichsmarschall went on leave for a month. The bureaucracy of Udet's procurement office was also a complete mess. He had no fewer than twenty-six departmental heads reporting to him, most of whom appeared to be paying him scant regard, and a staff of more than 4,000. Udet could not say what any of them were doing. 'Never have I been so deceived, so bamboozled and so cheated as by that office,' Göring thundered when he learned the extent of the mismanagement. 'It has no equal in history.' Very possibly he was right.

On the eve of BARBAROSSA, Göring had none the less ordered a quadrupling of front-line aircraft and now gave Milch special orders to oversee this new programme over and above Udet. Milch immediately asked Albert Speer, Hitler's favourite architect, to build three new and huge aircraft factories. Bottlenecks were to be ironed out, more workers recruited, which meant the disbandment of three divisions already in the East, and money and resources poured in. This was all well and good, but would need, at the very least, more than nine months before such an overhaul could take effect. What's more, once it was clear that the campaign in the East would take longer than six weeks, the plan to disband divisions was hastily scrapped; the quadrupling Göring had ordered appeared to be dead in the water already.

There were also still some forty new aircraft in various stages of production, including eleven being made by Messerschmitt. When Milch visited the Messerschmitt factory in August, he was horrified to see so little activity on the Me109 production line. Instead, Professor Messerschmitt wanted to show him an airframe being designed for new jet engines. These, as Milch knew, were far from ready. He rightly concluded that Messerschmitt was only really interested in designing new aircraft and ordered him off the Me262 jet and back on to the Me109F. Messerschmitt ignored him.

And then there was the lack of transport aircraft. As the lines of supply in the East lengthened, the need for Ju52s rapidly grew. As they had shown during the Battle of Crete, these hardy transports could be used as an effective airborne conveyor belt, but the 250 lost over the island had not been replaced – there were just over 150 available for BARBAROSSA, which was nothing like enough to make a difference across a 1,500-mile front. The truth was, the fleet of Ju52s had never really recovered from the losses suffered back in May 1940.

The Luftwaffe wasn't growing in size, but standing still – new production was merely replacing losses. Just as soon as numbers were built up they were squandered again in sideshow campaigns in which the Luftwaffe had been expected to play a starring role.

The victory on Crete was now looking even more pyrrhic than ever. Unless something dramatic could be done to turn the situation around and in quick order, the Luftwaffe – the trailblazer of German military might – was already staring down the barrel of terminal decline.

At the beginning of June, the British President of the Board of Trade, Oliver Lyttelton, had been summoned to dine alone with the Prime Minister in his small flat in the War Cabinet Offices overlooking St James's. On arrival he was confronted by a small dinner table, a bottle of champagne, one servant, and the PM looking fresh and relaxed in his all-in-one zip-up boiler suit. Churchill wanted to talk to Lyttelton about the Middle East, where he felt Britain did not quite have the grip on the theatre that it should. The C-in-C there not only had a vast command but was political as well as military master. Egyptian ports were becoming congested, the supply situation, so essential to the chances of successful military operations, was in some disorder, and it was clear that not enough was being made of local resources. The strain on shipping – naval and merchant – was close to breaking point. Furthermore, numerous political conundrums kept throwing themselves up that needed a political figure rather than a general to sort them out.

The American businessman and diplomat Averell Harriman, who had been in Britain for some months as Roosevelt's latest special envoy, had made a visit to the Middle East and quickly identified these issues. Also in Egypt was Randolph Churchill, the Prime Minister's son, and Harriman suggested to him that his father send a Minister of State out there. When the PM read his son's telegram, he immediately agreed. In short, he explained to Lyttelton, he wanted him to be his Minister of State for the Middle East, with a place in the War Cabinet.

Lyttelton, who had been put up as a Tory MP in a safe-seat by-election and won the previous October, agreed to accept the role and the following day Churchill put it to the Cabinet, who endorsed the plan wholeheartedly. At the beginning of July, taking his wife and two close staff from the Board of Trade with him, Lyttelton was off, pausing en route in Malta to see how the island was holding up. Their party reached Cairo on 5 July and Lyttelton quickly got to work, meeting the three service chiefs, as well as the Ambassador, Sir Miles Lampson, and the Egyptian Prime Minister, Hussein Sirry Pasha. He also quickly established a Middle East War Council and, as a sub-committee of this, a special Middle East Defence Committee, the latter of which would include the three service chiefs and the Ambassador.

Lyttelton was one of the modern breed of technocrats and cronies with whom Churchill had quite intentionally surrounded himself. A man of enormous good sense, business acumen, military experience and geo-economic understanding, he was a very sensible choice for this new Cabinet post, and someone who would do much to ease the burdens awaiting General Claude Auchinleck, the recently appointed C-in-C Middle East.

One of the biggest challenges was securing a peaceful calm throughout Syria, Palestine, Iraq and Iran. The war in Syria had only just ended; the Vichy French had sued for peace, a victory that the British had won with no small amount of help from the Free French. Now, placating the Free French there and assuring them Britain had no territorial intentions in Syria was one potential headache. The Spears Mission there, headed by the Francophile General Sir Edward Spears, was advising Général Georges Catroux, the new High Commissioner, and ensuring that the details of the armistice in Syria were carried out. Fortunately for the British, Spears and Lyttelton got on extremely well and formed a close and effective working relationship from the outset.

This, however, was more than could be said for Spears's relationship with Général Charles de Gaulle. Any satisfaction the leader of the Free French may have had about the defeat of Vichy in the Levant had been superseded by his suspicions about the intentions of the British, who, as far as he was concerned, were undermining his authority at every turn. Top of his grievances had been being kept out of the armistice negotiations, but the British were still treading warily as far as de Gaulle's position was concerned. Spears was convinced that de Gaulle trusted no one, which was probably true, but it was equally the case that the British did not trust de Gaulle and were reluctant to give too much authority to a man they knew did not yet have the majority support of those Frenchmen who opposed Vichy and Nazi rule. His over-sensitivity, Spears reckoned, 'amounted to the prickliness of a man with an itch.' When de Gaulle had demanded that Air Marshal Arthur Tedder, Air Officer Commanding Middle East Air Forces, transfer all French airmen in the RAF over to the Free French, Tedder had refused. He would not stop them transferring if they wanted to, he told de Gaulle, but he would not force them to do so. 'These Frenchmen are British officers,' Tedder told him. 'De Gaulle was furious,' noted Spears, who had accompanied the Free French leader, 'and I soon detected signs of his uncontrollable rage coming to the boil. His colour became that of a molehill.'

This was just one of many disagreements that erupted on an almost daily basis. For de Gaulle, however, any over-sensitivity was being provoked by mounting frustration at what he viewed as constant British interference. 'This persistent claim to meddle in our affairs,' he noted, 'and the incessant multiplying encroachments, were now reaching the limit of what we could tolerate.'

What de Gaulle was not recognizing, however, was that it was the British who were almost entirely responsible for the military defence of Syria and Lebanon as well as the wider Middle East. Furthermore, the Free French simply did not have the personnel to deal with the responsibilities they had now taken on in Syria. To get around the shortfall in personnel, Catroux had begun inviting former Vichy officials to join them in the Levant. This Spears understandably insisted was unacceptable and demanded they should be sent back again. Another storm looked set to blow, but by a combination of diplomacy and coercion on the part of both Spears and Lyttelton, and dignified acquiescence from Catroux, the Vichy officials were dismissed.

Before the fall of France, Britain and France had made largely ineffective allies. Dealings between de Gaulle's Free French and the British were proving every bit as fraught. Yet at least the Levant was now secure. So too was Iraq. Only Iran was causing concern. There had been a number of German nationals there, many of whom were working in Government services, but which the Tehran Government refused to expel. This made it a hot-bed for espionage and potential incitement against Allied interests in the region, and particularly threatened the crucial supply line from the Persian Gulf to the Caspian Sea, through which Britain hoped to send aid to the Russians.

A joint Anglo-Russian demand was sent to the Persian Government on 17 August, which was rejected. Iran actually now came under General Sir Archibald Wavell's remit as C-in-C India and so, with co-operation from Moscow, a joint Anglo-Russian invasion was launched on 25 August. It was entirely successful. By the end of the month the Persian Gulf was secured and by mid-September Tehran was occupied. Just a few months earlier, such an enterprise would have been utterly unthinkable. Now Britain and Russia were forming themselves into the bedfellows they could have been back in 1939 had Britain played a cannier diplomatic hand.

With East Africa and the Middle East secure and free from Axis forces, the British could now turn back to North Africa and, in particular, kicking General Rommel and his mixed German–Italian forces out of Cyrenaica, the eastern part of the Libyan coastline. Once again, Churchill, back in London, was chomping at the bit and itching to get his forces into action.

It was in dealing with the Prime Minister that Lyttelton could offer the new C-in-C the kind of help that Wavell had never enjoyed when he had been the top man in the Middle East. Recognizing that Auchinleck's tone was rather too brusque for Churchill's taste, Lyttelton asked to see all telegrams before they were sent to London. 'Auchinleck was not familiar with the workings of Whitehall,' he noted, 'nor had he any knowledge of the appropriate presentation of an argument to Mr Churchill.' Lyttelton was able to rework these messages in a way more likely to placate the PM.

Auchinleck was determined to build up the strength of his forces sufficiently before striking west – there could be no more half-cock attacks such as BATTLEAXE back in June, when the renewed British offensive in North Africa had so badly stalled. In September, his forces were entirely reorganized. In Iraq, Tenth Army was formed, and Ninth Army in Palestine. In Egypt, the Western Desert Force became Eighth Army, so numbered because the French had fielded seven armies while the British had just had the BEF. Eighth Army, it was felt, avoided any possible confusion. Its first commander was Lieutenant-General Alan Cunningham, victor of East Africa and brother of Admiral Sir Andrew Browne Cunningham, the commander of the British Mediterranean Fleet.

More men and more equipment had been flowing into Egypt. Between July and October, no fewer than 300 British cruiser tanks, 300 new US-built 'Stuart' light tanks, 170 infantry tanks, 34,000 lorries, 600 field guns, 80 heavy and 160 light anti-aircraft guns, 200 anti-tank guns and 900 mortars had safely reached Suez.

This was good news for Auchinleck and the newly formed Eighth Army and it was also good for the Nottinghamshire Sherwood Rangers Yeomanry, who had originally been posted to Palestine back in 1939 with their chargers, then humiliatingly told to send them home and ordered to retrain as artillery. Since then, they had been split up, with one part of the regiment sent to Crete and the other to Tobruk, which had then been besieged. Having been recently extricated safely from

Tobruk – and partially from Crete – they were now back in Palestine training to become mechanized at long last. Captain Stanley Christopherson had learned the news on leave in Cairo, when he had met the regiment's CO, Colonel Edward 'Flash' Kellett. Apparently they were going to be formed into a new armoured brigade along with the Staffordshire Yeomanry and equipped with mostly new American tanks. 'The colonel told me all this when I met him on the steps of the Continental,' scribbled Christopherson. 'He is most thrilled at the idea of becoming a tank regiment.'

Christopherson was also delighted to learn a couple of weeks later that he had been promoted to major and given command of A Squadron, although in between the new intense training at Karkur there was still time for partying and even cricket matches. None the less, the old pre-war part-time county regiment was slowly but surely shedding its skin. Christopherson was charming and easy-going but determined and ambitious too, both personally and for the regiment. Nor was he alone. Most of his colleagues were every bit as determined to learn the new ways of war. They had joined the regiment on horseback, had learned the rudiments of artillery and now faced the challenge of switching to tanks. They were part of a new British Army that was slowly adjusting to a very different kind of war from the one they had anticipated a couple of years earlier, and while there were still a number of pre-war Regulars at its core, most were, by mid-1941, already new soldiers – volunteers or conscripts who were wearing uniform because of the war and for no other reason.

In some ways, this was no bad thing. Those not reared in a military tradition were less likely to be constrained by those traditions. The British Army had received an influx of intelligent, worldly-wise and well-educated officers – men such as Stanley Christopherson – who were well placed to think open-mindedly. Britain's Empire and global reach was undoubtedly a huge advantage, because it meant there were large numbers of people who had travelled, had been colonial administrators, had done business overseas, and who had seen other cultures beyond the British and European norm. It had been British teams, for example, who had dominated desert exploration in the 1930s. Men like Ralph Bagnold, originally an officer in the Royal Engineers, had pioneered desert navigation, using motor vehicles for the first time to explore and map reaches of the Western Desert and Sahara previously thought impassable. It was Bagnold who had developed a sun compass and who had worked out that by reducing tyre pressure it became easier to drive over loose sand. Another was Bill Kennedy Shaw, a colonial administrator in Sudan, but also a skilled botanist, archaeologist and navigator who had accompanied Bagnold on several desert explorations.

These two, along with Pat Clayton, another pre-war explorer, had quickly offered their services once the desert war began, forming what became known as the Long Range Desert Group (LRDG). Driving far to the south, they made huge sweeps behind enemy lines, where they gathered intelligence and carried out occasional sabotage raids, all of which was very useful. Neither the Italians nor Germans had any such organization.

Now, in the late summer of 1941, a new unorthodox force was emerging, known as 'L Detachment, the Special Air Service Brigade' – soon to be known more simply as the SAS. The core of this new force were Guardsmen who had been detached from their regiments to join a Commando unit called 'Layforce', named after its commander, Colonel Bob Laycock. Layforce – or 8 Commando as it was also known – had been sent to Crete late in the day and had barely arrived before they were retreating south across the mountains. Back in the Middle East, underused and losing their sense of purpose, in July they had been disbanded.

One of Layforce's subalterns was Lieutenant David Stirling, formerly of the Scots Guards, a man known for his charm and slothfulness but not much else. None the less, with the end of Layforce he became curiously energized and convinced that Laycock's Commandos had failed because of their essential immobility. Learning that Jock Lewes, another 8 Commando member, had purloined a batch of parachutes mistakenly sent to Egypt, Stirling asked if he could join him in using them for an experimental jump. Using an ageing Vickers Valencia that was completely unsuitable for parachute drops, Lewes, Stirling and six others duly jumped out. They were lucky all to survive; Stirling was the only one to suffer injury, damaging his back in the process.

Whilst recovering, he drew up a memorandum for the Deputy Chief of the General Staff in Cairo, Major-General Neil Ritchie, outlining his ideas for a small specialist raiding force. The vastness of the desert could be an advantage, he explained, and landing grounds, especially, were very hard to defend efficiently. If they could get close enough, a handful of raiders could cause untold damage and mayhem. Bluffing his way into GHQ in Cairo, he managed to gain an audience with Ritchie and, much to his surprise, three days later he was called back to meet Auchinleck himself. The Auk – as he was widely known – thought Stirling's ideas were worth a punt. Promoted to captain, Stirling was told to raise six officers and sixty men. The name of this force – L Detachment, Special Air Service Brigade – was to be an intelligence bluff to suggest to the Axis the British had an entire brigade of airborne forces in theatre.

Among those who put his name forward was Johnny Cooper, a private in the 2nd Scots Guards who had been returned to his battalion following the disbandment of 8 Commando. Cooper was tall, dark-haired, with film-star good looks but, at only just nineteen, also still very young. Brought up in Bradford, Yorkshire, in the north of England to parents of Scottish birth, he had gone to grammar school but, having spent little effort on his lessons, had dismally failed his matriculation and been sent as an apprentice to Vickers and Wheelers instead. While schoolbooks may not have been to his taste, travel and adventure most certainly were and in 1939, having saved up, he had gone to Chamonix in the Alps to learn to ski and climb mountains.

Cooper had been on his way back when war was declared and, although he made it safely back to Bradford, he lost interest in his apprenticeship. When a fellow lodger suggested he was going to join the Scots Guards, Cooper decided he would do the same – after all, both his parents were Scots. On 2 April 1940, still two and a half months short of his eighteenth birthday, and without telling his parents what he was planning, he reported to the recruiting officer and was duly given a rail pass to Caterham in Surrey for enlistment.

Despite his obvious youthfulness, he was signed on, although the recruiting officer urged him to tell his parents. Cooper promised he would and so later rang his father and broke the news. There was a pause and then his father said, 'Be it on your own head, but look after yourself.' He quickly proved himself and even won his company's shooting medal. Army life suited him and when he saw a notice looking for volunteers for the Commandos he applied and was accepted for that too, and so had been part of Layforce when it was sent to the Middle East.

Most of his troop in 2nd Battalion Scots Guards had been part of Laycock's Commandos, and when Stirling arrived at their desert camp looking for volunteers for his new L Detachment, SAS, Cooper and most of 3 Troop immediately put up their hands. Swiftly accepted, he and the other recruits were posted to Kabrit in the Canal Zone for training – a desolate spot 90 miles east of Cairo on the edge of the Great Bitter Lake.

There was nothing there when they arrived apart from two lone marquees. Their first-ever raid was on the nearby New Zealand Division camp, which they pillaged by night for tents and other supplies. With their rudimentary equipment, training began under the control of Jock Lewes. They were, he told them, to learn to become entirely independent and to be able to operate either singly or in very small groups. They would have to develop self-confidence, acquire navigation skills, learn to survive on minimal rations and supplies, and to use their initiative. Night work was to be the most essential part of their training. They were also to learn the use of all small arms – German and Italian ones as well as their own.

And there was parachute training, something still new to the British Army. It was dangerous too, and on their first drop two men were killed when their 'chutes failed to open properly. Cooper had been terrified before he jumped, but once out and drifting downwards, with an incredible view all around him, his fear left him. 'Descending into a patch of soft drifting sand,' he noted, 'I felt a sense of stupendous elation as I wrapped up my parachute and trotted over to the waiting transport.'

L Detachment continued their training, along with the rest of the newly formed Eighth Army. Churchill might have been impatient for action, but this growing force needed to be ready for battle and that, Auchinleck recognized, meant ensuring his forces not only had the right equipment but knew how to use it too. As the Italians had shown, numbers counted for nothing if the training was poor.

A little over a year on from the BEF's humiliating defeat in France, the British Army was gradually rising again. The learning curve ahead of its men was enormous and, from such a tiny force just a year earlier, there was a limit to what could be expected in such a short time. But it was getting bigger and stronger. Soon Eighth Army would be put to the test. Great expectations rested on the coming attack on Rommel's Axis forces – an offensive Auchinleck had codenamed CRUSADER.

CHAPTER 4

The US Navy Goes to War

A T THE BEGINNING of September, Admiral Dönitz, the commander of the BdU, adopted a new system of moving concentrations of U-boats in the Atlantic. Frustrated by the dramatic fall in Allied shipping losses and problems of interception, he hoped that instead of fixing U-boats to one particular zone, they would have more success by drifting back and forth across the Atlantic.

His ploy seemed to work immediately, as a convoy, SC42, was swiftly picked up on 9 September and was soon under attack by a dozen U-boats. Although protected by five corvettes and a destroyer, these Canadian ships were lacking the latest anti-submarine warfare (ASW) equipment and were manned by crews still largely new to such operations. Fifteen ships were lost over two days but, all things considered, the Canadian escort group did better than might have been imagined against so many U-boats. Even so, SC42 was the hardest-hit convoy of this period in the Battle of the Atlantic.

The losses were still nothing like enough to disrupt Britain's war machine, however. Dönitz had reckoned initially that he needed to sink at least 500,000 tons a month to bring Britain to her knees, but the combination of U-boats and the Luftwaffe had achieved nowhere near that amount; in any case, that figure had been based on Britain's pre-war lack of self-sufficiency regarding food. Just forty-three ships had been sunk in July, forty-one in August, and eighty-three would perish in September. On Commander Donald Macintyre's watch with the 5th Escort Group, they had lost a mere handful of ships that summer. He noticed their attackers tended to withdraw if they came across a convoy that was well escorted.

In fact, Allied protection of shipping had improved greatly in all areas, not least in the much-enhanced aerial watch. German naval signals, transmitted by Enigma machines, were now being regularly decrypted by the code-breakers at the Government Code and Cypher School at Bletchley Park. The decoded signals – Ultra – ensured that RAF Coastal Command had a narrower area in which to search. There were now more than 200 aircraft dedicated to carrying out anti-submarine patrols from bases in the west of Britain and Iceland. None the less, even with Ultra, the Atlantic was vast and it was soul-destroying work for the crews, flying for endless miles across vast open tracts of grey ocean. Their Herculean efforts, however, ensured U-boats spent more time submerged and were forced to steer away from approaching convoys. U-boats were rarely spotted, but by keeping their watch over the Western Approaches and south from Iceland, Coastal Command made sure that by the autumn of 1941 no U-boat could hope to operate within their range. Turning large tracts of the ocean into U-boat no-go zones, especially parts that were easier to reach, was very helpful indeed to Allied trans-Atlantic shipping.

The addition of the Royal Canadian Navy and their Newfoundland Escort Force, which had been operating since May, had made a huge difference, but now, in September, the US Navy's Atlantic Fleet was also playing its part. In a change from the original ABC-1 agreement drawn up back in March by Britain and the US, it had been decided in June and then in August more formally agreed at Argentia, in Newfoundland, that the Americans would escort convoys across the Western Atlantic only as far as the Mid-Ocean Meeting Point (MOMP) that had been earlier agreed by the British and the Canadians. Indeed, the arrangement with the Canadian Navy had only ever been considered a stop-gap until the Americans entered the fray. Now that they had, the Canadians no longer came under Western Approaches Command but instead were answerable to the Americans and to Rear-Admiral Mark L. Bristol, commanding what was now called US Navy Task Force 4. Because, strictly speaking, the US was still neutral, Bristol would issue requests rather than orders, to which the Canadians would obligingly agree. Furthermore, they were still expected to play a full escort role, for while the Americans, with their quicker destroyers, would escort the faster convoys, the Canadians, equipped mostly with corvettes, agreed to escort the slower SC convoys.

Among those now joining Task Force 4 was one of the most famous movie stars in America, Douglas Fairbanks, Jr, who was as close to Hollywood royalty as it was possible to be. Impossibly dashing, with a fabulous white-toothed grin, pencil-thin moustache and a whole bucket-load of charm, he was known worldwide, as his father had been before him, for his swashbuckling adventure films. Now, however, he was going to be swashbuckling not on a make-believe pirate ship, but on a very real US Navy destroyer.

Fairbanks had been an interventionist from the outbreak of war. He'd heard the news on board a yacht he and his wife, Mary Lee, had chartered from Catalina Island, off the coast of California. With them were their friends David Niven, Laurence Olivier and Vivien Leigh. Hearing Chamberlain's voice announcing that Britain was at war had stunned them and, in their despondency, they had started to drink until Larry Olivier became so tight he clambered down into a dinghy and began rowing around the other moored yachts, shouting, 'You're all finished! Done! Drink up! You've had it! This is the end!'

After more sober reflection, Fairbanks, for one, decided to do what he could. Invited to become Chairman of White Committee's Southern California branch, an interventionist pressure group, he readily accepted the offer. He also got to know the President and spent a number of nights at the White House. A key message FDR passed on to Fairbanks was the need for the media and groups like the White Committee to put him, as President, under more and more pressure to support Britain. On one occasion in the White House, FDR told Fairbanks and others gathered there, 'Now go out and get the public to push me!'

Fairbanks had thought of joining the Navy before the war – he had always loved the sea – but it wasn't until April 1941 that he was commissioned as a lieutenant in the US Naval Reserve by Frank Knox, the Secretary of the Navy. His first task was to head to South America, outwardly to investigate the effect of American movies on Latin American public opinion, but in reality to get in touch with influential national groups veering towards Nazi ideology and to gauge their impact. Two and a half months later, after a successful trip, he returned to film a new movie for MGM, and then was finally called up for active duty.

He left for his first training post on a launch from Boston's Navy Yard.

His wife and small daughter had come to wave him off and it was then that he began to realize his embryonic naval career was for real. Clambering from the launch on to the ship, he glanced back and saw Mary Lee still waving. 'I damn near blubbered,' he wrote. 'What the *hell* had I got myself into?'

Meanwhile, in the east, German forces continued to win gargantuan victories. Hitler's decision to halt the drive to Moscow and reinforce the thrust into the Ukraine had led to the encirclement of four complete Soviet armies around Kiev, with the capture of 665,000 prisoners. Leading the change of direction had been General Heinz Guderian, who had turned south-east with the northern thrust of the encirclement while his old 1940 superior, von Kleist, had led the drive to the south.

This focus towards the south-east and away from Moscow had been the Führer's idea and his continued interference was very much true to form. Hitler tended to leave his senior commanders alone unless there was the slightest variation to the agreed plan, at which point he would fret, rant and begin micro-managing. Since the Soviet Union had not crumbled in six weeks and was turning into a modern-day hydra, the world's greatest military genius felt it was time to wade in and show von Brauchitsch, Halder et al. how to conduct a campaign properly.

It was certainly true that around Kiev there had been a major concentration of Soviet forces and that the subsequent victory there was a stunning one. None the less, for Halder it represented ongoing mission creep. 'Do we want to beat the enemy or go after economic objectives?' he had asked Jodl in a rare meeting alone with the OKW Chief of Staff.

'The Führer thinks we can do both at the same time,' Jodl had replied.

Halder disagreed. Moscow, he was convinced, was the key. Take Moscow, force Stalin and his Government to flee, and the rest would more than likely crumble. Neither Army Groups North or South needed any reinforcement – they had enough to hold their own. The focus of effort, in the centre, needed to be in the strike towards Moscow. Hitler, however, dismissed this strategy.

As it happened, this might well have been wishful thinking on Halder's part. After Stalin's brief crisis of indecision at the launch of the German invasion, he had acted with both swiftness and clear-headed pragmatism. On 24 June, he had ordered the establishment of a Soviet – or Council – for Evacuation. The vast bulk of the USSR's industry was to be moved, lock, stock and barrel, to the Urals, out of harm's way and more than 600 miles east of Moscow. Already by August 1941 this process was well under way. And not only was industry being evacuated. Soviet state archives had also been sent east to the Urals town of Ufa. In other words, Stalin recognized there was a good chance that Moscow might be captured, but he still had no intention of throwing in the towel. If there were still plenty of men and materiel, and the machinery of government was in place, the capture of the Soviet capital would not be the complete decapitation Halder hoped.

On 18 August, General Warlimont's Section L produced an appreciation of the situation for Jodl to pass on to Hitler, which once more outlined every argument for continuing the all-out drive on Moscow. The OKH staff produced a similar aide-memoire for the Führer, pressing the same. On 23 August, a meeting was held at the Wolf's Lair at Rastenburg. General Guderian was the only representative of the Army pushing for Moscow, but his arguments were unsuccessful as the phalanx of senior Nazis and Hitler's staff all fell in line with their Führer.

Stunning though the subsequent victory at Kiev was, it remained, as far as Warlimont was concerned, 'a tactical victory only', and in this he was surely right. Because of the huge numbers of men involved, there has been a tendency to lay more strategic importance on the various battles and envelopments of the war in the East than should be the case. Scale, however, does not necessarily equate to strategic importance, as Warlimont recognized. Nor did the Kiev victory alter the fundamental problems facing the Germans: that the Soviet Union was too vast for the Wehrmacht's operational system to cope with and that Red Army reserves were too inexhaustible.

With the Kiev victory, however, Hitler did finally agree to turn the focus back on the drive to Moscow. Three armies and three panzer groups, including Guderian's newly created 2. Panzerarmee, would strike towards the capital. This involved another massive redeployment of forces, which took time, not least because of the ongoing logistical difficulties. Operation TYPHOON, the drive to Moscow, was not ready to launch until 30 September. And by that time, it had begun to rain.

To begin with, this latest assault was once again stunningly successful. A further six Russian armies were captured in two surrounded pockets, yielding an incredible further 750,000 prisoners. However, with the lack of metalled roads, the incessant rain meant increasing amounts of mud.

Mud made rapid advance impossible. Russian autumn rain was also a well-known harbinger of Russian winter snow and dramatically falling temperatures. Despite the enormous successes and a staggering 2 million prisoners since June, the campaign had already been going on for three and a half months. Vehicles were breaking down, tanks were halted due to lack of fuel, while many front-line units were down to half strength. General Adolf von Schell, for one, was frantically trying to keep up with demand, but starting to fail badly. 'The problems began to increase suddenly from October 1941,' he said later. 'Motor vehicles could not cope with that kind of permanent strain.' At the same time, Oberst Hermann Balck was still desperately trying to conserve vehicles; it was a situation that was rapidly getting out of hand. Replacements of anything, whether men or machines or spare parts, were not to be found readily in the numbers needed.

Furthermore, Stalin had placed one of his very best and most experienced commanders, General Georgi Zhukov, in charge of the defence of Moscow and given him a newly created Army Group, the West Front. More and more men and equipment poured in. With every day that passed in which Army Group Centre battled through the mud, so Moscow's defences were strengthened. For the Germans, it had become a race against time – and one that was slipping through their grasp.

While the battle for Moscow raged, to the north German troops were still driving on Leningrad. By 8 September they were within 10 miles of the city and were confident that here, at any rate, they would soon have it in their hands, not least because they had crossed a small stretch of the River Neva to the south-east and reached the shores of Lake Ladoga. Meanwhile, further north still, Finnish troops were pressing south and had captured two-thirds of the lake's shores.

This meant that Leningrad, which stood on a 30-mile-wide isthmus between the Baltic and Lake Ladoga, was now almost surrounded. The only access point lay across the southern part of the lake via the railheads of Volkhov and Tikhvin and the roads that connected both towns. Capturing the Soviet Union's second city remained very high on Hitler's agenda, but taking it would also throw up a number of problems, as the Germans now realized. In Führer Directive No. 35 on 6 September the Führer had raised the issue of what should be done with the inhabitants should the city fall, and by 21 September the OKW had produced a number of options. '1. Occupy the city,' they listed, 'which was to be rejected, as the Wehrmacht would then be responsible for feeding the population.' Another solution was to ring the entire city with an electric fence guarded with machine-gunners. This too posed problems, though, because the weak would starve and there would be a danger of epidemics, which might spread to German troops. Another proposal was to allow free passage out for all women, children and elderly, but this was considered not feasible and might also cause epidemics. A fourth option was to withdraw and leave Leningrad to the Finns.

In the end, the OKW recommended that they announce to the world that Leningrad was being defended as a fortress and that, as a result, both the city and its inhabitants would be treated as military targets. 'Nevertheless,' continued the memo, 'Roosevelt should be permitted, with an assurance of safe conduct, to supply the inhabitants or remove them to his part of the world after a capitulation of the city. Such an offer could not, of course, be accepted and should be treated only as propaganda.'

The plan that was accepted was this: pound Leningrad to dust with artillery and bombing, then, once the city had been worn down by hunger and terror, they would let the defenceless out and deport them to the interior of Russia – the risk of epidemics would have to be taken on the chin – and then the Russian troops still inside would be left to fend for themselves through the winter. Come spring, German troops would then break in and capture the remains. They would then 'level Leningrad with demolition charges' and hand over the area of the River Neva to the Finns. Leningrad, one of the most beautiful and culturally rich cities on the planet, would be erased from the earth.

At the end of August, General Warlimont's staff produced an 'OKW memorandum approved by the Führer' on the strategic situation for Germany. In a nutshell, it accepted that the collapse of Russia might take a little bit longer than anticipated and that the East should remain the main focus before turning to the final objective. 'Our goal, as before,' noted Halder on receiving the memorandum, 'is to defeat and force Britain to sue for peace.' Siege and invasion were the means of achieving this, although mastery of the skies was accepted as still being a prerequisite. Also required was the mass production of 'first-class' landing craft, the creation of a powerful parachute and airborne force, and 'large-scale employment of all weapons that have so far been successful in sea warfare to eliminate effective British naval action against our transport fleet.' Presumably this meant U-boats and fast torpedo boats, but this was typically woolly, vague and, frankly, pie-in-the-sky stuff, as though writing it down meant it would magically happen. It would not.

The memo also accepted that 'siege warfare' now required the sinking of a million tons of British shipping a month. So far, they had sunk more than half that figure just three times and only once had they exceeded 600,000 tons per month. The Kriegsmarine was demanding far more air reconnaissance units and new aerial mines and torpedoes, more sustained attacks on British ports, as well as more U-boats. 'These plans cannot be fully realized in 1942,' the memo accepted. What it did not mention was that by that time Britain's defences would be even stronger and that even a million tons of shipping a month would not be enough. How Germany was going to find all these extra resources at a time when the Eastern Front was already absorbing far more men and materiel than they had expected was also not touched on.

The Mediterranean, unsurprisingly, was also seen as a crucial part of future strategy, although again it was accepted that little could be achieved there until the spring of 1942 at the earliest. Great hopes rested on attempts to bring Turkey into the war on the Axis side. Perhaps most tellingly, however, the memo claimed that, 'Of equal importance with the battle of the Mediterranean is the battle of the Atlantic. Russia's defeat is the prerequisite of victory in either.' This was an astonishing strategic misjudgement, as the Mediterranean theatre was nothing like as important as the Atlantic. Once again, German continentalism was clouding their view of the war and how best to defeat Britain.

Just two years earlier, Hitler had made his decision to invade Poland. A little under a year later, it had seemed as though the war was all but won and that Europe lay at his all-conquering feet. Now, just fifteen months afterwards, the German war machine was starting to unravel at an alarming rate.

In the autumn of 1941, victory in the Atlantic must have seemed even more of a far-off pipe-dream than ever to Admiral Dönitz. With the Americans and Canadians now covering much of the North Atlantic, the Royal Navy was partly freed up to send greater protection to the Gibraltar and West Africa routes. In September, a convoy, OG74, of some twenty-seven ships heading to Gibraltar was escorted by four corvettes, a sloop and one of the new escort carriers. This last was one of the most extraordinary-looking warships ever built, as, ironically enough, it was a former German banana boat that had been captured intact and converted into a carrier with a short 467-feet-long deck built on top. This made it look like a ship that had had its top sliced off. The bridge was stuck on the side, level with the flight deck; the aircraft, all six of them, had to remain on deck, shackled, and it was here that servicing and maintenance work had to be carried out, which might well prove easier said than done on the rolling Atlantic swell. Originally called *Hanover*, the ship then became *Sinbad* under a British flag, before being converted and renamed *Empire Audacity*.

Audacious it most certainly was, and when the CO of 802 Fleet Air Arm Squadron had briefed his pilots and told him they were to be the first pilots aboard this new kind of small escort carrier, they were dumbfounded.

One of those listening to this briefing was Lieutenant Eric Brown. Since escaping from Nazi Germany with his MG Magnette in the opening days of the war, Brown had made his way successfully back to Britain and, as a still-current member of the Edinburgh University Air Squadron, had been called up into the RAF and then duly posted to Drem in East Lothian. Soon after, however, a notice had gone up asking for volunteers for the Fleet Air Arm. 'I felt there was no action happening where I was,' he said, 'and I was keen to get back at the Germans – I was a bit piqued about having been locked up for a few days.' He was accepted and made the move across in December 1939. With over 100 hours' flying in his logbook, he'd been expecting to be thrown straight into action, but instead was sent off for more training in Northern Ireland. However frustrated he may have felt, it was no bad thing; by the time he was posted to 802 Squadron, he had well over 200 hours' flying to his name, a fair amount more than most newly trained pilots.

Now about to join *Empire Audacity*, Brown and his fellow pilots were told the ship would be carrying six US-built Grumman Wildcats, known as 'Martlets' in the Royal Navy. Four hundred feet was not very much for take-off – just over 100 metres – but more daunting would be landing again, for which the deck was equipped with two arrester wires. If they missed both of those, then there was a barrier and a further, third, wire. The CO called this the 'For-Christ's-Sake' wire; if they hit that, he told them, they would most likely break the aircraft. 'We sat speechless and aghast,' noted Brown. Before formally joining the ship, each of the pilots was to be given six deck landings and, assuming all went well, they would then join the ship and set sail.

Empire Audacity was steaming up and down south of Arran off the west of Scotland as Brown and his fellow pilots began their practice landings. They soon found her and, circling overhead at the very low height of just 300 feet, Brown couldn't help thinking how very small she looked. He had taken off with his flight commander, 'Sheepy' Lamb, and watched his friend safely land then take off again without difficulty.

This at least gave Brown some confidence as he now readied himself for his own turn. Rather than make a couple of circuits round the ship first, he decided to fly straight in. Filled with the calm of intense concentration, his earlier apprehension had gone. Throttling back, he came in at just 70 knots towards the looming deck, watching the batsman – the deck-landing control officer – and cut the throttle. The key, he had been told, was to land with the aircraft almost at a stall, which meant the pilot had very small margins within which to operate.

Fortunately, Brown had judged it near-perfectly. There was a bump and then he stopped – he had managed to catch the first arrester wire. Elation surged through him. In a trice, his Martlet was being man-handled back into position to take off. With the throttle open wide against the brakes, the signal flag fell, then off with the brakes and he was surging down the deck. He was airborne without losing an inch in height. 'After that,' he noted, 'it was easy.' He went through the rest of his practice deck landings concentrating on perfecting the procedure. There was, he recognized, an artistry to it that was very rewarding.

By the time they set sail on convoy OG74, *Empire Audacity* had been renamed yet again and become, more simply, HMS *Audacity*. It was quite a first trip. Brown and Sheepy Lamb were airborne when they first spotted a U-boat, *U-124*. They quickly swung around and dived on her, firing their .50-calibre machine guns, but although they could still see her as she submerged, their bullets made no impact on the boat's pressure hull. At least, though, the attack had forced her to dive.

Five nights later, on 20 September, Brown spotted a U-boat again, which encouraged the entire convoy to make several zig-zags. None the less, as darkness fell, the U-boats struck; Brown saw a huge flash of flame one moment and then a further eruption away to the left. Two ships were sunk. The following morning, the two rescue ships were still looking for survivors when they were attacked by Focke-Wulf Condors. Two Martlets were sent off to intercept but too late to save a third ship, *Walmer Castle*, which was hit and began to burn. Meanwhile, the Martlets caught up with one of the Condors and managed to shoot it down, blasting its tail section clean off. 'The only thing picked up from her,' noted Brown, 'was a pair of flying overalls.'

They eventually reached Gibraltar, but not before a Ju88, at the edge of its range, had bombed and sunk a further ship, and the U-boats had torpedoed three more. Five days after reaching Gibraltar, they turned around for convoy HG74, escorting no fewer than seventy ships back to Britain. After the losses suffered on OG74, the U-boats had all had to return to base to rearm; such were the ongoing problems with contact pistols – the mechanism that triggered the torpedoes' explosive charge – that U-boats were still firing twice as many torpedoes as they should have done. For the defenders, this meant the return leg was free of enemy sinkings.

Even so, the Martlet pilots were still frequently scrambled and it was on one such sortie, as Eric Brown was attacking a Condor, that his side window shattered and he felt a searing pain in his mouth as he was peppered by Perspex splinters. Heading back to *Audacity*, he was struggling to keep his wits about him and, to make matters worse, there was now a rough swell and the ship was heaving badly. Somehow he managed to touch down, but it was a treacherous landing – he missed the first and second arrester wires but caught the For-Christ's-Sake wire. As the Martlet came to a forceful halt, Brown was hurled forward and smashed his head on the gunsight, knocking himself out cold. Although he recovered soon enough, there was no more flying for him on that trip. On 17 October, they reached the River Clyde, *Audacity*'s first outward and homeward bound convoys completed.

Although the 'Führer-approved' OKW appreciation at the end of August had accepted that the Luftwaffe would need supporting in any renewed siege of Britain, there was no question they would have a tougher task than the one facing them in the summer of 1940 as Britain's home fighter strength continued to grow.

The RAF's night-fighters had increased in number and sophistication, with improved measures against German navigational beams, better onboard air interception radar, or 'AI', and much-improved armoury. Certainly, by early summer the difficulties of using AI, and cannons that repeatedly jammed the moment they were fired, had been largely resolved. AI was proving less effective at heights of under 5,000 feet, which made it harder to catch small numbers of enemy raiders swooping in to plant mines, for example, but new techniques were practised in which the British night-fighters would stay above their target until contact had been made. Guy Gibson, still with 29 Squadron and now a Squadron Leader, had shot down a Heinkel on 6 July in just such a way as it had attempted to lay mines in the Thames estuary. A two-second burst with his cannons had seen it explode and plunge into the sea, killing all on board. What a difference effective cannons might have made to Fighter Command the previous summer.

But no sooner had these techniques and technicalities been largely mastered than the Luftwaffe's night offensive had tailed off, which meant Gibson was now having a very good time socially down at West Malling in Kent, but seeing little action. The same, however, could not be said for the day-fighters, for with the launch of the German attack in the East, so Fighter Command made a much greater effort to draw the Luftwaffe up to fight in the West. The idea was to draw Luftwaffe units from Russia and to weaken German air defences in the West at the same time. As a result, from the end of June onwards, Fighter Command's day- and night-fighters had effectively reversed roles.

At the time, it was thought these 'circuses' and 'rhubarbs', as the fighter raids and sweeps over France and the Low Countries were called, were proving highly effective. In the six weeks from BARBAROSSA to the end of July, Fighter Command flew some 8,000 sorties, both escorting bombers and operating independently, and claimed 322 enemy aircraft destroyed in the air and on the ground for the loss of 123 of their own. In fact, the Luftwaffe lost just 81. Three hundred-plus enemy aircraft probably justified the effort; eighty did not, especially when there was such a need for even more fighters in the Mediterranean and Middle East.

In fact, Fighter Command was suffering in much the same way as the Luftwaffe fighters had over Britain the previous summer. First, there was the danger of flying over the Channel and running short of fuel; and second, there was the loss of home advantage. Those shot down over France were gathered up and dispatched to prison camps for the duration – and many of the RAF's best pilots suffered such fates, not least the legless Wing Commander Douglas Bader, probably Fighter Command's best-known ace.

Among those regularly flying over the Channel were the men of 609 Squadron, now based at Biggin Hill. Squadron Leader George Darley had been posted away and replaced by Michael Robinson, and so had the Americans and Poles, to the Eagle and Polish squadrons. However, 609 now played host to a number of Belgian pilots; the pre-war auxiliaries from Yorkshire were now the semi-official home of the Belgians in Fighter Command. On 17 June, Jean Offenberg, widely known to his English comrades as 'Pyker', was posted to join 609, and a few weeks later news arrived that he had been awarded a Distinguished Flying Cross (DFC) – the first Belgian pilot to win the medal.

That same day, one of the squadron's most popular pilots, Sidney Hill, was lost over France and that evening, in the Mess, the mood was sub-dued. Hearing of Offenberg's DFC, however, Squadron Leader Robinson tore off his own ribbon and pinned it to Pyker's chest, insisting they should all have a party to celebrate. Robinson had recognized that it did not do well for his pilots to dwell on the loss of their fellows; drinks and high jinks were means of taking their minds off such losses, and on this occasion a drunken evening ended with a nocturnal bathing party.

At the end of July, Robinson was promoted and posted away, and at the same time Offenberg was made a Flight Lieutenant and given com-mand of B Flight. The trips across the Channel continued, however – sometimes in pairs, sometimes escorting bombers; on other occasions they were attacking enemy minesweepers and shipping. Sometimes they found nothing; at other times they were engaged by a number of Messerschmitts. Offenberg even led the squadron several times towards the end of August, and found himself pirouetting and turning in the sky, duelling with the enemy. Confirmed hits were harder to claim over France – there was no wreck to examine, but he had two more 'probables' to his name.

Also still flying were Red Tobin and the American volunteers of 71 Eagle Squadron. In fact, by September, there were so many Americans now flying in Fighter Command that a second squadron, No. 133, was formed.

Among those who had arrived since the Battle of Britain was Jim Goodson, who had survived the sinking of the *Athenia* back on the opening day of Britain's war. Having eventually reached the US, he had gone over the border to Canada and joined the Royal Canadian Air Force (RCAF). By the end of 1940, he had returned to England with his pilot's wings and full of youthful excitement at the prospect of daily duels in his Spitfire. However, much to his chagrin, after completing his operational training unit (OTU), he was posted to 43 Squadron flying Hurricanes rather than Spitfires and carrying out endless patrols and scrambles after sneak raiders. After several bleak winter months of this, the novelty had most certainly worn off. 'We were frustrated and weary,' he noted of his time with 43 Squadron, 'a frame of mind popularly known in the RAF as being "browned off".' But then came a posting to 71 Eagle Squadron, winter made way for summer, and they began offensive ops across the Channel – and in Spitfires too – and Goodson's spirits rose. He also became firm friends with Red Tobin.

By September, Tobin had been flying a long time – more than a year in two operational front-line squadrons. So far, his luck had held, but it finally ran out on 7 September, when he flew on a sweep deep into northern France. The mission began badly when three of the nine had to return home with mechanical problems, but Tobin and the other five pressed on, crossing the French coast and flying some 75 miles inland. Suddenly, a mass formation of around seventy-five Me109s from Jagdgeschwader (JG) 26 dived down on them from 29,000 feet. As one Spitfire fell in flames, Tobin managed to break and turn after one of the attackers. Soon after, he was attacked by Joachim Müncheberg. Earlier in the year, Müncheberg had been based with his *Staffel* on Sicily, where in just a few weeks they had destroyed nearly fifty Hurricanes for no loss to themselves at all; Müncheberg personally had fifty-two kills to his name. He now added two more, one of whom, it seemed, was Red Tobin; at any rate, the American never returned from the raid and later news arrived that he'd been killed, identified and buried near where he'd crashed. He was one of three American pilots lost in as many minutes.

Tobin's loss was felt particularly keenly as he had always been a popular and larger-than-life character. When his friends gathered his belongings they discovered he had just one shilling and threepence – about $2 – to his name. 'The fortune of a hero,' it was reported in a US newspaper, 'who died in a foreign plane, riding foreign skies above a foreign land.'

The hot summer gave way to a wet autumn. On both sides of the Channel, pilots were feeling jaded and fed up. 'I no longer have much enthusiasm,' scribbled Siegfried Bethke in his journal on 21 October. The thought of flying over the Channel still stretched his nerves, but despite the flurry of activity over the summer, now that it was autumn, the inactivity was equally sapping. 'This quietness and readiness has made me somewhat soft. Also, I have very little ambition right now.'

A few days earlier, Jean Offenberg had returned from another sortie in the rain, the runway glistening and slippery as he touched back down. 'Biggin Hill is the fold, the lair to which you return after the hunt,' he wrote in his diary, 'where you can stretch your tired limbs and warm your numb fingers. Today it was bad hunting, we could not put up any game and we did not fire a shot . . .'

By November, 609 Squadron had been in the front line almost constantly since Dunkirk the previous May and Offenberg had been flying operationally for the best part of eighteen months too. This was too long; most front-line pilots were rested after around six months. Recognizing this, the squadron was posted to Digby, in Lincolnshire. It was freezing, the facilities were poor and everyone was fed up. 'After flying for about an hour and a half, Digby Control called me,' noted Offenberg on the 23rd. 'My hands were frozen in spite of my fur gloves and my feet were just as cold. In actual fact, I could not feel them at all.'

Clearly, there was going to be a lot less fighting now that the weather had worsened and the days shortened. It might have been better to send some of those increasingly under-used Spitfires where they might really make a difference – like the Mediterranean and Middle East, where the sun generally shone brightly and the skies were blue and where the RAF simply could never have enough aircraft. At any rate, the attritional grind of fighter sweeps over France was really not achieving a huge amount apart from mounting losses of aircraft and highly valuable pilots. Unfortunately, RAF Middle East was a long way away, and those in charge of Fighter Command, Air Chief Marshal (ACM) Sholto Douglas and Air Vice-Marshal (AVM) Trafford Leigh-Mallory, were closer to the corridors of power and the Air Ministry, where their claims could be heard in person. Ever since taking over from ACM Sir Hugh Dowding and AVM Keith Park the previous autumn, they had pursued an unimaginative and ineffective strategy. Very large numbers of Spitfires were now emerging from numerous factories all over the UK, but while it was a logistical challenge getting them to Malta and Egypt, it was not an insurmountable one. Spitfires were also a little harder to maintain than Hurricanes, but maintaining any aircraft in the desert or on a tiny island was difficult. What was absolutely clear was that nothing like the number now in England was needed either to protect British air space or tackle the Luftwaffe on the continent, and especially not in winter. They could and should have been put to far better use in the Middle East. The RAF was missing a trick.

CHAPTER 5

The Sinking of the *Reuben James*

AT THE END OF September, Lord Beaverbrook for Britain and Averell Harriman on behalf of the United States flew to Moscow for an aid-to-Russia conference; in fact, aid to the Soviet Union had already begun. This commitment, in terms of arms and many other supplies, put further pressure not only on US industry but that of Britain too, as well as adding greater strain to Allied shipping. The Royal Navy's Home Fleet had been given the responsibility for escorting convoys to Murmansk and Archangel, the former close to the Finnish border, the latter further east and south. Two routes were plotted – a summer one to the west of Iceland and south of Spitsbergen, and a winter route to the east of Iceland and further south. A naval raid on Spitsbergen destroyed coal installations, evacuated Russian and Norwegian inhabitants and successfully occupied the island, thus denying it to the enemy; it was a small but not insignificant operation. On 21 August, forty-eight Hurricanes had left Iceland on what was the first Arctic convoy; this amounted to two fighter squadrons, and the convoy reached Archangel ten days later. Despite its size, the Royal Navy had been feeling horribly overstretched almost since the outbreak of war. Adding Arctic convoys to its increasing number of responsibilities was not helping.

None the less, there was some cause for cheer for the British, and on the last day of September, as he outlined the war situation to the House of Commons, Churchill opened his report on that most vital of theatres: the Atlantic, where shipping losses had been dramatically reduced in recent months. Ever more supplies were reaching Britain, he reported, while home production had also greatly increased.

Something of a revolution was already taking place in British farming, with the emphasis on growing as many arable crops as possible and much less meat, and with greatly increased mechanization to achieve this. Changing eating habits and greatly increasing the amount of food produced at home meant that much of the shipping that before the war had been used for bulk food imports could now be employed for armaments and other supplies instead. Arable land, for example, had risen from 11.87 million acres in 1939 to 15 million for the 1941 harvest. The strategy for this change was directed by the Ministry of Agriculture, but the tactical management was decentralized, with a War Agricultural Executive Committee set up in each county. The 'War Ags' were largely made up of responsible and respectable county farmers and landowners, whose task was to ensure that Government demands were implemented. They had the capacity to categorize farms on their level of efficiency and could, if a farmer refused to co-operate or was struggling badly, exercise the right to commandeer the farm. There were, unsurprisingly, a few cases of War Ags unnecessarily throwing their weight around and requisitioning farms that perhaps, with greater care and understanding, need not have been taken, but for the most part their members worked efficiently and responsibly. Certainly, there was now all manner of help for farmers: financing schemes for tractors and other new mechanized equipment; deals on fertilizer; and plenty of advice from experts.

At the end of June, farmer, writer and broadcaster A. G. Street had welcomed the arrival of four experts for an inspection of his farm near Wilton, south-west Wiltshire – two to advise on arable and stock, one a seedsman and the fourth an expert on flax. 'For several hours we drove and walked and talked over Ditchampton Farm,' he wrote. Advice was given and there was much discussion about how best to improve yields. Overall, Street appeared to be doing all right. 'The farm,' he added, 'came through this ordeal satisfactorily.'

Much, of course, rested on the 1941 harvest. It was certainly the largest in Street's memory – in terms of acreage and in yield per acre, thanks to the new fertilizers and more efficient seeding. 'There is no doubt,' he scribbled on 3 September, the second anniversary of the outbreak of Britain's war, 'that home farmers have almost succeeded in doing the war job required of them, that is, fighting half the battle of the Atlantic by producing extra foodstuffs here at home.' Then he added, 'I say almost succeeded because although we have the best crop in history, we have been having the worst possible weather in which to harvest.'

A few weeks later, however, on the evening of 21 September, he could sit down happy in the knowledge that the harvest was, at last, in – and in no small part thanks to the huge collective effort involved. His fields had been filled with all manner of unskilled labour: schoolboys and girls, town-bred volunteers, soldiers and also Land Girls – members of the Women's Land Army – now working full-time on the farm. His wife, daughter and other women had also provided meals, driven soldiers to and from camps, taken newly threshed grain to buyers and a number of other tasks. For the first time, the harvest had also continued on Sundays. As Street looked around his farm, he could not get over how bare it looked. Never had he had so many fields devoted to arable that now lay empty and shorn. 'Everywhere one sees fields of cleared stubble and ploughs beginning to get busy,' he wrote. 'A few short years ago, I should have been thinking about cubbing and partridge-shooting at this moment, but today I can see only lots of work ahead of me.'

Still, this toil was not in vain. In Churchill's speech on 30 September, he was able to report that Britain's reserves of food stood higher than they had at the outbreak of war, and far higher than eighteen months previously. 'The Minister of Food,' he added, 'who has a pretty tough job, now finds himself able to make some quite appreciable improvements in the basic rations of the whole country, and in particular to improve the quantity and variety of the meals.' This was no small announcement. While food on the continent was becoming rapidly more scarce and rationing increasingly stringent, British people were able to get a more balanced and equally distributed supply of food than ever before. This in turn meant morale was improved, there was less illness and people were fitter. And more productive as a result.

On 11 September President Roosevelt had announced to the world that the US Navy had been ordered to destroy any Axis forces found in American waters, but, dramatic though this pronouncement was, in truth the US Navy was aggressively protecting Allied shipping from the moment it took over escort responsibility in the American zone of the Atlantic. It was therefore really only a matter of time before US warships came to blows with a U-boat; and when that happened, the descent into all-out war with Germany would be that much closer.

That moment duly came in the early hours of 31 October.

A group of eight U-boats were patrolling off the south-east of Greenland, including *U-552*, commanded by Erich Topp. He and his crew had only just reached their station when they spotted convoy HX156 of forty-four ships escorted by five American destroyers. Rather than immediately targeting the convoy, Topp lined up one of the US four-stack destroyers, the USS *Reuben James*, and at 8.34 a.m. fired two torpedoes, both of which hit on the port side and spectacularly split her in half. The bow then exploded and sank almost immediately; the stern, engulfed in flames, followed five minutes later, the destroyer's depth charges detonating as she did so, so that the sea erupted in a final enormous blast. In the water, survivors were black with oil and shivering from the intense cold. Some were choking and vomiting oil and seawater; others suffocated in the oil or were burned to death. Blackened bodies bobbed on the water amidst the debris. Hurrying to the scene came the other four destroyers, but it was too late for most of the men and only forty-five were picked up. A further 115, the skipper included, were lost in those treacherous seas.

At the time of firing, Topp had not realized the escorts were American, but a short while later heard the truth: that on his orders they had just sunk a warship from a country with whom Germany was not at war. He was keenly aware that Germany's resumption of unrestricted submarine warfare back in 1917 had brought America into that war, and very conscious of how politically explosive this sinking might be. 'Until we reached base,' he recalled, 'I was alone with my thoughts. As far as international law was concerned, I felt no qualms whatsoever. After all, I had attacked a British convoy screened by warships. Nevertheless, I felt bewildered. The tension a man endures when he thinks he is making history, however unintentional, is indeed enormous.'

And he had made history, because news of the sinking truly shocked and outraged the American public. Certainly Topp now had a long time to think about what he had done, as he and two others, including *U-567*, commanded by his great friend Bertl Endrass, continued to shadow the convoy and then had a sticky time dodging a British escort group. When they finally returned to Saint-Nazaire on 26 November, Topp was immediately summoned to Paris to explain himself in person to Admiral Dönitz.

*

In Rome, the Italian Foreign Minister and son-in-law of Mussolini, Count Galeazzo Ciano, heard the news of the sinking of the *Reuben James* that same day, Halloween 1941. 'It appears there were many victims,' he noted. 'I fear that the incident this time is of the kind that will provoke, or at least accelerate, the crisis.' The 'crisis' was not just the very real possibility of America's entry into the war, but Italy's drastically reduced status. Humbled and humiliated, Mussolini was feeling increasingly impotent, and trying to hide it with alternating moods of bluster and anger.

Il Duce had been stung at having been left out of the planning for BARBAROSSA. Yet again, Hitler had not informed his Axis ally at all about his plans, and had told Warlimont and the OKW that he only wanted partners who actually neighboured the Soviet Union or who had a particular score to settle; in reality this had initially meant just Romania and Hungary, which had joined the Axis back in November 1940, and Finland, which remained, officially at any rate, apart from the alliance. When news reached Rome that Russian opposition was stiffening, Mussolini had said, 'I hope for one thing that in this war in the East the Germans will lose a lot of feathers.' Yet a few days earlier he had insisted on sending Italian troops to the Eastern Front, even though the Germans had made it perfectly clear they did not want them. Despite this, the first division went at the end of July; it did nothing to sate the Duce's increasing anti-German mood.

How could it when Germany seemed to have it all and they had so little? At the end of October, Ciano had flown to Prussia and to the Wolf's Lair at Rastenburg. At the time, German forces were just 60 miles from Moscow. He found Hitler looking fit and well, and Joachim von Ribbentrop, the Foreign Minister, talking of Hitler's New Order in Europe lasting a thousand years. Ciano pointed out that a thousand years was a long time. 'Let's make it a century,' von Ribbentrop conceded. Ciano thought Germany seemed in fine shape, with all those he met apparently calm, well dressed and fed. 'When the Americans speak of an internal collapse,' he wrote, 'they are mistaken, or, to say the least, premature in their judgment. Germany can hold out for a long time yet.'

In contrast, at home Italy faced only long years of hardship and war – even Mussolini recognized that, which was why he had lost so much of his lustre. The country was being bombed by the RAF – Naples was badly hit in early July, for example, with the loss of 6,000 precious tons of oil – and rationing was becoming more stringent. Bread had been cut to 200 grams a day. Ciano noticed that morale amongst the people was low. In Sicily, conditions were worse, with poverty and lack of food increasing. In Greece, left by the Germans for the Italians to manage largely by themselves, the situation was even worse. There, the bread ration stood at just 90 grams a day. 'They have nothing else,' wrote Ciano. 'If a load of grain does not reach Piraeus tomorrow, the ovens will be cold. What is the solution?' Ciano was one of the men who were supposed to have the answers to that question. He had none. By the second week of October, the Under-Secretary of Food Administration was telling Ciano he needed to cut rations in Italy still further or risk running out of food for a month. It was easier for those in the countryside, but for city dwellers the shortages were becoming hard to bear; demonstrations were breaking out – including by women – which were difficult to suppress. Meanwhile, Mussolini appeared to be interested only in sending more men to the Eastern Front.

This was utter madness, because in Libya, still ostensibly an Italian possession, supplies were also running short and shipping across the Mediterranean was becoming more dangerous as Malta-based ships, aircraft and submarines continued to hammer Axis convoys. By the end of the first week of October, only 20 per cent of supplies set aside for the previous month had been sent, and 50 per cent of the men.

As if this wasn't hard enough to bear, Hitler had sent the Luftwaffe Feldmarschall Albert Kesselring to take command of all Axis forces in the Mediterranean. Kesselring was to pay lip service to the Italian Commando Supremo, but both Maresciallo Ugo Cavallero, the current Italian Chief of Staff, and Mussolini understood the significance of the appointment. 'Mussolini has swallowed the bitter pill,' wrote Ciano. 'He realizes the meaning of this within the big picture of the war and for the country, but, like a good player, he takes the blow, and pretends that he doesn't feel it.' How Mussolini and the Italians were paying for his terrible hubris.

The war in North Africa was about to erupt again after an uneasy stand-off since the fighting around the Egyptian–Libyan border in June. Rommel's forces had needed the breather to build up strength once more, although his campaign in Libya seemed little more than a tiny skirmish beside the fighting along the Eastern Front.

The scale of the fighting in the Soviet Union and the astonishing number of men involved are still hard to fathom, such is their enormity: some 7 million men had crashed into each other in the opening weeks of BARBAROSSA. None the less, this does not mean the war in the West was becoming a sideshow. The number-one enemy remained Britain: BARBAROSSA had been launched, after all, as a means of swiftly eliminating one potential enemy and enabling Germany to renew her strength and resources before turning back to deal with the British once and for all – preferably before the United States entered the fray.

The war in North Africa has often been portrayed as very small beer indeed compared to the gigantic battles in the East, and in terms of manpower this is, of course, perfectly true. Be this as it may, there was no doubting the strategic importance Hitler and his senior commanders placed on this theatre. It was one where they believed Britain could be successfully brought to heel and forced to the peace table. Such would be the earth-shattering shame of defeat there, they believed, Britain would have no choice but to seek terms. At the same time, Hitler was growing increasingly paranoid about a possible British attempt to invade Corsica or Sicily or even Sardinia. During his meeting with Ciano in October, the Führer offered further support in the Mediterranean, even though he could ill-afford to give it. It was from this rather myopic viewpoint that the Mediterranean and Middle East was seen by the Germans as being as strategically important as the Atlantic.

For the British, however, it remained what it had always been: a convenient theatre of opportunity, where advantageous victories could be won, Italy could be further brought to heel, increasing amounts of German resources could be drawn, and where, crucially, their ever-growing army could be tested and actually engage Axis forces properly in battle. No mistake, to lose the Middle East would have been a terrible blow, but the British Empire and Britain's global reach worked because of its possession of, and access to, giant amounts of shipping, something the Axis did not have. In other words, if North Africa and the Middle East were lost, it did not necessarily follow that British possessions in India and the Far East would fall too.

What was also true was that the fully mechanized armoured force of the Deutsches Afrikakorps would have been worth its weight in gold on the Eastern Front. As it was, Germany's and Italy's ability to keep supplying North Africa had been further tested during the autumn.

Because the Luftwaffe could not be everywhere, and because the Regia Aeronautica was nothing like as effective, Malta had been allowed to regain its offensive strength.

More British bombers reached the island – and others merely staged there from the Middle East – while the 10th Submarine Flotilla based in Malta also grew in confidence and ability. Two submarines in particular, *Upholder* and *Urge*, were amassing huge amounts of tonnage to their name. In September, for example, *Upholder* had sunk two troop liners, *Oceania* and *Neptunia*, both of 19,500 tons. These enormous ships were irreplaceable, as the Italians did not have the money, time or resources to build new ones on that scale.

In October, several fast and powerful surface vessels were temporarily posted to Malta. Rather like the German raiders earlier in the year, Force K, consisting of two cruisers and two destroyers, wreaked havoc on Axis shipping. On 8 November, an Ultra decrypt, supported by RAF reconnaissance, reported an enemy convoy off the toe of Italy. Force K immediately set sail and in the early hours of 9 November intercepted ten merchant vessels and six destroyer escorts. 'The result,' Admiral Cunningham noted with glee, 'was a holocaust for the Italians.' In a brief and violent engagement, nine of the ten merchant ships were sunk and the tenth, a tanker, left burning. Three of the destroyers were also sent to the bottom of the sea.

Ciano was horrified. Since the middle of September, they had been unable to run any convoys to Libya, but he was aware how desperately they were needed. 'All, I mean *all*, our ships were sunk,' he wrote. 'This will undoubtedly have deep consequences in Italy, Germany, and, above all, in Libya. Under the circumstances, we have no right to complain if Hitler sends Kesselring as commander in the south.'

Meanwhile, the war in the Atlantic continued. On 24 October, *U-564* was some 300 miles west of Gibraltar after a frustrating three and a half weeks on patrol. First, 'Teddy' Suhren, the captain, had been sent back up to the northern Atlantic, but after seeing nothing for a couple of weeks had asked to be moved on. 'Suhren to operate on the Gibraltar route,' had come the prompt reply. So they had set off on the long trip south and had reached their new station only to run into rolling sea mists. This was dangerous for U-boats, as they depended on sailing mostly on the surface and being able to spy both potential targets and any danger from a decent distance. As a result, they repeatedly had to dive and listen, then surface again, have a look around and, if visibility hadn't improved, sink below the waves once more, which massively slowed them down. Nor was it good for the crew's nerves. After six days of this, Suhren lost patience and signalled to BdU for permission to move further south. 'U-564 to maintain radio silence,' came the curt reply. 'It puts a strain on morale on board,' noted Suhren, 'to have to keep getting through fuel and provisions without any prospect of achieving anything. For we need success in the same way as a performer needs applause.'

Eventually, on the seventh day, a Condor had spotted a convoy heading towards Gibraltar – this was HG75. Suhren had been relieved and had hoped to make contact sometime around noon the following day. But, much to his mounting frustration, they had been too late. New orders arrived for them to patrol a different search line the following evening.

This time, they at last found the convoy. It was now early morning and they were lying to the starboard of the right-hand column of ships when the convoy tacked directly towards them. Suhren had already dived the boat to periscope depth, then suddenly the convoy was almost upon them, with the middle column about to steam directly over them. All five torpedoes were made ready to shoot. The lead freighter was now just metres away and looking as high as a house. With his eyes fixed on the periscope, Suhren felt it was so close he could almost touch it. Then he spotted a tanker.

'Bosun, what speed are we doing?' Suhren asked.

'A good 10 knots, Herr Oberleutnant. Bearing left thirty degrees, bearing changing.'

'Grünert, report state of readiness, please!'

'Tubes 1 and 2 ready!'

'Bosun, let me know when we have bearing sixty degrees.'

'Bearing fifty degrees,' said the Bosun.

'Grünert, rudder amidships.'

'Bearing sixty degrees – now!'

'Tube 1 – ready! Tube 1 – fire!'

Four more torpedoes followed in quick succession, the first three exploding with columns of red fire on three different ships. Billowing smoke from the sinking vessels now made periscope visibility impossible, so Suhren ordered them to dive deep; he had been less worried about being depth-charged than rammed by other ships in the convoy. The propeller noises above them gradually grew quieter and quieter. There was a chance an escort could have held back, waiting for them to surface, but as they rose to periscope depth and had a look around, it was still smoky and visibility was poor. They could see nothing. This was a tricky situation, and one in which Suhren was not prepared to chance his arm. He could have caught up with the convoy once more, but what if a destroyer were to creep up on them out of the smoke? 'I decided to turn off south,' he noted.

These Gibraltar convoys were, as Suhren ruefully acknowledged, well protected with escorts and increasingly hard to strike. A number of U-boats had been sent to intercept HG75, but despite a six-day effort of stalking and attempted attacks, only four ships were sunk – and Suhren accounted for three of them in his one attack. As the British escorts, especially, were increasingly well served with radar and Huff-Duff as well as ASDIC, the onboard sonar, U-boats were finding it more difficult to break through.

On the other side of the Atlantic, in the American zone, Lieutenant Douglas Fairbanks, Jr was now on board the destroyer USS *Ludlow*, a new ship and on its first duties as part of the US Task Force 34, escorting convoys as far as the MOMP. The first run was a bewildering time for this Hollywood star turned junior naval officer. Although he was an avid sailor and had never once been seasick, he spent his first few days feeling wretched as the narrow destroyer rolled and pitched on the Atlantic swell, constantly zig-zagging and darting in wide sweeps around the edge of the convoy. He tried to take comfort in the knowledge that Admiral Nelson had suffered from seasickness, but this provided little solace. The truth, he realized, was that his nausea was not just down to the sea. 'In fact,' he noted, 'I was scared of the unknown, scared because I didn't really know enough about my job yet, and scared of the war.'

Slowly but surely, however, he managed to find his sea legs. The petty officers, he discovered, tended to be more helpful than the Regular officers, and he soon caught on, learning more quickly than he had supposed about the rudiments of radio and visual communications, the basics of gunnery, the importance of keeping watch. He also got used to the constant ping-ping of the ASDIC. During his first convoy escort, the sonar suddenly picked up what appeared to be a U-boat. Bells clanged, while over the ship's tannoy came the order, 'Now hear this! All hands!

Take your battle stations! Take your battle stations! All hands to battle stations!' Fairbanks hadn't actually been given one yet, so stood on the bridge, binoculars glued to his eyes and hoping he looked as though he knew what he was doing.

The destroyer darted back and forth, fired off salvoes of depth charges and the rapid ping-ping of the ASDIC disappeared. They hoped they'd got a kill, but there was nothing to confirm this.

Some days later, during daylight, they crept into a thickening fog when they were ordered on a wild chase for a suspected U-boat. Heading out on an ever-widening search, they lost contact with the convoy and then began to suffer engine problems until, soon after, they stopped altogether. Surrounded by fog on a dead-calm sea, they drifted, a sitting duck. One day passed, then another and another, as the engineers frantically tried to repair the broken engines. The fog finally lifted on the third day and they were able to get their bearings from the sun. They discovered they had drifted well into the British zone; the Neutrality Acts, which were still in place, meant US ships were, in theory, protected inside the American zone but not in the British. Then, to everyone's relief, the engineers got one engine started and they were able to get going again. Three long days of unbearable tension were over. No U-boat had found them; they had got away with it and were able to make slowly for port in Iceland.

CHAPTER 6

Crusaders

THE FORCES IN North Africa might have been tiny compared with the enormous groups of armies battering each other in Russia, but the scale was still far larger than it had been a year before. Rommel's Afrikakorps had grown into three divisions, while the Italians also had two corps. Against this, British Eighth Army contained two corps. All were mechanized – that is, equipped with motorized vehicles, even though some were in static positions with their transports to the rear. Londoner Albert Martin, a recently promoted corporal in the 2nd Battalion, the Rifle Brigade, with more than a year's experience in North Africa under his belt, was very conscious of the change. The days of small-scale skirmishes were over – the build-up of supplies was, as far as he was concerned, incredible. He also knew, as October gave way to November, that action was in the air. Night patrols were becoming more aggressive, new tanks were assembling, dumps of supplies and ammunition were being established, and there was a noticeable increase in air activity. This, he and his mates agreed, seemed like a comforting edge in their favour.

Martin was not wrong. RAF strength in North Africa had grown. On the eve of CRUSADER, the RAF had 554 aircraft ready to fly, while the Luftwaffe had just 121 and the Regia Aeronautica had 192 that were serviceable. Perhaps more important than just superiority of numbers was superiority of method. Air Marshal Tedder had been not only doing all he could to get more aircraft to the Middle East, he had also insisted on a great improvement in serviceability at the front. Aircraft Replacement

Pools were established, with seven days' replacements, which were fed from Maintenance Units. Further forward were other pools holding two days' replacements. In four weeks in October, no fewer than 232 replacement aircraft were fed into front-line units. New methods, or doctrine, were emerging too, as Army and RAF together strove for a clearer understanding of the role of air support in a land battle. In achieving this, both Tedder and Auchinleck were keen to improve co-operation and had conducted a number of joint exercises to help determine the best targets for air attack and the most effective means of reconnoitring, attacking and destroying them.

Disagreements were also ironed out. The Army wanted greater protection from dive-bombers and a fighter umbrella directly above. This was not possible, however, as there were not enough aircraft nor was it an effective use of air power. Far better was to attempt to destroy as many as possible of the enemy air forces before they attacked the troops on the ground. A new directive on Army–Air co-operation was issued by Churchill at the beginning of September, based largely on the concepts of air support as outlined by Tedder. 'The Army Commander-in-Chief will specify to the Air Officer Commanding-in-Chief,' wrote Churchill, 'the targets and tasks which he requires to be performed, both in the preparatory attack on the rearward installations of the enemy and for air action during the progress of the battle. It will be for the AOC-in-C to use his maximum force on these objects in the manner most effective.'

A further development was the setting up of Air Support Control (ASC). An ASC unit consisted of a combined Army and RAF team equipped with trucks and radios and attached to each corps. Each brigade would also have attached a Forward Air Support Link – an RAF team also equipped with a vehicle and a radio. Ground troops would make requests for air support, which would then be passed much more quickly and directly to the ASCs, who would then decide whether to accept the request. If so, they would call up the appropriate air forces and be given an approximate time of attack and number of aircraft.

There were also changes in personnel. Now commanding the Desert Air Force was Air Vice-Marshal Arthur Coningham, a tough and charismatic leader bristling with ideas and energy. He was born in Australia – his father had once played test cricket there – but his parents were later exposed for trying to swindle and blackmail a local priest, so fled to New Zealand when their son was just five, and it was here that he was raised. During the last war, he served first in the New Zealand Army in Samoa and the Middle East. Discharged for poor health, he recovered and made his way to England, where he joined the Royal Flying Corps (RFC), flying with 32 Squadron on the Western Front. It was during this time that he gained his nickname, 'Mary', partly because it sounded like 'Maori' but also because of his association with a New Zealand nurse of that name. At any rate, it stuck, and brilliantly ironic it was too, because a more masculine person it would have been hard to meet. An unbridled force of nature, Coningham was both a natural leader of men and a fine pilot. Almost a double-ace from the Western Front, he had remained in the RAF, as the RFC had become, went on to pioneer the future Takoradi Route from West Africa to Egypt, and by the outbreak of war was in Bomber Command, where he had commanded 4 Group.

He had reached North Africa to take over one of the most important but challenging commands in the Middle East theatre, and now, in November, his strengthened and reorganized force was about to be tested. No one doubted the importance of air power, but Coningham was among those who devoutly believed it was essential to achieving victory on the ground.

Operation CRUSADER was due to launch on 18 November, and in the five weeks beforehand the combined efforts of the RAF Middle East, including bombers from Malta, amounted to nearly 3,000 sorties, which destroyed and damaged around seventy Axis aircraft – not a massive return, but certainly one that effectively chipped away at enemy air strength and gave cause for cheer to the troops of Eighth Army, such as Albert Martin.

Also part of the pre-battle preparations had been the SAS's first raid. The plan had been to parachute behind enemy lines and attack Axis air-fields, but the drop, on 16 November, coincided with one of the worst thunderstorms in living memory, which blew them off course and off schedule. Instead of attacking any landing ground, it took all their determination and stamina just to make their rendezvous with the Long Range Desert Group and, as it was, of the fifty-four who took off that night, only twenty-one ever came back – the rest were killed or captured. 'During the bumpy ride in the trucks we were all rather subdued,' noted Johnny Cooper, one of those who made the RV. 'In a small unit like ours, such losses are always hard to bear.' He was also keenly aware of the strained expressions on the faces of the officers. 'It was clear to David Stirling,' added Cooper, 'that he was going to have to rethink our operational methods and that the first SAS raid had been a disaster.'

On 21 October, Feldmarschall Milch, with his new authority over aircraft production still intact, had announced to 200 representatives of the aircraft industry that from now on the numbers of Focke-Wulf 190s compared to those of the Me109 would be ordered at a ratio of three to one; up until that point, the ratio had been four Me109s to one FW190. It was a shattering blow to Messerschmitt, but Milch was showing that he would put up with the Professor's arrogance no more. No longer was Luftwaffe procurement going to be pushed around by the industry moguls and their Nazi connections.

In the weeks that followed, however, Milch learned that Udet's office had falsified test data favouring the FW190 and it quickly became clear that to implement such a radical conversion in production would set back total fighter production for many months. At a meeting between Milch, Udet and Fritz Seiler, Messerschmitt's Deputy Chairman and Financial Director, the latter produced documents proving this doctoring of data.

'Not a very comradely action, Herr Seiler,' Milch commented.

'It's a game of chess,' Seiler replied. 'I am making the second move.'

With this bombshell, Milch had no choice but to promise Seiler he would try to reverse the production-ratio decision. It was a humiliation for him, and an even worse one for Udet. This aside, it was also no way to try to regain the initiative for the rapidly falling Luftwaffe.

In an effort to try to build bridges, Milch suggested to Udet that they both visit Paris for a few days' break in every German's favourite city. The two had once been such close friends; it was time, Milch believed, to rekindle that fellowship. To his relief, Udet agreed. They planned to fly together from Tempelhof on 17 November in Udet's own Siebel 104.

Thick fog prevented Milch from taking off from Breslau back to Berlin, so he drove instead and, having reached the Air Ministry, was about to set off for Tempelhof when he was told the devastating news: Udet had shot himself in his flat. Two empty bottles of brandy lay by the dead man's bed, but he had been addicted to various narcotics for some time. A black cloud had descended over this brilliant pilot: his mistress had left him and the humiliations he had suffered as head of Luftwaffe procurement had proved too much. Drugs and alcohol had done the rest. Milch was distraught when he heard the news.

At Udet's funeral – his death had been announced as a severe accident whilst testing a new weapon – Hitler took Milch to one side. 'Now there is another grave burden for you to take upon yourself.' Milch was to be officially Director of Air Armament with the brief to try to rebuild the Luftwaffe. The task facing him was, needless to say, monumental.

While the countdown to the resumption of battle was going on in North Africa, the United States was reacting to the sinking of the *Reuben James*. The folk singer Woody Guthrie even wrote a song about it. Certainly, most in America were deeply shocked, although Roosevelt was quick to play down its significance; nothing had changed, he told the press – the US was not about to declare war on Germany.

Few in the corridors of power would now bet against it, however, and the sinking coincided with the announcement of a new 'Victory Program' designed to double the present armaments plan.

For those running America's rearmament, 1941 had proved a difficult and frustrating year. Strike after strike had seriously hurt output; some projects had turned out to be flops; there were still horrendous raw material bottlenecks; and criticism of Bill Knudsen and those at the Office of Production Management (OPM) had been vocal and consistent. Knudsen, formerly CEO of General Motors and the man more than any other responsible for the rise of the automobile industry over the past twenty-five years, had been brought in by the President in May the previous year to help streamline US armaments production. Unlike the private automobile industry, however, armaments production came under the scrutiny of Washington's politicians and media. Knudsen had repeatedly told the President and anyone who was prepared to listen that mass production of tanks and aircraft could not happen overnight. Machine tools had to be made, factories built, assembly workers trained, and to get the largest number of arms, big business needed harnessing.

Despite this, the main gripes were still twofold: first, that production was too slow; and second, that too many of the raw-material supplies were still being siphoned towards civilian goods.

Knudsen, however, had quite deliberately instigated a policy of increasing military production on the back of continued civilian manufacturing; the change to all-out production would be gradual, as machine tools were built and companies gradually switched over. This, of course, all took time; Knudsen had warned that it would take eighteen months from when he and others were brought in to form the National Defense Advisory Commission (NDAC) back in late May 1940 to a point where ambitions were beginning to be realized.

Yet there was no doubt that, because the Office of Production Management (OPM) – as NDAC had become – had been set up to oversee military armament alongside other bodies such as the Office of Price Administration and Civilian Supply (OPACS), there would be friction and conflicts of interest. That was not Knudsen's fault, nor any of those working at OPM, such as his right-hand man, Don Nelson; it was the fault of the unwieldy way in which these bodies had been set up.

The increased bottlenecks and the fact that no one body had overall priority when it came to allocating supplies meant Roosevelt felt obliged to do something. His answer was to establish yet another organization: the Supply Priorities and Allocations Board, or SPAB for short. As part of a general shake-up of personnel, Don Nelson took charge of SPAB and the steel magnate Edward Stettinius took over the running of Lend-Lease. Knudsen remained head of OPM. The challenges facing all of them were still monstrous. Don Nelson had the unenviable task of somehow dividing available supply resources between military, civilian and overseas requirements – and this last was made even more of a headache by the pressing demands for aid now coming from Russia.

And yet, with the end of 1941 approaching, there were at last signs that American industry was kicking into gear as the all-important period of retooling was almost over. The steel industry had added facilities for 6 million net tons, which boosted its capacity to a whopping 88 million tons. The aircraft industry had increased its floor space from 9,454,550 square feet on 1 January 1939 to almost 54,000,000 square feet by the beginning of November 1941. The monthly expenditure for defence the previous September had been $200 million; now it was $1.36 *billion*. Since July, US factories had produced $2 billion of munitions; as it was, the aircraft industry had produced nearly 20,000 aircraft in 1941. The new British designed pre-fabricated Liberty ships rolling off Henry Kaiser's shipyards were also now taking to the seas. The first few had been launched in August. Henry Kaiser, the entrepreneur who had taken on the British challenge of trying to mass-produce 10,000-ton merchant vessels, had achieved all that had been asked of him and more. New ships were now being launched from shipyards around America almost daily.

Perhaps most remarkable of all was the number of machine tools now being produced. In 1932, the machine-tool industry had been worth $22 million a year, yet under Fred Geier, the head of the Machine Tool Builders' Association and another old friend of Knudsen's, this once small and highly bespoke industry had managed to build 110,000 tools in 1940 and 185,000 in 1941. By early 1942, the Cincinnati Milling Machine Company, for example, would be turning out a new machine tool every seventeen minutes each and every day – and it was these, the pieces of equipment that could create armour plate or wings or gun breeches, that were the keys to mass production.

Just as Knudsen had predicted, it had taken US industry eighteen months to wind itself up to produce the kind of numbers that had seemed fantastical back in 1940 and still beyond reach during the troublesome early months of 1941. Now, however, America's factories appeared to be poised to take war production to new, unprecedented levels. Still, though, there were plenty of doubters. 'Chief problems now and in the future,' wrote Hanson W. Baldwin in the *New York Times*, 'will be those of controlling the vast machine that has been started, supplying it with sufficient raw materials without wrecking the rest of our industry, and controlling prices and wages. It is the greatest task this nation has ever undertaken.' Baldwin was stating nothing less than the truth.

In the ongoing battle at sea, it had become clear by November that the Royal Navy's Western Approaches Command was expecting rather too much from their Atlantic partners. The Canadians, sailing in corvettes that were really too small for the mid-Atlantic, were becoming exhausted, and that went for their ships too. These corvettes were averaging twenty-eight days out of thirty-one at sea, which was much more than could be reasonably expected of young crews trying to learn on the job and with insufficient equipment, and on vessels where the open bridges were almost permanently awash from the cold grey Atlantic swell.

Their Royal Navy cousins tended to look down at their dubious signalling skills and roughshod escort discipline; but such condescension was entirely misplaced. The Royal Canadian Navy (RCN) were continuing to punch well above their weight and their presence in the western and northern Atlantic had proved a godsend to the British.

Western Approaches Command was then dismayed to learn that the

US Navy had brought out some printed escort instructions, in which the stated prime goal of escorts was to destroy enemy U-boats, rather than safely escort merchant ships to the MOMP. There was nothing the Royal Navy could do about it, however. The Americans were not officially in the war at all, and at no point had there ever been any attempt to draw up joint doctrine.

Fortunately for Allied shipping, at this stage, with the RCN almost at breaking point, Hitler chose to interfere. Once again, his paranoia about the Mediterranean and his southern flank clouded his judgement. Force K, operating from Malta along with the island's 10th Submarine Flotilla, continued to wreak havoc on Axis convoys to North Africa and when the British launched their CRUSADER offensive on 18 November, the Führer ordered Admiral Dönitz to send six U-boats from the Atlantic into the Mediterranean. Others were sent, at his direct behest, into the North Sea to act on an entirely fictitious belief that the British were about to invade Norway. By the middle of December, after nearly two and a half years of war, the only U-boats operating in the Atlantic, this most critical of theatres, were five patrolling the Atlantic mouth of the Mediterranean.

What Hitler singularly failed to understand was that, important though the Mediterranean was, he would never beat Britain so long as Allied merchant ships continued to flow back and forth from the UK.

In the Western Desert of North Africa, Alan Moorehead of the *Daily Express* and a number of other war correspondents had been called to the front to General Sir Alan Cunningham's Eighth Army headquarters at Bagush in Egypt on 16 November. 'I am going to attack the day after tomorrow,' Cunningham told them. 'Everything depends on how the battle goes.' The plan was for XXX Corps, with the bulk of the British armour, to advance and take on and destroy the German tanks of the Afrikakorps, leaving XIII Corps to hurry along the coast towards Tobruk, whose beleaguered garrison would at long last break out the moment the time was ripe. Another part of the pre-battle preparations was a daring Commando raid behind enemy lines on the night of 17/18 November on what had been Rommel's HQ. As it happened, Rommel had been in Rome and only arrived back the day CRUSADER was launched. Both SAS and Commando raids had thus been a failure.

None the less, the British attack caught the Axis off guard and, arriving back at the front, Rommel misread British intentions and sent his armoured divisions towards Bardia; in fact, XXX Corps was far further south and so the British armoured forces were able to advance to Sidi Rezegh, 10 miles south-east of Tobruk, while XIII Corps also drove on along the coast. After two days, General Cunningham felt the moment had arrived to order the Tobruk garrison to break out. However, having realized his error, Rommel had by this time ordered the Afrikakorps to do an about-turn. What followed was the largest tank battle so far of the North Africa campaign. By chance, Alan Moorehead saw the opening salvoes. Having travelled along the coast road following Cunningham's briefing, he had reached 4th Armoured Brigade, part of XXX Corps, on the evening of 19 November.

With dark, thunderous clouds building in the east, Moorehead and his fellows clambered on to their trucks and watched General Alec Gatehouse's light Stuart tanks, fresh from America, charge across the open desert like mounted cavalry of old towards Rommel's armour. 'It was novel, reckless, unexpected, impetuous and terrific,' wrote Moorehead. 'They charged straight into the curtain of dust and fire that hid the German tanks and guns.' And at that point he lost them. 'Dust, smoke, burning oil, exploding shell and debris filled the air. From a distance, it was merely noise and confusion.' As darkness fell, so the fighting died down again and both sides drew away.

The following morning, Albert Martin was in action too, advancing with 7th Armoured Division towards the landing ground at Sidi Rezegh, now littered with wrecked and burning aircraft. 'In all directions came the noise of battle,' he noted, 'twenty-five-pounders crashing away just yards off, a cluster of tanks in the distance firing at something but whether they were friend or foe was difficult to make out; neither could I work out what the target was.' Martin and his mates were in light tracked carriers, equipped with rifles and Bren guns; but this was an armoured battle of tanks and guns. They kept firing, but Martin was conscious they could hardly be achieving very much. At one stage there were panzers within 200 yards, but they squeaked and rumbled on past them. Again, only once dusk came was there any let-up.

The violent and confusing fighting that raged around Sidi Rezegh continued the following day, by which time the British armour had been halted in its tracks. German anti-tank guns, of higher calibre and velocity than the guns of the British tanks, had done most of the damage rather than the panzers themselves. Hoping to wrest back the initiative, Rommel, in typical fashion, had then personally led the Afrikakorps on a charge to the Egyptian border in an attempt to cut off Eighth Army from its forward supply depots. At the same time, XIII Corps continued its advance.

It is hard to appreciate how confusing desert battles were, and if, in the dust and mayhem of battle, General Cunningham misread the situation, it is not entirely surprising. Worried about his losses, and aware that Rommel was possibly about to outflank his army, Cunningham felt it best to call a halt to the operation and withdraw. Auchinleck, however, overruled him and immediately replaced him with Major-General Neil Ritchie, his Chief of Staff at GHQ, who was hastily promoted up a notch to lieutenant-general and dispatched to the front. This was to prove a terrible error of judgement.

In the meantime, Rommel had encountered problems too, as he found his own forces were now overstretched and being repeatedly harried by the Desert Air Force. Such was the intensity of the DAF's round-the-clock attacks, and the generally confused situation, that Rommel was forced to pull back once more. He had had a highly charged few days, moving from one unit to another, and even briefly overran a New Zealand Division field hospital, where, no matter that they were his enemy, he promised the startled patients and staff more supplies before driving on.

By this time, XIII Corps had managed to link up with the Tobruk garrison. With his forces now back together, Rommel tried to renew the siege, but his repeated counter-attacks were forced back; despite the losses at Sidi Rezegh, the British were too strong in defence. As both sides were discovering, defending against an attack across the open desert was often easier than taking the offensive. The Afrikakorps were also beginning to resent what they considered the weak performance of the Italians. The Italian Motorized Corps failed to join the attack on 5 December, then reported they were too exhausted and no longer fit enough to join Rommel's assault on Tobruk the following day. One last attempt was made on 7 December; again, it made no headway. 'I've had to break off the action outside Tobruk,' Rommel wrote to his wife on the 9th, 'on account of the Italian formations and also the badly exhausted German troops. I'm hoping we'll succeed in escaping enemy encirclement and holding on to Cyrenaica.'

After almost three weeks of fighting, he managed to extricate what was left of his forces from around Tobruk, with Eighth Army snapping at their heels. In fact, some British units had already set off across the desert in an effort to isolate Rommel's forces. 'We are off again,' jotted Albert Martin in his diary on 6 December. Such had been the casualties in the 2nd Rifle Brigade, A and S Companies were now combined. 'Our intentions are to isolate the pockets of enemy resistance and smash any supplies that try to get through to them.' Five days later, Martin joined the casualty list when his truck was strafed by an Me109 and he was hit in the arm and leg, although not badly.

He had more than played his part, however, because not only had Tobruk been relieved, but in pursuit British forces had broken through XX Italian Motorized Corps' lines, leaving Rommel with little option but to pull back out of Cyrenaica altogether. And thus, by Christmas, the two sides were pretty much back to where they had been the previous year, although there was a final phase of the CRUSADER battle still to be played out.

Much, however, had changed since then. In fact, much had changed since Rommel's final assault on Tobruk on 7 December.

CHAPTER 7

Unravelling

B Y THE END of July, Major Hans von Luck had been posted away from
7. Panzerdivision headquarters, where he had begun BARBAROSSA
as Adjutant, and given command of the division's reconnaissance
battalion. As part of 3. Panzergruppe in Army Group Centre, he had
been part of the encirclement of Smolensk, which lay on the River Dneiper
some 120 miles west of Moscow.

Two months later, he and his men were attacking the next town in
their path towards the Russian capital, Vyazma. Despite these successes,
however, von Luck was starting to worry. Their supply lines were becoming over-extended, time was marching on, and already-overrun Red
Army units were making trouble behind the lines. The whole point of
the *Kesselschlacht* was to surround the enemy and then annihilate them;
the problem was, they were not annihilating them. Smashing them, yes,
but totally destroying them – no. Sealing off a quarter of a million men
was not that easy and, repeatedly, large numbers of Russians were slipping away; a Soviet army or even group of armies might have been
surrounded and lost its central organization, but large numbers of troops
were managing to get away and either rejoin their own lines or escape to
the forests and join growing numbers of troublesome partisans.

Just before the assault on Vyazma, von Luck saw the divisional
commander, Generalleutnant Hans Freiherr von Funck. 'This war is
going to last longer than we would like,' von Funck told him. 'The days
of the blitzkrieg are over.'

They managed to encircle Vyazma in another *Kesselschlacht*, but the resistance was growing and the mopping-up process was taking longer. Von Luck and his fellows were astounded that, despite having captured over a million prisoners, there still seemed to be yet more Red Army soldiers ahead of them, and not only that, but with stiffening resistance. By now it was October and the next objective was Volokolamsk, only 60 or so miles from Moscow. The gap in time between their attacks was lengthening, however, as they waited for fuel, food and ammunition to be brought forward; the supply lines were getting ever longer.

By the end of the month, von Luck's recce battalion had reached the little town of Yakhroma on the Moscow–Volga Canal and had formed a small bridgehead. They were now almost within spitting distance of the capital. But then winter started to set in as the rain gave way to snow. They had no winter clothing at all, but as the snow around them began to pile higher, so the enemy started to counter-attack – and, to von Luck's dismay, on skis and wearing white camouflage snow uniforms, which enabled them to infiltrate the German forward lines with ease. 'We sensed catastrophe,' noted von Luck, 'and thought of Napoleon's fate.'

At the beginning of November, Oberst Hermann Balck had been posted to the headquarters of the OKH as General of Mobile Forces, although, despite the job title, he remained a colonel. After reporting to von Brauchitsch and Halder at their forward headquarters in the forests at Mauerwald in East Prussia, he went on to Orel to see General Heinz Guderian, his corps commander back in 1940 when Balck had been commanding 1. Rifle Regiment. From Orel, they then drove for three days to the front. It was now 25 November and on the road to Tula, the great railhead before Moscow, they witnessed a long line of Russian and German dead, where a Siberian division, which had broken out of the encirclement, had overrun two battalions of 25th Motorized Infantry Division and escaped, albeit at great cost.

They eventually reached one of Guderian's panzer divisions. The men seemed in good spirits. Guderian talked informally with many of them, but Balck could not help noticing that they seemed rather at the end of their strength. These were the elite of the Wehrmacht: motivated, well-trained, highly disciplined young men, but whose numbers were dwindling fast. 'As a result of their numerical weakness,' noted Balck, 'they constantly ended up in the most difficult crisis situations, which were then resolved by throwing in our best troops. But as those troops were killed, the toughest core of our army that we could not do without slowly but surely vanished.'

The following day, Balck saw his old friend General Leo Geyr von Schweppenburg, who was commanding XXIV Motorized Corps and whose men were about to attack Tula. His three divisions were now a tenth of their normal strength and he urged Balck to report the reality of the situation. They were at the limits of what they could now achieve. In a final meeting with Guderian, the General told Balck he hoped he could still capture Tula but that his forces were now all but spent. Like Geyr von Schweppenburg, he asked Balck not to hold back when he reported to higher headquarters.

Nor did he. On 30 November, Balck gave his very blunt assessment of what he had seen. Feldmarschall von Brauchitsch, the Army C-in-C, he thought, looked ill and broken. Hitler was still demanding more attacks and claiming that victory was yet within their grasp. Balck understood, though, that throwing understrength units into the fray was going to achieve nothing but a final erosion of their best young men. At this point, von Brauchitsch broke down. 'Why don't you go and tell him yourself? We are finished.'

'I was deeply shaken,' noted Balck.

That same month, November 1941, the Reich Minister for Munitions, Fritz Todt, sent a team of armaments manufacturers to see how the German advance towards Moscow was getting on along Army Group Centre's front and to talk to General Guderian at 2. Panzergruppe HQ. Leading the team was one of Todt's most trusted lieutenants, Dr Walter Rohland, aged forty-three, who now headed up a special committee created by Todt for panzer production.

Rohland's family had been in the metallurgy business for generations, but this had not stopped him from joining the Army and in 1916, when barely eighteen, fighting in the Battle of Verdun. He survived this ordeal, but his brother, Fritz, had been killed right beside him the following May, something that had left a profound impression.

By the time Hitler had risen to power, Rohland was a very youthful head of the specialist steel firm Deutsche Edelstahlwerke, which made armour plate and which was a subsidiary of the armaments giant Vestag. Rohland already had a reputation for clear thinking and as a superb organizer. He also passionately believed that Germany needed a strong military, and was a party member. He was unique among German heavy-armaments manufacturers in that he had served with panzers as well as making them; once Hitler had announced back in 1935 that the Reich was rearming, he had immediately decided to rejoin the Army as a reservist *Hauptmann*, and served with 11. Panzerregiment. His nick-name, inevitably, was 'Panzer' Rohland.

He was therefore an obvious choice to send to the front, although he found the trip a depressing one. The Red Army did not appear to him to be on the point of complete collapse; rather, they were well equipped with a sturdy tank, the T34, which had a decent 76.2mm gun and very thick forward armour, and which was not only manifestly superior to any tank in the German Army, but could still operate in the extreme cold. The cream of the *Ostheer*, the German Army of the Eastern Front, appeared to be in deep trouble, a shadow of the confident panzer force that had once swept all before them. 'Our troops were far too lightly dressed,' he wrote, 'in some cases wrapped in blankets! An assorted picture of frozen-up cars abandoned at the side of the road, with Panje carts drawn by Russian ponies doing their best to provide inadequate supplies.' The panzers, he reported, could not be used at all – even if the gearboxes and engines could be got to work, then the weapons were frozen solid and useless.

As soon as Rohland and his team returned to Germany, he fixed up a meeting with Albert Vögler, the chair of the supervisory board at Vestag, and other leading manufacturers, and recounted what he had seen. Then, on 28 November, they met with Todt. They all – even Todt, despite being an acolyte of Hitler's and an ardent party man – agreed that the war against the Soviet Union could now not be won. The day after that, Todt and Rohland flew to Hitler's forward HQ, the Wolf's Lair at Rastenburg in East Prussia, where they met with the Führer and with von Brauchitsch. Rohland described in some detail his experiences before Moscow and warned them that the combined industrial output of Russia, the USA and Britain was unbeatable. As a man who had visited Britain and the USA, who was a senior player in the armaments industry and who had both served in the panzer arm and witnessed the cream of the OKH in action in Russia, his prediction counted for a lot. Then, to really drive the point home, Todt turned to the Führer and said, 'This war can no longer be won by military means.'

Surprisingly, Hitler remained calm. 'How shall I end the war?' he asked. 'It can only be ended politically,' Todt replied. Hitler did not respond.

By the beginning of December, the German war in Russia was unravelling even more palpably, despite a front line that had moved far to the east and was now knocking on the door of Moscow. It was true that Army Group South had captured Kharkov and overrun the Crimean penin-sula, and by the end of November Rostov on the River Don, the gateway to the oil-rich Caucasus, had also been captured. In front of Moscow, however, the Soviet General Georgi Zhukov had a staggering eighty div-isions and 1.25 million men, 7,600 guns and 990 tanks. German forces continued to make ground, but ever more slowly and at terrible cost. The error of not preparing for winter was beginning to haunt them, and although they were now within 30 miles of Moscow, the conditions and mounting casualties made it appear a step too far.

What's more, there was still no sign that the Red Army was beaten. Since Stalin's formation of the Evacuation Soviet on 24 June, a staggering 2,593 industrial operations had been sent east, of which 1,360 were armaments manufacturers. Also shifted east had been around 40 per cent of the workforce, whether labourers, engineers or technicians. Some 1.5 million railway wagons had flowed far, far to the east, carrying with them the machine tools, know-how and key plant with which to ensure the Germans would be denied any swift and complete victory.

Also playing a part in these months of transition were British supplies, promised back in July, which had begun to reach the Red Army. In all, around 2,000 tanks and 1,800 Hurricanes were sent to Russia by the middle of 1942; needless to say, Stalin had demanded more and a second front as well, but these were not insignificant numbers. Around 30 per cent of the tanks opposing the Germans outside Moscow were British.

Meanwhile, at Rostov, as Russian forces launched yet another counter-attack, Feldmarschall von Rundstedt felt compelled to pull back. On 2 December, reports reached OKH headquarters from both Army Groups Centre and North that the troops were at the end of their tether: too hungry, freezing, ill and reduced in numbers to carry on.

At the OKW, senior staff were also struggling to keep the front anything like efficiently supplied, because the German economy was now in severe crisis. By this point, the stocks of food that had been built up before the war had been exhausted. So too had the fat that had been creamed from conquest. The granary of the Ukraine had not borne fruit and rationing was savage; officially, rationing provided 1,990 calories per day, only a little under what healthy women should be consuming, but some way short for men. In reality, however, it was invariably less. According to research by the Military Academy of Medicine, most large German cities were being forced to feed themselves the diet 'of a totally impoverished people'. In Essen in the Ruhr, for example, it was around 1,500 calories a day. The variations were because of distribution difficulties and because a large number of people simply could not afford the rations to which they were entitled. Research at the Krupp armaments manufacturers hospital in Essen showed that even miners, who were entitled to the maximum extra rations, had on average lost 6 kilograms in weight. Consumables had been reduced yet further and the black market was rising, which meant there was less and less on which to spend money. This in turn meant there was more currency in circulation, which, if the Reichsbank wasn't careful, could lead to rapid inflation, a massive decrease in productivity and then civil unrest – as had happened in the early 1920s.

At the same time, shortages were being keenly felt within Germany's war machine. The fuel situation was now so bad the Kriegsmarine's surface fleet was becalmed, lurking in ports and Norwegian fjords. It wasn't just the British blockade that was keeping them there – it was lack of fuel. Stocks of coal had also almost run dry, so further cuts were made to supplies to the occupied territories. This, of course, then made them less useful in terms of their own industrial output and more costly to maintain as part of the Greater Reich. It was a vicious circle.

Reduction in coal use meant a reduction in steel production too. Instead of producing 2 million tons per month, German steel producers were forced to accept a revised figure of 1.65 million tons instead, which had an inevitable knock-on effect on supplying the Wehrmacht. Feldmarschall Milch's planned massive increase in Luftwaffe production was the biggest casualty. He and Göring now had to settle for simply replacing losses: for the time being, there could be no expansion of the Luftwaffe, which was very bad news, as British and American factories were increasing their rate of aircraft production exponentially. Two of the Wehrmacht's armed services, the Luftwaffe and Kriegsmarine, were now in deep crisis – and at a moment in the war when British and American air forces and navies were rapidly growing in size and fighting capability.

As 1941 neared its end, however, the priority was the OKH in the East. Whatever cuts were required for the Army were swept aside. Hitler, especially, was in no mood to hear bleats about shortages of essential resources. 'He refuses to believe that there are not enough raw materials,' noted General Georg Thomas, the head of the Military Economic Office at the OKW. 'After all, he has conquered all of Europe.' Unfortunately for the Germans, however, such had been their own shortages they had had no choice but to bleed the occupied territories dry. As a result, these countries were now adding little to the German war economy. France, for example, had just 8 per cent of the vehicles it had had before the German victory of 1940. Back in 1940, it was the only main combatant in the war yet to impose rationing, but by this time its people were being brutally rationed. French factories couldn't run if all the vehicles, coal and oil had been sent to Germany, or if the young men had been coerced into becoming workers within the Reich. The Germans had been like locusts, sweeping in to the newly conquered territories and seizing everything they could: money, food, natural resources, amenities, machinery, vehicles, manpower – anything that could help their war effort had been greedily taken. Yet because of their own shortages, necessity had meant this booty be used immediately. Now, at this moment of deep crisis, the cupboard appeared largely bare.

And yet, despite these shortages, the Nazis were still astonishingly profligate and inefficient. Men were still issued with generously cut and beautifully tailored uniforms, given jackboots when ankle boots would have been much cheaper. Weapons were still engineered with extraordinary attention to detail. There were too many types of machine, too many factories, and not enough focus.

On 3 December, General Georg Thomas issued a truly extraordinary memorandum, signed by Hitler, demanding the 'simplification and increase in performance of our arms production'. From now on, he insisted, weapons would have to be mass-produced according to 'modern principles'. Only this would allow Germany to achieve a rationalization of manufacturing methods. 'What was demanded,' wrote Thomas, his frustration and anxiety all too apparent, 'was technically and aesthetically complete equipment made by the best craftsmen.' Henceforth, and immediately, engineering standards would have to be dramatically reduced. 'In principle,' he added, 'the usefulness and ability to be produced easily and the savings of materials is to be given priority over aesthetics and other exaggerated demands that are not necessary for the use of war and that are irresponsible.'

This was a truly astonishing admission. Ever since the end of the war, historians and combat veterans alike have waxed lyrical about the superb standard of German weaponry, rarely acknowledging the fundamental flaw in their ridiculous over-engineering that ensured a machine gun took three times the man hours of a British equivalent. The barrel alone of an MG34, for example, might have between six and nine different inspection stamps, each one utterly pointless and adding to the waste of time and unnecessary attention to detail. In the 1930s, as the Nazis were emerging, there was a point to having an excess of leather and overly tailored uniforms. Weapons could, justifiably, have aesthetic appeal. This approach was also, just about, understandable if wars were lasting no more than six weeks. By December 1941, however, Germany had been fighting for more than two years and yet no one had made any attempt to streamline production. Willi Messerschmitt, for instance, was still proceeding with plans for a jet aircraft while the Me109F languished. This was not the way to win a war – especially not a long war now being fought on multiple fronts, and especially not when precious resources were already in short supply.

Germany had many assets: the people were still behind their Führer; on the whole, her armed forces were imbued with an all-important sense of determination and, perhaps most importantly of all, iron-strong discipline. The Third Reich was also blessed with many clever and highly skilled inventors, scientists and engineers. Her military commanders were now, for the most part, smart, experienced, innovative and tactically adept.

And yet, there were so many obstacles too: the shortage of food, the lack of raw materials, the incompetence of Hitler, and the divide-and-rule approach that stemmed from the Führer and infiltrated almost every part of the Nazi machine. Only a little over a quarter of the Army was what they termed 'First Wave' – completely equipped and fully trained – and, inevitably, too much was expected of these men. The Luftwaffe was in disarray and no longer the pre-eminent air force in the world, while on the seas Germany's surface fleet had been neutralized and there were still nothing like enough U-boats. Nor was U-boat technology keeping pace with that of the British. Moreover, instead of making the absolute very best of what assets Germany did have, Hitler and the

Nazis were throwing up yet more obstacles at every turn. Really, it was incredible that they had achieved any successes at all.

As if to underline the disintegration of the entire German war strategy, on the night of 4/5 December temperatures along the Eastern Front plummeted to minus 35 degrees. Machine guns would no longer fire because the lubricants had frozen. Tanks became almost impossible to start and, once up and running, the engines had to be kept going, which meant they were using even more fuel – and so running out quicker. Men, still inadequately equipped, began to freeze to death. They could no longer function as armed forces. Meanwhile, Russian troops in their winter uniforms were moving through this arctic landscape with apparent ease. Even their tanks were working: the T34 was built with a compressed-air starter, enabling the engine to start in the coldest conditions, and lubricated with oil that did not freeze.

Hitler, as was his way, began intervening over and above the heads of the Army command. 'The most frightful aspect,' wrote General Halder, 'is that the Supreme Command has no conception of the state of the troops and indulges in paltry patchwork where only big decisions could help.' By then, however, the Russian counter-offensive had begun. On the night of 5/6 December, Fedor von Bock, the commander of Army Group Centre and now Feldmarschall, ordered a general withdrawal.

At the time, Major Hans von Luck and his men were still clinging to their small bridgehead on the eastern side of the canal at Yakhroma. On the 5th, he was summoned to see General von Funck once more. 'Hitler has overreached himself,' von Funck told him. 'Now we've all got to pay for it.' He ordered von Luck to 'disengage' – 'retreat' was not to be used. They would, inevitably, lose a lot of materiel, but the key, the General told him, was to get the men safely pulled back.

Von Luck's recce battalion was in the rear of the 'disengagement', and they soon found themselves forced to follow one of the main routes cleared through the snow. Harrying them all the way were the enemy air forces. At one point, a bullet from a Russian aircraft went clear through the windshield of von Luck's Mercedes. High piles of dirty snow lay either side of the road, alongside men, horses, equipment and other debris. Von Luck thought it a grisly sight, with dead horses and men piled beside each other. 'Take us with you or else shoot us,' he heard wounded men cry out. They took those they could, but soon they were having to abandon a number of their vehicles – due either to breakdown or lack of fuel. 'Only the will to reach safety in the prepared positions kept the men going,' noted von Luck. 'Anything to avoid being left behind and falling into the hands of the Russians.'

Meanwhile, far away in the Atlantic Ocean, Douglas Fairbanks, Jr was continuing his junior-grade officer training under instruction aboard the battleship USS *Mississippi*. Heading from Iceland to Norfolk, Virginia, they had been caught in a vicious storm and, although it had passed, one of the junior communications officers was still ill and Fairbanks had been ordered to help with the decoding of signals traffic reaching the ship. Most were routine or for other ships and forces, so were quickly discarded.

On Sunday, 7 December, however, late morning, Fairbanks decoded a message that said, 'AIR RAID ON PEARL HARBOR. THIS IS NOT A DRILL.' Initially, this made no sense to him so he discarded it, but then ten minutes later pulled it out again and took it to Commander Jerauld Wright, the ship's captain, on the bridge. Handing it to him, Fairbanks apologized for bothering him but wondered whether the signal was important.

'Is it important?' he snapped. 'Why, you damn fool, it means *our* war has started! The Japs have attacked our biggest base!'

CHAPTER 8

World War

THERE HAD BEEN plenty of indications that Japan was heading towards war, although none that suggested the US Pacific Fleet based at Pearl Harbor in Hawaii was the target. In fact, Admiral Husband Kimmel, the commander of the Pacific Fleet, had sent his three aircraft carriers west towards the Pacific islands of Midway and Wake in case hostilities broke out, which meant, crucially, they had not been in harbour when the Japanese struck.

Japan's move towards war with the West had been a long time in coming and, as with Germany's aggression, at its core lay the urgent need for resources. The herald for this change in Japanese ambition lay in the Meiji Revolution of 1868, in which practical imperial rule was restored and the old feudal shogunate thrown aside. While the Emperor was restored, practical government was handed to an oligarchy that was conscious that Japan was lagging industrially and commercially behind Britain, the United States, France and other global powers. In the decades that followed, Japan modernized very fast, with a massive growth in industry and infrastructure. Shipyards were built, so too was a national railway, and the largely rural population began to migrate rapidly to the cities. The trouble was, Japan was fairly resource-poor and her burgeoning urban population and growing middle class needed the food and comforts of a modern, industrialized nation. Britain, similar in size to Japan, had a large global trading empire and overseas possessions; clearly, Japan needed overseas possessions of her own.

Japan had invaded Manchuria in north-east China in 1931, but, while there were numerous engagements and sporadic fighting in the years that followed, it was not until 1937 that Japan and China fell into full-scale war. Despite sweeping Japanese victories – and merciless brutality towards many hundreds of thousands of Chinese civilians – the Chinese, under the military rule of Chiang Kai-shek, offered more stubborn resistance than Japan had anticipated. In fact, Japan's situation was not improving through war with China but worsening. In the summer of 1939, there was a drought and critical water shortage, made worse by a shortage of coal, which led to restrictions in electricity. The drought, which also extended to Japanese-controlled Korea, led to a drastically reduced production of rice. By early 1940, the trade treaty with the USA had lapsed with no hope of renewal. Fear that imports, especially those from the US, would be cut off, led to urgent purchasing of overseas war materiel, which in turn meant foreign-exchange reserves were being allowed to run low.

By the autumn of 1941, Japan held most of the eastern coastal area of China and Indochina (Vietnam), but at great cost and with ongoing resistance and guerrilla fighting with which to contend. Militarily, Japan was reasonably well equipped with soldiers, aircraft and a large Navy, but was dependent on America, especially, for steel, oil and other essential raw materials. Once the American source was cut off, her ability to build on that would be limited unless she could successfully tap the resources of the Far East, the best of which lay in the hands of Britain, the US and the Dutch.

As with Germany, there was also a pressing and increasing shortage of food. Japan was not self-sufficient and, as always happened when prosperity and urbanization grew rapidly, how to feed the burgeoning population was a major conundrum. The answer, Japan's leaders believed, was the creation of a Pacific bloc, but that would mean war with Britain, America and the colonial Dutch.

Britain and the United States had been watching Japanese aggression with increasing alarm throughout the 1930s. The Tripartite Pact between Japan, Germany and Italy in September 1940 was hardly an encouraging sign for the West, but it was the Japanese move in September 1940 into French Indochina, geographically close to Malaya, Singapore and the US Philippines, then the non-aggression pact with the Soviet Union in April 1941 that rapidly escalated matters. Japan and Russia had been old enemies and had clashed in the 1930s. So long as the two were at loggerheads, Britain and the US had correctly assumed that Japan would not risk further conflict with the West.

None the less, as Germany launched its offensive against the Soviet Union in June 1941, both Britain's and America's leaders still felt confident that Japan was unlikely to risk attacking their possessions in the Far East any time soon. Even so, tensions in the Far East continued to rise. By July 1941, with ever-more Japanese troops moving into Indochina, the United States finally imposed an embargo on all oil and fuel. The following month, on 17 August, President Roosevelt warned that the US would take steps against Japan if it attacked any neighbouring countries, including the oil-rich Dutch East Indies (modern Indonesia). American diplomacy then tried to warn Japan further by increasing aid to Chang Kai-shek's Chungking Government, and by sending a number of B-17 bombers to the US Philippines and transferring the Pacific Fleet to Pearl Harbor in Hawaii.

There were plenty in Japan who believed that, if it came to conflict, the combined might of the USA and Britain would be too great, especially since Japan was also still at war with China. One of those was Prime Minister Fumimaro Konoe, who preferred to find a diplomatic solution. Konoe offered to withdraw from most of China and even Indochina after peace had been made with Chiang Kai-shek's Nationalists.

These proposals were rejected by the Americans, however. Konoe also offered to meet Roosevelt for talks, but the President rejected this proposal too, despite the recommendations of the US Ambassador in Japan to the contrary. Roosevelt, unquestionably a great statesman, arguably demonstrated a lack of judgement in rejecting this offer. Tragically, the Americans had underestimated Japan's dilemma, and in so doing overestimated the strength of their own hand.

By October, Konoe's Cabinet was fatally split over whether they should continue to pursue a peaceful solution or risk war; there was, however, a growing realization that enough concessions had already been offered to the Americans. Thus, a diplomatic impasse had now been created. And the alternative to that was war.

Events now moved swiftly. After a self-imposed deadline for a diplomatic resolution passed with no progress, the Japanese Prime Minister resigned. His replacement, appointed by Emperor Hirohito, was General Hideki Tojo, one of Japan's leading hawks. Since Tojo not only retained his position as Army Minister, but also became Home

Minister, his power and influence was suddenly immense. At an Imperial Conference in early November 1941, his new Government concluded eventual war with the Western powers was unavoidable.

This was based on a number of assumptions. The first was that Germany *would* win in Europe, and the second that the British, already weakened, would be unable to defend her Far East territories successfully. The United States was more of a problem. Not only had the US provided most of Japan's resources for war, but Japan, still a growing nation, had lacked sufficient designers, engineers, draughtsmen, mechanics and pilots. Many had been trained in the US, while Japan had also bought designs from America. All this would be cut off the moment war was declared. The answer was to strike swiftly and decisively and in such a way as to give Japan breathing space to reap the benefits of new conquests. The plan was thus as follows: rapidly to grab British and Dutch possessions and eventually to come to a settlement with the Americans based on destruction of the US Fleet.

Ten days later, on 15 November, the basic strategy for war, the 'Plan for the Successful Conclusion of Hostilities with Great Britain, the United States, the Netherlands and the Chungking Regime', was agreed. Japan had crossed its Rubicon.

Out of this had emerged the attack on Pearl Harbor. The Japanese and US navies were of roughly equal size except in one area: aircraft carriers, of which the US had three in the Pacific and Japan had eleven. The aim of a stealth attack by Japanese naval aircraft flown off her aircraft carriers was to cripple the US Pacific Fleet long enough to allow Japan to get her foothold in the Pacific region. By the time America was strong enough to fight back, Japanese strength would have grown sufficiently to be able to resist. That was the theory, at any rate. Like Hitler's decision to invade Poland, however, it rested on a large number of ifs and buts, and, as such, was an incredibly high-risk strategy. The Tojo Government, however, had convinced itself not only that it had no choice, but also that it would succeed.

The subsequent attack on Pearl Harbor was brilliantly executed and certainly caught the Americans off guard. It was, however, flawed, because Pearl Harbor was quite shallow, which meant the ships attacked were grounded rather than comprehensively sunk, which would make salvage probable. Second, the all-important American aircraft carriers were not there. Third, the attack coincided with the moment US rearmament was about to accelerate.

Pearl Harbor stunned America and particularly her leaders, who had hoped recent measures would be enough to deter Japan. Logically, the risk to the Japanese had seemed too great. Henry Stimson, the Secretary of War, heard the news directly from Roosevelt, but his own reaction was one of relief that the long period of indecision was over and that a crisis had come that would at last bring the country together. 'I feel that this country united,' he wrote in his diary, 'has practically nothing to fear.' The drawn-out arguments in Congress were now a thing of the past; no longer would the administration have to produce arms on a wartime scale with a peacetime attitude; the strikes that had so blighted 1941 would surely be behind them too. The business of war would be easier now they were in it themselves.

In Britain that Sunday evening, 7 December, Churchill was at the Prime Minister's official country residence, Chequers, dining with John Winant, the US Ambassador, and Averell Harriman, Roosevelt's personal envoy to Britain. Quite casually, they switched on the radio to listen to the news and heard a small comment about a Japanese attack on US shipping in Hawaii. They almost missed the item, but Churchill's butler then came in and confirmed it. He had heard it on the wireless too. There was silence around the table, then Churchill got up and went through to his office to call the President.

'It's quite true,' Roosevelt told him. 'They have attacked us at Pearl Harbor. We are all in the same boat now.'

Churchill was overjoyed: while he had remained unshaken in his belief that Britain would be ultimately victorious, the route to that victory now seemed more clear. 'United we could subdue everybody else in the world,' he noted grandly. 'Many disasters, immeasurable cost and tribulation lay ahead, but there was no more doubt about the end.'

Hitler's response was, curiously, much the same as Churchill's. 'We can't lose the war at all,' he exclaimed. 'We now have an ally which has never been conquered in 3,000 years.' For him, Japan's entry into the war was no death knell, but rather a renewed cause for hope. With the United States doing more and more sabre-rattling, Hitler had accepted it was increasingly likely that America would, at some point, enter the war. His nightmare was that the US and Japan would resolve their differences, leaving both Britain and America to fight Germany without being drawn into conflict in the Far East.

Following the Japanese decision to prepare for war against the Allies, they immediately began contacting Berlin to find out what Germany's attitude might be. From Hitler's point of view, this was the best possible news, because they now had the chance to fight a joint war against the US rather than being left to fight it alone. Suddenly Germany had the opportunity to create a global strategic alliance, not just a European one. And so the Führer had immediately made it clear that if Japan declared war on the US, then he would follow suit.

He now had a revised strategy in mind, although it was not one he chose to share with his senior commanders. The British, he reasoned, would lose in the Far East, which would fatally weaken them. Collapse would then be inevitable – so that was Britain sorted. Without having to worry about Britain, German victory in the Soviet Union would be equally inevitable – they had learned the lessons, and this coming summer of 1942 they would complete what they had failed to do the previous summer. There was also hope that Japan would be able to help against the Soviet Union too; at any rate, Japan would certainly be able to tie down a substantial part of Anglo-US forces for a considerable period. With this in mind, a two-ocean offensive would be impossible for the United States and, clearly, the Far East would have to take precedence.

This was a strategy based on wishful thinking rather than any careful or considered appreciation. Hitler had never been to Japan – he had barely travelled outside the Reich – and apart from ambassadorial reports had no real understanding of the Japanese military other than what he was told or what could be studied on paper. As usual, he had made no effort at all to see others from their own perspective but continued to view them through the prism of his own exceptionally narrow and ideologically warped world-view. That the Japanese were – compared with his own view of Aryans – racially inferior, was not a concern. That this contradicted his racial ideology towards Slavs or black Africans, for example, does not appear to have crossed his mind.

So it was that while Britain immediately declared war on Japan, four days later Hitler and his entourage headed to Berlin. There, without any consultation with his senior commanders, the Führer declared war on the United States. Principally, this was to help bind Japan to the now global war, but also because he preferred to be the initiator rather than the recipient of a declaration of war. What Hitler failed to realize, however, was that his declaration of war was exactly what Roosevelt needed to persuade the American people of the policy that had already been agreed with the British in the ABC-1 talks at the start of the year, and again at the meeting at Placentia Bay in August: that the priority of the Allied war effort should be Nazi Germany not Imperial Japan. Without Hitler's declaration of war, persuading both Washington and the wider American public to this way of thinking would almost certainly have been a great deal more difficult.

On the eve of BARBAROSSA, Nazi Germany had just one enemy. Now, on the evening of Thursday, 11 December, just under six months later, it had three: Great Britain (and her Empire), the Soviet Union, and now the United States, each with access to vast pools of both manpower and resources. In contrast, Germany had neither. Already the Wehrmacht was in crisis: not enough planes, not enough men, not enough armaments, and certainly not enough U-boats. Germany was short of money, short of food, and short of coal, fuel and other crucial resources needed for all-out long-term war. In the last war, Germany had signed the Armistice in November 1918 because the country had run out of money and was no longer going to win. Men like Walter Rohland, Fritz Todt and even von Brauchitsch understood that the same moment had arrived in this war too, which was why they had urged Hitler to seek a way out.

That, however, was not Hitler's way. For him, the world was a very black-and-white place, and Germany would either be triumphant and there really would be a Thousand Year Reich, or it would fail in this struggle and Armageddon would follow. In this second week in December 1941, that the latter now seemed almost certainly the fate that would befall Germany was not something Hitler was ready yet to acknowledge.

His will and his iron grip on the German people ensured that, as a result, the war still had a long, long way to go.

PART II

EASTERN
INFLUENCES

CHAPTER 9

Battles at Sea

GENERAL WARLIMONT, the head of the OKW Operations Department, was at HQ Area 2 in Rastenburg and was just discussing Hitler's astonishing announcement in Berlin with fellow officers when General Jodl called from Berlin.

'You have heard the news that the Führer has just declared war on America?' Jodl asked.

'Yes,' Warlimont replied, 'and we couldn't be more surprised.'

Jodl ordered him immediately to begin an appreciation of where the United States was most likely to employ the bulk of her forces – the Far East or Europe. 'We cannot take further decisions until that has been clarified.'

This clarification is exactly what Churchill wanted too. Although the Germany-first policy had already been agreed, he was now anxious to reconfirm this strategy despite the imminent threat to Britain's own Far East possessions. As a result, he immediately suggested a conference in Washington, which was swiftly approved by both his Cabinet and the President.

By the time the PM and the British Chiefs of Staff set sail for Washington on the battleship *Duke of York* on 12 December, Britain had also suffered at the hands of the Japanese, when two of her three Pacific-based battleships were sunk in one day. The *Prince of Wales*, which had carried the British delegation to Argentia in August, had been suffering from defective radar when she was struck by Japanese bombers and torpedo bombers, so, as at Pearl Harbor, the Japanese attack had achieved tactical surprise. More than 800 men were lost from both ships, including Vice-Admiral Tom Phillips on the *Prince of Wales*. It was a big loss.

Life-and-death battles were continuing in the Atlantic. On 14 December, HMS *Audacity* sailed from Gibraltar on the home leg of a further convoy. For the pilots of 802 Squadron, the journey to Gibraltar had been a tough one as the CO had been shot down and killed as he overflew a Condor he had hit; it was a blow felt by them all. A further Martlet was lost over the edge of the deck in bad weather, but on the plus side they did shoot down at least three Condors, one of which was credited to Eric Brown, now stuck with the moniker 'Winkle'. Aware how well armoured the Condors were, Brown had realized the one weak spot was the cockpit. Flying towards one head on, he blazed away with his .50-calibre machine guns and saw the windscreen of the cockpit shatter and debris fall off the nose. Taking violent evasive action to avoid colliding, he looked back and saw the huge machine rear, then stall and spiral down into the sea. Circling overhead, he was surprised to see two men clamber out of the escape hatch and cling to a bit of broken wing still floating as the rest of the machine sank out of view.

Now, though, after a few days in Gibraltar, they were sailing back to Britain, with just four Martlets still serviceable, as part of a large escort force of some sixteen ships protecting thirty-two merchantmen in convoy HG76. Commanding the escort group was Captain Frederic 'Johnny' Walker, a pre-war sailor who had been on the early-retirement list before the war saved his career. This was his first command of an escort group.

Unbeknown to Walker, by the morning of 17 December there were already four U-boats in touch with the convoy. Two Martlets flew off for their dawn patrol and, just as fuel was getting low, one of them spotted a U-boat on the surface and, after reporting the news, opened fire, forcing the boat to dive. Walker, in his sloop HMS *Stork*, immediately set off towards the scene with three other destroyers and a corvette in tow. After rigorously depth-charging the area, they lost contact, then picked up an ASDIC pulse once more and peppered the area with another volley. On the receiving end of this deluge was a Mk IX boat, *U-131*, and on this second peppering it was badly smashed about inside. For almost two hours the crew attempted repairs, but eventually the commander surfaced her and was immediately sighted. Five escorts then began converging on the stricken U-boat, along with a Martlet flown by Eric Brown's friend George Fletcher. Circling overhead, he opened fire, but the crew were manning *U-131*'s gun, a powerful 105mm quick-loading cannon, and a single shell hit the cockpit. Fletcher and his plane plunged straight down into the sea. It was, however, all over for *U-131*. As the escorts descended, guns pumping, so the crew began abandoning the boat and leaping into the sea. At 1.21 p.m., the U-boat upended and sank. Forty-four of the crew were rescued.

The following morning, just after 9 a.m., 18 December, the destroyer *Stanley* spotted another U-boat, *U-434*, on the surface, some 6 miles away. Three more escorts hurried to the scene. Although the U-boat had dived, she received a pasting by depth charges and, like *U-131*, was forced to the surface, right in front of the destroyer HMS *Blankney*, which opened fire and prepared to ram her. At the last moment, *Blankney*'s captain decided to board her instead, but it was too late. *U-434*'s crew abandoned ship and her own demolition charges blew her to pieces. Forty-one of the crew were picked up.

The epic battle was far from over, however. Early dawn the following morning, *Stanley* spotted a third U-boat on the surface, but this time had barely signalled its position before *U-574* had dived and fired a torpedo directly into the destroyer, causing a sheet of flame several hundred feet high to whoosh into the air. Minutes later Walker was on the scene, depth-charging the U-boat and once again forcing the vessel to surface just 200 yards in front of him. Much to his frustration, the U-boat managed to avoid being rammed and *Stork*'s crew were unable to depress – lower – their guns to hit it. After cursing and shaking his fists at the still-surfaced U-boat, Walker ordered *Stork* to circle round for another attack, and this time he rammed and sank it.

While some sixteen Germans and twenty-eight British sailors were picked up, Winkle Brown was taking off as one of a pair of Martlets to intercept Condors patrolling from Bordeaux. They soon found them and Brown decided to try his head-on attack tactic once more. For a second time, he blasted the cockpit, ducked out of the way at the last moment and was able to watch an aircraft plunge down into the sea. Sheepy Lamb attacked another and saw bits falling off it, but it disappeared into cloud. A second confirmed Condor was shot down later that afternoon, with the pilot adopting Brown's head-on tactic. Only narrowly avoiding a collision, the pilot landed with one of the Condor's ailerons wedged into the tail wheel of the Martlet; it had been the closest of shaves and one from which the pilot was lucky to emerge in one piece.

The Martlets were in action again the following day, 20 December, and spotted and harried two more U-boats, firing at them and forcing them to dive; so far, despite interceptions by two separate wolfpacks, the U-boats had not destroyed a single merchantman – the combination of heavy and aggressive work by the escorts and aerial vigilance and aggression by Brown and his colleagues had shown just how hard it was for U-boats to get close enough to fire.

Early the next morning, 21 December, Brown was on the dawn patrol when, to his amazement, he spotted two U-boats on the surface side by side, a plank between them, some 25 miles from the convoy. With the death of his friend Fletch still vividly in his mind, he circled warily and realized the Germans could not elevate their guns above 60 degrees. Circling directly overhead, he could now see that one of the U-boats had a hole in her port and was badly damaged; the other, it seemed, was trying to help. Not wanting to miss such a golden opportunity, Brown rolled over and dived, firing his guns and seeing three men shot off the plank and into the water. Both U-boats then turned and headed off, away from the convoy. Keeping them both in his sights, he waited until he could see the escorts steaming towards them, then turned back towards the *Audacity*.

Just a few hours later, he was off again, flying a second sortie that evening, but, having seen no more U-boats, he and Sheepy Lamb returned to the ship. By now the light was fading but there was a heavy swell and the ship was heaving. As he was about to land, the ship fired two Very lights, a warning for him to climb and go round again. Brown did so, watching the ship alter course slightly and steady up. Then he turned in again, determined to make the landing; the deck had no lights and dusk was settling quickly. This time, he landed safely and, after lashing his Martlet securely, *Audacity* changed course. Unusually, the captain had moved her out of the middle of the convoy so that she was now alone on the starboard side, steaming at 14 knots.

Still the convoy ploughed on north, although by now a number of the escorts had turned back to Gibraltar or sped on their way. That afternoon, Walker had received an Admiralty signal warning him that six U-boats were still stalking the convoy. In an effort to draw them away, as it grew dark he attempted to stage a mock battle with gunfire and star shells, but it had the opposite effect as several of the merchantmen, not in on the plan, panicked and began firing snowflake flares, a disastrous action that served only to light up the real convoy.

Now on the scene was Kapitänleutnant Englebert Endrass in *U-567*, one of Dönitz's leading aces and great friend of another U-boat ace, Erich Topp. The snowflakes had guided him straight to the convoy and, at 8.33 p.m., he hit a British freighter, which sank with alarming speed. Sitting in the wardroom, Eric Brown heard the explosion, but a few minutes later it was *Audacity*'s turn. The blast as the torpedo struck was deafening, shaking the ship violently and making Brown spill his coffee on to his lap. He and the other pilots rushed up on to the deck, where they discovered the ship already down on the stern. It was still moving forward, but the rudder was jammed and the ship could no longer steer. Fearing he might ram another ship, the captain ordered the engines to be stopped, hoping that they might be towed to safety.

It was not Endrass in *U-567*, but *U-751* that had struck *Audacity*, with no fewer than three torpedoes, fired as the ship was silhouetted against the snowflake flares. The U-boat now drew near; up on the tilting deck, Eric Brown glanced over the port side and saw it surface just 200 yards away. 'It was an eerie sight,' he recalled. 'As it popped out of the sea it was covered in phosphorescence.' Brown could clearly see the commander, Kapitänleutnant Gerhard Bigalk, on the bridge, gazing at *Audacity* as though he was weighing up what to do. On the escort carrier, the Captain ordered everyone on to deck, realizing that if they were torpedoed again this would be their best chance of escape. 'And so we stood there,' said Brown, 'just looking at each other.' The stand-off was broken when one of *Audacity*'s sailors, his nerves clearly stretched, leaped over to one of the 20mm cannons and began firing at the U-boat. His shots had only one effect: to prompt Bigalk to finish off the job. Moments later, two white tracks were scything a path across the sea and then they hit. 'And literally,' said Brown, 'the bows fell off the ship.' In moments, *Audacity* began to tilt, stern-up, at an increasingly steep angle. As she did so, the lashings on the Martlets broke: the aircraft came sliding down and thundered into the massed group of sailors, killing many instantly and sweeping others into the water.

Meanwhile, Eric Brown had already jumped clear, realizing what was going to happen the moment the ship began to tilt, and taking with him his logbook and a pair of silk pyjamas he had bought for his fiancée. He hit the water, worrying whether he would be able to swim clear enough before the ship went down and sucked him with it. Still wearing his Irvine flying jacket and boots, he inflated his Mae West life jacket, frantically kicked off his boots and began swimming, but the logbook was restricting his movements, so reluctantly he let it go. He was, however, a decent swimmer and had managed to get about 50 yards away by the time the vessel slipped out of view, disappearing with a tremendous banging and grinding noise. Brown felt the tug of the undertow, but he was far enough clear and, for the moment at any rate, safe; and with his Mae West he had a better chance of keeping afloat than others.

'You all right, Winkle?' he heard Sheepy Lamb call out.

By this time, Brown was clinging to a rubber dinghy, but he swam away to join his friend and together they soon spotted a corvette picking up survivors. Swimming towards it, they were nearly within shouting distance when it suddenly turned and sped off. There were still U-boats about and although *U-751* had submerged, another was spotted on the surface and chased relentlessly by the sloop HMS *Deptford*, then depth-charged. This was Endrass in *U-567* and, although Walker's escorts were not aware of it at the time, they had just got their fourth U-boat of the battle.

While another U-boat ace was sinking to the bottom, Winkle Brown and around twenty others were still bobbing up and down in the sea. They had tied themselves together as a means of mutual support, but one by one the men began to fall asleep and drown. 'We couldn't wake them up,' said Brown, 'so we just had to cut them off and be ruthless and let them drift away in case they dragged us under.' After what felt like the longest three hours of their lives, Brown and Lamb were the only two still alive, but salvation was at hand. The corvette *Convolvulus* returned, and this time both men were able to shout and yell for all they were worth and were duly picked up. So too were the ship's captain and navigator, but as the skipper tried to pull himself up on the lifeline, it suddenly snapped and he fell back into the sea. In the dark, he was lost.

One final tragedy was still to play out, however. After the frantic night's sea battle, *Deptford*'s exhausted crew accidently smashed into *Stork*, crushing the after cabin and, with it, two captured German U-boat crew, who were, Walker reported, 'pulped, literally, into a bloody mess.' Both ships were badly bashed but still working, albeit without sonar.

By dawn on 22 December, the battle was over. After assessing the terrible losses to his U-boats, Dönitz called off the chase and HG76 reached Liverpool the following day. Two warships and two freighters had been lost, but thirty merchantmen had been brought into port safely. Walker's escorts were lavished with praise for having sunk an unprecedented three U-boats, though in fact they had sunk four. Dönitz was devastated, not least about the loss of Endrass, another of his celebrated aces, whose death he withheld until March.

The pilots of *Audacity* had also proved their worth, destroying at least three of the prized Condors. It was, however, a bittersweet return for Winkle Brown. He was to be married, but his best man, Fletch Fletcher, was dead and his second, Pat Patterson, was missing. He would never be found.

Meanwhile, the war in the Far East was going disastrously for Britain and the United States. They had underestimated both Japanese cap-abilities and their determination to risk war, and had been caught hopelessly short. Japanese forces had followed up their attack on Pearl Harbor with major strikes against British territories, and by the start of the New Year they were streaming into Burma and the American Philippines. The US island of Guam fell in half an hour, and Wake Island was also taken despite brave resistance from the small force of US Marines and construction workers; both these places were key stopping points and airfields in the Pacific. Borneo had been invaded, while at Britain's key port of Hong Kong some 40,000 Japanese troops had overwhelmed a garrison of 8,000. Manila, the Filipino capital, fell on 3 January.

It was against this maelstrom that the British war chiefs arrived in Washington for the Arcadia Conference. Despite the terrible and shocking run of defeats in the Far East, to the relief of the British delegation the Americans reconfirmed the Germany-first strategy. In truth, it still made sense despite the Japanese rampage: the threat to the Soviet Union, even with the German winter crisis, was still considered critical and the Japanese were seen as less of a threat to the US and Britain than Nazi Germany was. Moreover, if Germany and her European Axis partners were defeated first, then Britain would be far better placed to help the USA against Japan. None the less, it was a hurdle the British were glad to have got over. Both sides agreed that a joint Anglo-US force would invade mainland Europe as soon as possible. American troops would start being shipped to Britain right away, in what was called Operation BOLERO. The joint strategy was written up in the form of a Declaration of War Aims by the associated powers: Britain, America and the Commonwealth Countries, henceforth to be known as the United Nations. More commonly, they were now known as the Allies, although this was something of a misnomer, as no formal alliance was agreed; rather, they had formed a coalition.

While in Washington, Churchill, along with his current number-one international wheeler-dealer Lord Beaverbrook, met with Bill Knudsen, who had been invited to the White House. Just how much war materiel could be produced by the Allies had been the subject of much debate, Churchill arguing that since the USA was four times the size, it should produce four times as much as Britain. In fact, the USA was many more times larger than Great Britain, but certainly Roosevelt was now thinking of an even bigger programme than the one announced in November.

'Stepping up production to the limit,' the President asked Knudsen, 'how many planes can we make this year?'

Knudsen told him he had been discussing that very matter with his people and they agreed that, with increased facilities, 1942 could see US factories produce 45,000 aircraft. 'To be exact, Mr. President, 44,466 planes,' Knudsen said.

'How about tanks?' FDR persisted.

'On tanks we are just beginning to get production,' he replied. 'I can promise 20,000 and we shoot at 25,000.' These were huge numbers. In comparison, in 1942 Britain would produce an impressive 8,611 tanks, while by the end of the year Germany would have 6,842 armoured fighting vehicles of all types.

'And other stuff,' Roosevelt continued, 'ships, guns, and ammunition, all the other things. You can step them up too?'

'Yes, sir,' Knudsen promised.

A few days later, on 6 January, Roosevelt made his State of the Union Address to Congress and announced the United States would build 60,000 aircraft in 1942 and 45,000 tanks. In 1943, he said, American factories would build no fewer than 125,000 aircraft. 'These figures,' said Roosevelt, 'and similar figures for the multitude of other implements of war will give the Japanese and Nazis a little idea of what they accomplished in the attack at Pearl Harbor.'

While these figures horrified startled aircraft manufacturers and the staffs of SPAB and the OPM, Knudsen took a more sanguine view. 'Let's go ahead on what the President wants,' he told his staff, 'and adjust our plans so we can proceed on that basis.'

Now that the United States was at war, however, there was no longer any need to be quite so mindful of political sensitivities and even civilian requirements. This meant yet another reorganization of the administration of war production. On 16 January, the War Production Board was set up and SPAB abolished, but with most of its staff transferring to the new WPB – including Don Nelson as its director. Eight days later, the OPM was also dismantled. Roosevelt made it clear that from now on the WPB would be in charge of procurement and production and that Nelson's word would be final. Effectively, Nelson was the equivalent of Lord Beaverbrook, the British Minister of War Production. Efficient, personable and widely regarded, Nelson was a shrewd appointment.

If Knudsen was disappointed not to get the top job, he took the news well. As a leading 'dollar-a-year' man – a big-cat capitalist – in charge of the OPM during the troubled previous year, he did not have enough friends in Washington or the media to be given the post. He understood that and accepted it. He was, however, still a key figure in the new WPB and was appointed Director of War Production for the War Department. He was also now a lieutenant-general in the US Army. 'Bill, I want you to accept this commission,' Roosevelt told him. 'I want you to do that because when you go out into the field there may be generals who will try and pull rank on you – they can't do that because you will be over them.' Knudsen accepted and so became the first-ever civilian in the US to become a three-star general.

Knudsen may have been partially sidelined, but in truth he had already done his most important work; the foundations had now been set. He had got his way: big business had been harnessed to war production, regardless of the strikes and political shenanigans in the corridors of Washington, and was now primed to roll. Factories had been built, machine tools constructed and delivered, and the workforce put in place. The President had, at long last, got his building blocks neatly in a row and, while it was true that the gargantuan production figures he spoke about unsettled the manufacturers, his numbers were no longer purely fantastical but a very real possibility. The key now was for the burgeoning US armaments industry to pull together, think big and fulfil the enormous potential it so clearly possessed.

CHAPTER 10

Strategic Blunders

A ROUND 1 P.M. ON Friday, 19 December, General Franz Halder was summoned to see the Führer, who told him that Feldmarschall von Brauchitsch had 'resigned' due to ill-health. He might have had frayed nerves, but he had been sacked, as had von Rundstedt, as part of a purge for failure in the East. Hitler had never liked the old Prussian officer class and so used the opportunity to make himself C-in-C of the Army instead. Halder, the Führer told him, would remain as Chief of Staff, but General Wilhelm Keitel and the OKW would now take over the administration of the Army. This delineation of responsibilities was never properly worked out or written down, however. Hitler told Halder that anyone could deal with the operations of the Army but only he, the Führer, could educate the OKH to be more Nazi, which was why he had decided to take on the job. In reality, it would mean more micro-managing and less freedom of command for his generals. Only Hitler now had the power to move forces from one theatre to another, or to call up reserves. And with much of the day-to-day running of the Army in the hands of the OKW, rather than of Halder and his staff, that meant they would have even less time to do what they were supposed to do – which was to plan and prepare future strategy. General Warlimont was appalled by these changes. 'As a result,' he noted, 'any unified command of the Army ceased to exist.'

Warlimont's own section was disbanded and he became Deputy Chief of the OKW Operations Staff. It didn't mean much, but he now witnessed much more of the day-to-day running of the Army, including the arrival of Halder most mornings for his briefings with the Führer. Halder would come to the Führer's headquarters, looking impeccable, with just a few staff officers, and be confronted by Hitler's court: Keitel, Jodl, several leading Nazis and other staff. Keitel and Jodl would always demur to Hitler, who repeatedly revealed his ignorance and unsuitability for high command. Warlimont reckoned it was the constant meddling and interference by Hitler that Halder must have found the most intolerable aspect of the new set-up. 'The urgent concrete questions and proposals under discussion,' he wrote, 'would be drowned in this cease-less repetitive torrent of words in which matters, old and new, important and unimportant, were jumbled up together.' When Halder told him news he did not want to hear, Hitler would immediately call up his senior commanders in the hope they would give him better information. These often led to long interruptions. Ministers and other non-military figures would also be regularly summoned at a moment's notice, where they would be questioned, lectured and threatened. 'Hours and hours were spent every day in this fashion,' wrote Warlimont, 'a vast waste of time and energy.'

After a most welcome stint of home leave, Günther Sack faced the start of 1942 by making his way first to Koblenz and then to Gattschina air-field, supporting JG54 on the Leningrad front. He was not happy. It was horrifically cold, but his confidence in what they were doing had recently taken a big dip when he'd read a secret report about the number of shells fired as a ratio of enemy aircraft shot down. For light flak it was estimated at 2,000 shells per strike, and for heavy anti-aircraft guns, such as those he was now using, 500. 'When I imagine these enormous numbers of shots that were needed to shoot down one plane,' he scribbled in his diary, 'then this confirms the flawed shooting of the entire flak.'

Now, however, around Leningrad the situation was worse. More often than not, if Russian planes came over Sack and his fellows struggled to fire because the guns had frozen. In fact, German fortunes in the battle for Leningrad were mirroring those at Moscow: they had been close to breaking the city but not close enough, as the Russians inside the encircle-ment demonstrated an astonishing refusal to give in. No matter how great the suffering, the Soviet leadership was not willing to sacrifice their second city any more than they were Moscow.

For the Russians trapped inside, however – troops and civilians alike – the conditions in the city were now truly appalling. Bombing by the Luftwaffe had brought misery to the millions trapped within the encirclement; much of the city's food supplies had been destroyed back in September, for example, when several large depots were bombed and burned to a cinder. Further bombardments had followed during the second half of the month. Soon after, German troops had managed to press on east and on 9 November had captured the important railhead of Tikhvin. This did not mean Leningrad was entirely cut off, but initially it remained open only by building – at considerable human cost – a new road made of logs further to the north through the swamps and forests to the edge of Lake Ladoga and by creating a passage from the western edge of the lake to the city, known, not unreasonably, as the 'Road of Life'. In between, large numbers of ice roads ran across the frozen lake itself. Ingenuity and the Russians' grim determination to hold out were proving the German optimism of September badly misplaced.

Even so, by this time hundreds of thousands were dying from a combination of starvation, water shortage and disease, their bodies often left where they died. The survivors ate birds, then cats and dogs, then rats, then even humans. The paste from wallpaper was converted into a form of edible cellulose. Yet food was getting through, albeit usually at a rate well short of the 700 tons needed a day as a basic human requirement.

There were also still plenty of Red Army troops within the Leningrad front, and it was during these winter months, as the Germans froze and ground to halt, that they were able to regain a small initiative. A Soviet offensive to the south-east was launched on 9 December and the railhead of Tikhvin swiftly recaptured. By the last day of 1941, the Germans had been pushed back along a 90-mile stretch and, at its deepest, 60 miles to the west. This did not mean the siege was over – far from it, and for Leningraders there was still plenty more misery to come – but it did mean the main arteries from the rest of the Soviet Union to the shores of Lake Ladoga were clear once more, so allowing an improved passage of supply to the besieged city. The log 'corduroy' road, built at such cost, was not needed after all. It also meant that, like Moscow, Leningrad remained tantalizingly out of reach of the Germans while still continuing to soak up troops, materiel and a mass of other resources.

Oberst Hermann Balck had seen enough of the front on his travels to know how much German troops were suffering too, but he also thought

Hitler taking over direct command on a temporary basis was no bad thing – a view that was reinforced when he reached Smolensk at Army Group Centre's headquarters on 23 December, where Feldmarschall Günther von Kluge had just taken over command from von Bock after the latter had been sacked for wanting to retreat back over the Desna River. Clearly, there could be no more offensive action for a while, but Balck, who had been desperately trying to help the Army conserve vehicles, believed retreat would be fatal. Their troops needed to stay put and hold their lines; that was their only chance. Napoleon had retreated and had lost almost everything; and already vast numbers of panzers, vehicles and war materiel had been abandoned in the small distances they had already fallen back. As it was, many of the forward units were simply incapable of moving; the 160th Division, for example, had just eighty riflemen left. 'Everything was drowning in snow,' Balck noted. 'Communications were miserable. Lateral movements were impossible.'

On 30 December, Balck was back at the Wolf's Lair, Hitler's forward HQ at Rastenburg, and the following day, the last of 1941, he was allowed to brief the Führer on all that he had seen at the front. Hitler quite often preferred the opinions of fighting men over those of most of his senior staff, especially when they were talking the kind of language he wanted to hear. When Balck urged him not to withdraw under any circumstances, this was very much music to the Führer's ears, because since taking over direct command of the Army this was exactly what he had been ordering. However, while Balck believed more men and materiel would be saved by holding firm, for Hitler it was more a question of pride and, whether Balck was right or wrong, five days earlier even Guderian had been sacked too – for disobeying an order not to withdraw his men.

Guderian had been one of the key commanders and architects of the stunning victory against France in 1940, but the success of his panzer thrust had been largely due to his frequent ignoring of orders from above; had he not done so, he would have been forced to attempt a crossing of the River Meuse at an entirely different place and would have halted immediately afterwards rather than pressing on so successfully. The very effective air assault on Sedan would also have been conducted differently and quite possibly less successfully. One of the principles of Bewegungskrieg was 'mission responsibility' – that is, that commanders on the ground were best placed to read the situation and should be trusted to interpret orders as they best saw fit. This went hand in hand with flexibility and speed of manoeuvre, two other key principles.

Ignoring the orders of senior commanders, however, was all very well when victory was in the air, but before Moscow it had seemed as though the independent actions of individual commanders were only destabilizing matters further. On 26 December, Halder had stressed that from now on blind obedience to the orders of the Führer was essential if the crisis was to be overcome. 'We shall master it if we firmly seize the reins of command,' he wrote the day after Guderian's sacking, 'without consideration for inappropriate sensibilities, if the commands are entirely frank and truthful in their reports, and if a single will, the will of the Führer, prevails from the highest levels down to the soldier at the front.' So the hero of Germany's finest hour had been given the chop, and one of the key tactical principles of the German way of war had been shelved in favour of absolute obedience to a Commander-in-Chief who had only ever been a junior soldier in the last war, who had never before directly commanded troops in battle and who had no staff or command training whatsoever.

This was dangerous for German fortunes, to say the very least, and on a number of levels. In the past, for example, any grievances could be laid at the door of senior commanders. 'If the Führer only knew . . .' had been a common excuse and even slogan for when things did not go entirely according to plan. Hitler had been immune from criticism. Now, however, he was in the position to direct armies, divisions and even battalions, and that intermediate level of command – that of von Brauchitsch and the Army Staff – had effectively been stripped out. Confidence in the Führer would soon be eroded lower down the chain if things continued to go badly wrong.

Nor did this change of command and command style suddenly bring about honesty. Subordinates still told Hitler what he wanted to hear. Oberst Balck, in his briefing with Hitler on 31 December, had to insist that the numbers of tanks reaching the front lines was half the figure the Führer had been told. Hitler was horrified. Moreover, such was Hitler's will and iron grip, it was a brave man who turned down a direct request. Soon after taking over as Army C-in-C, Hitler asked General Adolf von Schell whether he had 10,000 trucks. Yes, Schell replied. 'Can I have them in Warsaw by December 22?' Hitler asked. 'Yes,' Schell replied, believing there was little room for negotiation. The trucks were found and loaded up, but there were not enough trained drivers so most of them ended up being driven by teenagers in the Hitler Youth. 'What actually reached the front lines,' wrote Balck, 'was junk. The ten thousand trucks had been wasted.'

Furthermore, the command process had now slowed down with Hitler as C-in-C. Snap decisions became almost impossible to issue because the Führer insisted on micro-managing. The flexibility of the German war machine, the independence of the subordinate commander and the ability to manoeuvre at speed – principles that had brought them their string of victories – had all been discarded.

'Führer holds forth at great length on the need of holding the line,' Halder noted in his diary on 20 December. 'A very bad day!' he jotted on 29 December, and 'Again a hard day!' two days later. 'Repeated talks with von Kluge,' he wrote on 2 January, 'who is at the end of his wits and talks of utter loss of confidence.'

It was hardly surprising. Casualties had been horrendous since the start of BARBAROSSA. By the end of July, the German Army had lost more men than all the campaigns in the West. By the end of August, the strength of the infantry divisions had fallen to just 60 per cent. By November, most front-line divisions were at just 50 per cent strength. At the end of that month, the Quartermaster General had to admit that, after five months, the OKH's manpower reserves had been exhausted. During the First World War, for every 1,000 German casualties, 226 had been killed, but in July 1941 the figure had risen to 236 and by the end of the year it was as high as 244. Since July, the Army had lost more than 40,000 dead every month apart from November, when the figure had been around 38,000. August had seen more than 60,000 killed. By 5 January 1942, Halder was recording in his diary that total losses were 830,903, 'i.e., 25.96 percent of the Eastern Army.'

The crisis was exacerbated because Germany was so under-mechanized compared with the Allies, which meant if Germany was to really pack a punch, there was no alternative to the man-heavy Army. This, though, then put a far greater strain on those manpower resources. Solutions of sorts, however, were being put into place. There were some 300,000 in the Reserve Army but, with transport capacity full just trying to keep those already at the front supplied, getting them there was impossible at the rate demanded. None the less, five new divisions were formed from this pool and were eventually sent exclusively east, although most of these were older men and only partially trained.

Another source was found by scouring prisons and paroling a large number of the inmates. Other men, previously exempt, were also called up. Most of these were industrial workers and were rather dramatically called the 'Valkyrie Divisions'. But there were now almost no men in their twenties still left: almost every single one had either already been called up or was now a casualty. Teenagers coming of age would amount to fewer than a million men a year, which just about covered current losses but did not allow for any expansion.

Thus Germany now faced a critical manpower shortage. The paradox, of course, was that by waging an ideological war against the Jews the Nazis were in effect shooting themselves in the foot; not only were they systematically executing large numbers of perfectly fit and able men – and women, for that matter – who might otherwise have been able to serve in the armed forces or in German factories and farms, they were also tying up manpower and capable staff officers, equipment and vehicles in the *Einsatzgruppen* – the SS death squads – set up to carry out such exterminations. Some 65,000 people were murdered in Poland in 1939, the equivalent of four divisions, while the numbers killed in the Baltic States, Ukraine and elsewhere were enormous: some 141,000 in the Baltic States alone; at Babi Yar, near Kiev, nearly 34,000 were executed in just two days. That these executions were barbaric hardly needs to be said. They were also utterly counter-productive, especially when a large number of the victims were as against Communism as the Nazis were and could easily have been a valuable asset, helping the Germans with much-needed manpower and fanning the flames of revolt against the Soviet Empire.

This was one of the many contradictions of Hitler and the Nazis. They were prepared to make alliances with the racially different Japanese and do deals with the Communist Soviet Union when it suited, but there was to be no compromise on the racial ideology against the Jews. What had begun as discrimination and segregation had morphed into horrific mass murder on an enormous scale. And it was all so utterly pointless. Because of warped and illogical racial hatred, an already very difficult task was now that much harder.

So it was that at the start of 1942, the German war machine, which had so dazzled and stunned the world in the first years of the war, was now in deep crisis, despite Japan entering the war and despite Hitler's renewed optimism. The truth was, the Nazi state was actually a rather fragile structure, built on lots of independent and rival organizations. The entire edifice was held together in a decidedly unstable balance. Divide and rule was Hitler's modus operandi. He mistrusted the Wehrmacht, the Wehrmacht mistrusted the SS, and every part of the apparatus of state was riven by factions, rivalries and mistrust. Nor were they making the most of their still-meagre resources. Aircraft manufacturers were allowed to get distracted with different projects, manpower resources were being squandered, Hitler was meddling in military matters that were well above his experience, knowledge or understanding, and the strategic focus was all over the place. Britain and especially America were modernizing in almost every single aspect of both the lives of their peoples and their war effort; Germany's modernization, however, was only partial. Yes, they had sophisticated radar and were developing rockets and jet technology, but they had an army that was largely dependent on horse and cart. And yes, they had developed effective panzer tactics, but their tanks were mostly obsolescent compared with those of the Red Army. It was also true they were pioneers of radio and communications, but they were acting with the barbarism of an earlier age as they plunged eastwards, lining up and grotesquely executing hundreds of thousands of innocents. These were paradoxes that were not only hard to square, but did not augur well as they now took on the largest, most powerful nations in the world.

On 15 January, Oberst Hermann Balck made some notes in his journal and blamed Hitler for the mess they were now in. As far as he was concerned, the Wehrmacht had exceeded its 'culminating point'. This was a term coined by the Prussian general and theorist Carl von Clausewitz in his seminal work *On War*, and to a student of warfare like Balck it was very familiar terminology. In a nutshell, the culmination point was the moment at which a force was no longer able to reach its objectives, whether because of supply problems, stiffening opposition or general fatigue. The aim, then, was to achieve an objective before the culmination point had been reached. Against Britain in 1940, in North Africa and against Malta, and now in the Soviet Union, the pattern had been repeated. 'Instead of completing one thing,' he noted, 'and taking it to the end, we already moved onto the next. So we exceeded our culminating point.' He was quite right. Germany simply did not have enough of what they required nor the strategic vision to fight the war they needed to fight.

'Do you know what "hubris" means?' General Halder asked Balck around this time. 'That is our problem.'

While Germany scrabbled to fill the supply holes, Britain and America continued to make sure no such shortages affected them. That America's industrial potential was, at last, looking as though it might be realized after all was good news for the Allies, but it would mean nothing if it ended up at the bottom of the Atlantic. So far, however, the vast bulk of British and Allied shipping had managed to get safely across the Atlantic. There had been some devastating attacks along the way and, by the beginning of 1942, 2,336 British, Allied and neutral merchant vessels had been sunk in all waters since the start of the war. That was no small number, but still equated to less than 2 per cent. To put this in perspective, at any one moment, on any given day, on average, there were around 2,000 such merchant vessels sailing around the world on behalf of the Allies.

Thus Dönitz could look back on 1941 as a year of enormous disappointment and wasted opportunity. Those dizzy days of 1940, the 'Happy Time' when his small band of brothers were sinking ships at will, must have seemed as though they belonged to another age. In the last seven months of 1940, Dönitz's few crews were sinking an astonishing average of 727 tons per U-boat per day. In sharp contrast, the best they had managed in 1941 had been 486 tons per day, and from May 1941 onwards that average had slipped yet further to just 220 tons per U-boat per day. In November, it was just 66 tons. That meant they were destroying nothing like the half million tons of Allied shipping a month he had originally reckoned was the minimum needed to have a decisive effect on Britain, and far short of the 800,000 tons per month he had decided was necessary by the beginning of 1942. They were not even getting close.

His most experienced crews had been killed or captured, while Allied anti-submarine equipment and tactics had greatly improved. In contrast, as more and more U-boats were built, so the training and experience of his crews diminished. It was in this area as much as any that Dönitz had cause to rue the lack of pre-war investment in the BdU. There was also a suspicion that the British had somehow broken their ciphers and codes, although this had been dismissed as impossible. It was not, however, and it has been estimated that as many as 300 ships were saved by re-routing as a result of Ultra intelligence. The other big problem for Dönitz and his men was the continued shortcomings of their torpedoes. While the British were producing ever-more effective radar, high-frequency direction finding – Huff-Duff – and other pieces of crucial anti-submarine warfare (ASW) equipment, the Germans were still using contact pistol torpedoes, which were not as reliable as they should be. A new homing torpedo and an improved proximity pistol were on their way, but they weren't available just yet. In this technological race, the British were currently winning hands down. It was the ding-dongs in the desert that were making the headlines in both the British and German press, but it was the grim battles out at sea, more often than not at night, on a rising swell in the cold, briny grey of the Atlantic Ocean, where the critical battles were taking place. Britain's war leaders understood this and so too did Dönitz. Hitler did not; not really, despite authorizing a major U-boat building programme that saw numbers tripling. Between June and the end of September 1941, fifty-three new U-boats had been sent out on first combat patrols; the previous year, that figure had been just six.

One of the major disadvantages for Dönitz was that the U-boat was not a true submarine because it could not operate under the surface for a protracted period. This was especially true of the Mk VII, the standard and most prevalent U-boat. When submerged, they operated on engines powered by batteries. These were capable of speeds of up to 9 knots, but only for a very short period of time – about an hour. Only by slowing speed to walking pace could they last longer and, when being stalked and depth-charged, having more than an hour of juice was important. On the surface, however, they could use their diesel engines, which not only charged the batteries, but gave them a range of some 10,000 miles and a maximum speed of more than 17 knots, which was plenty for hunting most Allied merchant ships.

This meant that U-boats did most of their sailing, stalking and operating on the surface; submerging was a short-term measure, used to avoid detection once in position to fire and for escaping a tight situation. This also ensured that most attacks occurred at night when, with their low profiles, they were harder to spot; and it also meant that U-boats were more likely to sink ships in winter, with the longer hours of darkness, than in midsummer.

It could have been very different, because, as it happened, the Germans had already invented the world's first proper submarine. Hellmuth Walter had created a submarine that could travel at 23 knots under the water and remain fully submerged for long periods at a time. This was an extraordinary speed for a U-boat and meant it could outrun any convoy by quite some margin. It could even outrun most of the fastest merchant vessels, which tended to sail independently. Walter's V-80 had been first launched in April 1940 and Dönitz had been an enthusiastic supporter of its development. It was powered, however, by hydrogen peroxide and the Naval Staff had concerns about its safe handling.

Repeatedly, Dönitz had urged further and rapid development – and did so again, most forcefully, on 18 January 1942 following his latest meeting with Walter. Yet every time, the Naval Staff demurred. The costs were too high; it might mean interrupting current U-boat production; and there was ongoing unease about its safety. All of these concerns could have been overcome, but it was symptomatic of how low a priority the Battle of the Atlantic was in the minds of the German High Command that the world's first modern, properly functioning submarine – a vessel that really could have had the potential to cause untold damage to the Allied supply chain – was met with such comparative indifference. As a result, a genuine world-beater was left languishing in development limbo and the task of winning at sea was left to ever-more Mk VII U-boats – an ageing design that was no longer really cutting the mustard for all its psychological menace.

Certainly, for the Allies, combatting submersibles like the Mk VII was a great deal more straightforward because of the U-boats' limited under-water capabilities. The key, then, to ensuring the safe passage of ships was not to destroy these U-boats – although that was unquestionably no bad thing – but to restrict their chances of attack. The further from home base a U-boat was, the less likely he was to risk damage, so what escorts had to do was either drive them off or force them to submerge. Either course would restrict a U-boat's ability to attack, which required huge amounts of skill in any case. The best chance for a U-boat to sink a ship was by getting as close to it as possible. Forcing U-boats to abort an attack actually did not require a huge number of escorts, and once a convoy had a sizeable escort group with half-decent ASW equipment, the U-boat's task became very, very difficult indeed.

The second key aspect of anti-submarine warfare was air power and ASW patrols. Having an air umbrella forced U-boats to re-route, evade and submerge. In the old days, a U-boat could cheerily cruise on the surface across the vast open tracts of the ocean without much concern. This had all changed now that the RAF's air umbrella off the western edge of Britain and Ireland had forced the U-boats far further west. What this meant was, so long as Allied shipping was put into convoy with some form of escort and a decent amount of air cover, the bulk of the vessels were most likely to get through.

Hitler had personally told Dönitz back in September that any incidents with the United States were to be avoided, but now that they were at war, the gloves were well and truly off: American ships were fair game. Really, it was just a question of getting U-boats across to the far side of the Atlantic.

On 1 January, Dönitz had ninety-one operational U-boats. Of these, twenty-three, much to his extreme chagrin, were still in the Mediterranean, with a further three on their way there at the behest of the High Command. Six were stationed off Gibraltar, and a further four were off the coast of Norway. Of the remaining fifty-five, 60 per cent were undergoing repairs and languishing in dockyards far longer than they might have done because of the absurd preferential maintenance treatment of the surface ships. This meant there were just twenty-two boats at sea in the Atlantic, of which at least half were either en route to or returning from their patrol stations. 'Thus, at the beginning of 1942, after two and a half years of war,' noted Dönitz, 'there were never more than ten or twelve boats actively and simultaneously engaged in our most important task, the war on shipping.' This was truly a pitiful state of affairs. If Dönitz was seething with frustration, it was hardly surprising.

On 2 January, he was able to order the first pack of five U-boats to make the long trek across the Atlantic to patrol off the US east coast. This was the start of Operation PAUKENSCHLAG – 'Drum-roll' – agreed by Hitler on 12 December. Off the Grand Banks of Newfoundland the weather was brutal, the swell horrendous and, for U-boat, merchantman and escort, the biggest battle was dealing with the appalling conditions. Further south, however, in areas where U-boats had rarely previously ventured, the waters were warmer and the seas calmer. Moreover, the shipping lanes off the coast of America, into the Gulf of Mexico and down through the Caribbean to Brazil and Argentina, were some of the most congested in the world as the passages across wide expanses of ocean were suddenly funnelled into straits between strings of Bahamian and Caribbean islands. They were also traditionally very important trading routes; just as Britain had had a very congested number of shipping routes around the United Kingdom, the same was true of the United States. Despite the network of US railroads, large amounts of freight were still ferried between Texas and New England, for example, and many places in between. Coal, bauxite, coffee, sugar, steel, iron, and especially oil from the Dutch West Indies, Venezuela and Texas, were all needed by the US itself as well as to transport across the Atlantic to Britain. All these supplies had been plying the seas, uninterrupted, for aeons; not since the Civil War had this trade been curtailed.

These shipping lanes were fast, well sailed and efficient, and the only enemy were tropical storms. Although U-boats had reached the east coast of the USA in the last war, preparation had not been made to deal with the arrival of aggressive U-boats now that America was at war with Germany once again. The bulk of America's Navy was directed to the Pacific, what remained was helping escort trans-Atlantic convoys, and no one had really thought to line these coastal routes with significant numbers of airbases and patrol aircraft.

As a result – and as Dönitz was well aware – at the beginning of 1942 American coastal shipping was continuing as it had always done: in the quickest and easiest way possible – that is, independently and un-escorted. For the U-boats, these represented rich pickings. A slaughter was about to unfold.

CHAPTER 11

Carnage Off America

'T HE USUAL NAVAL WOES,' noted Count Ciano on 13 December, as news reached him that two 5,000-ton cruisers and two large passenger ships loaded with tanks for Libya had been sunk off Cape Bon in Tunisia. This came on the back of the gloomy reports from the battle raging around Tobruk, in which Italian troops appeared to be receiving another kicking. None the less, a few days later, on 19 December, the Italian Navy finally had some small success, when three two-man manned torpedoes, released by a mother submarine, successfully managed to penetrate Alexandria harbour and severely damage two battleships, *Valiant* and *Queen Elizabeth*, and damage a further destroyer and tanker. All six men were subsequently captured but the damage would put both battleships out of action for some time. Admiral Cunningham, the gritty Commander-in-Chief of the Mediterranean Fleet, had been aboard the *Queen Elizabeth* at the time and was devastated. 'Thus our last two remaining battleships were put out of action,' he noted. 'It was a heavy blow.'

It also came at a time when news had arrived that II. Fliegerkorps had been posted to Sicily. With the fighting on the Eastern Front ground to a halt by the intense cold and snow, it made sense to deploy part of the Luftwaffe back to theatres where they could actually operate. Clearly, Malta was likely to face another hammering, which meant supplying the stricken island would be difficult. Cunningham was going to need all his fleet if he was to keep up the pressure on Axis convoys and escort British merchant vessels in their efforts to reach the island. It was no wonder he felt the temporary loss of his battleships so keenly.

Meanwhile, in the North African desert, Eighth Army's CRUSADER offensive had finally run out of steam. British forces had chased the Axis all the way out of Cyrenaica and back to El Agheila, where the British lost fifty out of ninety tanks in one final engagement, ensuring that, for the time being at any rate, that was the end of the line. There would be no further advances into western Libya. Incredibly, there were still a number of Italian and German pockets left behind around the Egyptian border. These had been cleared up one by one, so that by 17 January, CRUSADER was finally over.

The British had started the battle with slightly fewer men and a few more tanks than the Axis, but with the Germans' superior anti-tank guns – including the already much-feared dual-purpose flak and anti-tank 88mm – the two sides had ended up quite evenly matched. Only in the air had the British enjoyed anything like a significant advantage, one that had been made even more effective by the increasing levels of co-operation and improved organization; the Luftwaffe, in contrast, had not really developed at all in terms of tactical air-support doctrine. In fact, Rommel had a rather diffident attitude towards General Stefan Fröhlich, the Fliegerführer Afrika, and barely acknowledged Generale Vittorio Marchesi, the Italian Regia Aeronautica commander.

Overall, the British had lost about 15 per cent in casualties and the Axis 32 per cent, and CRUSADER had achieved most of its main aims, not least the liberation of Tobruk, but had failed to deliver a decisive knock-out blow to the Axis forces, so there was a feeling that Eighth Army hadn't done as well as it might. Neither Cunningham nor Ritchie had been willing to use massed formations of concentrated fire-power. Throughout the battle, Rommel had repeatedly been able to pick off small formations piecemeal.

On the whole, the armament of the British tanks was not really suitable for the wide, open spaces of the desert; they had been designed for closer European warfare. German panzers weren't much better armed, but their 88mm, 75mm and even 50mm anti-tank guns had far greater velocity than most of those in tanks, and in the desert it was velocity – the speed and distance at which a shell travelled – that really mattered. The 88mm, for example, could hurtle a shell several miles at around 2,750 feet per second. Even the 50mm anti-tank gun had a range of over a mile and a half and a velocity of not much less than the 88mm. Britain simply did not have any anti-tank gun that was remotely as powerful; the best on offer was the 2-pounder, or 40mm, which had a much smaller shell, and although its velocity was around 2,600 feet per second, its effective range was around 1,000 yards. At this distance or less, British tanks and anti-tank guns were reasonably effective, but as they discovered in the CRUSADER battles, it needed only a few German 88s and 75s and they had no answer – not on the ground, at any rate. It was air power that had done for Rommel's armoured charge in the early stages of the fighting.

'The role of our armoured forces is usually the destruction of those of the enemy,' observed a passage in *Notes from the Theatres of War No. 2* about the CRUSADER battles, produced by the War Office. 'This task can only be accomplished by direct attack if our tanks are better "gunned" than the enemy's, or if we are greatly superior in numbers. At the moment we are neither.' Actually, this was not quite true – on either point. The trouble was that those trying to learn the lessons of the recent fighting had not really worked out that it was the anti-tank gun, rather than the tank itself, that was emerging as the pre-eminent weapon in the desert. The slight worry was that the British were becoming just a little too impressed with German panzers, and with Rommel too, whose dash and flair were making him as well known within Eighth Army as he was in those of the Axis forces.

As if to prove the point, the German general made the most of a safely delivered convoy in January to push back into Cyrenaica. With British lines of supply once more overstretched, Rommel repeated his forays of a year earlier, pushing back the British defences, retaking Benghazi and driving on as far as Gazala, some 60 miles to the west of Tobruk. The loss of territory didn't hugely matter, but for the British it did rather take the gloss off the recent hard-fought battles. In the development of the British Army, it felt as though it was two steps forward and one step back.

There were setbacks in the Atlantic too. By the end of February, just a handful of U-boats, operating far from base on the opposite side of the Atlantic, sank seventy-one ships, of which all but ten were in the American zone and almost all independents. Two of those were sunk by Teddy Suhren and *U-564*. Setting off from La Pallice on the mid-Atlantic French coast on 18 January, America had seemed to Suhren about as far away as the moon. The Type IX U-boats could manage it with reasonable ease, but it was a heck of a distance for a Mk VII like *U-564*. They had left La Pallice with every bit of spare room in the boat crammed with hams, bread and other supplies.

Suhren had recently been promoted to Kapitänleutnant and been given the Oak Leaves to his Knight's Cross – and by Hitler in person – so he was in especially bullish mood when he set off on what was his fourth patrol with *U-564*. Travelling at their most economical speed, they reached Cape Hatteras off the North Carolina coast, where a series of small islands jutted out into the Atlantic. It was an obvious point where coastal shipping from the south turned on the run north to Boston and Halifax, Nova Scotia, and sure enough they soon sank the Canadian tanker *Victolite*. Frustratingly for Suhren, in thick fog, at dusk, they collided with *U-107* commanded by his good friend Harald Gelhaus. The crash struck *U-107*'s fuel tank and bent the doors of Suhren's four torpedo tubes. Both would have to head all the way back, while Suhren had to pump some of his fuel across to the other boat too. Even so, he and his crew managed to sink a second vessel en route with their gun. 'When I reported back, it must have been obvious that I was unusually meek,' he noted. 'Dönitz just looked down at me and said, "You mutton-head!"'

In March, the U-boats exacted an even bigger toll as ninety-two ships went to the bottom, of which only three had been in convoy. Italian submarines had also been sent across the Atlantic and were now operating off the Brazilian coast, catching meat freighters as they headed north.

Clearly, the answer was to get these merchantmen into escorted convoys and in double-quick time. The Americans knew and accepted this, but felt unable to do anything about it, and for a number of reasons, some justifiable, others not. The US Navy was unquestionably at fault for not anticipating this move by the U-boat arm; but once the slaughter began in January it was no easy matter to transform not only the shipping routes but the means of protecting them. Convoying was complicated and a logistical headache to the say the least; and it meant delivery of products was both slower and with greater gaps of time between shipment and arrival, which also had wider implications not for trans-Atlantic trade but certainly for US war manufacturing.

The second problem was one of command. Admiral Ernest King had stepped down as Commander-in-Chief Atlantic Fleet (CINCLANT) on 20 December on being promoted to Commander-in-Chief United States Fleet. Admiral Royal E. Ingersoll took over in the Atlantic, but because

CINCLANT was a floating, ship-bound command that lacked the necessary communications and facilities to direct something as complicated as protecting all Atlantic trade in the US zone, Admiral King effectively retained many of his former functions. King was sixty-three, brooked no nonsense from anyone, made decisions quickly and tended to be an immovable rock once his mind was made up. Experienced though he was, King was a hard, grim, determined man. He was also someone who believed the Japanese, not Nazi Germany, posed the greatest threat to the United States. This is not to imply a lack of concern about the Atlantic, but unquestionably he suddenly had a lot on his plate. It was, however, King's idea to shift the trans-Atlantic convoy routes south, which led to the creation of the Mid-Ocean Escort Force, which meant British and especially Canadian escort groups would be operating all the way across the Atlantic, between Argentia and Londonderry. King also suggested forming new Canadian short-leg escort groups, so freeing up US escorts further south. Both suggestions were accepted and adopted by the Canadians and British. It would mean more work for their escort groups, but with the trans-Atlantic routes being largely ignored by the U-boats, this was considered just about manageable – for the time being, at any rate.

The third problem, however, was one of doctrine. Since producing the *Escort of Convoy Instructions*, the US Navy had been wedded to the idea that a convoy without adequate protection was worse than none. 'It should be borne in mind,' noted Admiral King, 'that effective convoying depends upon the escorts being in sufficient strength to permit their taking the offensive against attacking submarines.' This was palpably not true: strong escorts were obviously better than meagre escorts, but meagre escorts and ships in convoy were better than sailing independently. The trouble was that, as prescribed in the *Instructions*, US doctrine argued that the role of escorts was primarily to destroy U-boats. It wasn't – it was to protect the convoy. Small numbers of escorts could do much to help drive U-boats away, as the British and Canadians argued, and they had the experience to prove it, not to mention the statistics.

The Americans were normally only too happy to learn from others and absorb new ways of doing things, but, as a coalition partner with Britain rather than a formal ally, there was no official exchange of doctrine and tactics. And on this matter of escorts, King was not to be swayed, even though the British had the Naval Control of Shipping

(NCS), which was able to cover the Eastern Atlantic and could easily have been used to help the Americans set up a convoy system.

The Americans were striving to set up a convoy system as quickly as possible, but on their terms and to a level that they thought was effective and based on their doctrine of the previous autumn – doctrine that had been written before they were in the war and before they had had much chance to absorb experience in the Atlantic.

None the less, plans for such a system were finally submitted on 27 March and approved by King on 2 April. In this, it was agreed that a 45-ship convoy would be needed every three days on two routes from Guantanamo in Cuba to Halifax, and from Key West in southern Florida to New York. This required forty-one destroyers and forty-seven corvettes or similar – a number that allowed for a minimum of five escorts per convoy.

They also needed greatly increased air cover. The proximity of the routes to land meant this should, in theory, be easy to implement. But again, the lack of preparation had caught the Americans short. Air patrols would grow, and swiftly over the ensuing months, but not fast enough to stop the carnage in the opening months of 1942.

In the Far East, the situation had gone from bad to worse for the Allies. Kuala Lumpur, the capital of Malaya, fell on 12 January, while Japanese troops were pressing into Burma. Fierce battles were continuing in the Philippines and Borneo, and Australian New Guinea had also been overrun, as were the Solomons and Bougainville, which threatened the vital shipping channel between the United States and Australia. All of the Dutch East Indies were lost. In February, the loss of Malaya was complete and was followed by the fall of Singapore, where on 15 February General Arthur Percival surrendered 130,000 British, Australian and Indian troops to General Tomoyuki Yamashita's force of a mere 30,000. It was the worst defeat in British history and, in terms of Britain's ability to keep fighting, a far worse blow than the defeat in France in 1940. Within a couple of weeks, the British and Dutch navies had also lost the Battle of the Java Sea, the worst Allied naval defeat of the war.

These were enormous humiliations, and especially the losses of Malaya and Singapore, because Yamashita's troops were not only considerably fewer in number, but also not especially well equipped. These losses have done much to perpetuate the impression of Britain as a fading power, rotten at its heart. In suffering defeat in Malaya, Britain lost its richest colony, with its crucial supplies of rubber and timber and quinine. These could be made up by expensive synthetic programmes – as the Germans had discovered – but Burmese oil supplied not only much of India but also Britain's interests throughout the Far East; shipping those supplies from the US, Venezuela or Iraq and Persia would, of course, place an extra strain on shipping. The only consolation was that by destroying the Rangoon oil-storage farms and refinery as they departed, the British at least denied them to the Japanese.

The Far East not only caused the loss of large numbers of men and materiel, but would also continue to suck troops and supplies there until such time as Japan might be defeated, and that was clearly unlikely to be soon. Churchill may have been overjoyed that the Japanese had brought the US into the war, but it was something of a double-edged sword, for while the Americans had agreed the Germany-first strategy, that didn't mean they would sit back and give the Japanese a free hand; far from it – both Britain and the US would have to pour enormous resources into the war against Japan and right away. In London, Major-General John Kennedy, the Director of Military Plans, was immediately faced with wrestling those very demands. 'The problem before us now,' he noted, 'is to decide how far we can strengthen our position in the Indian Ocean and in the Far East without weakening ourselves unduly at home and in the Middle East.'

Even before 1941 was out, convoys originally intended for the Middle East had been diverted. Troops, materiel and shipping that could have been used in the war against Germany were now sent east. Two Australian divisions and one British already active in the Middle East were withdrawn and sent to the Far East, including the Australian 6th. American supplies, for the time being, dropped to a trickle, and most US warships in the Atlantic were withdrawn to the Pacific.

The Soviet Union was fighting one war against one enemy. Britain and America were, like Germany, now fighting two, and the added demands of that war in the East had enormous implications for the war in the West.

Much of the slack from the US Navy's move east was expected to be taken up by the Royal Canadian Navy. Every Canadian now sailing in the Atlantic was a volunteer, and despite having less-well-equipped ships than their British cousins, and although they had not had the large pool of experience with which to rapidly build a new wartime Navy that the British had enjoyed, the RCN had done magnificently. Any criticism of their capabilities or lack of training had to be tempered by the knowledge that they had effectively started from scratch and flung themselves into the thick of the action and most debilitating Atlantic swells with grim determination and no small amount of fortitude.

In September 1939, the RCN had comprised just ten modern warships and had a complete strength of just 309 officers and 2,967 ratings, of whom fewer than half were full-time professionals. By the spring of 1941, it had grown exponentially, with more than eighty corvettes either in service or under construction. A huge naval base on Newfoundland had been constructed and ever-more corvettes and destroyers were being built. It was an extraordinary effort from a country with a population of just over 10 million. By the beginning of 1942, the RCN was being stretched to breaking point with over 90 per cent of its fleet in action – which really was too much.

Yet despite the huge strain being placed upon it, more young Canadians continued to volunteer, including Dick Pearce, who was twenty years old in January 1942 when he reported aboard HMCS *Arvida*, his first ship, as an acting sub-lieutenant. Born in Cannifton, Ontario, he had turned eighteen the day Britain entered the war. At the time, he had just enrolled at the Port Credit High School to complete his final Grade 13 subjects, but immediately wanted to volunteer. His father, however, had persuaded him to finish his studies first and even to think about starting university, which would then make him eligible for officer training.

Pearce did exactly as father had suggested, gaining his grades and enrolling at the University of Toronto to study engineering. He enjoyed university life well enough, but in January 1941 was determined finally to enlist. After an interview to join the Royal Canadian Naval Volunteer Reserve (RCNVR), he was accepted as a probationary acting sub-lieutenant. 'From then on,' he said, 'I went through the motions only at school.' Failing his first-year studies, he left university for full-time train-ing; in late August he was put on the active service list and sent to Halifax for a three-month intensive training programme. By December, he was trained and ready, and asked to choose in order of priority the part of the Navy to which he wished to be posted. Pearce marked corvettes and was granted his wish. *Arvida* was a Flower-class corvette that had begun duties the previous July.

As Pearce went aboard for the first time, he saluted the quarterdeck as he had been taught was the proper procedure, identified himself to the sentry and then was escorted to the tiny wardroom, down at the water-line and via a steep steel staircase. One of the officers there was John Clarke, an old schoolmate. 'Was I ever delighted to see a familiar face,' said Pearce, 'and have someone to show me the ropes!'

As part of the Mid-Ocean Escort Force, *Arvida* was soon back at sea and Pearce was forced to learn those ropes incredibly quickly. The *Arvida* was small – only just over 200 feet long – and had a crew of 110, including eight officers, all crammed together in extremely cramped conditions. Top speed was only around 15 knots; these small but sturdy escorts felt like little more than tin cans. In the north-west Atlantic, where the weather in the winter months was brutal, the corvette would roll like a barrel. 'The worst roll I recall,' said Pearce, 'was about forty degrees, as shown on the clinometer in our wheelhouse.' With its open bridge, Pearce and his fellow officers were lashed by waves and spray in even a rising swell. It was very hard to keep dry.

Nearly all the men were young, apart from the captain, a naval reserve officer, who was over forty and seemed like an old man compared with the rest of the crew. Pearce immediately learned to respect both his authority and seamanship, but noticed after a couple of trips that the skipper's nerves were beginning to fray. It was hardly surprising. The responsibility of command and the intensity of the relentless convoy work were immense. 'Corvettes,' said Pearce, 'like fighter aircraft and tanks, were designed for young men.'

Pearce learned fast, but such were the demands on the RCN and its youthful men, responsibility was thrust upon its young officers, especially, very quickly. By March, Pearce had qualified for his watch-keeping certificate, which meant he was judged capable of standing watch alone. For someone like Pearce, just feeling their way, to do so in the treacherous winter months was a particularly harsh baptism.

Even old salts like Commander Don Macintyre were struggling with the North Atlantic conditions. He had made the most of a refit for *Walker* the previous November and had got married, then had returned to his ship to discover she had been equipped with a new type of radar, one that was both more reliable and capable of picking up targets at up to

3 or 4 miles – a big improvement. Another new feature was the Plan Position Indicator – or PPI – which gave a continual visual map of the area around the ship on which any object detected by the radar showed up. This would transform night convoy operations, for at last they had a clear picture of all their ships and escorts. The biggest benefit was that at night the Watch Officer could now concentrate on looking out for the enemy rather than waste time keeping the convoy in sight.

In February, they were posted to Halifax as part of the general reshuffling of escorts following the US entry into the war. Here they were to lead the newly formed Western Local Escort Force, covering the passage of shipping from Halifax to Newfoundland. Further south, the battle was against the U-boats. Here, the battle was against the weather. 'The conditions off Newfoundland in winter,' noted Macintyre, 'were possibly more continuously foul than anywhere else I had served.' It was so bitterly cold, there was even a perpetual layer of ice on the inside of the ship. It got to everyone, Macintyre included.

After several long weeks of freezing cold and barely ever once being dry, Macintyre brought *Walker* back to Halifax to learn that he was being posted to the new US naval base at Argentia. Like *Arvida*'s captain, Macintyre was aware that he needed a break; he had been becoming short-tempered and overtired, his brief honeymoon not enough of a break after two years of almost continual active service. So, although he had little idea what his new job would entail, he was not entirely dismayed to be taken off the bitter North Atlantic. It would give him a much-needed chance to recharge his batteries.

CHAPTER 12

Fighters and Bombers

T HE FIRST CONSIGNMENT of American troops arrived in Britain on
26 January 1942. These were men from the 34th Red Bull Division,
although they were not shipped as one, but rather were sent over piecemeal, a regiment at a time. Sergeant Ralph Schaps had been given a day's
leave back on 7 December and had been with a buddy in a pool hall when
news broke of the attack at Pearl Harbor. In no time, military police
turned up and ordered all the GIs – general infantry – back to base. 'We
were at war!!!' wrote Schaps. 'Suddenly everything had changed. No
more playing at soldiering!!! Now it was for real!!' Within days the older
noncoms and officers had been weeded out and the old club atmosphere
of the National Guard vanished, almost overnight.

In January, the 135th Infantry was sent by rail up to Fort Dix, New
Jersey, to get ready to sail to Britain and, much to his relief, Schaps
and his fellows finally started to get modern equipment: new uniforms
and Parsons jackets, the new M1 helmet and the M1 Garand rifles,
half-tracks and weapons carriers, the new quarter-ton four-wheel drive
Jeep ('we went nuts over these,' noted Schaps), different machine guns,
radios and even new hand-held short-range radios called 'walkie-talkies'.
'Quite a change from the old WW1 junk we had been using,' wrote
Schaps.

The new kit was all very welcome, but the only heavy weapon Schaps
came close to was an already obsolete 37mm gun, which they would
occasionally fire at rough wooden targets. Facilities at Fort Dix were not
good either, and, just as those at sea in the Atlantic were suffering, so

were the Red Bulls as snow and perpetually freezing temperatures gripped a camp in which the men were still expected to sleep in canvas pup tents. The US Army was growing, more and more arms and materiel were hurrying from the factories and assembly lines, but the journey from tiny peacetime force to significant war machine was far from over. The US Army was now *in* the war, but whether it was ready for combat in those early months of 1942 was another matter altogether.

By the beginning of 1942, RAF Fighter Command had grown to seven fighter groups, and numbers of single-engine fighters were still on the rise. In the last quarter of 1941, the aircraft industry had produced 559 fighters, compared with 320 built in the USA and 221 in Germany. That was quite some lead.

For the fighter pilots, however, January brought another cold and miserable month where they seemed to be adding only a small amount to the war effort. Occasional sweeps over the Channel sometimes brought the Luftwaffe into the air, but these were largely indecisive engagements: a few Messerschmitts or even the new Focke-Wulf 190s might be shot down, but then a few Spitfires would be lost too. All in all, the balance sheet was fairly even. New pilots were arriving all the time too, which meant Fighter Command could still stick to its policy of rotating pilots from combat duty to instructing, and then perhaps they might be sent overseas for a tour. The key, as Dowding had identified, was to keep pilots as fresh as possible. Still, a few always fell through the net, not least Jean Offenberg, who was still with 609 Squadron, albeit at Digby in a quiet sector. He had been flying operationally now for the best part of two years.

None the less, his experience was welcome at 609 Squadron, because he was able to help the new Belgian pilots when they arrived. 'I take up the youngsters,' Offenberg wrote in his diary on 21 January. 'Blanco has arrived from Heston and has been posted to my flight. Lallemand has been promoted to Flying Officer.' The following day, with the air-field covered in snow and with an icy north wind blowing, Offenberg took off for some formation practice with Pilot Officer Robert 'Balbo' Roelandt, a young Belgian pilot who had just arrived. They had been practising for an hour when another Spitfire, from 92 Squadron, decided to perform a mock attack on the Belgian pair. Offenberg saw him too late, and the two aircraft collided, the other slicing his fuselage in two.

Offenberg's Spitfire continued to climb for a moment, then turned and plunged 1,000 feet into the ground. Offenberg and his friendly attacker were both dead, killed in a pointless and unnecessary accident. They were far from the first or last to die as a result of pilot error rather than at the hands of the enemy. 'I cannot explain to you all that Jean meant to us,' Jean de Selys-Longchamps, a fellow Belgian in the squadron, wrote to Offenberg's uncle. 'He was a symbol of integrity, a permanent example, an inexhaustible source of hope in the future, in our future, in the future of our country.'

A stone's throw from Digby were a number of airfields of RAF Bomber Command, whose men and commanders were also learning the harsh realities of war. So much had been written before the war about the power of the bomber that there was a very real fear in many quarters that bombers would bring Armageddon, devastating entire cities and killing millions. Britain had placed a great deal of emphasis on air power – it had been central to her war strategy – yet while fighters had proved their worth in the skies of southern England in 1940, and while Coastal Command was increasingly demonstrating its value in the Battle of the Atlantic, Bomber Command, by contrast, did not appear to be delivering decisive results.

The Butt Report, which had been launched to investigate the effectiveness of British bombing, had shown, by careful analysis of aerial photographs, just how inaccurate it was. Its publication the previous summer had been a devastating blow to Bomber Command, but until bombs could be dropped with greater accuracy the only alternative was to continue to strike at Germany with the means available. And so the scatter-gun approach would continue, even if that meant accepting a chilling disregard for the lives of German civilians. This was something the RAF seemed willing to live with. Near the end of 1941, Air Marshal Sir Richard Pierse, then C-in-C Bomber Command, told his audience in the Thirty Club that for a year British bombers had been quite intentionally targeting civilians. 'I mention this,' he told them, 'because for a long time, the Government, for excellent reasons, has preferred the world to think that we still held some scruples and attacked only what the humanitarians are pleased to call Military Targets . . . I can assure you, gentlemen, that we tolerate no scruples.'

In war, cold ruthlessness is often very necessary, but there was no real justification for being murderous if it was not achieving very much. The Luftwaffe's Blitz of Britain had neither broken British morale nor come close to dislocating Britain's war machine. Yet in an Air Ministry directive for Bomber Command in July 1941, it claimed there were many signs that 'recent attacks on industrial towns are having great effect on the morale of the civil population.' No one enjoyed being bombed and there was little doubt it was demoralizing, so on one level the claim was probably valid. However, crushing morale in this context was generally understood to mean inducing civil and political collapse. What had not been quite squared, however, was how British bombing could do this if the Luftwaffe had not managed it. There were plenty who understood this paradox and consequently wondered whether it might make more sense to abandon the strategic air campaign against Germany. It would certainly save a lot of bomber crews, as well as money, resources, time and effort. For what it was worth, it would save a lot of German civilian lives too.

This was not a view shared by Air Chief Marshal Sir Charles Portal, however, who since October 1940 had been Chief of the Air Staff. Portal was a fiercely intelligent and highly educated man, regarded for his straightforward character. Naturally shy, he liked to lunch every day alone in his London club, but he was certainly no shrinking violet and demonstrated a calm and iron determination to fight for what he believed. And Portal believed very strongly in the potential of air power and bombing in particular. Regardless of the Butt Report and the already considerable casualties suffered by Bomber Command, he was convinced bombing was a far more efficient way to wage war and was determined that Britain should continue the strategic air campaign against Germany. In this, he was not only an adherent of pre-war British strategy, but also at one with Churchill. It was part of a broader 'steel not flesh' policy, in which the number of young men at the coal-face of war was to be kept to an absolute minimum, with machines doing as many of the hard yards as possible. Aircraft, and lots of them, were part of this. Yes, they had to be crewed, but no matter how dangerous that was, it was believed they could bring about more destruction on Nazi Germany at a smaller cost in human life than by having vast field armies like the Germans or Russians.

Clearly, a small bomber force with inadequate navigational and bomb-aiming technology was not going achieve too much, however; yet that did not mean Bomber Command was finished. Far from it. The answer was greatly to increase the size of the force, bring in bigger, better bombers capable of carrying much larger payloads, and to ensure that much-improved technological advances in terms of navigation and the ability to drop bombs accurately were developed and hastily brought into service. This would not happen overnight, but Britain had always viewed the war in terms of a long haul. Portal fervently believed the RAF's bomber force would, before so very long, get to a point where they could make an enormous, possibly even decisive, difference.

The trouble was, critics of Bomber Command were mounting. Now at the Air Ministry was Wing Commander Sydney Bufton, who had relinquished active command to be Deputy Director of Bombing Operations. He was still only thirty-four. In a memo to his immediate boss, Group Captain John Baker, on 27 February 1942, Bufton warned that there was criticism of the strategic bombing offensive not only in the other two services but in Parliament too – just a few days earlier Sir Stafford Cripps, the Lord Privy Seal, had openly questioned whether Bomber Command's resources should be spread elsewhere. 'The criticism cannot be countered by promises of results which we expect to obtain in the future,' Bufton wrote, 'and rightly cannot be met by evidence of any decisive results which our bomber force has achieved in the past. These results so far have been nebulous, inconsistent and indecisive.' None the less, there *was* an expectation for the future, but a bridge needed to be built between the current lack of confidence and future potential. Portal rightly recognized that what Bomber Command urgently needed was a new chief who not only believed in the power of strategic bombing every bit as much as he did, but who also had the drive, bloody-mindedness and grim determination to fight tooth and nail to see it grow and develop into a force to be reckoned with.

As it happened, Portal believed he had just the man. Air Marshal Arthur Harris had been appointed C-in-C Bomber Command just a few days before Bufton wrote his anxious memo, and a more stubborn and bloody-minded individual it would have been hard to find within the upper echelons of the RAF. Bull-faced with piercing, pale eyes and light, greying, gingery hair and a trim moustache, he oozed charisma and an air of no-nonsense authority. Light-hearted and jovial at home, in the workplace he was altogether more serious and even austere. Harris was a man who suffered no fools and who was equally unafraid to say things as he saw them. And he was also a man who, like Portal, quite zealously believed that the best way to win the war was to destroy large numbers of German cities. Destroy them, and Germany's ability to produce war materiel would be destroyed as well. With no war materiel, the Germans would no longer be able to continue the war. Back in the autumn of 1940, when he was Deputy Chief of the Air Staff, Harris went on to the roof of the Air Ministry to watch the Luftwaffe's attack. Bombs were falling and London was aglow. 'Well,' he said, turning to Portal, who stood beside him, 'they are sowing the wind.' Now that he was chief of Bomber Command, he intended to let nothing stop him from fulfilling that prophecy.

When Harris arrived at Bomber Command HQ at High Wycombe, some 40 miles north-west of London, he was keenly aware that he faced a daunting challenge to say the least. One of his first challenges was somehow to improve the Command's standing within the armed forces. He needed to press continually for better navigational aids and, most important of all, he needed to ensure he got more aircraft – in the short term, whatever he could get his hands on, and in the medium and longer terms, more heavy four-engine bombers, and especially Avro Lancasters, which were now, in early 1942, finally reaching the squadrons, and which, in terms of carrying capacity, were in a league of their own compared with any other heavy bomber yet invented. 'On the day that I took over,' he wrote, 'there were 378 aircraft serviceable with crews, and only 69 of these were heavy bombers.' This was clearly a risible number with which to make any serious impact on Nazi Germany.

Despite this, the pressure on him to get on with the job in hand was immense. Having recently been in America and witness to the Arcadia Conference, he was fully aware of the pressure from Stalin on the Allies to take the attack to the enemy as soon as possible. Bombing was one answer. He also needed urgently to improve the Command's public relations. The best and easiest way to achieve that was to start delivering results, but again, this challenge would be easier to solve with more aircraft in the arsenal.

With this in mind, he asked his staff to throw the net wide and see if there were bombers that could be combed out from elsewhere, and they immediately concluded that RAF Middle East had more than their fair share. On 17 March, he wrote to Tedder, arguing that over the past twelve months the 'best part of a thousand' crews had been sent out to the

Middle East, but despite repeated requests for a number of them to be returned, only 'driblets' had been. 'We either alter this hopeless state of affairs, and at once,' he told Tedder bluntly, 'or we perish.'

After involving himself in a ding-dong of exchanges that were equally uncompromising at both ends, Tedder took the matter to Portal, pointing out that 280 Wellingtons and crews, not a thousand, had reached the Middle East from Britain in the past year. During that period, seventy-seven had been lost through casualties, thirty-four had become tour-expired and been sent home, thirty had formed a B-24 Liberator squadron, while others had been sent on to India and elsewhere. Only eighty-two had been absorbed into RAF Middle East.

As it was, Tedder's command was feeling incredibly pinched as the long shadow of war with Japan threatened to undo all the advantages gained by CRUSADER. The previous year, it had been Greece that had wrested hard-won initiative away. Now, it was the threat to Burma and especially India, both of which were perilously thinly protected by men, materiel and also aircraft. Being closer to the Far East than Britain, it was the Middle East that had to bear the brunt of the urgent reinforcements. Not only were divisions stripped out and sent across the Indian Ocean, but entire squadrons too. Tedder had dispatched 139 Blenheim bombers and 300 fighters – an enormous number. In a trice, air superiority in North Africa, built up so carefully, had been lost. This would be made good over the coming months, but part of Auchinleck's and Tedder's strategy had been to build up forces sufficient to ensure they never lost command of the air again. That strategy had undergone a massive setback.

In the end, Tedder was forced to send a handful of Wellingtons back to Britain, which was something for Harris, but the irony was that while Bomber Command were screaming for more bombers and thought the Middle East had more than they needed, Tedder was repeatedly demanding more fighters, specifically Mk V Spitfires, and believed, rightly in this case, that Fighter Command back in Britain had more than *it* really needed. As Britain was the current world leader in single-engine fighter production, and with new aircraft and repairs comfortably outstripping losses, Tedder's demands were more than reasonable – and especially since a new crisis threatened to overwhelm his command.

This was the arrival of II. Fliegerkorps on Sicily and their renewed air offensive against the tiny island of Malta, so key to the war being waged in North Africa.

The war in the Mediterranean and Middle East was curious in that it required equal efforts from all three services. The narrative of the war there has tended to focus both on the North African campaign and the Army, but when it came to the fighting on land, the air forces were every bit as important as the ground forces. None the less, the fighting on and over land was entirely dependent on success at sea, because it was only by sea that supplies could be delivered on the scale required. Paradoxically, however, and as Admiral Cunningham never failed to mention, success at sea was also dependent on air power and could not be guaranteed by naval vessels alone. Malta, for example, could not be supplied by air power, but without air power, those supplies could not be delivered.

In the spring of 1942, Tedder was deeply concerned about the island, as were his fellow service chiefs in the Middle East, and as were Churchill and the Chiefs of Staff in London. From its hopelessly inadequate defences back in June 1940, it had come through the early stages of siege, stepped-up assaults by the Luftwaffe and had, despite its position in the centre of the Mediterranean, 60 miles from Sicily and surrounded by hostile seas, made itself absolutely critical to the outcome of the war in North Africa.

In the previous autumn, the Mediterranean Fleet's Force K of destroyers and cruisers, as well as Malta's 10th Submarine Flotilla and RAF torpedo bombers, not to mention the reconnaissance aircraft of pilots like Adrian Warburton, had crippled Axis supply routes to Libya. Maltese aircraft alone had sunk some 350,000 tons of shipping – the same as had been sunk by U-boats in September and October 1941. While its position made it critical as an offensive base against Axis shipping, this also ensured it was incredibly difficult to supply. The Atlantic was vast and most convoys could cross it with impunity. The same could not be said for the Mediterranean: whether from Gibraltar or Alexandria, ships faced a combination of enemy submarines, fast torpedo boats, Italian warships and Axis aircraft with increasing intensity the closer they got to the beleaguered island. Five ships had reached Malta in January, but a further one in February was forced to turn back. Another – now desperately needed – convoy was planned for March, but with the Mediterranean Fleet's loss of battleships and with II. Fliegerkorps now on Sicily, giving it safe passage was going to be difficult, to say the least.

It was Hitler who had ordered the destruction of the island fortress, and by the end of December, with II. Fliegerkorps in place, Feldmarschall Kesselring was able to issue his directive. Neutralization of Malta was, he said, an absolutely indispensable precondition for securing their lines of supply to North Africa. This was indisputably true.

The start of this all-out air offensive had been delayed by terrible storms that lashed the island at the start of the year; the scirocco was working in Malta's favour. Fine weather returned in February, however, and with it the Luftwaffe were able to step up their attacks. None the less, losses soon mounted. The trouble for the Luftwaffe was that directives from the General Staff still insisted on dive-bombing and aiming for pinpoint accuracy. Malta, however, which was by now bristling with anti-aircraft guns and still a few fighter aircraft, was a lethal place over which to be a dive-bomber.

It was Oberst Paul Deichmann, the Chief of Staff of II. Fliegerkorps, who first suggested ignoring such orders and doing things their own way. With Kesselring's blessing, he devised a new plan, which did away with dispersed dive-bombing and promoted massed higher-level bombing instead. The first objective was to get rid of the RAF and particularly the fighters. Takali, one of the main airfields on the island, was singled out for an especially savage pasting on 20 March.

Admiral Cunningham, or 'ABC' as he was known, had assembled as big an escort force as possible for the March convoy to Malta, which set sail the same day Takali was blitzed. In Alexandria, Cunningham had to follow events from his office, waiting for signals to come in. 'Never have I felt so keenly,' he noted, 'the mortifying bitterness of sitting behind the scenes with a heavy load of responsibility while others were in action with a vastly superior force of the enemy.' This was not only Axis aircraft but also the Italian Fleet, which had emerged from harbour to try to intercept the British.

None the less, the Italians were fought off, aircraft dodged and blasted, and on 23 March two of the four-ship convoy passed into Grand Harbour. The third ship was sunk, while the fourth, a naval supply vessel, was hit and stopped dead in the water, but was towed safely to the south of the island. Precious supplies of fuel and ammunition had reached Malta in the nick of time.

What followed was a disaster entirely wrought by the ineptitude of the island's commanders. The arrival of the convoy coincided with another fortuitous and unusual downturn in the weather, which hampered

Oberst Deichmann's plans for the rapid destruction of the RAF on the island. During this time, however, no one on Malta had thought to put in place plans for rapidly unloading the newly arrived ships. Instead of calling on the help of RAF and Army troops, it was left to the Maltese stevedores. Nor had anyone thought to order them to work through the night and every hour of the day until it was done. Because of the low cloud, lighting the operation would have been more than worth the risk. Three days later, the clouds disappeared, the Luftwaffe returned, and all three ships were promptly sunk in harbour before a fraction of their cargoes had been unloaded.

In the early part of the war, Malta had been considered a decidedly second-tier posting and as a result its service commanders and governor were not exactly top-drawer. After the incredible damage the island's forces had caused to the Axis the previous autumn, however, both sides had woken up to its vital importance, but it was the Germans who had acted first. The very first few Spitfires, for example, reached Malta in March 1942 but, as things stood, it was too little too late. Tedder had sent one of his most trusted staff officers, Group Captain Basil Embry, to the island earlier in the year and Embry had reported straight back saying Malta needed better radar, a first-class ground controller and lots of Spitfires. The pilots on Malta had been demanding this all the previous year, but the Air Officer Commanding, Air Vice-Marshal Hugh Pughe Lloyd, one of those culpable for the fiasco of the March convoy, had never once asked specifically for any of these things. Having three squadrons of Spitfires on the island when the Luftwaffe launched their attack would almost certainly have dealt Kesselring's plans a decisive blow in swift order, for however overwhelming the Luftwaffe may have seemed to those suffering the Maltese blitz, II. Fliegerkorps began the air assault with just a couple of hundred aircraft. By the end of March they had over 400, of which 115 were single-engine fighters. These should not have been overwhelming numbers, but they were aircraft the Luftwaffe could ill afford to lose and their defeat would not only have massively helped the British situation in North Africa and the Middle East, but would have done much to help the Russians too.

A British strength was being able to see the wider strategic situation, but there is no doubt they missed a massive trick in not pumping Malta full of Spitfires and even more anti-aircraft guns. Admittedly, this would have been a logistical challenge, but it was one they would most certainly have been capable of putting into place the previous year, when the Luftwaffe was absent from Sicily and when convoys were getting through to the island with comparative ease. It was a big opportunity that had been missed.

As it was, by the third week of April, Malta was sinking. Its harbours and towns were wrecked, the airfields were barely functioning, and the RAF was all but destroyed. On five days in April, there had been just one fighter plane available; on two, there had been none at all. The 10th Submarine Flotilla's base was so badly hit, it was forced to abandon the island and sail for Alexandria, but not before its leading boats, *Upholder* and *Urge*, had been sunk.

King George VI announced the award of the George Cross, the highest civilian medal for valour, to the entire island of Malta on 17 April, but this was no substitute for aircraft, fuel and ammunition.

On 20 April, two Spitfire squadrons finally reached Malta – forty-seven had been flown off the US aircraft carrier, USS *Wasp*. Their guns had not been harmonized beforehand, the radios had not been properly set up and no plans had been put in place on the island to receive them, arm them, refill them with fuel and get them airborne again just as soon as humanly possible. Within forty-eight hours of their arrival, only seven were left, the vast majority destroyed on the ground before they could take to the skies.

By the end of April, Feldmarschall Kesselring considered the threat from Malta to have been neutralized. Few could doubt he was right.

CHAPTER 13

Steel and Strategy

O N 30 JANUARY 1942, Albert Speer, Hitler's favourite architect and the man in charge of the Reich's defence construction, was travelling east in a Heinkel 111 of the Führer's personal *Staffel*, which had been converted to carry passengers. Another of the passengers was Obergruppenführer Sepp Dietrich, commander of the Waffen-SS Panzerdivision Leibstandarte Adolf Hitler, which was currently being hard-pressed by the Russians near Rostov in southern Ukraine. They were flying to Dnepropetrovsk, Dietrich to rejoin his division and Speer to see his staff, who were hurriedly trying to repair damaged railway lines there.

As they huddled in this flying tin can, Speer gazed out of the window at the relentless landscape. Occasionally he saw burned-out farmsteads, but almost no roads. They were following a railway line, but there were no trains either. Speer was alarmed by the emptiness of this vast snowscape; it brought home to him just how cut off the armies at the front were from their supplies.

Within a few days of their arrival at Dnepropetrovsk, Speer was rather regretting venturing out into this desolation. The snow continued to fall and, more worryingly, the Russians were getting nearer. This was part of a major counter-attack by the Red Army around Kharkov, in which the Soviets had managed to punch a 50-mile hole between two German armies along the River Donets. Speer and his staff held frantic conferences over what they should do – the only weapons they had were a few rifles and an abandoned field gun with no ammunition. Inexplicably, however, having got to within 12 miles, the Russians appeared to circle around then call off a further assault.

After trying unsuccessfully to get away by train – the line was blocked by drifts – Speer eventually managed to leave on Saturday, 7 February in the same Heinkel that had brought him, by which time a short, sharp counter-attack by German forces out of Dnepropetrovsk had ended the crisis there for the time being. Speer's plane was not headed to Berlin, however, but to Rastenburg. Speer didn't mind – it was in the right direction and, in any case, there was a chance he might get to talk to the Führer, whom he had not seen since early December.

Hitler did not attend dinner, however, although the Armaments Minister, Fritz Todt, did. Speer and he got on well enough; in fact, increasingly well in recent times. Speer valued him as a prudent, more experienced colleague and respected his judgement. After supper, Todt was called away to speak with Hitler and did not reappear until much later, when Speer thought he looked tired and strained; the conversation with the Führer had obviously been difficult. They shared a drink together, but Todt said little, his mind clearly somewhat preoccupied, until he mentioned that the following morning he was due to fly back to Berlin and offered Speer a seat, which he gratefully accepted.

Soon after, Speer himself was summoned to see Hitler. The Führer looked every bit as strained as Todt had done. It was now after one in the morning, and Speer was shocked by the frugality of the Führer's study – there was not even a single upholstered chair. Hitler did, however, brighten a little once they began talking about their planned building projects for Berlin and Nuremberg – the capital was to be renamed 'Germania' and would include new avenues and even a vast domed hall that could seat more than 150,000.

After later giving Hitler a brief account of his impressions of the front, it was not until three in the morning that Speer finally retired. Todt had wanted to leave early and Speer, now exhausted, sent word that he would forgo the flight and instead get some rest.

Some hours later, the telephone in his small room rang, waking him from his deep sleep. It was 8 a.m. Dr Brandt, Hitler's physician, was on the line. 'Dr. Todt's plane has just crashed,' he told him, 'and he has been killed.'

The man in charge of Germany's all-important armaments industry, and who had been telling Hitler for months that the war could not be won, was dead. Speer was both stunned and saddened, but was soon to be shocked again. At around 1 p.m., Sunday, 8 February, he was summoned to see Hitler once more – and as the Führer's first caller of the day. Hitler was standing, formally, when Speer entered and, after hearing condolences about Todt, said brusquely, 'Herr Speer, I appoint you the successor to Minister Todt in all his capacities.'

Speer was dumbstruck and assumed Hitler meant he would take over all construction duties only. 'No, in all his capacities, including that of Minister of Armaments,' Hitler told him.

'But I don't know anything about—' said Speer, before Hitler cut him off.

'I have confidence in you. I know you will manage it. Besides, I have no one else. Get in touch with the Minister at once and take over!'

Speer insisted Hitler put that in writing, which reluctantly he did, then turned to other business. The close confidence of the previous night had gone; he had been dismissed. Just as he was leaving, however, Hitler's adjutant announced the Reichsmarschall, who had just arrived and was demanding to see the Führer, even though he had no appointment.

'Send him in,' replied Hitler sulkily, then, turning to Speer, added, 'Stay here a moment longer.'

Göring hurried in, having rushed the 60 miles from his own hunting lodge in Rominten, and immediately told Hitler it was best he took over from Todt within the framework of the Four-Year Plan, the armaments programme of which he was head. 'This,' Göring told him, 'would avoid the frictions and difficulties we had in the past as a result of overlapping responsibilities.' Göring's point was a fair one, but that was not how Hitler liked to run things.

So Hitler brushed the Reichsmarschall's suggestion aside. 'I have already appointed Todt's successor,' he told him. 'Speer here has assumed all of Dr Todt's offices as of this moment.'

Rumours and inconsistencies have surrounded Todt's death ever since. He and Hitler had argued over the continuation of the war the night before, yet it seems unlikely the Führer would have wanted him dead. Then there was Speer himself: conveniently there, and at the last minute deciding against taking Todt's flight. But again, it seems unlikely that Speer would have murdered a man he liked and admired, especially since he was, in every regard, so unready to take on the mantle. Most likely it was pilot error: flying in the snow and wind, in the aircraft of the day, carried risk.

Speer himself insisted he was incredulous and thought his appointment reckless. 'Never in my life,' he noted, 'had I had anything to do with military weapons.' Fortunately for Speer, Todt had had a number of very able men working for him and they remained in the Ministry. Furthermore, it has often been assumed that, from his accession, Speer became the armaments supremo in Nazi Germany. This was not quite the case. Rather, Speer inherited precisely the same brief as Todt: that is, his authority extended purely to the equipment needs of the Army and to those of ammunition – which amounted to around 45 per cent of the Reich's armament effort. The Kriegsmarine still retained its own procurement office, as did the Luftwaffe, which accounted for between 35 and 40 per cent of the armament effort. And since Udet's suicide, this had been in the hands of Feldmarschall Erhard Milch.

What did change in the weeks following Speer's appointment was the establishment of the Zentrale Planung, which was, as its name suggested, a central planning committee for all armaments production, and which was presided over jointly by Speer, Milch and Paul Körner, Göring's secretary, but with Speer in the chair. Of the three, Speer also had the greatest access to Hitler, but really, from the formation of the committee, German armaments production was not dominated by Speer, but Speer *and* Milch; Göring had not gained from Todt's death but had not lost ground either. And Milch was not only Göring's deputy and head of procurement, but his authority in the Zentrale Planung was unquestioned – and this was an overarching body that also regularly included Gauleiter Fritz Sauckel, the head of manpower; Herbert Backe, the new Minister of Food; and others like Paul Pleiger, the head of the coal industry. Conspicuous by their absence were Wehrmacht men from the General Staff, such as General Georg Thomas. In fact, it was the Military Economics Office at the OKW that really lost influence following the bitter winter of 1941–2, but this was as much to do with the emergence of the Zentrale Planung as it was with the rise of Speer.

The partnership of Speer and Milch, especially, and the very concept of the Zentrale Planung, was a major leap forward for German armaments production, which had for so long been riven by rivalries, a lack of co-operation, disparate committees and organizations, and inflated bodies and offices, all of which had led to both waste and inefficiency.

If this new and overarching body could, at long last, not only dominate the armaments industry, but also get some real grip on the situation, cut out much of the chaff and increase efficiency in the toxic and corrupt world of Nazi business, then the production of war materiel might yet improve.

And it had to, or else Armageddon would fall on Germany. Already, the violence and terrible treatment they had meted out to prisoners and civilians alike in the East ensured that, should the Soviet Union start pushing German forces back, terrible vengeance would follow, along with the dark cloak of Bolshevism. Nazi Germany could expect no mercy for what it had already unleashed in this war.

The solution was clear: in the summer, when the campaigning season resumed, they *had* to win the war in the East. Although General Warlimont and the Operations Staff at the OKW had been asked to prepare an appreciation, Hitler, it seemed, had swiftly drawn up his own vision for future strategy, one that he had put to the Japanese Ambassador back on 3 January. The oilfields of the Caucasus were to be the main focus of a resumed attack the moment the weather improved. 'This is the most important direction for an offensive,' Hitler said. 'We must reach the oilfields there and also in Iran and Iraq.' Once there, they could help the Arab 'freedom movement'. In North Africa and the Middle East, Axis forces would also mount what would be a giant pincer attack – the drive through the Caucasus in the north and another through to the Middle East in the south. It would be *Kesselschlacht* on a giant scale. At the same time, his armies would attempt to obliterate Leningrad and Moscow too. 'England remains our main enemy,' he assured the Japanese Ambassador. 'We shall certainly not go under in face of the Russians.'

In Hitler's mind, it followed that with the oilfields captured and the huge agricultural expanses of the Ukraine secured, these assets would be denied to the Red Army and would be of vital benefit to Germany. With the British beaten in the Middle East, the Soviet Union would inevitably collapse and then the Germans could turn back to Britain and the United States. Practicalities such as how they were actually going to transport oil from the Caucasus – or the Middle East, for that matter – had not really been thought through, but it would, at least, be denied to the Russians, and, as the Germans were only too well aware, without oil it was impossible to keep fighting a war.

This was, frankly, a pretty fantastical appreciation, but certainly everything now depended on ending the war in the East in 1942. That meant making sure the Army and Luftwaffe were equipped to do the job – and that, in turn, meant ensuring there was enough ammunition and shells, enough tanks, trucks, aircraft, artillery pieces, small arms, and that the equipment they did have was more than equal to the challenges demanded. Since their starting point for this was so far behind those of the Allies, it was an enormous challenge, to say the very least.

The biggest headache facing the Zentrale Planung, and the focus of many of their meetings, was steel – and how to get more of it. So far in the war, it was ammunition production that had dominated the allocation of this precious resource; whenever Hitler had ordered a drive to produce more shells, production of tanks and other war materiel suffered. Now, however, there needed to be an increase in ammunition *and* other weapons. It could no longer be a case of one or the other. Production needed to increase in both at the same time.

It was in the area of improving efficiency that the Zentrale Planung looked to make their first move, challenging a committee of steel magnates with the task of overhauling steel allocation. On 15 May, they presented their proposals. Any backlogs of steel orders – and there were many – were to be cancelled. In future, allocations of steel would be assigned to only 90 per cent of steel production and a reserve of 10 per cent would be kept for the highest-priority orders. Steel mills were not to take on more orders than they could reasonably expect to fulfil.

Later, the overall quantity of steel rations was to be cut to keep it in line with actual production. The axe would fall heaviest on exports, which was poor news for Italy, for example, but that was too bad. Military allocation was only cut by 7 per cent, but of the three services it was the Kriegsmarine, that most junior of German armed services, that took the biggest hit. The steel ration to the Army, on the other hand, increased. These measures were all quite sensible and did improve matters significantly, although the Zentrale Planung had no answer yet, in the spring of 1942, as to how best to improve steel output.

They needed to find solutions soon, however. The clock was ticking inexorably; time for the Germans was fast running out. The Soviet Union was still not beaten and all the while the Russians were building more tanks and guns, and pushing more divisions into the battle. At the same time, Britain was producing more bombers, more tanks, more of everything – and British output was now being outdone by what was starting to emerge from US factories.

This meant that even if Germany did beat the Soviet Union in the summer, it was likely that Britain and the United States would out-produce the Reich to a point where defeating them would become well nigh impossible. Germany had gambled on a swift victory against Russia in 1941 and it had failed. Now they were faced with trying to fight a war on multiple fronts when they barely had the resources to fight on one.

New equipment was on its way, however, including a new tank to combat the Russian T34. Both Daimler-Benz and MAN had been asked to produce designs for a 30–35-ton panzer with increased armour and a high-velocity 75mm gun, and in May 1942 Hitler chose the MAN design. It would become the Panzer Mk V, better known as the 'Panther', and, although it was a much bigger tank than the current stock, ease of build and comparative cheapness were expected to be key attributes.

Speer, who understood a thing or two about propaganda and who, from his position within the Führer's inner circle, knew Goebbels well, ensured that much was made of increased tank and weapons production. 'The best weapons bring victory', was the slogan, and one of those was the new multipurpose machine gun, the MG42, which, it was boasted, could fire 3,000 rounds per minute. This was nonsense, but it could fire 1,400, which made it comfortably the fastest-firing machine gun in the world, and it took only 75 man-hours to make rather than the MG34's 150. This was still more than the British Bren, for example, but there was not much aesthetic about it, so, to a certain extent, the designer at Mauser, Werner Gruner, had listened to General Thomas.

However, devastating though such a high rate of fire undoubtedly was, the MG42 had just the same practical issues as its predecessor, only more so. As it was also air- rather than gas-cooled, it overheated even more quickly, used even more ammunition, gave off a huge amount of smoke, and still needed its users to carry around a whole stack of spare barrels, all of which ate into that precious steel allocation. Bren-gun teams carried one spare barrel, whereas those on MG42s would need at least six.

The dilemmas facing Germany's war leadership were, however, now multiplying as they began their desperate effort to regain the initiative in the war. Suddenly they were faced not only with having to crank up rearmament with a shortage of supplies and cash, but also with a labour force that was overstretched. In addition, they had to find ever-more troops when the cream of German youth had already been exhausted. Finally, and perhaps most pressing of all, they needed to find more food, of which they were also already desperately short. These were all seemingly insurmountable problems. The fact they had captured gargantuan numbers of Russian prisoners, or could sink 400,000 tons of Allied shipping a month, or gain 2 miles of desert, or pound Malta into dust, did not really solve any of their difficulties. If anything, it made their situation worse.

The current predicament stemmed from the fact that they had never been as big and powerful as they had made out publicly before the war. They had invaded Poland with most Germans and certainly much of the rest of the world believing they were highly technological and mechanized, when in fact quite the opposite was true. One of the biggest conundrums was the paradox that their victories depended on lightning strikes, but for the most part they lacked the transportation to achieve it.

Going on the defensive over the winter had not done much to improve General Adolf von Schell's life, for example. Such had been the attrition on the Wehrmacht's motor vehicles, von Schell now had to keep back 40 per cent of the operating weight just for spare parts. By April, troops at the front had received around 210,000 new vehicles of all kinds and the repairs had risen to some 30,000 per week. These, however, made up only around 20 per cent of the required strength, while most already at the front were in need of replacement. A further complication was the North African front, as well as the demands from their allies, Finns, Romanians and Italians.

Von Schell had tried to streamline the number of different types of vehicle but had been only partially successful. By around this time, some 1,300 different models of vehicle were used by the Germans, a huge number and clearly massively inefficient despite his best efforts, but because the Wehrmacht was still dependent on requisitioned and captured vehicles, this was unavoidable. So too were the huge distances of the Soviet Union and the almost total lack of metalled roads or infrastructure. Even if he had had enough vehicles and spares, getting them to the front and then sustaining them, especially the further east they went, was an incredibly difficult challenge.

As it was, they did not have enough, and yet everyone in the German armed forces wanted vehicles and everyone wanted more spares. At the same time, Oberst Hermann Balck, still working as General of Mobile Forces at the OKH, was expected to be stockpiling vehicles for the summer offensive. There were, however, only so many vehicles that could be built, repaired and saved with the raw materials and labour that had been allocated. A more Machiavellian, unscrupulous and better-connected man than von Schell might have been able to worm his way into Hitler's inner circle and lobby the Führer direct, but there were always others whose demands went above those of the Plenipotentiary of Motor Vehicles. And still towering over almost all, despite his recent humiliation, was Göring, controlling much of German industry and the raw-material allocations, and regarding the requirements of lowly Adolf von Schell as quite far down the pecking order.

Just to make his life a little harder, in the spring of 1942 Hitler hired Jakob Werlin, a member of the board of Daimler-Benz AG and a good party man, as Plenipotentiary of Motor Vehicle Matters. It was yet another classic piece of Hitlerian divide and rule that only made von Schell's life even more difficult and served to undermine still further his considerable efforts in the face of never-ending obstacles.

Meanwhile, there was the mounting food crisis. The harvest of 1941 had been poor – Britain had done well only because of the massive increase in productivity, but that had not occurred elsewhere in Europe – and the Germans had not captured the large amounts of grain and other foodstuffs they had expected from the Ukraine and other occupied territories. In March, Hitler appointed Fritz Sauckel, the Gauleiter of Thuringia in eastern Germany, to the new position of Plenipotentiary General of Labour Mobilization. An acute political operator, Sauckel was deeply anti-Semitic and an ardent Nazi, and had made himself rich by ensuring he had holdings in key armaments industries within Thuringia, including Wilhelm-Gustloff-Stiftung, one of the Reich's leading manufacturers of small arms. He also made sure that the largest of the second wave of concentration camps was built on his home turf at Buchenwald. Ruthless, greedy and cunning, he was also a superb administrator and quickly set in motion a mammoth programme of bringing in forced labour, through a combination of prisoners of war and 'civilian' workers from the occupied territories. In fact, by the end of March, the numbers arriving in the Reich reached around 34,000 per week.

This helped solve the manpower shortage, but it had other detrimental knock-on effects. None of these men – and women – was capable of feeding themselves. The ever-larger armies also needed feeding, as did German civilians, who were already suffering from stringent rationing. As it was, Herbert Backe, who had been promoted to Minister for Food in April 1942 when Walther Darré was forcibly retired by Hitler, was wondering how he was ever going to feed the Soviet prisoners now being brought to Germany as slave labour. Göring had half-joked that he should give them cats and horsemeat. Backe had replied with no trace of irony that there were not enough cats and that horsemeat was already supplementing German rations.

To make matters worse, the winter had been bitterly cold throughout Europe, not just on the Eastern Front. On his estate in Prussia, land-owner Hans Schlange-Schöningen felt he had never suffered such a terrible winter, which had made the food situation even worse. 'We have had no chance of sending potatoes into the town to feed the people,' he wrote. 'And the worst is the widespread destruction of our winter grain – the grain we need for bread.' In April there was a further ration cut – for both the fighting troops and the population back in Germany. It was a disaster for the Nazi regime, who were paranoid that this, above all things, had the potential to cause revolution at home. It certainly was not received well, and in addition to the hunger there was now bomb damage; shops had fewer goods than ever before; more Sicherheitsdienst (SD – security services) men roamed the streets. Furthermore, troops back from the front looked emaciated and exhausted, and in the security of their homes they talked. Else Wendel was a young divorced mother of two living and working in Berlin. When her younger brother, Rudolf, returned on leave, he told her terrible tales of atrocities at the front. 'We behaved like devils out of hell,' he told her. 'We have left those villagers to starve to death behind us, thousands and thousands of them.' He also told her prisoners were shot on the slightest excuse. 'Just stick them up against a wall and shoot the lot,' he said. 'We order the whole village out to look while we do it.' She was horrified.

The combination of cold, hunger, shortages of everything, physical signs of the war and despair from the front was, the Nazi leadership was well aware, a potentially explosive combination. The biggest priority, however, was to stop Germans going hungry, whilst at the same time feeding enough foreign workers. If that could be solved, and if they started winning again, then the crisis would pass.

In the end the solution was a simple one, which combined the cold-hearted logic of the Wehrmacht-endorsed Hunger Plan, which had originally been devised to strip Ukraine and feed Germans at the expense of millions of Soviets, with the illogicality of Nazi racial ideology. Architect of the solution was Herbert Backe, who immediately set about a complete overhaul of the current food-distribution system and the introduction of a number of new measures readily endorsed by Göring and Hitler. From May onwards, all food deliveries from the Reich to the troops at the front were to cease. The Wehrmacht and Waffen-SS units were, from now on, to feed themselves from the territories they occupied – and with a ruthless disregard for the needs of the local population. At the same time, Ukraine and France would be expected to send a far greater proportion of the 1942 harvest straight back to Germany. While local populations were still expected to be left with some food on which to survive, the real benefit of Backe's new plan was the exclusion of some groups from getting any food at all.

In this way, Backe had found a means to kill two birds with one stone. Poland's Jews were to be completely eliminated from the food chain. That was 3.5 million people Germany was no longer responsible for feeding in any way whatsoever. They would, of course, starve, as would many other millions of people, but it was better, Backe believed, to starve Jews and the conquered Slavs of the East – and even Frenchmen, for that matter – than to allow Germans to die of hunger. Germany's need for food was starting to affect everyone in the occupied territories. For many, it would mean starvation and death. For others, such as those in the West who were not part of Germany's racial plans but who were still subordinate in the pecking order, it meant life was about to become noticeably harder. That, however, was the way it had to be as far as Backe was concerned. The interests of pure-blood Germans took precedence over everyone else.

Far away in the United States, there was also a new armaments supremo. Don Nelson, the head of the recently formed War Production Board, was an outwardly mild-mannered, pipe-smoking, balding and bespectacled 53-year-old with no industrial or manufacturing experience whatsoever – apart from, that is, what he had learned from Bill Knudsen during their time together on the NDAC and OPM, the War Production Board's precursors.

Nelson, however, had proved himself as a supremely successful businessman with that most famous of American retailers, Sears & Roebuck, the mail-order giants. From Missouri, and with a degree in chemical engineering under his belt and the intention of saving a few dollars so he could study for a doctorate at Harvard, he had joined Sears & Roebuck back in 1912. Somehow, he never quite left and after thirty years had steadily worked his way up the ladder until he was president of the whole caboodle. What his long career had taught him was how to make manufacturers give him the best prices and how to get a flow of materials from multiple sources out to the customer, and on time. Since joining NDAC back in 1940 as one of the 'dollar-a-year' men, or leading capitalists, he had impressed everyone with his cool, calm efficiency and good sense. Tall, rotund and bookish, people warmed to Nelson: he looked like a gentle giant, was affable and easy-going and very hard not to like. There was no barking and snarling, nor fist-thumping of tables; rather, he relied on charm, patience, imperturbability, razor-sharp analytical powers, gentle coercion and a voracious appetite for work. So far in his life, it had proved a disarming but highly successful combination.

When first offered the job of the new head of the WPB, Nelson had pointed out to Roosevelt that earlier boards had struggled because they had lacked any clearly defined authority. Accepting this, the President asked him to write out his own brief, which he promised he would sign. Nelson did as he was bidden and presented a draft that gave him the authority to exercise power in such a manner as he felt fit. The key line was, 'His decisions shall be final.'

This was what Knudsen had always lacked. From now on, manufacturers could be forced to accept contracts, private property could be forcibly requisitioned, and Nelson could also halt the production of civilian goods if he felt it necessary. He was the new war production Tsar. 'As I understood my job,' he wrote, 'it wasn't up to me to *tell* industry how to do its job; it was our function to *show* industry what had to be done and then to do everything in our power to enable industry to do it.'

That meant harnessing big business even more than Knudsen had been able to. It also meant doing away with normal peacetime business practices. Competitive bids, for example, were scrapped, even though fair competition practices – or antitrust, as it was known – had been at the heart of US business since 1890. Rather, Nelson convinced Roosevelt that the rules now had to be bent. Instead, a contract was negotiated on the basis of what the Government was willing to pay upfront, and while this was certainly open to corruption, Nelson saw it as a question of priorities: what was more important, mass-producing vast numbers of armaments, or clogging the production chain with lengthy bidding processes? Time and a profound sense of urgency dictated everything: every day lost to unnecessary legislation and red tape, or to maintaining ethical business policies, could mean the loss of more American lives.

No one had ever doubted the United States' potential to mass-produce armaments, but whether that potential would ever be effectively realized had been very much up for debate. Knudsen's vision of harnessing big business whilst maintaining civilian production, and stressing speed of process at every turn, had set the country on the right path: in the eighteen months since the formation of the NDAC, it had been Knudsen, above all, who had laid the foundations for America's war production. Now it was up to Nelson to try to deliver the increasingly high expectations not only of the President and America's war leaders, but also those of Britain and the Soviet Union.

The challenge of converting the US economy to an all-out wartime footing was a gargantuan one. Priorities were horribly tangled and urgently needed rationalizing. The conversion from civilian to military production now had to be sped up, although just how fast and to what extent was still being argued over both within industry and in the corridors of Washington. A mass of bottlenecks and some worrying raw-material shortages were also emerging, not least in steel, copper and magnesium, all essential if they were to get even close to the kind of production figures that were being talked about.

Highly capable though he was, whether Don Nelson could pull it off was another matter altogether.

CHAPTER 14

Seeds of Resistance

I N THE EAST, the sheer number of POWs had caught the Germans off guard the previous summer and so hundreds of thousands had been corralled into giant camps where they had been given little food or any of the courtesies and conditions afforded to Allied prisoners of war. Many had subsequently died. At the same time, the *Einsatzgruppen* had continued their murderous work. It wasn't only Jews who were lined up and executed, but Gypsies, the Polish intelligentsia and other minorities. On 31 July 1941, Göring had signed an order drafted by Obergruppenführer Reinhard Heydrich, the SS Chief of the Reich Security Office: 'I herewith commission you to carry out all necessary preparations with regard to organizational, substantive and financial viewpoints for a total solution of the Jewish problem within Germany's sphere of influence in Europe.' This expanded Heydrich's powers considerably, and by the end of the year he had realized that mass executions in the East and shooting hundreds of thousands of Jews was not an efficient way to achieve racial purity. In fact, even the head of the SS, Heinrich Himmler, after witnessing executions in the East first hand in August, had demanded Heydrich find another way. Shootings were, he said, too traumatic for those carrying them out.

By the end of 1941, Heydrich had come up with what he termed the 'final solution' as authorized by Göring on 31 July. The occupied territories were to be combed for Jews and they would then be sent to extermination camps. The fit and able would be used for labour, although it was acknowledged many would be 'eliminated' by natural causes. The remainder would simply be executed, mostly by gassing. This was all discussed, albeit euphemistically, with key administrators and officials in a ninety-minute meeting at the villa at Wannsee on the edge of Berlin on 20 January 1942.

While the plan for genocide clearly came from the warped minds of leading Nazis, it is a mistake to think that anti-Semitism was purely their preserve. Far from it: anti-Semitism was rife throughout Europe and the hounding of Jews found many willing collaborators in the occupied territories, and not least in France. The Vichy Government, for example, was under no obligation to introduce anti-Semitic laws. It did so not to curry favour with Germany but because its Chief of State, Maréchal Philippe Pétain, decreed it. In fact, Pétain brought in anti-Semitic laws in Vichy France before they were introduced in the occupied zone. These were designed to exclude Jews from public life rather than to kill them, but anti-Semitism in Vichy grew, rather than lessened.

In Paris, in the occupied zone, the arrests of Jews had begun in May 1941. One of the Jews living in Paris at the time was Freddie Knoller, who had just turned twenty. Having escaped from Vienna to Belgium before the war, he had been captured by the French and taken to an internment camp following the start of the German attack in May 1940. After escaping, he had made his way to Paris and was now living under a false identity, Robert Metzner from Metz, and working with a Greek friend, Christos, bringing in German soldiers to the clubs and brothels of Pigalle. He had been doing well enough financially to move out of Christos's flat and take his own digs in the Hôtel du Collège Rollin, one of the many small hotels in the area where prostitutes took their clients. Some 6,494 Jews were arrested that May, of whom 3,747 were then interned. Knoller witnessed many of the arrests and was horrified to discover that it was French policemen carrying them out. 'I saw not a single SS man or Gestapo officer in sight,' he noted. The German persecution of Jews may have driven him first from Austria, then from Belgium, but now here in France the situation seemed even worse: 'the willingness,' he added, 'of a defeated nation to do the dirty work of their so-called enemy.'

No German forced the French police to do this. It was the same in the Netherlands, where Dutch police did most of the rounding up of Jews. In Antwerp in Belgium, collaborators pillaged synagogues and burned down the house of a rabbi, and round-ups there were carried out in full collaboration, as, although there was a German military governor, the overall administration of the country was conducted by Belgium's ministry officials and civil service.

In Paris, Knoller found it impossible to hide his misery at witnessing these scenes and, having drunk too much one night, confided in Christos. For a moment his friend did not speak, then eventually he said, 'I just never thought of that.' He then looked at Knoller's forged ID card and exploded with anger. 'What do you think you're doing,' he exclaimed, 'going up to the Boches with a tinpot forgery like this? Are you mad?' His anger soon dissolved, however, and soon after another friend of Christos, a Corsican named Pierre Marcello, managed to secure Knoller a far better French identity card. Testing it when he visited the Mairie to obtain his ration card was a nerve-wracking business, but Marcello had promised him it would be foolproof and so it proved. 'Now,' he wrote, 'I could obtain rations again.'

The round-ups of Jews continued. Some 4,242 were arrested by French gendarmes in August 1941, then in March 1942 the first deportations to the East began – to a large camp complex that had been built near the IG Farben synthetic-fuel facility at Auschwitz.

Back in 1940, Churchill had vowed to set Europe ablaze by aiding and abetting resistance throughout Nazi-occupied Europe. This had been easier said than done, however, because resistance took time to evolve into any kind of meaningful movement. In the first instance, most of those in the occupied territories had been too stunned to resist or, as in the case of most Frenchmen, for example, too relieved that they would not have to suffer another slaughter on their soil similar to the deadlock of 1914–18. In Vichy France, many had genuinely believed Pétain would soon declare war on Germany.

Others had simply been relieved that the age of fractious politics and endless multi-party governments was over, and while there were plenty of French Communists at one end of the political spectrum, a very large number were also decidedly right wing and even pro-Fascist. One man to fall into that latter category was Paul Vigouroux, who before the war had been a young journalist and militant in the ultra-right-wing Parti français national-collectiviste. France, he had believed, was finished. There was too much alcoholism, too much decadence and too many Jews. Before the war, he had joined up voluntarily and had been posted to French Morocco. With the resignation of the Prime Minister Paul

Reynaud and the advent of Pétain, he had been exultant. Discharged and back in Paris, he felt more confident about France's future than at any time before the war. 'At last,' he noted, 'someone was leading France! We were going to negotiate – the winners would not fool us.'

He was wrong about that, but although Paris and the north were governed by the Germans not Pétain, Vigouroux welcomed the ideals of National Socialism and the strong leadership of the occupiers. He was also exhilarated by the German invasion of Russia and hurried to join the Légion des volontaires français contre le bolchevisme (LVF), made up of young men from several collaborationist and far-right parties. By October 1941, an LVF regiment of some 2,500 men was sent east and in December they had been flung into the battle for Moscow. Paul Vigouroux had been one of those men, although once he had reached Poland he had very nearly abandoned the idea and turned back – not because of the conditions, but because they had been expected to wear German uniforms. That had been a bad surprise; Vigouroux considered himself a profound French patriot. To admire the Nazis was one thing; to dress like a German was quite another. However, the fight against Bolshevism was even more important, so he had stuck with it, and at Christmas had been peppered with shrapnel during a Russian counter-attack. After a stint in hospital, he had been repatriated and sent to Colmar in Alsace.

There he had suffered another shock: all around the town was German anti-French propaganda, including a giant poster of a worker crushing a Gallic cockerel with the words 'Get Rid of French Ideas'. At the same time, he became aware that more and more French Alsatians were listening to the BBC and broadcasts by de Gaulle, begun back in June 1940. There would never be, he realized, a true partnership of equals between France and Germany. The French were too despised by the Germans: that was obvious. It left him feeling profoundly bitter.

Recovered from his wounds, Vigouroux returned to Paris, only to discover that most of the older pre-war Fascists had gone and that hatred was evident amongst every social class. The humiliation many Parisians felt was profound; rationing was severe; de Gaulle's radio messages were also stirring up resistance. The new breed of collaborators were black-market louts or wheeler-dealers without morals. Vigouroux despised them. He was finding that being an imperialistic French Fascist under the occupation was far from easy.

In truth, it was quite hard being French whatever one's political leaning, particularly in Paris and the cities of the occupied zone. Vigouroux was, however, quite right about the levels of hatred, which had grown rapidly over the past eighteen months. One young Parisienne, Andrée Griotteray, who worked at the Police Headquarters, still loathed the Germans who occupied her city every bit as much as she had the first day they had marched into town. Day-to-day existence, even for someone like her who still had a job, was made very much worse by the rapidly deteriorating conditions. 'We are unable to find any food at the moment,' she wrote in her diary on 22 January. A couple of weeks later she added, 'It is so cold in the flat. We have no coal.' That had been sent to Germany.

The only way to get any proper food was to go out to the country or befriend Germans. This latter course was the film star Corinne Luchaire's preferred method. After marrying a Frenchman she did not love the previous autumn, she had left him after a matter of days and returned to the capital. Initially, she had found Paris empty, but there were plenty of places open to Germans that were not freely accessible to Frenchmen. Luchaire was still a very young and beautiful woman, who not only craved attention but who had become used to the finer things in life. It did not bother her particularly who her admirers were if they could get her access to champagne and nightclubs or invite her to dine at Maxime's and La Tour d'Argent.

Corinne Luchaire was not the only Frenchwoman to be invited on dates by Germans. So too was Andrée Griotteray, but no matter how hungry or cold she may have been, it was a Faustian pact she was not prepared to make. Rather, she was becoming increasingly involved in her brother's resistance network. This now had a name – Le Réseau Orion – named after the Chateau Orion near Béarn in the Basque country in the south-west. This was the family home of Paul Labbé, one of Alain Griotteray's friends and fellow resisters. There was now a hard core of them working for the Orion network, but very sensibly their prime objective was not sabotage or murdering Germans, but rather gathering intelligence and developing an escape route across the Pyrenees. Andrée was helping by not only stealing blank ID cards from the Police HQ, but also occasionally heading south to deliver intelligence to her brother's network, which was then smuggled through Marseilles or through the mountains into Spain.

While it was unquestionably important for young resisters like Alain and Andrée Griotteray to feel as though they were doing something positive, the harsh truth was that their efforts amounted to very little in the larger scheme of things. In the summer and autumn of 1941, a number of *Jeunesses communistes* had gone on a shooting spree, assassinating Germans and even attempting to shoot Pierre Laval. In all, few more than a dozen people were killed, but retribution by the Germans was swift and savage, as hostages – men and woman snatched from the streets or political prisoners – were summarily executed. Ninety-eight, for example, were executed in revenge for the assassination of Oberstleutnant Karl Hotz, the military commander of Nantes. One of those was Guy Moquet, aged just seventeen and the son of a Communist deputy. 'Those of you who remain,' he said with immense courage before being shot, 'be worthy of us.'

For resistance to be meaningful, two things were needed. The first was a critical mass of people prepared to risk their lives. That condition had, by the spring of 1942, been met. Living under the Nazi yoke affected people in different ways, but the food and coal shortages, the loss of jobs, pay cuts, Allied bombing, loss of independence, coercion into forced labour, and even the treatment of Jews, as well as horror at the mass of executions the previous autumn, had all helped encourage pockets of resistance. A large and significant strike by French coal miners in the early summer of 1941 had also done much to fan the flames of early resistance. 'More and more now,' wrote one resister in October 1941, 'the population in France is beginning to become conscious of its strength of resistance and to yearn to shake off the yoke.'

That resister was the 42-year-old former Préfet of Eure-et-Loir, Jean Moulin, who had correctly recognized that what was also needed was organization and direction; collectively, resistance groups would add up to considerably more than the sum of their individual parts.

Moulin had parachuted into France from Britain in the early hours of 2 January 1942, dropping into the unoccupied zone between Avignon and Aix-en-Provence after what had been a long personal journey of enormous risk and fortitude, which began in June 1940. Back then, he had been arrested by the Germans for refusing to sign a document falsely blaming Senegalese troops for massacring civilians. So distraught had he been, he had attempted to kill himself by cutting his throat with a piece of glass. He had survived, however, and after being released from prison had been urged by friends to leave France and begin again in the United

States. Obtaining the necessary paperwork had taken long months, however, during which time he had travelled around the country talking to contacts in the fledgling resistance and trying to gather as much information as possible about what the movement needed and what might be realistically achieved.

By the time his paperwork for emigration finally arrived, he had written up a report and, on reaching Lisbon in Portugal in early September 1941, he had made his way straight to the British Embassy. Having decided he would not go to the States after all, he now asked to be flown to London. A month later, on 19 October 1941, after extensive grilling by a British Special Operations Executive agent, he finally arrived in London.

There, the SOE tried hard to recruit him, but after meeting de Gaulle Moulin decided to work alongside the Free French rather than directly with the British, even though politically he was far to the left of the Général. For the time being, this did not matter: what was needed, as Moulin had outlined in his report, was leadership – and de Gaulle was the best person to provide it. He would be the figurehead of the resistance. What was also required was moral support, money, arms and regular communication. Then, and only then, could resistance be properly co-ordinated. 'The object to be achieved,' he wrote, 'is first and foremost to intensify propaganda and to organize eventual collective action for the future.' He ended with a plea: 'Those carrying on the fight,' he urged, 'must not be left helpless.' It was in the interests of Britain and her Allies to help, and was 'the hope of a whole people enslaved.'

After landing in Provence, Moulin made his way to Marseilles using the *nom de guerre* Max. And there he began his mission: of coaxing and urging the various resistance movements, with their differing politics, opinions and egos, into one whole. It was going to be a gargantuan task.

Away to the north, across the sea, resistance was also growing. Norway's situation was different to that of most other occupied countries. The King and Government had escaped to Britain without ever surrendering: so as far as both parties were concerned, Norway was still at war with Germany. What's more, not only had they brought with them their sizeable merchant fleet, which continued to ply the trade routes on behalf of Britain and her allies, they had also managed to smuggle out their gold reserves in an epic journey through mountains and valleys, repeatedly passing under the noses of the Germans.

Like almost every country apart from Britain, Norway had made no provision for a resistance movement before their defeat. Despite this, a large number of officers and men who had slipped back into civilian life after the fighting was over swiftly organized themselves into the Militær Organisasjon, or Milorg for short. Their objective was to be able to spring into action the moment the Allies returned, but otherwise their policy was to lie comparatively low and do little that might unnecessarily antagonize the enemy. As if to prove their point, the Commando raid on the Lofoten Islands in March 1941 had prompted swift and savage reprisals on local fishermen. Despite this, Milorg insisted on sticking to its policy of long-term secret and cautious preparations – an approach that to many seemed like not doing anything very much at all.

One of those impatient to light the fire of resistance was 23-year-old Gunnar Sønsteby. Since escaping the clutches of the Germans after the battle for Norway, Sønsteby had never lost his determination to resist. By the summer of 1940, in Oslo, he had met up with three men, Harald Hanto, Max Manus and Kolbein Lauring, who all lived in a flat in a building that shared a courtyard with the building in Therese Street where Sønsteby lived. The three had already begun printing a resistance newspaper, *Vi vil oss et land* – 'We Want Ourselves a Country' – and Sønsteby started working for their group, writing reports for their paper.

By the autumn, Max Manus and a number of others had decided to head to the south-west coast hoping to get a boat to England, so Sønsteby decided to leave Oslo too and head back to his home town, Rjukan. It proved to be a good move, because just two weeks later several of the Oslo group were raided and arrested. By the spring of 1941, Sønsteby had made contact with Milorg and had begun recruiting for them, which took him back to Oslo. There would be occasional meetings, in which Milorg agents would carry out endless security measures, and Sønsteby successfully recruited a few people, but nothing much was actually happening. Fed up with the organization's exaggerated attention to security and what he thought was a lamentable lack of activity, he decided that he, too, needed to try to get to England, even though Max Manus's efforts had failed.

In October, Sønsteby left Oslo again, this time with his friend Knut

Haugland, a fellow resister and former Army engineer who was a trained radio telegrapher. They planned to build a transmitter so that they could communicate with Britain, but then they learned of an antique dealer in Oslo who was an 'exporter' who could arrange passage to Britain via Sweden. The whole venture turned out to be something of a fiasco for Sønsteby, for although they made it to Stockholm, only Haugland, with his radio skills, was told he would be going to England. Sønsteby, meanwhile, was advised to go back to Norway instead and get a boat from Ålesund, on the west coast, north of Bergen. Getting there from Stockholm was easier said than done, involving a long, difficult journey by train, cart and on foot over numerous mountains. He was ill-dressed and ill-equipped for such a journey, which was made worse by the snow and freezing temperatures. Before they reached Ålesund, Sønsteby was suffering from frostbite in his legs and was forced to go to hospital. News that a boat was leaving for England on 13 November made him decide to make one last effort to catch it, but after leaving hospital and attempting to start the journey, his legs began to hurt badly. Taking off his shoes and socks, he saw his toes were black. 'I knew I had to give up trying to get to England,' he wrote. 'All the ghastly trip from Stockholm had been in vain.'

But he did not give up for good. Once recovered and back in Oslo, he renewed contact with his resistance friends and agreed to become a courier. This meant heading back to Stockholm for money and supplies from the Norwegian and British legations there. On his second trip he was caught by the Swedish authorities and arrested on charges of espionage. After a couple of months in prison, he found himself in court, but was, much to his relief, acquitted and sent to a camp for Norwegian refugees.

So far, Sønsteby's resistance work had hardly been a great success. Organization was haphazard, travelling was fraught with risk and difficulties, and the Milorg seemed rather too risk-averse. His fortunes were about to change, however. Summoned from the refugee camp by the Norwegian legation in Stockholm, he first called on the British legation instead and suggested he work for them. By this time, he had realized he no longer wanted to get to England, but rather preferred to carry out resistance work in Norway – not with Milorg, but under an organization that could give him some much-needed direction, support and purpose. He hoped the British would provide him with this. Much to his relief, his proposal was accepted and Sønsteby was drafted into the SOE. After being fully briefed and given rudimentary training, he was assigned the codename Agent 24.

Gunnar Sønsteby may have decided a trip to England was simply not worth the risk, but there were a good number of Norwegians who were determined to get there no matter how hard it might prove to be. Twenty-two-year-old Jens-Anton Poulsson had been one of the few pre-war Regular soldiers, but it had counted for little once the German invasion began. Rapidly forced to retreat, after a week they had been ordered to cross the border into Sweden and had promptly been disarmed and interned. By summer, they had all been sent back to Norway and Poulsson had returned home to his family farm. He soon became restless, however, and wanted to do something to help his country. The King and Government-in-Exile were in Britain, and he and a friend decided that was where they should go too, to try to join the other forces gathering there.

On New Year's Day 1941, the two travelled to Sweden, skiing over the border and eventually catching a train to Stockholm. So far, all had gone to plan, but the Norwegians at the embassy there were, by now, tiring of young Norwegian men arriving and demanding help to get them to England. 'We had hoped they'd send us to England as soon as possible,' said Poulsson, 'but no.' There was neither a boat nor a plane they could take, and so, undeterred, they headed into Finland and worked their way down through the German-occupied Soviet Union to Odessa on the Black Sea – a mammoth journey across war-torn eastern Europe. From Odessa, they took a boat to Istanbul, then a train to Ankara. For two young men who had previously never left Norway, this was quite some adventure, but their long way round to Britain had only just begun. On they went – into Palestine and then to Egypt, gathering numbers of other young Norwegians who had had the same idea. From Egypt, they took a ship to Bombay. 'By that time,' Poulsson said, 'we were nearly a company.' From there, this extraordinary and epic journey continued: a ship to South Africa and then on to Canada, before finally crossing back over the Atlantic and arriving in Liverpool in October 1941. It has to rank as one of the most indirect trips to Britain from Norway ever undertaken.

From Liverpool, these hundred-odd Norwegians were sent to London, and to the London Reception Centre in the old Royal Victorian Patriotic School for clearance. Here, Poulsson and a few others were contacted by the former Norwegian actor Martin Linge. He was now a captain in the SOE-backed Norwegian Independent Company No. 1 and recruited them to join his unit. Training followed under British instruction, first at a camp outside London, then in Scotland and finally at the Parachute Training School at Ringway, outside Manchester.

It was whilst undergoing his parachute training that Poulsson injured himself – not leaping from a plane, but during physical training having already completed five jumps. As a result, he missed one of the first major raids by Independent Company No. 1 at the end of December 1941. A dozen of them had joined the Commandos for Operation ARCHERY, a raid to destroy the fish-oil production plant and stores used by the Germans to make explosives at Maaloy, on the island of Vaagso. It was pretty successful: four factories were destroyed, ammunition and fuel stores and the telephone exchange were blown up, as well as 120 German soldiers killed and ninety-eight captured. Furthermore, a complete copy of the German naval code was taken back to Britain. However, amongst those Commandos killed was Martin Linge – a particularly hard blow for the fledgling Independent Company No. 1.

In April 1942, Gunnar Sønsteby returned to Norway from Sweden. Unlike Jens-Anton Poulsson in Independent Company No. 1, his role for the SOE was principally one of intelligence: reporting on the movement of troops, the quantity and quality of their equipment, the activities of Kriegsmarine vessels and that of the Luftwaffe. He was also to get hold of timetables, telephone directories, police proclamations and other day-to-day information that could be passed on to other agents coming into the country. Another important part of his work was to arrange the reception of these agents when they were parachuted into Norway. He was expected to find them safe lodgings as well as jobs that they could use as cover. The men were to be made 'legal' as far as possible: given identity cards, ration books, health cards and so on – and not just in Oslo, but in Trondheim, Kristiansand, Stavanger and elsewhere.

Sønsteby's intelligence reports were sent back to his SOE contacts in Sweden via couriers whom he would meet roughly every ten days. He never knew their true identities nor they his, and his reports were always written in a code that was also unknown to the couriers. Writing these coded reports on a typewriter in his flat in Therese Street was no easy task, and he found his paperwork quickly mounted up.

Nor was it easy to carry out any of this work. Many of the resistance groups he had known had been broken up, and the Germans – particularly the Gestapo – had tightened their control considerably, both in Oslo and throughout the country. At the end of April, soon after Sønsteby's return, two Norwegian SOE agents were discovered by the Gestapo at the village of Telavåg on the coast. In the ensuing gunfight, two senior Gestapo officers were shot and killed. Soon after, in a brutally ruthless move personally overseen by Reichskommissar Josef Terboven, the village was razed to the ground, the villagers' boats all sunk, and the men either executed or sent to concentration camps and the women and children imprisoned.

After Telavåg, moving freely about Oslo was becoming harder. Sønsteby quickly discovered that he was actually well suited to this kind of nerve-wracking clandestine work. Clear-headed, quick-witted and pragmatic, he was also blessed with a rather unremarkable appearance: neither especially good- nor bad-looking, of medium height, with no obvious distinguishing features, but with an open and easy-going expression that did not court suspicion. He made sure he wore bland, unremarkable clothes, and began sleeping at numerous different places – family homes of those willing to help the resistance. He made sure his hosts never knew his real identity, tending to leave the house early in the morning and stay out all day. Knowing that the Gestapo liked to make raids in the early hours, he always slept with a pistol under his pillow. 'The point,' he said, 'was to be as unobtrusive as possible. I tried to be invisible.'

In France, in Norway and throughout the occupied territories, the light of resistance had been lit. It had taken time to emerge and there was much for the resisters to learn before this movement could become anything meaningful.

But, by early summer of 1942, the flames were beginning to grow.

CHAPTER 15

Heat and Dust

AT THE END OF February 1942, Oliver Lyttelton flew home from Cairo, his time as Minister of State in the Middle East over. His experience as a soldier in the last war, his understanding of resources and logistics, and his deft political nous and diplomacy had served both him and those trying to run Britain's war effort in the theatre very well indeed. The Middle East was an incredibly challenging command for its Commander-in-Chief and Lyttelton had been able to take away many of the political and economic headaches from Auchinleck. Had it not been for the diversion of so many Middle East-bound supplies to the Far East, the situation in Libya would most likely have been even more promising. As it was, Syria, Iraq, Palestine and Egypt itself were all reasonably secure, while ever-more supplies were once again reaching the front. Lyttelton had played no small part in that.

However, Churchill's great friend, the Canadian press baron Lord Beaverbrook, had resigned as Minister of Production after just twelve days in the post, in part because of a savage asthma attack but also because of one too many clashes with Ernest Bevin, the Minister for Labour and National Service. Churchill had wasted no time at all in ringing Lyttelton in Cairo and offering him the post instead – a job he accepted immediately. It was a challenge that excited him, but more than that it meant returning to England and seeing his four children again; unsurprisingly, he and his wife, Moira, had missed them desperately.

The Lytteltons left Cairo on 26 February for the long flight home via Brazzaville and Lisbon, and only finally landed back in a flying boat into

Poole Harbour at around 3 p.m. on 2 March. The heat and dust of Africa had made way for a biting wind, but their journey was not over yet. Waiting for them was yet another plane to take them to London and then, at long last, they reached the rooms booked for them at the Dorchester, where they were finally reunited with their children. It was now early evening, yet in a foretaste of what was to come, a secretary from the Cabinet Office now arrived with an invitation from the Prime Minister to dine with him that very night.

'I could have shot him,' noted Lyttelton. Prising himself away from his children, he reluctantly got changed and headed out to No. 10, finally crawling home, utterly exhausted, at two in the morning.

Over the next few weeks, Lyttelton realized what a huge challenge now confronted him. The Ministry was a new one, so he was effectively starting from scratch – there were just three men and two typists when he arrived. He swiftly set about gathering men of experience and knowledge around him: technocrats, mostly, who understood about production and logistics. The position also gave him a place in the now seven-man War Cabinet, while those older munitions ministries, of Supply and Aircraft Production, were not so privileged. This, he knew, could easily be resented. Nor would they take kindly to interference, and nor would other ministries whose areas he would inevitably have to invade, such as the Board of Trade.

None the less, while Lord Beaverbrook, for all his many skills, had not had the tact required for such a role, Lyttelton most certainly did. And his was unquestionably a really important undertaking – one that was to try to marry the complexities of production with the tactical requirements of the commanders in the field. Expectations at both ends were all too often unrealistic – the generals were demanding one thing, while those producing arms were railing against constant demands and modifications. For too long, the gulf between them had been too wide, as Lyttelton's time visiting the front in the Western Desert had shown him; it was one of the reasons why the British Army was lagging behind with a really good anti-tank gun, for example. He was also conscious that none of the Ministers of Supply had ever been in battle. One of these men had even once asked him whether a Bofors gun was a howitzer. Light anti-aircraft guns and field artillery were very different beasts. There had thus been a disconnect that urgently needed fixing.

There was, however, a further crucially important part for Lyttelton to play and that was to handle any discussions with his opposite numbers in the United States. Now that America's war production was kicking into gear, it made sense that they co-ordinate efforts as far as possible rather than doubling up. The US, for example, had designed their fighter aircraft primarily with a view to operations in the Pacific, where range and endurance were more important than manoeuvrability. For British fighters, however, operating at much shorter ranges, rate of climb, fire-power and manoeuvrability were of prime importance.

Similarly, RAF Bomber Command operated at night without fighter escort and the Lancaster now rolling out of the factories was designed for this. American heavy bombers, on the other hand, were designed with daylight operations in mind. Only in two-engine medium bombers was there much cross-over in terms of tactical plans, which was why Britain used predominantly American-built aircraft of this kind. Other areas of common tactical needs were in tanks – and US M3 Grants were now arriving in North Africa. It was Lyttelton's task to make sure Anglo-US war production continued to operate efficiently and smoothly and with as little wastage as possible.

The task ahead, he quickly understood, was enormous. Britain's fac-tories were now operating at near maximum effort. The number of contractors and links in the armaments chain was breathtaking. The complexity of what was being unleashed in this all-out effort to win the war was immense and, inevitably, this meant a staggering workload. 'The work was killing,' he noted. 'I calculated that a War Cabinet Minister at that time had to read the equivalent of one full-scale novel a day every day of the year.' Nor did Churchill's regime help. The PM started his working day early in bed, met at the House of Commons at 11 a.m., then had lunch. At 3 p.m. he took a nap for two or three hours. The War Cabinet would meet at 6 p.m. at the end of their ministerial day and often lasted until 9 p.m. Somewhere, a bite to eat would then be snatched before a meeting of the Defence Committee at 10.30 p.m., by which time Churchill was fresh and still raring to go. At 2 a.m. or even later, the PM would often call Lyttelton and Anthony Eden, the Foreign Secretary, into his private sitting room for a whisky and some further chat. 'In the middle of these discussions,' wrote Lyttelton, 'I sometimes used sadly to think of the meeting of – say – the Manpower Committee at 10am the next morning, and the massive schedules that wanted more study.'

Punishing though this workload unquestionably was, the need to streamline production, and to ensure that the very best balance between practical mass production and tactical requirements was achieved, was of vital importance. This was something all the major combatant nations now understood. And those who managed it most successfully would inevitably see that success transferred to the battlefield.

At the very end of April, Mussolini, with Ciano and Cavallero, the Italian Chief of Staff, in tow, took a train to Salzburg for talks with Hitler and his staff. The Italian delegation was housed in the Schloss Klessheim, a former palace of the prince-bishops of Salzburg, which was gratifyingly luxurious. The Italians found their German allies particularly cordial, which Ciano had learned was not necessarily a good sign. Hitler, he thought, looked tired and had many more grey hairs than when he had last seen him; the long winter had taken its toll.

Along the Eastern Front, even Hitler had recognized that his forces needed to go on the defensive. Subsequent counter-attacks by the Red Army in February had been successfully seen off, and earlier in April the Führer had issued his latest directive with his plans for the summer offensive, which had changed little since the beginning of January. There would be no further attempt on Moscow, but instead Army Group North would take Leningrad once and for all, while the main effort would be in the south, with a drive towards the Caucasus and the oil-fields there as the objective. The ice of Russia, von Ribbentrop assured Ciano, had been conquered by the genius of Hitler. The Soviet Union would be brought to her knees, then Britain would inevitably bow to save what remained of her battered Empire. It had all been worked out. But what if the English fight on, Ciano retorted? Aeroplanes and submarines, von Ribbentrop replied, and a return to the 1940 formula. 'But that formula failed then and was shelved in the attack,' noted Ciano later in his diary. 'Now they pull it out once more, and, after having dusted it thoroughly, they want to offer it to us again. I am not convinced by it and I say so to Ribbentrop.'

As regards America, the Germans claimed US boasts about the scale of their armaments were bluff and nothing more. Ciano thought the Germans were in denial on this score and wilfully blind to the reality, which was, of course, absolutely spot on. 'But this,' he added, 'does not keep the more intelligent and the more honest from thinking about what America can do, and they feel shivers running down their spines.'

While much of the talk was about the Eastern Front and how the Germans had the whole situation sewn up, there was also discussion on North Africa and the Mediterranean, the only other theatre of any consequence as far as the German High Command was concerned – and of vital importance to the Italians, who had been urging an invasion of Malta for some months but were particularly keen to press the point now that the island had been subdued.

So too, as it happened, was Feldmarschall Albert Kesselring, but from the outset this was seen primarily as an Italian venture, one being championed especially by Maresciallo Cavallero. Kesselring promised Luftwaffe support with both air forces and one airborne division, but apart from him and Jeschonnek, the Luftwaffe Chief of Staff, none of the German commanders was much enthused by the prospect. Hitler, though, assured the Italians of 'generous German participation.'

A few weeks later, however, the Führer changed his mind as he vacillated over what to do in the Mediterranean. He had gone off airborne ops of any kind, and Göring was against it. One advocate of an invasion, on the other hand, was General Kurt Student, the commander of the airborne forces, the *Fallschirmjäger*, but after he had presented his arguments for the operation to Hitler, the Führer was dismissive. The British Fleet would hurry to the island and the RAF would be over in a trice, he told Student. 'You can imagine how the Italians will react to that,' he added. 'The minute they get the news on their radios, they'll all make a dash for the harbours of Sicily – both warships and fighters. You'll be sitting all alone on the island with your paratroopers.'

The Italians had talked vaguely of the invasion taking place in the summer, but they wouldn't dare attempt it on their own, as Hitler well knew. The truth was, the summer offensive in the East was beckoning, and although some units had been left on Sicily, most of II. Fliegerkorps were now being sent back to the Soviet Union and across the sea to North Africa – for there, Rommel was preparing to launch a major attack on the British position at Gazala. His aim was to smash his way through and recapture Tobruk. Kesselring still wanted to take Malta first, but Rommel was determined that his attack should take place before the end of May. Thanks to the subjugation of Malta, supplies had, for once, been arriving in Libya largely unscathed, and although his Panzerarmee was still not at full strength, he wanted to strike before the British build-up of forces became too great. Since there was nothing like enough air power in the Mediterranean for both operations to take place side by side, and since Hitler was against the Malta invasion anyway, there the argument ended. Kesselring was overruled. Rommel would have his offensive at the end of May.

While these deliberations were going on, Allied plans to send a second batch of Spitfires to battered Malta were under way, combined with the run of a fast naval minelayer full of aviation fuel from Alexandria. Once again it was the USS *Wasp* that would be delivering them to the mouth of the Mediterranean. From there, the pilots would take off and fly the Spitfires onwards to Malta. This time, the defenders were determined not to repeat earlier mistakes and elaborate plans were being made for a number of Army and Air Force personnel to descend on each Spitfire as it came in to land and have it refuelled and ready to get back in the air just as soon as humanly possible.

On board the *Wasp* was Douglas Fairbanks, Jr, who had been posted to join Task Force 99 in April. Based at Scapa Flow, TF99 had been attached to the Royal Navy's Home Fleet to add support in escorting Arctic convoys to Russia. After flying to Prestwick and catching up with movie pals like David Niven and Ivor Novello, Fairbanks took a US Navy aircraft north to the Orkney islands, where he joined the TF99 commander, Admiral Robert 'Ike' Giffen. 'The first grey, misty sight of all those ships of two mighty navies lying there in that huge, landlocked sea shelter of Scapa Flow,' wrote Fairbanks, 'was breath-taking.' Here and there, small barges and gigs beetled from one ship to another, shortlived wakes following them as they criss-crossed on their errands. On shore were barracks and command buildings. Fairbanks thought it all looked invincible. Assigned to Giffen's flag staff as 'assistant staff gunnery and communications officer', he spent his first few weeks on fleet exercises with the British as he acclimatized to his new post, then Giffen called him over and told him he was posting him to *Wasp* for an important mission to help Malta. 'They're having a helluva time there,' Giffen told him, 'but are still holding off the bastards in spite of the losses. So we're sending the *Wasp* down again to help those poor kids.' He wanted Fairbanks to be his official observer, he said, and to keep a detailed log of the trip.

Wasp set sail for her second journey to the Mediterranean on 2 May, having sailed to the Clyde to pick up the Spitfires and pilots. As they steamed back down the estuary, Fairbanks looked out at the inviting landscape twinkling in the sun. 'We were all acutely aware,' he wrote, 'of our situation and wondered wistfully how long it would be before we would see green fields again.' Fairbanks had another reason to feel wistful: back in the States, his wife was pregnant with their second child. He was also struck by how young the British pilots seemed. He was now thirty-two, but most of these 'easy-going kids' were between eighteen and twenty-two. They were also rather agog to find an A-list Hollywood star on board. He'd been warned not to autograph things and had been routinely ticked off for showing a bit of white handkerchief in his breast-pocket – someone of his junior rank was not permitted such affectations. 'I blushed and stumbled over apologies and admissions of ignorance,' he admitted, and made sure that thereafter it was kept well out of sight.

On 6 May, a communiqué arrived informing them that US forces had surrendered to the Japanese at Corregidor in the Philippines. Although not unexpected, it was sobering to hear. They sailed on. The weather suddenly worsened and the great aircraft carrier rolled and pitched, but the Spitfires on the decks were well strapped down, and eventually they passed Cadiz and the Straits of Gibraltar and were into the Mediterranean itself.

On 9 May, the ship began to bustle with activity at around 4.30 a.m. In the wardroom, the American officers, Fairbanks included, wished the British pilots good luck and happy landings as they headed to their aircraft. Fairbanks experienced a palpable sense of nervous exhilaration. By 5.30 a.m., the crew were at flight quarters and gun stations, even though it was still dark. Outside, the air was hot, still and muggy. Slowly, dawn crept up on them and then, at 6.23 a.m., through the tannoy came the sound of the bosun's pipe followed by, 'Now hear this! Stand by to launch planes!' At exactly 6.30 a.m., the US Navy Wildcats were ready, the flag came down, the order 'Launch planes!' was given and one by one the escorting Wildcats took off, followed by the first Spitfire, whose pilot was a 21-year-old Australian Acting Squadron Leader.

By 7.30 a.m. all sixty-four planes had taken off from *Wasp* and the smaller HMS *Eagle*, and only one, having lost an auxiliary fuel tank, returned and landed again in what was a hazardous and difficult manoeuvre for a Spitfire. A further two were lost en route, but as the two aircraft carriers steamed back towards Gibraltar, a signal reached them that sixty-one Spitfires had reached Malta and had been airborne again within thirty-five minutes. In fact, some had been airborne in under ten.

As it turned out, there were few raids over the island that day, but the fuel arrived overnight via the minelayer HMS *Welshman* and the following day, when the last of the Luftwaffe's unit on Sicily arrived over the island they suffered a notable defeat at the hands of Malta's now drastically improved fighter force.

For Kesselring, it was too late to do anything about this sudden turn-around, as most of II. Fliegerkorps had already been posted back to Russia or to North Africa. By the middle of May, Sicily was largely left to the Regia Aeronautica. Of the German fighter units, only II/JG53 remained. All the carnage wrought on Malta by the Luftwaffe's blitz had come at a price. The best part of 500 aircraft had been lost over the island between January and May, including 100 in April to Malta's gunners. The heavy tonnage of bombs dropped had also used up a large amount of Axis ordnance, which then could not be used in North Africa. On the other hand, there had been – and remained – a huge imperative to neutralize this aggravating thorn in their side. The trouble was, all that huge effort would be for nothing if they now let the island recover once more. But what to do? With renewed offensives in the East and in North Africa brewing, there were no longer enough men and resources to finish off Malta.

And back in Rome, the Italians were also having doubts about the Malta operation. On 13 May, two days after the RAF's Spitfire victory, Count Ciano met with Colonnello Giuseppe Casero, an old and trusted Air Force *amico* who was now Chief of Staff to the Under-Secretary of State for Air, Rino Fougier. Casero was deeply worried about the planned invasion, which as far as the Italians were concerned was still very much on the cards. Malta's anti-aircraft defence was intense and effective, he told Ciano, the interior was a nest of machine guns and the landing of paratroopers would be difficult. A large part of their attacking air forces could be expected to be shot down and most likely a large number of seaborne forces would be killed too. Even Fougier had grave concerns, as had the Luftwaffe commander of II. Fliegerkorps, General Bruno Lörzer. 'The supporters,' noted Ciano, 'are Kesselring and Cavallero, the latter going through his usual tricks to place the responsibility on the shoulders of others.'

They all had to hope Rommel's offensive would be successful, because if they smashed Eighth Army and overran Egypt, then the failure to defeat Malta would be irrelevant. If not, it would prove a costly mistake, because more and more Spitfires would be flown to the island in the coming weeks, not from *Wasp*, which had returned to Scapa Flow, but in batches from HMS *Eagle*. In the air battle for Malta, the balance had swung, dramatically and suddenly, back in favour of the Allies.

On the far side of the Atlantic, Commander Donald Macintyre was now serving briefly as a staff officer at the US naval base at Argentia on Newfoundland. Before the arrival of the Americans, it had been little more than a tiny village, but now, just eighteen months on, it was a vast base. Just as Henry Kaiser and his men could make shipyards out of mudflats in record time, so, it seemed, could they create naval bases, complete with full port facilities, new roads, accommodation blocks, messes and other facilities. There was even an airfield there now too, and underground oil tanks were being planned.

Macintyre's role, he discovered when he got there, was to look after the interests of British escort groups now that, with the reshuffling into the Mid-Ocean Escort Force, Royal Navy escort groups were operating the whole way across the Atlantic, using Argentia on the western side. To begin with, he was treated with some suspicion, but soon trust was gained, so much so that not only did the US staff there permit him to see secret signals concerning shipping movements, but also built a vast safe in his office so that they could be securely left in his hands.

After that, nothing, it seemed, was too much trouble. In terms of welfare for arriving Royal Navy crew, the Americans were more than generous. Repair facilities were also second to none. When a repair ship, the *Prairie*, accidentally caught fire, Macintyre wondered how they would manage to replace it without causing a major backlog of work. 'I need not have worried,' he wrote. 'With a whisk of the magician's wand, the Admiral's staff pulled another equally well-equipped repair ship out of the bag.' He was discovering first hand the kind of energy and operational acumen the Americans were now bringing to the war. The zeal, the can-do attitude and the ability to move mountains at a staggering speed were unlike anything Macintyre had ever witnessed. Argentia, as an example of what the United States was capable of by the early summer of 1942, was impressive indeed.

What was less impressive, however, was the slow response of the US Navy to the ongoing slaughter off the American east coast. As a result of this, and because of demands from the Pacific, the Mid-Ocean Escort Forces were repeatedly cut back as more and more escorts were sent east. For the time being, this did not really matter, as the U-boats were continuing to wreak havoc further south rather than in the mid-Atlantic. This strip, beyond current aircraft range, was called the mid-ocean air gap by the Allies. Canadian corvettes were now escorting convoys between Boston and Halifax, while in April the British sent one of their Mid-Ocean Escort Forces to the Caribbean to run oil convoys, along with twenty-four anti-submarine trawlers, and one RAF Coastal Command squadron to base itself on the US east coast; the US Navy, however, was still stubbornly refusing to begin escorted convoys until it had what it felt was enough escort strength. None the less, that didn't mean the Canadians and British had to put up with this nonsense, and they quickly established their own convoy systems down the east coast and through the Caribbean.

The Americans were getting closer to starting a convoy system, however. Air patrols had increased and were now operating from twenty-six different bases as far south as Colombia and included airships, or 'blimps' as the Americans called them, as well as flying boats and long-range bombers. 'Bucket Brigades' had been instigated at the beginning of April, in which convoy ships sailed along the east coast escorted by coastal craft and then put into harbour every night.

Finally, on 14 May, the first southbound convoy set sail, and not before time. There were, however, still no convoys in the Gulf of Mexico or through the Caribbean.

By the beginning of May, Teddy Suhren and *U-564* were back across the far side of the Atlantic once more. Because of the distances, U-boats were being refuelled out in the Atlantic by larger U-boats being used as mobile tankers; they were known as *Milchkuhe* – milk cows. Having got his extra fuel, Suhren headed towards the Straits of Florida, a 100-mile stretch between the southern tip of the USA and the Bahamas.

They sank four ships in the Straits, and, although they had to be careful to avoid ASW aircraft and US coastal gunboats, the dangers were not as severe as they might have been had their targets been wrapped in a convoy system. In truth, they should have sunk more. Three freighters passed by Suhren off Key West, but, although he fired at each, the torpedoes failed to detonate. 'And,' he noted, 'they would have all made tasty morsels.'

As it was, in all a staggering 125 ships were sunk by U-boats in May, of which all but 14 were independents, while in June that figure rose yet again: this time 144 ships were sent to the bottom, of which 121 had been sailing independently. As if to underline this continued folly by the US Navy, the Canadian-escorted convoys for the precious oil tankers were passing through the lethal US coastal zone between Halifax and Trinidad in the Caribbean without a single loss – and nor would they lose a ship all summer.

This second 'Happy Time' for the U-boats was, in many ways, an aberration, however; it was largely a self-inflicted wound on the part of the US Navy rather than being down to any dramatic leap forward in technology for the U-boat crews. In fact, despite innovations such as the *Milchkuhe*, the capabilities of the U-boat had barely moved forward at all. A Type VII could do little more than it could when the war began; a Type IX offered not much more than greater size and range. Torpedoes for both had hardly improved either and there were ongoing troubles with contact pistols, as Teddy Suhren had discovered to his cost. Signals communication had improved, but not at a pace that was outstripping the Allies. Most importantly of all, Dönitz still did not have enough U-boats seriously to threaten Britain's lifelines. Monthly targets had risen from 500,000 tons of shipping to 800,000 tons. They had not managed to hit this increased target even once, not even in May and June when sinkings off America had risen to become the highest losses of the war to date. Losses in June, for example, around the United Kingdom coastal waters and throughout the Atlantic and off the US coast, had amounted to just over 650,000 tons of shipping. It was a lot, but it was no longer enough.

In war, proper training, and the right training, counts for a great deal, but so does experience, and by May 1942 Rommel was fortunate enough to have men in his staff and commanding the various components of the Deutsches Afrikakorps (DAK) who were well trained, highly motivated and had a wealth of experience. All those victories in Poland, France, the Low Countries, the Balkans, even the Eastern Front, were hugely valuable; so, too, were the bitter disappointments of the Russian winter.

Chief of Staff of the DAK was Oberst Fritz Bayerlein, who was forty-three, a career soldier from Würzburg who already had an enormous amount of experience behind him. One of the breed of young German commanders that had striven to embrace new tactics in the 1920s and 1930s, Bayerlein had become friends with Rommel during their time at the Infantry Training School in Dresden in 1929 and then in Hamburg the following year, and readily absorbed his unorthodox methods. By the outbreak of war, Bayerlein was a major and First General Staff Officer, 1a, of 10. Panzerdivision, serving in Guderian's corps in Poland and throughout the Battle of France. He had remained with Guderian for BARBAROSSA, and was promoted and served as his 1a in Panzergruppe Guderian during their string of victories. He had learned much.

In November, he had been posted to North Africa. Now an Oberstleutnant, he was appointed Chief of Staff to the DAK under General Ludwig Crüwell. Ambitious, driven and highly intelligent, Bayerlein had arrived in Libya determined to prove himself. During the CRUSADER battles he had avoided capture by a hair's breadth, had repeatedly found himself in the thick of the action, and had personally overseen much of the retreat back across Cyrenaica. For his part in the fighting at Sidi Rezegh, he had been awarded the Knight's Cross.

By April, he was promoted again to full colonel and helping with preparations for the coming offensive, which Rommel planned to launch on 26 May. The British positions were spread out over a distance of about 35 miles, with concentrations of infantry brigades and divisions linked by endless minefields and wire, and with the armoured brigades behind as a mobile reserve. At the bottom of the line was an outpost of Free French at an old, crumbling, wind-blasted desert fort called Bir Hacheim, 40 miles south of the sea and surrounded by a giant minefield and wire entanglements.

Rommel's plan was typically bold. Placing Crüwell in command of the Italian XXI Corps, his idea was to launch these infantry units against the northern British line on the opening day of the battle and the Italian X Corps at the centre of the British line. The aim was to make the British think this was the main assault. In fact, it would only be a feint, because overnight the massed armoured forces of the Afrikakorps, with the Italian Ariete Armoured Division in tow, would sweep around the bottom of the British line and drive in behind the British positions. The bulk of the British troops would be encircled in a large envelopment. In essence, it was very like the plan for the assault on France and the Low Countries two years earlier: two prongs, the first to draw off the attention of the enemy, the second to drive through the killer punch.

By the middle of May, daytime temperatures were regularly hitting nearly 50 degrees Celsius – that is, over 120 Fahrenheit – and with the heat came endless flies and fleas. Bayerlein, who had a naturally dark complexion, had quickly turned a deep brown and was glued to his *Feldmütze*, a peaked cotton cap issued to all members of the Afrikakorps. Rommel continued to wear his service cap with the captured British goggles resting above the peak, but Bayerlein and almost every other German soldier in Africa adopted a far more casual look: light shirts, trousers and even shorts, stained with dust and sweat, were the order of the day.

Rations at the front were generally terrible and mostly Italian: hard biscuits, olive oil, sardines, tubes of cheese and widely despised tins of dubious Italian meat known as 'AM'. The men joked that it stood for *'Alter Maulesel'* – Old Mule. Water was sparingly distributed, regardless of rank, and, combined with the millions of flies, dysentery was rife. The cure was simple: stop eating until it had run its course.

Also now part of the Afrikakorps was Major Hans von Luck. Rommel had personally asked for him to be transferred from Russia to take over command of the 3rd Reconnaissance Battalion. That had been back in October, but it had not been until January that he had been released. He had also left Russia with a newly introduced gallantry award to his name – the German Cross in Gold, which was ranked between an Iron Cross First Class and a Knight's Cross. He had been appalled. 'A large and clumsy star,' he noted. 'We at once coined a new name for this monstrosity: Hitler's fried egg.'

He reached Derna in Libya on 8 April, having flown over in a Ju52 and seen, from the air, the vast expanse of desert beneath him as he crossed the coast. A sense of longing for this huge bleached desert struck him immediately. 'What a contrast,' he wrote, 'to the icy snowstorms of Russia.' It was a contrast indeed. He was driven immediately to see Rommel, whose headquarters were hidden off the coast road and dispersed amongst folds in the ground and camouflage nets. Even the tyre marks leading to it were swept clear.

'Glad you're here,' Rommel told him. It was the first time they had seen each other since 1940 in France. 'I've waited long enough.' The previous commander, highly rated, had fallen sick and been sent back to Germany. The 3rd Reconnaissance Battalion, Rommel told him, was his pet unit. 'Let it be a credit to you.'

After telling Rommel about Russia, von Luck was briefed by General Alfred Gause, Chief of Staff of the Panzerarmee. Supplies were the biggest problem, Gause explained, most of them having to be shipped to Tripoli and then either brought down the coast by lighter or along the coast road. It was a journey of about 800 miles and they needed around 60,000 tons a month; the previous month, just 18,000 tons had reached them. Von Luck was surprised to hear that Rommel thought the chance of victory in North Africa had already slipped by, because although the British had to ship everything all the way around Africa, most of it was safely reaching Egypt and then being transferred to the front. Not enough effort was being made to bomb British ports, and U-boats were not sinking enough shipping. None the less, he hoped that in this new offensive he might yet be able to turn the tables.

Over the next seven weeks, von Luck immersed himself in his new environment and did his best to win over the men under his command; the legacy of his hugely popular predecessor hung heavy. He knew that this very tough environment could not be fought; rather, one had to embrace the desert: the intense heat by day, the cold at night. The millions of flies had to be accepted as part of daily life and, like Albert Martin in the 2nd Rifle Brigade and tens of thousands of other British, Italian and German troops before him, the way to survive was to learn how to deal with sandstorms, mirages and the tricks light played on distance. 'I learned to travel by compass and at the onset of darkness, to find my way back to the battalion with mutual light signals,' he noted. 'The reconnaissance trips into the desert held a great fascination for me.'

Meanwhile, now that the aerial blitz of Malta was over, the Luftwaffe had been reinforced in North Africa and by the middle of May had 704 aircraft directly ready to support Rommel's offensive, of which 497 were serviceable. There were also a further 739 serviceable aircraft in the wider Mediterranean, which could be drawn upon if necessary.

Among the fighter aircraft were one *Gruppe* – or section – of JG53, sent over from Sicily, and two *Gruppen* of JG27, who had been based in North Africa since the previous year. One of the pilots serving with I/JG27 was Hans-Joachim (known as Jochen) Marseille, twenty-two years old and the son of a general. A brilliant fighter pilot, he was something of an odd-ball, and a young man with a pronounced disregard for authority. This was usually not a particularly sensible trait to exhibit within the Wehrmacht, but his brilliance as a pilot had so far saved his neck, although not prevented him from getting into trouble.

He had, for example, lasted a little over a month in JG52, before his *Gruppe* commander, Macky Steinhoff, fired him for continued insubordination and repeated breaches of discipline. From there he had been sent to I/JG27, had flown briefly in the Balkans campaign and then, after staging in Sicily, had reached Derna along with the rest of the *Gruppe* in April 1941. Since then, Marseille had flourished, not least because his commander, Hauptmann Edu Neumann, had treated him with greater understanding and latitude than his previous commanders. By the beginning of May 1942, he had fifty-two victories to his name, as well as a Knight's Cross and Cross of Gold. By 16 May, that total was sixty, and every single one, except a lone twin-engine Maryland, had been an RAF fighter plane.

This was an exceptional score. In Russia, Luftwaffe fighter aces had been amassing even bigger personal records, but a large number of those victories had been won against inferior aircraft flown by poorly trained pilots. RAF fighter pilots, on the other hand, were all well trained and most were highly competent. They were also flying fighter planes that were mostly a cut above those of the Russians; at any rate, fighters were harder to shoot down than bombers. As Neumann had recognized, however, Marseille was a truly exceptional fighter pilot – possibly one of the finest ever. He had extraordinarily good eyesight, which enabled him to pick out enemy aircraft before anyone else, and was a superb shot, capable of deflection shooting – that is, aiming off – with an uncanny precision, so much so that he rarely used more than five or six cannon shells to bring down an aircraft, and about fifteen or so machine-gun rounds per kill. 'He was,' said Neumann, 'possibly the best deflection shot who ever flew a fighter.'

Marseille's technique was a simple one: spot the enemy early, fly into them, let off a few rounds, crippling or damaging several, then perform a climbing turn which enabled him to look back and assess the scene. Then he would dive down, have another crack and look around for any he had already damaged; if they were still there, he would try to finish them off. Because he was so good at naturally computing speed and distance, he was able to fire at angles and still hit his mark. Very few fighter pilots ever mastered deflection shooting.

Neumann had also recognized that, however unreliable he was on the ground, Marseille was a consummate professional when it came to flying.

He was one of the very few pilots who continually trained as hard as he could, and that meant exercise too – running, and particularly sit-ups to strengthen his stomach muscles, which he had realized was important when handling G-forces. As a result, Marseille could turn more tightly without blacking out than most.

Marseille and his fellow pilots in JG27 were also flying the improved and more powerful Me109F, which was only now reaching theatre in any kind of numbers. This was quite an improvement on the 'Emil' and certainly superior to the Hurricanes and Kittyhawks of the Desert Air Force, as RAF fighter pilots were discovering.

Early on 19 May, Marseille was flying a 'free hunt' with his wingman, Rainer Pöttgen, when they spotted seven P-40 Kittyhawks below them. Diving down, Marseille hit one, damaging it, then followed it down and, closing in, opened fire again at 200 yards, hitting the plane in the engine. The Kittyhawk was finished, but Marseille watched the pilot manage to land it safely, then jump out and run for it. Once the man was clear, Marseille returned and strafed the aircraft until it burned. He had never lost his feeling of guilt at killing others and made a point of trying to avoid doing so if at all possible.

He now climbed again, only to find another Kittyhawk on his tail. The 109F's faster climbing speed, however, enabled him to gain distance until eventually he cut his engine, stalled, gave his plane some right rudder and opened the flaps to enable a tighter turn, and then literally dropped back down towards his attacker, opening fire as the distance closed, hitting the P-40's wings and cowling. It was an extraordinary manoeuvre.

By 26 May, Rommel was ready, as planned. He had superiority in the air but not on the ground; and he had only 560 panzers, of which 230 were obsolete Italian types, against 850 British tanks, of which around 400 were brand-new Grants, large 30-ton medium tanks from America and armed with a much-improved 75mm gun as well as a 37mm and a machine gun. Even so, Rommel hoped that what he lacked in numbers on the ground, he would make up for in dash and skill. 'We're launching a decisive attack today,' he wrote to his wife, just hours before General Crüwell's Italians would make their assault in the north. 'It will be hard, but I have full confidence that my army will win it.'

His offensive had been intended as a surprise, and yet the British now strung out along the Gazala Line still had much in their favour. They had not only more men and more tanks but, once the battle was under way, they had shorter and better lines of supply, as Rommel was well aware. Crucially, thanks to Ultra and other intelligence sources, they also knew the Panzerarmee would attack that very day. In fact, on paper, it looked likely the British would see off this attack with comparative ease.

CHAPTER 16

Into the Cauldron

O N 13 MAY, Sergeant Ralph Schaps and a large part of the 34th Red Bull Division reached Scotland after a trip in convoy aboard RMS *Aquitania*, one of the biggest, most elegant four-funnel trans-Atlantic liners ever to have graced the seas. Those days were over for the time being, however, and now she was a grey, stripped-down troop liner. Schaps had felt as though he were a sardine in a tin and, with cramped conditions, bad food and the menace of U-boats, he and his pals had been mightily relieved to get on to dry land. This, however, had been shortlived, because they were then transferred to smaller vessels and shipped to Omagh, in Northern Ireland. 'To us,' noted Schaps, 'it was the most beautiful sight we had ever seen.'

Also reaching Britain was Brigadier-General Mark Clark, who had flown into Prestwick aboard a Boeing Stratoliner on 25 May along with his old friend Major-General Dwight D. Eisenhower, who, since February, had been head of the US Army's entire War Plans Division, soon renamed the Operations Division (OPD), and given the task of putting together plans for the Germany-first policy adopted at Arcadia. The key to this, as far as Eisenhower was concerned, was ensuring that Russia stayed in the war, which, in early 1942, was looking more likely than it had the previous summer, but still very far from guaranteed. With this in mind, at the end of March Eisenhower proposed a plan to invade northern France with forty-eight Anglo-US divisions by no later than 1 April 1943. The codename for the plan to establish beachheads around the Le Havre– Boulogne area was SLEDGEHAMMER, while the expansion of the bridgehead and breakout phase was codenamed ROUNDUP. The Americans promised to have thirty divisions and 2,550 combat aircraft ready by 1 April 1943, but pledged only three and a half divisions and 700 combat aircraft ready in Britain by 15 September 1942. The aim, therefore, was to cross the Channel in spring 1943, but to mount an emergency offensive in 1942 if the Russia position looked particularly desperate; effectively, this would be a suicide mission to France. In the meantime, more and more troops, aircraft and supplies needed to be hurriedly sent to Britain as part of Operation BOLERO.

These plans were approved by General Marshall and then Roosevelt, then presented to the British, who thought April 1943 seemed rather ambitious. Their caveat was that there needed to be, by then, signs that Germany was 'weakened in strength and morale.' This agreed, Churchill and the British Chiefs of Staff gave their approval too. At the time, Eisenhower was delighted. 'I hope that at long last,' he wrote in his diary, 'we are all definitely committed to one concept of fighting. If we can agree on major purposes and objectives, our efforts will begin to fall in line and we won't just be thrashing around in the dark.'

Eisenhower, known to all as 'Ike', had been born in 1890 to humble beginnings. From the age of two, home had been Abilene, Kansas, a modest town deep in America's Midwest. After working hard at school and doing well, he managed to get into West Point, the military academy, graduating in 1915. Unlike Mark Clark, however, Eisenhower did not see action in France. Rather, his career took him into a number of staff posts, in which he soon made a name for himself. By the end of the 1930s, he was in the Philippines, working under General Douglas MacArthur, but he returned in 1939 and joined the Third Army. His performance in the Louisiana Maneuvers in summer 1941 caught the eye of General Marshall. For those who made an impression in these rapidly changing times, it was possible to rise up the chain very quickly, as both Clark and Eisenhower were discovering.

Now he was making his first trip to Britain, to talk about plans and command structure. After trips to see troops training in Scotland and the newly formed US Rangers practising amphibious landings, they headed to London and to Claridge's Hotel, which would become a favoured base with the Americans. There they met Major-General James E. Chaney, currently commanding US troops in Britain. Marshall had big question marks over Chaney and part of Eisenhower's and Clark's brief was to talk to him and then make recommendations back to Marshall; certainly, the joint Anglo-US command structure in Britain was something that needed ironing out.

On 27 May, they went to see a large divisional exercise in Kent, part of Lieutenant-General Bernard Montgomery's South-Eastern Command. Invited to Montgomery's HQ, they sat waiting for him in his office, looking at walls covered in maps. Eventually, he came in and began lecturing them in his crisp, energetic, no-nonsense way. There were a number of other officers there and halfway through Eisenhower lit up a cigarette.

Montgomery stopped and glared. 'Who's smoking?' he demanded.

'I am,' said Eisenhower.

'I don't,' said Montgomery sternly, 'permit smoking in my office.'

Eisenhower put out his cigarette and Montgomery continued. 'We got a good laugh out of the incident,' noted Clark, 'but not until we were well out of Montgomery's hearing.'

With bitter fighting now going on in Burma, with India still under threat and with further losses in the Pacific, the Allies were struggling to stem the tide of Japanese advances. In fact, it now looked possible that the Japanese Imperial Navy might even stretch their reach across the Indian Ocean to take Madagascar, currently held by the Vichy French. If they established a base there, British shipping to both India and the Middle East would be threatened. As a result, the Chiefs of Staff decided to launch their first amphibious invasion of any scale since Gallipoli back in 1915.

On 5 May, Force 121, led by the Royal Marines and including two brigades of the 5th Division and a further Commando brigade group, landed on Madagascar. Defending the island were around 8,000 Vichy French troops, most of whom were poorly equipped local colonial soldiers. None the less, on the first day of the invasion their defence at the port of Diego-Suárez was surprisingly stiff. Only an outflanking manoeuvre by fifty Royal Marines into the Vichy rear area the following day broke the deadlock. The town surrendered the next day, with the Vichy forces retreating deep to the south of the island. The fighting would continue, but the island's main port had been captured and occupied. For the time being, at any rate, the crucial supply routes between Britain, the Middle East, India and Australasia were secure.

This was very much to the betterment of the British forces in North

Africa desperately trying to make good the losses sent to India and the Far East. Certainly by May 1942, the Desert Air Force, at least, was in reasonable fettle, even if it had not the superiority of numbers it had enjoyed the previous autumn.

Among those who had recently joined was Billy Drake, long since recovered from the wounds he had received in France back in May 1940 and now a squadron leader. In fact, after a stint instructing, he had rejoined a combat squadron at the tail-end of the Battle of Britain. By early 1942, he was posted to Sierra Leone, where for a month or so he languished until someone higher up the chain realized this was a waste of a very able pilot and commander, and so in March he had been posted to 280 Squadron as a supernumerary. On 25 May, he was posted again, this time to command 112 'Shark' Squadron, so called because of the vivid shark's teeth painted on to the cowlings of their Kittyhawks.

Drake was still only twenty-four years old, but an ace with over ten victories to his name and a stack of combat experience. He had learned the hard way: that to shoot anything down, he had to get in as close as possible, that he needed to watch his back at all times and to so thoroughly understand his aircraft that he knew exactly how hard he could push it. Flying had to be second nature so that he could concentrate on fighting. He also knew that pilots had to adapt quickly to any situation, which was just as well because the Kittyhawks were no longer being used purely as fighters in air-to-air combat. 'The first thing I saw,' said Drake on his arrival at 280 Squadron, 'was a Kittyhawk with a bloody great bomb underneath it.' The emphasis now for the Shark Squadron was on ground attack: flying in swiftly at low levels, dropping a single bomb, then strafing other targets. 'It was ground attack first and foremost,' said Drake, 'then occasional air-to-air work.'

The man behind this change of emphasis for the fighter squadrons was Air Vice-Marshal 'Mary' Coningham. Although he had led the DAF successfully since taking command the previous summer, his grasp had tightened considerably since the arrival of new staff, not least Air Commodore Tommy Elmhirst as his deputy. Elmhirst similarly had a long career in the RAF behind him, and had worked in both Air Intelligence during the Battle of Britain and later as a controller at Bentley Priory, Fighter Command Headquarters in north-west London. From here, he had been posted as a station commander in Bomber Command. This gave him, like Coningham, a very complete and rounded view of the differing components of modern air warfare, something that was invaluable out in the evolving North African theatre.

In many ways, Coningham and Elmhirst were chalk and cheese. As Coningham was tall and beefy, so Elmhirst was small and less imposing; as Coningham was boisterous, so Elmhirst was more softly spoken. Coningham was inspiring and charismatic, but somewhat haphazard in his methods. Elmhirst, on the other hand, was a superlative organizer and it was as chief administrator that he had joined Coningham's Air HQ at Gambut in Libya back in February.

There had been columns of smoke rising from burning aircraft destroyed on the ground when he first arrived at Gambut, but within a few days he had gained a pretty good idea of what was needed. The lull in the fighting had given him and his chief three clear months in which to reorganize the DAF completely. Gone were piecemeal units. In their place came a group of fighters, divided into three wings with their own administrative staffs and repair units, and, where possible, based on the same landing ground. This centralization of administration enabled wing and squadron commanders to get on with the job of leading their men rather than sweating over logistics, and by the same token halted the dangerous fragmentation of the DAF.

With the administration of the squadrons taken out of the hands of the squadron leaders and flight commanders, Coningham now had the infrastructure that enabled him to lick his air force into shape. Between February and the end of May, training was extensive and carried out between ongoing operations. First on his list was an improvement in the standard of gunnery. This was, understandably, a difficult aspect of air fighting in which to train, because there was no real means of practising live firing against a live target. In the desert, however, with its clear skies and blazing sun, it was quite possible to practise 'shadow firing' rather than pointlessly going after a towed drogue. Navigation was also improved and regular discussions held with bomber crews. Ground crews, too, were expected to up their game: rapid refuelling and rearming, as well as packing and unpacking bases, was drilled into every man. There were weekly conferences between Coningham and his wing commanders, in which tactics, training and administration were all discussed, analysed and refined. All this was designed not only to sharpen his force, but to help give them a renewed sense of purpose and confidence.

Coningham was also using this regrouping of his air force to hone his own ideas. Like Tedder, he believed the aim should be to win air superiority over the battle area. Once that was achieved, he could then more directly support the ground forces. Yes, the DAF *could* provide close air support, but they could do more than that, and while it was clearly important to form close working relationships with the Army command, it was essential that he was left to command his force how he, as an airman, thought fit. Sometimes, for example, he could best help the troops down below not by responding to a specific target request, but by neutralizing a threat further back behind the immediate front.

Coningham was also learning from the enemy. He had been impressed by how effective dive-bombing could be, but realized how vulnerable Stukas were as they came out of a dive, and how slow they were in all forms of flight. He had begun using US-built Kittyhawks in such a role. These lacked the rate of climb to be much use above heights of 10,000 feet, but below that were highly manoeuvrable as well as quick. Furthermore, they could out-dive both the new Italian Macchi 202s coming into service and the latest Me109s. They also had a very stable gun platform. With this in mind, he had started using them as 'Kitty-bombers'. With a bomb slung beneath them, they could hurtle in towards a target, diving down at speed, drop their load, then scurry out of the fray. The idea was to use them like a Stuka, but without the Ju87's increasingly obvious shortcomings.

Hurricanes, too, were being used more at low level. Like the Kittyhawk, they were no match for either the Macchi 202s or Me109s – and nor had they been for some time. Coningham's view was that if they were unlikely to compete against them at higher altitude, there was little to be achieved by trying. Far better that their strengths be exploited. A number had now been fitted with high-velocity cannons and were being used as low-level ground attack 'tank busters'. With a stable gun platform, high speed and a robust air-frame, they still had a very important role to play. Operating both Kittyhawks and Hurricanes at low height meant they would be vulnerable to being bounced by Axis fighters, but that was a risk that would have to be taken.

There was an obvious solution to this particular risk, and one that had been adopted successfully during the Battle of Britain. While Hurricanes – and now Kittyhawks – concentrated on targets below 10,000 feet, Spitfires could take on those troublesome Axis fighters. Ever since arriving in the Middle East, Coningham had been calling for Spitfires, and by

May, as had happened at Malta, he at last had a squadron of Mk Vs, complete with special Vokes tropical air filters to cope with the sand. And as on Malta, getting them into action, once the decision had been made, had not been anything like as difficult as the brass back in Britain had been suggesting.

In sharp contrast, the Luftwaffe was suddenly looking a little short of ideas. It is so often the case that trailblazers are caught up and then over-taken, and so it was proving with the air war. One of Rommel's failings was that he never got to grips with the operational art of war – logistics and supplies were, to his mind, someone else's problem – and nor did he understand air power. Again, he viewed it rather in the same way most British Army commanders did: as a direct support to the ground forces and therefore a junior partner to be held at his beck and call. General Otto Hoffmann von Waldau, the current commander of the Luftwaffe in the Mediterranean, disagreed with this view, and the relationship between the two was fraught, to put it mildly. In fact, Rommel was acting as British Army commanders had been acting the previous summer. The difference was that Tedder and Coningham had stuck to their guns and had then advanced their ideas of tactical air support, while Rommel and von Waldau had not remotely resolved their differences.

In terms of administration, so important in the vast emptiness and huge distances of the desert, there was no system comparable to the one being developed by the DAF. German and Italian squadrons could not rapidly move from one airfield to another; rather, they effectively closed down when on the move. In the air, fighters might carry out strafing runs, but their prime role was not even to shoot down enemy bombers, but rather enemy fighters – as Jochen Marseille was proving so spectacularly. The cult of the ace, or *Experte*, was as developed in the Mediterranean as it was anywhere and, as elsewhere, helping the leading aces shoot down yet more lay at the very heart of Luftwaffe fighter tactics. That, however, did not mean it was necessarily the right tactic.

The Desert Air Force might have been imbued with a very clear and dynamic sense of purpose, but this could not be said for Eighth Army. Despite the numerous advantages the British held in terms of new up-gunned Grant tanks, manpower and supplies, the tactical leadership was in a bit of a muddle. General Neil Ritchie, thrust into command during the CRUSADER battles, was a highly competent staff officer but had little combat experience; really, he was there as the Auk's man on the ground rather than as an independently minded Army commander, but Auchinleck was back at GHQ in Cairo and Ritchie, hastily promoted to three stars, did not have the respect he needed from his corps and division commanders, and neither the tactical experience nor the wherewithal to impose himself. As the British desperately tried to work out how to combat the dash and drive of Rommel and his Afrikakorps, decisions had started to be made by committee rather than with any sense of purpose and vision.

The net result was a line, just under 40 miles long, running roughly north to south, in which units and brigades were concentrated in what were called 'boxes' – areas in the desert marked out by entrenchments containing all arms of artillery, infantry and engineers, and linked only by minefields. The trouble was, the distance was so great, these boxes were too far apart to be mutually supporting. Even worse, the Free French Brigade, under Général Pierre König, were right at the very end at Bir Hacheim, cut off from their nearest neighbour by about 15 miles. Isolating – or, rather, abandoning – the highly sensitive French in such a way was politically not very smart.

One man despairing at this state of affairs was Major-General Francis 'Gertie' Tuker, who since December had been commanding 4th Indian Division. Having survived the First World War, he had briefly considered giving up the Army to become an artist. However, he remained in the Indian Army and saw further action in Iraq, Assam and northern Iran, as well as in border operations along the Northwest Frontier. Tuker was, and remained, an obsessive student of warfare, and spent a huge amount of time thinking and writing about the shape future wars might take. He was also, however, keenly aware that he was an unusual case in the inter-war Army, where talking 'shop' was largely frowned upon. In the 1930s he had also done much to develop new infantry training methods in the Indian Army and these had been so successful they had not only been adopted but he had been appointed Director for Training for the Indian Army, based at Quetta.

On his arrival in the Middle East, Tuker had met with Auchinleck, who promptly asked him for his views; the Auk was an Indian Army man too and knew about Tuker's highly regarded training methods. Eager to help, Tuker soon submitted a paper in which he emphasized the need for a mobile corps of two armoured divisions, supported by a lorried infantry division whose assault troops would be mounted in armoured fighting vehicles. This was much the same model as the Afrikakorps.

His suggestion, however, was not adopted. In fact, he was never given any feedback at all. Instead, Auchinleck split up his armoured forces into much smaller all-arms brigades, based on an earlier even smaller mobile column known as the 'Jock Column', named after Jock Campbell, formerly of the 7th Armoured Division. These smaller Jock Columns had worked brilliantly in helping to run rings round the static and hopelessly dispersed Italians, but were no good against larger mobile formations. Auchinleck was trying to ape the Germans but with smaller units, which, he thought, would give him greater flexibility.

Tuker, however, understood far more clearly what the Auk did not: that the way to beat the enemy was by concentration of force. By splitting Eighth Army's infantry and artillery into isolated boxes and the armour into small penny packets, Rommel would be able to bring his massed armour against them and pick them off one by one. As Rommel said to a captured British officer, 'What difference does it make if you have two tanks to my one, when you spread them out and let me smash them in detail?' That one sentence really did encapsulate the nub of the matter and the failure of the Auk's approach. Frankly, he and his senior commanders should have known better by now.

Back in February, 4th Indian Division had been sent forward to help build the Gazala Line, and Tuker, who had used the opportunity to have a thorough look around, had been appalled. He simply could not understand the logic of stringing Eighth Army out across the desert when a fairly small garrison in Tobruk had held out against all Rommel's best efforts for more than eight months. Tobruk could be comparatively easily resupplied: there were water pipes and supply dump facilities and it would have been easy to build up its now crumbling defences and stocks of water, food, oil and arms for six months. The fortress of Tobruk could have been reinforced with strong defences covering the landing grounds of Gambut, El Adem and Sidi Rezegh, and the main coast road blocked. The two armoured divisions and 4th Indian, fully motorized, supporting the armour, would provide the kind of mobile armoured corps Tuker had originally suggested to Auchinleck.

With these dispositions there would have been no need for a long defensive line that could so easily be outflanked and enveloped, for so long as Tobruk was held in strength, Rommel would be unable to invade Egypt. This was because Tobruk lay in the path of the Axis lines of supply, and even if successfully bypassed – and Tuker thought that would be unlikely – Rommel's forces would not get very far before the vanguard was severed from the main body of supply. And because superior Axis forces had been unable to dislodge the defenders of Tobruk the previous year, there was absolutely no reason at all why they would do so now that Eighth Army had superiority of supplies and troops.

Tuker suggested to Ritchie in February that he had grave misgivings about the Gazala position, but the Eighth Army commander told him he disagreed. In March, Tuker spoke at length to General Willoughby Norrie, the commander of XXX Corps, and outlined his idea for an alternative defensive position based around Tobruk. 'He did not accept the proposal as far as I know,' noted Tuker. On 15 March, Lieutenant-General Tom Corbett, Auchinleck's Chief of the General Staff (CGS), had also come to the front and Tuker spent the best part of twenty-four hours trying to open his eyes to the flawed dispositions. 'His final reply,' noted Tuker, 'was that he had put in about a million mines, or some such figure, at Gazala, and could not use more by filling up Tobruk.'

Tuker had been banging his head against a brick wall. What a tragedy it was for British fortunes in North Africa that he had not been appointed Eighth Army commander instead of Ritchie – after all, they had been the same rank. In fact, his self-confidence, calm logic and vastly superior tactical understanding were precisely what Eighth Army needed.

As it was, Auchinleck clearly felt undermined by Tuker and none of the other corps and divisional commanders at the front had much idea about what they were doing at all. If they had, they would have recognized that Tuker's plan not only made sense, but was self-evidently the right approach. Really, their unwillingness to adopt his obviously sensible plan to build up Tobruk beggars belief. What on earth were they thinking? The men of Eighth Army, many of whom were now tough, battle- and desert-hardened and experienced in the ways of war, deserved a lot better. The British people deserved better.

Instead, Tuker's 4th Indian Division was not even at the front. Rather, he was sent up alone to the front on 26 May to assume command of the left flank of the Army – that is, of the Free French, 7th Motor Brigade, 3rd Indian Motor Brigade and 29th Indian Infantry Brigade. It sounded piecemeal, and so it was, and ironic that Tuker, who was so against penny-packet static positions, should have been given such a command.

British tanks and British equipment have repeatedly come in for criticism in the narrative of the war. German tanks were better, German small arms were better, German troops were better trained. This is a massively distorted view. While, by the end of May 1942, Eighth Army lacked a powerful anti-tank gun, otherwise their equipment was broadly pretty good and their tanks were, for the most part, better than anything either the Germans or the Italians had in their arsenal. British troops were, overall, also a match in terms of training and fighting power.

The difference lay in the quality of the commanders. At Gazala, British tactical leadership had, sadly for the men, reached its nadir.

Meanwhile, in Rome, Count Ciano found Mussolini much improved after a bout of flu and now feeling bullish about Rommel's coming offensive. He told Ciano that the Axis armies in North Africa would reach the Delta, and even for the capture of Malta he was willing to make good forecasts. Of course, *Il Duce* was merely expressing his hopes rather than voicing a prediction based on sound military logic.

He made little mention of Russia, where he had just sent another seven divisions to join the three of the Italian Expeditionary Corps; the Corps had become Italian Eighth Army and the commander, Generale Giovanni Messe, replaced by Generale Italo Gariboldi, much to Ciano's chagrin, as he rated the outgoing commander highly but thought the latter too old and tired. Mussolini and Cavallero, however, had felt that Messe was becoming just a little bit too important out there and needed his wings clipping. 'Cavallero,' noted Ciano, 'is a faithful follower of the theory which calls for the decapitation of poppies that grow too high.'

Just a week earlier, Ciano had had a long conversation with Messe on his return to Rome. Messe was understandably furious at his ousting, but had warned Ciano that he thought there would be no 'total liquidation' of Russia before winter. 'Which,' added Ciano, 'raises some very serious problems for us since we shall soon have 300,000 men on the Eastern Front.' Three hundred thousand men they could barely equip and could ill afford to send.

On Tuesday, 26 May, Rommel launched his attack with General Crüwell's Italian Corps noisily approaching the line in the north and Stukas dive-bombing British positions there, occupied by men of the 1st South

African Division. That same afternoon, General Tuker flew up to the front, landing around 6 p.m. at El Adem and then heading to XXX Corps HQ, about 10 miles to the south and 25 miles south of Tobruk harbour. It was still quiet in the southern sector, but the bombardment of the north had increased. As daylight slipped away, Tuker watched a single searchlight beam up over the sky to the west. Outside the canvas tents and caravans, he spent a tranquil hour, chatting and watching the stars emerge. The night was now still and, from where he stood, not a gun could be heard. Even so, the battle was now under way and reports from the north suggested a major assault had been made on the South Africans' positions. The silence made Tuker and others feel suspicious and uneasy.

It was even quieter to the far south of the line, where the men of the 7th Motor Brigade, part of Tuker's new command, were dug in at the Retma Box, exactly 20 miles to the south-east of Bir Hacheim, waiting for something to happen. Among them were Albert Martin and his fellows in 2nd Rifle Brigade. For them, 26 May had been an 'ordinary day'; the only news Martin had heard was that the Japanese had made a fresh attack on the Chinese, and so he'd bedded down that night with no particular sense of expectation.

He was roughly woken, however, at 5 a.m. and told to get to his position right away as 'Jerry was on his way'. Minutes later, he was jumping into his slit-trench, 'fully alert and senses tingling'. He only just made it, because no sooner had he leaped in than a heavy artillery barrage burst down upon them, ripping apart the quiet and shaking the hard desert beneath them.

Rommel's Afrikakorps, with XXI Motorized Corps attached, had amassed some 10,000 vehicles for this main thrust and amongst the spearhead of the 21. Panzerdivision was Major Hans von Luck and his 3rd Reconnaissance Battalion. They had assembled overnight, when it had been pitch black, with only the southern stars to guide them. Navigation was done by exact compass bearings. 'It was a ghostly scene,' noted von Luck. 'Each man could just see the vehicle to his front or side.' They drove at reduced speed to avoid raising too much dust and risking losing sight of their neighbours.

As dawn spread, it was clear the British were not expecting them, which was surprising as numerous reports of enemy movement to the south had reached both XXX Corps and Eighth Army HQs through

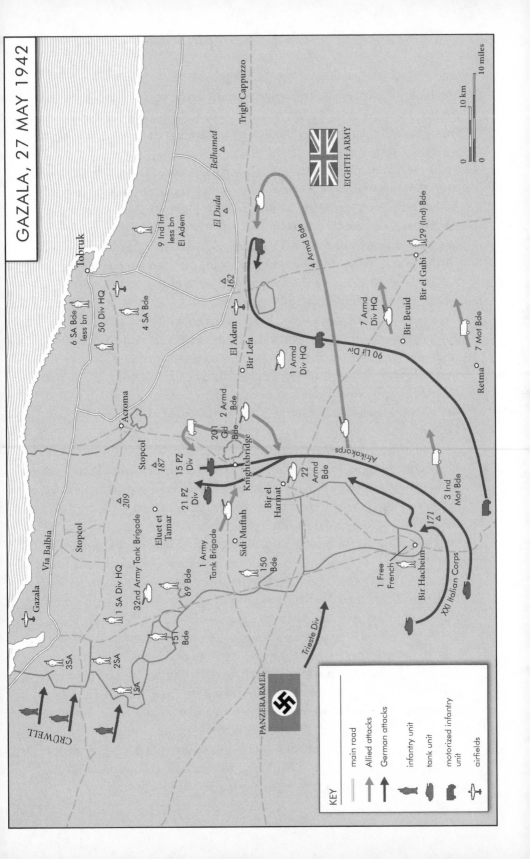

GAZALA, 27 MAY 1942

EIGHTH ARMY

PANZERARMEE

CRUWELL

Tobruk
Gazala
Via Balbia
Acroma

6 SA Bde less bn
50 Div HQ
4 SA Bde
9 Ind Inf less bn El Adem
El Duda
Belhamed
162
El Adem
Bir Lefa
El Lefa

3SA
2SA
1SA
151 Bde
32nd Army Tank Brigade
1 SA Div HQ
69 Bde
Stopcol
209
Eluet et Tamar
Stopcol
187
Stopcol
201 Gd Bde
15 PZ Div
2 Armd Bde
Knightsbridge
21 PZ Div
Bir el Harmat
22 Armd Bde
Sidi Muftah
1 Army Tank Brigade
150 Bde
1 Free French
Bir Hacheim
171
XXI Italian Corps
3 Ind Mot Bde
Afrikakorps
90 Lt Div
1 Armd Div HQ
Bir Beuid
7 Armd Div HQ
4 Armd Bde
Bir el Gubi
29 (Ind) Bde
7 Mot Bde
Retma
Trieste Div
Trigh Cappuzzo

0   10 km
0   10 miles

KEY
— main road
Allied attacks
German attacks
infantry unit
tank unit
motorized infantry unit
airfields

the night. These had been logged but not acted upon. Any doubt was finally dispelled at 6.30 a.m., however, when 3rd Indian Motor Brigade had signalled that 'a whole bloody German armoured division' was bearing down upon them.

By early morning, 21. and 15. Panzer had cleared the southern flank and were turning north towards a crossroads of desert tracks the British had named 'Knightsbridge', while the 90th Light Division had sped on north-east – it was this division that had stormed into most of Tuker's brigades. Meanwhile, the XXI Italian Corps had circled around Bir Hacheim and were attacking the French outpost from the rear. Hans von Luck was exhilarated by their drive. 'We were in the best of spirits,' he wrote, 'the surprise seemed to have worked.'

In fact, Rommel's attack had been launched with very sketchy intelligence to say the least. So strained were his relations with von Waldau, there had been insufficient Luftwaffe reconnaissance and, despite the best efforts of his own intelligence team, he had a very incomplete picture of Eighth Army's dispositions and was unaware both of the number of British tanks and that a large number of them were new US-built Grants.

None the less, the sheer scale of so many vehicles, concentrated into four giant columns, whipping up dust and blazing away with their guns and artillery, was certainly impressive to those on the receiving end. At the Retma Box, shells were screaming and whining and exploding, and between the smoke and dust Albert Martin could see hundreds of enemy vehicles spread out in front of him, as 90th Light Division charged north-east towards El Adem. Clearly, 7th Motor Brigade could not hold their ground. 'These wonderful defensive positions, which had taken so long to prepare,' scribbled Martin, 'were broken, smashed to the four winds.' Dashing for their vehicles, they sped away, firing as they went. By 9 a.m., the Retma Box was gone. One after another, as 90th Light continued its march, the brigades in the south were overrun and forced to fall back.

General Tuker, meanwhile, was still at XXX Corps HQ, where he had been waiting several hours to be taken to see the French at Bir Hacheim. Eventually, General Norrie turned to him and told him there was little left for him to command. Tuker asked what he wanted him to do instead. Norrie said he wasn't sure, but asked him to stay put for the moment. Tuker did as he was asked, twiddling his thumbs and wondering how such a fiasco could ever have been allowed to happen.

Meanwhile, the two panzer divisions thundered on towards Knightsbridge. By midday they were thereabouts, and at this point Hans von Luck and his men spotted a tank column heading their way. These were Grants, which the Germans had not seen before, and before long they had turned and opened fire at a range that was too great for von Luck's 50mm pieces. Halting the advance, he ordered the setting up of a defensive front to the north and, as his men were doing this, he left his command tank and ran towards the anti-tank guns. Shells were bursting all around and suddenly he felt a powerful blow to his right leg and fell to the ground. A shell had struck an armoured car and a piece of shrapnel had cut his upper right thigh. Blood welled from his trousers and he briefly lost consciousness. When he came round, a scout car had pulled alongside and men were picking him up and taking him back for medical help.

'You are lucky in your bad luck, Major,' the doctor told him. 'You've got a hole the size of a fist in your right groin. Another few centimetres and you would have lost your manhood, but no veins or nerves have been hit.' After having a tourniquet applied and being bandaged up, he was given several morphine injections and then returned to command his battalion, aware that he needed further treatment but unable, at present, from his position sandwiched between British infantry on the Gazala Line and two British armoured brigades on the right, to extricate himself. For the time being, he would have to grin and bear it.

In fact, despite the tumble of British positions that had been overrun, Rommel's position by later that afternoon was extremely precarious. Rather than folding up the British main line, they were now dangerously hemmed in, with infantry boxes and a mass of minefields on one side and the bulk of British armour on the other. British positions in the south might have been overrun, but the troops there had not been destroyed – rather, like 2nd Rifle Brigade, they had managed merely to fall back.

What's more, the Deutsches Afrikakorps had suffered serious losses and some units had broken in the dust and confusion. In fact, a third of their panzers had been knocked out, they were short of fuel and desperately fractured. Now it was the Afrikakorps that was almost surrounded and with their lines of supply all but severed. After the rout of the southern brigades, the tables had turned dramatically and suddenly it was the Axis forces, rather than Eighth Army, that were facing annihilation.

CHAPTER 17

Combined Production

'A N INTERESTING QUESTION is what are the Russians capable of doing in the spring?' Oberst Hermann Balck jotted in his journal on 3 March 1942. As usual, German intelligence on the true state of the enemy was pretty poor and Balck, for one, felt confident that having survived the winter crisis by the skin of their teeth, German forces could soon push the Red Army back.

Certainly, both sides were now preparing for a spring and summer offensive, and for both it was the south that was to be the focus. For the Red Army, it was to encircle and destroy the entire German forces around Kharkov, while Hitler and his staff continued preparations for Case BLUE, the summer drive to the Caucasus. Before that could be launched, however, a couple of preliminary operations were needed. First, the Izyum salient punched along the Donets back in January had to be straightened out; and second, the Crimea had to be conquered. Despite all that had happened, and despite Hitler still remaining as C-in-C of the Army, Balck was confident. 'One thing is clear,' he added, 'if we can grasp the initiative again, they will be finished.'

As it happened, the Red Army beat the Germans to it at Izyum, attacking on 12 May and taking the defenders completely by surprise as they drove hard towards Kharkov, to the north-west. Another big hole was punched in the German line, but the Russians again ran out of steam and Feldmarschall von Bock launched his own attack as planned five days later, thrusting northwards through the base of the salient with von Kleist's 1. Panzerarmee, so that by 20 May it had narrowed to just

12 miles and two days later was entirely sealed. The trapped Russian forces tried to break out, but by 28 May it was as though the German failure of the winter had never happened, as a further 240,000 Red Army prisoners were taken, along with 1,200 tanks and 2,600 guns. There could be no denying that this had been a very great German victory.

None the less, the essential problems now confronting the German war machine had in no way gone away, as the newly promoted Generalmajor Hermann Balck discovered towards the end of May. Fed up with being a 'pencil pusher' and with life as a staff officer at OKH headquarters, he had requested and been granted a posting to the front, to command 11. Panzerdivision. The division had been reduced to nothing more than a few battered remnants since the start of BARBAROSSA, and although the rebuilding process had begun and in terms of personnel it was back at full strength, they were still short of 40 per cent of their motorized vehicles, despite the best efforts of General von Schell and his staff to improve the supply and maintenance of vehicles to the front.

By reducing the number of artillery batteries and by transporting the infantry with motor column units, Balck managed to get his division functioning to a degree of combat efficiency. None the less, when one of his brigade commanders complained that the division had never been expected to launch an offensive so poorly equipped, he was speaking nothing less than the truth. Even so, after the shattering experience of the winter, Balck still felt it was a miracle that the German Army was able to plan to go on the attack at all. As things stood, Case BLUE was due to begin at the end of June, which was a week later than BARBAROSSA had begun the year before. They had run out of time then, and the danger was they would run out of time this year too – especially since the Red Army that confronted them now was, despite its staggering losses, older and wiser by a year.

In the meantime, however, there was a battle already raging in the sand and heat of North Africa.

In the north of the Gazala Line, the South Africans and infantry of XIII Corps had held firm – as had the beleaguered Free French Brigade at Bir Hacheim. One of those now defending the outpost was Lieutenant Jean-Mathieu Boris. A Parisian Jew, Boris had left his family and escaped France for England, where he had joined Général de Gaulle's fledgling Free French. Long months of training had followed, but finally, late the previous September, he and his fellows had been told they were to join the Forces françaises libres in the Middle East. By 4 October 1941 they were on board the *Chantilly*, a French pre-war liner which, coincidentally, Boris and his family had been on before, over Easter 1939, when they had gone on a cruise in the Aegean.

He had been one of six officers and thirty men, plus a number of civilians, and they had travelled in convoy to South Africa. Boris and his fellows had entertained the children by blowing condoms up into balloons for them, and he had passed the long journey by working on his own poetry anthology, copying out parts of poems by Baudelaire, Verlaine and others. They had eventually reached Suez on 18 December, then travelled on to join Général Pierre König. Boris had been placed in the 1st Artillery Regiment, one of 3,723 men and one woman in the 1st Free French Brigade; the woman was Susan Travers, an Englishwoman, who was the Général's driver – and lover.

They had headed to the front in January and had briefly been in action, then been posted to Bir Hacheim to relieve the British 150th Brigade. There, they had dug slit-trenches, added to the defences, patrolled extensively, and waited.

On 24 May, Boris was on patrol at Rotonda Segnali, some 50 miles to the west of Bir Hacheim and deep behind enemy lines. He was now signals officer for two six-gun mobile batteries and part of a Jock Column sent to harass Axis lines of communication. Suddenly, Italian aircraft appeared and strafed them, and one of his men got a bullet through the foot. It was a mess and, with no surgeon and miles from help, they had no choice but to amputate, dosing the man with morphine and whisky, while their medic followed instructions given over the radio.

The following day, they spotted German tanks and, after destroying one Panzer IV with their French 75mms, they hitched up the guns to their British trucks and hurried back to Bir Hacheim, where they saw Rommel's column outflanking the entire position as thousands of tanks, guns and vehicles rolled through. By the morning of 27 May, Bir Hacheim itself was singled out and, at around 9 a.m., some seventy Italian M13 tanks of the Ariete Division attacked, not from the west, but from around the back of their position. For two and a half hours the battle raged. Eighteen enemy tanks were knocked out by mines and by the defenders' guns, but then more tanks appeared in front of the perimeter defended by a demi-brigade of the Légion Étrangère – the French Foreign Legion.

None managed to breach the perimeter and, by the time the Italians withdrew, thirty-two wrecks lay burning in the desert around them. A number of prisoners were taken too, including the Italian commander. Boris saw him as he was brought in and immediately noticed the *Légion d'honneur* and *Croix de guerre* on his uniform. 'I fought with France in 1917,' the man explained, 'my wife is French and when I knew I was going to have to fight against them, it broke my heart. But I couldn't escape my duty and I didn't try to avoid death.' The Frenchmen rather liked him. 'He stayed with us for a few days,' noted Boris, 'playing the fourth partner at bridge.'

On 28 May, the bulk of the German armour was trapped in an area between several low ridges to the west of Knightsbridge, in a large hollow known as 'the Cauldron'. The Afrikakorps was being saved, for the time being, by its anti-tank guns, which had been thrust around this make-shift perimeter – what the Germans were calling a 'flak front'. Behind this were not only the surviving bulk of Axis panzers, but also most of the Panzerarmee's and Afrikakorps' senior commanders, including Fritz Bayerlein and Rommel himself.

A decisive thrust by British armour and artillery from multiple directions might have sewn them up there and then, but because of the confused nature of what was going on, and because Ritchie wanted to wait for reports from patrols, there were few serious engagements until the afternoon. Meanwhile, 21. Panzer continued forging north before turning back the following day, all momentum lost. The 90th Light Division, meanwhile, having equally over-extended and with the panzer divisions vulnerable, also turned back, heading west to support 21. and 15. Panzer. The British armoured brigades made attacks on both the Germans and the Italian Ariete Division, who, after calling off their attack against Bir Hacheim, had also headed north.

All along the front to the west, the Italian infantry kept up the pressure, firing their artillery relentlessly. Axis air forces also continued harassing the front line, even though they had completely lost contact with Rommel and so had little idea how they could help his endangered panzers. Meanwhile, to the south-west, Albert Martin and 2nd Rifle Brigade were regrouping with the rest of 7th Motor Brigade and protecting the huge dumps of stores to the rear. Rumours were rife. 'It's said we've knocked out 135 German tanks,' he jotted in his diary, then added, 'Probably an exaggeration, though losses in equipment are mounting for Rommel.'

This was certainly true, but rescue for the Afrikakorps was close at hand. During the day, the Italians had managed to drive into narrow gaps through the minefields on either side of 150th Brigade's box, which was roughly on a level with the Cauldron. This meant that, come nightfall, the panzers trapped behind the British line could now, potentially, be resupplied. Much depended on 150th Brigade's ability to close these channels.

Rommel spent the day trying to bring precious supplies in columns around Bir Hacheim and up the eastern side of the minefields, and, having insisted on leading the charge himself, was lucky to survive several narrow escapes. He also ordered Crüwell to try to break through in the north. Once again, the attack against the South Africans failed.

While this was going on, the armoured battle continued, although 1st Armoured Division was not attacking with anything like the vigour it should have had. 'Get a move on,' General Norrie urged Major-General Herbert Lumsden, the 1st Armoured commander. 'Hit them up the backside.' Lumsden replied that he would, but only when he had enough forces. This was not good enough – it echoed the slow response of the French back in 1940. This time, however, there were no refugees clogging roads, nor a lack of radios. Right now, the panzers were trapped and ripe for destruction, but it needed determined action straight away in a frenzied simultaneous assault. Gingerly firing from extremes and in piecemeal fashion was not the answer.

By the morning of 30 May, around 200 of Rommel's panzers were out of action and he had lost General Crüwell, who had been shot down behind enemy lines and captured during a reconnaissance flight over the battle. Wrecked tanks and vehicles littered the battlefield, many still smoking. Despite this parlous situation for the Afrikakorps, Rommel's efforts to reach his armoured divisions with his supply train had been largely successful, and more reached them during the day. Furthermore, his forces, once scattered, were now concentrated again and, while that had made them very vulnerable the previous day, now that supplies had reached them, the situation was slowly improving.

The panzers were still in dire trouble, however, and strong and decisive British leadership at this point could and should have seen the Afrikakorps finished off for good. This was not forthcoming, as the command-by-committee nature of Eighth Army once again reared its ugly head. Ritchie began working on a new plan, in which units from XXX Corps and even the Free French would swing round and attack from the south while General 'Strafer' Gott's XIII attacked from the north. This was a perfectly sensible idea as long as it happened right away, but this, it seemed, was not possible. Such an operation would take time, his corps commanders told him: they needed twenty-four hours at least, as well as reinforcements. In any case, Rommel's anti-tank guns were still causing problems; caution was needed, Lumsden informed Ritchie.

No it wasn't! If ever there was a time to throw caution to the wind and hurl everything, right away, at the ensnared panzer divisions, it was now, on 30 May. A stronger character would have told his subordinate commanders to pull their collective fingers out and get on with it, but Ritchie accepted Lumsden's increasingly pessimistic and defensive appreciation. Instead, Lumsden now suggested a night-time action by the infantry to destroy the enemy's anti-tank guns. In this, he was being woefully risk-averse. That a divisional commander was calling the tune rather than Ritchie himself says much about the weak command of Eighth Army at this crucial moment.

'The thousandth day of the war!' wrote Gwladys Cox in her diary on 31 May. Gwladys and her husband, Ralph, lived in north London and soon after she had heard the then British Prime Minister Neville Chamberlain announce that Britain was at war with Germany, she had decided, like so many others, to keep a daily journal of her experiences. So far, they had included a brief evacuation to Guildford in Surrey, having their flat bombed out and destroyed by the Luftwaffe, and a few months of attempted recuperation in the Lake District. Since then, they had returned to London, where they lived quietly in their new flat with what they had salvaged, as well as with Bobbie, their terrier. Gwladys read avidly – books or newspapers – and made sure she tuned in to any important speeches that were broadcast. How much longer this war would last, she had no idea, but like many Britons – and Americans too – she had been cheered by the news from Germany, where there were rumours of internal collapse. 'Some reports say Hitler and his Generals have fallen out,' she wrote, 'as is natural enough, the latter being trained men, who must see what is likely to happen.' While such rumours may have been premature, reports of Germany's dire food situation were closer to the mark.

On that thousandth day of the war, she also heard that Reinhard Heydrich, head of the Reich Security Office, had been shot at by Czech resistance fighters. 'Already six people, no doubt perfectly innocent, have been executed,' she scribbled, and she continued to report daily on the rising number being executed for the assassination attempt. Then, on 4 June, came the news that he had died. 'So passes in fitting manner one of the worst of the Nazi gangsters,' she wrote with venom, before adding, 'To date, more than 150 innocent people have been killed in connection with his assassination.'

A few days after that, she was able to jot down that six months after the United States had joined the war, the attack at Pearl Harbor had been avenged in the 'devastating repulse made by the US Navy to Japan's attack on Midway Island.'

The news from the Pacific certainly was better at long last; the US Navy's victory over the Japanese had been a stunning reversal. Thanks in large part to the work of American cryptanalysts breaking Japanese naval codes, the US Pacific Fleet was able to pre-empt the planned Japanese ambush and destroy much of their carrier fleet instead. Four Japanese carriers and one battle cruiser now lay at the bottom of the Pacific. These were catastrophic losses for the Japanese and would almost certainly prove to be a decisive blow. Japan's entry into the war had been predicated on crippling the US Navy so that it would be unable to threaten their military operations through the Pacific and South-East Asia for a considerable time. Six months was not time enough. After the crushing early defeats at the hands of the Japanese, Midway marked a crucial turning point. 'At a stroke,' noted Churchill, 'the dominant position of Japan in the Pacific was reversed.'

There were, however, concerns about the Russians, something their Foreign Minister, Vyacheslav Molotov, had been happy to stoke during his visits to London and Washington. 'I have a very strong feeling,' Roosevelt cabled to Churchill, 'that the Russian position is precarious.' Harry Hopkins echoed such thoughts in his own letter to the Prime Minister. 'We are disturbed here about the Russian Front,' he wrote, 'and that anxiety is heightened by what appears to be a lack of clear understanding between us as to the precise military move that shall be made in the event the Russians get pushed around badly on their front.'

That certainly had to be ironed out and quickly, but in the meantime more and more armaments were starting to emerge from America's rising number of production plants. Bill Knudsen had been making very good use of the plane Secretary of State Henry Stimson had made available. When Knudsen had been passed over as head of the WPB, Stimson had told him, 'You will have no set schedule. Bottlenecks in production appear to be everywhere, so use your own judgement which ones to break first.' Since then, he had flown some 55,000 miles and visited 350 factories in over 100 cities. He watched the making of weapons, talked to people from managers to assembly-line workers and ironed out one problem after another. Overall, production tended to increase by as much as 10–15 per cent after one of his visits.

None the less, the buck no longer stopped with Big Bill Knudsen, but with Big Don Nelson. Although he had been sticking to most of the production principles laid down by Knudsen, it was clear that for all the new powers invested in him, the challenges facing him six months on remained immense.

One of the first of these had been what to do about procurement. Up until the creation of the WPB, all military procurement – the requests for new guns, tanks, aircraft, uniforms and so on – had been in the hands of the military. The concern for many in Washington was that this meant the military would inevitably end up having control over virtually all the US economy, especially once the economy became almost entirely devoted to war production.

In Britain, the procurement process was very much a joint one between civilian and military. Requests for aircraft, for example, were made via the Air Ministry, which was headed by the civilian Minister of State for Air, but which included many leading officers in the RAF holding key positions. These would then be passed on to the Ministry of Aircraft Production and would be overseen by both the Minister of Production – Oliver Lyttelton – and the War Cabinet.

Germany, on the other hand, was a military state, and a totalitarian one at that. The head of the Luftwaffe, for example, Reichsmarschall Göring, was also the Minister for Air and thus a military and political head. Procurement, now in the hands of the number-two man in the Luftwaffe, Feldmarschall Erhard Milch, was overseen through a department of the Luftwaffe General Staff, which was also the Air Ministry.

In the United States, however, military procurement had, since the end of the last war, been a small part of the overall economy, and it had been seen as perfectly acceptable that it should be left in the hands of the military. Now that military procurement effectively *was* the economy, it was perhaps not surprising that there were many who wondered whether it was sensible to leave such a crucial role in the hands of military men, most of whom had little understanding or experience of how business and industry worked.

Against the wishes of both the Senate and the House, however, Nelson decided against changing things. To do so would have meant setting up an entirely new and single-functioning civilian agency and transferring a mass of complicated contracts from military agencies, with the legal minefield that would have inevitably come with it. The military were against the move, in any case, so this might take an eternity. Speed was of the essence. Quite simply, he didn't believe there was the time to implement such a dramatic change. And in any case, surely military men were the best placed to decide what was needed and whether the end product hit the mark? 'It was never part of my job,' Nelson wrote, 'to tell the military people what they wanted in the way of weapons. But if I had taken over the production function in its entirety I would have come very close to having such a job.'

His decision was almost certainly the right one, but it meant that, after the very briefest of honeymoon periods, there were a lot of people willing to criticize him and waiting for him to fail at every turn. Joy at getting the Munitions Tsar swiftly turned to frustration when not everything appeared to be going right.

And by the spring, that had certainly proved the case. There was not enough aluminium; nor was there enough copper. Most seriously, there wasn't enough steel. In January, there was a backlog of 4.5 million tons of steel plate on unfilled orders. What's more, President Roosevelt's production targets had been based on the assumption that the total output of armaments in the US would amount to $40 billion in 1942 and $75 billion the following year. However, by the time the orders had all been totted up, the figures were $62 billion for 1942 and $110 billion for 1943. These figures were so huge they would clearly never be fulfilled, particularly with shortages in key areas of raw materials. So now Nelson – albeit with Roosevelt's support – had somehow to reduce orders to a realistic level. That, however, meant neither the Army nor the Navy would get as much as it wanted. It also meant the British – and the Russians – would not get what they wanted either.

The truth was, now the USA was in the war everything had changed.

Their armed forces were expected to play a key role in beating not only Nazi Germany but Imperial Japan too. To do that, their young men needed to be adequately equipped so that it could be done as quickly and efficiently as possible with as few lives lost as possible. Britain had, from the start of the war, opted to use steel not flesh as much as she could. That mantra held true for Americans too; if producing huge numbers of ships, tanks, guns and aircraft saved lives, then that was what they would do.

In April, Nelson suggested to the British that, since the American programme had to be revised, it was the ideal time for a joint review of the armaments programmes for both countries. This way, as Nelson prepared his revision, he could try to make adequate allowance for British needs too. After all, they were now all in it together.

So it was that in early June, Oliver Lyttelton, Nelson's opposite number in Britain and even newer to his post as Minister of Production, arrived in Washington for talks about how best to go forward.

With the heartening news from the Pacific greeting his arrival, Lyttelton found himself sitting side by side with Don Nelson and facing a press conference. It was a hot and humid day in the American capital and far worse than any awkward questioning was having to sit for the best part of an hour as a mass of photographers clicked away right under their noses. Lyttelton was feeling hot enough, but Nelson, he noticed, was sweating through his shirt while a mass of press men, many of whom were smoking, seemed to be getting ever closer.

Eventually, the ordeal was over and Lyttelton was whisked away to the White House to see Roosevelt for a 'desk lunch' in the Oval Office of cold lobster and mayonnaise with both the President and Harry Hopkins, whom Lyttelton had already got to know and liked. 'Soon,' noted Lyttelton, 'there were lobster shells all over the desk, and not a little mayonnaise had found its way onto the papers, the commissions, the reprieves and the reports which littered it.'

He was utterly charmed by Roosevelt and glad to see Hopkins again, but the main focus of the trip was the creation of the Combined Production and Resources Board, which they announced on 9 June. Nelson and Lyttelton were to head this body, which was to try to ensure a pooling of resources as far as possible between not only Britain and the US, but Canada too. It was also agreed at the board's first formal meeting just over ten days later that Britain should have the same share of armaments and components produced in the US as American forces, so long as they were engaged on operations of equal strategic importance. With this in mind, both sides were to draw up their respective orders of battle – that is, the line-up of men, units and formations in their armed services. The trouble was, while the British Chiefs of Staff had already done this and had their spring 1943 predictions ready, the Americans, new to the war and still trying to work out their more detailed priorities, had not.

Events in the Western Desert and around Kharkov also served to remind everyone how uncertain the future was and therefore how difficult it was to plan. The result was that, by the time Lyttelton returned home, a Combined Production and Resources Board had been formed but no combined programme had been agreed. That was not ideal, but it was progress of sorts and showed there was the appetite for production co-operation even if in reality it was hard to put into practice. What's more, there were areas of cross-over: in tanks, in artillery, in a mass of components and in ships. Nor had the United States and Great Britain become formal allies; rather, they remained coalition partners. They were co-operating as far as they possibly could. In the summer of 1942, that was a lot more than could be said for the Axis.

CHAPTER 18

The Fall of Tobruk

THE LAST DAY of May was a Sunday and, back in Italy, Count Ciano allowed himself a day off at his family home in Livorno, where he tried to relax with a spot of fishing off the coast. It was, however, only the briefest of respites, because that day he still had to deal with grumbles and complaints from his staff about the food and wine shortages. His fisherman, Renato, complained to him that he had lost 30 lb in weight in just a few months; the rest of his family, he said, were also seeing their waistlines shrink.

Just about everyone in the Mediterranean was hungry, but what else could be expected with the war raging in North Africa and the entire region largely cut off from the rest of the world? In Italy, rationing was severe – most adults were reduced to around 1,000 calories a day – and there was a shortage of fuel for both vehicles and heating, although most private cars had been requisitioned in any case. Shoes, basic medicines and even soap had largely vanished from the shops. The young menfolk had been sent away to fight or as occupying forces, and for those left behind merely existing was a day-to-day struggle, especially since, traditionally, Italian women did not bring money into the family, but were kept busy bringing up children, cooking, washing and keeping house. Money sent home from the front, if it ever arrived, was a pittance. Compared with the sufferings of Italians – and it was even worse in Greece and the Balkans – Gwladys Cox and British civilians were swimming in the land of plenty.

Ciano had other problems, however. It wasn't only Generale Messe who was warning of bleak times ahead on the Eastern Front, but the journalist Lamberto Sorrentino, who wrote for the weekly magazine *Tempo*. Sorrentino had been shocked by the level of brutality meted out by the Germans. 'Massacres of entire populations, raping, killing of children,' recorded Ciano, 'all this is a matter of daily occurrence.' Against this, Sorrentino told him, was the Bolshevik insistence on resisting and fighting to the end. 'The coming four months,' the journalist warned him, 'may mark the beginning of a catastrophe the like of which has never been seen.' While Allied leaders in London and Washington were fretting over Molotov's bleak picture, so Italians, it seemed, were bracing themselves for disaster.

Then there was the current battle, which was certainly causing Ciano some anxiety, and the conundrum over Malta, which, as far as the Italians were concerned, was still very much on the cards. Later that day, having returned from fishing, Ciano spoke with Generale Giacomo Carboni, the commander of one of the assault divisions earmarked for Malta. Carboni told him flatly that he, too, was dead against an invasion of the island, and equally pessimistic about the Eastern Front. 'From this,' Ciano noted, 'he draws the most sinister conclusions for the German future.'

At the bottom of the British line at Gazala, Lieutenant Jean-Mathieu Boris and the French forces were still holding out. Since defeating the first major tank attack on 27 May, they had remained under fire, although they had sent out some harassing patrols of their own; but now, on the evening of the 31st, all seemed quiet and Général König had been told to get ready to move up the western side of the line. This, however, was swiftly cancelled and two days later they were still there, waiting, when two Italian officers approached with the white flag of truce. Rommel, it seemed, was offering them the chance to surrender. König thanked them but sent them on their way; there could be no question of surrender. 'You are brave soldiers,' the Italians replied as they departed.

By this time, they were already running short of water and ammunition, and within an hour of König's refusal, the first shells started to fall once more, followed by aerial assaults by Stukas. Bir Hacheim was proving something of a stubborn thorn in the Axis side, so on 3 June Rommel signalled them again, once more urging them to throw in the towel. Again, however, König refused, and pressed home the point by ordering all his guns to open fire.

Being out on a limb, Bir Hacheim was, however, an obvious target for the Stukas as it was easy to spot in its isolated position, and, the following day, Boris watched an intense aerial battle going on overhead; at one point he saw seven Stukas shot down in a matter of minutes. Then overnight a British relief convoy arrived, having broken through enemy lines, bringing with them precious supplies of ammunition, food and water. The following morning, Boris accompanied Capitaine Charles Bricogne on an inspection of the 75mm batteries, only for a shell to burst nearby. Boris immediately lay flat on the ground. 'I hope you haven't hurt yourself falling, M. Cadet,' said Bricogne. Boris hastily got to his feet again, feeling chastened. It was, he later realized, a good lesson, and from now on he became determined he would always remain on his feet, leading by example.

While the bombers were exhausting themselves against Bir Hacheim, the fighters were continuing their policy of hunting their opposite numbers. Early on 30 May, Jochen Marseille and his *Schwarm* – his four-aircraft flight – attacked a formation of British fighters from 250 Squadron and 450 Royal Australian Air Force (RAAF) between El Adem and Tobruk. Picking out Flight Sergeant Graham Buckland, one of the Aussie pilots, who was turning into a shallow climb, Marseille fired off a burst and crippled the plane. He then watched Buckland bail out, but his parachute never opened and the man plummeted to his death. 'Poor bastard,' shrieked Marseille in horror.

It was his sixty-fifth victory, but Marseille made a note of the coordinates and, after landing back down, headed off in a vehicle with his wingman, Reiner Pöttgen, and soon found the body, which still lay where it had fallen, behind Axis lines. The wreckage of Buckland's Kittyhawk was a few hundred yards away. Collecting Buckland's papers and confirming his identity and unit, they then hurried back to the airfield. There, Marseille clambered back into his Messerschmitt and flew back over Allied lines before swooping in low over 250 Squadron's landing ground and dropping a bag with Buckland's things and a note he had written. Once clear, he climbed and headed back to base. Over the British landing ground, no one had fired a shot.

It wasn't the first time Marseille had done this. Really, he was something of an idealist, a man fighting a war that was quite different to the one almost all other combatants were fighting. His number 14 Messerschmitt was known by both sides – a new Red Baron for the desert war, only his mount was painted sand yellow; after Rommel, he was already the most famous man in the North African theatre. For him, it was a duel, in which honour and respect for one's enemy was an essential part of the fighter pilot's role.

He was also obsessed with death and the thought of the men he had killed never being found, their mothers and families not knowing what had happened; in this, he had not changed a bit since his first victory. Perhaps it was because he was so close to his mother, who had divorced Marseille's father after learning of an affair. He wrote to her a great deal, always worrying that she should know where he was. 'He could have been viewed as a contradictory man,' said Ludwig Franzisket, one of his comrades in 3/JG27, 'killing and then trying to save, or inform and recover the dead. I would say that he was a humanist thrown into a very inhumane environment, and he was just trying to make the best of a very terrible situation.'

Certainly the Desert Air Force was taking hits – in three days, from 29 to 31 May, thirty-nine fighters were lost, but over a thousand enemy vehicles had also been destroyed. But in sharp contrast to the dithering leadership of Eighth Army, Mary Coningham had a very firm grip on his Desert Air Force. On the morning of 28 May, he had issued orders that no pilot was to engage enemy fighters or fly above 6,000 feet; rather, attacks on Axis supply columns were the top priority. Leaving his pilots exposed to Jochen Marseille and his fellows was a lot to ask, but he knew that supporting the Army in this opening move by Rommel was their prime objective and, apart from his few Spitfire Vs, he had no other fighters to spare as top-cover.

Operating from the landing ground at Gambut was 112 Shark Squadron, part of 239 Wing. Billy Drake had taken over command at a critical moment. Pilots were up before first light and expected to be at their dispersal tents ready to be scrambled at a moment's notice. 'Usually we knew roughly what we were about to do,' said Drake. 'On the whole, we were carrying out offensive operations. We'd find out what was cooking and then, depending on how many aircraft were required, I'd detail who would fly.' The ground crew would already be there waiting with the starter batteries and soon the airfield would be alive with the roar of engines. Swathes of sand and dust would be whipped up by the propellers; vision over the nose of the plane was difficult at the best of times, but with swirls of dust and sand, forward sight was terrible. The answer was to take off in a long line; space was one thing they were not short of in the desert.

Billy Drake had flown Hurricanes in France, then Spitfires over Britain, but was new to the US-built P-40 Kittyhawk. He rather liked it, though, and soon realized that under 10,000 feet it performed as well as an Me109 – although not when it had a bomb strapped underneath. Dive-bombing was tricky – Drake learned he had to dive down from around 8,000 feet at about 60 degrees, then drop his bomb and pull out at about 1,500 feet. 'You'd get in as close as you possibly could without hitting the ground,' he said. After a few days, he soon started to get the hang of it.

By 1 June, after four days of incessant dive-bombing and strafing attacks, he had lost three pilots. Low-level flying was particularly lethal because there was always plenty of light flak and small arms fizzing about and, if hit, there was little room in which to bail out or recover. Whether one was hit was purely a matter of chance. 'That's why the golden rule on any ground attack was to only attack once,' said Drake. 'You dropped your bomb and got the hell out. You always made sure you strafed a different target on the way back.'

The DAF's attacks were certainly working, however, and on average were accounting for some 150 vehicles a day. 'Low-level machine-gunning,' noted one German in a captured diary. 'RHQ dispersed. Some MT abandoned and lost. Chaos. Panic.'

Limited resources and aircraft were Coningham's and Elmhirst's biggest concern. Juggling what aircraft they did have was very much the order of the day. 'I am sure everything is being done to send a few more Spitfires to us,' Coningham wrote to Tedder on 1 June, in a tone more of hope than expectation. The difficulty was that it was impossible to know how long they would be expected to operate at such a high level of intensity.

On 1 June, Rommel and his senior commanders, still in the Cauldron, held a council of war. They all agreed that the situation remained desperate and that as soon as possible they should attempt a break out to the west through the British minefield. Soon after, however, Rommel's senior staff officer, Oberst Siegfried Westphal, was wounded and then so too was General Gause, Rommel's Chief of Staff of the Panzerarmee, when he was thrown backwards into a panzer by the blast from a British tank shell. Bayerlein was immediately told he would be taking over.

It was only now, as they prepared to break out, that they realized that within the minefield immediately to their west was another British box, in which 150th Brigade were still holding their positions. At the urging of Feldmarschall Kesselring, who had arrived at the front to lend a hand and take over from the captured Crüwell, Rommel now decided to hurl his armour at 150th Brigade. Rommel had faults, but indecision was not one of them, so he attacked at once with his panzers from the east and the Italians from the west. The battle lasted all day, but by dusk 150th Brigade had been destroyed. 'The defence was conducted with considerable skill,' Rommel admitted, 'and as usual, the British fought to their last round.' Bayerlein was certain it was the destruction of the 150th Brigade box that turned the battle. 'If we had not taken it on 1 June,' he said, 'you would have captured the whole of the Afrikakorps. By the evening of the third day, we were surrounded and almost out of petrol. As it was, it was a miracle that we managed to get our supplies through the minefield in time.'

It also enabled Hans von Luck finally to be evacuated from the battlefield, having been trapped in the Cauldron with much of the rest of 21. Panzer. For five long days he had remained in his command car, a tourniquet around his thigh, dosed up with morphine, and still attempting to command his battalion. At the aid station the doctor told him his wound did not look good and that he must get to the casualty clearing station at Derna as quickly as possible. With a heavy heart and close to tears, von Luck handed over command to his deputy and then was driven to Derna. There, the doctors told him his wound had become infected. He was cleaned up and put on a ship to Sicily, arriving the following morning and then taken straight into theatre for a small operation to stabilize the wound. From there he would be sent back to hospital in Germany. However, medical supplies were already so poor, the Italian surgeon began operating without any kind of pain relief. 'Clench your teeth, please,' the surgeon told him. Two nurses held him tight while the surgeon began to cut at his wound. 'I cried like an animal,' noted von Luck, 'and thought I would faint with pain.' His turmoil stopped only when General Gustav von Vaerst, the wounded commander of 15. Panzer, heard his screams and insisted the surgeon give him an anaesthetic.

*

That the Afrikakorps had been able to break out west from the Cauldron was not a miracle, as Bayerlein had thought, but rather came down to abject leadership on the part of Eighth Army's commanders. In fact, while this battle was raging, the rest of the British forces, with their still-large number of tanks and artillery, were doing very little. In the north, barely a shot was fired all day.

Ritchie had decided to take up Lumsden's idea of a night attack, however, and had they done so that evening, as had been his plan, they would almost certainly have succeeded. The Panzerarmee was exhausted after its battle with the 150th Brigade and was now short of everything: ammunition, food, water and fuel. Bayerlein had been among those who had pleaded with Rommel to call the attack off or surely face defeat in turn – the situation seemed to them that dire. But in a telling contrast of leadership styles, Ritchie acquiesced to his subordinates who wanted to hold off, while Rommel ignored his and drove his men on. By evening, 150th Brigade was no more, and a huge hole had been punched right through the centre of the line.

For three whole days Rommel's panzer divisions had been trapped in the Cauldron, ripe for destruction, yet the chance to close in for the kill had been repeatedly passed over. That Ritchie and his commanders failed to ram home the advantage was disgraceful. The desert was, effectively, a giant gladiatorial arena – a dust-swept expanse in which two opponents could slug it out without hindrance. Here, in the sand and heat, the skills and failings of each side were starkly exposed. Against Rommel, Ritchie was failing.

It was true that sandstorms, smoke and dust added to the fog of war – little flying could be done on 2 June, for example, because of sandstorms – but that was no excuse in this case. The various Eighth Army message logs show that Ritchie had a very clear picture of what was going on most of the time, and a far clearer one than Rommel was afforded. At his Tactical HQ at Gambut, tents and trucks full of radios and maps, clerks and telephonists dealt efficiently with the mass of messages, relaying them to the various members of staff, who hovered with coloured pencils waiting to plot the latest positions on to maps. Coningham had his own Tac HQ nearby and was available for conferral at any time. Since the start of the battle, the DAF had flown large numbers of ground attacks but also 'Tac Rs' – tactical reconnaissance flights, reporting on enemy movements.

Thus, Ritchie's picture of what was happening could not have been clearer. It makes his prevaricating even less excusable.

The British night attack was finally launched on 1/2 June, too late to save 150th Brigade, and was a fiasco. Two separate assaults were planned – one from the north, which achieved nothing, and one from the south by the re-formed 7th Armoured Division. Albert Martin and 2nd Rifle Brigade had been moved up as part of this attack, but then it was called off due to lack of reconnaissance. A new plan was devised, Operation ABERDEEN, which Ritchie delegated to Norrie, who in turn delegated it to his two divisional commanders. It was then discussed and argued over, each commander finding reasons why his own troops should not be committed. In the end, the plan for ABERDEEN was this: a night attack with a heavy artillery barrage followed by infantry and then armour. All the while, however, the Afrikakorps still in the Cauldron were being substantially reinforced and revitalized.

Back in Britain, while Eisenhower and Clark had been dashing about the country, the Soviet Foreign Minister, Vyacheslav Molotov, had been visiting London. Molotov was not a man either Britain's or America's democratic war leaders would ever have imagined they would have staying under their roofs. A long-term loyal supporter of Stalin, he had been personally involved in the purges of the Red Army of the 1930s that had seen some 25,000 officers executed. He was also the implementer of the programme of compulsory farm collectivization and the taking of Ukrainian grain that had led to an entirely man-made famine that resulted in the death of somewhere between 7 and 11 million Ukrainians. In May 1942, not even Hitler had the deaths of so many people on his hands. Molotov had also been the man who had negotiated the pact with von Ribbentrop in August 1939 that had directly led to the outbreak of war. Now he was in London as an ally.

Although there primarily to discuss the terms of a new Anglo-Russian Treaty, he was also determined to pin down the Allies to a new second front. He was quite frank with Churchill, warning him that the Allies needed to launch an offensive as soon as possible to draw off at least forty German divisions from the East. The PM replied with equal candour that it would not be possible in Europe that year – the Allies were simply not ready. He was quite right – they most certainly were not.

With this bombshell, Molotov then travelled to Washington, by which time Churchill had written to Roosevelt reporting on his talks with the Russian and reminding the President of a suggestion he had first made the previous October and again during the Arcadia conference – namely, a joint Anglo-US invasion of French North Africa. This, he had argued, would kill two birds with one stone, if not three: it would speed up the conquest of North Africa and clear the southern Mediterranean; it would help hustle Italy out of the war; and it would give the British and US forces a chance to act together in an operation where victory was likely before they attempted a cross-Channel invasion of Nazi-occupied France.

At Washington, Molotov stayed in the White House as a guest of the President, and when a valet unpacked his case he discovered a sausage, a loaf of black Russian bread and a pistol. Although the President's body-guards took a dim view of this when it was duly reported, no one said a word. The pistol – and bread and sausage – remained in his room. The Americans, perhaps more than the British, were determined not to get on the wrong foot with Molotov.

In the first of their meetings, Molotov wasted no time in pressing for the opening of a second front, warning again that the Red Army might not be able to hold out that summer and asking for a straight answer: would there be one or not? At this point, Roosevelt turned to General Marshall. Was the situation clear enough to say they were developing a second front?

'Yes, Mr President,' Marshall replied.

Apparently satisfied, Roosevelt then told Molotov to inform Stalin that they could expect the formation of a second front that year. That was not quite what Marshall had said, but he could not publicly contra-dict the President. At the same time, Roosevelt must have known, as Marshall had known, there was little chance of such a front being opened on the continent that year. That would have meant a cross-channel invasion in August or September at the latest.

Meanwhile, Major-General Eisenhower had returned to America impressed by British organization but depressed by their doubts about a successful invasion in the spring of 1943. The 'reservations' were, it seemed, the British way of euphemistically saying they did not like the plans at all. As General Alan Brooke, the Chief of the Imperial General Staff (CIGS), made clear, 'the prospects of success are small and dependent on a mass of unknowns, whilst the chances of disaster are great and dependent on a mass of well-established military facts.'

Nor had Eisenhower been much impressed by General Chaney and his staff, and, back in Washington, he had submitted to Marshall a draft of a 'Directive for the Commanding General, European Theater of Operations'. This was, Eisenhower told his chief, one paper he should read in detail. 'I certainly do want to read it,' Marshall told him. 'You may be the man who executes it. If that's the case, when can you leave?'

Just three days later, Eisenhower's appointment as commander of the European Theater of Operations was confirmed. And once more, Clark would be accompanying him, this time as his deputy and as commander of US II Corps, whose headquarters were about to be shipped to Britain. It was Eisenhower who had recommended Clark to Marshall. 'It looks as if you boys go together,' Marshall told him.

Back in the Libyan desert, the battle still raged. Axis air forces and the Desert Air Force had continued to fight hard over and around Bir Hacheim, where the French were still grimly hanging on and around which Axis supply chains were continuing to move.

On 3 June, seven Stukas from a flight of twelve were shot down by DAF fighters – cheered noisily by the Frenchmen below. The next day, Bill Drake dropped his bomb right on the middle of an Axis formation forming up for attack. On the 6th, he was leading a flight of his Shark Squadron over Bir Hacheim yet again when he spotted four Me109s below them. Making the most of his rare advantage, he led his flight into an attack and in the ensuing mêlée all four 109s were shot down, including one by Drake. They then bombed Axis vehicles, leaving one in flames and six more shot up. Later in the day, the squadron destroyed a further five vehicles and damaged twelve more. In all, thirty-eight sorties were flown by 112 Squadron that day, with most of Drake's pilots flying at least three times, including an attack over the Cauldron. This was entirely typical of all the DAF's squadrons.

No matter how valiant their efforts, however, it was not going to be enough to save Eighth Army from the disaster about to unfold on the ground.

By 4 June, the situation still looked horribly worrying as far as Count Ciano was concerned. Maresciallo Cavallero that day described the results of the Libyan battle as being 'considerable'. 'Which for anybody who knows the mysterious language of this mountebank general,' noted Ciano, 'means that things have gone very badly.'

Later, Ciano saw Generale Giovanni Messe again. He both liked and thought highly of Messe, so listened carefully to what he said. 'Like everybody else who has had anything to do with the Germans,' wrote Ciano later, 'he hates them, and says that the only way of dealing with them is to punch them in the stomach.' Messe then told Ciano that the Red Army was still strong and well armed and that any idea that they would suddenly collapse was pure fantasy. The Germans would probably still have some successes, but the winter would catch them once more and they would face an even greater shortage of supplies. It was hard, sometimes, to remember these two countries were allies, and that their troops were fighting together – and not least in Libya.

In the desert, ABERDEEN finally got under way in the early hours of 5 June. The initial infantry infiltration by the British swiftly achieved its objectives, but their intelligence had been wrong and all they did was overrun a few Axis outposts rather than destroy the anti-tank screen. When the main assault began, the mostly German anti-tank guns opened fire with devastating results. Because the one weapon Eighth Army was short of was a decent anti-tank gun, the South Notts Hussars, for example, were forced to use their 25-pounder field guns in an anti-tank role, for which they were totally unsuited. The South Notts Hussars were decimated. Then the 'I' tanks were thrown in, which were not as good as the Grants, and in very little time fifty of the seventy thrust into the battle were knocked out by the German 88s, 75s and 50mm anti-tank guns, all of which could fire multiple rounds per minute at high velocity and at ranges far exceeding those of the tanks.

To make matters worse, and unbeknown to the attackers, Rommel's forces had by now cleared a gap in the minefields to the south of the Cauldron, and through this had been able to retrieve and resuscitate a number of tanks knocked out in the earlier fighting. While 90th Light and 21. Panzer fought up the attack in the Cauldron, 15. Panzer moved out through this gap and began working its way up the east side of the British position. For the British, disaster loomed, while for the Panzerarmee, what had looked like almost-certain annihilation just a week earlier now looked like developing into a stunning victory.

With no troops or position to command, General Tuker had headed back to the Delta to rejoin his division, but not before he had witnessed the failed opportunities and heard the plan for the counter-attack in the Cauldron. On reaching Egypt, he had headed to GHQ and pleaded with General Tom Corbett, the CGS, to urge the Auk to head to the front immediately and concentrate all he could lay his hands on for a single heavy blow to rapidly seize back the initiative, otherwise, he warned, they were heading for the most unnecessary disaster of the war.

Corbett immediately went to see Auchinleck, but returned a short while later saying the C-in-C would not go. Having pushed it as far as he could, Tuker headed off to his division.

The Auk should have heeded the warning, because after the failure of the attack on the Cauldron, events rapidly started to slip out of Eighth Army's control altogether. The Gazala Line was being unpicked in stages, but after the Cauldron Rommel's next focus was to smash Bir Hacheim once and for all.

By 10 June, it was clear the French garrison at Bir Hacheim could not hold out much longer. They were heavily surrounded, supplies of every-thing were critically low and food had actually run out entirely. For Lieutenant Boris, it had been an astonishing baptism of fire. Just a few days earlier, on 6 June, he had seen a childhood friend, Lieutenant Jean-Pierre Rosenwald, killed right in front of him by a shell. It had greatly shocked him. Two days later, the battle had intensified further and the fighting around Bir Hacheim had lasted all day. Boris had been on duty at the regiment HQ when the field telephone rang. Lieutenant Gérard Theodore had been wounded but no doctor could be found, so Boris hurried off, found his wounded friend and tied a tourniquet, then was about to take over his command when he heard someone calling him from the HQ shelter. 'Message from the Commandant!' he called out. Boris crawled towards the radio operator, then a bullet fizzed, hit the man in the head and he dropped forward, dead.

Now, on 10 June, König decided they would attempt a breakout that night. Boris was told to get word to the captain manning the forward observation post, but since the field phone line was cut and using radio risked blowing their plan, Boris sent one of his gunners forward with a message. He had not gone more than 50 metres, however, when he was killed. Boris sent another, but he was shot as well. This time, Boris ordered a sergeant to go, but the man pleaded to be spared. He had a wife and children back in France, he said, beseeching him. Only when Boris threatened him with his pistol did he finally set off, and this time managed to make it there and back in one piece.

By midnight, a path through the minefields had been cleared and an armoured convoy of some forty vehicles assembled. Boris was in a car with Capitaine Bricogne and to begin with all went well, but then shots rang out, rifles then machine guns. They stopped to help some of the wounded who were running after the lorries to clamber on, then sped on themselves through a hail of bullets and tracers. One Bren Carrier hit a mine, while above them flares were whizzing into the air, bursting with a crackle and showering the desert with light. 'Not all bullets kill,' Bricogne said to him and then a split-second later one zapped through the car and struck the captain in the heart, killing him instantly. On the driver sped, and then, at last, they were through and among the British once more. 'I eat soup,' noted Boris, 'and sleep for twenty hours in the car that drives us away from the battle. The artillery regiment has lost sixty-six officers and men. Of the twenty-four cannons we had, there are only eight left.'

On 10 June, Churchill sent for Major-General John Kennedy, the Director of Military Operations at the War Office. The PM wanted to see him right away along with the Director of Military Intelligence, Major-General Francis Davidson, at No. 10 to discuss the strengths of the opposing forces in North Africa. Kennedy was forty-eight, a gunner in the last war but since then a staff officer and War Office man through and through. He and Davidson ran two of the directorates that served Brooke as CIGS. As DMO, Kennedy was a vital cog in Britain's war administration, involved in wider strategy but also distilling information from commanders in the field into appreciations of the military situation for both the CIGS and the War Cabinet. There was a strong element of planning too. At any rate, Kennedy was a man at the very heart of Britain's war machine and, other than those already out in North Africa, probably the person best placed to give Churchill a clear picture of what was going on in the desert.

It was around 11.30 a.m. when they were ushered into the Cabinet Room and found the PM sitting there already, his back to the fire and wearing one of his all-in-one boiler suits. After lighting a cigar, Churchill turned to a sheaf of papers on which were lists of British forces in the

Middle East. Rather to Kennedy's surprise, Churchill's and his own figures seemed to tally, but they then swiftly moved on to the nub of the matter. The Prime Minister had with him a telegram from Richard Casey, who had taken over from Oliver Lyttelton as Minister of State in the Middle East. Casey was reporting on a meeting of the Middle East Defence Committee, which consisted of himself and the service chiefs out there. They had been addressing what they should do were the Germans to break through on the Russian front and burst down into the Middle East. Should they hold the Delta or the Abadan oilfields? They had concluded they could not hold both.

Kennedy felt that considering a worst-case scenario was no bad thing, but it was clear Churchill had found this deeply frustrating. It suggested an overly defensive mindset; in fact, it hinted at a defeatist one. There was no conceivable way the Germans could achieve this over the comparatively narrow summer campaign season; such considerations, the PM believed, were horribly premature. He then held forth for about an hour on the situation in the Middle East. He had already been having serious doubts about Auchinleck – so too had Kennedy for that matter. Just under a month earlier, on 14 May and before Rommel's attack, the Auk had sent Brooke a long letter voicing his concerns about India and wondering whether it wouldn't be better to give up the offensive in the desert in order to strengthen the situation in the Far East instead. 'The possibility of having to relieve Auchinleck had been discussed in London for some time,' noted Kennedy. 'Now we began to feel that the change would have to be made fairly soon.'

It was a shame the concerns about the Auk had not been acted upon earlier and before he made such a hash of his command, but it would clearly have to come if and when this current crisis passed. In the meantime, Churchill was venting his frustration on Kennedy and Davidson.

'I don't know what we can do for that Army,' he railed. 'All our efforts to help them seem to be in vain.' New divisions had been sent out, Sherman tanks were being sent there and Grants were already in place. 'Nothing seems to help them. And I am the one who gets his neck wrung when things go wrong.'

Kennedy felt that there was some substance to the criticisms, but was not really sure what he could say.

'I doubt that Army's offensive spirit,' added Churchill. It wasn't the Army's fault, though, but its commanders'. Concerns about India, about the vastness of his command, about Germany driving in through the back door, were clearly distracting Auchinleck and clouding his mind. Ritchie was a desk-wallah and totally out of his depth. Personality clashes were infecting the cohesion and co-operation of corps and divisions, and neither Auchinleck in Cairo nor Ritchie at the front seemed able to grasp the situation, focus on what was needed and provide a clear, logical tactical approach. Fear of failure was leading to caution and indecision, which was, of course, leading to failure.

And failure meant defeat. Out in the desert, the British infantry in the north were still grimly holding their boxes, but the next, and decisive, clash was between the armour. The British armoured brigades – or what was left of them – had fallen back around the Knightsbridge cross-roads waiting for Rommel to make his next move. He did so on the afternoon of the 11th and, with his forces concentrated and confidence back to its normal sky-high levels, they destroyed many of the demoralized British armoured units they came up against. By the 13th, Ritchie had accepted the Gazala Line was finished, and the following day the South African Division – whose commander, General Dan Pienaar, had repeatedly refused to obey the orders of Gott, his corps commander, to go on to the attack – began pulling back to Tobruk. On the night of 16/17 June, El Adem, just to the south of Tobruk, was evacuated. Early on the morning of the 17th, with Rommel personally leading the charge, his panzers crossed the Via Balbia – the coast road – to the east of the town, and in so doing the town was once more effectively surrounded.

Much of Eighth Army was now racing to the Egyptian frontier in full retreat, but the 7th Motor Brigade was still operating south of El Adem, harassing enemy leaguers and columns at night. On the 19th, a resupply column reached them, which included not only food and ammo but letters too. Orders that day were vague – they were to carry on with their harassing activities, but they knew they were now out on a limb. 'Everything has been a jumble,' wrote Albert Martin. 'Does anyone at the top know what they are doing?'

Later that night, the British Riflemen attacked a German leaguer that was not yet napping and got a bad shock as a vicious fire-fight was unleashed across the night. It quickly became clear to Martin and his fellows that this was one harassing raid they could not win, so they

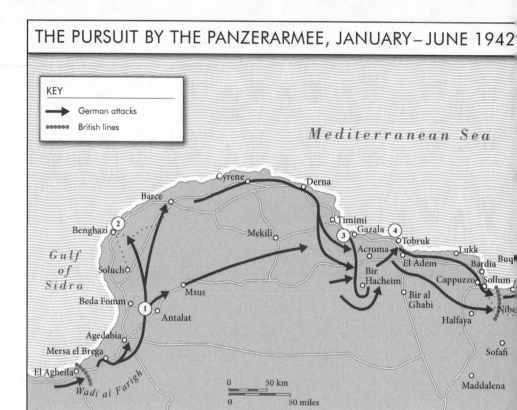

hastily pulled out, losing two men in the process. 'One of those suicide patrols,' Martin commented in his diary, 'when all we seem to achieve is annoying the enemy.'

Soon after, as they fell back into the safety of the desert, they heard distant guns and firing, and as dawn broke they looked northwards to see the ominous sight of rising plumes of thick black smoke.

By the evening of 20 June, Tobruk had been sliced in half, with the South Africans stuck on the western side. At 8 p.m., Ritchie signalled for them to fight their way out, but by dawn on the 21st they had not made much headway, their route blocked at every turn by Axis troops, guns and armour. As the first glint of sun appeared on the horizon, on this, the longest day of the year, the white flag was raised over the fortress of Tobruk.

While the midsummer heat had blasted down on the battle around Gazala and Tobruk, in Washington the heat was also stultifying. On 21 June, Churchill was in the American capital along with Brooke and other

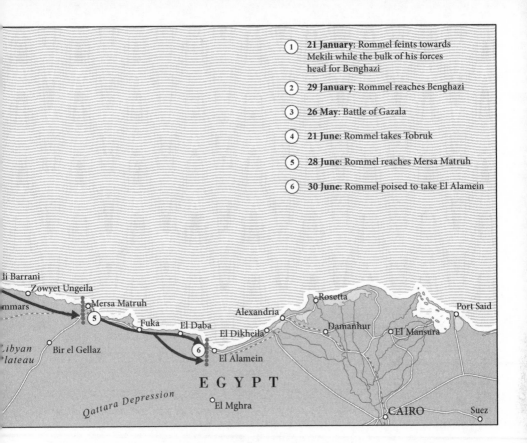

senior commanders for further talks about the direction of Anglo-US strategy. While General Marshall and Brooke had been agreeing that they were against a joint invasion of North Africa, Churchill had also been having private talks with Roosevelt at the President's country house, Hyde Park in New York. However, they were now back at the White House and were in the Oval Office when an aide entered with a pink slip of paper and, having glanced at it, silently passed it to Churchill. 'Tobruk has surrendered,' said the note, 'with 25,000 men.' In fact, it was worse than that – some 32,000 were in the bag. Utterly horrified, Churchill hardly dared believe it and asked for confirmation. It arrived soon after. 'This is one of the heaviest blows I can recall during the war,' he wrote later. 'I did not attempt to hide from the President the shock I had received. It was a bitter moment. Defeat is one thing. Disgrace is another.'

General Tuker put it even more tersely. 'This,' he wrote, 'was one of the worst fought battles in the history of the British Army.' It is very hard to disagree with either opinion.

CHAPTER 19

Sea and Sand

Iᴺ Nᴏʀᴛʜ Aꜰʀɪᴄᴀ, Eighth Army was on the run, its shattered and scattered remnants hurrying back across the border into Egypt. A blocking force was hastily forming near the frontier, but the mass were heading to a new position 60 miles to the west of Alexandria around the railway stop of El Alamein. Fresh troops were already preparing new defences here, including the 9th Australian Division, who had just been posted back to Egypt after their lengthy deployment in Syria. Among them was Ted Hardy of the 2/3rd Field Company, attached to the divisional headquarters, who now found himself a mile or so beyond the railway stop with orders to dig in furiously. 'We had the jack hammers out,' he said, 'spades and big picks. We put up wire, minefields at night and some even in the day.'

However worryingly close it might have been to Alexandria and Cairo, the Alamein position was none the less the best defensive position in all of Egypt and Libya, as here there was a natural limit to how long the line could be: around 40 miles to the south lay the Qattara Depression, a vast, low-lying stretch of ground with steep and dramatic sides. The depression could be outflanked by a handful of LRDG and SAS, but not an entire army. If Rommel was going to break through, he would have to do so head on.

As things stood, however, he was pretty confident he could. Promoted to Feldmarschall with immediate effect by an exultant Hitler, Rommel now intended not only to burst through the Alamein Line but then thunder on and take Cairo, Egypt and the entire Middle East. 'Soldiers of the Panzerarmee Afrika!' he exhorted them, 'Now for the complete destruction of the enemy. We will not rest until we have shattered the last remnants of the British Eighth Army.' To his wife, he confessed that the events of the past weeks 'lie behind me like a dream.' This was only possible because of the huge amounts of booty captured in and around Tobruk and included tanks as well as precious fuel, food and ammunition. Speed was of the essence. What was needed was classic Bewegungskrieg. The British, he knew, could not be allowed to recover. He had to smash the Alamein Line quickly before Eighth Army had a chance to regain balance.

Kesselring flew over on the afternoon of 21 June to confer with Rommel. The island fortress of Malta was still very much on his mind; Hitler had been unenthused by an invasion of the island in July, but his last word on the matter had been to postpone a decision until after Rommel's attack. Kesselring was still pressing for an invasion of Malta in July, but for this he needed the Luftwaffe that were now in North Africa. However, Rommel insisted he had Eighth Army on the ropes and needed to exploit his success. Now was not the moment to strip him of crucial air support. Kesselring countered that his chances of success were less if Axis supply lines across the Mediterranean were not secure – and increasingly, as Malta recovered, they were not. Neither man would give ground, but now that Rommel was a field marshal, he had the authority to appeal directly to Hitler – and Mussolini – and did so.

Mussolini, meanwhile, was lurching between euphoria and irritation. He was delighted with and admired Rommel greatly, but was unhappy that the battle was being identified as his victory and therefore a German rather than Italian one. Hitler's decision to promote Rommel to field marshal was, he told Ciano sulkily, clearly to underscore the German character of the battle.

On the other hand, *Il Duce* was now preparing to fly over with his best white stallion to lead the victory procession into Cairo. Before fifteen days were over, he expected the Italian commissariat to have been established in Alexandria.

At any rate, with all this excitement, Mussolini was no longer so worried about Malta – not that Hitler cared what he thought anyway. The Führer decided to back his new golden boy. The plan to invade Malta was shelved once and for all.

*

Both in the British press and in public opinion, the loss of Tobruk had been a huge blow, made worse because it came on the back of a string of other humiliations. In Burma, General Harold Alexander had been leading British and Indian forces back across the Irrawaddy and, after the losses of Singapore and Malaya, the threat to India was still severe. Gripes about the standard of weaponry continued. On 25 June, Churchill, still in Washington, faced a motion of no confidence in the House of Commons. It wasn't passed, but never in his two years as Britain's war leader had he faced such criticism.

At the War Office, Major-General John Kennedy was feeling concerned that Churchill placed far too much emphasis on the RAF, and especially Bomber Command. Harris had dreamed up a series of massed bombing raids on German cities – what became known as 'Thousand Bomber Raids' – and these had begun at the end of May, quite specifically to bolster support for his longer-term aims and to stop the bad press his command had been getting. This had rankled with Kennedy as well as with Brooke and the Chief of the Naval Staff, Admiral Sir Dudley Pound. Kennedy believed the problem lay in the employment of the RAF's bombers in an independent strategic role, when a better use of them would be to send them to support other operations. 'If we had diverted, say, 20 per cent of our long-range bomber aircraft to the Middle East,' he noted, 'it is doubtful whether Rommel could ever have started his offensive, and more than doubtful whether he could have sustained it at its recent tempo. I should like to take 50 per cent of the bomber effort off Germany even at this late hour, and distribute it in the Atlantic, and in the Middle East and Indian theatres. The price we pay at sea and on land for our present bombing policy is high indeed.'

He was, however, overlooking some key points here, not least that with the resources available, including the Desert Air Force and RAF Middle East bombers, had the Auk and Ritchie fought even a half-decent battle at Gazala then Rommel would have been stopped in his tracks. Furthermore, despite the Thousand Bomber Raids, Bomber Command was actually pretty weak at that time and especially so in the heavy bombers that Kennedy was suggesting should be sent to the Middle East. The number of bomber squadrons available to Harris through June was just thirty-five, and the average daily number of bombers only 402, of which only 141 were heavy bombers. Sending 20 per cent to the Middle East equated to seven squadrons; 50 per cent would have made Bomber Command completely ineffective.

Kennedy's comments overlooked another factor: that had the Americans implemented a convoy system straight away in the first few months of 1942, the real situation in the Battle of the Atlantic would have been more apparent – i.e. that the U-boats were losing already, and badly so. Finally, the monsoon had arrived in Burma and it was a more than reasonable assumption that the Japanese were not going to easily invade India any time soon. On the other hand, the Eastern Front was already rumbling into gear for the next round in this giant clash and, with the Germans already materially short, bombing targets in the Third Reich was one way in which Britain could use active operations palpably to help the Russians.

No, a lack of aircraft was not the reason Tobruk had fallen. Even Alan Moorehead, who had returned from a trip to India to witness the Gazala battles himself, had been unusually critical about both the superiority of German equipment and the British command. 'Quick-decision men,' he wrote, 'that's what we lacked most.' He was quite right: what had lost Tobruk was not a shortage of decent anti-tank guns, nor the poor per-formance of the troops on the ground, but bad generalship. So long as Eighth Army held Rommel at bay, however, the generalship could be sorted out. More Spitfires were arriving in the Middle East, and soon the first US Air Force squadrons would join the effort too. The latest American medium tank, the Sherman, a much-improved version of the still largely superior Grant, was also on its way – some 300 of them. The closer they were to the Delta and the Canal Zone, the shorter the lines of supply would be too. What's more, Britain's supply position in the Middle East had, after the immediate and dramatic change of fortunes brought by Japan's entry into the war, to a large extent been stabilized. In other words, it wasn't all bad, even if the cloud of collective gloom hung heavy not just over Cairo but over London too. So long as Eighth Army held out now, the situation could still be turned.

This, however, was very much on a knife-edge. 'Personally, I've had enough,' scribbled Albert Martin. 'When for heaven's sake are we going to stop running? Whatever is happening, we have all had enough. No fighting spirit left.' With morale shattered, with formations dislocated and with the Panzerarmee snapping at their heels, it was hardly surpris-ing that Rommel was sniffing blood.

While those in Britain were struggling to come to terms with the string of blows in the Far East and North Africa, there had been horror stories from the Atlantic too, where the U-boats had been enjoying their second 'Happy Time'. All in all, the Axis forces seemed suddenly resurgent once more.

On 9 July, Teddy Suhren's *U-564* slipped out of Brest and headed out across the Bay of Biscay in a westerly direction on what was her sixth patrol. The plan was to head back across the Atlantic and south of the Caribbean, but first there were reports of a convoy to intercept. Cruising on the surface at some 15 knots, they soon caught up with it and, as dusk fell, spotted mastheads in the distance on the starboard bow. Scarcely had they signalled their location, however, than the lookout was shouting, 'Plane!'

'Dive! Dive!' ordered Suhren, aware that they had probably already been spotted. Tank 5 was beginning to hiss with escaping air as he jumped down from the conning tower and into the belly of the boat. In a steep dive, they levelled out at 60 metres, expecting depth charges at any moment, but they never came. Cautiously, they climbed back up again, then had a look around through the periscope. All seemed clear, so Suhren ordered them to surface once more. Another quick look around, but the aircraft had vanished – and, frustratingly, so had the convoy. A moment later, however, they spotted another aircraft, so down they went again, Suhren cursing as they did so. 'Up and down the whole time,' he noted. 'It's like being in a lift! These fiendish air-patrols of the Allies.'

And that was not the end of it. Some time after midnight, they eventually spotted the convoy again, but by first light they were once more being harried by Allied aircraft and forced to dive. During the day they had to dive to avoid aircraft twice more, each one taking at least a quarter of an hour and threatening their chances of ever getting in position to attack. This was a game of patience that required nerves of steel; Suhren found his were beginning to be stretched, made worse by the fatigue of spending too long on the bridge, keeping an eagle-eyed watch.

After three days shadowing the convoy unsuccessfully, another U-boat joined them just after dusk. This was *U-751*. They were closing once more when yet again an aircraft came over, this time with a powerful search-light underneath it. As Suhren was leaping down the hatch of the conning tower and they began to dive yet again, he glimpsed the cone of light catch the other U-boat. 'No more was seen or heard of the other boat after that,' he wrote. 'Whether it survived this particular encounter I don't know, but it remained unaccounted for.'

Finally, on this fourth night of the chase, *U-564* overtook the convoy and Suhren brought her into position to attack, manoeuvring between the outer column of merchantmen and the escorts. Suhren stopped the diesels and waited. The tension was immense. No one said a word. The only sound from the boat was the crew's breathing. An escort swung out and, astern of him, Suhren now turned the boat until he was at long last in a good position to fire. At 800 metres, the first freighter slid into view and the first three torpedo tubes were fired, then a fourth torpedo as the fourth ship in line passed into view. Diesels back on, and they were away, full ahead, when they heard first one, then two detonations. 'At the same moment, all hell breaks loose behind us,' noted Suhren. 'Red, green and yellow jets of flame whizz through the air. A fireball of unimaginable size lights up the night and makes the ship stand out in silhouette.' But not for long: munitions exploding made the ship disintegrate moments later. The pressure-wave from the explosion swept over while an orgy of colours in the sky was reflected brightly on the water. Flying debris rained down on them, smacking into the sea around them. Suhren ordered the crew down, but he remained on the bridge, mesmerized. He had never seen anything like it.

Suhren had won that particular battle, but there was now only a narrow gap mid-Atlantic where the Allies had no air cover. The slaughter off the Americas was drawing to an end, as Dönitz had known it would, as a comprehensive convoy system came into being and as air patrols grew. Around Britain and south of Iceland, it was now almost impossible for U-boats to attack, such was the range of air cover. In addition to the flying boats and medium bombers, RAF Coastal Command had a squadron of Very Long Range (VLR) B-24 Liberators, four-engine US-built bombers that they used to very good effect.

New technology was transforming Coastal Command's ability to sink U-boats too. A much-improved radar, a 10cm set with very high definition, was entering service, as had, in May, a 250lb depth charge with a 25-foot setting – lethal for those U-boats caught on the surface. Another new addition was the searchlights, known as Leigh Lights, that had located and bathed *U-751*. On 12 June, Dönitz ordered his crews now to remain submerged until 12 degrees west – a further drain on time and fuel. In all, twelve U-boats were sunk on patrol that July, half of them by aircraft, the highest monthly score yet for the Allied air forces.

Teddy Suhren and his crew in *U-564* did eventually reach Caribbean waters and managed to sink a further three ships there, but with American shipping now in convoy and with the American planes also flying ever-increasing numbers of anti-submarine patrols, the second 'Happy Time' was now emphatically over. Even more ominous for Dönitz's U-boats was that, for the first time since the war had begun, the amount of new shipping being launched had overtaken losses to U-boats. In the Battle of the Atlantic, another crucial corner had been turned.

'Mersa Matruh fell yesterday,' Rommel wrote to his wife on 30 June, 'after which the Army moved on until late in the night. We're already sixty miles to the east. Less than 100 miles to Alexandria!'

Since the end of May, Eighth Army had now lost 50 per cent of its fighting force killed, wounded or captured. The Panzerarmee Afrika, on the other hand, had made good 50 per cent of its material losses with captured British equipment. In Cairo, panic gripped GHQ and staff officers began burning papers in what became known as 'the Flap'.

Just as the German war machine had appeared unstoppable to so many in the first years of the war, so Rommel's Panzerarmee appeared unstoppable now. The reality, however, was somewhat different after more than five weeks of debilitating battle and long, difficult charges across the desert whilst under constant attack from the RAF.

'Rock, wastes, arid, barren, desolate terrain interspersed with patches of sand,' wrote Oberst Fritz Bayerlein, the Afrikakorps Chief of Staff, 'where meagre clumps of desert thorn grow, where the African sun burns down mercilessly in July – that was the Alamein Front.' He had just thirteen battle-worthy tanks left in all the DAK and the only fresh-water well in the entire desolate area lay in the hands of the British. Overall, Rommel's supply situation was desperate despite the booty he had acquired. The 90th Light had only 1,000 motorized troops left; it should have had over 15,000. Overall, he had more than 300 guns, but his supply lines were horrendously stretched. Tobruk harbour was wrecked, the railway was no use because there was not a single working locomotive on the line and his stocks of water, fuel and ammunition were rapidly running out. Bayerlein was always, at heart, a realist, and in his heart he felt this was likely to be a nut that was simply too hard to crack.

None the less, in the early hours of 1 July, Rommel launched his attack on the Alamein position. By 3 July it was clear his attempt to batter his way through had failed. In the south, the freshly arrived New Zealand Division had shown particularly determined resistance, destroying the Italian Ariete Division's artillery.

With his divisions down to an average of just 1,500 men, a tenth of their strength, he was forced to call it off. All that momentum, all those dreams of glory, had been suddenly dashed – from triumph to bitter disappointment in what seemed like a click of the fingers. In truth, it underlined the Panzerarmee's persistent shortcomings: that they had never really had enough supplies to do the job in the first place, even before the attack on the Gazala Line. In this, the Panzerarmee was mirroring the overriding problem with both Germany's and Italy's wider war effort: a lack of resources, especially when compared with the Allies. Their forces might show some tactical flair and win a battle or two, but was that ever going to win them the war? 'Things are not going as well as I should like them,' Rommel told his wife. 'Resistance is too great and our strength exhausted.'

That Eighth Army had managed to make it successfully to the Alamein Line and regain some kind of balance was largely down to the brilliance, heroism and superb handling of the Desert Air Force.

While the Army commanders had been losing their heads, AVM Coningham had steadfastly held on to his. Air Commodore Tommy Elmhirst had always thought highly of him, but these past few weeks had been the first time he had seen him tested in battle. 'Mary's handling of the air battle was superb,' noted Elmhirst. 'He used his smaller and less modern air force with fine judgement which produced its maximum offensive effort.' He had pushed his men hard, but Elmhirst had seen for himself that the morale and fighting spirit of the Desert Air Force remained high. Billy Drake certainly thought Coningham a 'bloody good commander.' His authority and judgement were also unquestioned. As Elmhirst pointed out, while Coningham always listened to others' views, 'when the orders went out at night for the next day's fighting, there was never any question of discussion.'

During the retreat from the Gazala Line, the DAF had been fortunate that many of the Luftwaffe's bombers had been diverted to intercept an attempted convoy to Malta, but once Eighth Army was in full retreat, Coningham's force was very possibly the difference between Eighth

Army's survival and annihilation. Fritz Bayerlein certainly thought so. 'The Royal Air Force,' he noted, 'had reached unprecedented heights of strength and combat effectiveness. Against it, the air power of Kesselring gradually melted away . . . We were constantly menaced by the Royal Air Force.'

For this, Elmhirst was as responsible as Coningham, for it was he who had put the plans in place to enable the Desert Air Force to move back and forth rapidly. All the various fighter and bomber wings were split into two parties so that pilots, aircrew and aircraft would never be out of action and would be able to operate, at a push, for a couple of days with only half their men and equipment, while the other half was moving forward or backward to a new location. The two parties would then swap roles.

This leap-frogging began on 15 June and the workload of Billy Drake's 112 Squadron was typical of the fighter squadrons during these days. On that day, for example, they carried out thirty-four sorties, attacking the forward columns of 21. Panzer and scoring 'three flamers and 34 severely damaged vehicles.' In the evening, A Flight moved back to LG – landing ground – 75, while B Flight remained at Gambut. On 16 June, Coningham told Tedder, 'I have prepared landing grounds all the way back to the frontier and plan is steady withdrawal of squadrons keeping about twenty miles away from the enemy.'

It was also drummed into every man that absolutely nothing should be left behind for the enemy. Any aircraft unfit for service but flyable was flung into the air and taken to the next landing ground. One air-craft, for example, flew without its instrument panel. Others were towed by trucks, and only those that could not be moved were torched. One wing managed to salvage 260,000 gallons of fuel and 300 bombs, the last trucks heading off east as shells began falling around them.

Ground crews had been stripped of much of their equipment to enable them to move at a moment's notice. The aircrews were being pushed hard, but so too were the ground crews, working through the nights to keep up a high level of serviceability – in fact, as much as 80 per cent of the front-line strength was maintained most of the time through servicing on the spot and bringing up new replacements.

By 25 June, Coningham had begun round-the-clock bombing. Every hour of the day, the Panzerarmee was pounded by bombers and strafed by fighters. At night, Wellingtons, led by naval Albacores armed with flares, went out to bomb Axis columns and leaguers. That day, for example, 112 Squadron escorted bombers three times and carried out eight missions of their own, then the following day broke the record for the number of sorties flown by a fighter squadron – sixty-nine – in a day. Each pilot had flown five or six missions. The Desert Air Force was fighting at an intensity that far exceeded the hardest days of the Battle of Britain. On 3 July, the DAF chalked up no fewer than 1,000 sorties; in contrast, the Luftwaffe managed just 203. This was an astonishing number – flying was exhausting, but combat flying especially so – and demonstrated an extraordinary determination and level of commitment.

Just as superb organization, planning and the commitment of the men involved had taken the German panzer divisions to victory in France two summers earlier, so the same was working for the British as Eighth Army tumbled back to the Alamein Line. As Rommel's failure to break through the line showed, the gargantuan effort of the RAF had paid off. The Luftwaffe, by contrast, was lagging far behind the Axis forces on the ground, meaning time over target was at a minimum. Nor was their maintenance anything like as efficient as that devised by Tommy Elmhirst: the Luftwaffe could rarely fly at more than 50 per cent levels of serviceability. Rommel's advance had thus been carried out without much of the air support he had enjoyed in the opening stages of the fighting. One German artillery unit operating at full strength before the fall of Tobruk could barely move six days later. In a captured diary, a German officer described an attack by the RAF. 'It was then that I became really conscious of the horrors of war,' he had written. 'Tommy fired on us well into the night. We have had many attacks, but these bombs were the worst I have ever experienced.'

CHAPTER 20

Thousand Bomber Raid

B ACK IN BRITAIN, General Alan Brooke and Air Chief Marshal Sir
Charles Portal had been having an increasingly acrimonious spat
about the use of air power, with the Chief of the Imperial General Staff
arguing vehemently for a separate Army air arm independent of the
RAF. Portal had rebuffed such a suggestion, arguing there were not
anything like enough aircraft operating to justify such a move and
pointing out the by now well-trodden argument that airmen, rather than
soldiers, were the best placed to judge how air forces should most
effectively be used. Coningham's men had certainly proved that point
very clearly.

Things were also looking up for Bomber Command. At the end of
May, Air Marshal Harris had launched the first-ever Thousand Bomber
Raid against Cologne. Although the daily numbers in his squadrons had
still been only around 400, by scouring Training Command and
borrowing 250 aircraft from Coastal Command, as well as using aircraft
that really were almost obsolete, he had managed to reach the magic
1,000 mark – 1,047 to be precise. It was a high-risk *coup de théâtre*, but
one that proved, on the whole, pretty successful, inflicting heavy damage
on an important target. The German High Command had been pleasingly
appalled – in fact, as early as the end of April, well before the raid, they
had already been muttering to the Italian delegation at Salzburg about
the effects of bomb damage.

Most importantly, the raid was a terrific public-relations success,
which is exactly what Harris had hoped. Headlines about it were splashed

all over British newspapers. In her diary, Gwladys Cox excitedly quoted London's *Evening Standard*. '"This is the most glorious First of June in all our island's annals,"' it claimed, 'and all because "some 1,000 young British pilots have thwarted Hitler's strategy anew."' '1,500 PLANES IN BIGGEST RAID,' pronounced the *Daily Mirror*. '3,000 TONS BOMB STORM'. 'German radio began to wail last night about the great RAF raid on Cologne,' it added gleefully. 'A special transmission from Cologne said: "Much misery had come over our town."' That papers like the *Mirror* were blatantly exaggerating didn't bother Harris one jot. Two more similar raids followed in the ensuing weeks and, although it was not something Harris could mount regularly, they did much to stop the back-sniping and show all concerned that Bomber Command could, after all, pose a serious threat to Germany's war machine.

Harris was also now receiving increased numbers of two exciting new aircraft. The first was the twin-engine de Havilland Mosquito, which had been conceived as a light and very fast bomber but was proving its use in other ways as a reconnaissance and even fighter aircraft. Most, however, were heading straight to Bomber Command and, because they were largely – and incredibly – built of wood and had a maximum speed of over 400 mph, they were not only immune to most radar, but there was no German plane that could catch them. With the potential to carry bombs as well as cannons and machine guns, the Mosquito was a highly versatile and extremely fine aircraft.

The machine that Harris wanted as his workhorse, however, was the Avro Lancaster, which back in April had already dropped the war's first 8,000lb bomb. Numbers were only slowly rising, but gradually Harris was able to increase those squadrons now equipped with this big bomber. His aim was for the whole of 5 Group to be equipped with Lancasters and he was keenly aware that until then, and until navigational aids improved, little meaningful damage could be inflicted on Germany.

These difficulties and the logistical issues of converting a squadron of four-man crews into one of seven was just one of the challenges facing Guy Gibson, who was now a Wing Commander and the CO of 106 Squadron, one of the squadrons currently converting from the troublesome twin-engine Avro Manchester to the bigger and better four-engine Lancaster.

Gibson's Lancasters arrived five at a time from the Avro plant at Woodford near Manchester, flown in by the Air Transport Auxiliary

(ATA). Harris was planning to set up special Heavy Conversion Units, but Gibson and his squadron – which, including staff and ground crew, amounted to around 800 men – were to convert and train themselves. He was twenty-three.

Also still new to Bomber Command was a navigational device called GEE, first tested the previous year. This was a radar pulse system that enabled a navigator on board an aircraft to fix his position by measuring the distance of pulses from three different ground stations in England. It was hoped this would massively improve navigation and thus, in turn, bombing accuracy, but it was not proving as accurate as scientists had hoped. The Ruhr industrial heartland was about the limit of its range and it was nothing like good enough to aid blind flying. This meant Harris's bombers were still largely dependent on clear skies and preferably a half-decent moon – but that in turn made them easier targets for German flak-gunners and night-fighters. Furthermore, by the summer of 1942, as scientific and technological developments on one side were repeatedly answered on the other, the Germans had successfully worked out how to effectively jam GEE. As the British had trumped *Knickebein*, so the Germans had found an answer to Harris's latest navigational leap forward.

Although 106 Squadron contributed eleven aircraft to the Thousand Bomber Raid, Gibson was ill, much to his frustration, and so missed it. After recuperation and leave, he finally flew his first combat operation in a Lancaster on the night of 8/9 July. 'I'm always terrified every time I go on ops,' he later confessed to a fellow pilot. Standing around the crew rooms before the flight was the worst part. 'It's a horrible business,' Gibson wrote. 'Your stomach feels as though it wants to hit your backbone. You can't stand still.' He found he would smoke far too many cigarettes, laugh too loudly, and sometimes had to go to the lavatory because he felt sick. Somehow, once he was in the cockpit with the engines running, ready to take off, he felt better. 'Then it's all right. Just another job.'

That night, they attacked Wilhelmshaven, one of 285 aircraft. 'Very dark but good,' Gibson jotted in his logbook. 'Bombed from 12,000 feet. Bombs fell in dock areas but not sure whether submarine yards were hit. Opposition fairly accurate.' They had not hit the U-boat yards, as it happened. Rather, reports suggested damage to the dockyard buildings, a department store and a number of houses. Some twenty-five were killed and a further 170 injured. This rather insignificant return from so much effort underlined the problem of strategic bombing nearly three years into the war: that what was needed was very many more big aircraft with better means of achieving bombing accuracy.

The Thousand Bomber Raid had done severe damage to both the reputation of Germany's night-fighters and the Luftwaffe leadership. At the time of the attack on Cologne, Göring was entertaining Milch and Speer at Burg Veldenstein, his childhood home near Nuremburg, and that night he was rung personally by Hitler, who told him the Cologne Gauleiter – governor – had reported hundreds of bombers over the city. How could this be, Hitler wanted to know. Göring assured him the Gauleiter was mistaken – only seventy had come over, he told the Führer blithely; in truth, he had no idea. The following morning, Göring learned that around forty had been shot down, which then looked like a big victory until London announced that over a thousand bombers had indeed raided Cologne. When Hitler confronted him, Göring squirmed that this was a lie, and ordered Jeschonnek to play along. 'It is out of the question,' Hitler told his own staff, 'that only seventy or eighty bombers attacked. I never capitulate to an unpleasant truth. I must see clearly if I am to draw the proper conclusions.' That was rubbish, but it was also neither here nor there. Göring's and the Luftwaffe's reputation had taken a big dent.

Despite this, Milch's overhaul of aircraft production was going reasonably well. He had successfully removed Willi Messerschmitt from managerial control and had stopped the cosy up-front payments for air-craft delivery. This had been disastrous for the Heinkel company, which had enabled Milch to push Ernst Heinkel into a purely development role too. Junker was also brought under tighter financial control, which meant that three of the major aircraft producers, previously rather errant, un-focused and hugely wasteful, were now directly under Milch's eagle eye.

He had also put in a number of rationalization measures, which had seen production numbers rise while consumption of aluminium had stayed the same. Fighter production, for example, had risen from just over 200 a month at the end of 1941 to 349 per month by June – a trend that would continue to rise. None the less, Milch was still saddled with some projects that he could do little about. Aircraft, from first drawings to large-scale production, took about four years, and so in the middle of

1942 the Luftwaffe was still dealing with planes that had first been brought to the table before the war.

The Heinkel 177, for example, had not gone away, but was still being tinkered with and tweaked because it was too late to start afresh on a completely new four-engine bomber. Göring had only finally seen this monster in May on a visit to the aircraft-testing base at Rechlin and had been horrified to learn that its four engines had been coupled, one on top of the other, so that each pair powered one propeller. Incredibly, until then the C-in-C of the Luftwaffe had not known about this feature on the only major heavy bomber being developed. 'How is such an engine to be serviced on the airfields?' he railed. 'I believe I am right in saying you cannot even take out the sparking plugs without pulling the engine apart!' A few weeks later, on a visit with Speer to the Peenemünde research establishment, they saw an He177 taking off on a test flight with 4 tons of bombs. Soon after, it banked to the starboard, side-slipped and blew up. A coupling had broken on the propeller shaft.

There had also been problems with the FW190's engine, the BMW 801D, and with the Me109G's Daimler-Benz DB605. By the summer, these were being ironed out, but it meant the build-up of the Luftwaffe was still not as fast as Milch, Göring or Hitler would have liked. Milch was not only deeply shaken by the first Thousand Bomber Raid, but was also obsessed with production figures from Britain and the threat of American mass production. The attack on Cologne had given him a stark indication of what was to come. 'Comparison of German aircraft production with the figures available to us from Britain,' he told Göring in June, 'shows that the British are making both more bombers and fighters than we are.' Göring was dumbfounded.

With this inevitable bomber onslaught coming, it was the defence of the Reich that now dominated Milch's thoughts on strategy. Protecting Germany adequately was taken very seriously by the Luftwaffe High Command and the dressing-down Göring had received following the Thousand Bomber Raid had demonstrated that in this they were not alone. Luftwaffe flak units had in fact been fewer at the beginning of 1942 than they had been six months earlier due to the heavy losses over the Eastern Front. However, from April, improvements were made as concentrations of three flak batteries were attached to one radar detection unit, and by increasing the number of guns per battery from four to six for heavies, twelve to fifteen for light, with from nine to twelve searchlights per searchlight battery. Furthermore, heavy guns were gradually being upgraded from the 10.5cm models to the much harder-hitting and more powerful 12.8cm, which had a much bigger burst range, and from the 150cm models to 200cm. Overall, numbers of flak units would rise by 35 per cent in 1942 and within the Luftwaffe Command Centre, based in Berlin and responsible for the defence of the Reich, there were eight 'Air Districts', which included 838 heavy flak batteries in all and 538 medium and light flak batteries. That amounted to over 13,000 guns. Already, then, Bomber Command was making an impact, for that was a lot of German guns and manpower that were not being used at the front.

While the Luftwaffe was growing its flak defences, the night-fighters under General Josef Kammhuber had continued to achieve some notable successes, and none more than Helmut Lent. By May, he had thirty night victories to his name as well as a Knight's Cross, and was also now commander of his own *Gruppe*, II/NJG2, feted by Hitler and Göring and known throughout the Reich as the leading night-fighter ace. Like Guy Gibson, he had still been only twenty-three years old when he took command of the *Gruppe* back in January.

The Thousand Bomber Raid, however, had also underlined the need to improve radar both on the ground and in the air, as well as to increase the number of night-fighters, as Kammhuber had been repeatedly urging since the summer of 1940. The *Himmelbett* system used on the so-called Kammhuber Line worked because a night-fighter could be vectored to a lone enemy bomber in any one zone at a time. Back in England, Dr R. V. Jones, who had earlier cracked the *Knickebein* and *X-Gerät* beam systems, now worked out that if bombers crossed over into occupied Europe using the same route and in quick succession, not only would collisions be minimized but the *Himmelbett* zone over which they crossed would quickly become overwhelmed and no longer work – as Lent discovered on the night of the first Thousand Bomber Raid. Although he had been one of those who had taken off to intercept the attack on Cologne, even he had been unable to engage a single bomber. This new tactic by Bomber Command was known as the 'bomber stream'.

New radar and navigation technology was being developed in Germany, however. A 'giant' Würzburg radar had started to come into service, as had an improved Freya known as a Mammut. Both were essentially the same as earlier models but with larger reflectors, which gave them increased range. A further radar, the Wassermann, was the finest early-warning radar that had yet been developed anywhere in the world, with a range of some 150 miles and fully rotational. Finally, in early 1942, the Lichtenstein onboard radar set came into service. With a maximum range of 2 miles and minimum of 200 yards, Kammhuber had hoped this would be a crucial piece of equipment and had urged Hitler to give Lichtenstein the highest priority in production.

The first four sets were fitted to some of Helmut Lent's aircraft at Leeuwarden, where its shortcomings quickly became apparent. For Lichtenstein to work, large aerials and reflectors had to be added to the nose of the aircraft, which acted as an airbrake and badly affected the machine's handling. Most pilots, like Lent, would rather stick to the system of improved ground radar and being vectored to the target by ground controllers. Certainly he was managing just fine without Lichtenstein – in June 1942, he flew ten combat sorties and shot down nine, including a Halifax destroyed during a raid on Bremen. 'Once again, God mercifully looked after me when I was in action,' Lent wrote in a letter to his parents. 'The 40th was a hard, four-engined nut to crack. Praise be to God, he didn't succeed in dropping his bombs on Germany. He was forced to jettison them, and I was able to see just what the monsters can carry. Down below, a path of high explosives and incendiaries a kilometre long flared up.'

In the air, out at sea and on land too, British and German forces continued to battle it out that summer of 1942. In North Africa, however, the British had managed to avert annihilation. Along the Alamein Line, deadlock had been reached. After Rommel had put his Panzerarmee on to the defensive, the Auk had twice tried to turn the tables and break the position, but each time the Axis forces had held. Now, both sides were exhausted.

Eighth Army had been saved and the deep crisis at the beginning of the month had passed. None the less, while to the Germans it was clear that Rommel had once again overreached his forces, to the British it was also clear that change was needed. The first six months of 1942 had thrown a succession of bitter and humiliating blows at the British war effort. That trend needed to be reversed, and quickly.

Left: Hitler made it clear the war against the Soviet Union was an ideological one and told his commanders to fight without mercy. Villages were burned and the vast number of prisoners – more than they had anticipated – were treated appallingly.

Below: Operation BARBAROSSA was even more of a gamble than that of the attack on the West in May 1940, but to begin with, as hundreds of thousands of prisoners were swiftly captured, German commanders were confident victory was within their grasp.

Below: Meanwhile, British and Free French forces won the campaign in Syria against the Vichy French. In so doing, they made the Middle East more secure and, with the capture of Syrian airfields, rather cancelled out any benefits the Germans had gained from their costly victory on Crete.

Above: General Wavell (*centre*), with de Gaulle and Général Catroux (*right*). Tensions were already rising with the proud and temperamental Free French leader.

Above: The movie star Douglas Fairbanks Jr, who joined the US Navy and served in the Atlantic, Mediterranean and on the Arctic convoys. Even Hollywood was expected to play its part in this war.

Above: Another film star caught up in the conflict was the French actress Corinne Luchaire. She had links to Allies and Nazis alike.

Above: President Roosevelt and Prime Minister Winston Churchill meet for the first time as leaders at Placentia Bay. The Atlantic Charter they both signed that August was another important step on America's road to war and confirmed the US Navy's involvement in the Battle of the Atlantic.

Left: The US destroyer *Reuben James*, sunk by *U-552* commanded by Erich Topp. The first American warship to be sunk in the war, two months before Pearl Harbor, caused outrage in the United States and even prompted a song by the folk singer Woodie Guthrie.

Below left: In July 1942, General Claude Auchinleck, known as 'the Auk', was appointed as British C-in-C in the Middle East. He was expected to put the British swiftly back on the right footing in North Africa.

Below right: By October 1942 huge numbers of Soviet prisoners were still being captured, but after the three months the German command had predicted for defeating the USSR, victory was still well out of reach and what's more it had begun to rain. By this time, the wheels were literally coming off the German advance.

Left: A stripped-down 15-cwt truck like that used by Albert Martin (**above**) and his colleagues in 2nd Rifle Brigade.

Above: Home for these Afrikakorps soldiers was a towed wooden wagon roughly camouflaged.

Right: A Panzer Mk III. It was a myth that German tanks were superior to those of the British.

Left: The shock Japanese attack on Pearl Harbor finally brought the United States officially into the war and turned it into a truly global conflict.

Above: The view from a Heinkel 111 bomber over the Eastern Front. By the beginning of 1942, the Luftwaffe was in crisis and severely overstretched. It was the one arm of the Wehrmacht that had been in action almost continually.

Right and below: The German advance in the East was becoming increasingly bogged down. Still heavily under-mechanized, the vehicles they did have were breaking down. As the snow began to fall, they were as dependent on horses as Napoleon's army had been 130 years earlier.

Above: Hermann Balck, who was promoted to general in 1942.

Right: Feldmarschall Guderian, the genius of the Blitzkrieg, but sacked for disagreeing with Hitler in December 1941.

Above: The many unremarkable faces of Agent 24, the Norwegian Gunnar Sønsteby.

Below left: Jens-Anton Poulsson, one of the Norwegian leaders of the successful attack on the Vemork heavy-water plant.

Below right: The leader of the French resistance group Combat, Henri Frenay.

Above: The Axis did their best to neutralize the tiny but strategically important outpost of Malta. The bombing caused terrible damage, but the island never ceased entirely as an offensive base. The Axis failure to capture it would come back to haunt them.

Above: Rommel pauses to talk with his troops, Oberst Fritz Bayerlein beside him.

Left: General Ritchie (*centre*) scratches his head as he confers with his senior commanders. Hopelessly out of his depth, he commanded Eighth Army to the most embarrassing and unnecessary defeat of the war in the West.

Above: Walter Mazzacuto.

Right: Count Galeazzo Ciano, Mussolini's son-in-law, Italian Foreign Minister and increasingly at odds with his German allies.

Left: Billy Drake, one of the tough and imperturbable young fighter commanders now leading the squadrons of the Desert Air Force. The RAF was led as brilliantly as Eighth Army was poorly in the Gazala battles and the retreat to Alamein.

Below: Jean-Mathieu Boris, one of the many Free French who fought heroically at Bir Hacheim.

CHAPTER 21

Sea and Steppe

AROUND 2.30 A.M., Sunday, 19 July 1942. Kapitän Teddy Suhren stood on the bridge of *U-564* as first one then two explosions ripped through the night sky some 800 yards away. Red, green and yellow jets of flame flashed into the air, followed by a huge, rolling fireball, which lit up the sky like daylight, silhouetting not only the two stricken vessels, but much of convoy OS34 from Liverpool to Freetown in West Africa – supplies that were heading to the North Africa front.

Two ships had been hit, but it was the *Empire Hawksbill* that was now literally disintegrating before his eyes. All thirty-seven members of her crew and nine gunners were incinerated in the massive fireball. Now the pressure-wave from the explosion swept up towards the U-boat, as a mass of colours continued to light the sky and reflect in the inky Atlantic. 'Flying debris rains down from even more explosions,' wrote Suhren, 'smacks into the sea all around us, and makes fountains of water shoot up a metre high.' Suhren had already sent the crew down below and ordered the U-boat to speed away as swiftly as possible. In all his long years as a submariner, he had never seen anything like this; he found it curiously mesmerizing and could not bring himself to leave the bridge.

Then suddenly, black as a raven, a frigate swept past between them and the burning ship. Immediately, Suhren shouted down to the official photographer from the Propagandakompanien der Wehrmact, who had been forced upon him for the trip.

'PK man!' he shouted. 'Quick, quick, to the bridge!'

To his horror, however, instead of the photographer poking his head up, he heard air escaping from the dive chambers and realized the boat was starting to dip at the bow. What the devil was going on? Realizing they were starting to dive, he quickly clambered into the conning tower and only managed to pull down the hatch as a wave of water sloshed over him.

'Have you all taken leave of your senses?' Suhren yelled at the Navigating Officer. 'Whose job is it to give the alarm on board?'

'But, Boss,' stammered the man, looking completely taken aback, 'you gave the order yourself.'

Suhren now realized what had happened. Calling down 'PK man' had been misheard as 'Alarm'. He was still annoyed, but chose to take it out on the photographer instead. 'You stand around and get under everyone's feet,' he yelled, 'but if there is anything out of the ordinary to film, you're nowhere to be found.' It would have been, Suhren told him, the scoop of the war.

Meanwhile, they had now dived to around 100 metres when in the silence of the boat they heard the sound of propellers overhead and moments later the ASDIC began to ping, ping, ping rapidly. Suhren turned to the *Leitender Ingenieur* (LI), or Chief Engineer.

'Flying shit,' he said, 'they've found us. LI, down to 150 metres.'

From the listening room, reports were stated calmly, quietly. More than one ship was hunting them. A noise like a broom with iron bristles as one of the vessels swept overhead from astern. Three corvettes. Suhren couldn't understand why they hadn't attacked, and then in almost the same moment there were five explosions, not so very far away. *These damn depth charges*, thought Suhren, *they get more and more dangerous.* But *U-564* seemed to be all right – no leaks.

'Listening room,' said Suhren now, 'in a few minutes they'll attack again. To judge by the prop noise, they're coming from astern. When the escorts get close, let me know at once. LI, as soon as he makes his report, full ahead and hard to port. Pull the boat up then, and as soon as we're at 60 metres, blow tanks. Yes, don't look so worried; we'll chance it. We're going to surface and go for it. I'm not just going to sit here and get hammered.'

On cue, five more depth charges exploded a few minutes later, but further behind them this time, and now the boat was rising, as though pulled by a string. Suhren stood under the hatch and, as they surfaced, he opened it up and looked out. The freighter was still burning but he could see the three corvettes and it was clear they hadn't spotted them. The diesels fired up noisily and they were off, the distance growing. In no time they were doing 16 knots, but to get a bit more speed Suhren ordered the electric motors on as well.

They had now been seen and flares were fired, lighting them up. Beside Suhren, the 2WO ducked automatically. A star shell burst, casting another swathe of light before fading, then pitch blackness descended once more. More star shells followed, but the U-boat was now speeding away at 17 knots, too fast for the pursuing corvettes. Suhren was just beginning to breathe more easily when, to his horror, he realized the diesels were stopping and thick black smoke was coming from the hatch.

'Boat unfit to dive,' reported the LI.

'What do you mean, "unfit to dive"?' called down Suhren. 'Alarm! We must dive – there is no alternative. Take her down and let's get away.'

They managed to get her to dive, but as Suhren returned back down the tower he could not see his hand in front of his face; the boat was in darkness and everyone was coughing and choking. He couldn't under-stand why the emergency lights hadn't come on. Pressing a handkerchief over his mouth, he now heard, as they all did, the tell-tale sound of propellers again. Suhren looked up – they were right on top of them now – but then, mercifully, they swept on past until eventually the ping, ping, ping of the ASDIC was barely audible at all.

Playing safe, Suhren kept them down another quarter of an hour, then surfaced. The Atlantic was now still and clear once more: they had got away with it.

The emergency lighting flickered on and, with the hatch open and ventilators on, the smoke soon cleared, although it left a black film on everything. Suhren demanded an explanation, but the LI was unable to help; it was the mechanic who revealed all.

It turned out an oily rag had been left on a ledge above a bend in the exhaust pipe. With all the twisting and turning from taking evasive action, it had fallen off on to the exhaust pipe, which by then had been glowing red hot. The rag caught fire and fell into the bilge, where a fair amount of oil was swilling around; it caught fire in turn and developed into a full-scale blaze. They were able to open the ventilation valve, which flooded the bilge and put the fire out, but only with a mass of smoke filling the boat. One small oily rag had very nearly done for them all.

As it was, they had survived, and with two more sinkings to their names. Rather than point fingers, Suhren decided instead to hold a 'coffee party' regardless of the tight crew rations and to make a small speech. 'It's perfectly clear to me,' he told them, 'that God didn't just have a hand in this but an entire arm.' Everyone had kept their cool, no one had panicked and the LI had handled the boat in an exemplary way. 'It was,' he told them, 'a remarkable achievement. Now I can celebrate our success with the rest of the crew – even the mutton-head who left his cleaning rags on the ledge.' He was, he told them, proud of them all.

What he hadn't told them, however, was that this was to be his last combat patrol. After this, his sixth in command of *U-564*, he was to be given a rest and then to become one of Dönitz's trainers. Suhren, like his friend and fellow commander Erich Topp, had done enough; it was time for them to pass on their experience and expertise.

Even so, as the night's drama had reminded him all too clearly, serving in a U-boat was a dangerous occupation and becoming more so as Allied ASW technology steadily improved. And for Suhren and his crew, there were still many long days to go before this patrol was over.

For all the new technology, however, much still rested on human judgement, and for the British there was more terrible folly of leadership to come – this time at sea – which would add to the humiliations and tragedies of the Far East and the failure at Gazala.

Convoy PQ17 to Murmansk and Archangel, consisting of thirty-five merchant vessels, had sailed from Iceland on 27 June carrying 300 precious aircraft, 600 tanks, 4,000 trucks and trailers, and enough materiel to equip a force of 50,000 men. It was the biggest convoy ever sent to Russia, on what was already proving an extremely hazardous supply route. In winter, conditions were so bad a man would freeze to death in the water in seconds. By summer, the cover of darkness had gone; in June, there was daylight every hour of the day and the convoy route was within reach of the Luftwaffe.

To protect it was a naval force of two British and two US cruisers and three US destroyers, while the British Home Fleet had also sailed in support of the operation and was trailing it some 200 miles behind. On board the US heavy cruiser *Wichita* was Lieutenant Douglas Fairbanks, Jr, who had been asked by Admiral Giffen to carry out the same role he had performed on *Wasp* – that of report-writer and observer.

Unbeknown to those in the convoy, it had been quickly picked up and trailed by a U-boat and Admiral Dönitz swiftly dispatched two more. Icy fog protected the convoy as it inched its way across the Arctic, but then on 2 July it cleared and the first air attacks started. Late on the 3rd, Fairbanks recorded a signal that had been received: 'At 1900,' he noted, 'an Admiralty message, just broken down, confirms our previous report: the *Tirpitz*, the *Hipper*, and four large German destroyers have left Trondheim.'

Back at the Admiralty in London, the First Sea Lord, Admiral Dudley Pound, had already warned the escorts about the possibility of the German surface fleet emerging from the Norwegian fjords – it was a risk they faced with every PQ convoy – and had told them categorically not to engage any German force that included *Tirpitz*. Rather, should it venture out, they were to shadow it and try to lead it to an interception with the Home Fleet.

Now, Ultra decrypts suggested *Tirpitz* was on the move, which, as far as Pound was concerned, could mean only one thing: that the German battleship and other surface fleet had left port, would evade the Home Fleet, then soon catch up and slaughter the convoy.

Meanwhile, the convoy had been making good progress, and not until 4 July did the German attacks press home with much success. That afternoon, some twenty-five bombers arrived, including one piloted by Major Hajo Herrmann, now a *Gruppe* commander and operating from Kemi in northern Finland. There was cloud about as he and his men dived. They descended lower and lower, emerging into the clear from under the blanket of cloud. 'Small black, brown, and grey bursts of smoke on our starboard hand,' noted Fairbanks, 'are seen like sudden splatters of mud against an eggshell sky. Seconds later we hear the sound of gunfire. A new attack is on.' Then he spotted what looked like 'small fast bugs skimming just above the waterline.'

These skimming bugs were Herrmann and his *Gruppe* of Ju88s. They dropped their bombs, then swiftly climbed back into the sun, leaving the smooth white sheet of cloud over the convoy below them. 'Suddenly,' wrote Herrmann, 'it was pierced by a dark-coloured cumulus, which rose high into the sky as if from a fire-spewing volcano.' This was one of three ships that were hit.

Another attack developed later in the evening; by now two ships had been sunk and a third damaged. From the bridge of *Wichita*, Fairbanks breathlessly recorded: '1829: A plane is falling in flames – it crashes near us! Great blinding flash of fire – seems hundreds of feet high – then black smoke. Big cheer from *Wichita* crew. We think we are responsible. Now the cry, "Go get the bastards!" More explosions and the sickening "whoosh" of the fire. Looks like a merchant ship is hit badly. Fat smoke curling skyward. Another Nazi plane dives in flames.'

Then suddenly, when everything seemed to be under control, a signal arrived ordering the escort force to withdraw westwards. This was followed twelve minutes later by a further Admiralty signal: 'Because of threats from main enemy surface forces, Convoy PQ17 is to disperse and proceed to Russian ports.'

Fairbanks and all aboard *Wichita* were gobsmacked, but assumed *Tirpitz* must be about to appear at any moment. Without their knowing, Pound had called an emergency meeting of his operations staff and asked each one in turn what they would do in light of the limited intelligence they had about *Tirpitz* having left port. To a man, they were against dispersal, although Vice-Admiral Sir Henry Moore suggested that if they were going to order the convoy to scatter it was best not to waste any time. In fact, Pound had already made up his mind. And so the fateful order was given.

In fact, *Tirpitz* was not at sea; rather, had been merely moving berths. Why Pound acted in the way he did – why, frankly, he panicked – has never been understood. It has been suggested he was already suffering from the brain tumour that would kill him the following autumn; others have thought he was in the midst of some kind of breakdown. At any rate, it was the wrong order – a catastrophic decision.

'We hate leaving PQ17 behind,' noted Fairbanks. 'It looks so helpless now since the order to scatter came through. The ships are going round in circles, like so many frightened chicks.'

Without their escort and without the scale of the convoy to help protect them, the scattered ships could be picked off piecemeal. Whatever strength they had had in numbers was gone.

The inevitable slaughter followed. Learning the news, Grossadmiral Erich Raeder, C-in-C of the Kriegsmarine, then did order *Tirpitz* and his surface force out, but when it became clear that the U-boats and Luftwaffe had the task of PQ17's destruction in hand, he ordered the battleship back to port once more.

By the time the very last ship made port at Archangel on 28 July,

CASE BLUE: THE GERMAN OFFENSIVE IN THE CAUCASUS, JUNE – NOVEMBER 1942

KEY

→ German attacks
⇢ German retreat
— German front line
⇢ Russian retreat
⚑ oilfield

Tula

U S S R

VORONEZH FRONT
GALIKOV

Penza

Eletz
60
40
Don

Tambov

SOUTH-WEST FRONT
VATUTIN

Saratov

Kursk
2

Voronezh

Svoboda
6

DON FRONT
ROKOSSOVSKY

Belgorod
(1)

Pavlovsk
(2)

Kamishin

KAZAKHSTAN

Kharkov

2
HUNGARIAN

1 Guards

21

65   24

STALINGRAD FRONT
YEREMENKO

B
WEICHS

66

Izyum

8
ITALIAN

3

Stalingrad

UKRAINE

Donets

ROMANIAN

6
PAULUS

62   Baskunchak

Lugansk

Don

(2)

64

XXXX
SOUTH
BOCK

Novo Cherhassk

(2)
4
HOTH

57

Volga

Mariopol

Rostov

4
ROMANIAN

(3)

51

Yeisk

Elista

Ulan Erge

28   Astrakhan

17
RUOFF

LIST

NORTH CAUCASUS FRONT
BUDENNY

Caspian
Sea

Kerch
Taman
11

Krapotkin

Kuban

Krasnovar
47
56

Armavir

Maikop

Stavropol

Kuma

Novorossiysk

Tuapse

12

(3)

Piatigorsk
XXXX
1
KLEIST

Georgiyevsk

Mozdok

Kisliar

44

Grozny

Sochi

18

Sukhum

XXXX
9

Ordzhonikidze

Makhach
Kala

German Front Lines

(1) — June 1942

(2) -- 23 July 1942

(3) ···· November 1942

Black
Sea

37

Caucasus Mountains

Poti

TRANS-CAUCASUS
FRONT
TYULENEV

Kutais   Tiflis

Batumi

GEORGIA

0   100 km

0   100 miles

TURKEY

ARMENIA   AZERBAIJAN

twenty-four of the thirty-five that started the voyage had been sunk. That was more than two-thirds of PQ17, and included 120 men dead, plus 210 aircraft, 430 Sherman tanks, 3,350 vehicles and almost 100,000 tons of other cargo all lost. For the Germans, it had demonstrated that *Tirpitz* could cause the destruction of huge amounts of Allied shipping without even the risk of leaving port. For the British, it was yet another embarrassing and humiliating episode that was shaking the confidence of all – of the Russians, the Americans and those at home too.

It was time for the rot to stop.

On the Eastern Front, Case BLUE, the main German summer offensive, long in the planning, was launched on 30 June, more than a year after BARBAROSSA. On one level, confidence had been restored by the triumph at Kharkov, as well as by the preliminary operations to clear the eastern Crimea, which had gone well for the Germans – although Sevastopol did not finally fall until the beginning of July.

On another level, however, there were a number of signs to suggest Case BLUE was just a little bit too ambitious. To start with, the German forces amassed for the task were still short of just about everything. Generalmajor Balck's new division was not the only one expected to attack under-strength. In fact, at the OKW, General Warlimont had received a paper from his staff on 6 June called *War Potential 1942*. It was quite frank about the Wehrmacht's shortcomings. On 1 May, the armies on the Eastern Front were short of some 625,000 men and there was no hope of making good the losses of the 1,073,066 casualties so far. The panzer divisions in Army Groups North and Centre were so short of tanks they could field only one battalion each – that is, around 40–50 panzers per division. 'Mobility is considerably affected by shortage of load-carrying vehicles and horses which cannot be made good,' continued the report. 'A level of demotorization is unavoidable.'

In fact, Army Group South, the spearhead for Case BLUE, had only 85 per cent of the trucks needed. Luftwaffe units were now at only 50–60 per cent of their establishment, with 6–8 aircraft per *Staffel* – squadron – rather than the 12 they should have had. That meant total strength for the Luftwaffe was still lower than it had been on 10 May 1940. In terms of manpower, the 1923 class had already been called up – that is, men now as young as eighteen who at that age would normally have been expecting to be doing their Reichsarbeitsdienst – Reich Labour

Service; in other words, they were being thrust into action eighteen months ahead of time. 'Serious shortage of raw material for tanks, aircraft, U-boats, lorries and signal equipment,' it continued, before concluding, 'Our war potential is lower than it was in the spring of 1941.'

Even the plan for Case BLUE was more prescriptive, more detailed and more complex than anything that had come before it. There was no longer the strength to mount simultaneous attacks in the south and north around Leningrad, as had been originally envisaged. Instead, the attack in the south would happen first, then, once successful, men and materiel would be transferred north. What's more, because the forces available for Case BLUE were so tight, Hitler had decided they needed to be very carefully controlled. Panzer formations were not allowed to get ahead of themselves; there would be no more charging off like Rommel and Guderian had done in the past. Case BLUE had also been divided into four successive operations, each with a very precise timetable. Since timetables invariably went up the spout the moment a battle began because of the inevitably large number of variables brought by the fog of war, this was also a cause for concern. That flexibility of command and manoeuvre, such key features of *Bewegungskrieg*, were being stifled, in part by Hitler's micro-managing style and in part by the chronic shortages that appeared to leave them little choice.

Finally, the intelligence picture was once again woeful. Göring still had his Forschungsampt, his own private listening service with which he ensured he kept one step ahead of his rivals, and the SD still had an iron grip over most subjects of the Third Reich, yet when it came to the intelligence picture of their enemy, Nazi Germany was, bar some few notable exceptions, woefully bad. Underestimating enemy strength had worked against them during the Battle of Britain and now, two years on, they were making the same mistake again. For example, they estimated the Soviet Air Force had 6,600 aircraft when they had nearly 22,000; they thought the Red Army had 6,000 tanks when actually they had 24,446. In artillery pieces they were even further out: an estimate of 7,800 guns when in reality there were more than 33,000.

At around two in the morning on 28 June 1942, Generalmajor Hermann Balck was at his 11. Panzerdivision command post. They were on the left flank of Army Group South and were due to move towards Voronezh. Outside, all was calm – the night air was still and silent. Then suddenly, at 2.15 a.m., their own artillery barrage opened up. Even a man of Balck's experience was impressed as dust and smoke enveloped them and the night calm was shattered. Russian counter-battery fire quickly replied, but soon after his men were moving forward. By 9 a.m., the bridge across the first river obstacle had been set up by the engineers and, in an echo of Guderian at the Meuse, Balck was among the first to cross. While under fire, he went forward to see his infantry regiments before following on in his *Kübelwagen* with the panzers. 'It was an intoxicating picture,' he noted, 'the wide, treeless plains covered with 150 advancing tanks, above them a Stuka squadron.'

His own division was entirely successful and within a few days they had reached and crossed the Tym River, even though, to his annoyance, too many of the Russian tanks and guns appeared to have got away, pulling back and successfully withdrawing out of the fray. In Russia, as in North Africa, space could be readily ceded if it meant men and materiel could be preserved; the Russians were learning that. This time there were no vast encirclements.

None the less, all along Army Group South's front, Case BLUE appeared to be going well, as the main thrust now surged south towards the Caucasus. As news of these successes reached the Wolf's Lair, so Hitler became increasingly agitated. One moment he was dreaming of a vast link-up between Axis forces now in North Africa and those pushing south through the Caucasus. The next, however, he was worrying about his western flank and insisted both on keeping one of the precious panzer divisions in France and sending another now to join it on the Western Front. He was also micro-managing once more. Halder was tearing his hair out with frustration as the Führer insisted on interfering at every turn. Against Halder's direct advice, for example, he had concentrated too many panzer divisions against Rostov, leaving the flanks dangerously exposed. No sooner had these movements taken place than the folly of the decision became all too apparent. A fit of rage then followed. 'The situation is getting more and more intolerable,' noted Halder. 'This so-called leadership is characterized by a pathological reacting to the impressions of the moment and a total lack of any understanding of the command machinery and its possibilities.'

Hitler always interfered when he was anxious. With Rommel's success and with the early signs that Case BLUE was going well, it must have seemed as though ultimate victory really was possible. However fantastical this remained in reality, it felt tantalizingly close to Hitler –

which made every setback, small or large, seem that much worse.

As it was, by the end of July, German forces had smashed the Soviet South Front and, thereafter, the German advance was rapid. For Case BLUE, Army Group South had been further bolstered and so split into Army Groups A and B; huge German forces had been amassed for this renewed drive to the Caucasus. Maikop, a major objective, was captured on 9 August by General von List's Army Group A, although the significance of its capture was marred by the destruction of its oil installations by the retreating Russians. At the same time, the German Sixth Army under General Friedrich Paulus was advancing further east towards Stalingrad, on the major River Volga. By 10 August, after reinforcement by the Luftwaffe who had been supporting Army Group A, German troops had reached Stalingrad's outskirts.

By then, however, the advance south was beginning to slow as supply lines once again lengthened and Soviet resistance grew. Vehicles were breaking down, spares were harder to deliver, as too was fuel; the distance that Germany's mobile armoured units could operate was necessarily limited. Hitler could talk of creating a mammoth Axis link between Egypt and the Caucasus, but this was a pipe-dream; the Wehrmacht was simply not equipped to cover such distances. Rather in the same way that an aircraft had an operational radius, so too did the Army. Give or take, it was about 500 miles, but that was really stretching it; around 300–350 miles was a more practical limit – and that rough rule of thumb applied to the desert too. That was the culmination point, after which its speed of operation slowed down massively, giving the enemy the chance to regain its balance.

As it was, although they were within touching distance of those Eldorado-like oilfields at Baku, the Germans might as well have been a thousand miles away for all the good it would do them even if they did get there. Hitler's plans for an even larger Greater Reich, stretching from the Caucasus to the Middle East and into Egypt, were the stuff of fantasy, not least because of the logistical problems it would involve: the lack of roads, the lack of infrastructure, the absence of shipping, the inability to transport oil back to Germany. The world was not criss-crossed with oil and gas pipelines in 1942. There were pipelines, but most of those in the Soviet Union were still out of reach; there was one between Maikop and Grozny, but that was not much use to the Germans. There was another from the Guryev oilfields on the northern shores of the Caspian Sea, some 350 miles further east from Stalingrad, which led to Orsk in the Urals. And that was about it. There was none heading west towards Germany. How was the oil going to be transported, even if the wells had not been destroyed as they had at Maikop? The already overstretched Reichsbahn did not have the capacity to deliver it. Incredibly, no one within the Reich appears to have thought about this.

Rather, the best they could hope for was to disrupt Soviet oil and armaments production. The capture of Baku, the third largest oilfield in the world, would certainly have been a severe blow to the Soviet war effort, but their remaining oilfields – those at Guryev and at Beloretsk, some 600 miles further east of Moscow – still provided them with more than Germany received annually. What's more, because Hitler chose to accept over-optimistic appreciations, which in turn were based on faulty intelligence, he began Case BLUE truly believing the Soviet Union was at the limit of its military and economic strength. Little did he realize that Stalin had already ordered much of Russia's war industry to relocate further east, especially to the Urals. Here, those few oil pipelines and a comprehensive river and rail network had enabled Soviet armament manufacture to continue with far greater efficiency than German intelligence believed.

Furthermore, because the Luftwaffe did not have the aircraft either to spy on or to bomb those plants in the Urals and Siberia, they were, to all intents and purposes, blind to the reality. 'Russia, if it used its entire steel production for armament purposes,' reported the OKW's War Economy Department, 'would at best, temporarily, achieve approximately the same output figures as the German armament industry in the army and Luftwaffe sector.' This, in fact, was nonsense. Lend-Lease from the USA and Britain, the use of substitute materials and the highly effective industrial move eastwards all ensured that, far from being on their last legs, ever-more arms were reaching ever-more divisions of the Red Army. The gulf between German expectations and reality was enormous.

Nor was Case BLUE the only German effort. Hitler had not given up hopes of taking the still-defiant second city, Leningrad. The Russians, however, were proving equally determined to hold on. Grim though the situation remained inside the city – as many as one million had perished since the siege began almost a year before, a barely comprehensible number – the summer had meant the ice over Lake Ladoga had melted.

As the Allies were well aware and as the Germans were discovering, the most efficient way to deliver supplies of any kind was – and remains even to this day – by ship. More than a million tons of supplies were shipped across Lake Ladoga, while over half a million civilians were evacuated and 310,000 troops brought in, along with large numbers of guns and ammunition. It was these guns, together with those of the Baltic Fleet, that were able to silence German fire early in August during a defiant first performance in the city of Shostakovich's newly composed Seventh Symphony, 'Leningrad'. To all those who braved going out to watch this extraordinary performance, the Leningrad Philharmonic played in perfect unison with the Russian guns. At any rate, not a single German shell fell nearby that night and the concert was broadcast around the world.

For the planned renewed German attempt to take the city, General von Manstein had been sent north with his six-division-strong Eleventh Army and three massive siege guns. The intention was to attack towards the north coast to the west of Leningrad, neutralize the island of Kronstadt, from where Russian naval guns had been firing since the very start of the battle, then, with luck, sweep east into the city itself. Unusually since Hitler had taken over direct command of the Army the previous December, von Manstein was given a free hand to conduct the offensive as he saw fit. It was codenamed Operation NORDLICHT and was due to be launched at the end of August.

The Red Army, however, pipped the Germans to the post, launching their own offensive on 19 August and once more from the Volkhov front to the south-east – and in so doing proved they had still more depths to their manpower and ability to wage war on a massive front. No matter how many men, guns and tanks the Germans put into the field, the Soviets appeared to be able to produce more.

In terms of liberating Leningrad, it was not much more successful than the Red Army attack back in January, but von Manstein was forced to send most of his divisions south-east to help stem the Russian advance and his plans for NORDLICHT were completely scuppered. Hitler was furious. Red Army losses were over 100,000, but the Germans suffered another 26,000 casualties – the best part of two entire divisions, losses they could not afford.

And all the while, Hitler's micro-managing continued, making an already difficult series of operations even more challenging. List's essential air support, for example, was taken from him to reinforce General Paulus's drive on Stalingrad with the Sixth Army. This was mission-creep. The Caucasus oilfields, and particularly the largest site at Baku, had been the prime objective of Case BLUE, but now, it seemed, Stalingrad had become the Führer's most important target. On 24 August, meanwhile, Stalin ordered the city to be held at all costs and sent his favourite troubleshooter, General Georgi Zhukov, the commander who had defended Moscow, to co-ordinate the defence. By then, however, the German offensive was once more running out of steam.

CHAPTER 22

Gathering Strength

DESPITE THE SLOWING German advance along the Eastern Front, in Moscow, Washington and London, Allied war leaders were looking at their maps and seeing large swathes of the Soviet Union being absorbed by another rapid enemy advance. The fate of the USSR seemed more precarious than was perhaps the reality; and after Eighth Army's defeat in North Africa, it was hardly surprising the Allies were worrying.

They were also anxious about public perception and morale. In Britain, the people had already put up with almost three years of war and this first half of 1942 had been bruising. The successes had been all too often smothered by the disasters of Singapore, Malaya and Burma and by recent calamitous reverses in North Africa. Meanwhile in America, it was just as important to ensure that a public not so long ago dead set against war was now behind the war effort and not least the Germany-first policy. The modern world of mass media meant that news was received and digested quickly, and so far, after half a year of war against Nazi Germany, not a whole load seemed to have happened.

It was seen as vitally important that the American people understood the struggle, saw it in terms of a moral crusade and, most importantly, recognized it was a fight that could be won. Propaganda counted every bit as much in the USA as it did elsewhere, whether it be Britain, Nazi Germany or Italy.

It was for this reason that the dashing young men who had already been in the thick of the action were pressed upon the American public – men like Flying Officer Roald Dahl, who had miraculously survived the mayhem of the RAF's rather-too-small contribution to the Battle for Greece, and with several enemy victories to his name too. Since then, Dahl had briefly seen action in Syria but then had been declared unfit for further flying. An earlier flying accident had done for him; the headaches caused as a result had grown worse and worse until they had become unbearable. However, he was good-looking, charming and proving a dab hand at writing too, and so in April had been sent to Washington to take up a public-relations position at the British Embassy to fly the flag for the RAF in the United States.

After the rough life of a fighter pilot in the Mediterranean, and the austerity of wartime Britain, he was struck by the enormous difference he found in the States. Newspapers were forty pages long, people ate enormous ice creams and there was air conditioning, food galore and under-floor heating. The US seemed unspeakably modern.

His task was not necessarily to tell the truth, but to create an image of British pluck and determination. He gave lectures about his experiences, then began writing about them too – or, rather, fictionalized versions, which were then published in magazines. By July he had written a movie script and was being invited by Walt Disney to come to Hollywood, where he was wined and dined and introduced to movie stars.

He was also, however, carrying out other, clandestine, work for the British Security Coordination (BSC), which had been set up by the Canadian businessman William Stevenson. The BSC had been operating in the US since June 1940, partly to keep an eye on Axis activity over there but principally to encourage pro-British feeling in the States. Stevenson was the British Secret Service's senior agent in America, albeit one who was known to both Roosevelt and Bill Donovan, and was now in charge of all US Intelligence Services.

Dahl was in many ways an ideal recruit. He was well placed and because of his experiences and charm had the ear of those in Washington society. He was also eager for just a little more frisson in his life. 'I'd just come from the war,' he told Stevenson. 'People were getting killed. I had been flying around, seeing horrible things. Now, almost instantly, I found myself in the middle of a pre-war cocktail mob in America.' One of his first tasks was to befriend Vice-President Henry A. Wallace, who was an outspoken anti-imperialist, pro-Russian liberal. The British viewed him as something of a radical and, with Roosevelt's frail health, there was a real possibility that Wallace might one day take over as president. After an introduction was made, Dahl was able to develop a growing friendship with Wallace, and soon they were playing tennis together regularly and talking politics.

In the big scheme of things, this kind of intelligence work was decidedly low-grade, but the British weren't the only ones trying to carry out covert operations in the USA. So too were the Germans. For a totalitarian militaristic state like Nazi Germany, it was, in many ways, extraordinary how unsuccessful they were at running secret agents outside of their own territories. So far not one agent had successfully infiltrated Britain, for example, while their attempt to start a terror campaign in America in the summer of 1942 was equally a spectacular failure. Operation PASTORIUS was dreamed up by the Abwehr, the Wehrmacht's secret intelligence service. The plan was for eight Germans, all of whom had lived at some point in the US, to sabotage a number of targets with home-made bombs.

From the start, it was a cack-handed affair. The team leader, George Dasch, managed to leave compromising documents on a train, while another of the group got drunk in Paris before they set sail and began boasting that he was a secret agent. When they did finally reach US shores, via a U-boat, they were immediately spotted by a local coast-guard. Rather than killing him, they bribed him to keep his mouth shut, whereupon he pocketed the cash then hurried off to report to his superiors what had happened.

It then turned out that both Dasch and another of the team, Ernst Burger, confessed to each other that they hated the Nazis and wanted to compromise the mission – incredibly, Burger admitted he'd spent a year and a half in a concentration camp; how he was ever selected for this task is hard to imagine. Not only did they spill the beans to the FBI, they also handed over $84,000 dollars, PASTORIUS's entire budget. The team were quickly rounded up, tried and sentenced to death – Dasch and Burger included. These two later had their sentences commuted, but on 8 August the other six were all executed in the electric chair. It is hard to think how such an operation could possibly have been handled worse.

While such shadow operations and intrigues continued, no one could doubt that it was the blunt instrument of war that really counted: battles on the ground, in the air and at sea. That summer, Britain's and America's war leaders were still grappling with how best to defeat Nazi Germany. Yes, a direct invasion of north-west Europe was the main aim, but American and British strategy was not focused solely on an invasion of continental Europe; rather, a gradual tightening of the noose around Germany's ability to wage war, largely through air power and specifically strategic bombing, was also key to their plans. The British may have suffered a wobble over strategic bombing after the devastating revelations of the Butt Report the previous year and ongoing questions about Bomber Command's efficacy, but the Thousand Bomber Raids had seen Harris get past that, and it certainly remained a central part of US strategy, as outlined in AWPD-1, the Army Air Forces' prescribed war plans.

On 18 June, the recently promoted Major-General Carl 'Tooey' Spaatz had arrived in Britain to take command of the newly formed US Eighth Air Force. The plan was to build up a force of sixteen heavy bombardment groups, each with thirty-two heavy bombers, three pursuit – or fighter – groups of 75–80 fighters each, as well as medium and light bomber groups. The first units would start arriving that summer.

Spaatz held his first full-scale staff conference at Bomber Command's HQ at High Wycombe on 20 June, stressing the need for both cordiality and co-operation with Bomber Command. 'The Eighth must do well,' he said, 'otherwise our prestige will suffer at home as well as with the British who depend on the US effort.' He was quick, though, to stress that, while it was important for the Eighth to make the most of British experience, that did not mean aping British tactics.

In fact, Spaatz and his fellow Army Air Forces commanders were convinced that night bombing was always going to be too inaccurate ever to prove effective, and they had been singularly unimpressed with Bomber Command's efforts thus far. The answer, they believed, had to be day bombing, and they hoped that their heavy bombers, and particularly the B-17 'Flying Fortress' with improved armour and armament, would be able to operate without fighter escort. They would fly in mass formation, hoping that, rather like the convoy system, there would be safety in numbers. There was some ground for this confidence. Unlike Lancasters and Halifaxes, for example, which had a seven-man crew and were equipped with .303 Brownings, already proven to be little more than pea-shooters, the Flying Fortress had a crew of ten and was equipped with thirteen .50-calibre machine guns in eight different positions. The .50-calibre was everything that an air-to-air machine gun needed to be;

that is, it had a good velocity and rate of fire and could pack a hefty punch. The B-17 was, quite simply, designed for daylight, not night ops.

Perhaps the most important reason for pursuing daylight operations, however, was that Spaatz wanted the Eighth to operate independently of the British. He did not want them playing second fiddle to the British or to be sharing assets. Moreover, he and others in the USAAF, such as Hap Arnold and the AWPD-1 team, all genuinely believed in their theory of air war and were determined not to sing to the RAF's tune before testing their own carefully thought-through doctrine first. That this was more a matter of faith than of knowledge based on experience was neither here nor there. As coalition partners with their own doctrine, this approach was entirely fair enough. More to the point, it meant that at some stage in the not too distant future, they would, with the British, be able to deliver round-the-clock bombing. For the Germans, there would simply be no let-up.

One of the first units to reach Britain was the 97th Bombardment Group, whose crews flew in stages from the US all the way to Britain, where they made their home at Polebrook, to the south-west of Peterborough in central England. Bombardier of the *All American*, a B-17 in 414 Squadron, was 22-year-old Ralph Burbridge. From Missouri in the Midwest, Burbridge had joined the Air Force just before Pearl Harbor. He'd been disappointed not to be a pilot but reckoned so were a lot of other people, so decided to knuckle down to the role given him – one that carried a considerable amount of responsibility. Making sure he dropped their bombs on the spot was crucial, although he also had another task in the crew. When not bomb-aiming, he was expected to man one of the .50-calibre guns.

Eighth Air Force's first-ever operation over Europe was on 17 August, in a raid against the marshalling yards at Rouen in France, and the *All American* was one of the Fortresses taking part. For all of the crew, it was understandably a nerve-wracking experience, but they made it there and back in one piece. Overall, it was a good start – the bombers flew over together, dropping their loads from 23,000 feet and fairly accurately too. The rail network at Rouen was certainly put out of action for a while. The experience did, however, make Burbridge realize how under-prepared they were for war. 'We had a cover of Spitfires,' he said, 'but otherwise, I reckon we'd all have been dead.'

*

Also now in Britain were Major-General Dwight D. Eisenhower, the new commander of US forces in the European Theater of Operations, and Brigadier-General Mark Clark, his deputy and commander of US II Corps. The pair, and Eisenhower especially, faced a huge challenge. America was new to war, whereas Britain had been in for almost three years. Culturally, they spoke the same language, but in many other ways they were very different peoples. Moreover, they were expected to plan together and fight together, yet they had different approaches to warfare. Finally, Eisenhower was merely a two-star general, who was expected to work with vastly experienced and more senior men such as General Alan Brooke, General Hastings Ismay, General John Kennedy and others – and to more than stand his own.

To help his standing, he was promoted to Lieutenant-General on 10 July, but that same day, at a conference with Brooke, Ismay and Portal, it was made clear the British no longer believed SLEDGEHAMMER was remotely possible in the autumn that year. Since Eisenhower had been sent on his way to Britain with instructions to put into operation just that thing, this was a blow. There was a lack of shipping, the British told him, and failure would have disastrous knock-on effects for the proposed full invasion the following year. This was true. There was also a lack of landing craft – new Landing Craft Assaults (LCAs) were being built and bigger, flat-bottomed Landing Craft Ships too, but they were not ready yet. The Americans had never yet come up against a panzer division; most infantry had never seen even an American tank. Their combat doctrine, such as it was, had been tested only in a handful of manoeuvres in the southern United States. They were a long way from being ready to take on the Wehrmacht.

A week later, the US chiefs arrived in Britain along with Harry Hopkins. The Americans accepted that gaining a toehold in northern France would not be possible and SLEDGEHAMMER was scrapped. But something had to be done – the Americans had promised Molotov, after all, and by this time things were not looking at all good in the Soviet Union. Then, on 20 July, Churchill persuaded his Chiefs of Staff that an invasion of north-west Africa was the only viable option. Even Brooke, who had been dead against it from the outset, came round to the PM's way of thinking. Hearing this change of heart, the Americans initially refused to be swayed, but when deadlock was reached Marshall confessed he needed to talk to the President for instructions. By this time, however,

Roosevelt had begun warming to the North Africa venture, as he had intimated to Marshall before his Chief of Staff had left for London. His response was therefore to urge his delegation to reach an agreement whereby American troops could be used in land operations against the Axis powers sometime that year. Really, that left just one option open: North Africa. Admiral Ernest King, fresh from the US Navy's victory at Midway, now used this strategic window to press once more for realigning the US priority of operations to the Pacific and even sent the President a letter urging him to do just this. Roosevelt was not impressed. Calling both King and General Marshall, he asked for their detailed plans for the Pacific Ocean alternative. And he wanted to see them that very afternoon.

At that point, both King and Marshall had to admit they were no more ready to send a large army to the Pacific than they were across the English Channel. The problems were exactly the same – in fact, far away in the remote Pacific they were worse. Roosevelt had won an important battle with his Army and Navy chiefs.

None the less, the cancelling of SLEDGEHAMMER was a blow to Eisenhower. 'Well, I hardly know where to start the day,' he told his friend and aide, Commander Harry Butcher. With the terrible news from the Eastern Front, he feared Wednesday, 22 July could well go down as the 'blackest in history'.

Be that as it may, momentum had now swung in favour of north-west Africa, or Operation TORCH, as Churchill had renamed it. On 24 July, this was agreed in principle, with the British refusing to accept that it would rule out a cross-Channel invasion the following year. Together, the Joint Chiefs thrashed out a basic plan. A Supreme Commander was needed, which Brooke suggested should be an American. The Brits also proposed that the operation should be led by US troops, partly as a sop to the Americans but also because Vichy French antipathy to the British knew no bounds; France's former ally had become a hated enemy and in North Africa especially so: it was at Mers-el-Kébir near Oran in Algeria that the Royal Navy had blasted the French Fleet back in early July 1940. Thus any resistance would likely be stiffer against British than American troops. This was agreed. Two simultaneous operations were envisaged – one on the west coast of Africa, the other on the north-west coast. Planning would be conducted from Eisenhower's headquarters at Grosvenor Square in London, with the US team of a joint planning staff hurrying to the UK as soon as possible, because the date suggested for the landings was in October. That was a mere twelve weeks away.

Eisenhower had not been at this final session, but was briefed by Marshall as he scrubbed himself in his bath. He made it clear he hoped Eisenhower would command the whole thing, but in the meantime Ike was to be given the new title of Deputy Allied Commander in Charge of Planning TORCH, and was to get cracking right away.

A large part of the planning for SLEDGEHAMMER – and now TORCH – had been ensuring there were enough troops sufficiently trained for the job, and because the assumption had always been that a second front would jump off from Britain, that was where most of these men now were. In North Africa, Eighth Army remained, even in the summer of 1942, a force that had been drawn predominantly from Britain's Empire: Australians, South Africans, Indians and New Zealanders; and while there were plenty of Brits out there – men like Albert Martin and Johnny Cooper, for example – the vast majority of those now in the British Army were still in the UK, and had been ever since the retreat from Dunkirk two summers before.

Bill Cheall was one of them. Having joined the Territorial Army before the war, he had been posted to France with the 6th Green Howards and had managed to make his way back from Dunkirk. After spending much of the Battle of Britain on anti-invasion watch, he had been sent to join the 11th Battalion, which was a training unit of new recruits but which clearly needed some experience mixed in too. Cheall had not minded particularly, although he had begun to tire of moving from one camp to another; they had all been the same: all near the coast and all full of spartan Nissen huts.

Now, though, the battalion was based at Mareham-le-Fen in Lincolnshire, a few miles inland. Since arriving there in early 1942, Cheall had been relieved to discover training had been really stepped up. It was, he thought, not before time. Route marches became a regular occurrence, as did map and compass reading, weapons training was intensified, then so too were training exercises at section, platoon and company level. 'At last,' noted Cheall, who had been given the single stripe of a lance-corporal, 'the lads were beginning to realize that there was more to soldiering than guard duties.'

Meanwhile, American soldiers were swelling the numbers of

servicemen now in Britain, and not least the 34th Red Bull Division based at Omagh in Northern Ireland in yet another Nissen-hut camp. Sergeant Joe Schaps reckoned their quarters looked just like a barrel cut in half.

Another of those who had reached Britain with the Red Bulls was Staff Sergeant Warren 'Bing' Evans. From Aberdeen, South Dakota, Evans had been at college at South Dakota State when he'd volunteered to join the National Guard, and that was because a dollar a week for a bit of drill on Thursday evenings had seemed like a good deal to him. Evans had lost his father to cancer when he'd been four and he, his mother and younger sister had struggled to get by ever since. A much-valued newspaper delivery patch had brought in a few extra cents and he'd learned to fight trying to hold on to it. Later, he'd discovered he was pretty good at football too, which had got him a sports scholarship that included his college tuition as well as a room and two meals a day. The extra dollar from the National Guard had given him a bit of much-needed pocket money.

Being drafted into the Army had never been part of the game plan, but that was what had happened in February 1941 – and by that time Evans had been pretty certain America would be in the war before so very long. He wouldn't have minded so much had he not recently fallen madly in love. He'd met Frances Wheeler at a dance during Thanksgiving Weekend the previous November and sparks had flown immediately. The feeling was entirely mutual and both were distraught that, having found one another, they now had to be parted. Frances promised to wait for him – after all, his active service was only for a year – but that soon changed; after the Louisiana Maneuvers that summer, it was clear to Evans that he wouldn't be out of the Army any time soon.

With this in mind, Frances drove all the way to New Orleans, where the two of them were able to spend a precious weekend together. After dinner and a night of dancing, Evans proposed and Frances accepted. He'd saved $21 for the ring. After Pearl Harbor, when news arrived that he was heading overseas to Britain, they decided to get married right away, but it was now winter, snow was on the ground and driving anywhere was treacherous. On the long trip to New Jersey, where Evans was about to disembark, Frances was hit head-on by another car. Luckily, she only suffered a cut lip and broken arm, but by the time she was out of hospital it was too late – her husband-to-be had already set sail. Evans was heartbroken, but once again Frances promised to wait. Even so, one night while out on deck, Evans tore up his wedding licence and threw the ring into the ocean. 'I figured it was bad luck,' he said. He could only hope he'd make it back one day.

Now, however, six months on, he was not in Northern Ireland but in Scotland, having voluntarily left the 34th Division to join a brand-new elite force of troops called the 1st Ranger Battalion, based on the same principles as the British Commandos. This latter force came under the charge of Vice-Admiral Lord Louis Mountbatten, who was head of Combined Operations, the single headquarters that combined ground, naval and air forces to plan and execute hit-and-run raids on Nazi-occupied Europe.

During a visit to the UK by General Marshall, Mountbatten and the US Chief of Staff had agreed that a number of American officers should be sent to Combined Operations HQ. It had also been agreed that a number of American troops of all ranks would be attached to the Commandos, from which a nucleus of an American commando unit could be formed. The task of finding and forming these volunteers was left to Colonel William Darby, one of the aides on the staff of US V Corps in Northern Ireland.

On 1 June, Darby had put out his call for volunteers, all of whom should possess high leadership qualities with initiative and sound common sense. All were expected to have good athletic ability, stamina and no physical defects at all. Seeing the notice, Bing Evans had decided to volunteer right away. He thought it seemed like a good challenge, and he managed to become one of the first 300 to be accepted.

It was felt that a new and different name was needed, however – 'Commandos' would always have a British association – and so 'Rangers' was decided upon. On 19 June, the 1st Ranger Battalion was formally activated, with Bing Evans as First Sergeant of E Company. Immediately, they were sent up to Scotland, basing themselves at Achnacarry Castle, in the shadow of Ben Nevis near Fort William. And although they were trying to distance themselves from the Commandos, they were initially trained in much the same way and for similar purposes; even their instructors were the same. It was tough, both physically and mentally. As well as learning hand-to-hand combat, the Rangers were expected to climb mountains, carry out speed marches and river crossings, and swim in ice-cold water, in addition to developing scouting and small-unit tactics. There was also extensive amphibious training. Evans certainly thought both the training and their instructors were pretty thorough. 'They had their hearts set on discouraging us and didn't think we could take it,' he said, 'but, of course, we were just as intent on showing them we were up to anything they could do.'

It wasn't just the first few thousands of American soldiers who were arriving in Britain – there were Canadians too. In fact, the 1st Canadian Division had been the very first from Britain's Dominions to send troops to the UK, back in December 1939, but further troops were still being sent over, albeit in smaller numbers. Among those reaching Greenock on the River Clyde on a warm late-July morning was Lieutenant Farley Mowat, now twenty-one and bristling with impatience to get into the war after what had seemed to him to be a very long wait indeed.

Mowat was from Saskatoon and had been painting the front porch of the family home back in September 1939 when his father had told him the war had begun. Mowat Senior had fought in the last war, had returned with a damaged right arm thanks to German bullets, but had none the less remained in the Canadian militia, serving with the Hastings and Prince Edward Regiment, known to all as the Hasty Ps.

His son had greeted the news of war with an equal sense of fervour – after all, he may have been only eighteen at the time, but he believed that he and all other freedom-loving liberals were honour-bound to take up arms against the bestial Nazis. His intention, though, was not to join the Army, but the Air Force, so he swiftly signed up and some months later, in May 1940, was finally summoned for a medical – which he failed for being 4 lb under the required weight.

With his dreams of becoming a fighter pilot dashed at the first hurdle, he gave in to his father's steering, passed his Army medical and joined the 2nd Battalion – the militia – of the Hasty Ps instead, where, after a short stint in the ranks, he was offered a commission. Mowat had assumed that he would be transferred to the 1st Battalion, in Britain already, in quick order, but he was to be disappointed. 'Sorry, we just can't do it,' was scrawled on the bottom of his returned transfer request. 'He looks so damn young there'd be bound to be questions in Parliament about the Army baby snatching!' Mowat was incensed, but there was nothing he could do but return to the militia with its over-age soldiers and part-timers and hope he soon started to look more his age. Made a field-craft instructor, he reacted to this enforced stint with the 2nd Battalion by playing the fool, getting into trouble and generally proving why the powers-that-be had been right not to send someone so immature off to war.

Then, at long last, that July he and several others were finally posted for an overseas reinforcement draft. 'Thank heavens, this is it! It's worth two years of waiting,' he hastily wrote to his parents. 'Apart from you two, I don't in the least regret leaving Canada even though there is a chance I may not see it again. If we get a damn good lick in at the Hun, it'll be worth it.'

And now he was in England and a full lieutenant, although, much to his further frustration, still not with the 1st Battalion. Rather, it seemed the 1st Division was crammed with officers and the only casualties were from venereal disease, so until Mowat and his fellows were needed, they were to stay with the Reinforcement Unit, based near Guildford in Surrey. Put under the charge of Captain Williams, they were immediately taken on a pub crawl through the town. At one pub, Mowat found himself propositioned by a hefty Land Girl who invited him to take a walk along the river bank with her. There, in some bushes, she efficiently stripped him of his virginity, something he'd been trying in vain to achieve since the moment he joined the Army.

'There you are, luv,' she said as she fumbled with his fly buttons. 'Captain Willy said you needed doing . . . and there's nothink I wouldn't do for a Canuck!'

Mowat couldn't help feeling both set up and underwhelmed, and the following day told Captain Williams that if there was any more 'doing' to be done he'd rather do it himself. The Captain burst into peals of laughter and from then on insisted on calling him 'Do-It-Yourself Mowat'.

Meanwhile, Germany's war heroes were still being feted as much as ever. Upgrades of a Knight's Cross often involved the recipient's recall from the front and a trip to visit the Führer himself. If the winner was young, dashing, blond and blue-eyed, then so much the better; chances were, they would soon become very famous indeed. On 8 June, Helmut Lent had been on leave with his wife, the Russian-born Lena, and new baby daughter when he learned he had been awarded the Oak Leaves to his Knight's Cross, the first night-fighter to win such an honour. Soon after, a large piece about him appeared in the Wehrmacht newspaper, the

Wehrmachtbericht, describing one of his actions under the heading, 'Victory in the Night Sky'. After recounting how Lent had stalked and then shot down a 'Tommy' bomber, a vivid description of the crash was given. 'Fragments fly about like flaming torches,' wrote official war reporter Josef Kreutz, 'and then the mighty enemy colossus, many tons in weight, crashes into the earth with tremendous force. The bomber continues to burn for a long time. The instantaneous destructive effect of the German night-fighter's dashing attack gave the enemy crew no chance of escape. This was the 35th aerial victory of our most successful night-fighter, the first holder of the Oak Leaves in this new arm of the Luftwaffe.'

In the desert, Jochen Marseille had just notched up his 101st confirmed victory and promptly been awarded both the Oak Leaves and Swords to his Knight's Cross, the twelfth German serviceman to receive the honour. He was immediately summoned to Rastenburg to receive the award from Hitler in person, but was reluctant to go – he did not want to leave his comrades, nor did he want to be parted from his new friend, Matthias, a black South African they had captured in Tobruk. Since then, Marseille and Matthias had been bosom pals – ostensibly, Matthias had become his soldier-servant, but Marseille never thought of him in such terms. Rather, he called him the 'best friend and bartender one could wish for.' In Nazi Germany, such a friendship would have been impossible, but Edu Neumann, the *Gruppe* commander, didn't mind. He had always recognized that Marseille was a maverick, someone apart from the others.

Marseille left for Berlin on 18 June only after Neumann had promised to take care of Matthias, and he arrived at Tempelhof in Berlin only to find Hitler's favourite film-maker, Leni Riefenstahl, waiting for him with a film crew.

When he finally reached the Wolf's Lair to meet Hitler, he did not bother to change into his dress uniform and still wore his rough desert boots. At the lunch that followed he sat next to Göring, who said to him, 'So you now have, what, over a hundred conquests?'

'Herr Reichsmarschall,' Marseille replied, 'do you mean aircraft or women?'

Göring nearly choked on his food with laughing, but Marseille, completely unfazed by the entire experience, let it be known that he had little time for the Nazis. One of Hitler's staff officers asked him if he had considered joining the party. Marseille replied that if he saw a party worth joining, he would consider it, but there would have to be attractive ladies present. He also told Hitler flatly not to rely on the Italians, and when the Führer said to him that Germany would need men like him when the war was won, Marseille told him he thought neither he nor most of the men he served with would still be alive.

When he finally got back to the front in early August, he discovered three of his good friends had been killed and that his *Gruppe* commander and mentor, Edu Neumann, was desperately struggling to keep the men going as shortages of fuel, food, water, ammunition and just about everything were making it increasingly difficult for them to operate at all.

At the beginning of August, General Brooke and Churchill flew to the Middle East, landing in Cairo on the 3rd. Auchinleck had made his exhausted forces try for one more push along the Alamein Line, but still the Axis positions had held. Churchill had been cracking his whip from London, but at the back of the Auk's mind had been news of German advances in the Caucasus. Like Eisenhower, he feared imminent German victory in the Soviet Union, and was still fretting about an Axis link between the Caucasus and the Middle East.

He failed, however, to explain this to his commanders, who were all drained, understandably protective of their differing nations' troops and the responsibility their countries had placed in them, and were bickering badly after ten weeks of battle. The Auk had been unable to stop it, so Pienaar and Gott were still at loggerheads, while General Leslie Morshead, commander both of all Australian forces in theatre and of the Australian 9th Division, had openly quarrelled with the C-in-C.

By the time Churchill and Brooke landed, the PM had already decided that the Auk had to be given the chop, and Brooke, who had originally wanted to go alone, was by now rather agreeing with him. Any doubts were brushed aside when they visited the front a couple of days later.

Churchill went alone for a briefing from Auchinleck and repeatedly demanded he attack again. Auchinleck patiently explained why that was no longer possible, but the PM was in a foul mood and walked out of the C-in-C's caravan and stood alone, glaring at the desert, before being whisked away by Strafer Gott. Churchill had already decided Gott was the man to take command of Eighth Army. Gott, however, told the PM straight that he needed three months' leave back in England.

The Prime Minister's mood was lifted immediately by the startling difference in atmosphere at the Desert Air Force HQ at Burg el Arab. 'He arrived in an Air Commodore's rig,' noted Tommy Elmhirst, 'to our delight and honour.' Their party then flew to Fighter Group HQ, where lunch had been specially sent all the way from Alexandria. It all went down extremely well and Churchill gave them a stirring speech. The airmen were happy and so too was the PM.

Meanwhile, Brooke, too, had spoken with Gott. 'I think what is required here is some new blood,' Gott told him. 'I have tried most of my ideas on the Boche. We want someone with new ideas and plenty of confidence in them.' He was spot on.

Meeting back together in Cairo, Churchill and Brooke agreed that General Sir Harold Alexander should take over as C-in-C Middle East; he was now in England after successfully retreating British Forces in Burma back into India. In fact, he had recently met up with Eisenhower, as he had been earmarked to command British forces in TORCH. Brooke wanted General Montgomery to take over Eighth Army but Churchill insisted it should be Gott, even though the latter had almost begged to be allowed home.

The following day, 7 August, these changes were approved by the War Cabinet in London, but fate had other plans. British radio traffic in the field was not terribly secure at the best of times and it seems Axis intelligence learned that Gott was planning to return briefly to Cairo before taking up his new appointment. As he flew in a lumbering transport plane, he was attacked by six Me109s, shot down and the air-craft strafed on the ground until it was on fire – an uncharacteristically thorough and ruthless act in an air war in which pilots had so far aimed to destroy machines not men. By a twist of fate, the escape hatch jammed and Gott and his fellow passengers were all burned alive.

With Gott dead and the Auk flying home to India, Alexander arrived in time to be briefed by Brooke and the PM, and General Montgomery, Brooke's original choice for Eighth Army, arrived soon after.

In Cairo, the journalists were briefed about the changes. Alan Moorehead realized very clearly that an era of the war was now at an end. 'A new army of the Middle East was given birth,' he wrote, 'an army that for the first time was going to include Americans as well as British. A tide of reinforcement such as the Middle East had never known before was going to come in, and from it a better army was going to be built.'

CHAPTER 23

Last Chance in Africa

'GENERAL ROMMEL WAS our great hero of the summer,' noted Else Wendel in Berlin. 'In July he achieved the final victory in North Africa, or so we thought.' Once more a spirit of hope and even jubilation returned. Yet as the new field marshal was well aware, he had come close to a truly significant victory but had not quite managed it, and the difference between success and failure was massive. In fact, his sensational capture of Tobruk was looking like a smaller version of the German victories in the East – stunning and devastating on a tactical level, but strategically not enough to be decisive. It was no good winning battles if you didn't win the war.

In the old days, in Norway, France, even the Balkans, and even way back in Frederick the Great's day, these victories had been possible because, ultimately, the distances were slight and the general staffs knew their operational reach. Victory had been achieved in one surge forward. In the vast expanses of Russia and North Africa, that operational reach was no longer enough. The system could not cope: Germany did not have enough motorization, enough oil, enough shipping. They did not have reliable allies who could make meaningful contributions to final victory. They had reached their culmination point.

In Britain, the joint staffs, across the services, of two coalition partners were working together to launch the largest amphibious invasion the world had ever known. There was plenty to iron out, lots of doctrinal and cultural issues to resolve, and a fair amount of grumbling and grousing as well. None the less, there was also an atmosphere of co-operation, of determination to work together and to get the job done. The contrast with the hapless German planning for SEALION, the proposed invasion of Britain back in 1940, for example, could not have been greater. And there was the contrast of the German–Italian alliance.

Since the start of the war, Germany had repeatedly looked down her nose at her Axis partner. Occasionally, Hitler and von Ribbentrop could demonstrate a little bit of gracious charm towards the Italians, but only when it was felt absolutely necessary and when they wanted something from them. Kesselring had worked hard to be affable and accommodating to the Commando Supremo – the Italian General Staff – in Rome, but he was most definitely an exception; the rest of the time, Hitler, especially, repeatedly snubbed Mussolini, keeping him in the dark about plans, ignoring suggestions and advice, and regarding him with thinly veiled contempt.

Il Duce had hardly done much to earn greater respect, but now, in the North African desert, the German–Italian partnership was about to take another big dip. Following his failure to break through the Alamein Line, on 12 July Rommel wrote a report to the Army Operations Department and referred to 'alarming symptoms of deteriorating morale' in the Italian ranks. The Italian Pavia and Brescia Divisions had been all but wiped out in the recent fighting and Rommel claimed that 'several times lately' the Italians had deserted their positions. As a result, Rommel was pleading for more German troops.

When the Italians learned about this report it went down very badly indeed, not least with the newly promoted Maresciallo Ettore Bastico, the senior Italian commander in North Africa, and with Mussolini, who had given up waiting to march into Cairo on his charger and had gone back to Italy. During his three weeks in Libya, Rommel had not called on him once – justifiably, since he'd been in the thick of battle, but such excuses didn't really wash with Mussolini. 'Naturally,' noted Count Ciano, 'Mussolini has been absorbing the anti-Rommel spirit of the Italian commander in Libya, and he lashes out on the German marshal.' The attitude of German troops was also, apparently, obnoxious. 'The tone of the Duce's conversation,' noted Ciano a few days later, 'is increasingly anti-German.'

The truth was, everyone was exhausted – mentally and physically, Rommel included – and this was made worse by the sense of bitter disappointment and even panic at the current situation. Rommel's troop strength stood at 30 per cent, panzers at 15 per cent, artillery 70 per cent, and the all-important anti-tank guns at 40 per cent. He desperately needed new supplies of everything, otherwise he faced complete defeat; but his supply lines were now desperately stretched, while those of his enemy had been drastically shortened. Moreover, he was keenly aware that more Allied reinforcements were on their way. As it was, a US heavy bomber group, the 98th, was now operating from Egypt, while an American Fighter Group, the 57th, had been temporarily attached to Coningham's Desert Air Force. More Sherman tanks were also on their way, as were more guns, as well as additional British divisions and armoured units, including the now combat-ready Sherwood Rangers Yeomanry, who were part of the 8th Armoured Brigade.

Rommel viewed the next few weeks as a race against time, in which he needed to rapidly build up strength before the British forces became overwhelming. This being so, and with a shipping schedule firmly in place, he hoped to launch one last, decisive strike against Eighth Army before the end of August.

One of those now working to improve Rommel's supply situation was Leutnant Hans-Hellmuth Kirchner, who was just one of the pilots urgently now brought in to create an air bridge. Posted to Kalamaki, an airstrip south of Phaleron in Greece, he was given an He111 to fly that had had its bomb bays loaded with fuel containers. On 12 July, he flew directly to the landing ground at Fuka in Libya in a trip that took three hours. Once he had landed, the fuel containers were carefully unloaded with a pulley system and poured into the empty barrels waiting for him. On each flight, he managed around 1,000 litres. 'If you compare that to the amount that we needed for this long flight ourselves,' he noted, 'it was not much, but it had to be done.' Kirchner was somewhat taken aback by the chaotic scenes at Fuka: dozens of planes landing on a huge, flat, sandy clearing in the desert, literally in every direction. Army tankers and even panzers simply filled up right beside them as they unloaded. 'Everyone was very worked up,' jotted Kirchner. 'In Athens, the punishment for stealing or selling fuel was death and it was wasted and splashed around. It was insane.'

As soon as he had unloaded the fuel, he took off again and flew back to Greece, this time to Eleusis near Skaramangas. The next day, he was back again, and the scene at Fuka was even more chaotic. Now he flew to Heraklion on Crete, refuelled and remained there overnight before being diverted to Benghazi for his third trip to North Africa. There, both Kirchner and his Heinkel broke down – he with dysentery and the plane with battery failure. By butchering several wrecks at Benghazi, they managed to get the plane up and running again, and on the 16th Kirchner succeeded in holding his bowels in check just long enough to get them back to Eleusis.

Reinforcements of men were also on their way, including the 164th Light Division, currently on Crete, the Ramcke Fallschirmjäger Brigade, and the Italian Folgore Paracadutisti (paratroop) Division, one of the better Italian units. Among them was 22-year-old Luigi Marchese, a section commander in the 2 Regimento Paracadutisti, who had originally been called up as an ordinary soldier and posted to Libya in 1939, before Italy entered the war. Back then, he'd been based in Tripoli, working in the post room of Maresciallo Balbo's headquarters and then as a military map-maker. With the outbreak of war, however, he had volunteered as a paratrooper, hoping for a bit more excitement and a more soldierly role.

Two years on, and he and the division were posted to Yugoslavia, where occupation and maintaining the peace had been left to the Italians and, since January that year, the Bulgarian 1st Army. Yugoslavia had become a frightening place. One of the mish-mash countries created in 1919 after centuries of Ottoman and Hapsburg rule, it was ethnically and politically divided. Resistance had emerged almost immediately – from the Nationalist, Royalist but almost entirely Serbian Chetniks under Colonel Draža Mihailović, and from the more pan-Yugoslavian Communist and Soviet-backed Partisans under Josip Broz, known by his *nom de guerre*, Tito. Then there were the Ustaše, who were Catholic, ultra-nationalistic, right wing and Croatian, led by Ante Pavelić. They had been around since 1930, but after the Yugoslav surrender had declared Croatia an independent state, though they included Bosnia and Herzegovina within their new boundaries. Although they were then forced to accept the Treaty of Rome, which annexed part of Croatia into the Reich and part to Italy, they were left to govern this new state without much interference. Since then, their militias had been steadily cleansing their territories of Serbs with some of the most horrific violence yet seen in the war.

For the Italians, the Balkans and Greece had provided lots of territory, but they had proved an endless drain on resources that brought few, if any, benefits. There were no large reserves of natural resources, no wealth, no riches to plunder. All they were doing was ensuring Mussolini's territorial footprint was larger than it might otherwise be and preventing the Allies from reaching the precious Ploesti (and German-controlled) oilfields in Romania.

The Folgore had been based in Ljubljana in northern Yugoslavia, part of the territory annexed by Italy. Luigi Marchese found it a place of brooding menace. Posters had been pasted over almost every wall threatening reprisals for partisan action. 'From there,' he noted, 'we learned as much about the actions of the German and Italian troops as we did about the crimes that the partisans, including women, committed against unwary or lone soldiers.'

Marchese had been expecting a long posting in Yugoslavia, but they left this broken country of civil war and rampant partisan activity after only a few weeks, so that by the end of July they were now in another country reeling under the occupation: Greece. Marchese was shocked to find the civilian population so short of food; he had never seen so many beggars, all of whom seemed to be women and girls. He was struck that there were almost no men to be seen at all.

From Athens, they were flown by German and Italian air transports to Tobruk on 1 August and their battalion then sent to Jebel Kalakh at the southern end of the Alamein Line, where they began furiously digging in, and where Allied Air Forces seemed to bomb them almost continuously. Marchese wondered where their own Regia Aeronautica and the Luftwaffe were.

In fact, after a few days in the line, it was horribly clear that the division was under-equipped. Marchese could not see how they had any attacking capacity at all. Rations were poor and the flies were unlike anything he had ever experienced; millions of them swarmed everywhere. 'The absence of drinking water,' he noted, 'is like a scourging from God: not even a litre a day in temperatures of 50 degrees Celsius in the shade. The water comes in jerry cans, the taste and smell of which are the source of the disgust and ill-effects on our health that affects us all.'

The challenge remained getting supplies safely across the Mediterranean. In July, Air Vice-Marshal Keith Park had been posted to Malta and within a couple of weeks of his arrival the RAF had regained air superiority over the island. The 10th Submarine Flotilla was also returning there, while torpedo bombers from the Middle East were able to use the island as a staging post. Furthermore, because the Axis were sending convoys to Tobruk and Benghazi as well as Tripoli, those were well within range of Allied bombers. Crossing the Mediterranean was now a great deal more dangerous for Axis convoys than it had been back in April and May, when only a fraction of their supplies had been lost.

Now serving on the Italian destroyer *Corsaro* was the young sailor Walter Mazzacuto. In the middle of July he was part of an escort group consisting of four torpedo boats and four destroyers whose task was to shepherd just four merchant ships across the Mediterranean. Soon after leaving Brindisi in south-east Italy, they came under attack from RAF Beaufort torpedo bombers and one of the merchant ships was sunk. It happened to be carrying a number of troops heading to North Africa, but most were rescued by nearby air-sea rescue vessels. The convoy continued, pulling into port at Taranto and collecting another merchantman. No sooner had they set sail once more than they spotted a British reconnaissance Spitfire overhead and sure enough, not long after, a formation of Beauforts attacked them again. Another merchant ship was hit, but this time, after working to repair the damage, they were able to keep going and safely reach Benghazi.

The pattern, though, was repeated on Mazzacuto's next convoy duty. Leaving Brindisi on 3 August, on the second morning at sea they spotted a British reconnaissance plane overhead. Immediately, the alarm claxons were sounded and the men spent all day at their battle-stations, waiting for an attack. Suddenly, at around seven o'clock that evening, US Liberators from the 98th Bombardment Group appeared and began heavily bombing them. Fortunately for Mazzacuto and his comrades, the Americans attacked from far too high an altitude and their bombs fell wide, although spectacularly.

Further waves of aircraft followed, however. At around 11 p.m., another formation of enemy bombers came over, lighting up the convoy with flares and dropping both bombs and torpedoes. The convoy went into a defensive formation, splitting into three groups and covering themselves with a smokescreen. Another wave of attackers followed in the early hours but, much to the Italians' relief, not one ship was hit. 'The convoy reached Benghazi on the morning of 5 August around 11am,' noted Mazzacuto, 'and without a further attack.' This convoy, at least, had safely reached North Africa.

Supplying the Panzerarmee was principally left to the Commando Supremo, because the Germans had no shipping of their own and because supplies were going from ports in Italy to Italian ports in Libya. During July, on the insistence of Rome, most were being sent to Benghazi and Tripoli rather than Tobruk or tiny Mersa Matruh. This policy appeared to pay off because only 5 per cent was lost in July and 91,000 tons reached Libya safely.

This was not as good as it sounded, however, because the Panzerarmee needed around 100,000 tons of supplies a month at the front, not 1,300 miles away in Tripoli or 800 miles back in Benghazi. The supply chain was using half the fuel landed just getting these supplies to Egypt. As July turned to August, Rommel now insisted more supplies be brought direct to Tobruk and Mersa Matruh, and fuel was his most urgent requirement. For all his tactical flair, Rommel had a very large blind spot when it came to logistics. Fuel was so tight because he had overreached his supply lines. That limit of operations of around 350 miles still stood as true as it always had since the start of the war. Now he was overly reliant on excessive – for the Axis – fuel supplies.

'The battle is dependent upon the prompt delivery of this fuel,' Rommel told Maresciallo Cavallero.

'You can begin the battle now, Herr Generalfeldmarschall,' Cavallero replied. 'The fuel is already on its way.' On its way, yes, but whether it would safely arrive at the front was another matter, yet only if it did would Rommel have any chance of making the decisive breakthrough – a breakthrough he was now planning for the end of the month.

Another factor in building up the strength of the Axis forces in North Africa was making sure they held on to what they had once it was theirs and not allowing it to be frittered away. This, however, was becoming increasingly difficult for the air forces, as their workshops and landing grounds were being frequently attacked by marauding groups of the SAS, operating far behind lines. Eighth Army's senior commanders might have been tactically moribund but, in sharp contrast, this small band of unorthodox warriors were demonstrating a degree of dash, initiative and tactical flair that had not been evident in British forces since the days of General O'Connor, the C-in-C of British troops in North Africa until his capture back in April 1941.

Since their disastrous first attempted raid back in November 1941, the SAS had grown into an extremely effective force. They had done away with airborne drops and instead had been driven across the desert by

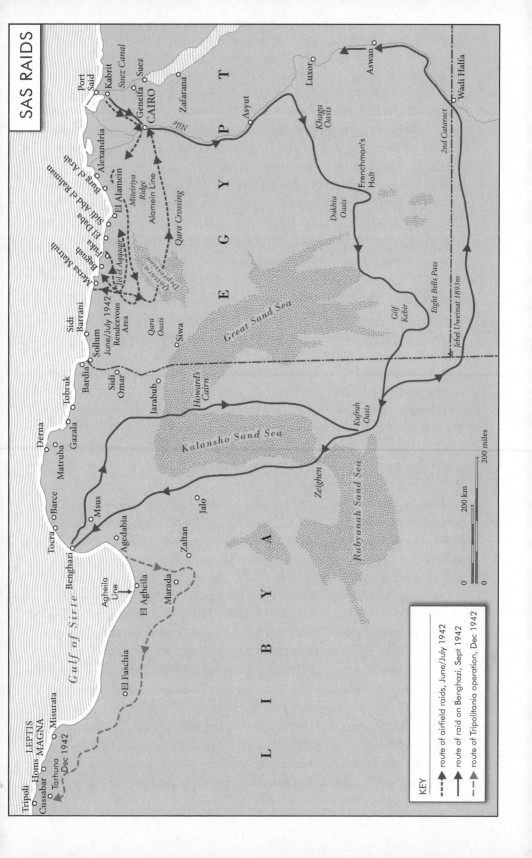

SAS RAIDS

Tripoli
LEPTIS MAGNA
Homs
Cussabar
Misurata
Tarhuna
Dec 1942

Gulf of Sirte

L I B Y A

El Faschia
El Agheila
Marada
Zaltan
Agheila Line
Agedabia
Benghazi
Jalo
Zeighen
Msus
Tocra
Barce
Derna
Matruba
Gazala
Rabyanah Sand Sea
Kalansho Sand Sea
Howard's Cairn
Jarabub
Sidi Omar
Bardia
Tobruk
Sollum
Sidi Barrani
Kufrah Oasis
Great Sand Sea
Qara Oasis
Siwa
June/July 1942 Rendezvous Area
Qattara Depression
Bagush
Fuka
El Daba
Tel el Aqqaqir
Mersa Matruh
Miteiriya Ridge
Alamein Line
El Alamein
Qara Crossing
Burg el Arab
Sidi 'Abd el Rahman
Alexandria
Port Said
Suez Canal
Kabrit
Geneifa
CAIRO
Suez
Zafarana
Asyut

E G Y P T

Nile
Luxor
Khaga Oasis
Dakhla Oasis
Frenchman's Halt
Gilf Kebir
Eight Bells Pass
Jebel Uweinat 1893m
2nd Cataract
Aswan
Wadi Halfa

0   200 km
0   200 miles

KEY

— route of airfield raids, June/July 1942
— route of raid on Benghazi, Sept 1942
— route of Tripolitania operation, Dec 1942

the Long Range Desert Group, whom the SAS now renamed the 'Desert Taxi Company'. During the CRUSADER battles, just twenty-one men had managed to destroy 109 aircraft at airfields near Sirte; the only dark point had been the loss of the inspirational Jock Lewes when he was strafed and killed by a Messerschmitt 109.

Other successful trips had followed. For the most part, the SAS men tended to operate in small teams. Johnny Cooper, promoted to sergeant, had been placed in David Stirling's team and in March they had destroyed a long column of fuel tanker lorries at Benghazi. A couple of months later, they had attempted to attack ships in port and had driven, in broad daylight, straight into the town, had holed up in an empty house and been thwarted only by broken valves on their inflatable rubber canoes. They had then driven out again. Accompanying them on that raid had been Randolph Churchill, the Prime Minister's son; it had been breathtakingly reckless, but they had got away with it. They also got away with a raid on the Luftwaffe repair depot at Benina, where, in June, they had destroyed aircraft, hangars and fuel dumps. Climbing the escarpment afterwards, they had paused to watch the fireworks as the time-fuses burned out and the explosions began. One Me110 had caught fire and its cannon shells then ignited, fizzing around the airfield like light flak. Then the petrol dump exploded and hangars caught fire. 'The effect,' noted Cooper, 'was stupendous.'

The SAS had expanded as a result of these successes to about 100 men strong, including a squadron of Free French, but their task now was even more pressing: to cripple Axis air forces as much as possible behind the Alamein position. That meant travelling down into the Qattara Depression, then up and out again behind enemy lines to the landing grounds at El Daba and Fuka. As had become usual, planning took place at Peter Stirling's flat in Cairo – David Stirling's brother was Third Under-Secretary at the Embassy. The idea this time was to take a number of trucks with them so they could be self-sufficient for several weeks. They also now had their own transports: new US-built Jeeps, quarter-ton 4x4 four-man vehicles, which they then stripped down and adapted by adding a .50-calibre machine gun and twin Vickers guns.

A column of some thirty-five vehicles headed out into the desert, and after a brief conferral at Eighth Army HQ they headed into the Depression. Around 150 miles behind enemy lines and some 60 miles south of the coast, they made their temporary base camp, camouflaging the trucks and taking good cover in a series of ridges around the north-west of the Depression at Qaret Tartura. This was their planned base for the next month. It was from here that they began making raids, usually in groups of three vehicles. The first set was on the airfields around Fuka and Bagush and was co-ordinated so that their bombs all exploded at 1 a.m. on 8 July.

Johnny Cooper had set off once again with David Stirling and, as a first, with Paddy Mayne. 'Young Cooper', as Stirling always called him, was the navigator, while Stirling tended to do the driving. While everyone else now had Jeeps, the commander's car was a much-loved Ford V8, which had been captured from the Germans and christened the 'Blitz Buggy'. On this occasion, they attacked an airfield full of Italian CR.42 biplanes, although they had clearly not destroyed them all, because at dawn the following morning, as they were approaching a long, wide wadi – a dried river bed – two CR.42s suddenly appeared and attacked them first with bombs – to no effect – and then with machine guns. 'Abandon ship!' Stirling called out as an enemy plane bore down on them. They all ran for it, but as Cooper hit the ground he heard the Ford erupt into flames. 'We shall have to get another Blitz Buggy, Sergeant Cooper,' Stirling said to him cheerfully once the planes had gone.

Of more concern to Cooper was the loss of his precious navigation logs and his theodolite, an important navigational tool. Gathered up by the other two Jeeps, they were safely back at the base later that afternoon, although because of reconnaissance planes spotted in the area they then shifted their base 25 miles further west to Bir el Quseir. All in all, the SAS teams had destroyed more than thirty aircraft and between thirty and forty vehicles, although, much to his annoyance, Eighth Army HQ had sent Stirling a signal not to touch the airfield at El Daba. This, it later transpired, had been a mistake.

While Paddy Mayne made another attack on Fuka, Stirling now planned an assault on the former British landing ground at Sidi Haneish, about 30 miles south-east of Mersa Matruh. Worried that if their attacks followed the same pattern, the enemy would prepare appropriate counter-measures, Stirling was always looking to try new attack methods and now decided they should hit El Daba en masse in two columns of ten vehicles each, with Stirling leading in the middle.

After a live-ammunition practice in the desert, which Cooper, for one, found excruciatingly deafening despite the distance from the enemy, and after carefully loading and preparing their Jeeps and weapons, they set off at dusk on 26 July, Cooper navigating the entire column. After a little more than two and a half hours, they had reached the edge of the airfield when suddenly runway lights came on and an aircraft came in to land. Switching off their engines, the SAS men paused and waited a moment, then Cooper stepped out and gave the two column commanders Stirling's orders, which were to follow him and form into their columns. Engines started once more and then they were off. Stirling drove straight into the middle of the airfield, heading right down the centre of the runway with aircraft lined up on either side. Then the blasting began.

In moments the entire airfield was ablaze. Italian machine guns opened up on them, but the aircraft obstructed their aim so only occasional bursts came anywhere near the SAS men. At the top of the airfield, they had turned and were heading back down on a different track when the Jeep came to a shuddering halt. 'What the hell's wrong?' Stirling shouted. Cooper jumped out and opened up the bonnet, only to discover a 15mm cannon shell had gone straight through the engine's cylinder head. A moment later, Captain Scratchley pulled up and they piled into his Jeep instead, Cooper clambering into the back next to Scratchley's rear gunner, who was slumped over with a bullet in his head – he was the SAS's only casualty. Then they were away, roaring after the rest, who were now disappearing back into the night, their departure covered by thick swirling smoke, dust and the darkness of a moonless night. 'The scene of devastation was fantastic,' wrote Cooper. Looking back he saw several aircraft burst into flames and then so did their abandoned Jeep.

They destroyed thirty-seven aircraft that night and most of them were those most precious of all German planes: the Ju52 transport, all of which were being used to airlift supplies to the front. It had been a triumph for Stirling's men.

On 10 August 1942, Churchill had scribbled a hand-written note to General Sir Harold Alexander, the new C-in-C Middle East. His prime aim, the PM wrote, was to 'destroy at the earliest opportunity the German–Italian Army commanded by Field Marshal Rommel together with all its supplies and establishments in Egypt and Libya.' Alexander felt elated. For too long he had overseen retreats – he had been the last man to leave Dunkirk, and had just returned from India where he had led British forces from Burma. Now, however, with more men and materiel arriving, he felt imbued with a sense of great confidence for the future.

Alexander had already had an extraordinary career and was unique in the British Army in having commanded men in battle at every rank apart from Field Marshal. Twice wounded in the last war, he had been repeatedly decorated and had been an acting brigade commander at just twenty-five. Then, in 1919, he had led German troops as part of the Baltic Landeswehr in the brief war against Russia – another unique distinction among his peers. In the 1930s, he also commanded a brigade of the Indian Army in Waziristan and the Northwest Frontier; during that time he had learned Urdu to add to a number of other languages, including French, Russian, Italian and German, all of which he had mastered effortlessly. Charming, witty, understated and utterly imperturbable, Alex, as he was widely known, had reputedly only ever lost his temper once and that had been during the Battle of Passchendaele in 1917, when one of his men had refused to give a wounded German some water. After three years' weeding out those not up to the task, the British Army was starting to get the right men into the right jobs.

While Alexander was a born diplomat, the same could not be said for the new Eighth Army commander, Lieutenant-General Bernard Montgomery. However, what 'Monty' lacked in people skills he made up for in no-nonsense common sense. Wounded early in the last war, he had then proved himself a superb staff officer and planner, and had demonstrated his clear-headedness and operational skills when commanding 3rd Division back in 1940. Since then, he had also emerged as a very good trainer of men. Together, Alexander and Montgomery made a rather unlikely couple, yet their experience and differing skills complemented one another perfectly. As the team to turn Allied fortunes around in North Africa, they certainly looked like a good bet.

And Alexander was quick to get started. He clearly got the impression that morale was low, that Rommel was held in far too much awe, and that in Cairo the many bars, restaurants and clubs were a distraction. Talking to a number of officers, this impression was quickly confirmed. 'They were bewildered, frustrated and fed up,' he noted. He immediately set up his new HQ on the edge of the city, at Mena, near the Pyramids. There, he and his staff could get a feel for the desert; moreover, it marked the start of the desert road to the front. He named it 'Caledon Camp' after his childhood home in Northern Ireland.

Montgomery, meanwhile, had appointed the Director of Military Intelligence, General Freddie de Guingand, as his new Chief of Staff, and together they quickly set up a new Tactical Headquarters in the desert – one that was cleaner, free of flies and, most importantly, right next to Coningham's Desert Air Force headquarters. On 19 August, Alexander gave Monty his formal directive, which included an order to stand and fight where they were with no further thought of withdrawal. This was to be relayed to the men. Montgomery, who agreed entirely, began his new role with a pep talk to his senior commanders. From now on, he told them, there would be no more bellyaching – and by this he meant the questioning of orders at any point in the chain of command. Anyone who did so would be very quickly given his marching orders. 'He gave an excellent talk on leadership and organization,' noted Tommy Elmhirst, who, with Coningham, was there to hear Montgomery's address. Elmhirst did not disagree with a word the new commander said. He thought Monty appeared to be 'a veritable little tiger'.

Montgomery then outlined his plan. Rommel, he said, would attack in two or three weeks. 'And we shall dig in and defeat him,' Monty told them. 'Then we shall do some hard training for two months. Every unit will go out of the line, one by one, to train, and on the beach if it is possible, to bathe and get clear of the flies. Then I shall attack with two corps in the line, a mobile reserve to come through the break, which we shall make in his line, and chase the remnants of his army out of Africa.'

'It was,' noted Elmhirst, 'quite clear as to who was now commanding Eighth Army.'

Back in London, planning was continuing for Operation TORCH, although the precise form it would take had still not been agreed. The Combined Chiefs of Staff wanted to launch it before 10 October. By the third week in August, that was looking very tight indeed. Certainly there were all number of potential stumbling blocks to be overcome, from the continued issue of shipping availability to the far thornier matter of how the Vichy French, and even the Spanish, would react.

While such considerations were being weighed up and agonized over, a plan had been also under way to raid Dieppe. Conceived by Lord Louis

Mountbatten's Combined Operations, to whom the Commandos were attached, it was to be the biggest raid yet proposed; SLEDGEHAMMER may have been discarded, but the Dieppe Raid would, it was hoped, achieve many of the aims of the original plan. Important lessons would be learned about amphibious operations, and about the nature of German defences; and it would answer those in Britain, America and even the Soviet Union who were impatient for action. Some 6,000 troops were being sent, mostly Canadians, although 4 Commando were also included, as were a handful of the new US Rangers. Tanks were being sent across the Channel and the raid would be supported by massive air cover.

It was clearly fraught with risk and Brooke, for one, was against it. Certainly, to land so many men and machines and then get them out again was very different to the lightning cut-and-dash operations the Commandos had carried out thus far. The odds on the Dieppe Raid being a success were not high and were made worse when the original date, 4 July, had to be abandoned due to bad weather.

Among those already on board ship ready to go was Sergeant Bing Evans, one of just seven officers and eleven enlisted men of the US 1st Ranger Battalion earmarked to take part in the raid. It was Independence Day for the Americans and Evans and his fellows were off the coast of the Isle of Wight. 'The weather was not at all decent,' said Evans. Postponed initially until the 8th, their cover was blown on 7 July when four German aircraft attacked the concentrations of shipping. The crucial element of surprise had gone and so the raid was called off again. The Rangers were sent straight back to Scotland, where Evans found himself promoted to battalion sergeant-major. Although Dieppe was once again rescheduled, with fifty Rangers now involved, Evans was not to be one of them; Colonel Darby did not want to risk his most senior NCO.

That the raid still went ahead was an extraordinarily foolhardy decision. It did so, though, on 19 August and was, predictably, a fiasco. Although the 6,000 men were disembarked, they never got off the beaches, and over half the force was killed or captured, while a staggering 106 aircraft were shot down. All it had done was underline how perilously dangerous and difficult amphibious operations were and teach the planners some admittedly very important lessons.

This, however, was small comfort to Generals Eisenhower and Clark, who were still struggling to get anywhere close to an agreed plan for TORCH. They both believed there should be several simultaneous landings, both inside the Mediterranean along the Tunisian coast, and at Casablanca, in French Morocco, which was outside the Mediterranean on the Atlantic. In other words, TORCH needed to be impressively big in scope – big enough to deter a strong, hostile French and Spanish reaction. At around 3 a.m. on the morning of the 25th, however, Clark was hauled out of bed to receive a cable from General Marshall. Over in Washington, the US chiefs were starting to worry seriously. If TORCH was mounted it *had* to succeed, Marshall said. A landing in Tunisia was just too risky. Instead, he now suggested landings at Casablanca and Oran in French Algeria.

Back to the drawing board they went again. 'This,' noted Clark, 'was the most depressing news of the summer.' That same night, however, Clark and Eisenhower were summoned to dinner at No. 10 with the Prime Minister. Both were in a gloomy mood as they headed over to Downing Street; they felt as though it was one step forwards and two back. Churchill, however, was in a far more chipper frame of mind, having just returned from his travels; not only had he been out to Egypt and overseen a change of command and renewed impetus, he had also flown on to Moscow to meet with Stalin. The Soviet leader was confident they could hold the Germans until the winter. He told Churchill his factories were now building 2,000 tanks a month – which was true enough. Furthermore, he professed to be 'entirely convinced' by the plans for TORCH – a huge personal relief to the Prime Minister.

In this buoyant mood, Churchill insisted to Eisenhower and Clark that TORCH should go ahead, no matter the concerns. Roosevelt was of the same mind, he assured them, and Stalin was behind the plan too – the Soviet leader had been disappointed there would be no invasion of France that year, but had warmed to the opportunities of a North African invasion. 'When Stalin asked me about crossing the Channel,' Churchill recounted to Clark and Eisenhower, 'I told him, "Why stick your head into the alligator's mouth at Brest when you can go to the Mediterranean and rip his soft underbelly."'

Clark told him that what was needed was firm decisions – there had been so many changes, he said, they and their planning team were feeling dizzy. 'The planners of TORCH,' he said to Churchill, 'are tired of piddling around. Every minute counts. What we need now is a green light.'

'The Prime Minister,' noted Clark, 'promised action.'

*

For the bomb-blasted and starving citizens and servicemen on the strategically critical island of Malta, it seemed as though the Axis had held most of the aces for far too long, yet for those in the Luftwaffe and the Regia Aeronautica, it was a terrible place over which to fly, because if hordes of Spitfires didn't intercept you then there was the intense flak over the island to contend with.

Reaching Sicily in early July was 23-year-old Tenente Francesco Cavalero, part of the 20 Gruppo Caccia Terrestre. Although he had joined the Air Force back in 1938, he had done so as a reserve officer and was still at the Air College when war broke out. By the time he joined his fighter group in 1941, they were still recovering from the mauling they had suffered during their brief foray in the Battle of Britain, and were based at Ciampino, near Rome, on defence duties.

All three squadrons in the group were short of aircraft by that time, so Cavalero had been one of those to travel separately by train, then across the Straits of Messina and on to Ponte Olivo airfield at Gela on the central south coast of Sicily. By the time he rejoined them it was almost a week after the rest of the squadron and in that time they had already lost five pilots over the island, four of whom had been killed. 'We had a lot of losses,' said Cavalero. 'You would fly back and in the mess another of the pilots would no longer be there. He isn't coming back.'

Within a couple of weeks, such were the losses, Cavalero had been promoted to deputy squadron commander. The greatest responsibility was trying to nurture the new arrivals; fighter training in the Regia Aeronautica focused very heavily on technical flying skills but offered almost nothing on tactical combat flying, and new pilots were simply not equipped to tussle with Spitfires or dodge intense flak. Cavalero would try to give them as much guidance as possible, warning them to turn their heads constantly, but the Axis air forces on Sicily were hamstrung by a lack of ground control and radar – and this even though Italy was the land of Marconi and despite German radar being manifestly the best in the world when the war began. Malta, on the other hand, had radar, ground control and a co-ordinated air defence system modelled on that back home in the UK.

Yet despite the recent ascendancy of the RAF on Malta, by August the island was suffering critical shortages. Its people were starving and fuel had been running desperately low. An attempt to run a convoy there in

June had failed, and unless the island was urgently resupplied it would be forced to surrender; the Axis would have won after all without ever having to conduct the much-debated invasion.

Operation PEDESTAL was to be the most heavily protected convoy of the war thus far – and for just fourteen ships, including one all-important tanker. The Axis forces were fully aware of the convoy, attacking and harrying it as it passed through the Straits of Gibraltar on the night of 9/10 August and continued its slow, tortuous route through the Mediterranean. A U-boat sank the aircraft carrier HMS *Eagle*, although not before more Spitfires had flown off towards the island; two cruisers were sent to the bottom and a destroyer, while one by one the escorted merchantmen were picked off by a combination of Italian torpedo boats, U-boats and, as they neared the island, aircraft.

The pilots from Gela were all involved, although their contribution proved slight. Cavalero was among more than sixty Macchi 202 pilots from the entire Italian fighter unit, 51 Stormo, sent up on 13 August, by which time three of the fourteen merchant ships were nearing Malta. He was flying as wingman to the squadron commander and, as they headed out over the sea, they were soon intercepted by Malta-based Spitfires. His commander turned tightly and Cavalero followed – even more tightly, with the result that he blacked out. When he came to once more he experienced that strange phenomenon common to fighter pilots during the war: a suddenly empty sky where seemingly moments before it had been a teeming mêlée.

'I remained in the sky over the battles for a long time,' he said, 'looking at the convoy on the sea under me.' He spotted lots of Hurricanes and Spitfires, but never had the chance to open fire – and this worried him, because he didn't want his fellows to think he had been scared and had avoided combat.

Eventually, he realized he was running short of fuel and so landed at Pantelleria, an Italian island to the south-west of Sicily. And not before time: as he touched down, his engine cut and the propeller stopped. He had run his fuel tanks dry. When he did eventually get back to Gela, there were no recriminations. Rather, they were overjoyed to see him still alive and in one piece.

Cavalero was alive, but so too was Malta. In what was one of the most bitterly fought convoy battles ever, the combined weight of Axis air and naval forces had still proved unable to stop five merchant ships reaching the island. Furthermore, one of the five ships was the all-important tanker *Ohio*, which, although repeatedly hit and despite a Stuka crashing on its decks, was towed the last 50 miles by three destroyers and finally limped into Grand Harbour on 15 August. With that, Malta was saved. It meant that in the weeks to come the island could once more return to its primary role in the Mediterranean war: that of offensive base for operations against Axis shipping.

Meanwhile, in North Africa, Rommel's concerns were mounting. He knew he had to strike Eighth Army before the end of the month and yet his supply situation had taken a downturn after the 91,000 tons received in July. Time was now running out. 'Unless I get 2,000 cubic metres of fuel, 500 tons of ammunition by the 25th and a further 2,000 cubic metres of fuel by the 27th, and 2,000 tons of ammunition by the 30th,' Rommel told General Josef Rintelen, the German attaché in Rome, 'I cannot proceed.' The Commando Supremo duly promised more ships. Nine vessels were to leave Italy over a period of six days, starting on 28 August. But if just one of those fuel ships failed to arrive safely, his forces would be in trouble.

For Rommel, the forthcoming attack was a last throw of the dice on which the fate of North Africa would almost certainly be decided. What a dramatic turnaround it had been from the dizzy heights of capturing Tobruk just two months earlier.

On all fronts, it seemed, Germany was suddenly running out of chances.

CHAPTER 24

The End of the German Dream

SINCE TAKING OVER as Armaments Minister, Albert Speer had become the pin-up for Nazi war production and, with Goebbels' help, was making sure that Germans believed a huge improvement in war materiel – in terms of both quality and quantity – was well under way. And to a certain extent it was, although not at the rate Hitler or anyone else would have liked. Overhauling an industry as messed up as that of the Nazi war machine did not happen overnight and there were still innumerable barriers to overcome, not least the thorny problem of steel shortages. Steel rationing may have been largely solved, but an even bigger issue was how to produce more of the stuff.

The root of the matter lay not with iron ore, but with coal, that essential ingredient needed for steel production. In a nutshell, Germany was not getting enough. Steel production had fallen dramatically in the winter of 1941 and then, in the first months of 1942, had reached crisis point, largely because the Reichsbahn, the German railway, had been overstretched by the demands of the Eastern Front and so nothing like enough coal had been delivered to the steel mills.

In many ways, the shortage of coal was another Nazi own-goal, typified by the French coal-miners' strike in the summer of 1941. Extracting coal was a dangerous and physically demanding job, and by stripping workers of food, money and transport, production had unsurprisingly dropped. By the summer of 1942, Speer had agreed with Hitler that steel production needed to be raised by at least 600,000 tons a month, but, for that to happen, supplies of coking coal also needed to rise to the tune of some 400,000 tons per month, and that would only suffice if more scrap metal and more skilled labour were thrown into the process.

Matters came to a head at a meeting between Hitler, Speer, Sauckel and leading steel industrialists on 11 August. Also attending was Paul Pleiger, the head of the coal industry, who was at a loss as to how to raise coal production. Germany's own pits were ageing, in need of modernization and at the limit of production. Productivity in the coalfields of northern France and Belgium had continued to fall, Norwegian and Swedish stocks were low, and the civilian populations of Germany and all the occupied territories were also suffering from the shortages. The misery of having to suffer intense cold through yet another bitter winter would have a profound effect on morale. On top of that, there were other demands: really large amounts of coal were needed for the production of synthetic fuel, which Germany desperately needed to make up the shortfall of real oil, and it was used to power the electricity grid too; it was also required for the increasingly hard-pressed Reichsbahn. In fact, coal was absolutely central to Germany's existence, let alone its war machine.

Pleiger could think of no way in which he could raise coal production without the urgent supply of tens of thousands of experienced miners from the Ukraine and Poland. Sauckel immediately told him this would be possible. Pleiger, however, was not convinced; it was one thing providing the men, but would they be well fed and strong enough to do the job?

'Herr Pleiger,' Hitler told him bluntly, 'if, due to the shortage of coking coal, the output of the steel industry cannot be raised as planned, then the war is lost.' Shocked silence descended on the room, and then Pleiger said, 'My Führer, I will do everything humanly possible to achieve the goal.' Whether that was going to be enough remained to be seen.

At every turn, Germany was being forced to squeeze her resources to the maximum. There simply wasn't enough of any of the key ingredients needed for war. At the end of June, General von Schell had approved a memorandum sent for Hitler's signature warning of severe penalties for anyone violating the strict fuel restrictions. 'The fuel situation does not allow such thoughtlessness or violations under any circumstances,' it warned. This meant vehicles could not be used for any kind of recreational purposes, service journeys at the front were to be limited to a bare minimum, speed limits were to be observed to keep fuel consumption as low as possible, and no one was to drive on any kind of journey longer than 200 kilometres. Anything further, then trains were to be used.

This, then, was the desperate situation facing Germany in the summer of 1942. A generation earlier, similar problems had brought the country to its knees. Nearly a quarter of a century after that, Hitler pressed on with the war, his black-and-white vision for the future undiminished: the Third Reich would last a thousand years or crumble into Armageddon. There could be no middle ground.

Meanwhile, in Britain and the United States, people were still able to eat well and healthily. Even in Britain, where rationing had been extended, there were still plenty of products that had not been rationed, bread included. 'The greengrocers,' noted Gwladys Cox that August, 'are full of splendid greengages.' They were fivepence a pound, half what they had been a year before. Although she wished she had a bit more sugar, she still bought 4 lb and made jam. There were also larger rations for those employed in physical labour, such as coal mining, which meant that the productivity of Britain's workers was greater than those poor emaciated souls being forced to work as slaves for Nazi Germany. In America, factories continued to operate without fear of bombing or blackouts. This made a massive difference.

Britain was also facing a bumper harvest, as a good summer, combined with the increased productivity of the land, was now bearing fruit. Once again, Land Girls, civilians from the towns and troops – American, British and Canadian – all helped. In Wiltshire, A. G. Street, for one, had regained much pride in British farming. 'Today I've driven the desert back to the very edge of the woods,' he noted, 'something that's given me more satisfaction than anything else I've done in my life. And thanks be, thousands of farmers all over Britain have done the same.' He was also penning the script for a short propaganda film that was being made, *The Great Harvest*: 'From the reborn countryside of Britain is coming the food on which we are going to live this winter and next winter,' he wrote, as the cameras filmed young girls driving tractors and carts brimming with corn. 'Farming never stops. The great harvest is in. The land and its people are in good heart. The countryside itself is alive again – alive with the vigour and defiance of a land fighting for its people.' Stirring stuff and, at its heart, perfectly true. Total grain harvested in 1939 had been 46 million tons; in 1942, it would be more than 80 million.

Troops and war materiel was also continuing to reach Britain, at around 200 million tons a month – a bounty rich enough to make the Nazis weep. Even during the second 'Happy Time' off the coast of America, total imports to Britain had barely dipped – 2,006,000 tons had arrived in January, and 2,214,000 in May, for example.

In fact, convoys to Britain were now crossing the Atlantic virtually untouched, as Commander Donald Macintyre had been discovering. Back in June, he had rejoined his old destroyer, HMS *Hesperus*, and had taken over command of the escort group B2, part of the Mid-Atlantic Escort Force. He had taken to his new crew immediately and, although only two officers were Regular Navy and the rest were all Royal Navy Volunteer Reserves, he quickly came to appreciate that not only were they a very happy team, but a competent one too.

Macintyre had rejoined *Hesperus* at a time when there was little U-boat activity in the mid-Atlantic. This was just as well, because early in the year the Kriegsmarine had added a fourth rotor to their Enigma coding machines and the boffins in Bletchley Park had been unable to crack it. There was, however, another means of tracking U-boat movement and that was by using high-frequency direction finding, or Huff-Duff, and *Hesperus* was not only equipped with ASDIC and radar but also with a Huff-Duff set.

These were able to pick up the signals sent by the HF radio sets used on U-boats. Although the signals were coded, the radio transmissions could be picked up so long as the Huff-Duff set was tuned to the right frequency. Provided there were a sufficient number of sets in an escort group, then all possible frequencies used by the U-boats could be covered. Reports would be intercepted and an estimated position worked out. Armed with this, an escort or aircraft would then go hunting for the U-boat safe in the knowledge that they would be operating in roughly the right area. It was almost certainly down to Huff-Duff, for example, that Teddy Suhren in *U-564* had had his last journey across the Atlantic so frequently interrupted.

On *Hesperus*, Macintyre was blessed with a particularly able Huff-Duff operator, Lieutenant Harold Walker, who was known as 'B-Bar' from the opening Morse symbol of the U-boats' signals. A former Marconi engineer, Walker had previously served in the Merchant Navy, had had his ship sunk from under him, and both his parents had been killed by Luftwaffe bombs. As a result, he had a passionate hatred of Germans, which gave him all the motivation needed to spend long hours glued to his Huff-Duff set. He was also sufficiently adept to be able to distinguish the Morse code styles of different German radio operators. 'Time and again,' wrote Macintyre, 'he gave warning of impending attack and we took suitable action to shepherd our charges away from the danger.'

Losses in escorts had been low in the Atlantic, which meant experience had been allowed to grow. More ships were being built and coming into service, but there was now a hard core of wartime personnel who could be spread throughout the escort fleet. This was also true for the Canadians, who were still more than pulling their weight in the battle to save Allied shipping, and who had been learning fast. At the same time, they were benefiting from improvements to technology; Macintyre's task had been transformed by such developments. What's more, this improved technology was being harnessed to experience – Lieutenant Walker on *Hesperus* was a case in point. Nor were these advances constrained to the escorts cruising the sea itself. In the skies up above, Allied air cover was also increasing and their ASW equipment improving too. The U-boats were finding it progressively hard, even in the vast expanse of the ocean, to find places to hide.

Ironically, it was only now that Dönitz was finally receiving the kind of numbers of U-boats he had been asking for since before the war – soon there would be more than 200 operational U-boats in service. But he was still not getting much support from the Luftwaffe. At the beginning of September, he sent a memo to Raeder asking 'for the development of a powerfully armed aircraft with a great radius of action, to help us in the Battle of the Atlantic in the more distant areas beyond the reach of the He177.' The answer was swift. Such a request 'cannot at the moment be met . . . Desirable as the possession of such an aircraft undoubtedly is, we have not, at present, the necessary technical data from which it could be developed.' So that was that: nothing doing.

Nor had the problems of misfiring torpedoes been solved satisfactorily. The new U-boats were thus entering the battle lagging behind in terms of technology and air support. By September 1942, however, it was already too late. They had had a chance, before the war, to prepare for this epic and bitter battle on the seas in a way that could have proved catastrophic to Britain's ability to wage war. That opportunity had been missed by Hitler and his land-centric commanders, and by a naval high command that had been, like the Führer, too easily excited by giant surface vessels. Now, as more U-boats entered service, so they were paying for having a U-boat force of just 3,000 men in 1939. So much of that hard-learned experience had gone, entombed in an iron coffin at the bottom of the sea. Unlike the British, the experience pool was dwindling rapidly and at a time when commanding a submarine was more dangerous than ever before. In the months to come, Dönitz's increasingly young force would suffer appallingly.

In the United States, the armaments revolution that Bill Knudsen had promised was now starting to bear fruit under Don Nelson's overall leadership. Bottlenecks were being ironed out and shortages solved. Steel production had been improved by the creation of a brand-new steel plant at Fontana in the San Bernardino Valley in California. This was another of the extraordinary Henry Kaiser's enterprises – dam builder, road builder and shipyard builder and a man never to turn down a challenge. Conscious that there were no steel producers west of the Rockies, he had proposed, as early as April 1941, to build a brand-new steel plant himself, even though he had no experience of building such a thing, had no financing and not even a site. What he had been after was $100 million from the Government, which was swiftly turned down. A year on, however, and with a 4.2 million-ton steel shortfall, Don Nelson had felt he had no choice but to reconsider Kaiser's proposal. On 19 March, the deal had been approved and Kaiser and his team wasted no time. By the end of April, the site at Fontana had been found and the ground broken up. It was a poor part of California, so they were quickly swamped with applications from potential workers. Seventy miles of railway lines were built to connect them to the main lines and new wells were dug, with methods devised to recycle the precious water they would use. It was due to be up and running by the end of the year and capable of producing some 470,000 tons of steel plate a year, enough to supply the shipyards up and down the west coast.

Meanwhile, Kaiser's shipyards were, by August 1942, producing Liberty ship merchant vessels at an astonishing rate. Here, the principles of the assembly line were now being applied to shipbuilding. It had been originally estimated that it would take 220 days to build a Liberty ship, but by the beginning of the year that figure had been slashed to 105 days.

At Richmond, California, Kaiser's partner Clay Bedford had been reducing that time even further. At the same time, Kaiser's son, Edgar, now
running the shipyard at Portland, Oregon, was viewing Clay Bedford's
efforts as a personal challenge. In May, the Richmond yards built the
James Whitcomb in seventy-three days. Two months later, in July, Kaiser's
men at Portland sailed the *Thomas Bailey Aldrich* in just forty-three
days. Then in August, Bedford's men built a ship in a staggering twenty-
four days. This was shipbuilding on a truly astonishing scale. No one
had ever believed in their wildest dreams that a 10,000-ton dry-cargo-
weight merchant ship could be built in such a ridiculously short time.
That record, however, would soon be beaten again. And again. How
could the U-boats, with their still-failing torpedoes and lack of sufficient
air cover, possibly compete? The answer, of course, was that they could
not.

Back in the Mediterranean, the amount of Axis shipping available was
falling. All the big ships in the arsenal had now gone, and there were
neither the shipyards nor the materials to build more. Getting supplies to
North Africa had become dependent on ever-smaller vessels, which
worked against economies of scale, as more smaller ships took longer to
load and unload than fewer larger ones.

Rommel launched his attack as planned on 30 August, by which time
the first three Axis tankers that had set sail from Italy two days earlier
had been sunk by a combination of Malta-based aircraft and submarines,
and Wellingtons from the Middle East. Despite this, he had decided to
go ahead anyway, praying that the next tanker due in, the *San Andreas*,
would successfully reach Tobruk with her 3,000 tons of fuel. By the time
the Axis barrage opened, however, the *San Andreas* was also lying at the
bottom of the Mediterranean. Malta-based torpedo bombers had once
again hit their mark.

Nor was Rommel a well man. His doctor had diagnosed 'persistent
stomach and enteric disorders', and side effects included very low blood
pressure and giddy spells. Rommel had asked to be relieved on 21 August
and had suggested Guderian should replace him, but this suggestion was
refused. So Rommel remained; he would fight this latest battle at least.

The Battle of Alam Halfa, as it became known, was, in many ways, a
carbon copy of Gazala: a bombardment and holding attacks in the north
designed to draw in the British, then a sweeping mobile attack with the

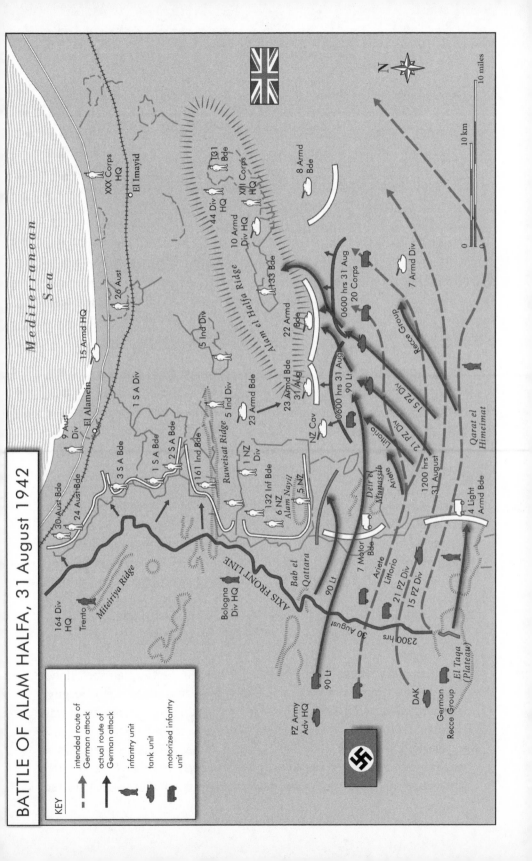

BATTLE OF ALAM HALFA, 31 August 1942

KEY

--- intended route of German attack

— actual route of German attack

infantry unit

tank unit

motorized infantry unit

Mediterranean Sea

El Imayid

XXX Corps HQ

26 Aust

15 Armd HQ

El Alamein

9 Aust Div

30 Aust Bde

24 Aust Bde

3 S A Bde

1 S A Bde

2 S A Bde

161 Ind Bde

1 S A Div

5 Ind Div

Ruweisat Ridge

5 Ind Div

23 Armd Bde

44 Div HQ

T 31 Bde

XIII Corps HQ

10 Armd Div HQ

133 Bde

Alam el Halfa Ridge

22 Armd Bde

8 Armd Bde

0600 hrs 31 Aug

20 Corps

7 Armd Div

132 Inf Bde

1 NZ Div

6 NZ

5 NZ

Alam Nayil

23 Armd Bde 31 Aug

90 Lt

0600 hrs 31 Aug

NZ Cav

Recce Group

15 PZ Div

Miteiriya Ridge

164 Div HQ

Trento

Bab el Qattara

AXIS FRONT LINE

Bologna Div HQ

90 Lt

7 Motor Bde

Deir el Munassib

Ariete

Littorio

Ariete

21 PZ Div

1200 hrs 31 August

Qarat el Himeimat

90 Lt

Ariete Littorio

21 PZ Div

15 PZ Div

4 Light Armd Bde

30 August

2300 hrs

DAK

German Recce Group

El Taqa (Plateau)

PZ Army Adv HQ

0   10 km

0   10 miles

N

Afrikakorps in the south, which would blast through the minefields and circle around to the north. This had been tactically suspect at Gazala because, having got around behind the British line, the Afrikakorps would then find itself cut off from its lines of supply. The ineptitude of the British commanders had enabled Rommel to get away with it, but only just, and not only would Montgomery not make the same mistake, he had also seen Rommel coming, thanks to a combination of Ultra decrypts of Enigma traffic and careful reconnaissance work by the Desert Air Force.

Rommel's armoured spearhead reached the British minefields at around two in the morning on the 30th, right opposite the 2nd Rifle Brigade, who were once again operating with the rest of the 7th Motor Brigade in the south of the line. Now equipped with new higher-velocity 6-pounder anti-tank guns, they made the most of easy targets as the German armour struggled through the minefields. The panzers were also clobbered by Wellington night-bombers, who left some thirty German tanks ablaze. 'Wave after wave of heavy bomber formations dropped their high explosives,' noted Oberst Fritz Bayerlein, 'while both sky and earth were intermittently made light as day by parachute flares and pyrotechnics.' He was witnessing this first hand and both he and Rommel were fortunate to survive the night. Other senior commanders were not. General Georg von Bismarck, the commander of 21. Panzer, was killed, while General Walther Nehring, commander of the Akrikakorps, was severely wounded by a bomb fragment. A British pilot appeared to have spotted Rommel's Horch command car too and Bayerlein watched it swoop down towards them. A bomb fell just in front, the blast killing several officers, including the corps supply officer Walter Schmidt, who was a close friend of Bayerlein's from back in Würzburg. 'Of the four generals leading the attack,' noted Bayerlein, 'three were killed.' He now took over temporary command of the Afrikakorps.

At dawn, Albert Martin and his fellow Riflemen-turned-anti-tank-gunners pulled back, having sufficiently slowed the German spearhead. Already Rommel's timetable was badly awry, and his slowly emerging panzers were saved from a further hammering by the RAF only by sudden desert winds that swirled into a brief sandstorm.

Fierce fighting followed all afternoon, but the Afrikakorps were barely making any headway at all. As dusk descended, they fell back, leaguering for the night. They were soon awoken, however, by flares that turned night into day and by wave after wave of Allied bombers. By morning, a pall of smoke hung over their positions from numerous burning vehicles. The night bombing had also disrupted attempts to resupply, and 21. Panzer was by now so short of fuel, its armoured formations could not move. The only spearhead now heading into action was 15. Panzer.

Moving forward to meet them was the newly formed 8th Armoured Brigade, which included the Sherwood Rangers Yeomanry in their first-ever action in tanks. In this, they rather showed what a lot they still had to learn. B and C Squadrons led the charge and they opened fire at 2,000 yards, achieved nothing, then pushed on to within 800 yards, at which point they were blasted by the tanks and anti-tank guns of the Germans. Seven tanks were soon knocked out and a further four were damaged. Stanley Christopherson's good friend Jack Whiting was killed and then they were ordered to withdraw. Fortunately for the Sherwood Rangers and 8th Armoured Brigade, however, 15. Panzer had by now also run out of fuel and so did not follow up their success.

Meanwhile, the RAF continued to pound the Afrikakorps, who were now caught in a large, wide-open expanse of desert that lay below the ridges of Alam Halfa and Alam Nayil, around 15–20 miles south of the coast. Medium bombers pummelled them without let-up, each bomb blast being made more effective as splinters from the stony desert floor lethally sprayed the air. Seven German officers were killed at Afrikakorps HQ that day.

The fighters were busy too. Billy Drake was scrambled at around two o'clock and led an entire wing to intercept a formation of some fifty Stukas and thirty Me109s. Ignoring the fighters, they tore into the Stukas, forcing them to jettison bombs early. Drake shot down two that day. This, however, was as nothing compared to the *seventeen* British fighters Jochen Marseille shot down that day out of a total of twenty-two. It was an astonishing achievement – yet it was bombers, not fighters, he should have been targeting. As it was, Billy Drake's wing managed to return to base without a single casualty, and Marseille's exploits completely failed to halt the RAF's bombers getting through. In fact, not one bomber was shot down by Axis fighters that day. As night fell, Rommel's forces were in disarray.

There was, however, to be no let-up. Soon it was once more the turn of the Wellingtons, who pasted the Afrikakorps until dawn; fires from these raids were still burning when the day-bombers took over. Rommel himself ventured into the forward area still held by his panzer divisions and came under attack six times in two hours between 10 a.m. and noon. 'Swarms of low-flying fighter bombers were coming back to the attack again and again,' he wrote, 'and my troops suffered tremendous casualties. Vast numbers of vehicles stood burning in the desert.'

Luigi Marchese had seen Rommel pass by in his command car that day. For much of the battle, Marchese and his comrades in the 2 Regimento Paracadutisti had played a static, defensive role, holding a low plateau of higher ground to the south of the line. Later that day, they learned the battle had not gone well; they all felt their morale take a big blow. 'Disappointment and dejection filled our hearts,' he wrote, 'and the thought that so many lives had been lost without achieving anything made the pain worse.' He was very clear about why they had lost: it was the shorter lines of supply for the British, combined with new tanks and artillery and the devastating power of the RAF. 'It was clear many things had not gone right during our attack,' he noted. 'Too many.'

'With the failure of this offensive,' wrote Fritz Bayerlein, 'our last chance to win in the Nile Delta had passed.' Rommel's dream of seizing all of Egypt and the Middle East was now over – and for good. There was a chance for Eighth Army to rise up and take the attack to the enemy, but Montgomery refused to be drawn. This had been a defensive battle. He would go on the offensive when he felt ready – and that would be soon enough but not yet.

Alam Halfa was, in many ways, a small battle, but it was a significant one. The tide had turned. More and more materiel – British and American – was reaching the Middle East. The build-up of forces was unstoppable, and now there would be no more distractions, no more tugs from other theatres. How long it would take to clear those southern shores of the Mediterranean was not clear, but the outcome was no longer in doubt.

In the East, the German summer offensive was also running out of steam, while the Battle of the Atlantic was already lost. In all these theatres, there would be setbacks for the Allies, and moments of hope for the Axis, but it was hard now to see how Germany could ever win the war.

Ever since the start of the Second World War, much of the world has been rather too dazzled by the achievements of the German military machine, and particularly the Wehrmacht of the opening years – those days of conquest and lightning victories. It was, however, all based on the very shakiest of foundations – foundations that went back to the days of Frederick the Great. The German way of war had shiny new weapons when it crossed the Polish border on 1 September 1939 and new tactics for using them, but tactical flair was not enough. Strategically, the mistakes and misjudgements had been legion. Operationally, they simply did not have the resources to take on the world.

What was more, key to those early victories had been the spectacularly successful harnessing of air power. The Luftwaffe had always been a tactical air force, designed to support the ground troops, and without that strategic capability it had always been somewhat incomplete. Yet air power had become a crucial part of modern conflict. 'An important lesson that was to influence all our later plans, especially the entire method of our conduct of the war, had been learned during this operation,' wrote Bayerlein of the aftermath of Alam Halfa. 'The operational and tactical capabilities are of little consequence if the enemy commands the air space with a powerful air force and can fly massive attack missions undisturbed.' This was nothing less than the truth: Germany had proved it so in the Blitzkrieg years and now the RAF was doing the same in North Africa. Whether air power alone could deliver victory as men like Portal and Harris were advocating had yet to be proved, but it was becoming crystal clear that winning this current war was very unlikely without it. What the first three years of conflict had proved was this: the bigger and better the air force, the fewer men would be needed on the ground. In Britain, the current priority for manpower was not the Army, the Navy or even the RAF; it was the Ministry of Aircraft Production.

The first three years of war, from 1 September 1939 to 1 September 1942, had witnessed the rise of Germany but also its fall – a failure that the slaughter off the Americas by the U-boats and the dazzling summer victories in the East and in North Africa could not hide.

For the Allies, the time had come at last to start clawing their way back and tightening the noose around the Axis. The first drive for victory was about to begin.

PART III

THE ALLIES STRIKE BACK

CHAPTER 25

A Brief Discourse on Tanks and Fire-power

B ACK IN JULY, on his return from the United States, the British Minister of Production, Oliver Lyttelton, had given an update on British war production to a Parliamentary Committee in the House of Commons. He chose to focus first on the suitability and quality of weapons that Britain was now manufacturing; he was also keenly aware that there were a large number of people within Britain's political and military establishment who believed that poor weaponry, especially when compared with that of the Germans, had played a significant part in Eighth Army's defeat at Gazala and Tobruk.

Lyttelton pointed out that the Army General Staff received a constant stream of tactical information from the front, all of which was carefully sifted and applied where possible. There were also a number of scientific observers who had been formed into Operational Research Sections which had been posted to the battlefront. They then reported directly to both the theatre C-in-C and the Ministry of Supply. He was confident this ensured that tactical lessons and production practice was a marriage that now worked pretty well. New enemy equipment was, whenever captured, given a preliminary investigation on site and then sent home. For this specific purpose, there was now a Weapons Development Committee under the Deputy CIGS at the War Office; it included officers from the Ministry of Supply as well as Professor Frederick Lindemann, now Lord Cherwell, as the Chief Scientific Advisor.

One of the main concerns coming from the desert war was the perceived disparity between British and German guns; no one seemed to feel very threatened by those of the Italians. Lyttelton pointed out that the Germans had a 37mm anti-tank gun, the Pak 35/36, which was equivalent to the British 2-pounder. 'The German weapon throws a projectile of 1.9 pounds,' Lyttelton told them, 'compared with the 2.4 pounds projectile thrown by the 2-pounder.' The Germans also had a 50mm anti-tank gun, which was roughly the same as the 6-pounder gun now in service, although, again, the British gun packed a slightly bigger punch than the German equivalent.

Then there was the German 88mm, about which, Lyttelton added, 'we have heard so much.' There was also the German 75mm, the Pak 40, which had a velocity that was comparable to the 88mm and was actually more numerous. At any rate, Lyttelton rightly pointed out that the British had the 3.7-inch heavy anti-aircraft gun, which looked and performed similarly to the dreaded 88mm. In fact, while the 88mm had a muzzle velocity of around 1,000 metres per second, the 3.7-inch was slightly better at 1,044 m/s. Because both were designed to be able to fire a shell vertically some miles into the sky, the range of both when fired horizontally was pretty impressive. To put it another way: both could penetrate up to 150mm of solid steel at 2,500 metres – more than 1½ miles. That was thicker than any armour on any armoured fighting vehicle on either side.

'There has been some suggestion that the 3.7 cannot be used in an anti-tank role,' continued Lyttelton. 'On mobile mounting exactly the same as the 88mm, it can be used very effectively.' Neither gun, he pointed out, was an ideal anti-tank gun because their profiles were not low enough. 'But when either of these guns gets a good target of tanks the effect will be devastating,' he added. 'These are exactly comparable weapons.' In fact, they were not *exactly* comparable, because the 3.7-inch was heavier and did not have the same quality of optics as the 88mm. However, be that as it may, the British had vastly superior pools of gun tractors and towing facilities than did the Axis, and perfectly adequate optics with which to spot, aim and fire at an enemy tank at ranges well in excess of one mile. In the Desert War, that was more than sufficient. It was more than sufficient pretty much anywhere, in fact.

One of the committee wanted to know whether Britain actually had any 3.7s available out there for the anti-tank role. Yes, Lyttelton replied –

large numbers of them. Actually, there were some 220 in Egypt, most in the Canal Zone, which was hardly the focus of fierce aerial attack, and around Cairo, of which the same could be said. Lyttelton then recounted a conversation he had been told of by a British artillery officer who had spoken to a captured German. The British officer had complimented him on the 88mm. 'Oh, yes,' the German had replied, 'but I prefer the 3.7. I was on the wrong side of it in France.'

Why 3.7s had not been used more readily at Gazala, for example, has never been sufficiently answered. They were quick-firing – up to twenty rounds a minute, but half that very comfortably – and very simple to load and fire. The 88mm had been put on a pedestal of weapon superiority and increasingly feared by Eighth Army troops. And yet there was, as Lyttelton rightly pointed out, an equally potent weapon within the British arsenal right under their noses out there in Egypt. The fault must lie once more ultimately with the leadership. If Auchinleck or Ritchie had insisted they be used in that role, they would have been moved up to the front and employed. If those at home were conscious of this perceived shortcoming in anti-tank guns, it is inconceivable that it would not have reached the attention of the army commander or C-in-C.

Then there was the issue of tanks. On 16 June, once it had become clear that Eighth Army had lost the Gazala battle, Major-General John Kennedy – the Director of Military Operations at the War Office – had written in his diary a very telling couple of lines: 'We fully realized the heavy disadvantage Auchinleck suffered in the poor quality of our tanks, which were inferior to those of the Germans, but quantity was no substitute for quality.' This perception holds true even to this day, but is utterly fallacious. The most common German tank was the Panzer Mk III. This was repeatedly being tweaked and upgraded, so that by the summer of 1942 they had reached the *Ausf. N* – that is, the fourteenth variant. The Mk III had originally been equipped with the 37mm gun, but had since been upgunned to a 50mm. The latest 'N' model had a low-velocity 75mm, but these had little effect over the long ranges of the desert – and they were in small numbers in the Panzerarmee too. The maximum armour any Mk III had was 50mm.

The best German tank was the Panzer Mk IV, which had originally been designed with the 50mm gun, then had a low-velocity 75mm gun added. Now, in the summer of 1942, new models were arriving with a longer and higher-velocity gun; this, however, was a mixed blessing, because the Mk IV had not been originally designed to hold such a gun and its length made it rather nose-heavy – so much so that it affected the forward suspension springs. This made it harder to drive and also led to increased wear – and then breakdowns. It had front armour of 80mm, which was reasonably good, but not enough to stop most anti-tank guns – although this rather depended on the range at which the anti-tank gun was fired, because the further away it was, the sooner the velocity and hence its penetrative power fell away. This was why the 88mm and 3.7-inch guns were so effective in the desert, where the ground was, for the most part, very open. Such a gun could blast any tank on either side over distances from which it was completely out of range of anything on the ground other than its direct opposite number.

Most Axis tanks in Rommel's army were inferior models to the Mk IV and Mk III, however, with less powerful guns and thinner armour. The main Italian tanks were the M13/40, equipped with a 47mm gun; the upgraded M14/41; and the newly arriving M15/42, which was supposed to be the even-better version, but which still had a 47mm gun and a maximum of 45mm. Rommel still had some old Czech models too – T38s, armed with a 37mm gun.

In contrast, Eighth Army had, by the summer of 1942, a mass of US-built M3 Grants, with a 75mm gun and 50mm of armour, and with new M4 Shermans on their way, also with a 75mm gun. Britain had its own equivalent of the Panzer Mk III and IV, which was the Valentine, with up to 65mm of armour and a gun that was, like the German equivalents, being upgraded, first from a 2-pounder, then to 6-pounder, and finally a 75mm was being produced. Most in North Africa still had the 2-pounder, however, much as most Mk IIIs still had the 37mm. There was also the Crusader, which was fast but under-protected and under-armed, and the Matilda, which was slow but well protected and had a 3-inch low-velocity howitzer. Certainly there were cases of Crusaders, armed with 2-pounders, coming up against a Panzer Mk III or IV armed with 75mm guns and finding themselves out-gunned. But, equally, there were panzers that came up against British tanks with larger guns too.

In other words, one to one, the qualitative discrepancy that Kennedy mentioned did not really exist. In fact, Eighth Army had considerably more 75mm tanks than did the Panzerarmee Afrika. Nor should the fact that Britain was now using ever-larger numbers of American-built tanks be seen as some kind of failing on the part of British tank manufacturers or a sign of weakness in the British war effort. Rather, the ability to purchase – or be given – large numbers of new tanks and have them shipped across the oceans was a sign of strength. What's more, both the Grant and Sherman had been developed on the back of British specifications. If the USA could build weapons such as tanks, which could easily be used in both British and American armies, then so much the better; it meant Britain could concentrate on building huge numbers of Lancaster bombers, Mosquitos, upgraded versions of Spitfires and other potentially war-winning aircraft, guns and other materiel.

What the fighting in the Soviet Union and North Africa had proved, however, was that Blitzkrieg-era tanks were no longer really cutting the mustard. The Germans had been horrified to discover the Russians had large numbers of T34s with its 76.2mm gun and 60mm turret armour, yet after the Battle of France, Hermann Balck, for one, had thought it was necessary then to build as many long-barrelled 75mm Panzer IVs and higher-velocity 50mm MK IIIs as possible. He had overheard a conversation between Hitler, who was advocating such a move, and Generals Adolf von Schell and Fromm, who countered that no main gun should ever extend beyond the edge of the tank's hull – because of balance and because it would make it difficult to move through the forests of the east with a longer gun. 'The consequence was that our tank guns at Moscow could not penetrate the Russian armour,' noted Balck. 'When we refitted our panzers with the longer-barrel guns during the winter of 1941–1942, the Russian tank superiority ended.'

This was true to a point, but there were many more T34s than there ever were long-barrelled Mk IVs. By June 1942, the Wehrmacht had only 681 of these 75mm Panzer IVs; some 6,000 T34s had already been built in the Soviet Union so far in 1942. However, the German panzer arm had not developed with heavy armour and fire-power in mind. Their prime role in *Bewegungskrieg* tactics had been to exploit breakthroughs, for which speed and manoeuvrability had been seen as key. What's more, as they had repeatedly proved in France when they destroyed the French 1st Armoured Division, for example, and again on numerous occasions during the desert war, panzers were often used as a bait to draw enemy armour into a hidden screen of anti-tank guns. Big, lumbering, heavy-gunned tanks could not fulfil that role.

Now, though, it was clear that a bigger, better-protected tank with a high-velocity gun was very much the order of the day, which was why

Germany was in the process of building two new battlefield tanks: the Mk V, to be known as the Panther, and the Mk VI, which would be called the Tiger. The focus of the Panther was to have been a high-velocity 75mm gun, but as with the Ju88 and Me210, it suffered from creeping design specifications. Originally a 20-ton tank, it had increased to 30 tons by the spring of 1942 when both MAN and Daimler-Benz had submitted their separate designs. On 5 March, Speer had told Hitler he thought the Daimler-Benz model was the one to back. However, MAN learned of this and altered their design accordingly to allow for more sloping armour, a design feature of the T34. The Führer then appointed a special commission to review both designs in May and the MAN version was selected – not least because it used an existing turret design and engine. This meant it could go into production sooner than the DB design, which required an entirely new turret and engine. That was the theory, but since then further tweaks and specification changes had been made, including several ordered directly by Hitler himself. Most concerned the level of armour, which rose from 60mm to 80mm and then again to 100mm on all vertical surfaces and on the turret plate. It was only now, in September 1942, that the MAN prototype was ready for testing, and it no longer weighed 30 tons but a colossal 45 tons. This was no medium tank but rather a heavy one. And heavy tanks used a lot of fuel and were difficult to manoeuvre.

Moreover, despite General Thomas's stark warning in December the previous year that German war production needed to abandon aesthetics and high-level engineering in favour of no-frills speed of production, this had been largely ignored. MAN's design included advanced torsion bar suspension and complicated interleaved wheels. If one of these wheels or the suspension needed repairing, the entire track and wheel system needed to be dismantled. In contrast, the suspension bogeys on the US-built Grant or Sherman were on the outside of non-interleaved wheels so repairs could be easily made in isolation. At any rate, the Panther was, by September 1942, both huge and incredibly complicated. It was hard to imagine how it could be mass-produced any time soon, let alone effectively maintained in the field, because its size meant much bigger hoists, wreckers (tow trucks) and tractors (low-loaders) would be needed too. Currently, these did not exist.

Meanwhile, the Tiger, a heavy tank, had also been designed and, again, there were two versions to choose from: one by Henschel and one by

Porsche. Like the Panther, the specification had also been repeatedly revised, so that what began as a 45-ton tank now had so much armour it weighed nearly 54 tons. It was the Henschel Tiger that got the nod and, with its thick armour of up to 120mm and an 88mm gun, it dwarfed any other tank in production. The first four were completed in August 1942. It was a beast that would certainly put the fear of God into those who came up against it. Witnessing this mighty tank for the first time, anyone would have been forgiven for thinking the Germans still had the best, most mechanized army in the world.

None the less, like the Panther, it had very complicated interleaved wheels, had double torsion bar suspension, was very difficult to maintain, and was so enormous it would not quite fit on the loading gauge of continental railways – which was the only practical means of getting it from A to B – so had to have a different, narrower set of tracks put on for travel, which would then have to be taken off and replaced with wider, combat tracks when it reached its destination. Not only was this time-consuming, it also meant building an extra set of tracks for each tank over and above what would normally be expected to be constructed in terms of spares.

Its transmission, meanwhile, was designed by Ferdinand Porsche and was a hydraulically controlled, semi-automatic, pre-selector, eight-speed gearbox, which sounds complicated – and was. Furthermore, because of its extreme weight, the traditional clutch and brake steering system didn't work, so an entirely new steering mechanism had to be developed, which included two fixed radii of turns on each gear. The Tiger therefore had sixteen different radii of turn. Sophisticated it most certainly was. It was also fearsomely big and lethal. Yet the opportunities for mass production were almost zero, the chances of it regularly breaking down were enormous, and it was gas-guzzlingly thirsty, using around 1 gallon per mile. In fact, for an oil- and fuel-starved nation like Nazi Germany, the Tiger was not really looking like the panacea for which Hitler had hoped.

Germany's priority for new tank design was therefore now armour and armament above all other factors. The trouble was, tanks, more than any other vehicle, were subject to defects. Some part, whether only a loose nut, was always in need of attention. Oil leaks would occur. Parts would wear out. This meant that the easier and simpler they were in construction, the easier they were to maintain. Simpler, smaller tanks ensured that a great deal of tank maintenance could be done by the crew, because the less complicated the tank, the less technical training, maintenance tools and spare parts were required.

Germany had begun the war with a low-level base knowledge in vehicle maintenance because it had not been a very automotive society and had not had a highly mechanized army either. Early panzer models were small and simple and, for the most part, the countries in which they were operating either had sufficient infrastructure or were close and small enough that large distances and mechanical strain were kept to a minimum. It also helped that victories were being won in a matter of days and weeks. General Adolf von Schell had tried to streamline production, and centralization of maintenance – that is, creating large maintenance depots at the place of manufacture within the Reich – had seemed the most sensible and logical way to proceed.

What had held true during the Blitzkrieg victories, however, most certainly did not in the Soviet Union or the vast, empty desert of North Africa. Having fourteen versions of the Panzer III was all very well, but each one needed different spare parts, which had to be made and then shipped. In the Soviet Union, maintenance was further complicated because the Soviet railway gauge was wider than that of Germany and the rest of continental Europe. Very little rolling stock had been captured and the Russians had destroyed all maintenance facilities, as well as bridges, as they had retreated. Railways had to be converted – and thousands of miles of them, which had a disastrous effect on the Germans' ability to maintain tanks and vehicles.

The other problem for Germany was that now tank factories were operating at full steam trying to build new models, there really wasn't capacity to repair those coming back from the fronts, so a huge backlog had developed. In North Africa, the priority was for fuel and ammunition. In fact, so precious was fuel, there was little left for maintenance trucks, and nor was there much shipping capacity for spare parts.

Despite these shortcomings, Hitler was now demanding that two brand-new, extremely complex and sophisticated tanks be mass-produced, while men like von Schell were still desperately trying to decentralize and further streamline the production and maintenance of existing models. Decentralization of maintenance was being put into practice, with new depots being built to support each of the Army Groups in the East and with maintenance units in Libya, but it was not something that could happen overnight.

On 10 September, von Schell was sacked by Göring. He had done his best, but he had always been doomed to fail. Getting rid of the one man in the Reich who now understood the myriad problems was unlikely to improve the situation much, however. 'Tanks and motor vehicles need maintenance like ships and planes,' said von Schell later. 'That was not respected enough.'

Britain, on the other hand, had learned back in 1940 the crucial importance of decentralized maintenance for tanks and armoured fighting vehicles. Tanks had been hastily designed and put into production before the war, rather in the same way that Germany was now doing with the Tiger and Panther. Because both France and Britain had assumed any war in the West would be largely defensive, neither country had really developed tank wreckers and transporters. French tanks were moved about by railway, while British tanks were returned to Britain for any major maintenance. This would have worked just fine had the campaign been largely static as they had predicted, but it had proved to be a war of manoeuvre instead and so for Britain, having survived and begun the process of rebuilding its army, maintenance of tanks and vehicles was very much at the forefront in their plans to grow and develop. Whatever doubts might possibly have remained on this matter were quickly kicked into touch by virtue of the highly mobile war against the Italians in both East and North Africa, where the distances, temperature extremes, sand and dust all underlined that maintenance of force capability, whether it be the health of the men or maintenance of equipment, was of absolutely paramount importance.

That meant factoring in plenty of spares, plenty of support vehicles and ensuring there were adequate facilities and men with the necessary know-how. Out in the Middle East there were now both fully functioning maintenance depots around Cairo, as well as plenty of mobile workshops, tractors and wreckers, both from Britain and, now more numerously, from the USA. For too long, criticism of Britain's tanks has focused on their tactical capability, not their operational one. The truth, though, is that if a tank could not be maintained effectively, it did not matter how big its gun was or how thick its armour. A broken-down tank was no good to anyone.

By September 1942, the British General Staff, after consultation with the Tank Board set up back in May, issued an 'Order of Priority of Requirement of Design'. Top of the list was reliability. The Army wanted tanks that did not easily break down. Second on the list was a high-velocity gun; in sharp contrast with Hitler's view on tank design, armour came fifth after speed and endurance. It was a priority list that was very much at one with the Americans'. The M4 Sherman was now coming off the production lines in good numbers. It had been designed with mass production in mind. This meant that it was fairly simple and uncomplicated, which in turn made it simple and uncomplicated to maintain. Not only did it have easy-to-change tracks, segments and accessible suspension, its transmission was a no-nonsense manual gearbox of four gears forward and one in reverse. Much of the hull and many mechanical features were the same as the M3 Grant, so many of the machine tools and parts were the same too, which made life easier. Access to the working parts was good, and engines and transmissions could be easily taken out and replaced.

The drawback was that, when going into action, inside it was stuffed full of ammunition and its armour was not sufficiently thick to stop a shell from a high-velocity anti-tank gun, such as a German 75mm or 88mm. If hit, it tended to burn quickly, with horrific consequences for the crew trapped inside. That, however, was true of most tanks in 1942.

Meanwhile, the British were developing their own tanks. The Cromwell was a medium tank with decent armour, a 75mm gun and good speed, while the Churchill, too hastily developed initially but now just coming into proper production, was slow but incredibly versatile; it could climb steeper terrain than any other tank in existence. It also had very thick armour and could withstand considerable punishment. While most were still in the UK, six were on their way to the Middle East.

In terms of small arms, the differences were comparatively small. The Germans favoured high-rate-of-fire machine guns – the theory was they could then be used in an anti-aircraft role as well – but the MG34 was over-engineered, took 150 man-hours to make, and there was a lot of material wastage in the manufacturing process, which the Germans could ill-afford. It was, none the less, a fine weapon. The new, less expensive MG42 was now coming into production, however. This took only 75 man-hours and had a rate of fire of an astonishing 1,200–1,500 rounds per minute. This certainly made it very lethal, but its high rate of fire meant the barrel overheated very quickly indeed, it produced a lot of smoke when fired and, when used in a light role on its bipod, it was hard to fire with anything like precision accuracy. In terms of range, effectiveness and maintenance, however, small arms were roughly comparable.

In other words, in the summer of 1942, in the war in North Africa, neither side had a qualitative superiority when it came to weaponry. Weapons were not the deciding factor when it came to battle.

CHAPTER 26

A Brief Discourse on Training and Morale

I<small>N</small> B<small>RITAIN</small>, <small>THE</small> K<small>ING</small> had called for a National Day of Prayer on Thursday, 3 September. It was the third anniversary of Britain's entry into the war; Rommel's drive towards the Middle East had been halted and the German advance in Russia was slowing, so there was now cause for hope. In London, Gwladys Cox and her husband, Ralph, decided to go to St Paul's Cathedral for the 12.15 p.m. service and made sure they got there early so they might secure a seat. It was the seventh such day of National Prayer called by the King, and Gwladys could well remember the first, during the retreat from Dunkirk. 'The bombing had not begun,' she noted, 'and London was still without her terrible battle scars of today.' By the time the service started, the cathedral was packed and there were many hundreds more outside, listening through loudspeakers. Gwladys found it hard to believe it had been only three years since war began. 'One feels years older,' she added, 'and many, we notice, are looking it.'

While Gwladys Cox and her fellow Londoners may have been feeling war-weary, there was, however, a very real feeling of renewed vigour and optimism among the British forces out in Egypt. Generals Alexander and Montgomery could, a month on from their arrival in the theatre, give themselves a light pat on the back. Their brief tenure had so far followed the path they had prescribed. Both men had warned there could be no more retreat. Nor would there be, for, by the end of the Battle of Alam Halfa, the Middle East was safe.

Inevitably, Churchill was impatient for Eighth Army to go back on to the offensive. This, Alexander had told him before Alam Halfa, would be the end of September at the earliest. Alam Halfa had changed that, however, and Montgomery put his foot down. Alexander now told the Prime Minister that the first week of October was more realistic and that they could expect the battle to last a week. But there would be no full moon until the third week of October and that would be needed for the sappers to make gaps in the extensive minefields that now separated the two lines. Alexander was pushing back the Prime Minister's demands with greater firmness than his predecessors.

Then there was the time needed to get more tanks and men into a mobile striking force. On 7 September, for example, Alexander went to the Base Ordnance workshops at Tel el Kebir to see the new Shermans that had just arrived. For the most part, they had travelled well, although seawater had caused some minor corrosion. These repairs, plus some desert fittings, meant they were being released at only twenty a day, but those tanks were most certainly all needed for the forthcoming battle.

Churchill was insistent, however, that the Panzerarmee should be defeated before the launch of Operation TORCH, now scheduled for November, in order to encourage the Vichy French to jump ship and the Spanish to remain neutral. 'I have carefully considered the timing in relation to TORCH,' Alexander wrote to Churchill, 'and have come to the conclusion that not only complies with military reasons but also to provide cover for TORCH, the best date for us to start would be minus 13 of TORCH.' That meant 24 October.

The Prime Minister was not happy, but Alexander was determined to shield Montgomery from any prime-ministerial interference and, in any case, he had an ally in Brooke. Churchill would have to lump it. Alexander agreed entirely with Montgomery's view on the state of Eighth Army. Alam Halfa, Alexander pointed out to Churchill, demonstrated the 'urgent need of intensive training.' During the battle, Eighth Army had still managed to lose more men and tanks than the Panzerarmee; as the Sherwood Rangers had proved, charging forward as though they were still on their horses and thundering towards lines of spear-wielding natives rather than screens of anti-tank guns really would not do any more.

Certainly, Montgomery had not been overly impressed with what he had found. It was, he noted, 'a regrettable fact that our troops are not, in all cases, highly trained.' That, he was determined to prove, was about to change.

A lot has been written about the standard of training in the war, and most of it has tended to highlight the superiority of the German soldier above any other. However, at its most basic level, training in the British, German, Italian and now US armies was much the same and broke down into three essential parts. The first was individual training – that is, basic training involving square-bashing (parade-ground drill); followed by weapons training; and route marches. This was designed to bring the recruit into a military environment where discipline was essential. German recruits had the added advantage that most had been in the Hitler Youth and all in the Reichsarbeitsdienst – the Labour Service – which instilled discipline but also provided political indoctrination. Much the same was true of the Italian armed forces, although young Italians were given even more paramilitary training and political indoctrination than young Germans; for Italians, it began at the age of six with *Figli della Lupa* – Sons of the Wolf – then progressed to *Balilla* and finally *Avanguardisti*, which took them up to the age of eighteen. It was not obligatory to join these Italian youth organizations, but it was very strongly encouraged.

In Italy, pre-military training did become compulsory at eighteen, when, for three years, they were expected to join the *Giovani Fascisti* – the Young Fascists. Every male was also liable for military service, which, before the war, amounted to eighteen months; year-groups were called up in the April of the year following their twentieth birthday. They then became reservists and most had been called up once more as soon as Italy entered the war.

The recruitment process of all the major combatant nations had a localized element too. In the case of Germany, the Third Reich was divided into a number of regional *Wehrkreise* – military districts – each of which was responsible for conscription in their area. A very similar organization was in place in Italy. In Germany, recruits were then posted to their *Ersatz* unit, which was part of the *Ersatzarmee*, or Reserve Army, commanded by General Fromm. *Ersatz* units were affiliated to a field division and were set up in much the same way – that is, in companies, battalions and regiments. Franz Maassen, a young baker's son from Düsseldorf, for example, was in the 9th Company of the 579th Infantry

Training Battalion of the 306th Ersatz Division, and would then, eventually, join the same unit in the 306th Field Division.

There were exceptions, however. The Kriegsmarine could recruit from throughout the Reich, as could the Luftwaffe, although there were a number of Luftwaffe *Wehrkreise* too and four naval *Wehrkreise*. What's more, as the war was progressing, the Reserve Army was finding it ever-harder to keep recruits in their corresponding *Wehrkreis* field units. For North Africa, for example, there was now only one field replacement battalion for all of the Afrikakorps. Training was also beginning to take place at centres outside both *Wehrkreise* and the Reich itself, resulting in the gradual breakdown of the local affiliation.

Much the same was happening in the British Army. At the start of the war, a recruit from Yorkshire, for example, would be placed in a Yorkshire regiment. Now, three years into the war, that was not necessarily the case. This was equally true in the United States and Italy; Bing Evans and Ralph Schaps were from the Midwest and had joined a Midwest National Guard division, the 34th, but there were now men in the Red Bulls who hailed from New Jersey, Maine and a number of other states along the East Coast.

After basic training, the second part was training within a small unit such as a squad or section, while the third stage emphasized higher-unit training such as platoon or company. Typically, training included map reading, patrol work, basic tactical principles, further weapons training, as well as unit exercises. What was needed was all-arms training, that is, joint exercises with artillery, armour and other arms of the services such as engineers, yet in no army did this happen before recruits joined their field unit. In other words, there was a practical limit to what could be taught during the early training process.

Franz Maassen, aged twenty-two in the summer of 1942, was one of the few German recruits to have avoided the Hitler Youth – getting up at 4 a.m. every morning to help his father in the bakery, he had insisted he didn't have the time. He had, however, volunteered before his call-up and had been sent for basic training in Detmold, in north-western Germany between Hanover and Dortmund. Maassen had been told initially that, because he was quite short, he would be going into the panzers, but for a reason that was never explained to him he ended up in the infantry.

Training involved endless route marches, large amounts of drill, as well as weapons training. 'It was very hard,' he said, then added, 'It was brutal.' This, however, was because their instructors pushed them hard and would punish them for the slightest misdemeanour. Basic training lasted three months and then they were posted to Belgium, where they were part of the occupying force but training at the same time. 'Basic training was rubbish,' said Maassen, 'but afterwards, when I went to Belgium, I learned a lot.' There was, however, almost no all-arms training, except for one battalion exercise, which involved live ammunition and artillery. They were taught how to assault a tank, but they never actually trained with tanks: they were too precious a commodity. By the spring of 1941, Maassen and his comrades were also practising amphibious assaults. 'We still thought we would be invading Britain at that time,' said Maassen. It had been part of the deception plan for BARBAROSSA. Now, after eighteen months in Belgium, he was about to be posted east.

Another recruit just entering the Army was Hein Severloh, aged nineteen. Young Germans could be called up for service to the Reich from eighteen, but annual classes, or drafts, were, before and at the start of the war, called up at twenty. Because of the shortage of manpower, however, the annual drafts had by this time begun to be called up a year or even two years early.

Severloh was ordered to report for service on 23 July 1942 and was assigned to Light Artillery Training Battalion 19 at the Scharnhorst Barracks at Hannover-Bothfeld. Even before basic training, he had to complete a short course of basic and mounted training on horses, as it was horses that remained the mainstay of the German artillery. Among his fellow recruits were a number of Poles and Upper Silesians – another sign of the emptying manpower pool. These were termed *Volksdeutsche*, or ethnic Germans, but none of them spoke a word of German. 'No one had taught these people the most important German terms,' noted Severloh. 'Despite the frequent comical situations, I found it really tragic.'

With this short course over, on 2 August they were posted to the Harz Mountains, where other replacement battalions assembled, then sent by train to Saint-Aubin, near Calais in France, where Severloh was assigned to the actual 3rd Battery of Artillery Regiment 321, part of the 321st Division. This was when his basic training began: as part of occupation forces and while attached to a reserve division. 'Our real training,' he noted, 'only actually began there.' Already, by the summer of 1942, the German Army was starting to cut some big corners when it came to training.

In the case of British infantry recruits, after basic training they were, from 1941 onwards, sent not to a regimental depot but instead to an Infantry Training Centre. From there, they were posted to their battalion. New to British infantry training, however, were the new Battle Schools, which had initially been an idea of General Alexander's when he had commanded I Corps in Britain after Dunkirk. He had recognized that large numbers of recruits were entering the army along with a great number of new and inexperienced officers. There was a limit to what could be expected from men who, in peacetime, would never, ever have put on a military uniform. His idea was to reduce the most common situations of infantry battles to a few basic rules. 'Better to know instinctively some orthodox line of conduct,' he wrote, 'than to be paralysed by the uncertainty of what to do.'

One of those now heading to battle school was Lieutenant Farley Mowat, who, on a patch of gorse-covered heathland, joined some thirty other subalterns for toughening-up. Their days began before dawn and lasted until dark, and everything they did seemed to be 'at the double' and weighed down by full battle equipment. They ran at least 10 miles a day and 20 on Sundays. 'We crawled, squirmed and wriggled for endless hours through gorse thickets,' he noted, 'while the training staff fired live ammunition under, over and all around us; threw percussion grenades between our outflung legs; or heaved gas canisters (which made us puke) under our noses.' There was unarmed combat too, with instructors who hit them in the windpipe, kicked them in the testicles and cartwheeled them over shoulders. Then there was the half-mile obstacle course with walls and endless barbed wire that had to be completed in four minutes flat. 'Before the first week was out,' wrote Mowat, 'we had lost eight or nine of our number, three of them wounded during live firing exercises.'

Accompanying this training was a vast array of written material, from specific training pamphlets to 'Notes from the Theatres of War' to Army training memoranda. The latest infantry bible, *The Instructor's Handbook of Fieldcraft and Battle Drill*, written by Lieutenant-Colonel Lionel Wigram and Major R. M. T. Kerr, was just being published; it was Wigram who had been largely responsible for setting up the Battle Drill programme that Mowat had just undertaken.

Although all officers were issued with most of the training pamphlets, they were by no means universally read. Inevitably, the keener the soldier, the more likely he was to read this material. The Americans were also now starting to produce large numbers of field and technical manuals, as well as training films – a much better way of disseminating key tactical information to recruits than pamphlets, not least because recruits could be shuffled into a screening and forced to watch a short film; it was not so easy making them read. The bible of the German infantryman was an unofficial and privately published guide known universally as the 'Reibert' after the name of the publisher. In terms of fieldcraft and tactical training it was remarkably similar to those issued to troops in Britain and the USA.

There were, however, differing approaches to creating and training officers and NCOs between the different combatant powers. Class and type of education counted for more in Britain than in other countries. Officer cadets were sent to Sandhurst Royal Military College during peacetime but to other Officer Cadet Training Units (OCTUs) now that the army was being rapidly expanded once more. Courses varied in length, but were seventeen weeks for infantry and thirty for more technical arms such as the Royal Engineers. Once these courses had been completed, the cadets would join their field unit and be expected to command a platoon of thirty-six men or its equivalent in the other arms.

In the United States, the army had grown from 267,767 in June 1940 to 1,460,998 on 1 July 1941, to 3,074,184 one year later. This was an astonishing rate of growth and in that time no fewer than forty-five new military camps had been built, including twenty-one replacement training centres. The Army was hurriedly trying to modernize, but it hadn't stopped the US Cavalry purchasing 20,000 horses in early 1941, nor had it prevented large numbers of men training without proper weapons and equipment. This, however, was unavoidable given the speed of expansion.

The quality of officers was the biggest concern. There had been officers in the National Guard and those from the Reserve Officer Corps, but all too often they had been as much as ten years over-age for their rank, outmoded in their thinking and physically under par. By the summer of 1941, more than 75 per cent of officers in the Regular Army divisions and half those in the National Guard had been reserve officers. Officer Candidate Schools (OCSs) had since been set up and involved a three-month course; its graduates were now mockingly referred to as 'ninety-day wonders'.

By the summer of 1942, the new 3-million-strong army was seriously short of officers, and this was because the Army Air Forces and Navy were siphoning off the best candidates. To get around this shortfall, enlisted men from the ranks were put forward for the Army General Classification Test (AGCT), the route of entry for the OCSs. The result, however, was a continued lowering of standards; far too many were admitted with lower AGCT scores than should have been acceptable. It was a situation that would improve, however. What's more, as matters stood, the vast majority were not being rushed into combat. Training could and would continue, and, as more and more equipment and weapons rolled off the production lines, so they would be increasingly better equipped. This was a luxury German and Italian troops could no longer afford: once trained, they were invariably hustled into the firing line. In contrast, most Canadian soldiers, nearly all Americans and the majority of British troops had yet to see any action at all. Some, like the Bowles twins from Alabama, or the former England cricketer Captain Hedley Verity, had been training for over two years already.

The Italian Army had also been rather dependent on out-of-date and over-age reserve officers at the start of the war. By 1942, a large number of these had been killed, wounded or taken prisoner. New officers were coming through, however, and were either volunteers for Regular service who were sufficiently educated to be selected as officer cadets, or those conscripted but of a higher educational standard who were compelled to be trained as officers.

Only in the German Army did all officers serve in the ranks first, although, as elsewhere, it was only those with higher educational standards who could be considered. Before the war, an officer cadet – a *Fahnenjunker* or the higher grade *Fähnrich* – would serve for around three-quarters of a year in the ranks before being sent to *Kriegsschule*, or War School. This was particularly rigorous and, at the end, the *Fähnrich* would be posted to his unit as a *Leutnant*. This process, however, had since been abolished because of the urgency with which new officers were needed. Now, a cadet had to serve for at least a year in the ranks and then, if he had proved himself to be suitable officer material, he would be sent to a shorter course at the *Waffenschule*. This, it was felt, still ensured the right men were being selected, but cut a lot of time. However, new changes were about to come in that scrapped the earlier academic standards. Soon, only bravery and leadership skills were necessary qualifications for becoming an officer cadet. Actually, to a certain extent this was also the case with the British Army, where a number of NCOs were being given field commissions or selected to attend OCTUs. It was a good idea, because war was rapidly breaking down many social barriers, and it meant that in most units there was a handful of newly arriving officers who already had front-line experience.

Training, of course, did not stop once a recruit or an officer joined his field unit – as Montgomery was now particularly keen to impress upon his new army in the autumn of 1942. There was also a difference between theoretical training and practical training, as Albert Martin had discovered on reaching Egypt back in 1940. 'The games were over,' he noted. 'This time, our very survival would be influenced by how well we learned our next lessons.' Finally, he and his mates were sent to the front, where they found themselves put into sections as replacements, filling the holes left by the dead, wounded and sick. Suddenly, they were among men who had actually been in action and soon they would be in action themselves. Pre-deployment training had given Martin a sound grounding, but his learning had only really begun once he was in the line, under fire and experiencing combat for real. It was only then that a soldier knew whether he could handle himself well and cope with the feelings of fear, exhaustion and stress.

That experience was the best trainer was axiomatic – and was as true for the British or American soldier as it was for the German or Italian. Yet while basic training was much the same, and while there was a commonality in the experience of war, there were fundamental differences all the same.

Much has been made ever since of the German soldier's ability to think on his feet and use his initiative. Since the war it has been taught as *Auftragstaktik* and given a translation of 'mission command'. Mission command is the concept of giving a subordinate commander an objective and then letting him use his own judgement on how that objective should best be achieved. However, that is not the *Auftragstaktik* that was first developed in the Prussian Army during the Napoleonic Wars; and certainly *Auftragstaktik* was a term only a very few in the German Army would ever have heard of.

What was encouraged was *Selbsttätigkeit des Unterführers* – the independence of the subordinate commander; this was promoted at every level, but was a particular feature at the higher command level – corps command or above. In the field, generals were absolutely expected to decide how, where and when they deployed their forces – this was part of the German way of war that had been practised for nearly 150 years. It was why Guderian disobeyed orders at the Meuse in May 1940 and why Rommel charged off across the desert in the spring of 1941. Since Hitler had taken over direct command of the Army, however, that no longer applied at the higher level.

Junior officers and NCOs were still expected to use their initiative, but then so were those in the British Army. 'Subordinate commanders must be trained to work on instructions rather than on detailed orders,' it was noted in a British *Army Training Memorandum* the previous year, 'to use their initiative, to think quickly, and to accept responsibility.' That neatly summarized the principle of *Selbsttätigkeit des Unterführers*. Really, there was no difference at all.

Thus, overall, there was no marked disparity in the quality of weaponry and there was not much difference in the method of training either. Both sides were also gaining a great deal from battlefield experience. None the less, there were differences, quite fundamental ones, between the Axis and Allied armies.

The biggest was that the Axis armies were from militaristic totalitarian states, whereas the Allies were from democracies. Discipline was vital in both, but was rigid in the German Army, especially, in a way it was not in those of the Allies. If a German soldier did not do what he was ordered to do, he was liable to be shot, whereas since 1930 there had been no capital punishment within the British Army for disobedience or cowardice. The US Army had capital punishment, but no one was going to be shot for desertion. They would suffer loss of face with their mates, and might end up in a military prison, but they would live. If some thought this was preferable to risking their necks in battle, then this was hardly surprising. Germany, in contrast, had executed just eighteen men for such felonies in the last war but had already shot thousands this time around.

Every part of the German state was focused towards the military. Culturally, the Nazis had tapped into earlier ideals of Prussian and Imperial German militarism, whereas in Britain that military apogee had long since gone; in the United States it had never been part of the American dream at all. Rather, anti-war isolation had been at the fore-front of American culture since the Founding Fathers. Before 1917, there had been a brief war against Britain in 1812, against Mexico, actions against native Americans and their own devastating civil war. Since 1919, isolationism and anti-militarism had grown. In Nazi Germany, after indoctrination at school, in the Hitler Youth and from the mass of militaristic propaganda that was simply impossible to avoid, it had become, quite understandably, the aspiration of a large proportion of its young men to join and then excel in the military. An example was the young fighter pilot Heinz Knoke. When he volunteered to join the Luftwaffe back in August 1939 all his classmates were volunteering for the Wehrmacht too. 'I am only one out of many millions of enthusiastic young people,' he wrote just before the outbreak of war, 'who have absolute faith in Hitler and dedicate ourselves to him without reservations.' It was his most 'ardent desire' to serve in the Luftwaffe and play his part in the war.

Combined with a desire to fight and become heroes of the Reich was confidence. Propaganda presented news and film footage of a Wehrmacht that was ultra-modern, mechanized and a cut above any other. Few doubted this. 'I believe in our strength and have a lot of faith in our Führer,' jotted Günther Sack, a young anti-aircraft gunner on the eve of war. 'I was young and gung-ho,' admitted Franz Maassen about joining up in 1940. 'We had our great victories in Poland, in Belgium, in Holland, in France. Next was Britain. I really wanted to be a part of that.'

And during those early campaigns, the casualties had been comparatively few; highly motivated, disciplined and increasingly experienced young men, the cream of German youth, had spearheaded one victory after another.

It was these men of the relatively small handful of elite divisions that had come to symbolize German military superiority. They were, however, and always had been, a minority. On the eve of war, only 38 per cent of the Army was considered fully trained, for example. Even for BARBAROSSA, only sixty-eight of the 208 divisions available in the OKH were considered First Wave – that is, fully trained and supplemented by the youngest recruits. And since then it was that group that had been taking a hammering in the Soviet Union and, albeit in smaller numbers, in North Africa.

It was also these men who were the most motivated, and with motivation comes the willingness to use initiative. Conversely, those older, less gung-ho, war-weary and not so well trained were less motivated and consequently not as likely to use their initiative. All, however, were subject to the same very strict discipline. If Hitler ordered them to stay and fight, and their commanding general opted to abide by that order, those men would have to stay where they were and do so – and on pain of death. That alone ensured there could be no easy walkover for the Allies. None the less, it is important that the German Army as a whole should not be put on an artificially high pedestal. There were, of course, still plenty of men within the ranks of the Deutsches Afrikakorps – and in the *Ostheer*, the Eastern Army, too – who had fought during the Army's apogee in the first half of 1941, but they were, inevitably, in decline. What was following could not hope to be as good.

For Alexander and Montgomery and those now responsible for turning around Allied fortunes in Egypt, however, there was no getting away from the fact that these similarly equipped, similarly trained and fewer in number Axis forces had nearly annihilated them at Gazala and had withstood everything that had been flung at them at Alamein in July. And, while Rommel's attack at Alam Halfa had been successfully stopped, Eighth Army had suffered more losses than the Panzerarmee.

The truth was, culturally, Britain really was very different to Germany. Few in Britain aspired to become war heroes; flying a Spitfire might be the wish of many a young British boy, but it was a minority who actually yearned to go and fight or put their lives on the line.

The make-up of the British Army fell into roughly four categories. At the top were those who craved adventure, loved the adrenalin-rush of combat and were keen to play an active role in any fighting going. These were the kind of men now in the SAS, for example, or those volunteering for the fledgling airborne forces being formed and trained in Britain. They were the men volunteering for the Commandos – and were pretty few in number. Next in line were those who did not want to fight but out of a sense of responsibility and duty would go the extra yard. Typically, these were particularly good junior officers or platoon and company sergeants – those who kept the men going and really were the backbone of the Army. There were more of them than of the first group, but they were still a minority.

Third up was the mass of soldiers: conscripts and reluctant volunteers – men who had no desire to be there at all, who would keep their heads down and try to get themselves through, but would not want to let their mates down, and who wanted to follow not lead. Finally, there was a very small proportion of men who simply could not cope at all and who were the first to crack or desert when the chips were down.

Those in the first two categories were more motivated and thus increasingly likely to use their initiative. They were also dependable, and could be relied upon even under extreme duress. The majority, however – those in the third category – were less steadfast. Morale in the Panzerarmee could be at rock bottom, but because of discipline and the threat of being shot were they to disobey an order, this fall in spirit would not so obviously manifest itself.

The same could not be said for Eighth Army. Before he was sacked, the Auk had lobbied hard for the reintroduction of the death penalty for desertion. As early as April 1942, he had produced figures showing that over the previous twelve months there had been 291 convictions for desertion in Eighth Army and nineteen for cowardice. After the fall of Tobruk, he raised the matter again and reported that sixty-three men had deserted in a single day during the fighting around Knightsbridge and that 907 absentees had been reported over the month up to the middle of July. There was also a feeling that Eighth Army men were becoming just a bit too willing to fling their arms in the air. Certainly, between 27 May and 4 August, Eighth Army suffered 11,400 killed and wounded, but 62,900 'missing', which meant nearly all had been taken prisoner.

Auchinleck did not get his way, because executing his men was hardly the way to turn around Eighth Army's fortunes; his lobbying was given short shrift. In any case, the problem was a comparatively simple one that both Montgomery and Alexander had recognized immediately: morale was terrible. On first arriving in Egypt, Alexander had talked to a number of officers and had been struck by how they lacked the usual air of confidence he had come to associate with British soldiers. 'They were bewildered, frustrated, fed up,' he wrote. And he was also troubled to hear that most believed there would be another withdrawal next time the Axis attacked in strength. The awe with which Rommel was regarded had been endemic for some time. Alex was appalled. 'That legend,' he commented, 'contributed a lot to the Eighth Army's widespread belief in the invincibility of the Afrikakorps.' The men had lost faith – in what they were doing there in this fly-infested scrap of desert, miles from home, and in the ability of the generals commanding them. After the utter hash they had made of the Gazala battle that was hardly surprising.

Now, in September 1942, with the Panzerarmee forced on to the defensive, they had the time to try to lick their forces into shape. Eighth Army needed to change; it had hit rock bottom. The only way for them now was up.

CHAPTER 27

Return of the Hero

ON 26 AUGUST, Colonello Publio Magini was on board a plane from Rome to Budapest along with his boss, Rino Fougier, Under-Secretary of State for Air, and Count Ciano. Magini, a former fighter pilot who had joined the Regia Aeronautica back in 1935, had also proved himself to be a fine air instructor. He had set up a specialist training school for flying in poor weather and another for night-flying, and since then had developed methods to improve night-time astral navigation. As a means of testing his methods, he had carried out a much-publicized flight to Tokyo, which included crossing the Gobi Desert. This was precisely the kind of heroic adventure Mussolini loved, so on his return Magini had been greeted and embraced by *Il Duce* in person, and promptly promoted and given medals too.

Magini couldn't help feeling both embarrassed and ashamed in equal measure. After all, his comrades had been risking their lives in battle and had got nothing like so much fuss. Nor was he a fan of Mussolini; every time he saw him, Magini thought he seemed more and more detached, not only from those around him but from reality, which was certainly true enough.

Since January, Magini had been working at the Air Ministry in Rome, which meant he could live at home with his wife and family. In April, his two brothers had been arrested for anti-Fascist activity, but this had not affected his career yet; after all, he was now sitting in a plane alongside Mussolini's son-in-law, the Italian Foreign Minister. Magini did feel somewhat conflicted, however. As they flew on to Budapest, he couldn't help thinking of his comrades fighting and dying at the front, or of his two brothers, in danger for their political activities while here he was with two of Italy's leading politicians. Whatever guilt he may have felt, however, was not enough to make him do anything about it. For the time being, Magini planned to remain in his comfortable staff post in Rome.

On his return from Budapest, there was bad news waiting for Count Ciano. The Greeks were starving, yet Germany was still insisting on 'astronomical indemnities', and although the Italian minister out there wanted Mussolini to intervene and plead with Hitler to reduce the degree to which he was bleeding Greece dry, Ciano warned him against it. *Il Duce* had already written one letter to Hitler, but the Führer had refused. 'One cannot fail twice,' noted Ciano, 'without losing too much prestige.'

Then came the bad news of Rommel's offensive, which put Mussolini in such a dark mood he could barely speak for three days and had a recurrence of his stomach pains. 'The sinking of our ships continues,' wrote Ciano on 3 September. 'Tonight there have been two.' The following day he recorded that two more had been sunk. 'Our supply problem,' he wrote, 'is difficult.' That was putting it mildly.

Meanwhile, out in the Atlantic, Teddy Suhren and the crew of *U-564* were continuing their long patrol. They had reached the Caribbean, had met up with the *Milchkuh* for more fuel and had even managed to take on some extra torpedoes from another U-boat; they discovered that by swathing a number of lifejackets around each tube, they could float them across with some of the men swimming alongside as guides.

One evening, they were cruising along the surface near Curaçao, hoping to run into a juicy oil tanker. Suhren was down below thinking that, for all the sunshine and beautifully blue sea out there in the Caribbean, there was also plenty of debris about – oil on the surface, flotsam and other signs of carnage. He always tried not to think too hard about such things or worry too much. Do that, he reckoned, and you'd had it.

Right on cue, someone shouted 'Plane!' and moments later two explosions were shaking the boat hard. As the men up above scurried down the conning tower, Suhren looked up and saw the wing of an aircraft loom overhead. 'Alarm!' he shouted and immediately they began to dive. At 50 metres another explosion lifted them all off their feet. But no leaks so far. They were still diving and Suhren could now hear the tell-tale crackling noise that told him they were below the 120-metre mark. Something was wrong. The crackling grew louder as the pressure on the hull intensified. 'Our hair stands on end,' noted Suhren. 'According to the meter on the trim-chamber, we're already at 160m, and the boat is still down at the bow. There's no stopping it.' They were well past the danger point, but still the boat continued to sink, the crackling and groaning so loud it was as though a giant hand were trying to crush them. They were now at 200 metres.

Then slowly, painfully slowly, the bow began to lift. Checks showed damage to some of the instruments and the depth-gauge pointer had come adrift from the drive shaft. 'Consequence,' wrote Suhren, 'nearly total destruction in the depths.' But luck was once more with them and they were able to rise to the surface again. The plane, however, had not been spotted earlier because it had flown at them out of the sun. Generally, it was too bright, Suhren reckoned, and what with the blistering heat and the brightness, concentration could easily seize up. From now on, he decided, they would avoid taking risks and dive by day.

Back in Britain, the RAF's Bomber Command was still feeling its way in this war, although at least now the criticism had largely abated – publicly, at any rate. Neither of the Thousand Bomber Raids that followed the one on Cologne had quite reached the magic one thousand mark, but they had been close enough to be legitimately rounded up and collectively they had done wonders for the Command's image; it was clear they had more than just rattled the enemy. Air Marshal Harris was a man who always preferred action over words, but he was quite prepared to use rhetoric and propaganda when required. That summer he had put his name to a leaflet that was dropped over Germany, then translated and printed on both sides of the Atlantic and cited on the BBC. 'We are bombing Germany, city by city, and even more terribly,' he had written, 'in order to make it impossible for you to go on with the war. That is our object. We shall pursue it remorselessly.'

The trouble was, with a strength of just thirty-two squadrons, it was proving difficult to be quite so remorseless and terrible as he had threatened. Two hundred aircraft on a single raid was quite a good effort, but very often operations amounted to just twenty or thirty. This was why it was important to continue to mount a few really large raids every so often. On 10 September, some 479 aircraft attacked Düsseldorf, for example. Three nights later, 446 aircraft were sent to Bremen, of which once again training aircraft from the OTUs were included.

Among those flying to Bremen was Wing Commander Guy Gibson, still commanding 106 Squadron ever since taking it over in April. As squadron commander, he wasn't flying quite as much as he used to, but he still tried to go out one night in five. It was a lot on top of his other responsibilities, which were considerable. As he was discovering, plenty of those with whom he'd started at 106 Squadron had gone already, shot down, blown up, crashed on take-off or ditched into the North Sea. He felt the burden of those losses very keenly. He was also finding it increasingly difficult to get into a plane himself.

That night of 13 September, he took off twenty minutes before midnight. Cloud was light, but there was a thick ground haze. They found the city by following the River Weser and bombed from comparatively low – just 11,000 feet. Bomb bursts were seen over the town but it was impossible to tell how accurate they had been. 'A VERY HOT TARGET,' Gibson wrote in his logbook that night. 'LOST 10% ATTACKING FORCE.' That translated as three of his crews, all of whom were long-standing and experienced members of his squadrons; privately, he was consumed with grief. He thought the raid a failure, yet local newspapers reported that Bremen's industry had suffered considerable damage. The Focke-Wulf plant was badly hit, as was the Lloyd dynamo works. Some 848 houses were destroyed, 70 people were killed and 371 injured.

The key questions in Bomber Command's chequered existence continued: were enough targets being successfully hit, was it worth the already considerable sacrifice, and was the inevitable cost to the German civilian population having any effect on Germany's determination to wage war?

Harris, as well as Portal and Churchill, believed it most certainly was worth it, but accepted that in its current state Bomber Command was not going to make a decisive impact. On 17 September, Churchill insisted the force be raised to fifty squadrons by the end of the year – but there were other factors, too, that were preventing the RAF's bombers from having as great an effect as Britain would have liked.

Harris had known from the moment he took command that his bomber force was a work in progress and that before he began his all-out bombing offensive against Hitler's war machine a number of blocks needed putting into place. None the less, expansion had been painfully slow, although this was largely due to factors beyond his control. Not only was Bomber Command still a small force, but he had been obliged to use what crews and aircraft he did have for a number of other purposes besides the strategic bombing of the Third Reich. Some bombers had been needed for the Battle of the Atlantic, then in the first half of 1942 further resources had been sucked up by the escalating and worsening war against Japan in the Far East and then by the needs of RAF Middle East. Not only were bombers needed in the Mediterranean and Middle East, but Harris was expected repeatedly to attack U-boat pens and to use vast numbers of his meagre forces laying sea-mines.

In addition to the diversion of resources, there were also issues of training crews and rebuilding morale after the mauling the Command had received in the first years of the war. The four-engine Rolls-Royce Merlin-powered Lancaster was now in production, but getting to the point where they were being built in large enough numbers all took time. None the less, Harris was convinced that he now had the kind of heavy bomber he needed – an aircraft that could carry not just a handful of light-weight incendiaries, but really big bombs – bombs as big as 10,000 lb in weight, possibly even bigger than that. Bombs that could cause really large amounts of destruction.

Nor did Harris have enough airfields, or even airfields that could handle four-engine heavies – either operational stations or those needed for Heavy Conversion Units. New airfields and runways were being built, but a number of the new ones had had to be given over to the American bomber units now starting to arrive in England. No one was grumbling at the arrival of the Americans, least of all Harris, but this still had a knock-on effect on the speed of expansion of Bomber Command.

Yet perhaps the biggest stumbling block of all was the inability of Bomber Command to bomb accurately. The GEE radar pulse system tested the previous year and fitted in planes in early 1942 had proved insufficiently accurate, and although better devices were now being worked on – including a more sophisticated system codenamed 'Oboe' – they were not ready to be put into aircraft just yet.

Still Deputy Director of Bomber Operations (DDB/Ops) at the Air Ministry in London was Group Captain Sydney Bufton. He was one of the Ministry's staff officers with practical operational experience, having both flown bombers and commanded 10 Squadron in Bomber Command. By the time he took up his position in November 1941, he had been as aware as anyone that the Command was in bad shape. Since then Harris had done much to improve its standing, but Bufton was convinced that, even with GEE and the further advances that were currently being developed, there was a comparatively simple way of ensuring targets could be much more effectively identified. That was the creation of a Pathfinder Force.

The idea of having a specialist squadron or group that would operate ahead of the main bomber stream and then lay target-markers as a guide to the others following behind had been discussed as early as the summer of 1941, well before Harris took over Bomber Command. It had been discovered that during the Blitz, the Luftwaffe had done just this with two specialist bomber groups, KG100 and KG26, and so it had been suggested that several 'fire-raising' squadrons might be developed along similar lines to the Germans.

This was a tactic that Bufton believed, very strongly, was absolutely essential. He had flown too many bomber operations himself where the target had been almost impossible to find and, although navigational aids were surely going to improve further, he knew from practical experience that these were unlikely to be enough. So, on taking up his role at the Air Ministry, he had immediately set about writing a paper in which he urged the formation of a 'target finding-force', whose aircraft would be the first to be equipped with GEE and the still-being-developed Oboe.

Whilst stirring interest, there was little sign that anyone was prepared to push Bufton's ideas. So, at the end of February, and with Harris newly ensconced as C-in-C Bomber Command, Bufton had written another memo, which was circulated around the Air Ministry. 'We should immediately form a Target Finding Force,' he wrote, 'cut out the dead wood from Bomber Command, and so tighten the sinews of control that the bomber force may be wielded and directed as a sharp, flexible, hard-hitting unit.' He also suggested that a target-finding force would enable precision attacks to be made on specific targets and even listed a few, such as several synthetic-fuel plants and the ball-bearing factories at Schweinfurt.

Bufton's report received rather more enthusiasm within Air Ministry circles this time around and eventually wound up on Harris's desk. This, however, was precisely the kind of paper Harris really disliked: unasked for and unwanted and written by a junior officer, who, despite his combat experience, did not know or understand the whole picture. In any case, he fundamentally disagreed with the idea of creating a specialist target-finding force by creaming off the best crews of all the bomber groups into what would be a *corps d'élite*. This, he believed, would not only be bad for morale, it would never really work because, human nature being what it was, the groups would want to retain their best crews, and the best personnel themselves would also object to leaving squadrons in which they had half-completed tours and were looked up to in order to be sent to new squadrons and have to start all over again.

These objections were more valid than Bufton was prepared to acknowledge. Bomber Command was still small, and there was no doubt that taking away the best crews would be keenly felt. Harris also reckoned that bombing techniques would improve by appointing certain crews as 'raid leaders' or giving the honour to the squadron that achieved the best bombing results each month.

These arguments didn't wash with Bufton, however. After all, better results were an obvious way to improve morale dramatically, and creating a target-finding force would be the best way to get those results, because by putting the best crews together they would then have an opportunity to discuss, develop and co-ordinate their technique. Furthermore, they could operate with the best and latest navigational aids, which could be quickly introduced to these few aircraft without waiting until there were sufficient supplies for the entire Command.

Bufton's determination ensured that this was a debate that would not go away. Harris therefore decided to try to deal with it once and for all by organizing a conference at Bomber Command and inviting all his five bomber groups and two training Group Commanders and their SASOs – all of whom he knew he could rely on to back him – along with Bufton and his immediate superior from the Air Ministry.

The conference opened with Harris reeling off his arguments about morale and then arguing that if crews were collected into a target-finding force they would inevitably lose their chance for promotion. At this Bufton, who had had two brothers shot down, lost his cool and, banging the table with his hand, said, 'Sir, you will never win the war like that! These people don't know if they will be alive tomorrow and they couldn't care less about promotion.' This was extraordinary behaviour in front of the C-in-C, and it says much for Harris's *sangfroid* that he merely looked at his watch and suggested it was time for lunch.

When they reconvened, the C-in-C suggested a vote. Needless to say,

Harris's men all voted against the idea. And that, as far as Harris was concerned, was an end to the matter.

Bufton was not to be so easily put off, however, and decided to go behind Harris's back and canvass opinion himself. Having sent out copies of his proposals for a target-finding force, together with a short questionnaire, to a dozen squadron and station commanders, the response was as he expected: all agreed it was an urgent requirement. Copies were sent to Harris.

His survey, however, was every bit as loaded as the conference Harris had convened. The dozen people questioned were all known to Bufton and like-minded. There were plenty of squadron commanders he did not question. And squadron leaders did not fully appreciate the paucity of aircraft and crews that Harris was having to juggle in the first months of his command. He was not disagreeing with a target-finding force *per se*, but, rather, its form and structure.

By June, there had still been no response, but then Bufton had been visited by Air Marshal Sir Wilfrid Freeman, at the time standing in for Portal, who was away on leave. Bufton told him that he was frustrated by the lack of progress with the Pathfinder Force and lent Freeman his folder on the matter.

'This last letter, have you had a reply?' Freeman asked.

'No, Sir,' Bufton replied.

'Do you know why?'

'No, Sir.'

'Because there isn't a reply,' said Freeman. 'You've beaten Bert at his own game. CAS will be in on Monday. We've got to have a Pathfinder Force and I'll talk it over with him.'

Events moved swiftly after that. A letter was drafted for Portal to send to Harris. 'In the opinion of the Air Staff,' ran the note, 'the formation of the special force would open up a new field for improvement, raising the standard of accuracy of bombing, and thus morale, throughout Bomber Command.'

Harris could ignore junior staff officers, but not the Chief of the Air Staff. Meeting with Portal the very next day, he was forced, reluctantly, to concede, while Bufton was asked to draw up a list of crews for this new force. The Pathfinder Force – or PFF as it would be known – came into being on 15 August 1942. It was a humiliation for Harris and a reminder that he was still very much Portal's subordinate.

A few days later, the PFF was put into action and one of its first operations, on 1 September, was Saarbrücken. Guy Gibson and the Lancasters of 106 Squadron were among those following their new guides. It was also the first time Gibson's crew had carried a mighty new 8,000lb bomb – that is, some 4 tons. Sure enough, they spotted the flares as planned. 'The bombs, incendiaries first, began to fall thick and fast,' he noted, 'about 1,000 tons of them. Soon the whole area was one mass of flames.' His bomb-aimer saw their 4-ton 'cookie' fall and said it caused 'an expanding mushroom of blue-red flame which seemed to cover an area of about half a mile square for a full five seconds.'

The Pathfinders, however, had targeted the wrong place and so Bomber Command hit Saarlouis, 13 miles to the north-west and not an industrial centre at all. A week later, during a raid on Frankfurt, they hit Rüsselsheim instead. The Pathfinders were certainly helping the bombers hit a marker. All they needed to do now was ensure they found the right target in the first place. Yet that required better navigational aids, something that was out of the Pathfinders' control. Those improved navigational aids were coming, as were more heavy bombers and more squadrons, but it was all taking a frustratingly long time. For Harris, and for all of Bomber Command, progress was two steps forward, one step back.

Out in the Atlantic, Teddy Suhren and the crew of *U-564* were now almost back at Brest. They had hit two more ships on 19 August and a third, a large Norwegian freighter of some 8,000 tons, on the 30th. They had, however, missed two when the torpedoes they had transferred so carefully earlier in the trip had proved to be duds. And then they had set off for home.

On 1 September, Suhren had just sat down in his wardroom when he became conscious that the diesels had suddenly stopped and that the boat had become eerily quiet. Hurriedly entering the control room, his fears swiftly vanished as he saw his LI beaming. All the crew, he told Suhren, had gone up on deck to congratulate him. 'Why?' Suhren asked as he hurried up on to the bridge, where nearly the entire crew stood grinning from ear to ear. Then his LI read out the signals he clutched in his hand. 'In recognition of your proven heroism,' he said in his most dignified voice, 'you are the eighteenth member of the German Armed Forces to whom I grant Crossed Swords to your Knight's Cross with Oak

Leaves. Adolf Hitler.' Then he read a second, announcing that Suhren had been promoted to KK – Korvettenkapitän.

Suhren was overjoyed. His men had even managed to make new rings for him from tin cans and had fashioned a set of swords and oak leaves for his cap too. Back down below, and with the engines on once more, Suhren took the chance to speak on the tannoy and thank them. After all, a boat was only as good as its crew, he told them. Together, they had explored the limits of all that was possible. As he spoke, he remembered what Dönitz had said to him: 'Suhren, make sure you bring your boat back again in one piece.'

He was determined to do so, but the last test was getting through the Bay of Biscay. In the past they had simply sped through and hoped for the best, but now that was too risky. There were too many planes – aircraft that Suhren was convinced must now have onboard radar of some kind – and so they surfaced by night and dived by day. Even then, they spotted a huge flying-boat coming towards them at just 500 feet.

Finally, on 18 September, they reached Brest, where on the pier waited an Army band, a naval guard of honour, the town mayor and a crowd of officers, soldiers and port workers, waving and clutching flowers. As Suhren stepped ashore, the band struck up and he was met with handshakes and congratulations. The U-boat arm was a small brotherhood within the Wehrmacht, and the enthusiasm and relief that Suhren had made it was genuine and heartfelt. So many of the aces had gone; so many crews were now lying at the bottom of the sea. Suhren, however, had come through. He was one of the BdU's heroes, and he had survived.

He was one of the lucky ones.

CHAPTER 28

Getting Ready

IN PARIS, THE Austrian Jew Freddie Knoller was still living as Robert Metzner from Metz and working alongside his friends Christos and Pierre as a pimp in the Pigalle district. For much of the time, life was as good as could be expected: he had his friends, a bit of money in his pocket, he was continuing his sexual awakening and, most importantly, he was free. This was more than could be said for a lot of other Jews living in Paris. In May, the German Army had handed over police operations to the Reichssicherheitshauptamt (RSHA) – the Reich Main Security Office – which up until that point had played a small part in the occupation. Newly arriving to take charge was Gruppenführer Karl Oberg, who set himself up in a spacious townhouse on the Boulevard Lannes, while establishing the RSHA across nine separate buildings in the Avenue Foch with some 2,000 men, as well as the existing Field Police. Oberg could also call upon around 8,000 full-time French agents.

The RSHA was divided into seven areas of operation across France in units called Kommandos der SiPo-SD, better known as KdS. Most Frenchmen came to know both the RSHA and the KdS units more simply and generally as the Gestapo. They certainly did not wait long to get into their stride. At the end of May, it was the turn of all French Jews to start wearing a yellow star. Soon after, Knoller was leading a group of German officers along Pigalle to the Rue de Provence when two young men wearing yellow stars walked towards them, then hastily crossed to the other side of the road. 'I felt this as a terrible rebuke,' wrote Knoller. 'I was once again seized by that urge to declare myself, to live again as a Jew, to be Freddie Knoller once more, not this person sedulously courting the enemy for money.'

In July, the arrests began, although deportations from France had already begun back in March. The latest Paris round-ups had been planned by Haupsturmführer Theodor Dannecker, the head of the SD's Judenreferat office, in co-ordination with the Vichy police chief René Bousquet, and took place on 16 and 17 July. At the suggestion of Pierre Laval – who had returned as Vichy Prime Minister in April – women and children were now to be included as well as men. Up to that point, Jews had been able to convince themselves that the men had been taken away to work; that was harder to explain now. What's more, after some wrangling with Bousquet, it was agreed that French policemen would carry out the arrests. In all, 3,031 men, 5,802 women and 4,051 children were rounded up; 6,900 of these were held for a week with little food or water in the Vélodrome d'hiver, a French showcase cycling stadium, before being forced on to trains and sent east to Auschwitz.

Also still living in Paris was Andrée Griotteray. Bored, fed up and with her hatred of the occupiers growing ever more intense, she was, none the less, still working in Police Headquarters. Life in Paris – and throughout much of Nazi-occupied Europe – was now pretty grim. There were soldiers, swastikas, the dreaded Gestapo; even for those of a more accepting nature, it was hard not to feel the palpable air of menace and the heavy shroud of oppression. Shortages were really starting to kick in. People in the cities were hungry, all the time. One man in Paris recorded his efforts to buy food:

7h30 – To the baker's. Buy bread. There will be biscuits at 11h00.
9h00 – It is a meat day today but the butcher says there won't be any until Saturday.
9h30 – To the dairy shop. No cheese before 5pm.
10h00 – To the tripe shop. My ticket is number 32, I will be served at 4pm.
10h30 – To the grocer's. There will be vegetables at 5pm.
11h00 – Back to the baker's. There are no biscuits left.

Wages had gone down, consumables were all but gone, vehicles had been requisitioned and it felt as though Germany was bleeding the land dry, which, of course, it was. Just existing had become a challenge, albeit one that most people met. But few were enjoying it much, not even Corinne Luchaire, the film star, who was now living a quiet life in Paris, occasionally going out with German officers, but depressed by the blackout, the shut restaurants and the gloom hanging over the city. Even she was experiencing the shortages. When her car ran out of petrol she asked a German general for some more, but he refused to give her any. He, like all the Germans, seemed to her tenser than before; they were no longer so cheerful. 'Times of sacrifice had come,' she wrote, 'and although none of them would dare say it, they knew they might be defeated.' Also a concern was her weakening health, for she was starting to suffer from tuberculosis. That summer, she left Paris and headed to a sanatorium in Megève in the Alps. She was relieved to get away.

There was no such opportunity for escape for Andrée Griotteray, who was none the less doing what she could to help her brother, Alain, who was still down south in the foothills of the Pyrenees trying to foment the spirit of resistance with the Orion circuit.

Resistance, though, remained disjointed, disparate and, for the most part, disorganized, although two years after the armistice there were some signs that the flame was beginning to catch. Certainly, the early enthusiasm for Vichy had waned and, while there was still widespread respect for Le Maréchal, the same could not be said for Laval, who on 22 June had announced the *Relève* scheme, under which French workers were encouraged to volunteer to go to work in Germany. In return for every three volunteers, three POWs were to be released. The rather spurious theory was that freed POWs would be farmers while those heading to Germany would be industrial workers; in reality, the Germans were not prepared to be quite so rigorous in their picking of prisoners to release. The scheme very quickly became unpopular with almost everyone. Take-up was poor, and most people quickly recognized that it was also deeply unfair. Families of prisoners not released turned their anger towards Vichy rather than the Germans.

Laval had ended his speech announcing the *Relève* saying, 'I wish for German victory, because, without it, tomorrow Bolshevism will be installed everywhere.' It was fear of the westward spread of Communism that had led many, like Paul Vigouroux, to join the Légion des volontaires français (LVF) the previous year.

One of those listening to Laval's speech with a mixture of fear and anger was Henri Frenay, the founder and leader of the resistance movement Combat. Frenay was thirty-six, lean, handsome and serious-looking, his brow forever slightly furrowed, reflecting, no doubt, the seriousness of the task he had set himself. A former captain in the Army, he was naturally right-wing but deeply anti-German. Captured in June 1940, he had managed to escape to the south and had initially supported Pétain, believing, mistakenly, that the Maréchal would fight back against the Germans. He had even worked for the Vichy intelligence, the Deuxième Bureau, for several months. He had, however, quit in January 1941, having become disillusioned and already having begun recruitment to his embryonic resistance movement.

Frenay had drawn people to his early movement simply by starting up a conversation, sounding out their views about Germany and Britain, then dropping in his belief that the Nazis would eventually lose the war. He would then pause to gauge their response and, if encouraged, would continue. Eventually he would say, 'Men are already gathering in the shadows. Will you join them?' It wasn't particularly safe, but neither was it recklessly dangerous in those early days of Vichy. By Christmas 1941, he had not only followers but some 15,000 francs stashed away in his 'war treasury', and a few months later he was using these funds to help get an underground paper off the ground. Originally, *Les Petites Ailes de France* had been started up in the north, in the occupied zone, but Frenay had taken it over, changed the title to *Verité*, then *Verités*, then finally *Combat*.

Steadily, Frenay's resistance movement had continued to grow. Combat, the group, had fused with Liberté, and Frenay had become, in effect, the *de facto* head of resistance in the unoccupied zone. However, although he had believed in the need for a unifying command of the resistance movement, it was not until he met with Jean Moulin in early 1942 that he became prepared to nail his colours to de Gaulle's mast.

After hearing Laval's speech introducing *Relève*, Frenay stayed up late into the night, working on two directives: one for their regional chiefs, the other for *Combat*'s editorial board. 'Every worker who remains in France is one less prisoner in German hands,' he wrote. 'Frenchmen! Frenchwomen! With us, against misery and slavery – fight! For your daily bread – fight! Against pillage and oppression – fight! For your freedom and your children's freedom – fight! For liberation, for

Victory – fight! For France – fight!' Some 80,000 copies of this edition
were printed and distributed.

For men like Frenay, Laval's announcement and his comments about
hoping for German victory provided another step towards a more
concerted resistance. As it happened, Laval's speech also coincided with
one made by Général de Gaulle, now back in London, the following day,
which was something of a timely rallying call.

These had been testing times for de Gaulle. The British expedition to
Madagascar in May had been launched without his prior knowledge and
since then a former Vichy official had been put in place as Governor
there. Time and again, he had felt marginalized, although the recent Free
French heroics at Bir Hacheim had done much to bolster his confidence
and belief in his movement. He had also realized, however, that he needed
to try to more obviously bring the scattered resistance movements under
his single banner. For most Frenchmen, he had remained a nobody – the
most junior general of 1940 opposite Pétain, the most senior and respected
military figure in all of France. The British recognized his passion and
potential, yet he tended to blow hot and cold, and his arrogance ensured
that he had remained a man on the sidelines, to a large extent, rather
than an obvious banner to which all freedom-loving Frenchmen would
naturally flock.

A succession of resistance leaders had, however, visited him in London
on what became known jokingly as the 'Thomas Cook agency' after the
well-known British travel company. The first had been Christian Pineau,
leader of Libération-Nord, who had spent several weeks in March 1942
having a long series of discussions. Part of the problem was that de Gaulle
still knew very little about the resistance and had somewhat authoritar-
ian views about how a future France might look. As far as he was
concerned, the old political way of the 1930s with multiple-party
coalitions was as toxic as Vichy; rather, he told Pineau, what was needed
was a strong leader of a strong state. This, Pineau knew, was the kind of
talk that would make many in the fledgling resistance run a mile and he
told de Gaulle so in no uncertain terms. 'Tell those brave people that I
will not betray them,' the Général told Pineau, brushing off his
concerns.

Next to arrive, in April 1942, had been Emmanuel d'Astier de la
Vigerie, leader of Libération, who arrived armed with numerous proposals and ideas, and whom de Gaulle sent on to America. Finally, Pierre

Brossolette reached London, a left-wing journalist, former army captain and, along with Henri Frenay, one of the very first resisters in the occupied zone. These conversations, and the ideas that flowed from them, as well as the candid portrayal of France and what they believed was needed, showed the Général the importance of harnessing the resistance. 'The resistance,' he wrote, 'was not only the rebound of our self-defence reduced to extremities. It was also arousing the hope of a national revival.'

Pineau had left de Gaulle believing that not a word he had said had sunk in, but it had, and by the time of his manifesto in June the Général was promising the French people a future national assembly elected by the whole people, including, for the first time in France, women.

Meanwhile, Jean Moulin was working hard to try to bring the various groups together into some kind of cohesion. Moving between Lyons and Nice, where he helped run a small art gallery selling Impressionist and early twentieth-century paintings, he lived a humble, spartan existence. Most days, he would meet with members of Combat, Libération and le Franc-Tireur – the largest groups in Vichy – either in safe houses or in parks. A joint information service had been set up in April for circulating resistance press within France and abroad. Then, in July, Moulin established the Général d'Etudes, a group of bureaucrats and administrators who would advise the Government at the moment of liberation. It was a clever idea: hope was essential; and giving voice to a future beyond the war helped persuade others that there was a light at the end of the tunnel and that the France of the future was one worth fighting for.

Soon after his return to France, Moulin had met with Henri Frenay in a safe house in Marseilles along with another Combat leader, Maurice Chevance. Standing in the kitchen, next to the sink, Moulin had taken out a hand-written letter from de Gaulle urging them to unite and fight. He had then produced microfilmed orders from a matchbox which required a magnifying glass to read. Frenay had been ecstatic. For eighteen months, he and his fellows had been working alone, but from that moment on there was a direct link to de Gaulle and the Free French movement. Moulin offered him a direct radio link, through him, to London, and gave him a wad of notes amounting to some 250,000 francs. From now on, Moulin told them, he was to be known as 'Max'. Frenay was to be 'Charvet'.

Frenay agreed entirely with Moulin that closer co-operation and unity was needed between the various resistance groups. However, he had founded Combat to take military action and now, under the orders Moulin had shown him from de Gaulle, that power was to be ceded to the Général in London. There was to be complete separation between the military and political wings of the resistance movement. Neither Frenay nor Chevance, however, could see how this would work in practice; after all, they were the men on the ground, who knew and understood the nuances of day-to-day life in France. London might provide them with predetermined targets, but to Frenay it had seemed crazy to suggest that any action should only be taken under London's direct control as well. The issue, of course, was one of trust; what neither de Gaulle nor the British Secret Services wanted were disparate, ill-trained resisters committing acts of violent resistance in an uncontrolled, ill-disciplined manner. None the less, trust cut both ways. Moulin was zealous in his determination to bind Combat et al. more firmly to de Gaulle's single leadership, yet he recognized that he needed to apply coercion not orders. Or rather, a combination of carrot and stick: cash and radio links on the one hand, gentle threats and control on the other. His time as a regional prefect had been the ideal training.

Meanwhile, in the Western Desert of Egypt, that September General Francis Tuker was back with his 4th Indian Division, who were now at the front once more and on active operations. They had been given a static role along the Alamein Line – much to Tuker's chagrin, as he had been training them as motorized infantry. Even so, he issued a stirring Order of the Day to all his men as they moved into the line. 'The eyes of the Army are upon us,' he told them. 'Dominion and American troops are closely watching us. Let us show the Italians that it is of no avail to struggle against us; the Germans that they can never hope to stand our fury in battle.'

Tuker now had his own HQ in the desert with the divisional support units nearby. These included a mobile workshop company, units of the Indian Army Ordnance and Royal Indian Army Service Corps. There was also the Divisional Signals Regiment, split into separate companies and sections, each with a distinct role. A division had many components; organizing and supplying such a formation was no small matter. Just the headquarters alone needed rations – including different ones for the various Indian, Gurkha and British troops – tents, mile upon mile of wiring, telephones, paper, radios, tables, chairs, maps, trucks, motor-cycles, new US Jeeps, anti-aircraft guns; the logistics were mind-boggling and that was just one divisional headquarters.

Among those now at Tuker's HQ was Corporal Mangal Singh, of C Section, No. 1 Company. He had already been out in the Middle East for some three years, ever since August 1939 when the 4th Indian Division had been sent to Egypt. Mangal Singh was one of a huge number of men who had volunteered for the Indian Army. From a small village in Ferozepur in the Punjab of northern India, his family were farmers, producing cotton and keeping a few buffalo and goats. They lived in a one-room mud house with no running water or electricity. Even so, Mangal Singh did go to a local school some 3 miles away, which he walked to and from daily.

At seventeen he was married and soon after joined the Indian Army. Some friends told him a recruiting officer was visiting Moga, the nearest town, so, believing this might be a chance for some regular income and even prospects, he decided to sign up. Without telling either his new wife or any of his family of his intentions, he walked the 6 miles to Moga and so began his army career. Immediately put into the Signals, he was given five rupees, made to swear an oath and then put on a train to Jabalpur, nearly 1,500 miles away. He had not even had a chance to tell his wife and parents – instead, they learned he had gone when they received his hast-ily scribbled note the following day.

At the Signals Training Centre, he learned to be a lineman, laying telephone cables. He enjoyed it very much, and in turn became an instructor himself. He missed his family, but at least he had begun send-ing some money home. Not until two years had passed did he finally go home again; it was then that he saw his son for the first time. Now based at Karachi, he was able to take his wife and son with him, but after a couple of years he joined the 4th Indian Division and was posted over-seas. He'd not seen them since; after eight years of marriage, he had been with his wife for just two.

Since June 1940, he had been up and down the Western Desert, served in East Africa and in the Middle East, laying cables, mending broken lines and ensuring the division's signals functioned efficiently. He was not a fighting man, but it was still dangerous creeping forward at night laying lines. He had been fired at, shot at by aircraft and shelled, but so far Mangal Singh's luck had held.

Now, with the division back in the line, there was plenty to do. Division HQ had to be linked to the forward brigades and, despite intermittent shelling and the odd Stuka raid, he had to make sure they remained linked.

All the front-line units were now being rotated in and out of the line for training and recuperation. Albert Martin and 2nd Rifle Brigade were moved back to Burg el Arab, near Montgomery and Coningham's Tactical HQs. There they underwent more training, rigorous PT and swimming in the sea, which was both warm and a beautiful twinkling turquoise. Monty, as he was already known by the men, even came to visit them. Martin, for one, was impressed. 'The impact of Monty's visit stayed with us,' he noted. 'We also liked his scathing comments about Rommel and his repetitive and unenterprising battle strategy.' Equally uplifting was the good military sense Monty spoke. Albert Martin had been fighting in the desert long enough to know what worked and what did not, so to hear that there would be no more defended boxes with their inflexibility and negative connotations, no more penny packets of troops and cavalier tank charges, but rather troops operating in strength, was very much music to his ears. 'It sounds heresy, I know,' he added, 'but by the time Monty had finished with us we were almost looking forward to the coming showdown.'

This talk was one that Montgomery repeated over and over and one that, as with Albert Martin and his fellows, did much to bolster morale. None the less, Monty did not have a particularly high opinion of the British Army. Despite its growing superiority in tanks and fire-power, he did not think the men were either well trained or well motivated. Certainly, a largely civilian conscript army was not the same as a professional one, and the defeat at Gazala combined with the palpably low morale he had found on his arrival were colouring his view. With morale improving appreciably, however, he should have had few concerns about the infantry: the Australians, the New Zealanders now in the line, 7th Motor Brigade and Tuker's 4th Indians, for example, were experienced, generally well led and as good as any now in North Africa.

There were still some mediocre generals within Eighth Army, however, and there was no doubt that Monty was right to consign penny packets, boxes and Jock Columns to tactical history. The problem of the commanders could largely be dealt with by Monty himself, who immediately showed he was going to be no pushover like Ritchie and made it crystal clear there could be no more bickering or 'bellyaching' as he called it. Men he had known from England, and whom he knew would toe the line, were brought over: Lieutenant-General Sir Oliver Leese to take over XXX Corps and Lieutenant-General Brian Horrocks to take command of XIII Corps. Both were fairly unimaginative – Tuker was appalled by their lack of tactical knowledge – but both were solid, dependable and would do Monty's bidding. Whether that would always be a good thing was debatable, but it was certainly the right approach at this particular moment.

Where Montgomery was more justified in his concerns was with the armour. By mid-October he would have over 1,000 tanks, but the challenge was getting the various units of cavalry, tank regiments and yeomanry to work to the same prescribed tactics and hand in glove with anti-tank screens – something that was most definitely not the case at present. Tank regiments tended to be plodding and work alongside the infantry; cavalry units still tended to charge off as though they were on horseback; and the yeomanry regiments like the Sherwood Rangers were new to mechanization and still learning the ropes.

Monty believed the best policy was to make a simple plan, then stick to it. That way, every man, from the top to the bottom of the chain, would know exactly what was expected of them. Then they would rehearse it over and over until the lines were learned. This applied to the supply chains as well as the troops.

Stanley Christopherson and the Sherwood Rangers were sent back some 30 miles along with the rest of 8th Armoured Division. A dummy minefield was created with lanes marked out by perforated petrol cans with lights inside. Over and over, the regiment practised going through these lanes at night. To add a sense of realism, flares were shot up into the sky and explosions set off.

As the weeks passed, so Eighth Army was gradually being transformed into a very well-supplied, well-oiled and highly mechanized machine. This new-look force might have lacked a bit of flair, but it was increasing in size, increasingly well supported and increasing in confidence – which was exactly what Alexander and Montgomery intended.

One of those who had seen this vast military machine spread out beneath him had been US Army Air Forces fighter pilot Lieutenant Dale Deniston, who on 12 August had flown over the Western Desert en route to Palestine along with the rest of the 66th Fighter Squadron. 'Flying over the British Eighth Army was an experience I shall never forget,' he wrote. 'Spread out before me on the desert sand was an army of many personnel in groups, with great numbers of tanks, armored cars, supply vehicles, ambulances, machine guns, artillery pieces, all spread out.'

Deniston had graduated back in March and, much to his delight and relief, had been posted to fighters – and specifically to the 66th Fighter Squadron in the 57th Fighter Group. Deniston caught up with his new group at Mitchell Field, New York, where seventy-five brand-new P-40 fighter planes were lined up waiting, all painted a dusky-pink colour that he and his fellows quickly reckoned had to be desert camouflage. A further clue had been the large aircraft carrier he had spotted docked at Quonset Point, Rhode Island, during his test flight.

Sure enough, he and his fellow pilots soon found themselves aboard USS *Ranger* heading across the Atlantic to West Africa. After one anxious U-boat scare, they were nearing the African coast and were ordered to fly off. Deniston was the twelfth in line. *Ranger*'s decks were 700 feet long, but because of the number of aircraft, they only had just under 400 feet. It wasn't a lot for young pilots like Deniston who had never done such a thing before. 'I set the flaps,' he noted, 'the trim tabs, held the brakes, ran up full throttle, released brakes and was airborne well before reaching the end of the deck and had to push the nose down to avoid a stall.' After cheekily buzzing the flight deck, he joined the rest of his flight and set off towards the Gold Coast – present-day Ghana.

This was the Takoradi Route, pioneered by AVM Mary Coningham, among others, back in the twenties, and it involved plenty of refuelling stops across the dense jungle of central Africa before turning north through Sudan and then into Egypt. It was certainly a good way of building up flying hours. Their journey eventually ended not in Egypt but at Beit Daras in Palestine, where they were to acclimatize, get their machines in order and carry out some essential training. Then the plan was for them to join the Desert Air Force and take part in the forthcoming battle.

The 57th were the first US fighter group to go to war in North Africa, but a detachment of B-24 heavy bombers was already operating from Egypt. The decision to send USAAF units to the Middle East had not been one General Hap Arnold had accepted lightly. He agreed with

Roosevelt and Marshall in the Europe-first strategy and was eager to get as many US Air Force units into battle as soon as possible. However, British requirements in the Middle East had been swallowing up a lot of his aircraft and equipment. On the other hand, with the loss of Tobruk and the whole of Egypt apparently under threat, that was going to make the task of winning in Europe much harder.

Arnold reckoned he had a stark choice: either he could allow the RAF to continue to consume many of his resources, or he could send his own units – American aircraft manned by American aircrew. He decided upon the latter, confirmed with Air Chief Marshal Portal on 21 June. Nine groups – what the RAF called wings of three squadrons – were earmarked for the Middle East. One heavy bomber group and two fighter groups were due to be ready to fly and fight by October. By the end of August, the 57th FG were already back in Egypt, their training over. However, before they were let loose to operate together, it was felt it would be a good idea for the pilots to get a bit of combat flying under their belts attached to a Desert Air Force squadron. It was Mary Coningham's idea and a good one too. Young pilots like Deniston had some 300 hours in their logbooks, double what a German or British pilot would have at the time of going operational, but there was always a huge difference between flying and combat flying. The more proficient the pilot, the less he had to think about flying the machine and the more he could concentrate on learning to fight, so there was every reason to think the Americans would learn quickly. None the less, the chance to learn from those who had a bucket-load of experience was invaluable.

Deniston was posted to join 2 Squadron, Royal South African Air Force, and for his first-ever combat mission he was given a 50-gallon auxiliary fuel tank. He had spent his training time practising dog-fighting and fancy manoeuvres, but there was none of that on this mission. Rather, they flew for about two hours, and low – really low – then swooped in over an Axis landing ground. 'We made one pass, fired at them, surprised them, and ran for home right along the deck,' wrote Deniston. 'The mission was hairy and the leader was a tiger.' He found it exciting, though. His adrenalin had been really pumping.

It also took time to adjust to the strangeness of flying in the desert, and for those unused to spotting enemy aircraft – often just pinpricks in the sky until it was too late – the guiding hand of those more experienced could make all the difference. Billy Drake, for example, still commanding 112 Squadron, had not only honed his own ground-attack techniques but had also taught his men how to deal with attacks by enemy fighters, who nearly always had the advantage of height.

The three-aircraft 'vic' – or 'V' – as used by the RAF in the days of the Battle of Britain had long been discarded. 'The basic formation was the finger-four,' said Drake, 'well-spaced apart and working in pairs, leader and wingman.' This had always been the German system; vics were often better when defending because they were tighter and so easier to manoeuvre together, but when on the offensive the four was best. 'This way,' continued Drake, 'everyone had a bloody good sight of what was happening. Whoever saw the enemy first would inform the leader.' Timing the break – the moment at which pilots suddenly turned their aircraft on to their sides and pulled into a tight turn or dive – was key, and was always the leader's decision. 'The trick was to leave it to the last minute,' said Drake, 'so the 109s would overshoot us.'

Like almost everyone in the Desert Air Force, Drake was impressed with the Americans. He had a number from the 65th and Deniston's 66th Fighter Squadrons attached to him and he was impressed by the speed with which they caught on. 'They were a great bunch,' he said, 'and I think they respected us. Certainly the feeling was mutual.'

While British and Americans were starting to rub along well together, the same could not be said for the men of the Luftwaffe and the Regia Aeronautica, who tried to have as little to do with one another as possible. Nor was there much co-operation between Rommel and General von Waldau, the Axis air forces commander, who disliked each other intensely. Rommel had unrealistic expectations of what the air forces could achieve, while within the Luftwaffe a certain degree of complacency had crept in. It was all very exciting that Hans-Joachim Marseille was able to shoot ever-more British fighters, but in fact it was the bombers they needed to be hitting hardest.

The Luftwaffe was facing not only a production crisis, but also one of aircrew. Training had suffered because of the shortage of fuel. There were also fewer bombers because many of the instructors had been pulled from the training schools to fly transports over the Eastern Front and Mediterranean, so as one leak in the system was hastily plugged, others emerged. Furthermore, ground crew, so necessary for maintaining the mobility and efficiency of aerial units, had also begun to be stripped out and the men put into the Luftwaffe Field Divisions, which were, in essence, army units still under Göring's control.

The knock-on effect in North Africa was that ground crews were struggling for lack of parts, aircrew were struggling for lack of fuel, and the numbers of bombers, which used more fuel and were harder to maintain, had also been reduced. Their landing grounds were being bombed and strafed and when the RAF wasn't harassing them, it seemed the SAS were; the LRDG had also managed to destroy sixteen Italian aircraft during a raid at Barce.

Morale was, inevitably, suffering and, now that they were on the back foot, losses were mounting too. At JG27, Hans-Joachim Marseille lost two of his best friends in the squadron on the same day, 6 September; he and Fifi Stahlschmidt had been especially close. The pilot was seen going down with smoke trailing, pursued by three Spitfires, but although Marseille went out to look for him, he could not be found. Marseille was distraught.

Despite his astonishing seventeen victories in one day, Marseille was clearly struggling. He had always had difficulty sleeping, but now, when he was finally able to rest, he had begun increasingly to sleepwalk. It had started soon after his beloved sister had been murdered in Germany nine months earlier, but in North Africa, as his own scores rose and more of his friends were killed, so the sleepwalking increased. So mentally and physically exhausted had he become, he often needed his friend Matthias, the black South African, to help him out of the cockpit. Matthias would get him to his tent and on to his bed as though he were a child.

Marseille had been awarded the Diamonds to his Knight's Cross – the highest award of all – but he barely acknowledged the accolade. After Stahlschmidt's death he retreated further, eating alone and chain-smoking. It was clear he was burned out. He needed a long rest, but there was no chance of that happening while he was still shooting enemy planes out of the sky and while the Luftwaffe was so short of pilots. Once again, immediate and short-term needs were getting in the way of longer-term common sense.

On 26 September, Marseille was flying yet again, one of nine Me109s from I/JG27 ordered to escort Stukas. Just before 5 p.m. that afternoon, as the Stukas were making their dive-bombing run, Marseille spotted six Spitfires climbing to intercept them, rather than the Stukas – something they rarely did.

'*Indianer!*' called out Marseille, flying on over the Spitfires, then suddenly rolling into an almost vertical dive, leaving his comrades behind. He met the first Spitfire almost head-on, fired, and the enemy plane broke apart. The Spitfire's wingman hurtled past, but Marseille pulled back the stick, half-rolled and then cut the throttle, extended the landing flaps to enable him to pull a tighter turn and so cut in on the Spitfire's own turn. Opening fire, he saw the Spitfire burst into flames and fall away streaming smoke.

Marseille now climbed again, clear of the smoke, then heard a warning of a Spitfire below at nine o'clock. Throwing the Messerschmitt over hard to the right, he pulled back into a dive as the third Spitfire banked away to the left but continued to climb, exposing its underside. Marseille fired again, riddling the Spitfire, and saw it plunge towards the ground. That was three down. Immediately, however, he came under attack in turn from the third Spitfire's wingman. The Spitfire, and bullets, were coming straight towards him, so Marseille rolled and dived, then pulled up once more and looped as he tried to get on to the Spitfire's tail.

What followed was some eleven minutes of aerial duelling as Marseille in his Messerschmitt and the highly skilled RAF pilot in his Spitfire turned and pirouetted around the sky. Eventually they sped towards each other, less than 300 feet off the ground, and each opened fire. Both slewed their aircraft to avoid being hit and hurtled past each other. By now, Marseille's fuel light had come on; he needed to shoot down his pursuer or get out of the fight and get home – and quickly.

Climbing up into the late-afternoon sun, Marseille now hoped to use it as a blind and get away, but the Spitfire had turned to follow and was starting to close the distance, when suddenly his plane erupted into flames. At the same time, Marseille finished his climb and cut the engine, before rolling and diving back down on to the Spitfire's tail. At just over 100 yards, he opened fire, saw the Spitfire's wing rip off and the remains of the aircraft plunge into the ground. It was Marseille's 158th kill.

By the time he landed back down again, Marseille was so exhausted he almost fell asleep as the engine cut. Ashen and soaked in sweat, his hands trembling, he could barely get out of the plane and needed Matthias to help him. Only when he was told he was finally being given some leave and sent home to receive his Diamonds did his spirits seem to improve.

Three days later, on 30 September, Marseille was flying another sortie over enemy lines using a brand-new Me109G-2 when he suffered engine problems and radioed in to say he had smoke pouring into the cockpit. 'I am blinded,' he called out, 'can't see a thing.'

With two of his comrades drawing up alongside him, they escorted him back across their own lines, by which time Marseille was struggling to breathe even with his oxygen mask. Back on the ground, Edu Neumann, the group commander, now called him up and ordered him to bail out.

'I have to get out now,' agreed Marseille, '. . . can't stand it anymore.' Releasing the canopy, he flipped over the plane and dropped out from 1,500 feet, but as he fell the nose of the plane fell forward and he was struck by the stabilizer on the tail plane, which knocked him over on his back before he could open the parachute. Seconds later, he hit the ground.

The Star of Africa, as he had become known, was dead.

CHAPTER 29

The Vicious Circle

BRITAIN AND THE United States may not have been formal allies but General Eisenhower, now promoted from Deputy Commander to Allied Commander-in-Chief for Operation TORCH, had made it a central tenet that unity between the two nations was of paramount importance. Time and again he reiterated to his staff the need to work together. There would be testing moments, undoubtedly, but whatever the problems, he told his subordinates, they had to be overcome, and especially at the start of this joint venture; it was essential, Eisenhower correctly believed, to get the foundations right and parameters established from the outset. When Major-General Mark Clark, also promoted and now overseeing the planning for TORCH, mentioned the difficulties of getting American and British personnel on his planning team to gel, Ike told him to make changes until the right personalities were found.

Eisenhower also recognized that British public perception of both him and all Americans was very important, and even sought the advice of an American academic at Oxford University. 'The relations between the American Army and the English people is a problem of outstanding importance,' Professor Arthur Goodhart told him, 'because it will affect not only the immediate conduct of the war but also Anglo-American co-operation in the future.' It was imperative, he told Ike, that US troops should be happy in Britain and that British people liked them.

A booklet was written and issued to every US serviceman arriving in the UK. *A Short Guide to Great Britain* was full of explanations of British currency and practical advice about how to come to terms with this strange – and tiny – country and its even stranger people. 'Britain may look a little shop-worn and grimy to you,' it wrote. 'The British people are anxious to have you know that you are not seeing their country at its best.' It might look like it needed a lick of paint, the guide continued, but this was because the paint factories were making aircraft instead. There was also a list of important dos and don'ts. They were not to rub it in that they were better paid than British servicemen: 'Play fair with him. He can be a pal in need.' It was also important not to 'swank', as the British called it. 'Don't try to tell the British that America won the last war,' it advised, 'or make wisecracks about the war debts or about British defeats in war.' And most importantly, 'NEVER criticize the King or Queen.'

As it happened, American troops were proving rather popular in Britain. Most were well-mannered and friendly. Henry Bowles, now training in Britain with the US 1st Division, certainly tried to behave in such a way. 'And we were there for a purpose,' his brother, Tom, pointed out. They were generous, too, with their cigarettes and chocolate. 'Oh yes,' added Henry, 'you could go and get cigarettes and different kinds of candy bars' – which were scarcer in Britain.

It was higher up the chain where potential tensions were more likely to express themselves. There was the British perception that Americans were loud and brash and boastful, and the American one that the British were repressed, condescending and stuck in the past. Broad-brush prejudices were just that, however, and for the most part any clashes tended to derive from personality and differences in the way of doing things, rather than along national lines.

Tensions between Americans and British have repeatedly been played up, but the reality was that for every searing Anglophobe or ardent Americaphobe there were many more examples of courtesy, mutual admiration and burgeoning friendship. And under Eisenhower's diligent insistence, anyone displaying obvious xenophobia tended to be moved on pretty swiftly. As Ike put it to his American staff, 'You can call a man a son-of-a-bitch, but if you call him a *Limey* son-of-a-bitch, you're out!'

In marked contrast, there had never been a similar determination from Germany to find unity and mutual respect with any of its allies. Rather, mutual mistrust had been the basis of their working relationship. On 22 September, Count Ciano had had a gloomy meeting with Rino Fougier, the Under-Secretary of State for Air, who had described Italian aircraft production in 'dark colours'. Between them, Fougier told him, Italy and Germany now produced less than one-fifth of what the Allies were producing. Numbers of pilots were also declining dramatically. This meant that before long the Allies would have mastery of the skies, which Ciano was well aware meant the Axis could no longer win. Italy, though, Ciano confided, would find a way out – it was why, behind the backs of the Germans, he had maintained what he believed was a 'measured policy' towards Britain and America. 'It is because of this policy that Ribbentrop especially, and the Germans in general, hate me.'

Another bone of contention was the enormous reparations Germany was insisting upon from the occupied territories, and especially, in the Italian sphere, the Balkans and Greece. In Greece, for example, monthly payments had amounted to 4,000 million drachmas, which, at exchange rates set by Germany, came to 80 million Reichsmarks – that is, around $32,500,000, or, in today's money, around half a billion dollars every month. This had been reduced to 1,500 million drachmas a month in March, plus interest-free credit from the Bank of Greece, but these were crippling sums which the country could simply not afford. It was the same in Yugoslavia. In both cases, these were countries that had hardly been well off in the first place. Mussolini had already complained about this once to Hitler but had been knocked back. 'If we lose the war,' *Il Duce* railed, 'it will be because of the political stupidity of the Germans, who have not even tried to use common sense and restraint, and who have made Europe as hot and treacherous as a volcano.'

A few days later, now back in Rome, Ciano attended a dinner for the Tripartite group of Germans and Japanese from their respective embassies and noted that the atmosphere was decidedly heavy. Cavallero then made an enormous *faux pas* by telling the Japanese Ambassador that Axis forces had been successful at Stalingrad. The Ambassador assumed this meant Stalingrad had fallen, when it most certainly had not, but the damage had been done: the rumour of victory there spread through the hall until the Germans openly denied it, much to Cavallero's 'great shame'.

Rather, General Paulus's Sixth Army was becoming horribly bogged down at Stalingrad, while in the Caucasus the advance was slowing alarmingly and the Germans were still a long way from the El Dorado that was Baku. In the northern part of Army Group South's push,

Generalmajor Balck's 2. Panzerdivision had been pulled out of the line at Veronezh, having been on the defensive for the past few weeks. Their casualties had been heavy. Between Second Panzerarmee – to which they had been attached – and Paulus at Stalingrad, a distance of nearly 600 miles, were the Hungarian Second Army, the Italians and the Third Romanian Army, none of which was as well equipped, trained or motivated as their German allies. This meant that with the bulk of the German troops now in a giant bulge south of Stalingrad in the Caucasus, they were vulnerable to being entirely cut off by a Soviet drive through these weaker Axis forces. Currently, however, the Red Army was starting to pour the weight of its effort towards Stalingrad, the city Stalin had declared could not fall. At any rate, it was now the autumn, winter was approaching, and once again it looked as though Axis forces on the Eastern Front had gained vast amounts of territory for not very much benefit and a great deal of loss. Certainly, the killer knock-out punch against the Red Army was as far away as it had ever been.

On 15 September, Halder had recorded in his notes that a grand total of 1,637,280 German men had been lost since BARBAROSSA began. Nine days later, he was fired by Hitler. 'My nerves are worn out,' he wrote in his final diary entry as Chief of Staff of the German Army. 'Also his nerves are no longer fresh. We must part. Necessity for educating the General Staff in fanatical faith in The Idea. He is determined to enforce his will also into the army.'

Meanwhile, back in Germany, Nazi technocrats were trying to keep Germany's rapidly failing war effort going, even though they were now losing the production battle so dismally. The biggest challenge of all remained the shortage of food. Herbert Backe had returned to the principles of the Hunger Plan of the previous year. Ukraine and France were to be the main provider of new food deliveries, while Poland would, from now on, be expected to be a contributor to that flow of food into Germany rather than a receiver. How they were supposed to feed themselves was no longer of any concern to the Nazi leadership. 'The Führer repeatedly said and I repeat after him,' Göring declared in a speech announcing Backe's new measures, 'if anyone has to go hungry, it shall not be Germans, but other peoples.'

While these brutal measures would, it was hoped, improve the food situation in Germany, the manpower crisis was hardly abating. Every day, thousands of workers, both forced labour and POWs, were arriving in Germany's industrial centres. The system could not cope – there was not enough food or housing for them. Nor was it possible to keep this mammoth migration of workers under lock and key all the time, and the forests and German countryside were now awash with escaped Russian prisoners in numbers that were putting the efforts of British and French escapees into the shade. Some 42,714 foreign workers escaped between April and August 1942, all of whom were hunted with varying degrees of success by the Gestapo. This meant the Gestapo needed to keep up its own numbers, who then could not fight at the front. So the vicious circle continued.

By now, in the autumn of 1942, the Germans were having to send back tens of thousands of ill and emaciated workers; so neglected had they been they were no longer able to work. Precious freight capacity was thus being used, achieving nothing but misery and death – and large numbers inevitably died en route. Treating workers appallingly badly was not conducive to high productivity, but there was barely enough food for wholesome pure-blood German citizens, let alone Soviet POWs and other *Untermenschen*. Rumours about the terrible conditions in Germany soon spread; it was no wonder so few Frenchmen were taking up Laval's *Relève*.

Meanwhile, in Britain, young men and women fed with well-balanced diets filled the factories. What's more, they were more motivated, knowing that their efforts were helping those of fellow citizens, brothers, lovers, friends and family fighting overseas. If there was any motivation for a Polish worker being treated abysmally in the factory of his enemy, it was either to sabotage or simply try to survive the hell in which he found himself.

In the Western Desert, the myriad problems of home were making themselves felt at the front too. At the southern end of the Alamein Line were the men of the Italian Folgore Division, still living in their fox-holes and mostly wishing they were anywhere but in this scrap of desert. The lack of food was bad enough, although Luigi Marchese found eating immensely difficult because of the thousands of flies that swarmed around them. Worse, though, was the water shortage. Daytime was now not quite so blisteringly hot as it had been when they first arrived, but it was still pretty warm and none of them was even remotely able to quench their thirst. Marchese had found one of his men crying. The man confessed he had been so thirsty he had drunk his own piss, which had made his throat swell up.

On 15 October, there was, miraculously, a cloudburst, so Marchese grabbed a piece of soap, leaped out of his dug-out and began scrubbing himself. His chest was covered in a 'carapace of sand and sweat' and the soap was so hard it took him a while to work up a decent lather. Then as soon as he had done so, the rain stopped, and the mist that had shielded him from the eyes of the enemy lifted too. Still filthy, he dashed back into his fox-hole, feeling even dirtier than before.

Like Marchese, Giuseppe Santaniello had also recently reached North Africa from Yugoslavia. Just turned twenty-two, Santaniello was a lawyer from Avellino in the south near Naples and had joined up the year before, believing war was a glorious business. His initial training, however, had done much to disabuse him of that perception. At the barracks, thieves were rife, while the facilities had been awful, including communal lavatories that had been covered in a layer of stinking piss and excrement. 'An inventor of tortures,' he wrote, 'could not have dreamed up anything worse.' The uniforms they were given were ill-fitting. He had been utterly appalled. 'Very soon,' he noted, 'our hopes and dreams crumbled, replaced by the awful reality of having to live in the midst of this filth and surrounded by criminals.'

Having survived this ordeal, he was eventually commissioned as a gunner, joined the 48th Reggimento Artiglieria in the Bari Division and was posted to Brindisi. There he was billeted in a house that was, at least, clean, although in this case there were not even toilets at all – rather, he was expected to use a chamber pot. 'And we presumed to bring civilisation to Abyssinia,' he snorted.

By July, he had been in Yugoslavia and, like Luigi Marchese and countless other Italians, had found the Balkans a nerve-wracking experience, where partisans lurked on every corner and where even a friendly smile might mask a knife beneath the cloak. Fortunately for him, they had not stayed long and soon were on a slow train chugging its way south to Athens. At every station, he saw people crowding around the train, asking for cigarettes and drink, but, curiously, refusing any money, which because of the enormous reparations demanded by the Germans had become worthless. 'The mountain people no longer have faith in the paper of whichever government now rules over them,' noted Santaniello in his diary. 'They've gone back to barter, and misery is visible on the faces of everybody. That's war!'

He and his comrades eventually reached Athens in early August, where they remained for three weeks waiting to be shipped to North Africa. Again, he found a people struggling to exist. The citizens were starving and the women forced to prostitute themselves in return for food. Santaniello had heard there were more than 4,000 girls who had been 'ruined' by unwanted pregnancies with Italian and German troops. 'I'd say that Athens now keeps going,' he jotted, 'thanks only to the legs of its women.'

At the end of the month they sailed for North Africa, safely crossing the Mediterranean to Tobruk, and by 20 September had reached the front at Alamein, where he joined the 9th Battery of the 21st Artiglieria Reggimento of the Trento Division, in the northern part of the line. Unlike Luigi Marchese, he found his men to be in reasonably good spirits. 'Morale here is very high,' he noted. 'I get the feeling that I'm with people who really know their business.' Within a couple of weeks, however, he was not quite so upbeat. He had spent much of his time as a forward observation officer, which involved long hours on watch. Soon, the conditions, the sandstorms, the endless bombing and strafing from the RAF began to play on his nerves.

Meanwhile, in the unoccupied zone of southern France, the three major resistance groups were forging ever-closer ties. Back in early July, Combat had agreed to co-ordinate efforts with Libération and Franc-Tireur, and it was also agreed in principle to create a new Armée Secrète (Secret Army). The issue of control of any military effort, however, had still not been resolved with de Gaulle and London, and while the creation of the Secret Army was very much in tune with Henri Frenay's aims and ambitions for armed insurrection, there was still a big question mark over leadership of this new paramilitary formation.

Frenay was now pressing for a complete fusion of the three movements and also unity for the proposed Secret Army. At a meeting in late July, Jean-Pierre Levy, the head of Franc-Tireur, expressed his agreement with Frenay, but Emmanuel d'Astier disagreed; he felt that co-ordination of efforts was enough. He did, however, accept the need to merge the proposed Secret Army, but with one proviso: the commander should not also be in any of the three movements. This was a blow to Frenay, who felt he was the obvious choice. However, he took it on the chin and soon learned of a reserve lieutenant-general, Charles Delestraint, who was apparently vehemently anti-Vichy and had the necessary gravitas and status to be the titular head of the Secret Army. In practice, Frenay still hoped that he could control the strings.

In early August, Frenay travelled to Bourg-en-Bresse, to the north of Lyons, to see Général Delestraint in person. Presenting himself at Delestraint's modest apartment, he was confronted by a moustachioed, bald-headed man in his undershirt. Frenay explained who he was and his admiration for de Gaulle. It turned out Delestraint had been de Gaulle's commanding officer before the armistice. 'I've great admiration for him,' the Général told him, 'as much for his quick mind as for his tactical skill.'

Frenay then talked about the Resistance and patiently answered the Général's questions, realizing as he did so how hard it was to explain, briefly, all that he had learned over the past two years. Eventually, he came to the purpose of his visit. 'Général,' he said, 'the Secret Army must become a well-armed, perfectly trained instrument of war. It must play a large role in the battle for our liberation, and so its actions must be integrated with the Allied battle plan.' An experienced senior commander was needed who could deal confidently with de Gaulle and the Allies, he explained. 'Général, I've come to ask if you could accept such a responsibility.'

There was a long silence, then Delestraint stood up, paced the room and told Frenay that he would need both time to reflect and also, if he were to accept, a written order from de Gaulle. This, Frenay told him, went without saying. 'I must warn you,' Frenay continued, 'that an acceptance on your part would entail your exposure to mortal danger, a far greater danger than you've ever met on the battlefield. The Gestapo does not spare—'

Delestraint cut him off. 'Monsieur,' he said, 'mortal danger is the career officer's lot.'

Back at the front was Major Hans von Luck, who in early September had been pronounced 'fit for limited combat duty' and given a week's leave. He had gone to see his mother in Berlin and found a city that was war-weary. Berliners were naturally cheery souls, but he saw only drawn, grey faces. 'With their sense of reality,' he noted, 'they had no illusions.' His leave over, he had been sent to a replacement section and by now was itching to get back to rejoin his unit. He did not have to wait long – by the middle of the month he was on his way to Rome, then on a flight to Tobruk via Sicily in a large Blohm and Voss flying boat, which came into the harbour alongside a half-sunken British freighter. Moments later, he was out on the dock, breathing in the hot, familiar desert air. He was rather glad to be back.

A car met him and he was driven straight to see Rommel himself at his HQ in Mersa Matruh.

'I'm glad you're here again,' Rommel told him. It seemed von Luck's replacement had done well enough but had recently become ill. 'He's only waiting for your return to be posted back home.' Rommel explained he was about to head back to Germany himself for a brief bit of leave and to see Hitler, then handed him over to General Gause, his Chief of Staff, who had also now recovered from his wounds at Gazala, and who put von Luck in the picture and explained the chronic shortage of supplies. Rommel was very disappointed in the 'slack conduct' of the OKW and Hitler, and the half-hearted efforts of the Italians to ensure adequate supplies. Von Luck was struck by how tired and depressed both men seemed. Gause told him about the failure to deliver the promised supplies and the shattering blow of the failure at Alam Halfa, which, the General said, had been down to the shortages and the almost 100 per cent air superiority of the RAF.

Gause also told him about Rommel's interview with Brigadier George Clifton of the New Zealand Division, who had been captured and brought before him. Clifton told him the Allies would now win the war, something Rommel had become convinced about too. He told Clifton that the Allies would, like Germany, have to get used to the danger coming from the East, from Russia. 'So, Luck,' Gause told him, 'now you know why Rommel is so disappointed.' The Feldmarschall was going to see Hitler and planned to tell the Führer, frankly, that unless his Panzerarmee began getting sufficient supplies, and soon, North Africa could not be won.

Gause then told him where to find his old reconnaissance battalion, still part of 21. Panzerdivision. They were based at Siwa Oasis, around 200 miles to the south, guarding the southern flank beyond the Qattara Depression. The following day, 23 September, von Luck was given a ride in a Stuka and after an hour landed and was with his men once more. 'I felt as though I were in a fairy tale from the *Thousand and One Nights*,' he wrote, 'blue skies above me, hot sun, and endless groves of palms with ripening dates.'

*

In France, the disparate nature of resistance was not being much helped by the equally disparate number of intelligence agencies now operating in the country under the control of various bodies in London. This was making Jean Moulin's task of uniting resistance even harder because he was telling resistance groups that he was the representative of de Gaulle and the Free French, only to discover that some other agent had already claimed that supposedly unique position. In August, he had fired off an angry message to London. 'Inform you that only serious difficulties have encountered in my work have come from Gaullist agents,' he signalled. 'If issue not settled immediately will regretfully ask you to accept my resignation. In this field disorder is extreme.'

The trouble was, the Free French had set up three separate intelligence bureaus. Two had been combined back in January to form the Bureau Central de Renseignements et d'Action Militaire (BCRAM) led by Major André Dewavrin, known under his codename as 'Colonel Passy', but that still left a second intelligence network known as Service d'Action Politique en France, run by the Free French Department of the Interior. Both were quite independently operating agents inside France.

Then there was the British Secret Intelligence Service, of which MI6 dealt with foreign intelligence and also had agents operating in France. On top of that, there was the Special Operations Executive, set up in the summer of 1940 specifically to foster resistance and sabotage in Nazi-occupied territories, and which came under the Ministry for Economic Warfare headed by Hugh Dalton.

SOE had different sections for different countries, but there were five separate sections operating in France. There was DF, which was the escape section; AMF, which operated from Algiers; and EU/P, which operated amongst the half million Poles still in France. Then there was F Section, run by Maurice Buckmaster, which had initially been hidden from de Gaulle and which had at first sent agents to look into what opportunities there were for subversion, but which was now sending agents to co-ordinate and co-operate with the resistance. Finally, there was RF Section, which was primarily SOE's bridge to the Free French agencies and which included French rather than British agents. There was a common overall purpose, but also rivalry between F and RF Sections and between SOE and the BCRAM.

The truth was, all wartime intelligence agencies operated in a certain amount of disarray – and German intelligence was certainly no exception. The thinking behind the creation of SOE had been sound enough, however; it had not been designed to be a purely intelligence-gathering agency, but in essence a terrorist organization, based more on the Irish Republican Army that had proved so effective during the Irish rebellion two decades earlier. SOE was, however, a work in progress. Two years was a long time for those suffering occupation, but not for those trying to set up a subversion organization from scratch. Agents had to be found, then trained, and trained by trainers, who also had to be found and recruited. Methods had to be worked out and new technologies developed. Contacts had to be established. Those subdued peoples in Europe had to realize life was not going to improve in any way under the draconian occupation of the Axis forces. What's more, SOE had to overcome resistance to its very existence from MI6, who, not unnaturally, felt they were a bunch of upstarts who were not only treading on their own feet but who could very easily compromise their own work.

Nor was SOE the only new subversion organization operating in French territory. On 13 June, President Roosevelt had formally ordered the creation of the Office of Strategic Services (OSS), run by his old friend General Bill Donovan. Its genesis had been a year earlier, when the President had asked Donovan to draft a plan for an intelligence-gathering organization. The US had code-breakers and for domestic intelligence-gathering they had the FBI, whose field of influence extended to South America, but they had no equivalent to MI6 and SOE. In July 1941, Donovan had become the Co-ordinator of Intelligence (COI), although as his new organization developed, much of his information came via British intelligence services.

In June 1942, however, the OSS had come into being. Its task was to spy, subvert, sabotage and wage a propaganda war, and by that time it had already begun recruiting agents and had a string of contacts both in Vichy North Africa and in France itself.

By the autumn of 1942, these various agencies, of which SOE was one, and the different resistance movements were just beginning to work out what needed to be done and what could plausibly then be achieved. The worry for the Allies in the case of France was that, no matter what their various merits, there were simply too many of them. Greater co-ordination was needed – and for the sake of those now risking their lives, the sooner the better.

This was one of the reasons why, in September, plans were put in place for a summit between the principal resistance leaders and de Gaulle's and his intelligence chief Passy's operation in London. Henri Frenay received his invitation from Jean Moulin; both he and Emmanuel d'Astier were to head to the Riviera and from there be picked up and taken to London. By the 14th, he and d'Astier were in Marseilles and there picked up a signal via the BBC that they were to embark from the tiny cove of Port-Miou. Standing on the pebbly shore, they flashed their torches into the darkness as instructed, but not until an hour had passed did they hear the sound of oars and then a voice call out in English, 'How are you, gentlemen?'

In fact, the men were Poles, and as soon as Frenay and d'Astier had been rowed out to a waiting fishing boat they were offered proper coffee and then British cigarettes. 'I can honestly say that in my whole life no gift ever seemed more exotic,' Frenay wrote. 'Oh, that first puff!' The real coffee was like nectar too.

After some days waiting beyond the limit of French territorial waters, they were picked up by British warships and taken to Gibraltar, then from there by seaplane to Bristol and on to London, where they met Colonel Passy. It was by now 26 September.

Both Moulin and Levy had been delayed getting to London, so Frenay spent a few days wandering around the city, eating and drinking well, and buying a few clothes. He wondered where all the ruins caused by the Luftwaffe were – he had expected to see much more damage. He was also surprised to see shops still well stocked. 'To one arriving from France,' he wrote, 'they were overflowing with luxuries. And the restaurants and dance-halls were packed.'

There was also a lunch with de Gaulle at his country house, 50 miles north of London. There, both spoke frankly. Frenay told de Gaulle about Général Delestraint, explained that he thought Jean Moulin was becoming a barrier between Free France and the Resistance and asked for more arms.

'I know,' de Gaulle replied to this last point. 'Try and explain that to the English.'

Frenay returned to London feeling neither disappointed nor especially comforted. There had been no exchange of human warmth, but he did feel de Gaulle had at least listened.

Moulin never quite made it to the summit – fog, cancelled planes, long train journeys and a missed boat all conspired against him, but a number of matters were agreed none the less. A Co-ordinating Committee was established that would meet regularly in France with Moulin as chair and with the casting vote. This helped further unify resistance, but also brought it under closer control of London – it was agreed that, in military terms, the Co-ordinating Committee was under direct command of de Gaulle. It was, however, accepted that the Secret Army should remain in being and come under command of Général Delestraint. Large-scale military action was forbidden, except in conjunction with an Allied invasion, whenever that should be. In the immediate term, only sabotage was allowed – that is, disruption to infrastructure and material used by the Germans – and only upon instruction from London. These were considerable constraints upon Frenay's original vision and yet the Secret Army was now sanctioned, as was its commander. From those many first seeds, the resistance movement had come a long way.

Meanwhile, the British Special Operations Executive was, like OSS, rapidly extending its influence, and not least in Scandinavia. It now had agents in Norway and Sweden, including their Agent 24, Gunnar Sønsteby. His role was not, and never had been, to kill or harm German troops, but rather to gather intelligence and carry out subversion wherever possible. He was becoming rather good at it. 'I had an unremarkable, forgettable face,' he said. 'I wasn't the sort of person people noticed.' He made sure he kept a number of different identity papers and that he never stayed in one place for more than a few nights at a time, nor gave any new contacts his real name. He was also methodical and had a meticulous attention to detail. These attributes had so far served him well.

At the end of August, his SOE handler in Stockholm, Tom Nielsen, asked him to get printing plates for the 5-, 10-, 50- and 100-Crown notes from the Bank of Norway's printers. Names and contacts were given to him and soon he was meeting with a man who had a friend who was managing director of the Bank of Norway's printers. London had told Sønsteby that casts would do, but they also needed a large specimen of the paper used. The risks were, of course, enormous, and first the printers wanted proof that London was behind the plan. What they asked for was a signed letter from Toralv Oksnevad, the BBC radio announcer known in Norway as 'the voice from London'. Sønsteby duly reported this to Stockholm, who informed London and a short time later the letter arrived.

This satisfied the printers, but the next hurdle was letting someone within the bank in on the picture, as it would have been impossible to borrow the plates without them knowing. Fortunately, the bank played ball, although with every person who knew about the plan, so the risks increased.

None the less, all went to plan. Sønsteby received the plates and paper, and that same evening took a taxi, hiding the plates in the bottom of the coal sack used in the car's gas-generator, and began the journey to Stockholm.

All was going to plan until around 20 miles east of Oslo the car's lights suddenly failed and, in the dark, they skidded and crashed into a ditch. For a while, Sønsteby was at a loss as to what to do, as they were still some way from the border. Then a large, six-wheeled German truck rumbled along, so Sønsteby and the driver flagged it down and asked for assistance. The young soldiers seemed only too happy to help, and within quarter of an hour had pulled the car from the ditch. Fortunately, it was largely undamaged, the lights were got to work once more, and they were able to continue to Kongsvinger on the Swedish border. There, Sønsteby handed over the plates, which were taken to Stockholm, copied, and returned by courier the following day. It had been an entirely successful operation.

SOE was planning a far more ambitious operation in Norway, however. Back in May 1941, intelligence reached London that the Germans were significantly increasing production of heavy-water at the Norsk Hydro works at Vemork in southern Norway. By the summer, the scientist who had overseen the development of the heavy-water plant, Professor Leif Tronstad, had fled to Sweden and then flown to London, where he became head of Section IV of the Norwegian High Command, responsible for co-ordinating intelligence and sabotage operations with SOE. Taking his place at Vemork had been Dr Jomar Brun, who, unbeknownst to the Germans, continued to send intelligence reports back to London, including via microphotos smuggled in tubes of toothpaste to Sweden.

It was in 1938 that German scientists Otto Hahn and Fritz Strassmann had successfully split the uranium nucleus and in so doing released atomic energy. By the eve of war, it had been widely recognized by scientists that an unprecedentedly powerful bomb created by atomic fission was not only possible, but would, one day, become a reality. On

Churchill's visit to Washington in June, he and Roosevelt had discussed pooling resources to accelerate work to create such a bomb, although both accepted this was still some way off. They were, however, both concerned that German scientists might get there first. 'However sceptical one might feel about the assertions of scientists,' wrote Churchill, 'much disputed among themselves and expressed in jargon incomprehensible to laymen, we could not run the mortal risk of being outstripped in this awful sphere.'

As it happened, the Germans did have an atomic research programme – or rather, they had several, because as with most areas of the Nazi state, atomic physics was also riven with jealousies, disagreements and rival operations. Albert Speer, however, was very interested in this potentially war-changing field of science and on 4 June, the same month that Roosevelt and Churchill were discussing such things, he called a meeting of leading physicists to try to learn more. Also attending this meeting were Feldmarschall Erhard Milch and General Fritz Fromm, the commander of the Reserve Army. Among the physicists were Fritz Strassmann, as well as Carl-Friedrich von Weizsäcker and Werner Heisenberg, one of Germany's leading scientists and head of the Kaiser Wilhelm Institute for Physics (KWIP), the important research facility in Berlin. A further physicist was Dr Kurt Diebner, who was not only an ardent Nazi but also a passionate believer that atomic weapons were the panacea Germany needed and that they could be developed in a realistic timescale.

These were all very clever people, but unfortunately for Germany, many of their leading physicists had been Jewish and had been forced to leave the country before the war began; Otto Frisch, for example, was now working for the Allies in the US. The development of atomic weapons was not only incredibly complicated and difficult, it was also phenomenally time-consuming, which was why some 125,000 people would soon be working on the Allied project and why huge sums were being pumped into it. Success depended on pooling all possible resources in a co-ordinated effort. Atomic research was not the area in which to impose the usual Nazi approach of divide-and-rule so favoured by Hitler. As it was, however, atomic research lay in two camps. Dr Diebner had his own facility in Gatow, a suburb of Berlin, having been ousted as President of the KWIP for being too political. His place had been taken by Professor Heisenberg, who was not a Nazi and who divided his time between labs at the KWIP in Berlin and his own facility in Leipzig. Needless to say, Heisenberg and Diebner did not get along.

At Speer's symposium, it was Professor Heisenberg who gave the main lecture. He used his speech to point out that creating an atomic bomb was theoretically possible, but that it would take Germany at least two years to develop one – which, in June 1942, was felt to be beyond the end of the war. He also stressed that in the USA the Americans faced similar difficulties and were no nearer than the Germans to creating such a weapon. He asked for incredibly modest funding. Whether he was being deliberately disingenuous or simply had not thought through what was needed for a full-scale German atomic weapon research operation is not entirely clear.

On the back of this conference, Speer recommended to Hitler that Göring be put in charge of the Reich Research Council and that greater funding be given to the rival research projects. He was excited by its potential, but also recognized priorities had to be made when it came to resources; with this in mind, he also warned the Führer that the development of a successful atomic weapon was not about to happen any time soon. However, atomic weapons research was to continue and did so, with both Heisenberg and Diebner building a number of experimental nuclear reactors.

They were also using heavy water, or deuterium oxide, which they believed was a potential key ingredient in creating atomic energy. It was why, when the Allies discovered the Germans were massively increasing heavy-water production, major alarm bells began ringing. It was still felt certain that Germany was some considerable way off creating an atomic bomb, but, unlike the German approach to Allied atomic research, there was to be no complacency whatsoever. For the Allies, German atomic research had to be taken very seriously indeed and all efforts made to restrict their progress.

With this in mind, they realized it was essential the heavy-water plant at Vemork be wrecked, but how this was going to happen was another matter. The Norsk Hydro plant there was some 150 miles inland and the same distance from Oslo. There was only one road in and the plant itself was halfway up a cliff above a steep gorge that led up to the Hardangervidda, a vast plateau wilderness which for half the year was covered in snow and ice.

At first, it was thought that bombing the dam at the head of the valley was the answer, but that was not going to be easy and, in any case, the resulting tsunami as the dam broke would kill thousands. Direct bombing also risked destroying one of the liquid-ammonia tanks in the plant, which could have terrible consequences for those living in the valley. Eventually, after much soul-searching and endless debate and discussion, it was agreed that a sabotage mission was the only option.

The SOE-trained Norwegian Independent Company No.1, now renamed 'Linge Company' in honour of Martin Linge, was still training in Scotland when Lieutenant Jens-Anton Poulsson and his radio operator, Gunnar Sønsteby's friend Lieutenant Knut Haugland, were called to London and briefed about the mission. They were to be part of a four-man advance party codenamed Operation GROUSE. Once landed, they would carry out a reconnaissance of the area and prepare a route to Vemork. A little while later, two gliders carrying the pilots and fifteen Royal Engineers from the new British 1st Airborne Division would land on the Hardangervidda at a point prepared by the GROUSE team in what was to be the first-ever British glider operation. The team would then lead them to Vemork and the engineers would destroy the plant. The glider landing was codenamed Operation FRESHMAN.

In London, Poulsson learned that he was to be the team leader. A tall, imposing figure, he was not only a highly experienced mountaineer, but was also, like Gunnar Sønsteby, from Rjukan, the town closest to Vemork. 'As a boy and young man,' he said, 'my main interests were hunting and fishing – the outdoor life – and I knew the area.' Nor was the sabotage of the heavy-water plant their only objective. Afterwards, the plan was for them to recruit and train guerrillas in the Telemark region around Vemork.

Poulsson had been told of the importance of the mission and how vital it was to destroy the heavy-water plant, but he hadn't really believed it; he thought that had been a ruse to make them eager for the job. He had needed no incentive, however. For too long, they had been hanging about in England, waiting to be sent back to Norway; it had been deeply frustrating. Now, though, they would soon be heading back. Whether the importance of the mission had been exaggerated or not, Poulsson didn't care: he was just relieved to be finally doing something against those now occupying his country. It was time to strike back.

CHAPTER 30

Lighting the Torch

A CROSS THE ATLANTIC, and over on the far side of the United States, extraordinary feats of engineering and production were taking place at Henry Kaiser's still-new shipyards. August had seen Bedford's Yard No. 2 at Richmond, California, build a Liberty ship in just twenty-four days, but in September that astonishing feat had been bettered yet again by Kaiser's son, Edgar, at Portland, California. Albert Bauer, his assistant general manager, had found a way to increase the production of every worker in every department. 'More men and equipment are swung into the job,' he explained. 'We simply program the erection on a faster schedule.' He made it sound so simple. Perhaps it was; at any rate, on 23 September, the *Joseph N. Teal* was finished in just ten days.

FDR flew in after having been to see the Boeing plant at Seattle, meeting the Kaisers, Henry and Edgar, and Clay Bedford too, who had come up under sufferance from Richmond. The President's car toured the shipyard then came to a halt on a ramp that overlooked the glistening *Joseph N. Teal*. Some 20,000 people had come to watch the unveiling – although the honour of breaking the champagne bottle was given to Roosevelt's daughter, Anna Boettiger. It took three attempts but eventually smashed, rather showering her and other dignitaries in the process. The crowd simply cheered and kept on cheering.

The President spoke, saying how inspired he was by what he was witnessing: 'I wish that every man, woman and child in the United States could have been here to see the launching and realize its importance in winning the war.' Henry Kaiser then stepped up to the microphone. In a few days' time, he said, the *Joseph N. Teal* would be at sea, bearing supplies to America's troops and allies. 'It is a miracle, no less,' he told them, 'a miracle of God and of the genius of free American workmen.' Few of those standing there that day would have disagreed.

Yet nor was the ten-day ship the only staggering feat of production that September because, out to the east, what eighteen months before had been a sleepy, rather featureless creek west of Detroit was now home to a mind-bogglingly huge factory – a giant L-shape more than a mile long. *Time* magazine called it 'the most enormous room in the history of man.' It was called Willow Run. The project to construct this factory to build Consolidated B-24 heavy bombers had been the brainchild of Charles Sorensen, one of Henry Ford's production chiefs and the man in charge of the company's defence contracts. After Knudsen's appeal to the auto industry at the back end of 1940, Ford had been approached about helping to make warplanes. Ford Senior had given both his son, Edsel, and Sorensen free rein to get involved, although he refused to let them make Flying Fortresses. Instead, Sorensen had visited San Diego to look at the Consolidated plant.

He had not been impressed and, having quickly thought through a production plan, had offered to build the entire aircraft or not at all. Unlike other auto manufacturers, he was not prepared to be a bit-player. Sorensen had quickly realized he might have bitten off more than he could chew. A Ford car required some 15,000 different parts, but a B-24 had 488,193. However, he and his team soon enough worked out that the B-24's half a million parts could be broken down into 30,000 components and into nine separate pre-assembly compartments.

Repeatedly, obstacles were thrown in his path – by old man Ford, by the Government, by innumerable production issues along the way. None the less, just nineteen months on, not only had Sorensen overseen the building of the world's largest single factory, but the first completed fully built B-24 rolled off Willow Run's assembly line. That was as much of a miracle as the ten-day Liberty ship.

'Those who delay us keep reminding us that TORCH must be carried out at the earliest possible moment,' recorded Major-General Mark Clark in his diary on 2 September. 'However, we're still waiting for the mission directive. And there is an urgent need for time to plan, time to train, time to assemble for the assault.'

The very next day, however, the plan was finally, at long last, agreed. A proposal was received from Roosevelt suggesting simultaneous landings at Casablanca in French Morocco and at Oran in Algeria, but also at Algiers, so three in all. US troops would lead the way at Casablanca and Oran, and the British at Algiers. Eisenhower and Clark were once again summoned to Downing Street, where they discussed Roosevelt's proposals with the PM and British chiefs and then, after an hour's consultation, accepted them. Having dictated his reply, Eisenhower turned to the Americans. 'It's great not to argue when you get into a tight place,' he said. 'It makes you appreciate the accord between us. I know we all want to get the plan and get going.'

The Casablanca task force was to come directly from the USA, while the troops for Algiers and Oran would come from Britain. All three landings were to be simultaneous, if possible. After securing the beaches, beachheads were to be expanded rapidly with a view to securing French Morocco and western Algeria. Ground bases and airfields could then be quickly established to support the push towards Tunisia. 'Hurrah!' came the one-word reply from Roosevelt. 'Ok, full blast,' Churchill answered in turn.

'Mission planned for early take-off,' recorded the 97th Bombardment Group's war diary on 4 September, 'postponed twice and finally washed out at 1330 much to the disgust of the combat crews.' Two days later, Ralph Burbridge and his crew in *All American* and twenty-six other B-17s bombed the Potez aircraft factory in France the day the US Eighth Air Force lost its first two bombers. On the 16th, the next planned mission was cancelled – as was the next. 'Proposed mission for the day scrubbed,' noted the diary three days later, 'due to weather conditions.'

In all, the US Eighth Air Force would launch only four missions in September as it struggled its way towards full operational readiness. General Hap Arnold had promised Tooey Spaatz he would have 500 heavies by January and by the end of the month he would have 178 in England, but nothing like that number would be airborne in one go. Back in the States, Arnold was firing off increasingly irritated messages asking why so few raids were being mounted. Training requirements, serviceability and bad weather were the reasons, but from a sun-drenched Washington Arnold was looking at statistics and numbers and expecting more. In Britain, meanwhile, Air Chief Marshal Portal was still frustrated by the Americans' insistence on daylight bombing, which he maintained would inevitably lead to unacceptable losses and an inability to strike much beyond the Ruhr. However, he had accepted the joint directive for the development of the day-bomber offensive. Initially, US bombers would fly with combined US and RAF fighter cover. As Eighth Air Force grew, so US fighters would take over escort duties while the British would mount diversion raids. Finally, the Americans would operate entirely independently from the RAF, albeit in co-operation.

As part of this build-up and transition, the American fighter pilots serving with RAF Fighter Command were to be moved across into the US Eighth Air Force too. Jim Goodson, who had been flying Hurricanes with 416 Canadian Squadron, had found himself posted to 133 Eagle Squadron towards the end of August, along with two of his fellow Americans, Ray Fuchs and 'Whitey' White, and none of them had been particularly happy about it.

Taking a train to Audley End, a lonely halt south of Cambridge, they eventually got a ride to Debden in Essex, a sector station, only to be told that 133 Squadron was at a satellite, Great Sampford, a rough grass field with a small collection of wooden huts. 'There was nothing great about Great Sampford,' noted Goodson. 'We were dumped off in front of the barracks reserved for officers and the van immediately headed back for the civilization of the main base at Debden. We couldn't blame it.'

The place seemed rather deserted. Eventually they found Don Gentile, one of the 133 pilots, who confessed that he was all alone there.

'Where are the others?' Goodson asked.

'Don't you know? None of them came back.'

Gentile explained. The squadron had only just moved to Great Sampford. Earlier that day, 26 September, they had been escorting B-17s but had been bounced by German fighters on the way back when they were already short of fuel. Pilot Officer Roy Beaty had managed to reach England and had crash-landed in a small field, but all the other eleven had either been shot down or had landed in France and been taken prisoner. It had been a shattering day. 'I guess you can take any room,' Gentile told them. 'They're all empty.'

Goodson chose a room with Ray Fuchs. The kit of two of the pilots killed earlier was still there. Opening a locker, Goodson saw a bunch of well-thumbed letters, and the beginning of a reply on a new sheet of paper. 'Dear Mum—'

'I feel like an intruder,' muttered Fuchs.

It was perhaps not surprising that morale in 133 Squadron had gone dramatically downhill. The loss of so many pilots in September, the sudden influx of new pilots and the depressing facilities at Debden combined to create a bad atmosphere. 'There was no *esprit de corps*,' noted Goodson. 'There was no enthusiasm or spirit and without these no fighter squadron could survive.'

It was at this point, as the Eagle squadrons were switching over to become the US 4th Fighter Group, that Red McColpin, the old CO, was posted home and Don Blakeslee took over. Like Goodson, he had been reluctant to join the Eagle squadrons in the first place and had only done so to avoid being made an instructor and to keep combat flying. 'He was a great believer in the RAF tradition of hard drinking and high living,' observed Goodson, 'and never permitted either of them to interfere with constant readiness to fly, and fly well, at any time.' This was certainly the case on his first full day on the job: a long night in the bar with the drinks on him, followed by an early start the following morning at 6 a.m.

He then informed the squadron that all sixteen of them would take off together. On a small grass airfield like Great Sampford, this was a crazy idea. Goodson had occasionally seen a section of four fighters scrambled at the same time and only twice had seen sixteen, but those times had been at much bigger sector stations. Blakeslee, though, was quite nonchalant about this dramatic squadron take-off. 'We'll form up this way on the east perimeter,' he told them casually. 'When I give the signal, the squadron will take off in formation.' There was an audible intake of breath, cut short by Blakeslee saying, 'Move!'

It was barely daylight when they began taxiing into position. Goodson was at the back and as they began thundering across the grass he was having to throttle back to keep formation when at the same time he needed all the power and speed possible to get airborne. When he saw the fence and trees looming, he pushed the throttle open and managed to get clear with only inches to spare, then had to swerve to avoid the trees.

'Tighten it up,' he heard Blakeslee call through his headset. 'Let's show these bastards.'

They now hurtled over Debden at 500 feet in perfect formation, watched by the other two squadrons and most of those on the base. It was a dramatic sight: sixteen Spitfires and sixteen Merlin engines appearing to rise out of the ground and sweep over them. Goodson, though, was sweating and straining, as he knew every pilot in the squadron was sweating and straining, desperately trying to keep as close as possible without colliding with the next plane. They were even tighter on the return sweep and as they landed back down again Goodson realized what that madcap exercise had been all about. 'There was excitement, enthusiasm, boasting, and pride,' he wrote. 'That evening Blakeslee wasn't the only 133 pilot with the belligerent swagger as we arrived in the officers' mess at Debden.'

When Rommel reported to Hitler at the very end of September he told the Führer that the Panzerarmee's supply situation was still extremely critical, and urged him to use all available cargo space, both air and shipping, to get supplies urgently across the Mediterranean. Their men, he said, were now opposed by the best elements in the British armed forces. He also had some stinging criticism for his Italian partners. They were, he made clear, only good for defence, while only German troops were capable of attack. He then gave Hitler a list of requirements necessary before he could consider going back on the offensive: German reinforcements and a senior German staff officer to oversee transport in the entire Mediterranean. The Führer told him pretty much what he wanted to hear: forty of the new Tigers would be sent, as well as assault gun units and improved supplies. None of these had even the remotest chance of being fulfilled in the immediate term. An air of surreal optimism pervaded Hitler's headquarters. Göring, especially, pooh-poohed any talk of the difficulties the Panzerarmee Afrika was now facing. When Rommel told him there were now RAF Hurricanes armed with 40mm cannons knocking out his panzers, the Reichsmarschall ridiculed such a notion. 'Quite impossible,' he told Rommel. 'Nothing but pilot's lies. All the Americans can make are razor blades and refrigerators.'

'I only wish, Herr Reichsmarschall,' Rommel replied, 'that we were issued with similar razor blades.'

Before he left the front, Rommel had thinned out and deepened the line, so that one battalion of 800 men now held about a mile. More and more mines were being planted and wire entanglements put in place, but rations had been cut and more and more men were falling sick, largely because of under-nourishment and the poor quality of food. Not only was any offensive now utterly out of the question, it was hard to imagine how the Panzerarmee could possibly hold out in such a weakened state. And all the time, they were bombed, strafed and harried by the Allied air forces.

Nor was the situation helped by a sudden dramatic change of senior personnel. General Gause soon followed Rommel home, as did General Friedrich von Mellenthin, another of his senior staff officers. Oberst Siegfried Westphal, his operations officer, was also sick, while Fritz Bayerlein, who had taken over as Chief of Staff, was given leave at the end of September. There was a new man in charge of the Afrikakorps – Generalleutnant Wilhelm Ritter von Thoma – after General von Vaerst had been relieved, and, of course, a new temporary commander of the Panzerarmee in General Georg Stumme while Rommel was away. Stumme, however, had previously been relieved of his corps command on the Eastern Front under a cloud and had even been court-martialled, convicted and given five years' fortress detention. Göring had recommended clemency, to which Hitler agreed; he had been sent to Afrika to prove himself. None of this augured well at all, and although Stumme threw himself into the task with great alacrity, he had no control at all over those precious supplies.

The problems of shipping capacity were only worsening for the Axis, as Rommel had been well aware. Large stocks were mounting at Italian ports, but with neither the big shipyards nor the means of producing ever more merchant vessels, they were dependent on a rapidly depleting number, while those ships still afloat were getting smaller and smaller. This in turn meant loading and unloading took longer and was less efficient.

This was why the Italian sailor Walter Mazzacuto, now serving on the frigate *Calliope*, was escorting small merchantmen like the 300-ton *Creta*. On 7 October, *Creta* was sailing from Tobruk to Benghazi and *Calliope* was to provide protection while carrying out an extensive anti-submarine sweep at the same time; it was British submarines, more than aircraft or surface vessels, that were sinking most Axis freighters. At around 8.30 p.m., their sonar picked up what appeared to be two submarines off the coast near Derna. Immediately, *Calliope* began a hunt, but after two hours' searching they had still found nothing. Then an alarm was given as planes had been spotted and at 10.45 p.m. the aircraft even dropped flares. *Creta* was now under threat from below the waves and from the sky above and *Calliope*, despite her guns and torpedoes, was badly outnumbered.

Dawn arrived – they had survived the night. On they went, hugging the coast, but then at about 7 a.m. Mazzacuto and his comrades heard a huge explosion. Looking out across the sea, he saw that *Creta* had been hit and was broken in two. The bows sank almost immediately, but the stern remained, dead in the water, for a further painful thirty minutes. Hurriedly, *Calliope* began collecting the crew, who were mostly Greek, and fortunately all but one survived.

But another ship had gone to the bottom. Feldmarschall Kesselring was aware that a resurgent Malta was the base from which most of the British submarines and torpedo bombers were operating and so, making the most of the lull in Egypt, decided to launch a renewed aerial assault on the island. There would be no invasion, but he hoped he could reduce Malta's ability to function as an offensive base once more. By the second week of October, he had amassed some 700 Axis aircraft on Sicily, including the battle-hardened and experienced II. Fliegerkorps.

The attack was launched on 11 October and, although Kesselring kept going for two weeks, the most intense effort lasted just three days. '82 IN FOUR DAYS – Malta's Answer to Luftwaffe's New Bid,' boasted the *Times of Malta* on 15 October. The daily newspaper had kept going through the darkest days of the siege so perhaps was entitled to a bit of gloating. Two days earlier, the thousandth Axis aircraft since the start of the war had been lost over the island, shot down by Canadian ace George 'Screwball' Beurling, a pilot almost as prodigiously talented as Jochen Marseille had been. That small island, which had endured so much at the hands of the Luftwaffe in particular, had certainly exacted a heavy price for its suffering. By the time Kesselring called off the assault, some 350 planes had been destroyed – that is, half his attacking force – and by then it was too late: the British had attacked at Alamein and nine ships, amounting to 41,409 tons of supplies, almost half what had been dispatched, had been sunk. The mighty Luftwaffe seemed all but broken.

On Saturday morning, 17 October, Major-General Mark Clark walked into Norfolk House in London, Allied Force's Headquarters, and was immediately met by Brigadier-General Al Gruenther, Eisenhower's new Deputy Chief of Staff under Major-General Walter Bedell Smith; both had arrived in mid-September.

'I've got a message for you,' Gruenther told him. 'It's red hot.'

He handed it to Clark. It was a cable from Marshall addressed to Ike and he had just begun to read it when the red telephone on his desk rang. This was the direct scrambled line to Eisenhower.

'Come up,' he said. 'Come right away,' then hung up without waiting for an answer.

Clark already had an idea of what Eisenhower wanted to discuss. The cable from Marshall was, for the most part, the text of a message from the American diplomat Robert D. Murphy, then in Algiers. Murphy had long-established relations with the French, having served in Paris before the war and in the American Embassy in Vichy. Recalled to Washington by Roosevelt, he had then been sent to Algiers in December 1940, officially as Consul General, but in reality as Roosevelt's personal intelligence agent. And he had done well, having formed strong relationships with a number of Vichy French political and military leaders and even negotiated an aid pact. This had enabled him to continue to foster good relations and brought him access to some of the key players, not least Amiral François Darlan, the Governor of Vichy North Africa, and Général Henri Giraud.

In September, Murphy had gone to Washington to confer with the President and had then visited Eisenhower and Clark in London to give them a thorough briefing on the size, state and political temperature of the French forces there, as well as the mood of the civilian population. The main aim of TORCH was to get Allied troops into Tunisia and help drive all Axis forces from North Africa. The landings in Vichy French territory were supposed to be a stepping-stone only, and neither Britain nor the United States wanted to fight their former friend and ally. Murphy reckoned stiffest resistance was likely in French Morocco and, although there were plenty in Algiers who would support the Allies, his best guess was that the landings would be met with resistance in some areas and swift submission in others.

The scale of the proposed landings was, however, exactly what Murphy's co-conspirators in Algiers had been hoping for, and he had then briefed Eisenhower and Clark on his dealings with Général Henri Giraud, who in August had sent word that the Allies could count on French Army support so long as there were landings in Metropolitan France as well. Giraud had been a far more senior general than de Gaulle back in 1940 and, although taken prisoner, had dramatically escaped.

On his return to Vichy, however, he had sworn loyalty to Pétain. Unlike de Gaulle, who was seen as divisive and lacking any influence within Vichy, it was crucial, Murphy told them, that they won over the Vichy French *in situ*; de Gaulle, he argued, would only throw a spanner in the works. At any rate, what was clear was that, while there was a chink of light that could be potentially exploited, it was a very thin political tightrope they needed to cross.

Those talks had been on 16 September. A month later, the message from Murphy was suggesting that if a senior US military figure were to go clandestinely to Algeria to discuss Allied intentions with Général Charles Mast, the Vichy commander in Algiers and close to Giraud, it would demonstrate serious intent. This person could then also brief these French friends about activities that might help the landings, such as silencing coastal guns, seizing radio stations and providing signals to the approaching armada. There was more, however. The Vichy Government had learned from both Japanese and German sources that the USA was planning operations at Dakar and Casablanca. Vichy was convinced that Axis aggression in North Africa was imminent. Murphy also warned that German spies were flooding into North Africa. Meanwhile, Amiral Darlan had expressed willingness to co-operate and bring with him the French Fleet, but only on the condition that he be made C-in-C of French Armed Forces in North Africa and that the USA assured him of economic aid on a large scale. On the other hand, Général Mast still favoured Giraud and was suggesting the Allies pick him up by submarine from southern France. Murphy believed they should encourage Darlan with a view to securing his co-operation with Giraud. 'Mast asserts,' he wrote, 'we can gain entry practically without firing a shot through Giraud's command.'

The risks of such a mission were clearly huge – the entire operation might be compromised. On the other hand, if it gave TORCH a chance of quick success, then it might well be a risk worth taking.

'When do I go?' Clark asked Eisenhower as he entered his office.

'Probably right away,' Ike replied.

He was not wrong. After thrashing out the details and then conferring with Churchill and the British War Cabinet, Clark and his party set off that very night – flying in two B-17s to Gibraltar. From there, they would take passage on a British submarine to Algeria.

They were due to make their rendezvous on Wednesday, 21 October.

*

Meanwhile, over Norway, Operation GROUSE was finally under way. There had been one delay after another due to bad weather or technical glitches, but on 18 October Jens-Anton Poulsson and the three other members of his team were aboard a Halifax four-engine bomber and preparing to parachute on to the glacial Hardangervidda. They had been given new IDs and papers, had bought themselves arctic clothing and equipment, and were carrying newly developed Rebecca-Eureka homing equipment, which they would use to bring in the gliders to the correct location – one that had been pinpointed beforehand by Poulsson.

It was a four-hour flight, but the night was bright and clear. Then they dropped and soon were over the Hardangervidda, a vast wilderness of lakes, rivers and now, in October, snow and ice. It was as barren and forbidding an area as anywhere in all of Europe; only reindeer, a few hardy birds and foxes lived here. Few humans would dare venture here during winter. As they neared the dropping zone, the four men stood and readied themselves. Then, through the bomb bay, canisters of supplies were thrown out, followed by Poulsson and the other three in quick succession. 'I think we were all nervous when we were jumping through the hole in the bottom of the aircraft,' said Poulsson, 'at least I was – but then it was a very happy feeling to see Norway coming up to greet us.'

While Eighth Army was making its final preparations in the desert, the troops earmarked for TORCH were busy training in both Britain and the United States. The Bowles twins, Tom and Henry, were now together in the same 2nd Battalion of the 18th Regimental Combat Team (RCT) of the 1st Infantry Division. Henry had managed to get himself transferred so he could be near his brother. He was now in Battalion HQ company, while Tom remained part of the mortar team in Company G. The 18th RCT was made up with three battalions and was the equivalent of a British brigade; it was also still part of the US 1st Infantry Division, known as 'the Big Red One', after the single large red number one that formed the centre of the divisional crest. The division was due to spearhead the invasion. Also now attached to the division were Bing Evans and the 1st Ranger Battalion.

They were all now up in Scotland practising amphibious assaults and, on 18 October, General Eisenhower headed north on a long train journey to see their progress for himself – and on a night-time exercise. He then watched some more manoeuvres the following morning. All the men looked fit and agile, but he was really worried by the lack of direction and leadership given by the officers, all of whom seemed horribly unsure about what they should be doing. 'It is in this level of command that we have our most glaring weakness,' he reported to General Marshall, 'and it is one that only time and eternal effort can cure.' The trouble was, there simply wasn't much experience above battalion commander either, not in terms of battlefield command at any rate.

Ike returned to London feeling pretty low. He was getting a head cold, perhaps not surprisingly after stomping about in the wet and cold in Scotland, and confessed to his naval aide, Harry Butcher, that he was struggling with a 'state of jitters'. Who could blame him? America was so new to large-scale modern warfare. So much seemed to be at stake. Other armies had hard-won experience to draw upon, but this US Army had grown from almost a standing start and was increasing in size exponentially, yet already so much was being expected. A few months earlier he had felt the bitter pill of disappointment when SLEDGE-HAMMER had been cancelled; now this planned invasion of north-west Africa seemed a truly mammoth undertaking.

There was just so much to think about: grand strategy, tactics, procurement of landing craft and a huge fleet of ships, the allocation of supporting naval forces, the organization of the air forces, provisions, staging areas, adapting from training in the UK and US to North Africa, the composition of each element of each assault force, and the choosing of the right commanders. No one had ever attempted such an operation on this scale before. Another handicap was the lack of information about north-west Africa. A lot of people now involved in the planning had never even heard of Casablanca or Oran. They had no good maps, little intelligence and were planning largely on supposition. What was crystal clear, however, was that the political situation with Vichy North Africa was a highly delicate and complicated one, and he had just sent Major-General Mark Clark into the lion's den. The fate of his friend and trusted colleague – and indeed the fate of the entire operation – was preying on his troubled mind this third week of October.

In Egypt, the air battle had already begun with an intensification of bombing and strafing of enemy landing grounds, lines of communication and positions along the front line. 'If there is anything I have not yet done,' wrote Tommy Elmhirst to his wife on 21 October, 'it is too late now.' Montgomery had also now given his commanders and officers their final briefing.

Both Monty and Mary Coningham were in good spirits that night, however. The two commanders and their principal staffs had taken to having dinner together as a means of forging closer bonds. Elmhirst enjoyed these and had begun introducing topics for discussion as a means of taking everyone's mind off their responsibilities just for a short time. The subject this night was, 'The young married officer is the curse of the services'. The conversation soon evolved into what things were likely to make a successful marriage. 'It was,' jotted Elmhirst, 'the first time any of us had seen Montgomery REALLY unbend and be very human.'

The next day, Monty told his Army that the battle would start the following night, 23 October. He wanted every man to be in no doubt as to exactly what his task was. Throughout the day, up and down the line, briefings were being given about the battle and what each unit's role would be.

Back in London, Churchill was also waiting anxiously for news of when the battle would begin. 'Let me have the word ZIP when you start,' he wrote to Alexander on 20 October. Alexander had skilfully and patiently protected Montgomery from Churchill's impatience and haranguing, but the Prime Minister did not have long to wait now. The battle was about to begin, and then, in two weeks' time, TORCH would be launched too.

This time, the Allies meant to knock the Axis out of North Africa for good.

CHAPTER 31

Lightfoot

THE ALAMEIN LINE was now a mass of wire entanglements and extensive minefields, most of which were of the anti-tank variety. The ground varied over the 40 miles from the coast to the Qattara Depression – stony sand and vetch to the north, and utterly flat to the untrained eye, although there were a number of low ridges that it was sometimes hard to notice until directly on them. Further south, the desert developed into strange lunar valleys with sudden escarpments, over which it was hard for vehicles to cross, but then it levelled out again into a broad gravelly plain.

Montgomery's plan for the battle was to punch two holes through the Axis defences, one in the north and one further to the south, although it was the one in the north that was to be the main breach. This was also the strongest part of the enemy line, but Monty believed that any attack in the south would still have to wheel north at some point and so concluded it would be best to hit the strongest point head-on first along a 10-mile front. This was to be called Operation LIGHTFOOT. It was XXX Corps who were going to make this main hole and their objective was an imaginary line some 3–5 miles beyond the British front line and codenamed 'Oxalic'. The hole would not be 10 solid miles wide, but rather would be through two channels, each of three lanes each just 8 yards wide, which would be cleared by the engineers during the night. Through these impossibly narrow lanes, the weight of British armour – hundreds of tanks, trucks and guns – would travel, then burst out into the wide, open desert beyond the minefields. The tanks would then hold the

EVE OF EL ALAMEIN, 23 OCTOBER 1942

Mediterranean Sea

Trieste →

El Daba

Ghazal

PZ Army HQ

Ras Gibeisa

Sidi Abd el Rahman

El Alamein

El Imayid

El Hamman

90 Light Div

21 Corps and 164 Division

15 PZ

15 PZ and Littorio Groups

164 Div

Trento Div

Littorio Div

Tel el Eisa

9 Aust Div

51 (H) Div

NZ Div

1 SA Div

Miteiriya Ridge

Deir el Abyad

Bologna Div

El Mreir

DAK Corps HQ

Deir el Qattani

21 PZ

Qattara Track

El Mreir

Ramcke Bde

Bab el Qattara

21 PZ and Ariete Groups

21 PZ

Ariete Div

Brescia Div HQ

Ariete

Jebel Kalakh

Pavia Div HQ

Folgore Div

El Taqa Plateau

Naqb Abu Dweis

10 Corps

Qattara Depression

1 Armd Div

Assembly area

X Corps

10 Armd Div

Assembly area

Alam el Halfa

XXX Corps

14 Ind Div

Ruweisat Ridge

Springbok Track

50 Div

Deir el Munassib

February

XIII Corps

44 Div

7 Armd Div

Fighting French

Qaret el Himeimat

KEY

- - - - - inter-corps boundary

0   10 km

0   10 miles

panzers at bay while the enemy infantry was destroyed in a process Monty called 'crumbling'.

At the same time, XIII Corps would break through the line to the south through which 7th Armoured Division would pass, and the Fighting French, as they were now renamed, would attack the Italians at the extreme south. That was the plan, at any rate.

Much depended on Mary Coningham's Desert Air Force and the other air forces now in the Middle East. There were concerns about numbers, as ever; on paper the Axis had 595 fighters to call upon, while the Desert Air Force had 506. The difference – and it was a big one – was that the Allies had plenty of fuel, ammunition and workshops close to the rear, and the Axis did not.

Montgomery was also staking much on his artillery. On the eve of battle, he had 908 field guns compared with the Panzerarmee's 200. The opening bombardment by the British gunners was to signal the start of the battle. For twenty minutes they were to concentrate on counter-battery fire; that is, they would try to destroy the enemy gun batteries, most of which they knew about thanks to extensive aerial photography by the RAF. They would then provide a creeping barrage, lobbing shells over the advancing infantry and moving their range forward at a rate of 100 yards every three minutes. The differences between the start of this battle and those of the Western Front in the last war were negligible.

On the other hand, innovative tactics were not Monty's game. Rather, he was offering firm leadership, fire-power and careful handling of his largely conscript Army. There would be three phases: the 'break-in' – the initial moves; the 'dogfight' – that is, the crumbling process; and then the 'break-out', by the armour when the battle would be wrapped up. He warned of bitter fighting and suggested it would last around a week. There was no doubt that the Panzerarmee was weakened, but the line was a naturally strong defensive position, there were millions of mines, and the German troops, especially, were highly disciplined and unlikely to throw in the towel at the first sign of trouble.

German and Italian units were rather mixed up. Infantry were dug in but the Afrikakorps was split. Part of 15. Panzer and the 164th Light were in the north along with the Italian Trento Motorized Division and the Littorio, one of just three armoured divisions in the entire Italian Army. A long, narrow minefield then extended roughly east–west for around

10 miles, separating the two halves of the line. To the south of this were 21. Panzer; the Ariete, another of the three Italian armoured divisions; and the Folgore, one of two Italian airborne divisions.

Tenente Giuseppe Santaniello and the gunners of the Trento Division were roughly in line with the Miteiriya Ridge in the northern half of the line. For weeks he had been living in his fox-hole, occasionally firing the guns but mostly watching, waiting and trying to preserve ammunition. Over the past week, enemy air activity had increased, which suggested something was up, but even so, the start of the battle, when it came, was a shock.

Santaniello had been in his dugout looking up at the most beautiful moon when suddenly, at 10 p.m., the entire horizon burst into flame. 'An infinite number of flashing tongues of light,' he wrote, 'intersecting one another and spreading in an immense semi-circle which stretched as far as I could see. Then a whistling, whispering inferno exploded on top of us.'

The ground was trembling under the continued pounding. Santaniello felt as though his guts were being crushed. His comrade, Petolicchio, was grimacing next to him, shaking quite uncontrollably and jabbering at the same time, congratulating himself on reinforcing their dugout that very morning. Santaniello crouched, thinking of the ordeal that lay ahead, then realized that he too was shaking and that his mouth was full of saliva. 'As hard as I tried,' he noted, 'I couldn't get a grip on myself.'

On the other side of the line, Albert Martin saw the barrage open like sheet lightning before thunder, the flash coming before the sudden eruption of noise. He had never heard anything like it. The 2nd Rifle Brigade were now in 1st Armoured Division as part of X Corps, the recently created *corps de chasse* of Montgomery's plans, and he had spent the day feeling nervy and edgy, smoking incessantly. Now the battle had started and the shock waves of those guns pulsed through the ground. Also watching was Ted Hardy, with the 6th Australian Division to the north. He had spent every night of the previous week creeping forward and clearing mines. Now, though, he was watching from a shallow sand hill as shells poured on to the enemy positions. 'I felt a bit sorry for them,' he admitted.

As the gunners' loading rhythm changed, so the sky became a kaleidoscope of flickering colour. Among those now manning the 900 guns was Jean-Mathieu Boris, who had been ill and in hospital, then convalescing, and had only just joined his comrades near Himeimat at the southern end of the line at 9 p.m. Forty minutes later, he had watched hundreds of aircraft attacking the enemy positions and at 10 p.m. he was beside one of the 25-pounders in the French sector as they fired one shell after another over to the Italian lines.

One of those on the receiving end of the French shells was Caporale Luigi Marchese. As soon as it began, he decided to move into one of the better-protected dugouts and had just reached it when a stream of shells rained down on to their position and several hit the dugout. The canvas covering the hole was struck by a hail of shrapnel, stones and grit, transforming it into a colander, but at least he was uninjured. 'Now there was nothing to do but wait,' he wrote, 'because outside the inferno raged on.'

From his caravan at Air HQ, Tommy Elmhirst started writing to his wife. 'The battle started five minutes ago,' he scribbled, 'and even here, up wind, there is no mistaking the thunder of the guns.' The air battle had been going well apart from problems caused by bad weather on the 21st. On the 22nd, Allied fighters had cruised back and forth over the Luftwaffe airfields at El Daba, challenging the 109s to come up and fight. The tactic worked: German fighter pilots were scrambled to take on the intruders. Billy Drake had been leading his own squadron as well as Dale Deniston and the Americans of 66th Fighter Squadron over El Daba when they spotted four 109s below them. Diving down, they hit all four, Drake claiming one of them. 'I think we have definitely set Rommel back,' Elmhirst had written. 'His Air Force was hardly seen in the air today.'

Fifteen minutes after the guns began firing, they stopped as suddenly as they had begun and, in Cairo, Alexander signalled the Prime Minister: 'ZIP 2200 hours local time today.' For five minutes, the gunners re-set their guns, then opened up the creeping barrage, and so the infantry began advancing. From where he stood, in the brief silence Jean-Mathieu Boris could faintly hear the bagpipes of the 51st Highland Division to the north.

The opening night of battle at Alamein was marked by both confusion and the mounting sense that not all was going to plan, although that was, perhaps, inevitable with a nighttime assault through very narrow lanes of the desert. When Albert Martin finally set off, the situation seemed to him to be incredibly confused. For all the space of the 40-mile length of the Alamein Line, all the British armour was now trying to channel itself into six narrow passages. The infantry divisions in between and either side could advance freely over the minefields, but not so the tanks, gun tractors and carriers, who were desperately squeezing themselves into a passage narrower than a tennis court. White tape marked the way, while posts had been thrust into the ground and on them were empty petrol cans, each holding an oil lamp with a moon, star or sun cut out of the metal, depending on the track. Amid the noise and mayhem, Martin couldn't help wondering who had prepared all these cans and how they had miraculously appeared there.

The trouble was, very quickly neither Martin, nor anyone for that matter, could see the lanterns or anything very much, as the air swiftly thickened with smoke and fine, cloying dust. The sand was becoming crushed into powder and clouds of it were swirling into the air, clogging eyes and throats and hindering visibility. The fog of war had descended. Tanks and vehicles began bumping into one another and the enemy's guns, albeit limited in number, had opened up too. As in the First World War, the opening barrage appeared to have had only limited effect.

Not that Tenente Giuseppe Santaniello would have agreed. He was among those trying to fire back, but all around him now were apocalyptic scenes as shells continued to explode and the casualties mounted. Dust and smoke filled the air, mixing with the bitter stench of burned explosive. A sinister light glowed over the battlefield and through it bursts of fire could be seen. 'The layer on the third gun didn't want any help,' recorded Santaniello, 'and despite his back being laid open to the lungs and his legs mangled, he got down from his seat himself.' Santaniello tried to shout orders but he could hardly hear himself speak. When his men did yell back their confirmation, their voices 'seemed to come from beyond the grave.'

Opposite Santaniello, a few miles to the west and also covered in dust, were the men of the Sherwood Rangers, now mostly equipped with the new American Shermans, although Major Stanley Christopherson and his men in A Squadron, spearheading the Rangers' attack, were in the lighter, faster and less well-armed and protected Crusaders. Christopherson had already had to send one of the Crusaders leading them back with a water leak and they had been halted before they'd even reached the start line. Christopherson ordered his men to refuel their tanks and, while they waited, to get a cup of coffee made from water in tins above the engine. 'When the engine runs for any length,' he explained, 'the water invariably gets heated up.'

They eventually got going again, but it wasn't until 4 a.m. that they finally reached the first enemy minefield, passing through the New Zealand Division's sector of the corridor. Halfway through, as they passed by the northern end of the long, narrow Miteiriya Ridge, they were stopped again. Jumping down from his tank, Christopherson walked up to the front of their column, which had halted by a hastily set-up control post. There he learned they could move no further for the moment because the lane head still hadn't been properly cleared after all. Up ahead, he could see the muzzle flashes of enemy guns and tracer reaching out across the desert.

They'd been there a short time when a message came through from division to push on regardless. With mounting apprehension, Christopherson ordered his squadron on, following behind the Crusaders and expecting to hit a mine at any moment. To his enormous relief, they were all still in one piece when a sapper informed them they had made it through. Anti-tank and machine-gun fire soon started pouring towards them. They had no choice but to keep going, however, because a dangerous bottleneck was forming behind them at the mouth of the route through the minefields. Turning southwards, they had gone about 200 yards when they ran straight into German anti-tank positions, some as close as 50 yards. Mayhem ensued. Armour-piercing shells screamed across the gap and, in moments, five of Christopherson's Crusaders had been knocked out and were burning brightly in the last darkness of the night.

'EDWARD,' radioed Christopherson's friend Sam Garrett in the leading tank, using what he thought was the right codename, 'I have been hit twice. Tank on fire – am evacuating.' Before Christopherson could reply, the CO, Colonel 'Flash' Kellett, radioed, 'Get off the bloody air and your name is KING not EDWARD!' As Garrett's crew bailed out, they were machine-gunned, but despite being wounded three of them made it to safety.

'It was quite one of the worst moments of my life,' wrote Christopherson. 'I couldn't go forward, but all the heavy tanks were behind me so I couldn't go back on account of them and the minefield . . . We just had

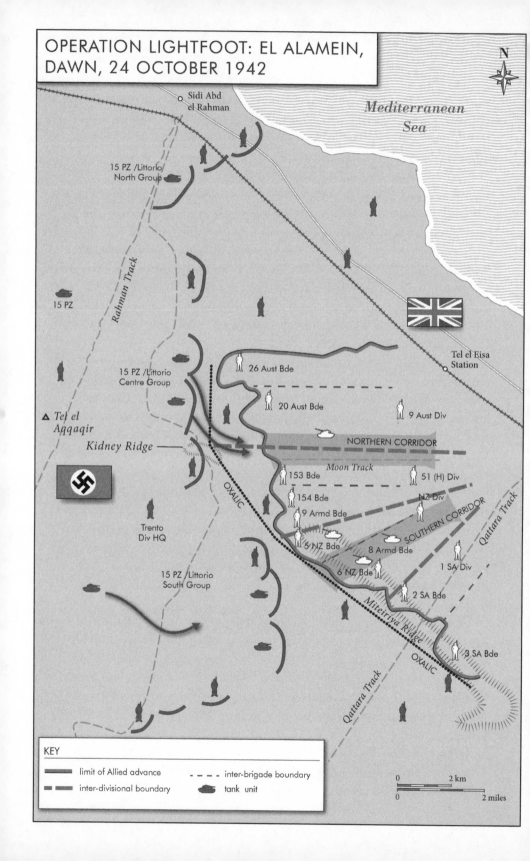

OPERATION LIGHTFOOT: EL ALAMEIN, DAWN, 24 OCTOBER 1942

N

Sidi Abd
el Rahman

*Mediterranean
Sea*

15 PZ /Littorio
North Group

15 PZ

Rahman Track

15 PZ /Littorio
Centre Group

Tel el Eisa
Station

△ *Tel el
Aqqaqir*

26 Aust Bde

20 Aust Bde

9 Aust Div

Kidney Ridge

NORTHERN CORRIDOR

OXALIC

Moon Track

153 Bde

51 (H) Div

154 Bde

NZ Div

Trento
Div HQ

9 Armd Bde

SOUTHERN CORRIDOR

Qattara Track

5 NZ Bde

8 Armd Bde

15 PZ /Littorio
South Group

6 NZ Bde

1 SA Div

2 SA Bde

Miteiriya Ridge

OXALIC

3 SA Bde

Qattara Track

KEY

― limit of Allied advance

- - - inter-brigade boundary

▬ ▬ inter-divisional boundary

🛆 tank unit

0   2 km

0   2 miles

to sit there.' They were, however, now firing back and two enemy panzers were soon burning.

As dawn crept over the battlefield, so the enemy fire increased. Amongst the Italian gunners was Giuseppe Santaniello, who could see British tanks advancing towards their position. His battery opened fire and then they saw German tanks moving up to support them. This was 15. Panzerdivision launching its counter-attack. A number of the men started cheering, '*Viva il Re!*' and '*Viva il Duce!*' 'The battle is filled with the noise of tracks on the move, of machine-guns, of armour-piercing rounds, of 88s,' Santaniello jotted in his diary, 'everything covered in the dust thrown up by the tanks, like the wake of ships in a sea of sand.'

Not far away, four Grants of B Squadron of the Sherwood Rangers were hit and began flaming – or 'brewed up', as the crews termed it – then another four and three more Crusaders. Ahead, German, Italian and British corpses already littered the ground, some dark with blood and thick with flies.

From the Italian lines, Giuseppe Santaniello could no longer really tell who was who, but every time a tank went up in flames, his men cheered. 'For them,' he jotted in his diary, 'everything that burns is British.' Then one tank that had been hit continued to roll forward before finally coming to a halt in a sea of fire. Santaniello could see one of the men trying to get out, but the flames were too much. 'Soon all that remains,' he wrote, 'is a blackened mass which bubbles and burns.'

Later, he saw some of the Italian infantry begin to get up and start falling back – their flanks were now open, they explained. Then one of the battery commanders asked to withdraw, explaining that his guns were low on ammunition. His commander told him to stay put. Fall back, he told him, and he would personally see he was shot in front of his men.

Meanwhile, the remains of the Sherwood Rangers' A and B Squadrons held firm as the rest of the column withdrew through the minefield gaps. Now that it was daylight, however, further gaps in the enemy's minefields were apparent, so on the orders of Colonel Kellett, Christopherson was at last able to bring the rest of the regiment back over the Miteiriya Ridge without any further losses. It had been a difficult night.

'A tense day here awaiting developments,' wrote Tommy Elmhirst at Desert Air Force HQ. 'Good and indifferent news coming in but the Army have not achieved the hundred per cent success they planned.' The infantry had managed to get within 1,000–2,000 yards of the Oxalic objective, but progress had not been so good in the narrow channels of X Corps. The experience of the Sherwood Rangers had been repeated at the mouths of both corridors and, because of the delays, there had not been enough time to get sufficient armour clear by dawn.

A lull developed. Scraps of news reached Albert Martin and the other riflemen still in the thick of the minefield. They were used to beetling about in their wagons, spotting the enemy, engaging, then moving on again, but here they were rather pinned down. 'We were surrounded by all the trappings of a major battle,' he noted, 'it had all the tension, stuff was exploding onto our patch, casualties were occurring, but there was no target for us to have a go at.' He and his mates couldn't understand why there had been no counter-attack.

Despite some elaborate deception plans that Montgomery had put in place – including a magician using smokescreens, amplified sound and fireworks – the Axis command had not been fooled. Panzerarmee intelligence officers had also managed to get fairly accurate appreciations of British dispositions and had guessed that the October full moon would be a likely time to attack. With this in mind, it was bizarre that the Panzerarmee should have so many senior officers away at once; with a handful off sick, was it really necessary for others to be given rare periods of leave at the same moment? As it happened, there was plenty of confusion amongst the Axis forces that morning, but not because of any magic shows further up the coast.

General Stumme, Rommel's stand-in, had left Panzerarmee HQ that morning to have a look at the front line and the level of enemy minefield penetration in the Australian sector. He was just getting out of his car when he was fired upon. Panicking, his driver sped away with the General still clinging to the side of the car. Stumme then suffered a massive heart attack, fell off the car and died, although his body wasn't found until the following day.

General Ritter von Thoma, the commander of the Akrikakorps, took over, but for a while the Panzerarmee had been rudderless. He quickly gripped the situation but, as a panzer man, was all too aware of the shortage of fuel, too much of which was still at Benghazi. A tanker was due to dock in Tobruk on 26 October, but if that failed to materialize, then the situation would once again be desperate. With this in mind, von Thoma decided it was pointless wasting fuel on a counter-attack when they could stay put on their containing line and blast any oncoming attack from fixed positions.

Meanwhile, Montgomery was trying to piece together what information he could. In the far south, the French assault by the Foreign Legion had failed, and the 7th Armoured Division had been unable to breech the minefields but had done enough to keep 21. Panzer and the Ariete Divisions pinned down. By the evening, however, he had learned that infantry casualties were quite high and that the armour was bogged down. He now issued new orders. The Aussies were to carry out a crumbling operation that night to exploit their pretty impressive gains; the New Zealanders were to push south from the Miteiriya Ridge; and X Corps were to renew efforts to clear the corridors and burst into the open desert beyond. In the south, 7th Armoured was also to make another attempt to break through.

The Australians couldn't believe they had to attack again. It meant another long night for Ted Hardy, who would have to creep forward and help clear mines. It was tricky and dangerous enough in the comparative calm of a lull, but under fire and with flares crackling overhead, and with tracer arcing and shells exploding, it was no fun at all. The 51st Highlanders were also pushing forward, trying to open a gap for 1st Armoured Division, and once more playing their pipes. Albert Martin watched them, the eerie sound of the pipes cutting across the sound of battle as the men disappeared like spectres into the smoke and dust.

The Sherwood Rangers, meanwhile, were also on the move once more, having fended off a localized counter-attack by German panzers late in the afternoon. That evening, Stanley Christopherson was just climbing back into his tank when a shell burst overhead. The blast hit his head, closing his eye, giving him a nosebleed and concussion and a few splinter wounds. Really, it was a lucky escape, but he was sufficiently injured to need attention. After being patched up he was taken back to Alexandria.

Later, the Sherwood Rangers formed up again but soon got stuck, nose to tail, unable to move. At this point, they were attacked by Stukas and much of the B Echelon, the 'soft-skins' with their ammunition and fuel, was hit. Twenty lorries were blazing. It was one of the Luftwaffe's few successes and caused pandemonium. Meanwhile, the sappers were finding the minefields denser and deeper than they had thought. It was another disappointing night.

At 3.30 a.m. on 25 October, crisis talks were taking place at the Army Commander's headquarters, as it was clear X Corps were starting to baulk at the lack of progress and rising casualties. Montgomery stuck to his guns, however: they had to press on, whatever the casualties. Nor were XIII Corps doing much better in the south. Only the Australians, it seemed, were making much progress, so at General Freyberg's suggestion, Monty decided to switch tack and reinforce the Aussies with armour and motorized artillery. It was a good move: that night, they surged forward, sweeping through the Axis positions, then holding and consolidating a key feature near the coast called Point 29.

While the battle was raging in the desert, Major-General Mark Clark had been making his clandestine trip to Algiers. For three days, General Eisenhower, still in London, had heard nothing and had been worried sick, but then, at around midnight on Saturday, 24 October, he finally got word that his friend had made it safely back to Gibraltar. The following afternoon, the man himself was walking through the door of Eisenhower's rented cottage on the edge of London and, all things considered, looking well.

Sitting down, Clark then told his tale. They had met the British submarine HMS *Seraph* and had reached their rendezvous point off the coast of Algiers without a glitch, but had then waited thirty-six hours, watching through a periscope for a white-light signal from a secret house on the shore. As stipulated by Général Mast, his party had included four other staff officers with specific expertise in planning, supply and civil affairs and had included Clark's right-hand man and Head of Plans, Brigadier-General Lyman Lemnitzer.

At long last, the signal came and Clark, his team and three British Commandos set off to the beach in folbots – collapsible canvas canoes.

Général Mast and several of his staff officers were there waiting for them, as was Bob Murphy. Clark opened the discussion by telling Mast that they had to trust one another and that it was essential they were frank and honest. Clark admitted he then lied like hell – he made no mention, for example, of any dates; as far as Mast was concerned, TORCH was still some way off and remained hypothetical only. Mast gave him exact details about the location of troops and batteries along the coast. The problems, Mast suggested, would come from the French Navy; he did not trust Darlan and advised the Allies against dealing with him. Clark, however, made it clear that Giraud could never be overall Allied commander, but he did suggest he could be Governor of French North Africa and that Mast could be Deputy Chief of Staff of the Allied Expeditionary Force. Mast seemed happy with these proposals and also accepted British involvement.

Clark and his party had landed at 10 p.m. and were still talking well into the following morning, at which point Clark excused himself for a pee. As he did so, word arrived that the police had become suspicious after local Arabs had reported footprints on the beach and were on their way to the house. The Americans and the three Commandos were hurriedly bundled into the cellar, Clark clutching his carbine, and soon after the police arrived. While the owner of the house was assuring them nothing was wrong, one of the Commandos was seized with a coughing fit. Clark then offered him his chewing gum, taking it from his own mouth and handing it over to the slightly perplexed Commando, who began chewing nervously; it seemed to do the trick. 'Have you another piece?' the man asked soon after.

'Why?' whispered Clark.

'Because this one has no flavour.'

Fortunately, the police went away again without checking the cellar. It was clearly time to go, but as they hurried down to the shore they realized quite a swell had developed. Clark stripped off and sat on his clothes in his folbot, but they were all flung into the sea and so headed back to the shore again. Completely naked but for his cap, Clark persuaded the owner of the house to let him back in and to give him some clothes. They all then hid in nearby woods until the swell calmed down. They were nearly spotted by some locals, but managed to get into their folbots and head back out to the submarine, which had now manoeuvred just half a mile from shore. Once safely aboard, they made it back to Gibraltar without mishap.

Mast, Clark believed, had committed himself so far that there was now no chance he could possibly be double-crossing the Allies, so Eisenhower agreed that on 4 November he should be told the landings would take place four days later. A question mark still remained over Darlan, but it looked as though this extraordinary high-stakes mission had paid off. They would know soon enough.

CHAPTER 32

Supercharge

MONDAY, 26 OCTOBER 1942. At his caravan at his Burg el Arab head quarters, General Montgomery had much to think about. About 300 of his 1,200 tanks had been knocked out, although most of these were recoverable, and he still had 900 left. This meant he could use them to win by sheer force of numbers. This was why he had insisted resolve was needed. They could bludgeon their way through. It was not pretty and there would be casualties, but battles were not for the faint-hearted. There was no other way.

Or was there? General Francis Tuker, for one, thought Montgomery's battle plan had been poor. The enemy's greatest strength had always been in the north, along the main supply routes, which suggested this was the area they were most concerned about. With this in mind, Tuker thought it made sense to strike a heavy blow with artillery in support on a narrow front in the north, around a feature or ridge that the Panzerarmee simply had to counter-attack. Whether the minefields were breached or not was irrelevant. The key was to draw in the bulk of the Axis armour in the north.

While most of the Panzerarmee's armour and artillery was caught up with this attack in the north, Tuker would have liked to have made a second thrust simultaneously in the centre of the line, along the Ruweisat Ridge. Once the British were through, the enemy would be split in two. With most of the enemy forces distracted in the north, British armour could deal with the Panzerarmee's forces in the south before turning into the enemy's flanks to the north. Tuker believed that, regardless of the levels of training, once free of the minefields the sheer weight of numbers of the British armour, combined with motorized infantry, would ensure a speedy and decisive victory.

The ground around the Ruweisat Ridge was certainly better than it was in the north – it was stony, not sandy, and while there would have been dust, it would not have been as bad. Furthermore, that finger of a minefield extending west would have helped protect the British armour as it broke into the enemy positions and dealt with the southern half.

Tuker's biggest beef with Monty's ideas, however, was over his fire plan for LIGHTFOOT. Of the 900 field guns available, only 400 were used in support of the main thrust in the north – that is, less than 50 per cent. That meant over 500 guns were not being used in the main thrust, while more than 300 were available to support the feint thrust of XIII Corps to the south. Giuseppe Santaniello and his fellows had had a bad time of it, but he was still alive, his guns were still firing and the damage caused by those 400 guns in the north had been limited. Certainly, 750 guns, for example, would have been more effective.

Perhaps more inexplicable, though, was the way in which they were used. A central tenet of war is the concentration of force. One of the failings of the Gazala battle had been the dispersal of Eighth Army, but for all his new stamp and fighting talk, Montgomery had dispersed his firepower not only in terms of its spread along the length of their line, but also in the way the guns were fired. Those 400 in the north were spread over 10 miles, with just 100 guns supporting each of the four attacking divisions. That meant one gun every 45 yards and, unfortunately, they were mostly firing straight ahead. A far better plan would have been to have attacked over, say, 5 miles, with 750 guns firing in concentrations and systematically sweeping the length of the proposed breech.

At Alam Halfa, Montgomery had rightly acknowledged the devastating power of artillery and air forces working in tandem. By October, however, he appeared to have forgotten some of these basic principles of concentration of fire. The overall standard of British artillery was high – they were very well trained and their skill was second to none, just as it had been by the end of the last war, but their potential had not been properly harnessed.

Nor was there any sign of a 3.7-inch gun anywhere near the battlefront, despite Oliver Lyttelton's comments just a few months earlier. Axis bombers had not seriously threatened airfields or installations in the

Delta for months and so these considerable numbers of guns were largely standing idle. Even if just half of the 200 guns in the Delta and around Cairo had been brought up to the front, they could have made a huge impact. The Panzerarmee, after all, had just 200 guns in total. Montgomery had brought much to Eighth Army, but certainly not tactical innovation or flair.

On hearing the news that the British offensive had begun, Hitler had telephoned Rommel at his sanatorium in Semmering and asked him whether he was capable of returning to Egypt. Rommel was certainly not well enough, but still checked himself out and flew straight back. He reached the front on the evening of 25 October, and from von Thoma and Bayerlein received a full briefing. All the reserves had been committed, von Thoma told him, and 15. Panzer had been counter-attacking that day. 'They suffered heavy losses,' von Thoma told him, 'under the fearful artillery barrage and systematic bombing by the Royal Air Force. This evening, only thirty-one of their tanks are still operational. Only small supplies of fuel remain available close to the front.'

Despite this bleak report, Rommel was determined to try to push the enemy back and then stabilize the front once more. The north was clearly the focus, so he ordered his remaining armour up from the south. So too did Montgomery, who after his period of quiet cogitation in his caravan had decided that the crumbling process would continue, that artillery and the air forces would contain any Axis counter-attacks, and that he would then prepare for a new all-out assault. The southern battle was, for the moment, over. Seventh Armoured Division was taken out of the line, as was the entire New Zealand Division and over half of X Corps' armour.

Since the Australians were doing so well in the north, they were ordered to continue their drive. This could leave a bit of a gap, so the 51st Highland Division were moved up to cover the old Australian sector. The South Africans, left out of battle to begin with, were moved into the gap left by the Kiwis and the Scots, while Tuker's 4th Indian, so far with nothing but a holding role, was to continue in that vein but over a long distance of some 15 miles. These moves were to be completed by the morning of 28 October.

In the meantime, 1st Armoured Division had been ordered to keep going through the northern corridor towards the tiny feature known to the Axis as Hill 28, but as Kidney Ridge to the British. And playing a key part in this continued northern drive were the men of the 2nd Rifle Brigade.

Meanwhile, Tenente Giuseppe Santaniello and his men were delighted to hear that Rommel had returned. 'How much faith is there in that man?' he jotted. 'Why? Because we saw him pass through our batteries in his tank, in the midst of the battle. Doesn't that tell our generals anything?'

Yet it was clear the situation was now desperate and, as far as Santaniello was concerned, it was the RAF that was the enemy's greatest weapon. The relentlessness of the air assault was stupefying. The RAF, he thought, appeared to be everywhere. At one point, he had heard the tell-tale whistle of a Messerschmitt only to see a British fighter hurtle over, drop a bomb, then turn and head back west.

The only slight morale-boost was the sight of some Stukas appearing that evening and bombing the enemy positions. Vast amounts of tracer poured up towards them as one bomb after another dropped and exploded. His men were delighted to see them and a number jumped up out of their trenches and, as the Stukas dived, began imitating them with plunging hand movements. As they flew back over, their attack finished, the men counted them – and much to the Italians' jubilation, on this occasion all had survived.

The gunners were in trouble, however, as there was now no infantry at all in front of them – only they and their guns were holding their stretch of the line. Santaniello had been taking his turn to keep watch – it was known that the Australians were now opposite them and might launch an attack at any moment. Then, at around 10 p.m., a message arrived that threw them into a terrible dilemma. British tanks, it seemed, had broken through the line. Panzers were due to counter-attack through their own positions, but it was now being left to the battery commanders to decide whether to stay put or withdraw back into the desert. After the officers were gathered together, they decided to remain where they were. Santaniello headed back to his fox-hole for what he called his 'tragic and oppressive vigil'. 'The RAF,' he noted, 'always wins!'

It was on the afternoon of 26 October that Albert Martin and his mates learned that their role as part of the Minefield Task Force was over and that they were now to take part in a night attack to capture and then consolidate one of two enemy strongpoints near Kidney Ridge. The following morning, two armoured brigades would move up and, using these strongpoints as a firm base, would then blast their way further west and sever the crucial Sidi Abd el Rahman track, which ran down the length of the Alamein Line and was a major supply route for the Axis rear positions. The 2nd Rifle Brigade were to take a feature codenamed Snipe, a mile south-west of Kidney Ridge, while the King's Royal Rifle Corps (KRRC) would take Woodcock, a mile to the north-west.

However simple the plan may have seemed on paper, however, it was clear to Martin and all his fellows that they were very likely going to have one hell of a fight on their hands. And so it proved. They were shelled heavily during the night advance, found themselves in a firefight in which over a hundred enemy sappers caught between the Rifle Brigade and a leaguer of Axis tanks were decimated, but as dawn slowly crept over the battlefield they realized they had pushed really quite a long way into the Axis positions. In fact, they had moved into the heart of the enemy armour's assembly area, which was massing for Rommel's intended counter-attack later that day. Their little depression in the desert was a miserably exposed outpost.

Shelling began early in the morning. The promised British armour soon came forward, but in fifteen minutes seven Shermans had been knocked out and were burning fiercely. Equipped with their 6-pounders, the Riflemen were now completely isolated, nor did they have a proper forward observation officer to direct fire or a medical officer to tend the inevitable casualties. A small party of Carriers was sent to try to find both, but one was hit and the others could make no headway at all, such was the weight of enemy fire.

As the morning wore on, it was clear the Rifle Brigade was now facing a major trial of strength. Shells screamed down on them unceasingly as their own guns answered furiously. Burning hulks of tanks, often with their mangled and charred crew nearby, already littered the ground; black, angry smoke billowed upwards and mixed with the grey fog from the smoke canisters laid by both sides. Small arms chattered while choking dust and the bitter stench of cordite, oily smoke and rubber fouled the air and made breathing difficult. 'From the squaddies' point of view,' said Albert Martin, 'the scene was one of utter confusion and mayhem.' He had very little idea of what was going on, except that it felt as though half the Deutsches Afrikakorps was heading straight for them.

The enemy armour was, in fact, trying to mount its counter-attack and so was moving across their front to engage the British tanks of the 1st Armoured Division. Waking to find the Riflemen set up with their 6-pounder anti-tank guns was therefore a big blow to Axis intentions. Clearly, the panzers needed to deal with this particular thorn and in quick order. German and Italian tanks now started moving directly towards Snipe, but the gunners fired back and soon eight more panzers were hit. The Riflemen were suffering too, however. By mid-morning, only thirteen guns were still in action, while six of their Carriers were also now burning furiously.

A lull followed, but then, around 1 p.m., a number of Italian tanks attacked from the south-west. There, the Riflemen were now very low on ammunition, so only one of the 6-pounders could be brought to bear. Six enemy tanks had been knocked out when Lieutenant Toms made a dash for it in a Jeep, speeding across Snipe to one of the destroyed guns; he collected some more shells, then sped back in time to feed three more rounds to the sergeant manning the gun. One after another, the three remaining Italian tanks were hit.

Later in the afternoon, British armour once more pressed forward and suddenly a number of panzers again moved directly across the front of the northern side of Snipe. Albert Martin, watching this, could scarcely believe their luck. They could hardly miss, and nor did they: nine more panzers were knocked out and, although two further 6-pounders were destroyed, by half-past five the panzers were beginning to withdraw.

The battle at Snipe was not over yet, however, because now a further fifteen panzers attacked from the south-east, towards where Albert Martin was stationed alongside three guns, each with no more than ten rounds. Waiting until the German tanks had ground their way to within 200 yards, the Riflemen then fired. Three panzers were hit and came to a standstill amidst thick smoke and flames. Martin and the other Carrier crewmen fired at the enemy tank men as they bailed out of the burning hulks, then a third tank was struck by a 6-pounder round and began backing away before suddenly erupting into flames. When a further two brewed up, the remaining nine panzers withdrew, pulling back into hull-down positions. From there, they continued pounding the Snipe position, but by now dusk was falling. Soon after, darkness descended once more, and at 10.30 p.m., their ammunition spent and with no sign of the promised relief, the Riflemen pulled back, taking with them the lone 6-pounder still capable of firing.

'Is it possible, I wonder,' noted Martin, 'to put into words the emotions of soldiers who have now reached safety after long hours when death or a crippling wound could happen in a second, any second, during those interminable hours? The usual words of pleasure, relief, happiness, thankfulness, are totally inappropriate. Substitute bewilderment, incomprehension, drained, numbed or disbelief.'

Left behind were the remains of seventy tanks and self-propelled guns. Just seven of these were British. At Snipe itself, the dead were surprisingly few: fourteen and one missing. They lay where they had died, next to the smashed guns and discarded ammunition boxes, the piles of spent shell cases and contorted remains of Bren Carriers. Through the night, Axis troops managed to recover some of their tanks, but by morning thirty-two wrecks remained, of which twenty-two were German panzers. Snipe had proved that experienced and well-trained troops were invaluable. It also proved once again that in the desert war a high-velocity gun was the most important weapon.

Those on the ground also had much for which to thank the Allied Air Forces. As 21. Panzer had been trying to form up for their counter-attack that morning, they had been repeatedly carpet-bombed. 'Our best effort yet,' noted Tommy Elmhirst, 'with our two light bomber wings putting in 200 sorties and hitting enemy panzer divisions while they were trying to concentrate for an attack.' Billy Drake and his 112 Squadron had been in action throughout the day, shooting down an Italian Macchi 202 on one sortie and escorting bombers. Their air superiority was almost total, their attacks relentless, and the effect they were having was devastating and demoralizing, as Giuseppe Santaniello, for one, was all too aware. 'The RAF always wins,' he wrote in his diary for the second day in a row.

By nightfall on the 27th, it was clear Rommel's counter-attack had failed; what's more, he had used up precious fuel in the attempt and lost far too many panzers. There had been some successes, and there would continue to be more: the following day, for example, the entire 4th Royal Sussex Regiment was overrun at Woodcock and 342 taken prisoner. But the Australians were still pressing forward along the coast, the crumbling was continuing and the Panzerarmee was slowly but surely being ground down.

The battle Montgomery had planned had not worked out as he had intended, but the pattern was much as he had expected: cussed, bloody attrition, in which fire-power, both from the artillery and especially the Air Force, slowly but surely ground down the enemy.

On the morning of 29 October, General Alexander and Dick Casey, the Minister of State, visited Montgomery at his Tac HQ at Burg el Arab – prompted by anxious messages from London about rumours of Monty withdrawing troops. Alexander managed to have a quiet *mano-a-mano* talk with his Army commander, who was preparing the next phase of his assault, which he had codenamed SUPERCHARGE and which he hoped would end the battle. The plan was much the same as LIGHTFOOT: a night-time infantry attack supported by a barrage and with the bulk of his armour, now refreshed once more, following behind and then passing on through. This time, however, the punch was only 3 miles wide and there were no longer so many mines to clear. This meant more guns could be brought to bear as well, which was going to please General Tuker.

This tighter, more focused plan, was pretty much the right one, but Alexander was concerned that Monty was intending to send it through the Australians to the very north of the line. Alexander was Ultra-cleared and decrypts had indicated that the German 90th Light Division, having been held in reserve, was arriving in this very same part of the line. Alexander had made a point of not interfering with Montgomery's plans – it was not his role to micro-manage, after all – but did now suggest that his Chief of Staff, Dick McCreery, have a quiet word with Monty's COS, Freddie de Guingand, and gently try to persuade the Army commander to change his mind. The trick to making him do so was to try to make Monty believe the idea had been his all along. It worked. 'I decided,' wrote Montgomery later, 'that I would blow a deep hole in the enemy front just to the north of the original corridor.' Alexander was relieved; it was, he thought, the key decision of the battle. At any rate, he wrote to Churchill the following day, assuring him all was well.

Meanwhile, the three great armadas of Operation TORCH were now at sea. The Bowles twins, as well as Bing Evans, were part of the first wave, making its way from England, while the third was crossing the Atlantic.

Since Major-General Mark Clark's return from Algiers, he had barely stopped as last-minute plans were put in place. He also found he was much in demand to tell the story of his daring mission. On 29 October, he and Eisenhower went to visit King George VI, who wanted to say goodbye before they flew to their new Gibraltar headquarters for the invasion. 'I know all about you,' the King told Clark. 'You're the one who took that fabulous trip. Didn't you, by the way, get stranded on the beach without your pants?'

Clark had also made arrangements to transport Général Giraud from southern France to Africa. He appeared to be co-operating, although insisted an American submarine pick him up. The US Navy did not have one in the Mediterranean, but it was agreed an American naval officer could, for the purpose of the trip, be put in charge of the Royal Navy submarine HMS *Seraph*, whose crew had done so well taking Clark et al. to and from Algiers.

Meanwhile, messages continued to flow from Robert Murphy, still in Algiers. He had not yet spoken with Darlan's agent, but, he reported, Darlan had told Vichy officials that there was little chance North Africa was about to be attacked. That was definitely a good sign.

Perhaps inevitably, there was a glitch. On 1 November, a message arrived from Murphy saying that Giraud, with Mast's backing, was insisting he could not now leave France until 20 November. Murphy was going to suggest to Roosevelt that TORCH be delayed.

This, was, of course, completely out of the question at this late stage and with the armadas already out to sea. Murphy was told that TORCH would go ahead come what may and that the submarine would wait for as long as was needed for Giraud. The next day, 2 November, Clark and Eisenhower lunched with Churchill then boarded a train to Bournemouth. Just as they were leaving, a message arrived with good news. Giraud would board the submarine waiting for him right away; they would meet in Gibraltar as originally planned. 'We set off,' noted Clark, 'in an optimistic mood.'

Back in the Western Desert, on 1 November Operation SUPERCHARGE was pre-empted by another blistering aerial assault by the RAF over Axis positions around Tel el Aqqaqir along the Rahman Track. This was where most of the Axis armour was concentrated. For seven hours they pummelled the enemy. Their efforts produced six massive explosions and a number of fires. They also hit the Afrikakorps Advanced HQ, wrecking their telephone communications system. Oberst Fritz Bayerlein reckoned they were attacked some thirty-four times that afternoon. 'The sky,' he noted, 'was simultaneously filled with hundreds of British fighters, while innumerable fighter-bombers strafed our supply vehicles moving up the coast road.' They reckoned they had just 90 panzers and perhaps 100 Italian tanks left. Eighth Army had over 800.

The opening barrage of SUPERCHARGE began at 1.05 a.m. on Monday, 2 November. Albert Martin and the 2nd Rifle Brigade were once more in the Minefield Task Force, and pretty unhappy about it too; after Snipe, they felt they'd earned some relief from the fighting. They emerged from the chaos, dust and congestion at around 9.30 that Monday morning, the din of battle shrieking overhead and booming in front of them. They then took up position with their Carriers and a new batch of 6-pounders just north of the Tel el Aqqaqir trig point.

Around half an hour later, the Sherwood Rangers and the rest of the 8th Armoured Brigade also rumbled clear of the minefields, although there was so much smoke and dust they struggled to work out where they were. Major Stanley Christopherson, recovered already from his wounds and back leading A Squadron, paused to ask some gunners. They couldn't help, but did offer him 'a most acceptable' mug of tea.

They pushed on forward, past bodies of dead British and Italian soldiers covered in a layer of fine dust, then made contact with the Staffordshire Yeomanry and paused again. Ahead of them, an ambulance beetled about picking up the wounded. Knocked-out tanks belched smoke into the sky. A strange, yellowish fog descended over the battlefield. Enemy tanks cranked into view and the Rangers opened fire, hitting two.

They remained roughly where they were until the afternoon, when they were ordered to turn back to their start line to rearm and refuel. In A Squadron, they all made it, but back at the start found themselves being shelled. Two Crusaders had sprung leaks and two men had also been killed earlier in the day when a shell exploded above their heads. Their tank was all right, but the turret was spattered with blood; someone would have to clean it up before it could be used again. However, there would be no more fighting for them that day. As evening fell, they leaguered for the night.

SUPERCHARGE had done what Montgomery had hoped. Against this renewed assault the Panzerarmee was all but broken. 'The day of death,' jotted Giuseppe Santaniello in his diary. At the village of Sidi Abd el Rahman on the coast, where he had set up his Tactical HQ, Rommel realized the game was now up and that the main British thrust was not in the northernmost part of the line after all. On the morning of the 2nd, he called off his assault by the 90th Light, and in so doing the exhausted Australians, isolated out on a limb, finally found some relief. In an area known as the Saucer, the fighting had been especially bitter; in an old building they called the Blockhouse, both German and Australian medical teams had been working together, treating the wounded from both sides.

The Afrikakorps had been moved south and two counter-attacks attempted, but both failed. A hundred and seventeen German and Italian tanks were knocked out, including seventy of the ninety that had remained the day before, most destroyed by massed formations of Allied bombers. By the time dusk fell, the entire front had taken a big leap forward. The battle was almost over. 'Monty now has Rommel by the pants,' noted General Tuker that evening.

Rommel realized this too and ordered a general disengagement. It was that or face annihilation but, realizing his orders to retreat might be mis-interpreted by the Higher Command, he decided to put his aide-de-camp, Leutnant Berndt, into a plane with instructions to head straight to Hitler's HQ at the Wolf's Lair. 'Explain our situation clearly to the Führer,' Rommel told him, 'and suggest that the African theatre of operation is probably lost to us. Ask for complete freedom of action for the Panzer Army.'

Meanwhile, the retreat had already begun. In the south, the Folgore were moving out of their positions. Luigi Marchese was heading back across the desert when he and his comrades heard loudspeakers urging them to surrender; they ignored them, however, and kept moving, heading towards Jebel Kalakh. Giuseppe Santaniello and his gunners received the retreat order at around 10 p.m. Not only their battery but the entire Trento Division was to pack up and move that night, back in the direction of Fuka. Trucks arrived around 3 a.m. – far later than had been hoped. Santaniello looked back at the patch of desert they had occupied since the start of the battle. 'Your sand,' he mused, 'has known the bitter taste of our sweat, has tested the blood of our best soldier, and witnessed an epic struggle.'

'Dearest Lu,' Rommel wrote to his wife that morning, Tuesday,

3 November. 'The battle is going heavily against us. We're simply being crushed by the enemy weight . . . At night I lie open-eyed, racking my brains for a way out of this plight for my poor troops. We are facing very difficult days, perhaps the most difficult a man can undergo. The dead are lucky, it's all over for them.'

At 9 a.m. he drove east along the coast road to his Tactical HQ. Large numbers of vehicles were jammed along the road. At 10 a.m. he heard from von Thoma and Bayerlein. They had just thirty panzers left and the British were now lying in a semi-circle in front of them around Tel el Aqqaqir. The Afrikakorps, they hoped, would hold the British armour at bay while the Italians made good their escape.

Not far away were the 2nd Rifle Brigade. They had been asked to put in another night-time attack, this time at Tel el Aqqaqir but had been too hastily assembled and so were recalled. They were still hurrying back across the Rahman Track when over twenty Stukas appeared on one of their brief forays. So too did a dozen Hurricane tank-busters, who immediately swooped in to attack. They shot down two, but more importantly hustled the Stukas into jettisoning their bombs – and right over the Axis positions.

By late morning, the entire German front was collapsing fast, but at around midday Rommel received a reply from Hitler. 'In the situation in which you now find yourself,' he signalled, 'there can be no other consideration save that of holding fast, of not retreating one step, of throwing every gun and every man into the battle. Despite his numerical superiority the enemy too will reach the end of his resources. It would not be the first time in history that the stronger will has prevailed against the stronger battalions of the enemy. You can show your troops no other way than that which leads to victory or to death.'

Thus spoke the world's greatest-living military commander. It was madness. 'When we read this order,' wrote Bayerlein, 'we felt as though we were criminals who, though condemned to die, had been granted a reprieve of forty-eight hours.' 'We were completely stunned,' added Rommel. They now made an effort to re-form on a line some miles to the west of the Rahman Track, but there could be no calling back those already heading west. The retreat had begun, regardless of Hitler's order.

The Trento Division, along with the rest of the Italians, were now heading west. Giuseppe Santaniello had been moving all through the night, which had been lit by endless tracer and explosions from Allied air forces. 'All is chaos and confusion,' he scribbled in his diary. 'Nothing is clear. From time to time we stop. Lorry follows lorry in a cloud of thick black dust.' He couldn't imagine the desert had ever seen a more dramatic sight than their column fleeing headlong into the darkness. Where they were going, Santaniello had no idea. He only knew they were escaping the enemy.

That morning, Oberst Fritz Bayerlein met with his chief, General von Thoma. The Deutsches Afrikakorps commander was, for the first time that Bayerlein had ever seen, wearing a proper uniform with all his general's insignia, orders and medals. There was a *Götterdämmerung* atmosphere of impending doom. 'Bayerlein, Hitler's order is a piece of unparalleled madness,' von Thoma told him. 'I can't go along with this any longer.' He now ordered Bayerlein to their command post further back at El Daba. He would remain and command what was left of the Afrikakorps at Tel el Mampsra.

As the endgame of the battle was played out that morning, so General Tuker's Indians finally entered the fray. He had been champing at the bit throughout the battle, but when Montgomery heard the news that the Italians were pulling out from their positions in the south, he had ordered Tuker's 5th Brigade to join the Highlanders and cut a line through the minefields south of Tel el Aqqaqir so that the armour could pour through.

The operation was a complete success. Advancing behind another barrage, they were through the minefield by 7 a.m. For a moment, the desert was quiet but for the crackle of small arms. Then from the British lines came a low rumble that grew louder and louder. Suddenly, British tanks emerged through the dust and, plunging out through the gap, began to wheel north.

At 11 a.m., Bayerlein heard that the Afrikakorps was all but destroyed. Clambering into a small armoured reconnaissance car, he sped off eastwards. Suddenly, armour-piercing shot was whistling about him. In the haze up ahead, he saw a number of British tanks and, jumping out, he ran as fast as he could towards Tel el Mampsra. It looked like a place of death – of burning tanks and smashed flak guns, without a living soul. He lay down and looked around, then saw a man standing ramrod straight about 200 yards away near a burning tank, apparently impervious to the intense fire that still criss-crossed around him. It was General von Thoma. Bayerlein saw Shermans closing in – they were the tanks of the Sherwood Rangers and of 1st Armoured Division. He wondered what he should do. To run clear of this carnage felt like cowardice, yet to scamper through the curtain of fire would be suicide.

Suddenly the firing stopped. Von Thoma still stood there, a canvas bag in his hands. A Bren Carrier was driving straight towards him with two Shermans just behind. The Tommies signalled towards the General and then, like a flood, a mass of armour and vehicles swept across the desert. At this point Bayerlein ran, as fast as his legs would carry him. His car had gone, but he managed to hail another and they sped west. To the south of his command post, he could already see clouds of smoke.

The Battle of El Alamein was over.

CHAPTER 33

Cutting Losses

THE CAREER OF Albert Speer continued on the rise. He might have been thrown in at the deep end after the death of Fritz Todt back in February, but Hitler's favourite young architect certainly appeared to have risen to the challenge. By the autumn, armaments numbers were most definitely on the up: more tanks, more ammunition, more guns, more submarines and more aircraft – only by around 30 per cent on average, but the line on the graph was definitely heading in the right direction.

Speer, however, was not responsible in any way for either U-boat or aircraft production; rather, his remit was for the armaments needs of the army only – that is, around 40 per cent of total armaments production. Furthermore, over and above his Armaments Ministry there remained the Zentrale Planung. He had also benefited from the earlier rationalizations that both Todt and even General Thomas had put in place, and from the fact that Fritz Sauckel, the man in charge of German labour supply, favoured Speer over the Luftwaffe's and Kriegsmarine's requirements.

However, this was frankly neither here nor there, because the perception was that Speer had single-handedly taken the armaments industry by the scruff of the neck and given it a good shake. What's more, unlike his colleagues in the procurement offices of the Kriegsmarine and Luftwaffe, Speer had access to Hitler – which was one of the reasons Sauckel was favouring his ministry over other demands. This meant he could become the public face of the new armaments drive – and take much of the credit – without anyone spoiling the illusion. As the Nazis had proved very cleverly before the war, projecting an impression of military might was very important even if it belied a somewhat different reality. Speer recognized that this still held true.

Promoting this renewed armaments drive was, he understood, an important part of the job. After the setbacks of the previous winter, both the soldiers at the front and the German people as a whole had to believe that this new armaments drive would bring about a change in German fortunes, and so he had moved very quickly to make himself its public face. Unlike Todt, Speer painted no picture of doom and gloom but one of unbridled optimism, even though to do so was simply encouraging the Führer to continue with a war that could no longer realistically be won. Hitler, who always liked being told what he wanted to hear, lapped it up. So did the German people.

Propaganda was key, and in pushing the armaments drive to the forefront he found a willing collaborator in Joseph Goebbels, whom he knew well from his time in Hitler's inner circle. Suddenly, tank and shell factories were given plenty of air time on *Die Deutsche Wochenschau* newsreels, with the dashing young armaments minister pinning medals to foremen and factory workers and making rousing speeches. When the new, cheaper machine gun, the MG42, was launched that autumn – a direct result of Thomas's demands for simpler weapons the previous December – it was done so with a flourish. 'The best weapons bring victory,' was the mantra, along with a claim that this new miracle weapon could fire at a staggering rate of 3,000 rounds per minute. This, of course, was nonsense, but even at 1,400 rounds per minute it was still the world's fastest. That such a rate of fire was still way more than British and US equivalents, or that such a rate of fire brought as many problems as benefits, was understandably kept very quiet.

The truth was, those fundamental shortcomings of Germany's situation three years into a war they had intended to fight as a series of short, sharp campaigns had not gone away. German industry was still hopelessly short of the resources needed, it was still over-engineering, and although Speer was attempting to make savings and increase efficiency, there was much that counted against that: a lack of space, a largely inefficient workforce based increasingly on forced labour and a culture of production that was changing only very slowly.

*

At Debden in Essex, in eastern England, a grand ceremony had been held on 28 September to formally transfer the American volunteers of 133 Eagle Squadron RAF over to the embryonic US Army Air Force 4th Fighter Group. 'It is with great personal regret that I today say goodbye to you whom it has been my privilege to command,' said Air Chief Marshal Sir Sholto Douglas, the C-in-C of RAF Fighter Command. 'You joined us readily and of your own free will when our need was greatest.' Yet despite this formal handover and although they had officially become 336 Fighter Squadron, the switch from RAF to USAAF had, in reality, been a little more gradual. Through October they continued flying the RAF Spitfires, although the roundels were gradually replaced with the white star used by the USAAF, and in ones and twos they trooped off to London to pick up khaki green jackets and A2 leather jackets to replace their RAF blues and Irvin sheepskins.

The first two Spitfires to be given US markings were those of Dixie Alexander and Jim Goodson. They had not stopped flying, but the new squadron had not been on an official USAAF fighter mission yet, so Goodson and Alexander started badgering the CO, Don Blakeslee, to let them head over to France on a 'rhubarb', or nuisance raid, as a pair. Blakeslee liked the idea well enough and so put it to Brigadier-General 'Monk' Hunter, the C-in-C of Eighth Fighter Command, the US Eighth Air Force's fighter component. Hunter, who expected the 4th needed to harness a bit of identity and spirit, agreed.

On 29 October, at around 2.25 p.m., Goodson and Alexander took off and headed out down the Thames estuary and under the grey clouds over the Channel. They were so low it felt as though they were almost skimming the waves, but it was important to keep below German radar. Alexander was leading and Goodson following and they made landfall exactly where they had intended at Gravelines, then turned east, so that almost immediately they were over Dunkirk. Hurtling down the big canal, they fired on a large barge they guessed would probably be carrying coal. Then they saw Ostende, but kept going until they reached Bruges. It was off-limits for bombing but not strafing and they soon spotted a train with its steam up. Flak was rising up and they had to do a lot of jinking and stomping on the rudder as they lined up their targets. Gun button to fire, the judder of the plane as bullets and cannon shells spat from the gun ports, and in a flash they were over, still hugging the deck, the flak arcing over them harmlessly. They turned north, roared over a cyclist on a quiet country road, which made him topple over, then in a flash they were back over the sea and heading home. They touched back down at 4.10 p.m.

Both men gave the intelligence officer an appropriately modest report, forgetting this was the 4th's first mission and there was a host of newly arrived press men hungry for news. 'At dawn today,' ran a piece in the US forces newspaper, *Stars and Stripes*, 'fighter planes of the US Eighth Army Air Force carried out daring low-level attacks on rail, road, and water transport in Northern France and Belgium, leaving behind a trail of destruction.'

Blakeslee was furious. He'd been in the RAF long enough to know that a fighter pilot should never boast, or 'shoot a line'. Seeing Goodson, he said, 'All right, where's the other half of the Eighth Air Force?'

Both Goodson and Alexander protested their innocence. 'All I claimed was one bicycle damaged,' Goodson told him.

It hadn't been quite the glorious level of destruction claimed by *Stars and Stripes*, but the 4th Fighter Group was now up and running, with its first combat mission under its belt.

Also now over in Britain was the recently promoted Captain Gabby Gabreski. Back in the summer, while still stationed in Hawaii, he and his fellows had been visited by a number of US Navy fighter pilots, including Butch O'Hare, who had won a Medal of Honor. Talking to them, Gabreski had realized the US Navy had it pretty much sewn up in the Pacific and that the USAAF was not going to get much of a look in. That had set him thinking. He wanted to get involved. More than that, with his Polish roots, he wanted to get over to Europe; he felt very strongly about what the Nazis had done to Poland. Furthermore, having read about the Polish squadrons in the Battle of Britain, he now wondered whether maybe he could get himself assigned to one of their squadrons in the RAF in England. It was a long shot, but he reckoned it had to be worth asking the question.

Much to his surprise, his squadron commander thought it a good plan and agreed to pass it up the line. Months went by and Gabreski had pretty much given up hope, but then a wire arrived from the War Department telling him to report to Eighth Air Force HQ for further processing to a Polish fighter squadron. He was to stop en route in Washington and take a week's leave, then head over the Atlantic.

For a reason he never quite understood, in Washington he was issued with a civilian passport then put on a Yankee Clipper to Lisbon, from where he flew to neutral Ireland before finally reaching England. Heading straight to Eighth Air Force Headquarters in Bushy Park, south-west London, he was slightly surprised to discover only about twenty people there and in what appeared to be complete confusion. No one seemed to know anything about him or his assignment to join the Poles. Instead, they gave him a pass for a hotel in town and told him they would be in touch. At the hotel, he was in for another surprise. One of its walls was completely missing: his room consisted of three walls and a tarpaulin. He had come from Hawaii to England in October: a cold, damp land of three-walled hotels.

Back at Eighth Air Force HQ, they still couldn't sort out his transfer to the Poles, so he was made a ferry pilot instead and told to go to Prestwick in Scotland, where aircraft from the States were being received. He flew a P-38 twin-engine fighter, a P-39 and B-17s and B-24s too. It was all quite interesting and good experience, he supposed, but wasn't the reason he'd come over to Britain. Gabreski hadn't given up yet, however. By hook or by crook, he was going to join those Poles.

Across the Channel, Siegfried Bethke, now a Hauptmann, was still one of the few Luftwaffe fighter pilots to have been based continuously in the West. His Jagdgeschwader JG2 had, from time to time, moved up and down the Channel coast, but now he was back in Cherbourg, a place for which he had no affection at all.

The summer had been marked by an invasion scare, but since the Dieppe Raid the heightened alert had been downgraded. Bethke was struggling, however, and had been for some time. Although he was continuing to shoot down enemy aircraft, his love of flying had been replaced by fear; Bethke was losing his nerve. 'I have a proper fear of the Channel and Spitfire "fantasies",' he had jotted in his journal. 'I can no longer lead the squadron, because I get alarmed at even the smallest group of enemy fighters. I have a proper fear, and I am afraid that my pilots will find out. But mainly it is the water. Defensive fighting over land would not be so bad, but the moment I start thinking about water, it is over for me.' That had been back in May, but somehow he managed to continue to dig deep, to fly and lead his men; a few weeks after that confession, he shot down two Spitfires in one sortie. Then he was posted briefly to Paris for some courses, flew numerous missions during the Dieppe Raid and by the autumn was still both flying and leading his *Staffel*. It was typical of the Luftwaffe that someone should still be leading a front-line squadron in Bethke's condition. And he had been in JG2, at the front, since May 1940. It was inconceivable that a British or American pilot would have had such an excessive tour.

By September he was utterly sick of the war, praying constantly for bad weather and panicking more than ever over water. 'I will call the group today,' he wrote on 6 September, 'and ask to talk to the group commander. I can no longer lead the squadron with the necessary enthusiasm and courage. I can't look at the water any more, and I get all worked up when I hear the word Spitfire.' His case went all the way up the chain to General Adolf Galland, the C-in-C of Fighters, and finally, in October, he was posted to south-west France as an instructor at a replacement training unit where fresh pilots were prepared for combat. He could not have been more relieved.

Also still in the West was Leutnant Heinz Knoke, who had been stationed in Norway with JG1, but back in June had been posted to Jever, near Wilhelmshaven, with his *Gruppe* and there placed under the command of the Fliegerkorps XII Experimental Unit as a test pilot. This was so that he could test the new 'Y' System ultra-short-wave radios. This was a greatly improved long-distance radio, which would massively enhance both in-flight communications and those with ground controllers down below. Finally the Luftwaffe were creating the kind of air defence system Britain had developed before the war – one in which a more centralized control could follow any approaching enemy formation through a combination of radio interception, radar and ground observers. This information was then fed out to a series of regions rather like those of RAF Fighter Command and to both flak units and fighter ground controllers.

As with the British system, there were now concrete bombproof shelters with large map tables, a raised dais on which the controllers sat, and female plotters. Knoke was given a detailed tour. 'A glance at the map,' he noted, 'is all that is required to obtain a complete picture of the changing situation at any given moment.' He had been mightily impressed. Had the Luftwaffe known the RAF had much the same system back in 1940, perhaps they would not have begun the Battle of Britain with quite the same level of over-confidence.

In terms of night defence, the *Himmelbett* system seemed to be working well too. A newer, more efficient ground radar system, Würzburg-Riese, had been put in place, and by now Hauptmann Helmut Lent, the leading night ace, and nearly all the Nachtjagd pilots were using onboard Lichtenstein radar. Because the Germans had not developed the cavity magnetron, Lichtenstein was not as sophisticated as the British and American sets. The Mk VIII AI (Air Interceptor) used by the British had a range of around 5½ miles and a sharply focused beam that meant it avoided ground reflections even at pretty low levels. Nor did it really have a minimum range. Currently being developed were an improved Mk IX version and a British variant of the US SCR-720, which could pick up a scan of between plus-50 and minus-20 degrees and, like the Mk VIII, in a very focused way.

Lichtenstein, in contrast, had a maximum range of 2 miles and minimum range of around 200 yards, and still meant having enormous and complex antennae, which caused terrible drag and acted like an air brake. British and American radar was onboard and so presented no such problems.

Even so, Lichtenstein was certainly helping. Of the 531 RAF bombers that had been shot down between June and August, the Nachtjagd had claimed 349 of them.

There were also new aircraft coming into service. By the beginning of October, Heinz Knoke was testing the new Messerschmitt 109G, the 'Gustav'. This was the same aircraft that had dramatically caught fire and killed Jochen Marseille, but Knoke jotted in his diary on 2 October that it was 'definitely superior' to the Spitfire. Later that day, Knoke learned of the death of Marseille and the circumstances in which he had died. Then, at around 12.15 p.m. they had an alert: a Mosquito was reported in the Oldenburg area. With Feldwebel Hans-Gerd Wenneckers as his wingman, off they flew, climbing quickly, but Knoke noticed Wenneckers falling behind. By the time they had reached 12,000 feet, he had lost sight of him altogether. Knoke called him on the radio, but got no reply, then noticed the flaming wreckage of an aircraft on the plain below. Was this Wenneckers, he wondered.

Knoke never caught up with the Mosquito on this occasion and so, descending in a handful of wide spirals, he headed back to Jever. On landing, however, there, much to his surprise, was Wenneckers, laughing at Knoke's shocked expression. The sergeant-pilot then explained that his Gustav had suddenly caught fire mid-air for no apparent reason – in exactly the same way as the plane Marseille had been flying had done. They were all baffled. And apparently, a Gustav in 4/JG1 had also caught fire in the same way. 'I begin to look at my plane,' jotted Knoke, 'with some misgiving.'

Back in 1940, the Me109E – or 'Emil' – had been unquestionably the finest fighter aircraft in the world. It could do the three things a modern fighter needed to do better than any other: it could climb fast, dive fast, and with its fifty-five seconds' worth of ammunition and combination of cannons and machine guns, it had better fire-power than any other operational single-engine fighter at that time.

By 1942 standards, however, its airframe design was beginning to creak. The enclosed cockpit, cut into, rather than above, the fuselage, and straps of metal between the Perspex meant the pilot had poor visibility. The biggest problem of all, however, was that the Me109E had swiftly been overtaken in terms of performance. The 'Friedrich' had redesigned wings, improved overall aerodynamics and beefed-up Daimler-Benz 601 engine, but still only managed 1,300 HP, so that, although it had an improved performance on the Emil, it still wasn't enough. What was needed was a bigger engine, and that came in the form of the Daimler-Benz 605, which gave it 1,455 HP. Since the Friedrich, all armament had been moved to the central engine cowling area: two machine guns were placed between the cylinder banks and a single cannon was placed so that it fired through the centre of the propeller hub. This was a bit of a fiddle to mount. Furthermore, the DB605 was some 250kg heavier than the DB601 and also performed poorly at low speeds. Flying straight and level, the Gustav was quick enough and it could fly up to 40,000 feet but had lost some of its agility.

And then there were those fires that kept breaking out. In almost every way, the Gustav was more complicated and difficult to build than the Emil, yet one economy was the switch from ball bearings to plain bearings in the engine. It was, on the face of it, a small thing, but was typical of the somewhat haphazard approach the Germans had: excessive over-engineering on one hand, but corner-cutting on the other; there never seemed to be a happy medium between practicalities and high design spec. This meant the bearings were roller-bearings rather than cylindrical, which in turn meant there was more friction. These would overheat more quickly; with half-decent lubricants this would not have necessarily mattered, but with poor synthetic lubricants, the bearings and metal around them would get so hot the oil within the engine would combust. Hence the engine fires.

The truth of the matter was that the Me109 had peaked with the Emil and Friedrich and, because of its early 1930s designed airframe, had no real development scope left by the time the Gustav was being proposed. What was needed was a new fighter entirely, but at the time, the FW190 had problems of its own and Feldmarschall Milch had been forced to climb down on making it the priority Luftwaffe single-engine fighter. To meet the rising aircraft production in Britain and the USA, time had been very much of the essence, and there certainly had not been enough of that precious commodity to go back to the drawing board.

So the Gustav had got the nod and had been a central part of the rationalization of the Luftwaffe that he was now overseeing. This, Milch had realized, was absolutely essential because it was the only chance they had of implementing any kind of mass production. Two projects that had already absorbed far too much time, money and effort were the Me210 – the planned replacement of the Me110 twin-engine fighter – and the Heinkel 177 four-engine heavy bomber. Both projects were now scrapped; painful though this was, Milch believed they had no choice but to cut their losses. From now on, all available capacity was to be focused on just a few models that had already been tried and tested. In the case of the bombers, it was the 1934 vintage Heinkel 111 and the Ju88. The Ju88 was renamed the Ju188 – 'so that the enemy gets the impression it's something new,' admitted Milch.

Yet there were other battles to be fought in Milch's drive to increase production, not least Sauckel's favouring of Speer's and the Army's requirements, so that Milch's factories never had as many workers as they might otherwise have done. Then there was the problem of materials allocations, which were never enough. This was a particular source of frustration because, as with most other areas of the Nazi armaments production, there was always wastage, even now at a time when the industry was supposed to be economizing and becoming more efficient. He had, for example, sent inspectors around some of Germany's shipyards and at the end of August they had reported seeing large quantities of steel lying about doing nothing at Wilhelmshaven, Kiel and Hamburg. When asked, workers said these had been there for years.

None the less, by November 1942, German aircraft production was significantly on the rise. Costs were plunging as manufacturers became more efficient. And as costs fell, so unit numbers rose. In the second half of 1941, Germany had produced, on average, a total of 870 aircraft per month. During the second half of 1942, that average had risen to 1,341 per month and the line on the graph was still going upwards.

The trouble, though, was that greater quantity was coming at a qualitative cost.

Out at sea, the invasion fleets were steaming towards North Africa – one travelling 3,000 miles from the United States and two travelling more than 1,000 miles from Britain. In all, some 370 merchant vessels and a further 300 warships had been assembled for what was the world's largest armada ever and the biggest seaborne invasion in the history of the world. The plan for TORCH had been agreed only two months earlier, yet miraculously the three task forces were out at sea and all appeared to be on schedule after what had been a truly breathtaking planning operation; just working out and writing all the various orders was a feat in itself and one that had taken four days of near-continuous dictation to two teams of stenographers.

Commander-in-Chief of the Naval Forces was Admiral Cunningham, the former C-in-C of the Royal Navy's Mediterranean Fleet. After long years of evacuations and attrition in the Mediterranean, it made a good change to be commanding such a mighty force and yet, as he was well aware, there was much that could go wrong.

He arrived at Gibraltar on 1 November and installed himself in the recently built tunnels under the Rock – a feat of engineering in their own right. Here were map rooms with wall charts on which the progress of the three task forces could be monitored. U-boats had been more active on this side of the Atlantic again in recent weeks, and such huge forces were vulnerable to attack by enemy submarines. Both British and American bombers had been attacking U-boat bases and extra ASW patrols had been carried out in the Bay of Biscay. The convoys had hefty protection from their escorts too, but even so, it was a worry. On 30 October, for example, eight merchantmen had been sunk as their convoy passed by the Canary Islands. They had been nothing to do with TORCH, but the attacks had been only 100 miles south of where the Western Task Force from America would be passing.

The other worry was the weather, especially for the Western Task Force, which would be landing in French Morocco outside the Mediterranean; it was now November, after all. Sure enough, on 2 November the weather over the Atlantic began to roughen. By the following day it was worse; and by the 4th, the Western Task Force was sailing through a full-blooded Atlantic storm – precisely the kind of weather ABC and the planners had most feared.

'Ring out the bells!' General Alexander signalled to Churchill on 6 November. 'Prisoners now 20,000, tanks 350, guns 400, MT several thousand. Our advanced mobile forces are south of Mersa Matruh. 8th Army is advancing.' Despite this euphoria, however, bad weather had struck the Western Desert too, and air operations, so crucial for harrying the retreating enemy, had been brought almost to a standstill that same day, 6 November. On the ground, Eighth Army's spearhead had also become bogged down in the downpours. 'We got soaked to the skin,' said Albert Martin, who was now back in his truck once more, 'and freezing cold. We were bogged down in mashed, gritty sand and had to stop.' Further along the coast, the Sherwood Rangers had also ground to a halt as their B Echelon – the regiment's support troops – had tried to follow the tanks across the desert and had now become stuck. 'The rain continued practically throughout the night,' noted Stanley Christopherson. 'We slept in our tanks. Not a very comfortable night.'

Because the remnants of the Panzerarmee had given themselves a head start and because they were mostly using the metalled coast road, the rain was not proving the hindrance it was to Eighth Army. Montgomery had intended to pursue Rommel's broken forces, catch them and annihilate them. But they were slipping away, just as Eighth Army had done after Tobruk. Unlike Eighth Army, however, there was no obvious place to stand and fight until they got to within spitting distance of Tripoli and the Panzerarmee's main supply base. That, however, was still a very long way away.

What's more, the Panzerarmee remained in complete disarray, as Adolf Lamm was discovering. Lamm was thirty-two and an *Unteroffizier* – sergeant – and panzer radio operator who had flown to Tobruk from Athens as a replacement earlier in October. That alone had been hairy enough, as their transport had been attacked by enemy aircraft en route. Fortunately for all on board, they had managed to get away, but on reaching Tobruk he had immediately been told to head to El Daba, further east down the coast towards Alamein.

Lamm had then been sent up to the front just as the Alamein Line was collapsing and the Panzerarmee was streaming back. Hastily assembled into a tank crew with men he had never met before, they joined the retreat as the defeated Army began hurrying back westwards. The situation was utterly chaotic. No one seemed to know where Lamm should be or what he should be doing. He was now in 15. Panzerdivision, or what remained of it, but had not the faintest idea where he was; he had no map, had not served in North Africa before and, as far as he was concerned, the desert all looked pretty much the same. Nor did he have any orders for radio operations, any radio-code table, and no wavelength and no ciphers. The tank commander was equally in the dark, but they followed the others and tried to keep going.

Yet not everyone was getting away. On that Friday, 6 November, Luigi Marchese was keenly aware that the British were hot on their tails. There were no trucks, so he and his comrades were forced to march across the desert. Around noon, they paused briefly and, sitting on a rocky outcrop, Marchese decided to eat the last bit of food he had with him – a tin of meat still in his haversack. Opening it with his bayonet, he realized immediately that it had gone rotten. Despite this, he was so hungry he would have eaten it anyway, but it was horribly salty and he had run out of water; and so he remained hungry.

They soon got walking again, aware that the enemy guns had stopped firing and that the skies were now blissfully clear. 'Our group had been reduced to a long, straggling line of a few hundred men,' he wrote. Then, at around three o'clock, Bren Carriers appeared from the north. They all knew what this meant and understood why they had been left in peace by both aircraft and guns. They were now surrounded. One of the officers now ordered them to destroy their weapons and ID cards, which they did with tears in their eyes. The British troops fired a few volleys from their machine guns over their heads and approached them, while the Italians stood and waited. 'Then, in that sandy defile,' wrote Marchese, 'no more shooting was heard, and there fell on us a deathly silence.'

The same day, Major Hans von Luck and his 21. Panzerdivision Reconnaissance Battalion were in action, easily seeing off tentative British patrols far to the south. He had been brought up from Siwa early on 3 November to help support the Italian XX Corps, but had been able to do little with their armoured cars, low-calibre anti-tank and machine guns. As Tuker's Indians and the follow-up British armour had destroyed the Italian corps, von Luck had watched the thin-skinned tanks of their allies burning. 'It was heart-rending to have to witness how the Ariete Division,' he wrote, 'and the remains of the Trieste and Littorio Divisions, fought with death-defying courage.' But von Luck was still in radio contact with Rommel's headquarters and had then been sent back south-west to patrol the desert above the Siwa and Giarabub oases and prevent any outflanking.

Like everyone else, he and his men suffered in the rain and wind, but on 7 November his troops made contact with General Hermann-Bernhard Ramcke and his brigade of *Fallschirmjäger*, now only 700 strong. 'I shall never forget the sight of Ramcke's men coming towards us, exhausted, out of the desert,' wrote von Luck. 'For reasons of space, they had left everything behind except for weapons and water, but their morale was astonishing.'

Ramcke asked to be taken to Rommel, but the Army commander flew down to see him and von Luck instead, early the following morning. There he briefed them both, telling them of terrible scenes that were taking place on the coastal road: columns shot up and bombed, vehicles left burning, men desperately trying to keep going on foot. 'Through Hitler's crazy order to hold out,' Rommel told them, 'we lost a vital day, which cost us losses that cannot be made good.' He could no longer hold Cyrenaica, he explained. He intended to set up a defence line at Mersa el Brega, on the edge of Tripolitania, some 800 miles away. He was worried about the southern flank and so had decided to send von Luck reinforcements.

Von Luck thought Rommel remained unbroken, but couldn't help but notice his profound disappointment. 'What had become of Rommel's proud Africa Army?' he noted. 'How depressing it must have been for him to have to give up in a matter of days all that had once been conquered in unprecedented operations.'

Yet while Hitler's order had undoubtedly brought nothing but greater casualties, the defeat at Alamein had been because Rommel had urged his superiors to allow him to press on into Egypt. In so doing he had gone way, way past his operational reach. The responsibility for that – for putting tactical dash over sound operational reality – lay primarily with Rommel.

*

The bad weather had been buffeting southern England too and had delayed Eisenhower's and Clark's departure so that it wasn't until 5 November that they finally left Bournemouth for Gibraltar in their fleet of B-17s. That same night, the Eastern Task Force began passing through the Straits of Gibraltar, still in complete radio silence and with the ships all blacked out. Between 7.30 p.m. on 5 November and 4 a.m. on the 7th, the entire Eastern and Central Task Forces successfully passed into the Mediterranean. It was a vast armada: together, in all three task forces, there were 107,453 men heading to the North African shores in 107 troopships protected by 350 warships.

Despite the size of the escort force, at 5.35 a.m. on the 7th, Allied headquarters learned that a ship in the Western Task Force, the USS *Thomas Stone*, had been torpedoed. There were 1,400 on board, but soon after another signal arrived with the news that the ship – with the men all still on board – was not only still afloat but being towed. She would make the landings, albeit a little late.

Meanwhile, Eisenhower and his team still had plenty of other things to worry about: the reaction of the Spanish, for one, and the whereabouts of Giraud for another. Since *Seraph* had gone to fetch him, there had been just one message and a cryptic one at that: 'Task gone, radio failing.' At the Rock, Ike had called a meeting to discuss how they should handle Giraud should he baulk at their plans. Cunningham tried to reassure them. 'He's thrown his coat over the fence,' he said. 'He will do what he's told.'

Also that day, 7 November, Ultra decrypts revealed that the Germans had sighted the convoys; and Luftwaffe reconnaissance planes were spotted shadowing the Eastern Task Force. None the less, there was, incredibly, no indication that they suspected an invasion of north-west Africa, even though Berlin was aware of the massive increase in traffic at Gibraltar; rather, they seemed to think it was a large convoy to Malta or a landing aimed for Libya or even Sicily.

The weather in the Atlantic was also improving, and then came some further good news: Giraud had been safely picked up and was on his way. A Catalina flying boat was sent out to meet him and brought him to Gibraltar at around 4 p.m. that afternoon. At 5.20 p.m., Eisenhower gave the operation the final go-ahead. 'Warning order,' he signalled. 'H-Hour confirmed November 8. For East and Centre, 1 a.m. For West, about 4.30 a.m.'

*

Evening, Saturday, 7 November. At Allied headquarters in Gibraltar, Eisenhower and Clark were finally talking face to face with Général Giraud. Eisenhower explained the Allied plans and told him a message had been prepared for all the French people in North Africa, to be signed by the Général, calling on them to support the invasion.

Giraud sat up stiffly. 'Now let's get it clear as to my part,' he said. 'As I understand it, when I land in North Africa I am to assume command of all Allied forces and become the Supreme Allied Commander in North Africa.'

Clark gasped audibly; both he and Eisenhower were thunderstruck. This was arrogance or stupidity, or both, of the highest order. How a French general, still bound to the pro-Axis Vichy, could possibly imagine he would be given command of combined Anglo-US-Franco armed forces is hard to fathom. Taking a deep breath, Clark explained that no, Giraud would not be Supreme Commander.

'But what would the French people think of me?' Giraud asked. 'What about the prestige of Giraud; what about my family?'

Clearly, neither Clark nor Eisenhower could give a damn about that. Clark patiently explained that he could command French forces in North Africa but that was all.

'Then,' replied Giraud, 'I shall return to France.'

'Oh, no,' Clark replied. 'That was a one-way submarine. You're not going back to France.'

It was clear Giraud was stalling and waiting to see how the invasion would pan out. All that effort and trouble in getting to him and then bringing him from France appeared to have been for nothing. The discussions continued, but Giraud wasn't budging. Some time after 11 p.m., Clark said to him, 'Old gentleman, I hope you know that from now on, your ass is out in the snow.'

It was, frankly, about time Giraud was brought down to earth. Henri Frenay had learned how insufferable he was earlier in the summer when one of his Combat members had met with the Général at the latter's house in Lyons. 'He'd been very unfavourably impressed,' noted Frenay. 'To be sure, the man was deeply anti-German and hostile to Vichy, but he was also unduly respectful of the Maréchal. Moreover, he acted idiotically self-important.' It had also been abundantly clear that he knew nothing at all about the Resistance and that his motives were rooted entirely in self-interest rather than in any altruistic desire to help liberate the oppressed French people.

While these talks were going on, the task forces were approaching their invasion zones. Off Algiers, near the coastal towns of Oran and Arzew, the Central Task Force successfully rendezvoused with their beacon submarines. In the darkness, the men huddled together, packs on their backs and weapons slung over their shoulders. The Bowles twins in the 18th Regimental Combat Team and Bing Evans with the Rangers were in Z Sector, where they were to storm Arzew. On land, the lights of the towns twinkled in the night sky as the troops prepared to clamber on to the nets and down into the landing craft now bobbing on the water below. And from the shore, not a shot had yet been fired. Miraculously, it seemed the invasion was still a secret.

It was now Sunday, 8 November 1942. The first major Anglo-American military land operation of the war was about to begin.

CHAPTER 34

Invasion

GENERAL WALTER WARLIMONT had spent a long, two-day railway journey from the Ukraine to East Prussia on 31 October–1 November polishing up an OKW appreciation entitled 'Survey of the Overall Situation in Autumn 1942'. He and his planning team had concluded that the Wehrmacht and their allies had shot their bolt in the Soviet Union. They had run out of steam in the Caucasus, did not have their hands on the Baku oilfields, and still had not been able to take Stalingrad. Losses had once again been horrendous.

The survey also contained a detailed examination of the most likely area for attack for the Western Allies, which had to be imminent. Warlimont was convinced – and had been for some time – that French North Africa was as good a jumping-off point as any for further attacks against Fortress Europe. A mass of intelligence had been assembled: from Spain, from Switzerland, from Lisbon, from Budapest, all pointing to an imminent second front and, collectively, a growing weight of it pointing towards north-west Africa. There was, however, no hard evidence to support this and so, despite strategic and operational logic, it was rather swept to one side. In fact, for all the time and effort that had been put into it, Warlimont's appreciation never got beyond Jodl and Keitel; Hitler certainly did not see it.

Just a few days later, Warlimont was out of a job. At HQ Area 2 at Rastenburg, his staff had received Rommel's first signal of 2 November warning that he must fall back or face annihilation. They were not told, however, that Hitler had replied telling Rommel to stand fast.

Consequently, when, a day later, Rommel signalled that he had now given the retreat order, Warlimont's duty officer thought this was in accordance with the message of 2 November; quite understandably, he had no idea Rommel had gone against the direct wishes of the Führer. When this was discovered, the duty officer was summarily sacked by Hitler, reduced to the ranks and posted to a detention battalion, which was pretty much a death sentence.

Warlimont had tried to stick up for the unfortunate man and had been fired too. Although Warlimont had been Jodl's principal staff officer for three years, all Jodl said was, 'For us, the Führer's will is the supreme law of the land.' Rudolf Schmundt, however, Hitler's military advisor, immediately managed to convince the Führer of the injustice of both dismissals. The duty officer's punishment was reduced and Warlimont was begged to return. Still incensed, he replied that he needed to think it over; he had been looking for a way out and a posting elsewhere for a long time.

With Warlimont dismissed and his appreciation left unread, it was left to Hitler alone, with his lackeys Keitel and Jodl, to assess the strategic situation. Italy's Secret Service, the Servizio Informazioni Militari (SIM), now warned of an invasion of north-west Africa, but this was dismissed. Hitler, once again, was viewing possible Allied intentions through his own narrow world-view and preconceived attitudes to strategy; he was now most worried about Norway and north-west Europe and had, earlier in the year, ordered the construction of the Atlantic Wall – defences that would run all the way from the Arctic Circle in northern Norway down to the Spanish border. Even if the Allies were to land somewhere within the Mediterranean, he thought Libya or even Sicily more likely. The build-up of shipping was known about and on 6 November Göring, bypassing the OKW entirely, told Kesselring in Rome of Hitler's view on the matter. Kesselring protested that north-west Africa should not be written off; he insisted that the Allied convoys should be attacked and destroyed by continuous action by day and by night. Of course, there were neither the air nor the naval forces for such attacks; the Regia Aeronautica and Luftwaffe were concentrated on trying to help Rommel's retreat and, frankly, not doing very well.

On 7 November, Hitler then personally intervened, demanding that defences in Tripoli and Benghazi should be urgently shored up and ordering further reinforcements to Crete, an island so far out of the

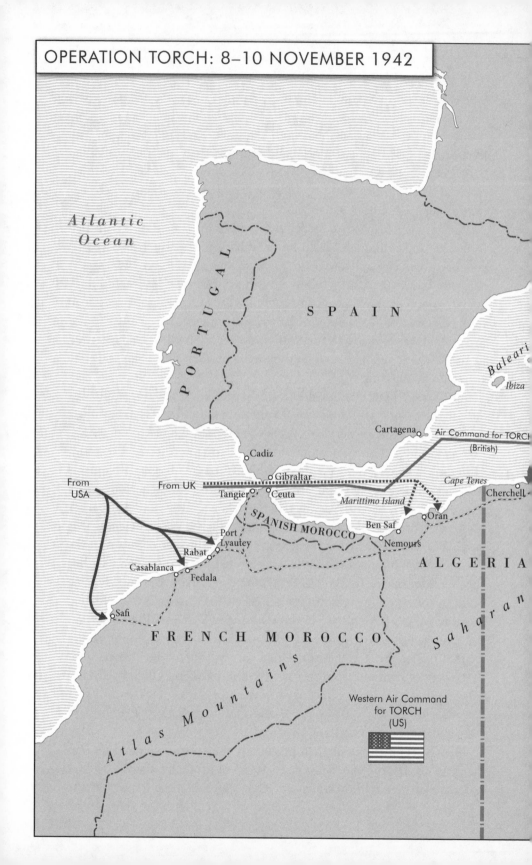

OPERATION TORCH: 8–10 NOVEMBER 1942

Atlantic Ocean

PORTUGAL

S P A I N

Baleari

Ibiza

Cartagena

Air Command for TORCH (British)

Cadiz

Gibraltar

Cape Tenes

Cherchell

From UK

Tangier   Ceuta

Marittimo Island

Oran

From USA

SPANISH MOROCCO

Ben Saf

Nemours

Port Lyautey

Rabat

Casablanca

Fedala

A L G E R I A

Safi

F R E N C H   M O R O C C O

S a h a r a n

Western Air Command for TORCH (US)

Atlas Mountains

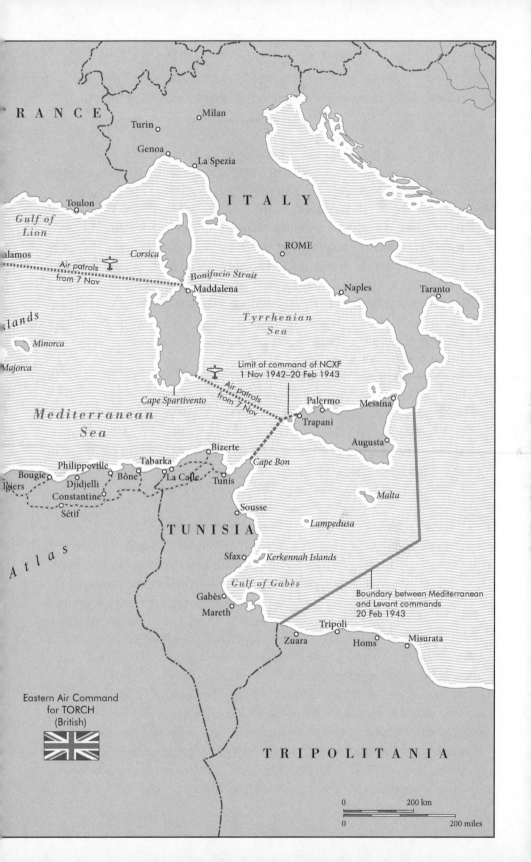

F R A N C E

Turin○ ○Milan

Genoa○
La Spezia○

Toulon○

Gulf of Lion

I T A L Y

Corsica

ROME○

Bonifacio Strait
Maddalena○

Naples○

Taranto○

Tyrrhenian Sea

alamos

Air patrols
from 7 Nov

lands

Minorca

Majorca

Limit of command of NCXF
1 Nov 1942–20 Feb 1943

Air patrols
from 7 Nov

Cape Spartivento

Palermo○

Messina○

Mediterranean Sea

Trapani○

Augusta○

Bizerte○

Cape Bon

Tabarka○

Bougie○
lgiers○

Philippeville○
Djidjelli○

Bône○

La Calle○

Tunis○

Malta

Constantine○

Sétif○

Sousse○

T U N I S I A

Lampedusa

Atlas

Sfax○

Kerkennah Islands

Gulf of Gabès

Boundary between Mediterranean
and Levant commands
20 Feb 1943

Gabès○
Mareth○

Tripoli○

Misurata○

Zuara○

Homs○

Eastern Air Command
for TORCH
(British)

T R I P O L I T A N I A

0   200 km

0   200 miles

Allies' reach as to not even be worth considering. The ineptness of the Führer's strategic appreciation beggars belief.

The three task forces made their landings pretty much on schedule in the early hours of Sunday, 8 November 1942, along the three invasion fronts in north-west Africa. The first of the Central Task Force to land at Arzew were the Rangers, spearheading the attack. Capturing this port swiftly was considered essential, as landing heavy equipment would be impossible without it. Overlooking the port were two gun batteries and it was clear that destroying them was the first priority. The first, at Fort du Nord, was on top of a hill dominating the harbour, while the second, Fort de la Pointe, was at the foot of the hill at the north-east corner of the port.

Colonel William Darby had decided to split his force into two. Major Herman Dammer would take two companies and capture both the harbour and Fort de la Pointe, while the rest, including Darby himself and Sergeant Bing Evans, would land on a small beach around the headland and then climb the hill to take Fort du Nord from the rear.

Dammer's force was in the harbour, unchallenged, by 1.30 a.m. and, clambering up on to the quay, swept past one sentry then opened fire on another. These were the first shots fired. Sirens then began wailing, but the Rangers were now already at the gates of the Fort de la Pointe and successfully charged the gun positions. Inside the fort, the French had been caught napping and forty-two men were swiftly captured, including the commandant, who had been in bed with his mistress.

Meanwhile, Darby and the rest of the Rangers had set off in just two LCAs. Bing Evans had made sure he had studied and memorized sand-table models and aerial photographs and now, as they sped towards the shore, felt a mounting sense of exhilaration. 'This is what we had trained for,' he said, 'and I felt anxious to get on with it.' Their beach marker was a buoy, but Evans reckoned they had missed it and told Darby. And so they had but, swiftly turning back, they soon found it. 'That,' said Evans, 'was the only hitch we had.'

By 1.30 a.m. they were ashore and an hour and a half later reached the fort, where they quietly set up some heavy mortars and began cutting the wire around it. When the defenders in the fort opened fire, the Rangers fired their mortars, rushed the battery and were in among the French before they knew what had hit them. After preparing the guns for demolition, they sent up a green flare, which informed those watching out at sea, including Major-General Terry Allen, commander of the 1st Infantry Division, that the battery and fort had been secured. Soon after, the two Ranger forces made contact. The port and both forts had fallen.

Commanding all US ground forces for the Western Task Force was Major-General George S. Patton. He had been aboard the USS *Augusta* with the Western Task Force, and at 2 a.m. on the morning of the 8th had been up, dressed and looking immaculate, as was his way, and out on deck. Patton had waited all his life for a moment such as this. It was, he believed, his destiny to achieve military greatness, and this war was going to help him reach it. Already one of America's best-known generals, his first taste of fame had come in 1916 when he led a raid that killed three of Pancho Villa's Mexican bandits. A year later he had been sent to France, where he had become the first officer assigned to the US Tank Corps. Badly wounded in the groin, he had still been recovering when the armistice was signed.

He had remained in the US Army – it was his life, not just a career – and spent the 1920s and 1930s thinking deeply about the future of warfare. Like General Tuker, he had also written a number of far-reaching papers, including a prophetic piece on the possibility of a Japanese attack on Pearl Harbor. While the US Army had been stagnating – especially America's armoured capability – Patton had been one man desperately trying to buck the trend. For him, these had been long, frustrating years.

Patton was a man of many contrasts and contradictions. Tall, with fierce, pale eyes, he none the less had a high-pitched, rather squeaky voice at odds with his bullish demeanour. A noted horseman and champion swordsman, he had come fifth in the pentathlon at the 1912 Stockholm Olympic Games. He was also something of a poet, was utterly devoted to his wife and family, and to God, and yet was also, despite his obvious charisma, prone to bouts of self-doubt. As a leader of men, he was tough, uncompromising, but utterly inspiring.

Now, as he stood and watched the lights of Casablanca and Fedala, he sensed a great crusade was beginning. 'The eyes of the world are watching us,' he'd written to his troops from *Augusta*, 'the heart of America beats for us; God is with us. On our victory depends the freedom or slavery of the human race. We shall surely win.' He urged them to remember their training, to attack with 'speed and vigor' and told them retreat was unthinkable. 'Americans,' he added, 'do not surrender.'

*

Back at the Rock, Eisenhower, Clark and Cunningham were waiting anxiously for news. At 2.38 a.m. a signal arrived saying the Eastern Task Force assault had been successful and that landings had been made on three beaches at Algiers. Around half an hour later, it was announced that Sidi Ferruch had been captured too, another objective for the Eastern Task Force.

However, there had been more resistance there than at Arzew. In fact, the entire TORCH landings were a strange combination of bitter but brief resistance in certain places, utter fiasco in others, and of almost no opposition at all elsewhere. In Algiers itself, for example, the fighting had been really quite heavy, as Sergeant Ralph Schaps soon discovered. He had been aboard the British destroyer HMS *Broke* for the assault along with the rest of the 3rd Battalion, 135th Infantry. Shore batteries had opened fire as they approached, and another ship, HMS *Malcolm*, had been badly damaged. Then the *Broke* had rammed the harbour boom, although Schaps, crammed on board with the other assault troops, had barely noticed it. However, the ship was taking hits. 'We were getting a little uneasy,' recalled Schaps. 'In fact, we were scared shitless.' Soon after, however, they managed to berth and hurriedly disembarked. Daylight was spreading from the east and small-arms fire was coming in towards them.

They moved on to the Mole Louis Billiard, where there were large piles of wood and baled straw, and, rather than try to go on the offensive, immediately prepared for defence instead in the hope that those landing to the west of the city would soon come to their rescue. However, those troops had landed further west than intended and so now had a greater distance to travel into Algiers. Meanwhile, the unfortunately named HMS *Broke* was hit several times more and sounded the recall siren. Schaps and his fellows, however, had no intention of reboarding under the current fire. French tanks appeared and, although the Americans had some bazookas, the range was too great for them to be much use. Casualties were mounting; Schaps lost one of his buddies, a medic named PFC Mel Lien, who was killed trying to tend a wounded officer.

In the circumstances, the battalion CO, Lieutenant-Colonel Edwin Swenson, who had not been privy to Patton's assertion about never surrendering, decided it was best to do just that and raise the white flag. 'The French treated us real good,' wrote Schaps. 'We stacked arms in a park and in a couple of hours we were drinking wine in a bistro.'

Despite this rather surreal scenario, their captivity – for want of a better word – did not last long. Général Mast had managed to mount a successful coup in the city, rounding up key Vichy officials, including, most importantly, Général Alphonse Juin, the Vichy C-in-C in all of North Africa.

Back at the Rock, more signals were arriving. By 6 a.m., the Western Task Force under Patton was reported to be landing successfully and in calm waters, while by 7.45 a.m., General 'Doc' Ryder, commander of the 34th Red Bulls, signalled that the all-important Maison Blanche airfield near Algiers had been captured.

Elsewhere, Oran harbour itself was the scene of brief but bloody and bitter resistance. There, Mast's resistance operation largely failed, while the harbour had been far bigger and better protected than that at Arzew. Not only was it bristling with guns, but the Royal Navy ensigns fluttering from the two assault ships, *Walney* and *Hartland*, had only stirred bitter memories of the destruction of the French Navy at the hands of the British back in July 1940. Although both ships had crashed through the boom, they had been met by heavy fire at almost point-blank range. In the carnage that followed, 364 American and nearly 200 British troops were killed or wounded.

Further to the west of Oran, however, the Bowles twins landed without trouble with the 2nd Battalion, 18th RCT, as part of the second wave, and followed behind the 1st Battalion towards Saint-Cloud, a village 7 miles inland. Whatever nerves they may have felt soon melted away; they had simply stepped from their landing craft on to the beach and kept going. Not a single bullet had whizzed past their ears or one shell exploded.

One of the day's fiascos was with the airborne operation, which had been due to capture La Senia airfield south of Oran. Both the British and US airborne arms were still in their infancy, but both countries had seen what the Germans had achieved in May 1940 and were rather dazzled by this exciting new form of warfare. That large numbers of transports had been destroyed in the process and that for every success there had been a high-casualty failure had been rather glossed over. Airborne troops were all volunteers, young, keen, highly motivated and definitely among the best-trained in both armies. Unfortunately, no concurrent plan had really been thought through as to how they would be transported. The result was hastily adapted civilian aircraft such as the DC-3, now renamed C-47 or 'Dakota' by the British, which were flown and navigated by the bottom tier of aircrew emerging from the flying schools. In other words, the best-trained troops were being delivered to the battle zone by the least-trained and skilled aircrew.

The dangers of this approach were demonstrated with alarming clarity on 8 November. Of the thirty-nine aircraft that had set out from southern England, seven never reached Algeria at all; of these, one landed in Gibraltar, two in French Morocco and four in Spanish Morocco. Twelve dropped their men at least a day's march away, while sixteen landed in the Sebkra Salt Lake, some way to the south-west of Oran. A further four aircraft dropped their men in Algeria, but too far away to be any use at all; they were promptly taken prisoner.

None the less, as Clark and Eisenhower at Gibraltar were consoling themselves, they had prepared for greater resistance and, all things considered, the landings had got off to a pretty good start. What's more, by evening Algiers was in Allied hands – and Joe Schaps and the men of the 3/135th Infantry released once more – so Eisenhower told Clark he should fly over the following day and establish Allied headquarters in the city right away. First, however, they had another tête-à-tête with Giraud, and this time he was starting to co-operate. Not only did he agree to become C-in-C of all French forces in North Africa, he also offered to fly over right away and play his part in stopping any further resistance. Suddenly, now that the landings were proving successful, Giraud was becoming a little more helpful.

'Darling B,' Patton wrote to his wife, Beatrice, later that morning. 'We have had a great day so far. We have been in a naval battle since 0800 and it is still going on.' Patton had feared there would be no fighting at all, but he need not have worried. In Morocco, French guns had opened fire from Safi at 4.55 a.m., while there was also fighting at Mehida. The third landing, at Fedala, had gone a little awry, with many of the LCAs landing as much as 6 miles from where they should have been. Meanwhile, off-shore from Casablanca, the USS *Massachusetts* had been shelling the French battlecruiser *Jean Bart*. Although immobilized since 1940, there was not much wrong with her 15-inch guns and so the US Navy was keen to make sure they were not brought to bear. Then, at around 7.15 a.m., seven French destroyers had emerged but, seeing the invasion fleet out to sea, quickly turned around and hurried back to port for reinforcements. Half an hour later, a cruiser and two larger destroyers appeared and so had begun the naval battle Patton had written to his wife about.

In fact, on board *Augusta*, General Patton had just placed his kit in the landing boat – including his brace of pearl-handled revolvers, which was swinging from its davits – when the ship suddenly surged forward and opened fire. The blast rocked the landing craft and the General's landing party lost all their kit except the precious six-shooters – a huge relief to all concerned; if his revolvers had gone overboard there would have been hell to pay. Shortly after, an enemy shell landed close to *Augusta* and Patton, still on board, was drenched from the spray. The naval exchange continued until around 11 a.m., when the French ships moved back into Casablanca harbour. Coastal batteries had also been firing, but a bridgehead had, by now, been established and by the afternoon the battle was all but over. General Patton finally stepped ashore around 1.20 p.m., his pistols now safely strapped to his waist.

By mid-afternoon, the French coastal guns had been silenced all along the invasion front and the first two US squadrons of Spitfires from Gibraltar had landed at La Senia and Tafraoui airfields. Yet the battle was still not entirely over, even despite the fall of Algiers. South-west of Arzew, the 18th RCT were held up at Saint-Cloud. Tom Bowles spent the night in a cemetery; he'd also now seen his first dead American soldier. 'I saw him lying there,' he said, 'and that made a big impression on me. I thought, this is for real now.' The following morning, all three battalions of the 18th RCT launched an attack, but the defenders were proving dogged. Unable to break through, it was not until the afternoon of the 9th that the 2nd and 3rd Battalions were able to bypass the town and advance on towards Oran.

Meanwhile, the political situation was rapidly evolving. The previous evening, word came from Robert Murphy that Amiral Darlan wanted to negotiate. He also wanted to meet Eisenhower face to face. 'Kiss Darlan's stern if you have to,' Admiral Cunningham advised Ike, 'but get the French Navy.'

Clark and Giraud, heavily escorted by Spitfires, flew low – and separately – over the Mediterranean to Algeria. Clark's departure, however, was delayed by bad weather and so he didn't get going until nearly noon. Travelling in a B-17 called *Red Gremlin* at just 500 feet over the sea, he decided to open the panel above the radio area and, in goggles and helmet, stuck his head out and watched the approach to Africa. They landed at 5 p.m., just as a dozen German Ju88s flew over at around 6,000 feet. Anti-aircraft guns, already in place, started pumping shells into the sky as the bombers dived on the harbour. As Clark clambered out of his plane, he could hear the dull crump of bombs exploding. Then the Spitfires were upon them. 'Everywhere around us,' noted Clark, 'Americans and British ran out onto the field, yelling and cheering the Spits on.' He watched one of the Junkers belch black smoke and plunge down, then ran into the aerodrome building just as a stick of three bombs landed within a few hundred yards of *Red Gremlin*.

Clark now hurried into the city and made for the St George Hotel, conscious of a very palpable sense of uncertainty and turmoil in the air. At the hotel, he met a grim-faced General Doc Ryder, who said, 'I'm glad you're here. I've stalled them off about as long as I can.' Robert Murphy appeared, urging a greater demonstration of force throughout the city. He wanted tanks, but these had yet to arrive; air power would have to suffice. Clark also quickly learned that neither Darlan nor Juin, nor a number of other French commanders, were willing to see Giraud; his standing was falling rapidly. Rather, it was crystal clear to Clark that it was Amiral Darlan who was the pre-eminent Frenchman in Vichy North Africa.

Formal talks, however, did not begin until the following morning, 10 November. The meeting was long and protracted. Clark thought Darlan seemed nervous and uncertain, anxious about which peg he should hang his coat on. He was also worried about taking responsibility for the inevitable German occupation of the rest of France. Eventually, however, late in the morning, he agreed to issue an order for all French troops in North Africa to observe an immediate ceasefire.

Soon after came word from Vichy that Darlan had been sacked as C-in-C in North Africa, which then prompted an immediate change of heart from the Amiral on his earlier pledge. 'You will do nothing of the kind,' Clark told him firmly, and placed him under immediate house arrest. Uneasy peace now reigned in Algeria, but fighting was continuing in French Morocco, where Général Charles Noguès had been named by Pétain as Darlan's successor. 'The only tough nut left is in your hands,'

Eisenhower signalled to Patton on the 10th. 'Crack it open quickly and ask for what you want.'

Now armed with Eisenhower's signal, Patton decided it was time to do just that. Sherman tanks from Safi approached the southern outskirts of Casablanca, while his infantry were to the north. Offshore, US warships and aircraft carriers waited. He was prepared to reduce the city to rubble early the following morning. 'God favors the bold,' he scribbled in his diary that evening, 'victory is to the audacious.'

Patton was in his hotel in Fedala when, at around 4.20 the following morning, 11 November, news arrived that the airfield at Port Lyautey had finally fallen and that a dispatch had arrived from Général Noguès announcing that a general ceasefire had been ordered. Patton's staff wanted him to call off his planned attack on Casablanca, but he was having none of it – not until the French Navy made it clear they would honour the ceasefire too.

The French took it to the wire. US Navy dive-bombers had already taken off and the American warships' guns were primed and ready, when, at 6.40 a.m., the French Navy finally surrendered. Soon after, US troops marched into Casablanca. 'A nice birthday present,' noted Patton. He was fifty-seven.

With that, the invasion was over. French North Africa was now in Allied hands once more. The fighting had been patchy and, at times, a little sticky, but as a feat of logistics and planning, it proved the Allies were already in a league of their own. It had been achieved in an incredibly short time and over truly astonishing distances. Nothing like it had been attempted by any force ever before, and yet in little over three months an embryonic plan had evolved into an operation involving nearly 700 ships, 70,000 troops and over 1,000 aircraft. Unquestionably, many hard lessons had been learned, but it was a monumental achievement by new coalition partners working together in a way that two independent nations had never attempted before. The level of co-operation and the sheer scale of troops, but particularly materiel, involved was a warning to the Axis of what was to come.

PART IV

CRUSHING THE WOLFPACKS

CHAPTER 35

The Blackest Month

IN JUNE 1942, U-boats out in the Atlantic had sunk a whopping 636,926 tons of Allied shipping, most of which had been off the Americas. This was the most the U-boats had destroyed so far in the war in a single month but was only the third time they had exceeded 500,000 tons a month, Admiral Dönitz's original estimate of the tonnage they needed to sink every month to bring Britain to her knees.

That figure had originally been based on Dönitz's pre-war estimates, which in turn had been worked out on the assumption that Britain would continue importing most of the food she needed. Since then, however, food imports had halved, another million acres of land had been reclaimed and the 1942 harvest had yielded more than 80 million tons, up from 53 million the previous year. In contrast, in Germany each harvest had been down on those of 1935–9.

Despite the dramatic rise in tonnage for the British harvest of 1942, the weather had not been especially kind: a lovely June had given way to rain and insufficient sunshine in August. In September, the weather had continued to be mostly unfavourable. On his farm at Ditchampton, near Wilton in Wiltshire, A. G. Street had to watch from his sickbed with phlebitis in his thigh. Taking over the mantle was his daughter, Pamela, who managed to get compassionate leave from her job as a nurse in the ATS. 'Barley carting – six ricks now – terrific,' she noted in her diary on 9 September. 'Quite a lot of volunteers from the Signals.' They continued to turn up in good numbers until the harvest was completely gathered in. The weather might not have helped, but many hands certainly did.

At any rate, Britain was not facing a food crisis as Germany was, and the shipping space created by fewer food imports could be used for other war-related materials and supplies. Dönitz had realized some time earlier that his half a million a month figure was way off and so had now revised the figure to 800,000 per month.

In July, Dönitz had decided to transfer the weight of his U-boats back to the mid-Atlantic. Now that the US had introduced the convoy system at long last, there was not much point in going to such efforts to send the bulk of his U-boats all the way across the far side of the ocean. Furthermore, the B-Dienst, the Kriegsmarine's code-breaking unit, had managed to penetrate the British convoy cipher, which meant it was once again possible for wolfpacks to operate together by lying in wait for convoys to appear. Even better for the U-boat crews, in the mid-Atlantic they still remained out of range of Allied aircraft.

None the less, the 'Happy Times' were now well and truly over. Dönitz was finally getting the numbers of U-boats he had been demanding for years, but all the experienced crews had gone. Even Erich Topp and Teddy Suhren, survivors both, were no longer available to him; quite rightly, he had accepted their immense experience was of even greater use in helping to prepare the rookie captains now heading out to sea. This was another of the legacies of not building a larger U-boat arm before the war; now that expansion was finally happening, there was not enough experience to make the increase in numbers really count. A pitifully small number of the 3,000 men of the 1939 BdU remained to take these new boats out to sea.

At the same time, the technological gulf was widening almost on a monthly basis. Eleven U-boats were sunk in the Atlantic in July, ten in August, a further eleven in September and sixteen in October. After his final patrol, Teddy Suhren was ordered to Berlin to receive his Swords to his Knight's Cross from Hitler in person. He was part of the same awards ceremony as Rommel and after the Feldmarschall had emerged from Hitler's inner sanctum at the Reich Chancellery, Suhren was called in.

Suhren was not a man to be easily cowed, and he was also someone who liked to talk pretty straight. The Führer clearly wanted to sound him out about his hopes for the BdU, so when Suhren was asked whether he thought the U-boats could increase the number of enemy ships they were sinking, he pulled no punches. 'The enemy, I am quite convinced,' he told Hitler, 'has radar in its planes. That means he can detect us much

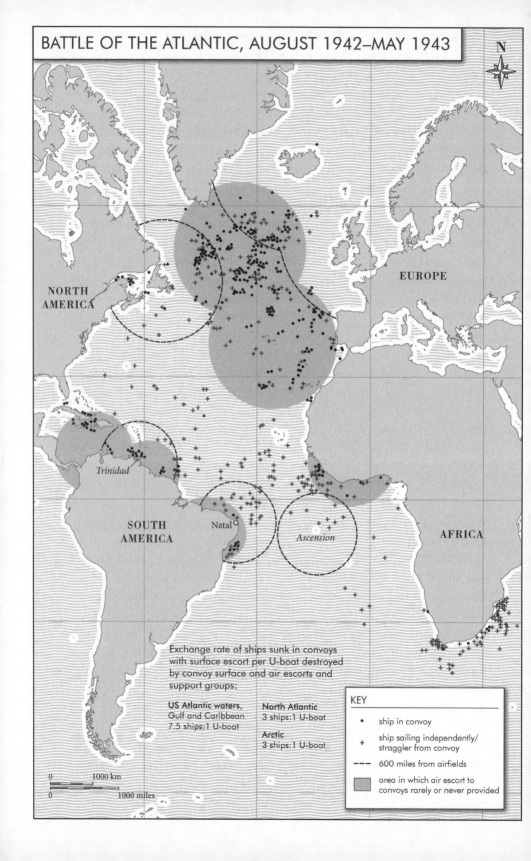

BATTLE OF THE ATLANTIC, AUGUST 1942–MAY 1943

N

NORTH
AMERICA

EUROPE

Trinidad

SOUTH
AMERICA

Natal

Ascension

AFRICA

Exchange rate of ships sunk in convoys
with surface escort per U-boat destroyed
by convoy surface and air escorts and
support groups:

**US Atlantic waters,
Gulf and Caribbean**
7.5 ships:1 U-boat

North Atlantic
3 ships:1 U-boat

Arctic
3 ships:1 U-boat

0   1000 km

0   1000 miles

KEY

•   ship in convoy

+   ship sailing independently/
    straggler from convoy

--- 600 miles from airfields

▓   area in which air escort to
    convoys rarely or never provided

earlier; trying to get ahead of a convoy by day is getting very difficult, and it just about rules out the sort of surface attacks by night that we have made up to now.' Hitler seemed taken aback. Couldn't they defend themselves, he wanted to know? Suhren explained that their guns were not ideal – they jammed easily and the platform, bobbing about on the sea, was hardly very stable either. They talked on, so that by the time Suhren was dismissed twenty minutes had passed. He left convinced that the Führer had only the shakiest grasp of naval warfare. 'He found submarines a bit of a mystery,' Suhren commented. 'In the past, this had made it difficult for the BdU to push through its demands. On the other hand, both Party and State left us in peace. And this was no bad thing.' Suhren's assessment was spot on, and was why the U-boat arm had been so terribly under-strength at the start of the war. Hitler simply had never understood naval power; he had chosen to build a surface fleet of capital ships largely because enormous battleships more obviously projected strength and power. After all, submarines hardly looked very impressive. U-boats, however, had been his best chance of crushing Britain in the first year of the war. Had he had the numbers available to him now in 1939 or even by 1940, the war may well have developed very differently. But in the autumn of 1942 it was too late.

Of course, Suhren was quite right about onboard radar, and said as much to Dönitz too. He and others had been slow to realize it because they were not aware that the British had developed the cavity magnetron. Not one agent had yet successfully penetrated Britain and so they were dependent on radio listening, aerial reconnaissance and cipher decryption. None of those forms of intelligence gathering had yet revealed the cavity magnetron or, indeed, a host of other inventions, or even Allied intelligence breakthroughs of their own.

As it was, small, onboard radar was only one of a number of technological developments now available to the Allies. In addition to ASW radar and Huff-Duff, the Americans were now developing Magnetic Anomaly Detectors (MAD). These were able to pick up changes in the earth's magnetic field caused by large metal objects – such as U-boats – and could do so from the air. The Americans were also developing air-launched acoustic homing torpedoes and also air-launched sonobuoys. These were disposable sonars that were dropped into the sea and could then detect the precise whereabouts of a U-boat and relay radio pulses back to the aircraft. On top of that, the British were starting to equip aircraft with rockets that had an armour-piercing warhead that could puncture a submarine pressure hull. These would all be coming into service soon and were really sophisticated, advanced bits of kit, which demonstrated the vital importance the Allies attached to the trans-Atlantic sea-lanes.

And there were new weapons that were already in place, such as the British 'Hedgehog'. This piece of weaponry threw out a pattern of twenty-four small contact-fused bombs, each containing 15 kilograms of TNT, ahead of a ship that was hunting a U-boat. The big drawback of ASDIC was that its beam was thrown out in an arc, which became deeper the further away it was from the sonar, and which meant that directly under an escort vessel, a U-boat could not be detected. This meant that more often than not, depth charges were thrown blind, on a guess as to where the U-boat was likely to be. Hedgehog, however, threw the charges forward, where a detected U-boat was still in ASDIC range, which in turn meant Hedgehog could be fired more accurately. It was not easy to use, but crews were training hard with it and it promised a much-improved increase in strike rate.

For Commander Donald Macintyre, still plying back and forth across the Atlantic and commanding B2 Escort Group, these improvements had massively reduced the risks to both themselves and the ships they were protecting. Nearly all the convoys he escorted into the autumn of 1942 crossed the Atlantic unscathed. U-boats, he now realized, could attack only at very great risk to themselves. From the Allied perspective, this was all to the good, but for the escorts it meant very long days and nights with little or no action, which in turn chipped away at morale. 'Boredom and monotony,' he wrote, 'were a very real problem to contend with.'

As autumn now, in November, gave way to full-blown winter, so the greatest danger for the Navy became the grey Atlantic itself. Once more, they had to battle high winds, rain and rough seas. On one occasion, Macintyre's ship, HMS *Hesperus*, was trying to top up her fuel from one of the tankers they were escorting, but in a worsening gale and at night. During this difficult operation, one of his crew was swept overboard. At once the alarm was given, but in the swell there was no chance of putting down a lifeboat. Instead, Macintyre ordered a searchlight to be trained on the man, then they brought the ship alongside him. David Seeley, one of his officers, was lowered on a rope with a lifebuoy around his waist to try to pull the man aboard. After successfully grabbing the fellow, Seeley hauled him up only for the man to slip from his grasp at the last moment. He was never seen again.

Also now steaming across the Atlantic on escort duty was Lieutenant-Commander Vere Wight-Boycott, who had been given command of the destroyer HMS *Ilex* in the summer, picking it up in Charleston, in South Carolina, in early August. After refitting and working up, Wight-Boycott and his crew were on their way to Trinidad for refuelling before joining a convoy in the mid-Atlantic that was heading from the UK to Brazil.

Wight-Boycott was pleased with his officers, who were, three years into the war, typical of the disparate and wide-ranging backgrounds found in a wartime destroyer. His No. 1 – first lieutenant – was a Regular, young but 'very sound'. His navigator was RNVR, a chemist for ICI before joining up, but 'keen'. He also had a young red setter puppy, which Wight-Boycott had allowed on board and which kept them all amused. The sub-lieutenant had just had his twentieth birthday and was a good Dartmouth College entrant; Wight-Boycott rated him too. His temporary sub-lieutenant was another RNVR man, who had run a jewellery shop off Bond Street in London before being called up. 'A nice chap,' noted Wight-Boycott, 'and he has the business of cyphers well weighed off.'

However, this first escorting voyage was also marred by tragedy. One of the ordinary seamen became sick with a lung infection. The RNVR doctor on board did his best to help him but realized the man needed an operation there and then. The doctor did not have the skills to use proper anaesthetic, so gave the lad a local instead, which knocked him out all right – but only for a bit. Halfway through the operation, the man awoke and in his shock and agony knocked all the doctor's paraphernalia off the table. It took them three-quarters of an hour to sterilize everything again and the doctor then managed to finish the operation. Sadly, however, the patient died the following day. Even when not plagued by U-boats, life on the oceans could be very tough and very cruel.

Despite the heightened tension in the Mediterranean, and despite the known massed Allied convoys steaming into those waters, on 8 November Hitler left the Wolf's Lair at lunchtime to visit Munich, where he planned to give his annual Beer Hall Putsch speech to the party faithful in the

Löwenbräukeller. After flying to Berlin, he boarded his train, *Amerika*, but this was halted in Thuringia for him to be given news of the Allied landings, which came as a complete and shocking surprise. After berating the Luftwaffe for their lack of planning and, of course, overlooking his own unwillingness to take the threat to north-west Africa seriously, he gave orders for the defence of Tunis and rapid build-up of forces there.

Further down the track, von Ribbentrop joined the Führer's train and urged Hitler to allow him to put out peace feelers with Stalin via the Soviet Embassy in Stockholm. This, Hitler dismissed. Later, in his speech in Munich, he was even more emphatic. 'From now on,' he told them, 'there will be no more offer of peace.' In fact, the speech was dominated by the same uncompromising view he had always maintained. There could be no alternative to complete success. Final victory was certain. Only a few pockets of resistance remained in Stalingrad; it would soon be entirely in German hands. In North Africa they were in retreat, but so what? It was only desert – they would soon be charging eastwards again. The gulf between rhetoric and reality was huge.

General Warlimont heard the news of the Allied landings on his radio at home and very soon after received a call from the OKW ordering him to go to Vichy to organize the defence of north-west Africa in collaboration with the French. Hurrying to Munich, he located the Führer's train but it seemed empty. He wondered where everyone was, then eventually found Jodl, who told him he was not after all to go to Vichy; Hitler had decided the French could no longer be trusted. Instead, he was urgently needed back at his old job. 'In a crisis like this,' noted Warlimont, 'I could do no other than conform.'

Installing himself in a small sleeping compartment on the train, he collected what information he could and began working out the initial orders for the creation of a bridgehead around Tunis and for the occupation of all France. Both operations would be, it went without saying, a further drain on resources and manpower.

In Rome, Count Ciano was woken at 5.30 a.m. on 8 November by a call from von Ribbentrop telling him of the Allied landings. Ciano thought he sounded nervous. He asked Ciano what the Italians planned to do. 'I must confess,' wrote Ciano, 'that, having been caught unawares, I was too sleepy to give a very satisfactory answer.'

Later, having freshened up and got his wits together, he met with

Il Duce, who was 'lively', then with Generale Cesare Amè, the head of SIM. Amé was not only possibly the best-informed senior Italian but also one who had repeatedly demonstrated a firm strategic grasp and a healthy dose of realism, and he now told Ciano in no uncertain terms just how bad the outlook had become. As matters stood, he said, they could expect the Allies to rush eastwards, take Libya, then press into Tunisia. Once North Africa was in Allied hands, Italy would inevitably become the next focus of their intentions. 'Amé says that army morale is dramatically low,' added Ciano.

The following day, Ciano was summoned to Munich, where Hitler told him his plan to occupy France and build up the bridgehead in Tunisia. From there, they all moved on to Berchtesgaden, where the Führer had unhelpfully decided he needed to retreat for some strategic contemplation. This meant that large numbers of staff officers also had to move there, around a secondary Reich Chancellery that had been built on the edge of the town. The main meetings took place over 10–11 November. Pierre Laval had also been invited, but was not told of plans to occupy France; that came on his way home, by which time the occupation process had already begun. Ciano thought Laval seemed utterly out of his depth.

While there were those urging Hitler to abandon North Africa entirely, the Führer was having none of it. He had always been obsessed with the Mediterranean because of his paranoia about the Allies striking from the south – the soft underbelly, as Churchill had called it – and taking the Ploesti oilfields, but also threatening the southern Reich. This was why he had intervened in the Balkans, Greece and on Crete; it was why he had sent Rommel to shore up the Italians back in February 1941. These interventions had always come at a really bad time, when men and materiel were more urgently needed elsewhere, but the truth was, the cracks were multiplying and there was no longer enough of anything to fulfil the ever-increasing commitments.

For the most part, wars tend to end because one side realizes it can no longer win. Hitler had refused to accept this the previous December and he again refused to accept it now at this moment of crisis. However, having decided they must fight on, then reinforcing Tunisia was an obvious course of action. Geographically, Tunis and Bizerte were further north than southern Sicily and the stretch of sea between the two was only around 100 miles. Of all the places in North Africa for the Axis to reinforce, Tunisia was the easiest. By doing so, Hitler hoped to avoid any Italian collapse, which would have been truly catastrophic. Tunisia had become, in his mind, 'the cornerstone' of Germany's conduct of the war on the southern front. It was another place on the map that was to be held at all costs. That meant sending forces in strength. Now that it was winter once more in the East, and despite the ongoing fighting around Stalingrad, the timing was at least better than it would have been in high summer.

Responsibility for overseeing this rapid build-up lay with Feldmarschall Kesselring, who wasted no time at all. Bomber units were ordered to Sardinia and Sicily, from where they could attack ports in Algeria newly secured by the Allies. In addition, he sent a team to negotiate with the French authorities in Tunis, along with a parachute regiment, his own HQ Battalion, and a number of Me109s and Stukas. These landed at El Aouina airfield on the edge of Tunis and – although the French commander hastily flew to Algiers, where he reported that over forty German aircraft had landed unopposed – the French forces there simply sat back and watched. Two days later, German *Fallschirmjäger* took over Bizerte airfield on the north coast as well.

Within two weeks of the Allied landings, some 11,000 Axis troops had reached Tunisia, hastily drawn from Sicily and France, including not only *Fallschirmjäger* but also panzer grenadier units – that is, motorized infantry and armour. The Italian Special Brigade was shifted from Tripoli and partly made up from remnants of the battle-hardened Ariete Division. On 14 November, General Nehring, wounded at Alam Halfa but now recovered, arrived to take command. He was still living danger-ously, though, because his pilot crash-landed their plane; but this time Nehring survived unscathed. By 24 November, 10. Panzerdivision had also reached Tunisia, along with a number of brand-new Tiger tanks. This rapid build-up proved what German and Italian logisticians could achieve when there was full support from Hitler and considerably shorter lines of communication. What's more, Kesselring, unlike Rommel, had always had a very good operational understanding, and had also con-sistently worked hard to keep his Italian peers on side – again, a contrast with Rommel. This was now paying off.

Back in 1940, the French military leadership had been indecisive, slow to act, and had been caught out by a German Army and Air Force operating with far greater speed and singleness of purpose than they were. It seemed not much had changed in the intervening years. First Giraud had chopped and changed and prevaricated. Then Darlan had blown hot and cold. In Tunisia, the French commander at El Aouina had fled at the first sign of Germans arriving. The French governor, Amiral Jean-Pierre Esteva, also failed to act decisively, unsure how to respond to contradictory instructions from Algiers and Vichy, and instead he opted for neutrality. Général Georges Barré, the commander of the Tunisian Division in northern Tunisia, quickly retreated with his troops away from the plains around Tunis and into the hills between Medjez el Bab and Béja.

Allied efforts to persuade the French in Tunisia to hold firm and resist the Axis build-up had fallen on entirely deaf ears, the situation exacerbated by disunity and dithering on the part of Darlan and others. Darlan, especially, was continuing to prevaricate – refusing to order the French Fleet in Toulon and Tunis to come over and join the Allies, then changing his mind, then switching it back again and saying he could not do so until Général Noguès arrived from French Morocco. Finally, on 13 November, with Eisenhower and Admiral Cunningham now arrived in Algiers – and also Noguès – a deal was agreed. In an atmosphere that Cunningham for one found electric, Darlan announced he would head the civil and political government of all French North Africa, while Noguès would remain Governor of French Morocco. Giraud would become C-in-C of all French forces, which he would mobilize to help fight the Axis. Eisenhower and Cunningham then headed back to Gibraltar, while Clark, newly promoted again to lieutenant-general after his crucial part in the invasion and the negotiations that had followed, was left to give a press conference. 'The past four days,' he told reporters, 'have been difficult. We have had to keep looking back over our shoulder instead of to the front in Tunisia. Now we can proceed in a business-like way.'

The Darlan Deal, however, did not go down well, especially in Britain but not in the American media either. 'Are we fighting Nazis or sleeping with them?' asked Ed Murrow on CBS. Darlan was anti-Semitic, a known Anglophobe, and had willingly cosied up to the Axis. And while these political machinations had been taking up far too much time, the baton of initiative had been passed back to the Germans, whose supply lines into the Tunisian bridgehead were now shorter than those of the Allies.

Algiers to Tunis was 560 miles; Casablanca to Tunis was 1,500. Admiral Cunningham, for one, had been a strong advocate of landing at Bizerte, but during planning that extra 500 miles into the Mediterranean had seemed a risk too far. None the less, the time to nip the enemy build-up in Tunisia in the bud had been in those very same first few days, and that opportunity had been missed. The Allies, whose every item had to come from overseas and who were still unloading in the Algerian ports, now faced some tough fighting ahead – fighting that was likely to be a lot harder than they had faced from the Vichy French.

None the less, now that the Darlan Deal had been struck, there was an acceptance, as Clark had made clear to the press, that there was no longer a moment to lose. The landings may have been made by mostly American troops, but overall command of the land battle now reverted to Lieutenant-General Kenneth Anderson, the British commander of the newly formed First Army, who had flown to Algiers with Clark on 9 November. Patton's forces were mostly to remain in French Morocco for the time being, but the rest – the Rangers, the 34th Red Bulls and the Big Red One included – were part of US II Corps, now attached to the British First Army. Yet as General Anderson was quick to point out, First Army had not arrived in Algeria 'fully formed like Aphrodite' but, rather, grew steadily as fortnightly convoys arrived. This meant the initial thrust into Tunisia had to be made by a cobbled-together mixture of British paratroopers, Commandos and the first elements of the British 78th Division, which were starting to arrive.

No one, however, had doubted the important part air power was going to play, while capturing airfields and ports and building up strength as quickly as possible were also crucial in the race for Tunis that was about to unfold. Allied air forces had been stacking up at Gibraltar, so much so that the place resembled a giant aircraft carrier crammed with pilots and planes. With Maison Blanche and other airfields now clear, however, squadrons were beginning to arrive in quick succession.

Among those now at Maison Blanche were 225 Squadron RAF, designated as tactical reconnaissance. This meant they operated at low heights, carrying out important photographic and general recon- naissance work but also shooting up any targets they might spy during the course of a sortie. As such, they were among the first to fly over. Equipped with brand-new Hurricanes, which were robust, provided a sturdy gun platform and were better at lower heights, most of the squadron had flown straight to Maison Blanche from Gibraltar. Four, however, had escorted some Dakotas to Oran, and among those pilots was 21-year-old New Zealander Ken Neill.

Neill was a farmer's son, brought up on a large farm on South Island in the 1920s and 1930s, a world away from the turbulent events brewing in Europe and elsewhere. But the war, when it came, caught up even with people like him, living as he was in a degree of isolation in the stunning, open farmland of rural New Zealand. 'I wasn't one of those people dying to get into the fray,' he admitted, 'but I could see that I was going to have to get involved.' With the support of his father, who had survived being a soldier during the First World War, he decided to wait until he was nineteen and then join the Royal New Zealand Air Force, despite having never even seen an aircraft airborne before.

Training in New Zealand had been followed by a long sea voyage to England, where, after completing his Operational Training Unit, he had finally been posted to 225 Squadron. Neill had been delighted – he had been desperate to fly fighters. He had arrived just as the squadron was converting on to new American Mustangs, which he liked well enough, but no sooner had they done so than they were told they were being posted overseas and would have to convert again, this time to Hurricanes. They had travelled up to Glasgow ready for shipping out, but first had been given a briefing in a large hall. 'And in came these ex-Battle of Britain pilots,' said Neill, 'all wings and gongs. Fellows you'd heard of and admired all these years.' It had been hard not to feel a little over-awed.

After a long sea voyage, a couple of days in Gibraltar and a flight low over the Mediterranean, he touched down safely at La Senia, to the south of Oran. But it was getting dark and it was too late to fly on to Maison Blanche. Facilities at the airfield were sparse, to say the least, and so they ended up bedding down in a joinery next to the airfield. This, they soon discovered, was full of out-sized rats and so, not wanting his ears nibbled as he slept, Neill spent his first night on African soil sleeping in a coffin. 'But,' he added, 'we were soon to discover there were a lot worse than rats in North Africa.'

Further airfields were swiftly taken. British airborne troops seized Souk el Arba in the north-west of Tunisia on the 16th, while US paratroopers were also sent to the front. After the fiasco of 8 November, and now all together once again, they successfully captured Youks-les-Bains airfield further south on the Algerian border; there was not much wrong with the troops – it was the transportation that was the issue. A day later, on the 17th, they occupied the landing ground at Gafsa in southern Tunisia. These were all very important and entirely successful operations. None the less, Bône, on the coast near the western Tunisian border, was the only one with all-weather runways. This was where 225 Squadron moved on the 17th, but by then the weather was starting to close in, with days of wind and rain. Like southern Europe, winter can be cold, wet and pretty grim.

Hurrying into northern Tunisia were elements of the newly arrived 78th Division, advancing on three different roads towards the port of Bizerte and to the towns of Béja and Medjez el Bab. These troops clashed with German *Fallschirmjäger* at Djebel Abiod on the Bizerte road on 17 November. The Germans were pushed back, but with heavy casualties on both sides. British paratroopers then destroyed a German armoured reconnaissance force near Sidi Nsir the following day. Général Barré's French troops also clashed against German forces for the first time since 1940.

But while the Allied troops were holding their own against the Germans, they were not making much headway either. By 21 November, they were within 25 miles of Tunis and 50 of Bizerte, but a feature of the fighting was how many Luftwaffe aircraft seemed to be supporting the German troops on the ground. And it was making all the difference.

Nor was the terrain helping much. While the southern half of the country dipped into the Sahara, the northern half was very Mediterranean. Along the north coast were dense cork forests, while further inland were rolling hills and valleys lined with olive groves, wheatfields and vineyards; nearly 2,000 years earlier, the Medjerda Valley had supplied much of Ancient Rome's wheat. French colonials occupied most of the coastal towns, but further inland and to the south the area was peopled mainly by Arabs. Two ranges of mountains ran through the country: the Grande Dorsale, running diagonally north-east to south-west, and the Eastern Dorsale, north–south inland but to the east of the country and roughly parallel to the coast. Between the sea and the Eastern Dorsale, it was flat and rather relentless. Needless to say, the hills and valleys of the north and the two chains of mountains most definitely favoured the defender, not the attacker.

General Anderson now prepared to make a further push to take Tunis and Bizerte, but with the worsening weather, increasing numbers of Axis troops and aircraft, that final push was looking as though it might, for the time being at any rate, prove a push too far. How the Allies would rue those early missed opportunities.

November 1942 was turning into a terribly black month for the Axis. They had been caught napping by the TORCH landings, and in the Caucasus had managed to get within one mile of Ordzhonikidze, the gateway to the Georgian Military Road and the great oilfields of the southern Caucasus, but then had been smashed back by a major Soviet counter-attack. They were caught short again on the Eastern Front on 19 November, when the Red Army launched Operation URANUS. Back in September, Stavka, the Soviet High Command, had realized that while General Paulus's German Sixth Army was tough enough, the flanks were much weaker. To the north, the Third Romanian Army was struggling through attrition and the onset of winter. To the south, the Fourth Romanian Army was just as weakened.

Poor German intelligence once again let them down. The build-up of Soviet forces to the north and south of Stalingrad had been hidden from them. When those troops attacked, in freezing fog and through thick snow-clouds like apocalyptic spectres, and with a kind of speed and fury that aped the German glory days of 1940, they caught the Axis completely off guard. Smashing through the two Romanian Armies, in just four days the two Soviet thrusts linked arms some 35 miles west of Stalingrad. Now trapped in the *Kettelschlacht* were Sixth Army and elements of the Fourth Panzerarmee. Some 250,000–275,000 men had been encircled. By the following day, 24 November, the Fourth Romanian Army had been destroyed, the Third Romanian pushed back more than 50 miles to the River Chir and a massive gap opened up between Army Group B to the north and Army Group A still in the Caucasus.

What was Hitler, still the German Army C-in-C, to do? Feldmarschall Erich von Manstein, now C-in-C of Army Group Don along the Stalingrad Front, understandably felt it imperative to get Sixth Army out. Frantic explorations were made as to whether the beleaguered German forces could be supplied by air until von Manstein could counter-attack with a relief force. Paulus reckoned he needed 750 tons of supplies a day. Göring ordered his commanders to supply 500 tons, and they informed him the maximum they could airlift was 350 tons, although that was weather permitting. In fact, Göring now had only 298 planes available and in the days that followed managed only around 100 tons a day. In the meantime, General Paulus had been ordered by the Führer to stand firm. There would be no withdrawal. Catastrophe beckoned.

CHAPTER 36

Setbacks

A T SHIPYARD RICHMOND NO. 2 in California, Clay Bedford had been a little bit sore to have been bested by Henry Kaiser's son, Edgar. With this in mind, he had sent round a flyer to his workforce titled, 'What's Oregon Got That We Haven't Got?' In it, he asked for ideas about how Richmond might regain the record of the fastest-ever-built ocean-going ship. He received more than 250 letters and suggestions about how construction might be speeded up. And so they set themselves a new challenge: to build one in half the time of the ten-day miracle ship. Theirs would be the five-day vessel.

Construction began on 7 November, with all the parts already pre-assembled and the workforce working round the clock. Twenty-four hours on, the keel was laid and the shell of the hull welded. Forty-eight hours in, the engine had been installed and the upper deck finished. By the end of the third day, deckhouses and masts were in place and the ship was already looking pretty well done.

The fourth day was spent wiring, finishing off the welding and paint-ing. Then, at 3.27 p.m. on 12 November, the latest Liberty ship, the *Robert E. Peary* – named after an intrepid American Arctic explorer – was launched into the sea. It had taken four days, fifteen hours and twenty-six minutes.

This was truly miraculous and was some solace for the shipping losses the Allies were to suffer that month. In all, 128 ships were sunk, 117 by U-boats, amounting to a staggering 802,160 tons, which was the first time Dönitz's crew had managed to reach the magic 800,000-ton monthly target. It was a significant number of losses, but most were independents and stragglers, plying their trade primarily to the United States; the majority had been sunk in the south-east Atlantic and Caribbean, where too many ships were still travelling out of convoy.

Even so, thirty-nine had been sunk in the Atlantic, and most of those along the mid-Atlantic air gap, and that was a worry at a time in the war when there could be no let-up in the supply of war materiel to Britain and North Africa.

There were a number of reasons for this dramatic surge in sinkings. The first was technological. A new radar receiver had been developed in Germany called *Metox*. It was pretty crude, but gave U-boats warning of airborne metric wavelength radar. By the autumn it had become safe again for U-boats to operate on the surface. What's more, new Ju88c long-range aircraft were getting the better of Allied planes operating over the Bay of Biscay, which meant that was a safer area for U-boats too. *Metox* was also able, however, to pick up transmissions of metric radar on ships. Most British escorts had long since done away with such old-school radar equipment, but not so the Canadians, and they were responsible for 35 per cent of the escorts operating in the mid-Atlantic.

From the moment the Royal Canadian Navy entered the Battle of the Atlantic, its ships and crews had been horribly over-stretched, and that was perhaps more the case than ever in the autumn of 1942, when so many British and US warships were involved in the TORCH landings and so not available for normal Atlantic escort duty. Lieutenant Dick Pearce was No. 1 on HMCS *Arvida* even though he was still only twenty-one and despite having only joined his first ship earlier in the year. The captain was also only a lieutenant. The strain on Pearce, his fellow officers and crew was immense. 'In my year-plus in *Arvida*,' he said, 'I saw more sinkings and picked up more survivors than I can begin to count . . . The carnage was dreadful.'

At one point, *Arvida* had the somewhat unwanted record of having picked up more men from the water than any other ship. *Arvida* was part of Escort Group C4 during Convoy ON127 when they ran into a large U-boat pack in the mid-Atlantic air gap on 10 September. Despite having ASDIC, it was not enough to sweep the entire convoy area at all times and before they knew it, *U-96* had sunk three ships in broad daylight. The escorts began furiously sweeping the area, but only one of the ships had Huff-Duff and the set was defective. For four days the battle raged.

Just after 2 a.m. on the 14th, the destroyer *Ottawa* was hit amidships by *U-91* and blew up, the ship silhouetted against the night sky by the orange glow of the fire-burst, the air suddenly rich with the stench of smoke and explosives, like a particularly bad rotten egg. *Ottawa* went down almost immediately. *Arvida* hurried to the scene to look for survivors but steamed through a large group of them. By the time Dick Pearce and the officers on the bridge heard their cries it was too late to stop, so they had to make a large circle around and come back for them. By that time, the combination of the freezing water and suffocating film of oil had already killed a number of men. Several of *Arvida*'s crew took ropes and dived into the oily water to help the rescue. Nets were also thrown over the side. In all, *Arvida* and her fellow escort *Celandine* picked up only sixty-two of *Ottawa*'s crew and just seven men from *Empire Oil*, who had been saved earlier in the convoy when their ship had gone down. 'It was a tragedy that haunted us all,' said Pearce, who gave up both clothing and his sleeping space for the survivors. By the time *Arvida* finally reached port, they had over 150 on board a vessel designed for eighty-five. In all, ON127 had lost seven ships on that hellish run.

Experience and decent equipment, of course, made a massive difference, which was why during the entire autumn of 1942 Commander Donald Macintyre did not lose a single ship in convoy. For the embattled Canadians, however, continuing above and beyond the call of duty, more Huff-Duff was needed, and newer radar, and some slack taken from their overworked crews. This would come, but it was not there in October and November when escort carriers and other shipping was tied up with the TORCH landings.

Allied shipping could materially cope with these losses and, with Liberty ships being built with such astonishing rapidity, new boats were outnumbering those sunk, but a greater concern was for the crews. Winter had arrived and with it not just the fear of U-boats but also the perils of the cruel sea. The dreaded Arctic convoys had resumed as well now that summer was over. That more than 80 per cent of all convoys were getting through entirely unscathed and that only a tiny proportion of the total number of ships that sailed were being sunk did little to bolster the morale of crews who were repeatedly hacking back and forth across these terrifying seas. The thought that a U-boat might strike at any moment or that one might die a horrible and lonely death in the middle of the grey Atlantic worsened when large numbers of Allied ships were being sent to the bottom. Admiral Dönitz now wondered whether he could push merchant crews to the point of mutiny.

Something had to be done. Western Approaches Command had a new C-in-C. No one could doubt the achievements of Admiral Percy Noble since taking command back in 1940, but, as with the removal of Air Chief Marshal Sir Hugh Dowding from RAF Fighter Command after the Battle of Britain, it was felt it was time for some new blood and fresh ideas. These were to come from Admiral Sir Max Horton, a submariner of exceptional experience and a man who was ideally placed to understand the mind of the U-boat commander. Full of drive and energy, he knew he had to inject some new ideas and new approaches into the Battle of the Atlantic and in quick order. Dönitz now had as many as ninety U-boats operating at one time; the technological gap had, in part, briefly closed; and winter was the best killing time for submarines. The weak links, Horton swiftly realized, were the mid-Atlantic air gap and the training and technological gap between the Royal Navy escorts and those of the Canadians. The outcome of the Atlantic battle was not in doubt – superior Allied production, technology and, for much of the time, intelligence ensured that – but suddenly it was threatening to set the Allies back, with a knock-on effect in all other theatres. That could not be allowed to happen. Somehow, then, both these issues had to be solved. And soon.

On 8 November, Henri Frenay had been in the midst of shaving when he was rung by Colonel Passy's BCRAM headquarters to tell him the Allies had landed in French North Africa. The situation, he was told, was confused. Soon after, the telephone rang again. It was Sir Charles Hambro, one of the directors of SOE, who wanted to know whether Frenay would be willing to fly to Algiers that very night to try to build a bridge between Giraud and de Gaulle. Frenay replied that he would gladly go, but only if sanctioned by de Gaulle.

The Free French leader was having none of it, however. If Frenay was to go, it would be with others, as part of a delegation. 'We must show Giraud that the French freedom fighters have formed a united front,' de Gaulle told him, 'that the Resistance and the Free French are marching in step under de Gaulle's leadership.'

When Frenay returned to his hotel, he rang Sir Charles Hambro. 'Ahhh,' came the icy reply. 'That's not exactly what I had in mind.'

Rather, it had been hoped that Frenay might play the lone and under-stated representative of de Gaulle, demonstrating respect and helping to inflate Giraud's ego. As it happened, Darlan had then stepped into the ring and Giraud had been relegated.

However, both Giraud and Darlan had been courted by the Allies purely for political expediency. They, rather than de Gaulle, had been far better placed to help win over resistance to the Allied landings than the Free French leader. Furthermore, Roosevelt had taken a sharp dislike to what he had heard about Général de Gaulle; the outbursts, the perceived arrogance, the endless demands for arms, for money, for respect had all sat badly with the President.

That Giraud had managed to get away from France on HMS *Seraph* in the first place, however, had only been possible because of the risks taken by the Alliance circuit in southern France. Yet in transmitting details about Giraud to London, the Alliance resistance group fatally com-promised themselves and in the following days the entire leadership was arrested. Now, it seemed, it had been all for nothing, because Giraud had been cut adrift in favour of Darlan.

For the Americans, especially, the Darlan Deal had been *Realpolitik* and nothing more, yet while the liberation of France had taken a step closer with the Allied landings, in the short term life was about to become a greater deal harder for most French citizens. German troops now swept into the unoccupied zones, adding to the sense of oppression. When Henri Frenay heard that the enemy had crossed the demarcation line and started occupying the southern zone, he realized that, for him and his friends in the resistance, the battle was about to change radically. And so it was.

Without delay, the RSHA sent a KdS of six sections to Lyons, known to the Germans as a hot-bed of the French resistance movement. Commanding the SD in Lyons was Hauptsturmführer Rolf Müller, but leading Section VI – Intelligence – was a particularly zealous Nazi and anti-Semite, Obersturmführer Klaus Barbie. From Godesberg in the Rhineland, Barbie had been born out of wedlock to two teachers. They married three months later, but his illegitimacy was a terrible badge of shame that meant he could never legally inherit. His had been a hard childhood; being the son of teachers, he was expected to set an example. His father was also an alcoholic and abusive; the young Klaus was regularly beaten. Shy and studious, Barbie had been raised a devout

Catholic and had thought of becoming a priest, but then, having left school, developed aspirations to study theology and become an academic. As he was about to go to university, however, first his younger brother died of a chronic illness and then his father too. Because he was a bastard, his grandfather refused to give him any kind of family inheritance, so there was no money for university after all.

Instead, Barbie found himself drawn towards the Nazis. He was nineteen years old when Hitler came to power. 'The mighty national uprising,' he said, 'drew me, like every German youth, along in its wake.' While serving in the Reichsarbeitsdienst – Labour Service – he was recruited into the SD and by 1940 had become an Obersturmführer in the SS, the equivalent of a lieutenant. It was by no means a senior rank after five years in the SD, but he had worked his way up through the ranks from nothing and was now an officer. His record was exemplary and he had earned both status and authority over others. Proving himself a particularly diligent 'referent' – that is, an intelligence-gathering officer – in Amsterdam, he had then been posted to Dijon in May 1942, in the occupied zone. Now, in November, he was commanding his own intelligence section in Lyons, with 200 men under his command, nearly all of whom were French volunteers. 'I was only a lieutenant,' he said, 'but I had more power than a general.' Henri Frenay's prediction was about to be realized.

Frenay and Emmanuel d'Astier finally left London on 18 November after two earlier attempts at the end of October had been aborted by bad weather. Before they left, however, they had one last dinner with de Gaulle, Colonel Passy and others, including the resister Pierre Brossolette. Frenay and d'Astier would not be eating a dinner such as the Savoy could provide for some time to come, but as they ate and drank well they discussed the creation of an organization that could bind both resistance movements and the pre-war political parties. They might call it the Conseil national de la résistance – the National Council of the Resistance – or CNR for short. Frenay considered it a bad idea – he'd thought the fractious politics and useless coalitions of the Third Republic had been disastrous. The last thing France needed, he argued, was everyone endlessly arguing and disagreeing with one another.

'In that case,' said de Gaulle, 'we'd just have to try and find a way to work things out.'

'And if we failed,' Frenay retorted, 'we'd be up a one-way alley.'

'No. In that case, I'd just issue orders.'

It was de Gaulle's autocratic approach that lay at the heart of any unease on the part of men like Frenay, d'Astier and other young resistance leaders, and at this an uncomfortable silence fell over the table.

At last, Frenay said, 'We are resisters, free to think and do as we choose. Our freedom of choice is an inalienable right. It is up to us to decide whether, in the political domain, we shall carry out your orders or not.'

De Gaulle thought for a few moments, then said, 'Well then, Charvet, it seems that France must choose between you and me.'

Far away, in the glacial Hardangervidda in Norway, things were not going well for Jens-Anton Poulsson and his GROUSE team. In fact, it had started to go wrong the night they parachuted in because, having safely landed without mishap, they quickly realized they had been dropped not on the drop zone, but on a mountainside 10 miles west of where they should have been. Normally, this would have been no great setback, but between them they now had some 700 lb of equipment, food and other supplies. Some of it they stored, but compounding the problem was damage to their Primus stove. They needed heat – for food and for drying clothes – and that meant working out a new route, along lower slopes where there were still some trees and thus wood for making fires. Then, three days after their arrival, they were hit by a violent snowstorm. Temperatures plunged.

A mountain hut Poulsson and Haugland knew from childhood had gone, and their wireless was unable to make contact with London. Back in Britain, their superiors were growing anxious about what had happened to them. There were fears the entire mission had been compromised.

On 24 October, they finally reached a hut where they were able to have their first proper meal. Also inside the hut was a toboggan, which, by a bizarre coincidence, belonged to Poulsson. He had lost it at the start of the war, but there it was, in this hut in the middle of the Hardangervidda. He could not understand it, but it was, none the less, a very welcome discovery and certainly made their lives easier.

It was not until ten days had passed that they finally made radio contact with London. By that time they had also been spotted by local men looking for lost sheep. The GROUSE team had been ordered to shoot anyone who saw them, but Poulsson felt the men were true

Norwegians and so asked them not to breathe a word and let them pass. 'We knew the operation was very important,' he said, 'but it is difficult to shoot a man – to kill him.' It was a risk, but one, on balance, Poulsson felt was the right decision.

It had always been intended that the GROUSE party would be dropped on to the Hardangervidda just a short while before the gliders of FRESHMAN, but their delay in reaching the right drop zone as well as in making radio contact with London, and the need for clear weather and a moon, meant that it was not until an entire month later, on 19 November, that FRESHMAN was launched.

It was a disaster. The weather worsened suddenly and one of the Halifax tugs crashed into a mountain. Although the glider had been able to cast off in time, it crashed nearby, injuring a number of men; they would soon be picked up and taken prisoner. The other Halifax and glider pressed on, but although the weather suddenly improved and although they were actually where they should be, there was a failure between the GROUSE team's Eureka beacon on the ground and the Rebecca on the Halifax. Running low on fuel, the pilot decided to abort.

After being dazzled by the dash and elan of the German glider assault on the Belgian fort of Eben-Emael back in May 1940, the British had been determined to create their own glider force, but this first-ever British glider operation had been an unmitigated disaster. FRESHMAN had failed and proved just how difficult such operations were in anything other than extremely calm and balmy weather.

'It was a sad and bitter blow,' said Poulsson, 'not least because the weather was splendid over the following days.' They were told to stay on the Hardangervidda but were warned it was vitally important to ensure they remained safe; German troops and the Gestapo would now be on the alert. That meant retreating further into the wilderness and hunkering down. Poulsson and his team signalled for more information. 'Keep up your hearts,' came the reply. 'We will do the job yet.'

Meanwhile, over 2,000 miles away, the scattered remnants of the Panzerarmee continued to head west. As far as Adolf Lamm was concerned, it was still utter mayhem. At Sidi Barrani, near the Libyan border, his tank broke down. While they were trying to repair it, their *Leutnant* was posted somewhere else and the new tank commander was a sergeant Lamm disliked immediately.

Having got the tank going again, they trundled on up the Halfaya Pass, where they were strafed by enemy aircraft. Fortunately, they were not hit, but they saw a number of dead beside the road and realized the bodies had already been stripped of boots, clothing and other possessions. Thousands of flies swarmed over them.

They managed to reach Tobruk, but then ran out of petrol. Not far away was a camp with some provisions and also petrol, but part of the petrol was on fire, sending angry flames and thick black smoke into the air. They did spot a pile of intact jerrycans, but these, they discovered, were full of aviation fuel and so no use to them. 'A Panzer III needs about 300–400 litres of fuel per 100 kilometres,' wrote Lamm. 'A tank without petrol is worth shit.' And so they had to drive it off the road and ditch it. They all grabbed what clothes they had, plus blankets, and then Lamm, the loader and gunner were sent on their way to find an alternative means of transport while the sergeant and driver immobilized the tank.

Soon after, Lamm came down with diarrhoea and became detached from the rest of his crew. Eventually, and still only partially recovered, he caught a ride on an artillery gun mount, and so the flight west continued.

Major Hans von Luck was still to the south of the main retreat, watching out for any outflanking manoeuvres from their pursuers. Attached to his recce regiment was the Italian Nizza Armoured Reconnaissance Battalion. At first, he'd not been pleased as, like most Germans, he had a low opinion of Italians as fighting troops, but he was to be pleasantly surprised. They appeared to know what they were doing, and proved brave and fearless. Keeping his entire formation going was difficult, especially so far down to the south, although somehow von Luck's supply officer performed miracles in getting small convoys of fuel down to them. It meant very strict discipline, however. Half a litre of water per man per day – that was all – and minimal rations. It meant no washing and no shaving for a ten-day stretch, but that was a hardship they had to endure. By day it was still hot, but freezing cold at night. Deluges of rain and vicious sandstorms pummelled them too.

In between, however, they were able to keep one step ahead of the enemy, even luring some British reconnaissance patrols into a trap and capturing them. They also found themselves in occasional radio contact with their pursuers. One evening, von Luck's intelligence officer called him over.

'The Royal Dragoons are on the radio,' he told him, 'and they would like to speak to you.'

Von Luck picked up the headset and heard a crackly British voice. 'I know it's unusual to make radio contact with you,' said the officer, 'but Lieutenant Smith and his scouting party have been missing since this evening. Is he with you, and if so how are things with him and his men?'

'Yes, he is with us,' von Luck replied. 'All of them are unhurt and send greetings to their family and friends.' He then asked them if he might call them too if he had anyone missing.

'Sure,' came the reply, 'your calls are always welcome.'

On 13 November, the British had retaken Tobruk, that battered, beaten-up shell of a town that, just under five months earlier, had been the nadir of British fortunes in North Africa. A week later, they were in Benghazi and storming across the rest of Cyrenaica. Hitler still hoped this largely empty tract of land could be taken back, just as it had in the past, but Eighth Army were no longer in 1941. Everything was different now, not least because the Panzerarmee was still being pursued by the Allied Air Forces.

This included the US 57th Fighter Group, now operating independently but part of the Desert Air Force. Lieutenant Dale Deniston was in action almost every single day and had been since the opening of the Alamein battle – only bad weather was stopping him, which was why, when the rains came down on 16 November, he was able to catch up on his rest and get thirteen hours' solid sleep. It did him the world of good.

But once the skies cleared, they were off again, leap-frogging forward to one landing ground after another; Air Commodore Tommy Elmhirst's system was working just as well in pursuit as it did in retreat. 'Went on a mission at 10.15,' noted Deniston in his diary on 17 November. 'Flew over Jerry airdrome several times, like poking a hornets' nest with a stick. Three to four enemy fighters finally came up after us. Jackpot blue flight jumped one, but he pissed off. I led an element; we kept our tails clean.' Later, it rained again and a wind got up. After he went to bed at around 8 p.m., Deniston's tent nearly blew away.

None the less, as far as Mary Coningham and Tommy Elmhirst were concerned, they were not pursuing Rommel's scattered and defeated forces as hard or as quickly as they should be; in their view, they should have been annihilated on the eastern side of the Halfaya Pass. Montgomery had blamed poor weather and that had undoubtedly played a part, but the Desert Air Force was beholden to the Army for bringing forward supplies of food, water and fuel, and by the time they had reached Tobruk, they had run out of these. Only through the great efforts of Elmhirst's rear headquarters was it possible to supply the forward units, such as Billy Drake's 112 Squadron or Dale Deniston and the 57th FG. Motor columns hurried back and forth, while airlifts from Egypt brought just enough supplies to enable them to operate over Cyrenaica and continue to harry the Axis retreat. Keeping the fighters going was one thing, but there were simply not enough supplies for the bombers.

Montgomery was following hard now, but there could be no doubt that a golden opportunity to finish off the Panzerarmee had gone begging. This chance had been there on 4 November, when the Panzerarmee had broken and the battle had been won. Instead of ordering his spearheads into hot pursuit, Montgomery had briefly called off the chase in order to bring his entire army forward in strength. There was a time for the methodical approach and a time for unreserved dash, but he was simply not prepared to take the risk, no matter how small. There could be no more reverses – not even a small one.

And yet, and yet . . . Montgomery was aware of intelligence reports about the state of Rommel's forces, and there were still plenty of fresh troops for the pursuit – General Tuker's 4th Indians, for one. The total number of German troops on 4 November had been under 10,000 men; 21. Panzer had just eleven tanks left, 15. Panzer none at all. Adolf Lamm had joined a fleeing 15. Panzerdivision that had utterly shot its bolt. The Luftwaffe had also left much behind – including sixty-three aircraft they destroyed themselves rather than let fall into enemy hands. At the end of June, Eighth Army's bacon had been saved by the brilliance and relentlessness of the RAF. As the Panzerarmee fled westwards, they had no such close air support. It is impossible not to conclude that Montgomery had both been over-cautious and had misread the situation.

General Tuker was not impressed. He had been incensed when his 4th Indians were withdrawn from offensive operations on only 7 November. 'A victorious army in pursuit,' he noted, 'must fling seeming discretion to the winds and seek to bring the weakened and demoralized remnants to battle and either to destroy them or force their surrender. They must be held and dealt with.' This did not mean a wild goose chase and over-reaching supply lines; rather, with Eighth Army's material superiority, he believed the remnants of the Panzerarmee could be caught and destroyed swiftly.

Wandering about the battlefield around Tel el Aqqaqir, he found it a heart-rending experience to look upon so many young dead, and the bloody shapelessness of many more. 'We were reflecting,' he wrote, 'how much less painful for both sides it is when one captures one's enemy rather than fights him to bits.' Eighth Army, supported so brilliantly by the RAF and with such a material advantage over the Panzerarmee, had squandered an opportunity to annihilate Rommel's forces in a matter of a few days. Montgomery, he believed, had mismanaged his battle. Concentration of fire-power, used in co-operation, Tuker felt certain, would have made a massive difference, and he was surely right. It was no wonder he was angry. And despite the rain, his men tidied up their part of the battlefield in a sixth of the time they had been allocated. He then took them off for more training.

Now, ten days on, and with the remnants of Rommel's forces scuttling back across Cyrenaica, what was particularly frustrating Mary Coningham and Tommy Elmhirst was Montgomery's refusal to support the Allied air forces' efforts to keep at the enemy. 'Mary and I had just one idea,' wrote Elmhirst. 'To go forward quickly so that the Germans should never be out of striking distance. I know the Army supply position was difficult, but so was ours. But, whereas we were stretching ourselves to the limit and making our lorries and their drivers do double their normal stint, the Army was holding themselves to a normal seven-hour day.'

Giving up on Eighth Army, Coningham turned to the Americans and specifically to General Lewis H. Brereton, commanding what had originally been a detachment of bombers, but which had now grown and been designated US 9th Air Force. He was happy to oblige and immediately arranged a 'flying pipeline'. On just one day, forty-nine Dakotas ferried some 48,510 gallons of fuel from El Adem, near Tobruk, to Agedabia, a distance of 425 miles by road. What would have taken at least three days by truck took a few hours.

None the less, the lack of co-operation from Montgomery had incensed Coningham, especially after the unceasing support his aircrew had provided since Gazala. Montgomery's intention now was to attack the enemy at El Agheila in mid-December. In an appreciation that reached

Coningham, it was also suggested that First Army rather than Eighth should be the one to take Tripoli. Coningham immediately sent a copy to Tedder, pointing out that it looked as if Monty had no intention of pressing on beyond El Agheila. 'The whole tone of the past weeks has borne this out,' he wrote to his boss. 'Any competent general with overwhelming force can win a positional battle, but it requires the spark of greatness to do well in pursuit or in retirement.' Tedder was of much the same opinion.

Montgomery has always been a divisive figure. When he arrived in the desert, he brought a firm grip, gave his army a much-needed boost in morale and made sure his forces were properly and sufficiently equipped before launching his battle. He understood the operational level of war and the vital importance of maintaining supply lines, and, crucially, he also recognized the vital role of air power and how it should be integrated into the land effort. His caution was born from the need to save the lives of his men and from the recognition that there could be no more reverses; in many ways, it is hard to criticize him for that. His weaknesses, however, were largely twofold. Petty jealousies and an inherent insecurity complex made him intolerant of any questioning of his orders or of his approach to war; he was also, in modern parlance, a control freak: he had to be always in control. It was absurd that he was so unwilling to use 4th Indian Division in a greater role, but it was almost certainly due to his dislike of the Indian Army, which had rejected him when he applied to join them as a cadet; past slights were rarely forgotten. Insisting he would not tolerate 'bellyachers', as he called anyone who disagreed with him, was all well and good back in August, when Eighth Army's senior corps and divisional commanders had all needed a collective rocket up their backsides, but it was a dangerous policy to insist upon at all times. A bit more flexibility was needed, plus a willingness to listen to others.

His second shortcoming, however, was more serious. His intolerance might have been more acceptable had Montgomery been a general of dazzling tactical flair, but he was not. Tuker was right: Alamein was a poorly directed battle with a truly terrible fire plan. Now, as they pursued the Panzerarmee, Monty was showing the same lack of imagination and flair. But the British were stuck with him. He had already proved Britain's first media-savvy general of the war. He had adopted a distinctive tanker's black beret and an understated appearance that the press loved. He told them what was going to happen and then did it. He talked in certainties. The Battle of Alamein would take at least a week, he had said, but by the end Rommel would be smashed, and so it had proved, give or take a few days. After all the setbacks of the first half of 1942, in the Far East and in the desert, Britain had a general adored by the media, who took a terrific photograph and who dealt only in victories. Tuker, Coningham, Tedder and others now starting to recognize the monster in their midst would simply have to put up with it. Montgomery was, for now at any rate, untouchable.

CHAPTER 37

Year End

WHILE IN LIBYA the Desert Air Force still had command of the skies, for those now struggling in the rain and mud of north-west Africa it was a very different story. Ken Neill and the pilots of 225 Squadron were finding both the conditions and the flying pretty grim. One of their most respected pilots, Peter Rodwell, had been killed. Word reached them that his body had been found and buried with full honours, only for his grave to be robbed and his body stripped. That did little to improve morale. Then there were the attacks by the Luftwaffe, often at night. Neill and his fellow pilots could always tell German planes because they made a different sound, so as soon as they heard them they would dash from their tents and take shelter in slit-trenches. 'They started dropping anti-personnel mines called Jumping Jacks,' said Neill. 'They were horrible things.'

Bombed at night and shot at by day. It was nerve-wracking, to say the least, flying at zero feet – they were operating over unfamiliar territory and with no idea when someone might start shooting at them. On one occasion, flak suddenly opened up and moments later there was a blinding flash in front of Neill and something hit his propeller. Tracer was flashing past, and Neill shouted, 'Break! Break!' to his fellow pilot. Frantically, he tried to adjust the revs, but the Hurricane was shaking badly. Somehow, he managed to nurse the stricken plane back to Souk el Arba and when he finally touched down again and came to a halt, he saw that a large chunk of one of his propeller blades was missing. He'd been lucky – very lucky.

*

Meanwhile, General Tooey Spaatz reached Algiers on 13 November, the day he was appointed Theater Commander United States Army Air Forces. Under his command was not only the Eighth Air Force in England, but also the Western Air Command, now designated the Twelfth Air Force, in North Africa. It was a promotion, but Spaatz was not ambitious in that kind of way and had accepted the post both reluctantly and with significant misgivings. Like Eisenhower and Clark, his prime objective when he'd arrived in Britain had been to get bombing Nazi Germany just as soon as possible. The build-up had been slower than expected but now, just as he was laying down a firm logistical base in England for the Eighth, much of his bomber forces, especially, were instead being siphoned off to support TORCH and the unfolding Tunisian campaign. In fact, Eighth Air Force lost some fourteen units of fighters, bombers and transports – amounting to more than half its strength – all of which had been painstakingly built up over the preceding months. The worry was how much this would set back the Eighth Air Force's operations – which right now were limited to regular raids on U-boat pens and bases along the Atlantic Coast.

Spaatz was also worried that, in creating this new command and a new headquarters, he would only be diluting even more the already overstretched staff officers that were available. However, General Arnold had pressed the point, Eisenhower had wanted it too, so really he'd had no choice but to accept.

There was, however, a further concern, and that was doctrinal. The Eighth was a strategic air force designed to operate on its own, and they had worked out and agreed their doctrine for daylight operations in coordination with, but separate from, RAF Bomber Command. The duties for Twelfth Air Force in North Africa, however, were very different: part strategic, part coastal and part tactical in support of ground operations. For this Spaatz had good numbers of aircraft, but inexperienced crews, an untested logistical organization and no doctrine at all for close air support. What's more, unlike the RAF, which was an independent armed service, the US Air Forces were part of the Army. Eighth Air Force could operate – and was doing so – without interference from the ground forces, but North Africa was already proving a different kettle of fish.

As if to complicate matters further, nor was there a unified command.

The Americans were doing their thing in Twelfth Air Force, and the RAF was doing its, and was also split up between Eastern Air Command in Algeria and Tunisia, the Desert Air Force and other units of RAF Middle East. It had been designed in this way to support the landings and on the assumption that Tunisia would be swiftly captured, but with that already looking like wishful thinking, the current set-up and total lack of any co-ordinated close air support doctrine was threatening to undermine the material strength being thrown into the theatre.

The lack of doctrine, however, was hardly surprising: both the British and US troops in north-west Africa were mostly new to war and the air forces had never before directly supported ground troops. Even in Libya, where Mary Coningham had been developing his Desert Air Force into a finely tuned tactical force offering close air support, he and his men were still feeling their way and working out methods on the hoof. What's more, they only had Eighth Army to support, whereas in north-west Africa there were American, French and British ground forces, all new to fighting and each with different structures and attitudes to air power. Joined-up thinking on air power was decidedly lacking.

That they were feeling their way was completely understandable, however. After all, just three years earlier the US had an air corps amounting to only just over seventy fighter planes; it had come an incredibly long way already in what was, in the grand scheme of things, no time at all. In any case, it was also far better that they worked such matters out now, in North Africa, than crossed the English Channel en masse and tried to find their way of war in Nazi-occupied Europe.

The challenge for Spaatz, then, was to guide and mould his command and help turn them from greenhorns into operationally and tactically seasoned air forces that could very soon win the air war not just in North Africa, but beyond into Europe. Right now, however, with the rain lashing down, with airfields turning to mud, with a massive trans-ocean supply chain, and with ever-more enemy air forces flooding into Tunisia, that was looking like a mighty challenge indeed.

On the ground, meanwhile, the race for Tunis was still on, although during the last week of November things hardly went to plan. The three-pronged attack by the British 78th Division was over-extended, on too wide a front, and without enough men or sufficient equipment. Detachments of US artillery and tanks had been hurriedly sent forward too, but none of these troops had trained together, it was the first time they'd operated shoulder to shoulder and inevitably there were issues of teething. Axis resistance was fierce, but it was really the Luftwaffe that made the difference. Reaching a crescendo during the last days of November, their relentless pounding of the Allied positions proved once again that it was virtually impossible in this modern war to attack successfully against overwhelming air superiority. On 30 November, General Vyvyan Evelegh, the 78th Division commander, recommended to Anderson that he now pause his attack and wait for reinforcements. Anderson had little choice but to agree.

Meanwhile, in Libya, Rommel's forces continued to press on westwards. Giuseppe Santaniello and the shattered remains of the Trento Division were transferred into the Trieste instead – an unpopular move made worse by the lack of praise from the Trieste for all the past achievements of the now disbanded Trento. Santaniello was not impressed.

Then again, he was hardly in the best of spirits in any case. Endlessly marching in retreat, with little food or water, and being shot up by Allied aircraft was demoralizing to say the least. Every evening he would listen to the radio. As always, the Italian newsreader put on a far more positive slant than was the reality. The response of the Axis, Santaniello heard, would be powerful and terrible; it would show itself at the right moment and then they would strike back. 'Idiots!' he grumbled. 'Last year, when I heard the same words coming from the loudspeakers in the courtyard of the military school at Nocera, I believed them. Now that I have experience of the desert and of war, I would tell them to shut up.' He found such propaganda nauseating.

Unteroffizier Adolf Lamm, meanwhile, had recovered from his dysentery and managed to rejoin his tank unit in 15. Panzerdivision, where he was put with a new crew in a new tank. They were part of the rearguard and were now in action repeatedly. On 14 December, they were holding their makeshift position at Nofilia, trying to hold off and delay the enemy while the rest of the Panzerarmee continued west towards El Agheila. Two days later, aerial reconnaissance warned that a British column was trying to outflank it and so, along with other elements from the Afrikakorps, including Hans von Luck's recce force, they counter-attacked and, with a combination of panzers and 88s, knocked out around twenty British tanks. For the time being, the danger had been averted.

*

Rain, wind and mud. By the beginning of December, Pilot Officer Ken Neill and the rest of 225 Squadron were at Souk el Arba – a low, flat oval plateau surrounded by mountains and filled with forlorn-looking fighters and medium bombers, aircraft wrecks, bomb craters and windswept tents. Apart from one battered, square, once-white house, there were no facilities to speak of. The conditions were bad, but 225 had been struggling in the air too: casualties were mounting. They carried out their Tac R – tactical reconnaissance – sorties in pairs, often as low as 50 feet off the deck. 'The idea behind it was that you were going too fast for anyone to get a gun on you,' said Neill, 'but it didn't work out that way. The small arms was lethal, really.'

On the 4th, they'd lost two pilots in a day. That was a big hit for a single squadron. On one occasion, Neill was about to take off with Graham Stewart, another of the 225 pilots, and had begun taxiing when they got a call to hold on and let two Spitfires take off first. Sitting in his cockpit, Neill saw a number of enemy bombers, escorted by fighters, swinging around the far end of the airfield and then, moments later, bombs fell as the Spitfires took off. Neill now watched the station commander walking across the field, calm as anything, as though he were on a Sunday-school picnic, but telling everyone to get under cover. Then a bomb hit one of the hangars and a bit of iron shot across the tarmac and sliced off both his legs, while the Spitfires were shot up and exploded. Then the enemy planes were gone. 'For Christ's sake,' Stewart called over to Neill, 'let's get airborne.'

Everyone was struggling, though, the bombers included. Before the campaign, the Allies had thought it unlikely they would come up against the Focke-Wulf 190 in Tunisia, but they had been sent over, along with the Me109s, and many of them were flown by men brimming with experience of the Eastern Front, Malta and the Western Desert. On the same day that 225 Squadron lost two pilots, twelve Bisley medium bombers took off from Souk el Arba and headed off, unescorted, to bomb an Axis airfield. One returned with engine trouble and crash-landed, but as the others approached the target they were pounced on by more than fifty enemy fighters. Not one made it back.

The 97th Bombardment Group were also now in Tunisia, having been posted away from the Eighth Air Force back in England to help in North Africa instead. They had flown several missions already and, on the 3rd,

Ralph Burbridge and the crew of *All American* had flown over Bizerte and at some 20,000 feet had been attacked by Axis fighter aircraft. Their escorts, American twin-engine P-38s, were hammered; nine were shot down. The next day, General Jimmy Doolittle, the US Air Commander, complained to Eisenhower about the problems his men were encountering: Axis radar when they had none, poor levels of maintenance and the excessive distances his men had to fly to reach targets that were just a stone's throw away for the Luftwaffe.

'Those are your troubles?' Eisenhower retorted. 'Go and cure them. Don't you think I've got a lot of troubles too?'

He certainly had and, to make matters worse, the Germans now launched another attack on the British and American troops in the Medjerda Valley, this time coming in around the back and catching the Americans unawares. Tanks of Combat Command B, 1st Armored Division, were now at the front and were sent forward without any artillery support. They swiftly found themselves coming up against the usual screen of anti-tank guns and were shot to pieces. 'The day's lessons were deeply disturbing,' wrote the 1st Armored's historian. 'The enemy's armament and tactics had been extremely effective. American armament and tactics had failed.'

Now arriving at the front was Lieutenant-General Charles Allfrey, commander of British V Corps, of which the 78th Division was part. Although the Allies still held the Medjerda Valley, Allfrey took one look and realized they were in no position to attack again imminently, and in fact suggested they pull back. Eisenhower and Anderson agreed they should try to consolidate around a prominent hill called Djebel el Almara, soon renamed Longstop Hill. This took place over two nights and was a further fiasco, as rain began falling once more, turning the valley into a thick, glutinous quagmire. Then the Germans attacked again and their superior fire-power made short work of the American Stuarts sent in to stop them. Nineteen were knocked out, the Allies fell back further, and Longstop, so obviously the key feature of the western end of the Medjerda Valley with its commanding views and dominating position, had fallen into German hands. From there, they would be able to shell the Allied advance, destroy supply lines and use it as a base from which to launch counter-attacks. Taking Tunis was going to be impossible for the Allies until they had captured the Medjerda Valley in its entirety, and that wasn't going to happen until Longstop was taken back again – which was precisely why the Germans had been swift to attack and move on to it in the first place. Nor would they readily give it up again. Longstop was destined to become one of the most fought-over outcrops of rocky hill of the war so far.

By mid-December, both sides had run out of steam in North Africa. Eisenhower reported to the Joint Chiefs, warning another pause was needed before the offensive in Tunisia was renewed. Planning for TORCH had been quite brilliant and miracles had been achieved, yet no one had really prepared either for such a rapid and determined build-up by the Axis nor such appalling weather. In the mind's eye, North Africa had been perpetually hot, with palm trees, sand, olive and citrus groves. Few had expected to be operating in conditions more akin to the Ypres salient of 1917.

Combat Command B of the 1st Armored Division had been so badly mauled it had to be withdrawn and its place at the front was taken by the 18th RCT of the 1st Infantry Division, the Big Red One. Meanwhile, Ralph Burbridge and the rest of the 97th BG were moved forward to Biskra, a flat, palm-lined town sitting in the desert beneath the Atlas Mountains and a much better place from which to fly heavy bomber operations. Burbridge and the other officers were quartered in hotels in the town. They quickly appreciated the improved ambience: more places to eat and drink, less rain and fewer marauding Luftwaffe.

Then came a break in the weather, and by 19 December British 78th and 6th Divisions were almost at full strength – some 20,000 men, supported by 11,000 US troops and 39,000 – albeit poorly equipped – French. On the other hand, Kesselring's build-up of forces had also been continuing unabated. Newly arrived was General Jürgen von Arnim, fresh from the Eastern Front and now commanding what had become the Fifth Panzerarmee. Von Arnim had around 40,000 troops, nearly all German, as well as control of the skies.

None the less, General Allfrey launched his V Corps attack on Longstop Hill on Christmas Eve, with the recently arrived Coldstream Guards attacking and the 2nd Battalion of the 18th RCT supporting. It started raining again as they began and, although the Coldstreams took the heights, the Americans, when they took over, were subjected to a heavy counter-attack. This was eventually repulsed and, with further help from the French, by Christmas Day most of the feature was in Allied hands. Then came the second German counter-attack and the Coldstreams began pulling out. Tragically for the 2/18th RCT, that news never reached them and they were left isolated, outgunned and out-numbered. By the time the message did get through and they were able to extricate themselves, they had suffered 356 casualties. The attack on Longstop, renamed yet again as Christmas Hill by the Germans, had failed.

'The passage of convoy HX219 followed its, by now, usual peaceful progress,' recorded Commander Donald Macintyre, seemingly oblivious to the losses back in November; after all, nothing had been sunk on his watch even then. It was Boxing Day, and they had passed the lonely out-crop of Rockall off the Outer Hebrides when Macintyre heard the shrill sound of the bell from the Huff-Duff office and moments later he was being urgently called to the bridge. A U-boat had just transmitted a message reporting the sighting of their convoy from a position astern – behind – them. Analysis of the ground wave of the transmission suggested it was only 10–15 miles away. Macintyre was licking his lips. The following day, the convoy would be divided up and its various parts would head on to their final destinations; as Macintyre was well aware, no U-boat would risk attacking this close to the UK, which meant they did not have to worry about evasion tactics or looking after their charges any more. Ordering the escort ship *Vanessa* off in hot pursuit, Macintyre then signalled the convoy commodore his intentions and ordered his own ship, *Hesperus*, to head off hunting too.

It was a clear, sparkling winter's day and calm too, although there was the usual Atlantic swell. As they surged westwards, the green Atlantic spray washed over their bows. David Seeley, his navigator and a keen horseman, commented that normally on Boxing Day there would be a hunt; now they were carrying out their own version of that tradition. Signals began arriving from *Vanessa*: 'U-boat in sight on surface. Bearing 235 degrees.' Then came another warning them the submarine had dived. *Hesperus* was now about fifteen minutes from the last sighting. Would they get there in time to take part?

But *Vanessa* failed to make contact and, as *Hesperus* arrived, Macintyre organized a combined hunt. They began slowly, and on the bridge Macintyre was listening as they probed the depths with their ASDIC. Then, suddenly, he saw a periscope emerge from the water no more than

50 yards away and trained towards *Vanessa*. It was too close for *Hesperus* to turn quickly enough, but none the less Macintyre yelled, 'Full speed!', then ordered the ship to swing sharply to stern. They released a bevy of depth charges, more to startle the U-boat and spoil its aim than expecting to deliver a fatal blow. As the charges exploded, the U-boat dived.

'The next half hour,' wrote Macintyre, 'was a desperately anxious time.' The return ping on the ASDIC lessened, then disappeared entirely. It seemed they had been given the slip. Relations between Bill Williams, Macintyre's No. 1, and himself grew strained, each conscious that blame for losing the U-boat lay at both their doors. Then from the ASDIC operator came, 'Contact!' The echo was back. Another set of depth-charge attacks, but nothing. Daylight was fading, but Macintyre ordered that more depth charges be brought from the magazine. A further sweep from both ships and by now darkness had fallen. Then came another signal from *Vanessa*: 'U-boat on surface. Am ramming.'

Surfaced the U-boat may have been, but it was still operable and set off at full speed to try to out-turn its pursuers. At one point, *Vanessa* managed a glancing blow and also began shooting at it, but Macintyre ordered them to stop – they were in danger of being hit themselves. Now *Hesperus* took up the chase. 'The U-boat turned and twisted,' noted Macintyre. 'Every dodge I had ever learnt about ship-handling was brought into play to keep him ahead and in a position to be rammed or depth-charged.' He could hear and feel the destroyer shudder and growl as an engine was put into reverse in an effort to claw an ever-tighter circle. Two signal search-lights were trained on the sub at all times and very possibly these blinded the U-boat commander because, suddenly, there she was, crossing directly in front of *Hesperus*'s bows. Stopping the engines to avoid over-running, Macintyre called out, 'Stand by to ram.'

It was all over in a moment: the U-boat disappeared from view, then came a grinding crunch as it was cut in half. *U-357*, commanded by Kapitänleutnant Adolf Kellner, was on its first combat patrol. It sank almost immediately, leaving a widening spread of oil and just six survivors. After congratulations and hand-shakes all round up on the bridge, *Hesperus* picked up the survivors then assessed the damage caused by the ramming. Nearly a quarter of the length of the ship's bottom had been ripped off, compartments were flooded and a large stash of Christmas turkey brought back from Argentia was now floating around in oily brine.

None of this damage much affected *Hesperus*'s ability to catch up with the convoy. As they passed through, giving the 'Submarine sunk' signal, the ships responded with noisy blasts on their whistles and sirens. For Macintyre and the crew, it was a thrilling moment. There was also much to be learned from the prisoners, who explained they had been forced to the surface after draining their batteries. They also revealed details of a deception device called *Pillenwerfer*, a chemical bomb that effervesced on contact with water and which provided an area that returned the ASDIC's sound beam. While the pursuing destroyer believed it was right above the U-boat, the submarine could use the *Pillenwerfer*'s shield to sneak away.

They reached Liverpool to a great welcome and a well-deserved stint of leave while the damaged hull was repaired. It was a good start to the New Year.

Macintyre's latest U-boat-killing voyage had proved once again, as if proof were still needed, the benefit of highly skilled, very experienced and well-equipped escorts. Preventing U-boat attacks and even destroying enemy submarines was no easy matter; it needed mutual support born of well-earned trust, confidence and self-belief, and an innate sixth sense. The Royal Canadian Navy had grown exponentially from a standing start in this war, and remained short of both experience and the latest ASW equipment. Their collective resilience, stoicism and bare-faced courage could not be faulted, and they were absolutely blameless for whatever shortcomings they had. None the less, it clearly made much more sense that the Royal Navy should take on the lion's share of shepherding convoys through those perilous waters of the mid-ocean air gap.

Before Christmas, at the behest of the Admiralty, Churchill had specifically broached the matter with the Canadian Government and suggested the Royal Canadian Navy relinquish escort duty mid-ocean. Perhaps unsurprisingly, this went down very badly; the Canadians retorted that it wasn't rapid expansion and inexperience that were the problem but insufficient modern technology and equipment, too many corvettes and not enough destroyers. Unfortunately for the beleaguered Canadians, their next major convoy was the southern route – through the widest part of the air gap – and a slow, and hence more vulnerable, convoy too. Hammered by massed U-boats mid-ocean, the C1 Escort Group was outnumbered four to one and utterly unable to deal with so many submarines attacking literally like wolves. On the second-to-last day of that very long year, Convoy ONS154 lost thirteen ships and that very same day most of the escorts had to hurry to the Azores for refuelling because the tanker that should have replenished them was one of those now lying at the bottom of the ocean. Fortunately, the wolfpacks left them alone after that, but by New Year's Eve, the Senior Officer Escorts was so mentally and physically shattered, he was ordered straight to bed by the medical officer.

It was true that 80 per cent of all convoy losses since the summer had been on the Canadians' watch, but it had not been their fault they hadn't been given the same high-calibre tools as the Royal Navy; nor was it their fault that they had been running slow convoys across the mid-ocean gap at the moment large numbers of U-boats were finally entering the fray. None the less, after ONS154, the RCN conceded, but with a caveat: they would relinquish the mid-ocean air gap for training in British waters, but they also insisted on being re-equipped too.

Meanwhile, Eisenhower and Clark had yet further problems on their hands, this time in the form of their troublesome new allies. Giraud, predictably enough, was being insufferable, demanding greater military control than the Allies would grant him in a million years, while neither Clark nor Eisenhower was much more impressed by the weasly Noguès. The short-term fix – ensuring the invasion worked – was proving to be a Faustian pact that was not so easy to unpick. In an effort to escape Algiers, Eisenhower took a trip to the front. The weather was too bad to fly, so he and his party went by road. On Christmas Eve, they were 20 miles south-west of Béja. A little further on, they went to inspect American troops, who all seemed to be struggling in the mud. One scene particularly caught Eisenhower's eye: 30 yards off the road, four men were trying to pull a motorbike from the mud but in doing so were only managing to slither in the mire themselves. This pathetic scene seemed indicative of the bigger mire in which his forces now found themselves. Hopes of a swift victory in Tunisia had been dashed; even in North Africa, and even in a modern, technological war, it seemed there was a natural campaigning season, and it was not during December.

At V Corps headquarters at Souk el Khemis, General Anderson told Eisenhower what he already knew: the attack had to be postponed, and for at least six weeks. It was the right call, but no less disappointing for that. Roosevelt, Churchill and the Joint Chiefs would not be happy and Eisenhower would have some explaining to do – but that, as he was rapidly discovering, was the burden of high command.

He was still pondering the issues of command, and what to do about Giraud's refusal to allow any French troops to serve under Anderson and the British, when Clark rang him and told him to get back to Algiers right away. Amiral Darlan had been assassinated. Driving all night, he reached Algiers by 6 p.m. on Christmas Day, by which time Darlan's murderer, a youthful anti-Fascist member of the Resistance called Bonnier de la Chapelle, had already been tried, sentenced and executed by firing squad.

Darlan's death solved more problems than it created. The Allies had been embarrassed by the Deal, and the British, especially, had been unimpressed, no matter how valid the political expediency of the decision at the time. 'His removal from the scene,' noted Clark, 'was like the lancing of a troublesome boil.' Now he was gone, so Giraud could take his place, which meant he would no longer be vying to command Allied armies in the field.

Then, on the last day of the year, came the news that the Allied war leaders were coming to North Africa: President Roosevelt, Churchill, the Joint Chiefs of Staff – the whole shooting match. This was to be the Casablanca Conference. There was much for them all to discuss.

Heinz Knoke (**top left**), Hans-Joachim Marseille (**top right**) and Helmut Lent (**left**). The Luftwaffe had begun the war as the finest air force in the world and as a beacon of Germany's new military might. Despite the undoubted heroism – and brilliance – of men like Marseille and Lent in particular, the Luftwaffe was already in terminal decline.

Clockwise fom top left: A Liberty ship being built. The increasing speed with which these prefabricated vessels were being constructed almost defied belief. Neither raw courage and discipline nor the iron will of the Führer was equal to this level of production.

Right: Willow Run, built by Ford to build B-24 bombers, was the largest single factory in the world.

Below left: Don Nelson, who in January 1942 became the new production Tsar for the USA.

Below right: The extraordinary Henry Kaiser. No single individual better encapsulated the new energy and imagination with which the US was now embracing war production.

Above left: By August 1942, the British badly needed a change of leadership in the war in North Africa. In the imperturbable and deft General Alexander (*left*) and the no-nonsense Montgomery (*right*) they finally found a winning combination.

Above right: David Stirling behind the wheel of a loaded Jeep. Under his eccentric leadership, the SAS began to cause havoc behind Axis lines.

Right: German troops move into the Caucasus in the summer of 1942. Despite more swift victories, this was another campaign that lacked strategic focus or operational possibility.

Below: Milch (*centre*) and Speer (*arms folded*). It was these two men together, not Speer single-handedly, who began the process of increasing German armaments production. In doing so, however, they were forced to sacrifice quality for quantity. For Speer, this went hand-in-hand with a renewed publicity drive that was misleading to say the least.

Top: French Jews rounded up and awaiting deportation at Drancy. French authorities and police were entirely complicit. The unfolding Holocaust was certainly not the sole preserve of Nazi Germany.

Right: The aptly named Hedgehog on a British destroyer. This was just one of a number of advances that ensured the Allies won the technological battles in the Atlantic.

Above: A Panzer Mk IV – the best tank the Axis could field at Alamein, although very few in number.

Left: Panzers loaded for shipping to North Africa from an Italian port and on to an Italian ship. Axis shipping losses in the Mediterranean were catastrophic and made much worse by the failure to defeat Malta.

Top left: General Mark Clark (*left*), a superb planner who played a crucial role in the Allied invasion of north-west Africa.

Top right: US Ranger Bing Evans with his fiancée, Frances.

Above: Major Stanley Christopherson (*seated*) with men of A Squadron, Sherwood Rangers, by their Crusader tank.

Right: Tom Bowles, who with his identical twin brother, Henry, fought all through the Tunisian campaign.

Left: Teddy Suhren receives his Oak Leaves to his Knight's Cross from Hitler. A brilliant U-boat commander, he was one of the lucky ones to survive the Battle of the Atlantic.

Below: HMS *Hesperus*, commanded by the indefatigable Donald Macintyre, arrives into Liverpool to cheering crowds. The success of *Hesperus* proved what could be achieved by harnessing experience and rapidly improving technology.

Left: Fritz Bayerlein (*left*) confers with General von Thoma (*right*) during the Battle of Alamein.

Right: A German wartime poster spinning a whopping lie. German agriculture was hopelessly under-mechanized and inefficient and one of the reasons why food shortages were so debilitating the German war effort.

Left: Roosevelt and Churchill hold court with journalists sitting obediently at their feet during the Casablanca Conference.

Above: The B-17 *All American* still flying on 1 February 1943, despite being nearly sliced in half. How this aircraft ever made it home was something of a miracle.

Left: Italian troops in Tunisia. Poorly equipped and repeatedly sneered upon by their German allies, many Italian troops none the less fought both bravely and determinedly.

Below right: General Eisenhower (*left*) standing next to the brilliant but under-promoted General Francis Tuker, commander of the 4th Indian Division.

Below: Coningham (*left*) with Kuter (*next*) and Elmhirst (*right*) at 'Morning Prayers'. These three air commanders were pioneering new Allied theories of close air support and proving the vital importance of Allied tactical air power.

Right: The Avro Lancaster heavy bomber. This could lift double the tonnage of any other bomber and was identified by Air Marshal Harris as the main weapon with which to launch his all-out strategic air campaign against Germany – finally under way at the beginning of March 1943.

POWs captured at Stalingrad (**above**) and in Tunisia (**right**). The first months of 1943 were very costly for the Axis. In terms of men and materiel, defeat in Tunisia was even worse than at Stalingrad.

Left: A U-boat under attack from the air. Increasingly out of date, by the spring of 1943 they really did have nowhere to hide.

Below: Guy Gibson (*on steps*) and his crew pause before boarding their specially adapted Lancaster to attack the German dams on the evening of 16 May 1943.

CHAPTER 38

The Critical Theatre

O N 18 December, Count Ciano arrived at the Wolf's Lair in Rastenburg for meetings with their German allies. He found an atmosphere that was predictably heavy. 'To the bad news there should perhaps be added,' he noted, 'the sadness of that humid forest and the boredom of collective living in the barracks of the command.' He couldn't spot one bit of colour nor a single vivid note. Waiting rooms were filled with grey-looking people smoking and chatting quietly. Pervading the entire complex was the smell of kitchens, tobacco smoke and soldiers' boots. Ciano found it life-sapping and oppressive. Italy's war effort might have been in dire straits and its people struggling, but at least Rome still looked fabulous.

Also at Hitler's HQ was Pierre Laval, the Vichy Prime Minister. His visit, Ciano thought, was an utter waste of time, because he was barely allowed to open his mouth, and even when he did, the Führer cut him off. 'I believe that at heart, Hitler is happy at being Hitler,' jotted Ciano, 'since this allows him to talk all the time.'

Ciano had reached Rastenburg as news arrived that the Italian Eighth Army north of Stalingrad, at the southern end of Army Group B's front, had been attacked and overrun. The broken Italians were falling back in disarray. Meanwhile, von Manstein's forces had managed to get within 16 miles of Sixth Army, who were holding out in their pocket in and around the city. Paulus, however, refused to break out, holding his men to Hitler's order to stand and fight to the last. In so doing, he ensured that he and his army were doomed.

*

Before Korvettenkapitän Teddy Suhren had ended his leave, he had gone to visit his parents in Dresden and while there was encouraged to make a courtesy call on Gauleiter Martin Mutschmann. Mutschmann was interested to hear about the BdU, but was astonished to learn that after the extensive and much-publicized U-boat building programme of 1942 there were only 130 or so submarines in the Atlantic and not quite fifty elsewhere. 'But surely,' he said to Suhren, 'we have more submarines than that?'

Suhren shook his head. 'I wish we did have more, Herr Gauleiter,' he replied, 'but that's all we do have.' He then explained about the rule of thirds. 'That's how it works out: a third in dock for repairs, another third on their way out and back, and a third actually at the front.' Mutschmann then placed his hand on Suhren's sleeve and in a conspiratorial tone said, 'You wouldn't believe what the Führer has got up his sleeve.' It would all be all right; further production miracles were about to be unleashed, along with wonder weapons and other war-winning secrets. 'Afterwards,' noted Suhren, 'I could only shake my head and wonder what on earth was going on. That's what they all thought: the Führer will sort it out, he's got everything under control.'

Soon after Suhren had taken up his new training post at the 2nd Submarine Training Division (2ULD) at Gotenhafen – the Polish port of Gdynia – Grossadmiral Erich Raeder resigned as C-in-C Kriegsmarine. He had been subjected to one of Hitler's more bruising tirades, outlining in graphic detail the failures of the Kriegsmarine, most of which were little to do with Raeder and a lot to do with the chronic shortage of resources and the failure to build a large U-boat fleet before the war when there had been the chance. During his rant, Hitler declared his intention of scrapping the entire surface fleet, moribund as it was and mostly skulking, inactive, in the Norwegian fjords. Its failure to prevent Allied Arctic convoys reaching Russia had been one of the main reasons for Hitler's ire.

In the middle of January 1943, Raeder rang Dönitz at BdU headquarters in Paris to tell him of his intention to retire and to find out whether he could propose the U-boat chief as his successor. The choice was between him, Raeder said, and Admiral Rolf Carls. Dönitz was caught completely off guard but assured Raeder he was fit enough and willing to take the post. Sure enough, Hitler chose him, not Carls, and, although Dönitz managed to persuade the Führer it would be better not to scrap the surface fleet and hand the Allies a powerful psychological advantage, it was clear that the principal focus of the Kriegsmarine now lay with the U-boat arm.

Dönitz was delighted by the appointment. It meant greater influence and greater control. 'I had repeatedly suffered during the past war years under the continental-mindedness of our political leadership and of Supreme Headquarters of the Armed Forces,' he wrote. 'Neither the one nor the other had clearly realized that Britain was our chief enemy.' The question, however, now he was top of the pile, was whether it was too late for him to be able to influence events in that most critical of theatres, the Atlantic.

In Casablanca, US and British war leaders were gathering. Roosevelt and Churchill had hoped Stalin would join them, but the Soviet leader had told them he could not spare himself even for a single day. As it was, bringing both President and Prime Minister, as well as all service chiefs, closest governmental colleagues and advisors together in one place across thousands of miles of ocean, and even over enemy-occupied territory, was risky to say the very least. Churchill had travelled with Portal on a US C-46 Commando equipped with heating points to keep them warm. These, however, started overheating alarmingly, so much so that they burned the PM's toes. Realizing they were being kept on by a petrol heater, he immediately ordered them to be turned off, accepting it was better to be cold than risk a fire or even explosion. Eisenhower also had a fraught trip from Algiers, where they were now based with Allied Forces headquarters (AFHQ), when the engines of his B-17 started playing up and he saw oil spewing over one of the wings. He and his fellow passengers were even ordered to put on parachutes.

Roosevelt, however, the most infirm of all the chiefs, thoroughly enjoyed his trip, as he and Harry Hopkins, sitting side by side, took the *Dixie Clipper*, a Boeing 314 Flying Boat, from Miami to Brazil and then across to West Africa. 'He acted like a sixteen year-old,' was Hopkins' verdict on the President's delight at flying over the ocean. The final stretch up to Casablanca was taken in a C-54 named *The Sacred Cow*. In the run-up to the conference, FDR had confessed he was looking forward to getting out of Washington for a few weeks. He was regarding the whole adventure as something of a holiday.

Despite the anxious moments for some, they all made it in one piece. The purpose of the conference, which began on 14 January and which was to last ten days, was a face-to-face discussion about future Allied strategy. Once again, the Americans found themselves outmanoeuvred by the British, who had come better prepared. Right at the very top of the agenda was the Battle of the Atlantic. That January, there were around 100 U-boats at sea in the Atlantic and, although sinkings were down considerably from the carnage of the previous November, among the U-boats' few successes had been an attack on a special nine-tanker convoy from Trinidad to Gibraltar. German intelligence had failed to pick up this convoy, TM1, but, unfortunately for the Allies, the tankers crossed the path of *U-514*. The SOE, the escort commander, then made a catastrophic error of judgement. Instead of taking the rerouting offered, he decided to press ahead because the calmer waters on the current course would make refuelling easier. A few days later, on 7 January, the tanker convoy ran into a wolfpack and seven were sunk with the loss of a mammoth 100,000 tons of fuel, which had a terrible knock-on effect for the Allies in North Africa. On the other hand, this entirely avoidable calamity certainly focused the minds of British and American war leaders in Casablanca.

What they realized was that, from now on, defeating the U-boats had to take first precedence when it came to resources. The drain on supplies caused by the North African landings and increased effort before Alamein had been startling. Up until that point, Britain had managed fairly well – superbly well in comparison with Germany. No one in Britain had gone hungry, and factories were running at full tilt. Fuel, by Axis standards, was positively gushing forth. But Britain's war effort had increased hugely, as had that of the United States. They were fighting in the Far East, in the Pacific, and attempting to build up a truly monstrous strategic air campaign against the Third Reich. Aircraft, manpower and shipping were now needed all around the world.

And now there was the two-pronged North African campaign as well, which was already lasting longer than had initially been foreseen; the rapid build-up of Axis forces in Tunisia had not been predicted before TORCH was launched. Extra shipping was required to nourish North Africa and still the Mediterranean had not been opened up, which meant too much shipping was still being routed all the way around South Africa, with all the time hindrances that imposed. What's more, over the course

of the eighteen meetings, the net strategic outcome was the abandonment of a cross-Channel invasion in 1943 and an agreement that an
assault on Sicily – now codenamed HUSKY – should be next on the list
once North Africa was finally in Allied hands. Germany remained the
priority theatre, but it was also agreed that American forces should
mount new operations against the Japanese. In the Pacific, the Americans
were making progress and at Guadalcanal, a large and strategically
important island in the Solomons, US forces were within spitting distance of driving the Japanese out for good. This victory clearly had to be
exploited – the drive against Imperial Japan had to continue. The British,
too, were already now on the offensive in Burma. All these operations,
however, whether against the Axis in Europe or against Japan, required
shipping – lots and lots of shipping. Another crucial decision, and one
that was made a proclamation at Roosevelt's insistence, was that the only
terms the Allies would accept from Germany, Italy and Japan were 'uncon-
ditional surrender'. Only emphatic and complete victory would do.

The trouble was, the war leaders and chiefs of staff had a surprisingly
sketchy understanding of the available shipping, because while they
could look at figures and see what was available on any given day, and
what was likely to emerge out of the shipyards, this did not allow for
potential losses.

Over the course of the previous year, the U-boats had sunk a total of
7,790,697 tons of Allied shipping. At the same time, the Allies had built
some 7 million tons of new shipping, so overall the balance sheet was
down. Between October and December, for example, Britain had gained
626 new merchant ships, but had lost 1,334 so far in the war; in the USA,
however, with Kaiser's men churning out new Liberty ships by the week,
the losses had been 287, but 1,727 new ships had been launched.
Collectively, this meant the Allies were in credit over that three-month
period by 732 ships.

On one level, this was quite healthy, but there were some very lofty
plans being set out at Casablanca for Allied operations in 1943, and every
single one required shipping: shipping to supply Britain across the
Atlantic, shipping to continue the build-up of US forces in Britain,
shipping for North Africa, even more shipping for the planned invasion
of Sicily, and gargantuan amounts of shipping to keep US forces island-
hopping in the Pacific and to keep Britain going in India and back into
Burma. What's more, most of the burgeoning US Navy was now in

operation in the Pacific. Admiral King had never thought much of the Germany-first policy; after the Battle of Midway the previous June, he had believed – and with some justification – that it was best to exploit success and hit Japan hard now that they had been knocked off balance. Guadalcanal was, as far as he was concerned, further proof of the rightness of his argument. At the Arcadia Conference in December 1941, it had been agreed that just 25 per cent of combined Anglo-US resources would be allocated to the war against Japan until Nazi Germany had been defeated, but by January 1943 a great deal more than that was being siphoned off to the US effort there. Nor was the US Navy just about ships: it had its own air force and, in the United States Marine Corps, its own infantry too. In the Pacific, Admiral King's Navy was the complete package: a tri-service organization operating almost entirely independently from the US Army. Just how many ships were heading to the Pacific was also something of mystery. At Casablanca, the chiefs had lists of shipping and figures for projected production too. How much was likely to be lost in the Atlantic and elsewhere, however, and how much was heading to the Pacific, was not at all clear.

Thus, while attempts were made at Casablanca to estimate just how much shipping would be needed and how much might be available, these could only be guesses, and guesses were not really much use. Logistical planning required certainties as far as was possible. During the discussions, the Chiefs of Staff, and particularly Admiral Pound, the British First Sea Lord, expressed grave concerns about the increase in U-boat numbers now at sea. What's more, the North African campaign was taking longer than had been hoped and there was a concern that, for all the ambitious talk of future amphibious operations, they could easily end up putting an unacceptable strain on shipping. Even now, there was a danger that the battle raging in the mid-Atlantic would badly affect the supplies needed for the front; the loss of seven tankers on the eve of the conference was a case in point. As it was, Britain was already starting to break into reserve stocks, while its merchant fleet, comfortably the world's largest in 1939, was now the smallest it had been since the war began. What was needed was urgent action to reverse this downward trend.

This moment in the Battle of the Atlantic has often been painted as a moment of extreme crisis. However, a bit of context and perspective is needed. The tipping point in the shipping war had happened much earlier, back in May 1941, when Britain had taken the technological and intelligence lead over the U-boat arm and by which time the Kriegsmarine had suffered a series of irreparable losses; the second 'Happy Time' off the coast of the Americas in the first half of 1942 had been largely self-inflicted by the American refusal to establish a convoy system from the moment they entered the war, and October and November had been aberrations caused by the combination of TORCH and the increase of German U-boat construction. Everything Pound had said was absolutely correct, but compared with Germany, the Allies were still in a very comfortable position. It was true Britain had delved into reserves, but in the case of fuel, for example, this meant a reduction from 5,800,000 tons stockpiled down to 5,300,000 tons. That latter figure was more than Germany used in one entire year.

The Allies were not even remotely about to lose the Battle of the Atlantic, nor indeed the North African campaign. What was at stake here was time and, by extension, the lives of Allied servicemen. Both Britain and America wanted to continue to fight an efficient war, in which the numbers of men at the coal-face of battle were kept to a bare minimum. The aim was to win the war as quickly as possible and at the least cost. That meant depending heavily on machines, the best medical care, decent rations, and plentiful supplies of ammunition and equipment. This was absolutely the right approach, but it did mean the Anglo-US armed forces were far more dependent on their supply chain than the Axis forces, who, from the outset, had deployed the more old-fashioned approach of putting vast numbers of boots on the ground and expecting their troops to operate with far less.

Unlike the USA, which was both newer to war and had a population three times the size of the UK's, Britain could also foresee a day, possibly as soon as in twelve months' time, when the country would have reached the end of her available manpower. But again, this needs contextualizing. As it stood, Britain had almost 10 million in either the armed forces or essential industries – that is, nearly half the available workforce. Of those 10 million, slightly more than half were involved in war production. In other words, there wasn't a shortage of manpower, but a risk that the existing planned means of conducting the war might be threatened. Unlike Nazi Germany, where the factories had been stripped and the men sent to the front, Britain was simply not prepared to risk slaughtering another generation of young men.

The crisis, then, was over the Allies' ability to win swiftly, without any significant reverses along the way, and to ensure they could continue to wage war in the technology- and machine-driven manner they had chosen. The foundation of this strategy, however – and of all long-term planning – was shipping. Even so, while increasing numbers of U-boats were massing in the mid-Atlantic and Allied merchant ships were continuing to be sunk, it was also a strategy that was under threat.

The situation, then, was serious enough to warrant extremely firm action indeed in the Atlantic. If the U-boat threat could be eliminated, then supplies could flow undisturbed; there would be no more conflict about the support given to amphibious operations such as HUSKY. Campaigns like the one raging in North Africa would no longer be held up by oil tankers being sent to the bottom of the ocean. This would ensure campaigns were fought with greater efficiency and material protection, and that proper, realistic planning could be carried out with appropriate shipping allocations. This would mean victory would not take so long and that more young men would be able to return home when it was all over.

Thus the imperative to smash the U-boat force once and for all could not have been greater for the Allies. In November, Churchill had set up the Anti-U-Boat Warfare Committee, which was answerable to the British War Cabinet. Among its members were Roosevelt's special envoy, Averell Harriman, and the US Admiral Harold Stark, but also a number of scientists, ministers and service chiefs. Another member was the scientist Professor Patrick Blackett, the head of Operational Research at the Admiralty. Churchill hoped the committee could find not only solutions to defeating the U-boats but also the means of rapidly applying those answers. Everyone was clear that the air gap had to be reduced, but Blackett, for example, produced careful analysis that suggested some 64 per cent of all losses in the mid-Atlantic could have been avoided if there had been air cover. He also provided research showing that the larger the convoy, the safer it would be. 'The people of Britain can tighten their belts,' he said, 'but our armies cannot be let down by failure to provide equipment, guns and tanks. This means ships and more ships, and safe escort for them.'

It was from this work and the conclusions of the Anti-U-Boat Warfare Committee that the British were able to set down a resolution at Casablanca on how the Battle of the Atlantic was to be won. This was accepted by the American Joint Chiefs. Intensive bombing raids against

U-boat bases and construction yards were to be stepped up. The shortfall in escorts was to be found by scrutinizing existing dispositions and allocating as much new construction as possible to the campaign. Escort carriers were to be added to the Atlantic battle as soon as possible. More Very Long Range (VLR) aircraft were to be provided and the very latest technology issued as widely and as swiftly as possible. And this was to be put into place in quick order because, in a nutshell, the entire grand strategy of the Allies depended on the swift defeat of the U-boats. It was as simple as that.

In northern Germany, everyone had taken the news of the disaster at Stalingrad badly, although for Leutnant Heinz Knoke it had been a particularly hard blow because many of the men of the Sixth Army had come from the same area around Hamelin as him; he had been class-mates with many of those now dead or taken prisoner. 'The war,' he jotted in his diary, 'has imposed upon us unbelievable hardships.' Knoke was no longer the same gung-ho idealist he had been on the eve of war.

On 27 January, Knoke was leading a training course for NCOs organized every year. At noon, however, he learned that his *Staffel* back at Jever had been scrambled to intercept the US Eighth Air Force's first daylight attack on Germany – a raid by fifty-five bombers targeting the naval base at Wilhelmshaven. They had been expecting it for weeks, and had been greedily absorbing the flow of information about the American bombers that had been arriving from their intelligence service. Knoke had spent hours in lectures and discussions trying to work out the best tactics and manoeuvres. Models had been built for demonstrations and every minute of spare time spent making calculations of angles and speed. 'Long target tabulations are compiled,' he wrote, 'sketches and plans are drawn, new models are hurriedly constructed.' In between time, a number of these bombers had been shot down, doing much to break the myth of invincibility. Wrecks had been further analysed, while radar screens and additional ground control had been put in place. Rather like RAF Fighter Command in 1940, now that enemy bombers were on their way, Knoke felt ready and prepared to take them on.

It was frustrating for him not to be there with his men on this momentous day, so that afternoon he requested permission to rejoin them. This was granted. 'At a time like this,' he wrote, 'I feel that my place is with my comrades. I leave for Jever the same night.'

As it happened, the American attack on Wilhelmshaven wasn't terribly effective – bad weather and poor navigation put paid to that – but that wasn't really the point. Rather, it was a reminder in this dark week for Germany that the Allies were getting ever stronger and that the noose was slowly but surely tightening.

Nothing, it seemed, was going right for Germany, not least at Stalingrad where the Sixth Army was now on the point of annihilation. Saturday, 30 January, was the tenth anniversary of Hitler's accession to power, and it was Göring to whom the Führer and Goebbels entrusted the task of broadcasting to the nation. He had been due to broadcast at 11 a.m. over every single radio station in the Greater Reich, but the RAF got wind of the fact and so sent three of their new, very fast Mosquitoes to bomb Berlin and force both the Reichsmarschall and the population of the city to hurry to their shelters.

After a delay of an hour, he finally got going. It was, in many ways, a funeral oration for the Sixth Army. Defeated they may have been, but they were heroes – and their heroic stand was right up there alongside the Spartans at Thermopylae. 'Even in a thousand years,' he said, 'every German will still speak of this battle with religious awe and reverence and know that, despite everything, Germany's victory was decided there.' Göring had been chosen for this speech because, despite being the butt of jokes, he was still popular and because his speech for the October Harvest Festival the previous autumn, when he had promised an improvement in rations and subsequently delivered on it, had gone down well. That, however, had been when there was still hope of victory in the East. The rhetoric suddenly sounded tired and, worse, hollow too. A few days later, on 2 February, when the final defeat at Stalingrad was announced, the public were told the generals, officers and men had fought shoulder to shoulder to the last bullet and had died so that Germany might live.

This had been Hitler's intention. He had even promoted Paulus to Feldmarschall, aware, as Paulus was unquestionably aware, that no German field marshal had ever surrendered. He had been supposed to take the 'honourable' way out and kill himself, but instead Paulus, along with fifteen other generals, chose captivity. Hitler was incensed, but so too were the German public, who remembered the Führer's promise on 8 November, the day of the TORCH landings, that Stalingrad was as good as captured. This string of defeats and setbacks had proved a terrible shock. Stalingrad had now become a word that represented doom and despair.

When Hans Schlange-Schöningen heard Göring's speech to mark the 'National Resurrection', he was appalled. 'What a dull, stale, flat joke of world history,' he wrote. In Berlin, Else Wendel knew plenty of young men now at the Eastern Front – everyone did – but most tried not to talk about them to each other. After all, what could they say? However, when her old friend Edith Wieland wrote begging Else to visit her as she had just lost her husband at Stalingrad, she felt she had no choice but to go.

Edith Wieland had always been a proud, confident and robust woman, but a greatly aged, thin lady in black opened the door and began crying as Else stepped inside. Her friend showed her her husband's last letter, and heartbreaking it was too. 'He asked her to forgive him for anything he might ever have done to hurt her,' wrote Else. 'It was for her alone that he was now living and he loved her more than his life. This was no empty phrase he wrote because they were now facing death, and it would only be a matter of days or weeks.' He begged her to bring up their children – the youngest was just a few months old – in the spirit they had agreed upon and urged her never to give up hope. Apparently, his death had been instant – a single bullet – but then it was always that way, rather than a slow, agonizing death from a festering wound that had not been sufficiently treated, or blown to bits, or death from gradual but inevitable loss of blood.

'There is one thing that haunts me,' Edith told her. 'I have heard a rumour that they could have escaped but that Hitler forbade it.'

'No! Impossible!' Else replied. It took all her powers of persuasion to convince her friend that Hitler would have done no such thing. She had to still believe in the Führer.

In all, some 110,000 had been killed in the fighting for Stalingrad. Sixth Army had been the Wehrmacht's largest and now it was gone. 'A hush fell over the country,' noted Else Wendel, 'in the press and the radio.' Not long after, she caught up with an old college friend. Two of Gerda's brothers had been killed, but her eldest brother had been wounded at Stalingrad and had survived, although his hip had been smashed and he could no longer walk freely. 'I may as well say it,' he told Else, 'it's no use you trying to cheer us up. Germany must lose the war.'

In Prussia, Hans Schlange-Schöningen noted grimly that casualty lists were no longer issued as they were too long. Meanwhile, the conditions in Germany were now almost unbearable. 'The shops are literally empty,' he wrote. 'The simplest necessities of daily life are no longer obtainable. Even the illegal barter system no longer operates as it did, for there is nothing left to barter.'

Food was also once again scarce. Despite this mounting sense of despair among many Germans, and despite the realization of most that the war could no longer be won, there was to be no talk of an armistice as there had been at the similar point in the last war back in 1918. The Nazi elite were certainly in a state of panic. In terms of propaganda, Goebbels now began preparing the German people for what was being called 'total war'. On 13 January, Hitler announced a Führer Decree for the complete mobilization of the German people. A triumvirate of Martin Bormann, Feldmarschall Keitel and Hans Lammers, the head of the Reich Chancellery and President of the Cabinet, now organized themselves to do the Führer's bidding, although it was Bormann, once Hitler's secretary but increasingly controlling every detail of the Führer's day-to-day life, who was emerging as the most trusted of disciples. Every man and woman in the Reich was to be registered for war work, including the call-up of 500,000 boys born in 1925 and all women between the ages of seventeen and forty-five. Any businesses not directly contributing to the war effort were to be either made to do so or closed down.

Meanwhile, Speer was ordered to increase production even further. Germany still held much of Ukraine, including the coal and iron-ore fields of the Dontz. What was also needed was a big and positive production story to lift spirits and energize the home front. This had come in the form of the Adolf Hitler Panzer Programme, announced by Speer on 22 January, in which it was declared that production was being doubled to 900 tanks and 2,000 self-propelled guns per month. This was on top of the planned 1,400 armoured fighting vehicles agreed between Speer and Walter Rohland the previous September. The programme was going to have priority for steel; workers in tank factories were exempt from being called up; 72-hour weeks were imposed; and extra rations and clothing were allotted to the workers. Lots of photos and newsreels were taken of Speer smiling and shaking hands with factory workers. Another now thrust back into the public eye was the hero of 1940, General Heinz Guderian, who, it seemed, had been forgiven and was back as Inspector General of Armoured Troops.

The Wehrmacht had certainly lost a staggering number of tanks and armoured vehicles, not just in the East but in North Africa too, although most of these had been to fuel shortages and abandonment – as had been experienced by Adolf Lamm and his crew near Tobruk, for example. The fuel shortage was not about to be improved with a sudden and dramatic increase in the number of tanks. Hitler's plan in January had been to see production of the new Tigers and Panthers rise dramatically, and these, he announced, were to be the priority. The trouble was, they were huge, very complicated and, in terms of man-hours and materials, hardly conducive to mass production. The alternative was to improve existing Mk IIIs and Mk IVs, but that also required new machine tools and retraining, and meant a lessening of efficiency. Krupp's plant in Magdeburg, for example, had been told in October 1942 to produce nothing but Panzer Mk IVs and to increase output from sixty to eighty a month. By January, this had been raised to 150 per month as a result of the Adolf Hitler Panzer Programme. Almost immediately, they were ordered to switch over to Panther production instead.

By now, there were seventeen different tank guns in production, all requiring different manufacturing processes and assemblies and differing logistical headaches; in 1940, there had been just six types. And the Panther was still not really ready – design had been hurried and its complexity was not ideal for battlefield maintenance. Also, like the Tiger, it was spectacularly thirsty. Twenty-one synthetic fuel plants were now manufacturing fuel across the Reich. The largest, at Pölitz near Stettin in northern Prussia, was producing 700,000 metric tons of fuel a year, but only by using ever greater amounts of coal. It was both incredibly wasteful and expensive to make. In other words, while panzer production was unquestionably set to rise now that the much-publicized Adolf Hitler Panzer Programme had been announced, production was still not very efficient, and the increase looked likely to cause as many problems as it solved.

Nor was the panzer programme the only big construction project under way. At the same time, the Atlantic Wall was being built – the largest military fortification to be built since the Great Wall of China. Also included in this programme were massive fortifications on the Channel Islands, the only bit of British territory conquered by Germany. These small isles off the coast of Brittany were of very limited strategic value, which is one of the reasons why the British had let them go back in 1940; the Government had recognized they would prove a terrible and costly burden that was not equal to their psychological, morale or strategic value. None the less, Hitler had ordered that the Channel Islands be massively fortified and so they were, in what must be one of the most ill-judged construction projects of the war. Most of the materials had to be imported, along with 16,000 labourers of the Organization Todt. In fact, during 1942, the Channel Islands had swallowed up 12 per cent of all resources poured into the Atlantic Wall, while the entire project was now absorbing 260,000 labourers building more than 15,000 concrete bunkers and shelters.

Meanwhile, the defeats in the East had not abated. By 18 February, the huge swathes of Soviet territory that had been captured by German forces in the summer and autumn had all been reversed. Army Group A had been pushed out of the Caucasus and was desperately hurrying back across the Kerch Strait between the Black Sea and the Sea of Azov. To the north, Army Group B was only just holding certain parts of the front, while Army Group Don looked to be in danger of being entirely encircled against the northern shores of the Sea of Azov. Maikop, Rostov, Kharkov and even Izyum, fought over in May the previous year, were all now back in Red Army hands.

That same day, Goebbels delivered a speech at the Sportpalast in Berlin. It was packed with some 15,000 Berliners, including party officials, Red Cross workers, soldiers home on leave and ordinary civilians. It was a ticketed event, although Goebbels had made sure there was plenty of canned applause linked up to the speakers around the arena. Copies of his speech had already been given to newspapers, and it was to be broadcast live as well, blaring from the many hundreds of thousands of radios that still filled the Reich, both in homes and public places.

The speech included ten rhetorical questions. 'The English claim that the German people have lost their trust in the Führer,' he said. 'Are you determined to follow the Führer through thick and thin and shoulder even the heaviest burden?' The answer was a massed cry of 'Yes! Führer command, we obey!' As the crammed audience in the Sportpalast was further whipped up into near-hysteria, he asked the last of his questions: 'Do you want total war? Do you want more total, if need be, and more radical than we can even begin to conceive of today?' For anyone listening on the radio – and millions were – the answer to this final question was so loud it nearly burst the speakers.

The speech was supposed to rally Berliners and the German people, and to shore up ailing support for Hitler, and certainly agencies of the SD – the secret police – primed to eavesdrop at railway stations, cafés and other public places reported back that the speech had been very well received. However, what Goebbels had really got from his hysterical audience was tacit support for the continuation of war – total war, as Goebbels was now referring to it. A war that promised only even greater levels of destruction.

In North Africa, in Tunisia, Rommel was about to deliver an attack that caught the Allies, albeit briefly, completely off guard. At the same time, in Britain, Air Marshal Sir Arthur Harris, the Commander-in-Chief of Bomber Command, was, after a long year of preparation, finally about to unleash his all-out bomber campaign against Germany. Compared with the brief setback Rommel was about to inflict, the bomber war was going to bring destruction on a truly unimaginable scale.

CHAPTER 39

Living Dangerously

Now in North Africa was the American journalist Ernie Pyle. Since his time in London covering the Blitz, he'd been back in the States and had sailed across the Atlantic again with no great enthusiasm, although on reaching Algeria he had decided to focus on what interested him most: other people, and particularly the American boys and girls out in North Africa doing their bit for Uncle Sam.

At the beginning of January, he had taken a trip to the airfield at Biskra to see how the bomber crews of the 97th BG were getting on. It was exactly how he'd imagined North Africa: blue skies, palm trees and, at night, a million twinkling stars. Apart from his time in London, this was the closest the 43-year-old Pyle had ever got to the front line and within three hours of his arrival he witnessed an air raid. Since there was no air-raid siren, the alarm was called by ringing a dinner bell, augmented by sentries firing shots. He was struck by the randomness of the attackers' firing – one man had the sights of his rifle knocked off by a bullet and another had his water bottle holed.

He also watched the 97th take off on a mission on 12 January, including Ralph Burbridge and the crew of the *All American*, to attack the Axis airfield at Castel Benito near Tripoli – in support of Eighth Army rather than First. By late afternoon, the bombers began returning. 'The sun was lazy, the air was warm,' noted Pyle, 'and a faint haze of propeller dust hung over the field, giving it softness.' A red flare was fired by one of the approaching Fortresses. As it landed and came to a halt, Pyle hurried over and watched as the crew lowered their dead pilot through the hatch.

No one said very much but the crew looked grave. Pyle, who had not seen a dead person before, noticed how white the lifeless man's hands were. 'Everybody knew the pilot,' he wrote. 'He was so young a couple of hours ago. The war came inside us then, and we felt it deeply.'

Also back out in North Africa was the Australian journalist Alan Moorehead, who was still writing for the British *Daily Express*. He had been in the States and then in London, where the people he spoke to had been incredulous about the Darlan Deal. Nor could they understand what was happening in North Africa. If such a large Allied army had landed there, why was it being held up by a few Germans in a tiny corner of Tunisia?

And so he was out there with First Army to find out for himself. After a few days at the front, he began to understand. 'It is no exaggeration at all,' he wrote, 'to say that the average citizen in New York and London had not the remotest idea of what fighting was like, of who was doing it, of what weapons were being used, of the numbers engaged on both sides, of what local objectives were being sought or of the prospects for the future.' Moreover, as he pointed out, in the States it was widely believed that the majority of the Allied troops doing the fighting were Americans, when in fact, in early 1943, it was predominantly a British operation. Most also assumed it was flat and sandy. That their boys were struggling through hills, mountains and thick syrupy mud, in driving and frequently freezing rain, was incomprehensible.

It also took Moorehead time to get used to the Tunisian battlefield, so different from the vast open Western Desert. In Tunisia, he could lift his binoculars and see German soldiers moving about. Here, one looked down on positions, or even up to them, the combatants seemingly on top of one another. He was struck by the sense of congestion at the front, and the fact that every yard of it was dangerous: landmines and booby traps were everywhere. From behind rocky crags, snipers might shoot, while hurtling down valley roads were fighting planes, hammering those vital supply lines, so that all driving had to be done at night, on rough, winding and often precipitous roads and with no headlights. And the mud – thick, slippery, impassable mud, devoid of vegetation – was everywhere. 'This perishing cold,' he wrote, 'this all-invading mud and this lack of hot food could exhaust and kill a man just as thoroughly as bullets.'

Now stuck in this mud were the 18th RCT. The Bowles twins in the

2nd Battalion had not been part of the slaughter on Longstop, although some of the lessons learned on that bloody ridge had been swiftly absorbed by the entire regiment. One of those lessons was that the 37mm anti-tank gun was not big enough or powerful enough for warfare in early 1943. As Henry Bowles pointed out, however, that was what they'd trained with, so they had not thought twice about trying to use them. It had been something of a shock to discover how ineffective they were.

The 18th RCT had been kept in the Medjez sector and were now attached temporarily to the British 6th Armoured Division. Tom and Henry Bowles now found themselves in the front line in Tunisia for the first time, after the remnants of the 1st Battalion had been withdrawn. The 2nd Battalion took over from some British troops south-east of the town on positions near what was now called 'Grenadier Hill' and which overlooked the Medjerda Valley and a crossroads called 'Peter's Corner'.

Under British command, they were given British rations and even British clothing when new uniforms were needed. Pretty soon, all Tom Bowles had left was his helmet; the rest of his uniform was British. He wasn't bothered; nor was Henry. Of much greater concern was the food. 'The volume was somewhat less than American rations were, you know,' said Henry, although he quickly took to drinking tea. 'That tea they had,' he said, 'really was beautiful.'

At Medjez, the 18th RCT dug themselves in, got soaked, went out on patrols and learned to tell which enemy aircraft was which and the kind of evasive action they needed to take. Soon, they had a complex of zig-zagging trenches rather like those of the last war.

This lull, however, did at least give the many green Allied troops – both British and American – a chance to experience living and surviving at the front without having to take part in an all-out assault. Valuable lessons were being learned. Desultory shell and mortar fire and air attacks gave them experience of being under fire. The 18th RCT, for example, had arrived in North Africa having had no live ammunition training at all. What's more, pre-war doctrine, for what it was worth, had emphasized light warfare and mobility, which was why they had arrived in North Africa with small guns like the 37mm. It was also why, until the British started ordering new medium tanks, most of their armour had also been small and light. And it was also why horses had still been a part of the US Cavalry right into the spring of 1941. The United States Army had traditionally fought small, light border wars. Their entry into the

First World War had been an aberration and had initially been fought with the same light, manoeuvrist approach until the slaughter had begun and they had quickly abandoned such notions. Otherwise, however, apart from the catastrophic Civil War, the United States Army had only ever really operated as a border constabulary, for which the light tactics were ideal.

The Army's commanders were also now under scrutiny and most were untested, although some, admittedly, had seen action in the First World War; Mark Clark was one and General Terry Allen of the 1st Division another, but neither Marshall, Eisenhower nor Fredendall, for example, had ever commanded troops in combat. As it was, no fewer than thirty-one of the forty-two divisional and corps commanders who had taken part in the Army's Louisiana Maneuvers back in 1941 had already been given the chop. Whether that cull had been enough was still largely unknowable, however. The point was, the US Army forces now in Tunisia were very much feeling their way. It was not their fault and entirely understandable, given both their history and the exponential growth of the past couple of years. Most, however, were willing to learn – a fact reflected in the sheer number of 'Combat Lessons Learned' memos that litter the records of the American units in North Africa. Yet unfortunately for them, there were a few more hard knocks to be taken in the weeks to come.

Still part of Eighth Army were the Fighting French, although at Derna in Libya they had been halted for re-equipping and retraining. Lieutenant Jean-Mathieu Boris was still with his artillery battery, but now that they had paused for breath, he discovered he was struggling, haunted by his experiences at Bir Hacheim, the brushes with death he had experienced and his sending of two men to their deaths in an attempt to deliver a message. It was this, especially, that was giving him nightmares, and he began to worry he was not capable of commanding his men any more. His state of mind was hardly improved when he was suddenly given an unusual and disturbing mission. Capitaine René Gufflet had been killed at Bir Hacheim and a message had reached the Fighting French that Gufflet's widow wanted her husband to be found and given a proper Christian burial. As Boris had been the one who had buried him back in June 1942, he was asked to go and find the body and bring him back. And so off he went, with a burial party and three trucks, back to Bir

Hacheim. Wrecks and debris still littered the desert. Setting up camp, they started digging where Boris remembered burying the captain, but more than six months had passed and it was difficult to recall precisely. They found a lot of bodies and many of them had been half-eaten, but after three days they eventually discovered the withered remains of the captain and began the journey back across the desert to their camp. Such a visual reminder of death and the fate of so many of his comrades had done little to improve his already frayed nerves.

Everyone was losing friends and comrades. It was impossible to keep serving in the front line and not either lose a close friend or be killed oneself at some point. That was simply the barefaced statistics of it. On 11 January, Dale Deniston's good friend and tent-mate Bill Williams was killed. They had been out on a fighter sweep as a group of thirty-six P-40s when they were attacked from above and behind by Messerschmitt 109s. The Americans turned into their attackers and very quickly the fight became a confused mêlée. 'There was a lot of excitement,' recalled Deniston, 'frantic calls on the radio . . . a lot of quick dives, climb, turns, and blackouts.' Then, as was so often the case in such aerial fights, the sky suddenly cleared. Deniston found himself heading back to base on his own. When he got back to their landing ground he learned Bill Williams was missing. No one saw what had happened – he just disappeared in the fighting. A few days later, there was still no sign of him, but then the desert was such a vast place. He could have come down anywhere.

On the 14th, Deniston and his flight flew top cover for Billy Drake's 112 Squadron as they dive-bombed and strafed an enemy column. Drake had been leading his squadron almost without a break since the previous May and in that time they had shot down 199 enemy aircraft. The 200th came two days later, on 16 January – no small achievement. Drake's own score in that time was seventeen confirmed, which made him an ace more than three times over. He was still only twenty-five years old.

As he was aware, though, it wasn't about getting personal scores but about working together, as a squadron – as a team – and destroying as much of the enemy as possible, whether in the air or on the ground and whether aircraft, trucks, tanks or soldiers. That also meant there could be no weak links, and over the course of his command he had had to sack several pilots who had lost their nerve. This was called 'LMF' in the RAF – Lacking Moral Fibre. 'I had no compunction about it whatsoever,' said

Drake. 'We had a fair idea of how far we could go on, and that we were under a considerable amount of strain.' If someone started to look washed out, Billy would give him a rest, but if that didn't sort him out, then he would quickly send the fellow back to Cairo. 'Particularly in the desert,' he said, 'we relied on each other so much that we couldn't afford to have a weak link.'

Just after the 200th squadron kill, Drake was finally posted away; for the next few months his huge experience would be put to use helping to train the new pilots arriving in the Middle East. One airman who had been sent home to Britain, however, was Air Commodore Tommy Elmhirst, although not for reasons of either fatigue or discipline; far from it, as he had excelled in his post. Before he left, however, he had drawn up the administrative plan for the next 500 miles' advance to Tripoli – an advance that, as far as Air Vice-Marshal Coningham was concerned, was still taking far too long. As Coningham had feared, Rommel had slipped away from the El Agheila position before Eighth Army had been able to begin their frontal assault.

Another who was battling hard to keep his nerves in check was Wing Commander Guy Gibson, who, ten months on, was still CO of 106 Squadron – and, more to the point, still flying operationally. By mid-January, he had flown sixty-three bomber raids as well as ninety operational sorties during his time as a night-fighter. A normal tour for aircrew in Bomber Command was thirty ops, then after a break and period as an instructor, a further twenty. No one was expected to fly more than fifty bomber missions; such were the dangers, it was considered that fifty was more than enough. Gibson, however, had comfortably surpassed that and there was no sign of him stopping there either.

In recent weeks, however, the burden of responsibility had increased. In December, Gibson and the Station Commander at Syerston, Group Captain Gus Walker, had been watching aircraft taking off when Walker spotted that a parked Lancaster of 61 Squadron had its bomb bays open and that incendiaries were dropping out and some igniting. Also on board was a 4,000lb 'cookie', so Walker dashed off to warn them and try to avert catastrophe. He hurried over in his car, then Gibson watched him get out and wave his hands. He was only 20 yards from the Lancaster when the cookie went up. 'There was one of those great slow explosions,' noted Gibson, 'which shot straight into the air for about 2,000 feet and the great Lancaster just disappeared.' Gibson thought his friend had been torn apart in the blast, but in fact he had been blown some 70 yards backwards – albeit without one of his arms. He was, however, still alive.

A surgeon and two nurses hurried over from the military hospital at nearby Rauceby, and Gibson helped them tend the wounded man. It was a huge blow to Gibson, because Walker – older, wiser – had been something of a father figure to him and, as a highly proficient station commander, had shouldered many of the responsibilities that might otherwise have fallen to the young squadron commander.

On 11 January, he led a mission to bomb Essen in the Ruhr industrial heartland of Germany, and specifically the Krupp works. Only twenty-five were going – a dangerously small number – but they were trying new marking techniques. The plan was to take off and climb as high as possible, then set course for Ijmuiden. At this way point, they would change course and fly straight to Point X, where two yellow flares would be burning in the sky straight ahead and where they would be 25 miles from the target. From here, they were to press straight on, with no evasive action at all, until Point Y was reached, where they would find two red flares either side of their wing tips. Then straight on again, keeping a bearing of 170 degrees towards a cluster of green flares, the marker for dropping the bombs. 'But it is very important,' they were told, 'to bomb on that exact heading; if you are ten degrees off either way, your bombs will go about ten miles from the target.'

Gibson and his crew took off at 4.30 that afternoon. 'We set off,' he wrote, 'we saw our flares and we bombed them, and we came back, having been through the worst flak of all time.' He and his crew had somehow made it, but two others from 106 were not so lucky. To make matters worse, they were two of Gibson's best crews. One of the pilots, Gray Healey, had been a particularly close friend, while Maurice Phair, an American, had nearly finished his tour. Gibson waited up all night hoping they might return. The following day he wrote the usual raft of condolence letters – another of the duties, and strains, of command.

Five days later, the target was Berlin for the first time in over a year, and on this occasion Gibson was asked to take with him the well-known journalist and broadcaster Richard Dimbleby. This was part of Harris's ongoing efforts to keep his command at the forefront of public consciousness. They crossed the Dutch coast with German flak opening up and jolting the great aircraft, then flew on, eventually reaching the capital of the Reich. Searchlights criss-crossed the sky and intense flak began bursting all around them. One was close enough to make the bomber lurch upwards dramatically, but they went on. Ahead of them incendiaries were being dropped. 'And where a moment before there had been a dark patch of the city, a dazzling silver pattern spread itself,' said Dimbleby. 'A rectangle of brilliant lights, hundreds, thousands of them, winking and gleaming and lighting the outlines of the city around them.'

Gibson's Lancaster was carrying just one, massive 4-ton bomb, but on the first run the bomb-aimer could not see the target, so Gibson decided to go around again. This required nerves of steel, because it meant taking a wide circuit all around the outside of the city and going through the bomb run all over again. It was the bomb run, when the pilot had to fly straight and level and through the most intense flak, that was the most dangerous part of the raid. The bomb-aimer still couldn't see the target on the second run, however, so Gibson went around for a third time. This was pushing luck to the extremes, but at last the target was spotted, the bomb released and immediately the Lancaster climbed and Gibson corkscrewed the bomber away into the night. It was all too much for Dimbleby, who promptly threw up. At 1.50 a.m., they landed down again at Syerston, after over seven hours in the air. 'Good trip and fairly successful,' Gibson noted in his logbook.

Later that day, he drove over to the RAF hospital at Rauceby. Since the night of the exploding Lancaster, he had become friends with Maggie North, one of the nurses who had helped, and had taken to driving over to see her whenever he got the chance. Gibson was married, to Eve Moore, a dancer eight years his senior, with whom he had become infatuated back in the winter of 1940, but he barely saw her. His mother, an alcoholic, had managed to set herself on fire and been killed around the same time, while his father was entirely estranged – a colonial administrator still in India. There was a brother, Alec, to whom he was close, but Gibson, a highly sensitive person, was in many ways rather alone in the world; he was not alone, however, in finding it impossible to speak to others about his experiences. On the station and in front of the boys, he had a carefully constructed personality that was quite at odds with what he really felt: larger than life, one of the lads, a bit of a martinet, and gung-ho.

Maggie North, however, understood him: she saw the trauma and violence of bomber ops on a daily basis. With her, he no longer had to play the cheery and indefatigable leader.

On this occasion, he arrived at Rauceby unannounced, asked for Maggie and told the sister he would be waiting outside for her in his car. When Maggie joined him, he was sitting staring out through the windscreen and chewing on an unlit pipe. He was also shaking quite uncontrollably.

'Please hold me,' he asked her. She did so, until the shaking eventually stopped.

'Ops last night?' she asked. Gibson nodded but said no more. Soon after, she returned to her work and Gibson drove back to Syerston to take command of his squadron again. He needed a rest, and urgently, but perhaps only he and Maggie were aware just how close to the edge he was. To his squadron, he was the press-on, imperturbable bomber leader he had always appeared to be.

It had been all very well thrashing out future strategy at the Casablanca Conference, but there had been much to discuss about the current situation too. Not a huge amount was going to plan and General Eisenhower found himself not only under the spotlight but rather under the cosh as well. Clearly, he was overstretched, trying to command his forces in Tunisia and juggle the demands of running Allied Forces HQ in Algiers. General Clark was now effectively out of the frame because he was setting up Fifth Army, which was being formed from the troops now assembling in French Morocco and Western Algeria, so Eisenhower had lost his right-hand man and number-one political handler. He also needed someone to command US II Corps, which was now being formed and moving up to the central Tunisian border, and so he chose Major-General Lloyd R. Fredendall, who had commanded the US landings at Oran.

Eisenhower had not known Fredendall before the war but he had caught the eye of General Marshall. As far as Eisenhower was concerned, that had been good enough. Fredendall had also performed perfectly well during the landings. Since then, however, there had been warning signs that he had just a few screws loose. As Acting Governor of Oran he had issued a number of building contracts and appointments to well-known Vichyites, a story that had been picked up by Ernie Pyle, for one, and which had caused quite a stir. When Fredendall had been taken to task, he had reacted angrily. 'Lay off that stuff!' he yelled. 'What the hell do you know about it?' It turned out he was equally loud and rude to his staff, was prone to jumping to conclusions from which he could not be swayed and was rather too fond of a drink. He was also pathologically Anglophobic. These were not good attributes for the commander of the first US Army corps to serve in action, and especially one that was expected to do so under British command, yet he managed to tone down these characteristics in front of Eisenhower and together they drew up a plan to strike across central Tunisia to ensure that Rommel's forces never linked up with von Arnim's in the north.

This Eisenhower had presented enthusiastically at Casablanca, and was rightly quickly taken to task. Fredendall's force included some French units and British airborne troops and amounted to some 38,000 men, but Rommel had around 80,000 and von Arnim 65,000. As the Chiefs of Staff pointed out, it was more likely that II Corps would be swallowed whole. General Brooke also informed them that Ultra decrypts had revealed that Rommel was sending a re-strengthened 21. Panzer up into Tunisia and, with that bombshell, Eisenhower's plan was shelved. The following morning, Marshall gave Eisenhower a talking-to and then, in a quiet tête-à-tête with the President, Ike offered to resign. Roosevelt waved this notion away, however, and instead asked him to name a date when the campaign might be over.

'May 15,' Eisenhower told him.

Also attending Casablanca had been General Alexander, who glided in looking tanned, healthy and every inch the suave fighting commander. He brought good news: Tripoli was about to fall and soon they would be cracking the Mareth Line, the next major defensive position in south-east Tunisia. His confidence was contagious and the contrast with Eisenhower could not have been more obvious, prompting Brooke to suggest a further change of command. Eisenhower was clearly carrying too much responsibility and had neither the tactical nor strategic experience required for a battlefield commander. Perhaps, Brooke suggested, Eisenhower should be further promoted and Alexander brought in as his deputy and overall Allied field commander of both First and Eighth Armies. At Alexander's suggestion, these could be called Eighteenth Army Group, as it combined the numbers of both. Eisenhower could be Supreme Commander, allowing him to concentrate on the political issues and inter-Allied challenges, leaving Alexander to provide the much-needed drive and co-ordination that had been lacking so far.

The Americans liked the sound of this. They also further agreed to Brooke's suggestion that Air Chief Marshal Tedder become the overall Allied Air Commander. Cunningham was also promoted to Admiral of the Fleet and took back his old job of C-in-C Mediterranean.

Unifying the Mediterranean Allied Air Command was a vital step forward. Tooey Spaatz had already brought all bombers under the umbrella of the Twelfth Air Force, but now he was given yet another appointment: Commander-in-Chief of the Northwest African Air Forces, which were split up into further commands including Coastal and Training, as well as the Strategic Air Command under Doolittle. The biggest part of Northwest African Air Forces, however, was to be Air Support Tunisia, which was to consist of the majority of fighters and medium bombers already operating over Tunisia as well as the Desert Air Force. There was really only one man to command this new combined force: Air Vice-Marshal Mary Coningham.

His new deputy was to be Brigadier-General Larry Kuter, who had helped write AWPD-1, the USAAF's plan for a strategic air offensive. He had also worked alongside Hap Arnold as Deputy Chief of the Air Staff, before being posted to Britain to command 1st Bombardment Wing of the Eighth Air Force. Then, in the New Year, he had been summoned to North Africa to become Spaatz's Chief of Staff.

Kuter had been at Spaatz's forward base at Constantine only a few days when he realized there were serious strains between the Army and Air Forces, and especially between the fighter groups and US II Corps. The fighters, it seemed, were flying purely at the behest of the Army. 'Fredendall had them parceled out here and there,' noted Kuter, 'flying umbrellas and other piecemeal defensive chores.' He confronted Fredendall, but the II Corps commander angrily dismissed his concerns and insisted it was the right of the Army to demand when and where fighter cover was used. This was nonsense and betrayed a total lack of understanding of how air and land should co-operate. 'Talking to Fredendall,' wrote Kuter, 'might make any airman delirious.'

Kuter was now given temporary command of Allied Air Support Tunisia until Coningham could take over, and quickly realized that Fredendall was not alone in his misguided view of air support. At a planning conference with Anderson and his divisional commanders, Kuter outlined his plans to knock out Axis airfields and carry out reconnaissance work while they were about it. These ideas were dismissed out of hand. What was needed, he was told, were standing patrols over the battle zone. Ground troops, they said, could not withstand even one attack by a German Stuka and tank combination. 'It appeared to me,' noted Kuter, 'that our troops had fallen victim to some very effective propaganda.' What he and Coningham now faced was not just a battle against the Axis air forces, but also the rigid mindset of many of the army commanders.

General de Gaulle had been brought over to Casablanca, too, as Churchill and Roosevelt attempted to build a rapprochement between the Free French and those Vichy leaders who had come in from the cold. This 'unity' was demonstrated in the announcement of the formation of the Committee of National Liberation, of which Generals Giraud and de Gaulle were to be joint heads. Both men were then paraded before the Western media alongside Roosevelt and Churchill. Witnessing this extraordinary charade was Alan Moorehead, who, along with other reporters, had been invited to the Anfa Camp outside Casablanca. Once there, they were all kept waiting for a couple of hours, then led up the road to meet the President and Prime Minister.

While Moorehead and other journalists squatted in a semicircle of damp grass, Churchill and Roosevelt sat before them with Giraud and de Gaulle on either side and a plethora of diplomats and ministers behind them. Both Frenchmen looked painfully uncomfortable. De Gaulle was still smarting from being kept out of the TORCH operations, while Giraud regarded the Free French leader as little more than a dangerous upstart. Roosevelt beamed in an avuncular fashion, then urged the two Frenchmen to stand and shake hands. They did so, teeth gritted. 'It was all rather embarrassing,' wrote Moorehead, 'like the rehearsal of an amateur play.'

While Rommel was preparing for his renewed strike into Tunisia and Eighth Army were moving up towards the Mareth position, the SAS were launching a new offensive of their own and hoping to help Eighth Army with further operations behind enemy lines. Since their successes the previous autumn, the SAS had been expanded, given full regiment status, and David Stirling promoted to lieutenant-colonel. Among their number now were some Greeks, known as the 'Sacred Squadron', and a Free French squadron too. There was also a Special Boat Section for amphibious operations.

Stirling's plan was to penetrate deep into southern Tunisia by moving around the Matmata Hills and well to the south of the coastal strip, then turn north and link up with First Army. He also hoped to meet with his brother, Bill Stirling, who now commanded 2nd SAS, which had been recently formed in Algeria.

By 22 January, Stirling's own raiding party of five Jeeps had reached the vast saltmarsh of Lake Djerid and found it totally impassable, while further east there were mountains equally difficult for their vehicles to cross. Growing impatient, Stirling decided they should throw caution to the wind and head back towards the coast. He suggested they simply drive straight through the Gabès Gap, the comparatively narrow coastal strip that allowed easy passage to the more open northern half of the country.

As dawn broke on 23 January, Stirling's party sped towards the Gap. As ever, Johnny Cooper was driving Stirling and, with the accelerator pressed to the floor, they hurried through a large German armoured formation just waking from their night's leaguer. 'The tank crews were savouring their first cups of coffee and stretching themselves in the early morning sun,' noted Cooper. 'Many of them looked at us curiously but we just stared back and motored on.' And it seemed as though their bluff had succeeded, because no one fired a single shot. The SAS men kept going and then after a short while, with the sun continuing to rise, they decided to pull over and hide up for the day, camouflaging their Jeeps and themselves within a wadi surrounded by the sides of a steep ravine and covered with small trees and bushes.

By this time it was around 10 a.m., and Cooper and his good friend Mike Sadler, a former member of the Long Range Desert Group, volunteered to climb up on to the high ground and keep watch. From their vantage point they looked south-east towards the town of Gabès on the coast and could see long columns of enemy traffic heading east towards the Mareth Line. It all appeared to be heading one way. Then they spotted two vehicles climbing towards their escarpment and stopping; Cooper and Sadler assumed they were German soldiers just pausing to relieve themselves.

Around 1 p.m., both men returned to the SAS camp, gave Stirling a report, then decided to get some rest; they'd been on the go for over forty-eight hours and were by now utterly exhausted; Cooper, for one, was soon asleep. A couple of hours later, however, he was awoken by a sharp kick to his feet and opened his eyes to see a German soldier, an MP40 sub-machine-gun slung across his chest, staring down at him. He indicated to Cooper to stay where he was, then hurried off, running away with a fellow soldier.

Hurriedly, Cooper woke Stirling and the others. Stirling immediately ordered the signallers to destroy their signals logs and codes, but now shots were ringing out from another part of their makeshift camp. Cooper, along with Sadler, the two signallers and a French SAS man, Freddie Taxis, ran uphill and out of their camp, while Stirling headed off in another direction. Near the top of the hill, they reached a defile and found a low depression covered by dense, thorny scrub and hid themselves, their hearts hammering, cursing themselves for their earlier complacency. Clearly, their stunt of driving directly through German positions had aroused suspicions; and equally clearly, the men Cooper and Sadler had later seen had not been taking a break but had been looking for them – and had found them. The chances of escape looked slim.

Luck, however, was on their side, as an Arab and his herd of goats suddenly appeared and surrounded them, the animals munching at the shrub and, in so doing, hiding the SAS men even more fully. After around half an hour, the goats moved on, but by then so had the Germans, although they had taken the Jeeps with them and all the SAS men's supplies. 'All we had,' wrote Cooper, 'was a 1:1,000,000 map and a compass.' Taking stock, they realized they had two options: to walk back through the Gap towards Eighth Army, or to make for the Free French base at Tozeur, an oasis on the northern side of the salt lake. Not fancying chancing their arms in the Gap a second time, they set off for Tozeur.

They made good progress and at dawn the following morning came upon a Berber encampment where they were given much-needed food and water. They then trudged on, before finally pausing for a rest. Soon after, they were woken by a Berber tribesman armed with a shotgun and demanding Cooper's clothes. Reluctantly, he handed over his Battledress and jerkin, only to be attacked by a number of Arab children who started throwing stones. One struck him on the side of the head, causing a bad gash, but, throwing caution to the wind, Cooper and his fellows made a run for it and were able to make good their escape.

The following day they finally reached the oasis and the Free French *Beau Geste*-style fort, which shimmered in the sun. Gazing upon the palm trees, deep blue sky, white-washed fort and the Senegalese troops approaching them, Cooper wondered whether he had stumbled on to a filmset, but they were all real enough and soon after they were being ushered inside, given food and water, and Cooper was having his head wound stitched up and bound. Signals were also sent and later that afternoon a US II Corps patrol arrived to pick them up and take them to Tébessa. They had finally linked up with First Army, but not in the way they had at all imagined.

Cooper, Sadler and his colleagues were safe, but unbeknown to them, David Stirling had been captured. And with that, the SAS's run of remarkable successes in support of Eighth Army came to an abrupt end.

Guy Gibson and his crew weren't the only ones lucky still to be alive. So too were the men of the *All American*. On Monday, 1 February 1943, at around 10.50 in the morning, they took off from their base at Biskra in Algeria as part of an attack by the USAAF's 97th Bombardment Group on the northern Tunisian town of Bizerte. Pilot Ken Bragg pulled back on the control column as the bomber climbed steadily into the sky, then circled as it formed up first with the other bombers from the 97th, then with the other groups that were joining them, until there were no fewer than fifty aircraft in all, droning through the clear blue sky towards Bizerte. Major Robert E. Coulter, squadron commander, was leading. The *All American* was flying on his right wing.

Up front in the bombardier's section was Ralph Burbridge. He always felt apprehensive as they took off; they all did. 'No-one felt too brave when starting a mission,' he admitted, although the intense camaraderie among the crew helped. 'It was just like family – there really was a bond there,' he added. They had been to Bizerte before; the flight would take around two hours. Burbridge took the opportunity to test his gun, firing a few rounds harmlessly into the air. The whole sky appeared to be full of bombers, steadfastly heading on their way, white contrails streaming behind them.

It was 1.40 p.m. when the almost circular Lac de Bizerte came into view. Beyond was the wide arc of the coastline; below was Bizerte, its jetties and wharves jutting out into the sea. Almost immediately, they saw groups of 109s climb into the sky, just as they'd done for the past six weeks. In the *All American* no one spoke, each member of the crew concentrating intensely on the task expected of him. Burbridge was managing his machine gun, waiting for a target to slip into range.

Now the 109s were upon them, diving out of the sun, machine guns and cannon spitting fire. Their own machine guns began to reply, reverberating and clattering through the B-17s as they did so. A couple of 109s spiralled earthwards, black smoke trailing behind, but four of the Fortresses had been hit and were struggling to keep in formation, their only real hope of survival.

As the formation began the bomb run, the 109s left them alone, not daring to venture into the flak that would open up at any moment. Instead, they circled high against the sun, waiting for another chance to attack once the bombers turned for home. Burbridge took up his position over the bombsight, peering down, waiting for the target to appear. Thick black bursts of smoke peppered the sky as pilot Ken Bragg ordered the bomb bay doors to be opened. They now had to fly absolutely straight and level, with the fused bombs exposed to the tiny shards of shrapnel from bursting ack-ack fire. On they went, the Fortress jolting from the endless flak, until at last Burbridge saw the target line up. Pressing down his thumb on the button, he called out, 'Bombs away,' on the intercom.

With the bomb bay empty and half their fuel now spent, the Fortress rose higher into the sky, weaving from side to side, making the anti-aircraft gunners' task ever more difficult. But they still had to face the fighters again. Burbridge had moved to take position by his .50-calibre. Away from the rest of the attackers were two 109s, climbing high into the sun; then they dived from twelve o'clock high, seemingly straight for the *All American*. As Burbridge poured bullets towards them, he watched the Messerschmitts hurtling bullets ever closer, their own lines of tracer spewing from their noses and wings.

The first 109 drew towards them and half-rolled just as Major Coulter's plane started pouring smoke and spiralling uncontrollably towards the ground. The second fighter was riddled with bullets, but instead of turning away seemed to be heading straight into the *All American*. Ken Bragg rammed the control column forward in an effort to take evasive action. The Messerschmitt passed straight over his head, the Fortress jolting slightly.

'Pilot from top turret!' came an urgent voice over the intercom. 'Pilot from top turret!'

'Come in top turret, what's the matter with you?' replied Lieutenant Bragg.

'Sir, we've received some damage in the tail section. I think you should have a look.'

Both Bragg and the co-pilot, Lieutenant Geoff Engle, found the Fortress was still flying okay, but the trim was not working and the plane wanted to climb. But by throttling back the engines, they could keep her fairly steady, so Bragg handed over to Engle and went back to see what had happened. He was stunned by what he saw: nearly three-quarters of the fuselage had been sliced in half. Jagged metal and wires were flapping in the air. Part of the wing of the Messerschmitt was still embedded in the tail of the plane.

When Burbridge heard the skipper call everyone into the radio room, he clambered up from the nose to join the rest of the crew. Once gathered, Bragg told them they had a choice: either they bail out now, over enemy territory, or they could stay and hope the Fortress would keep intact. Bragg had already decided to keep going, and Burbridge and the rest of the crew agreed to remain with the stricken plane too, although they were all sent to an emergency exit ready to jump should they have to. 'It was terrifying,' admitted Burbridge, 'wondering whether we were ever going to get back.'

But the trusty Fortress held fast and, still leading the formation, they were the first to reach Biskra. Firing three emergency flares, they circled while the rest of the bombers landed; then, with the runways cleared, they readied themselves to try to get her down. Miraculously, she made it, her tail scraping along the ground until finally they came to a grinding halt. 'No business, Doc,' Lieutenant Bragg called from the cockpit as the ambulance hurried to them. Not a single member of the crew had been injured. As one of the 97th staff noted, 'A Fortress really can take a beating and still fly.'

A crew member of another of the bombers took a photograph of the crippled *All American* as they flew back to Biskra, a picture that made the front page of the forces newspaper, *Stars and Stripes*. 'UNKINDEST CUT OF ALL, BUT BOMBER BEATS RAP,' ran the headline. Boeing officials looked at the plane as it landed and said it was 'aerodynamically impossible to fly'. But flown it had, to the ever-lasting gratitude of Ralph Burbridge and the rest of the crew of *All American*.

CHAPTER 40

Frühlingswind

DESPITE AN UNCOMFORTABLE day at Casablanca, Eisenhower had returned to AFHQ with a weight lifted from his shoulders. He was pleased with the new command arrangement and had been relieved to have the President's backing. Even so, neither Alexander nor Tedder would be taking up their new roles until Libya had been wrapped up, which, realistically, meant sometime in February. In the meantime, the plan was to continue to bring forces forward but to keep First Army largely on the defensive until Eighth Army had reached the Mareth Line. Only Général Juin, the new commander of the French forces in Tunisia, offered a word of caution. His men were now positioned in the Fondouk area, guarding two passes through the Eastern Dorsale, the north–south spine of mountains to the east of the country. They were dangerously strung out and pitifully short of equipment too. 'The Germans,' he warned, 'will not remain inactive.'

There were, in all, four passes through the Eastern Dorsale, and these were the only real means of moving an army from the Tunisian interior to the coastal plain or vice versa and, as Juin had predicted, Kesselring had also registered their importance, recognizing that while German and Italian troops held these gateways, they would not lose Tunisia. With this in mind, he ordered von Arnim to mount a series of attacks to push the Allies clear and take control of them. These operations began on 18 January with 10. Panzerdivision making a diversionary attack in the north around Bou Arada. Mines, mud and good shooting by the British artillery ensured 10. Panzer didn't get very far, but further south Axis infantry and several of the new Tiger tanks burst through the Ousseltia Valley, where the French XIX Corps were holding the line, and swiftly captured more than 3,500. The British 36th Brigade and Combat Command B – effectively a US armoured brigade – were sent to stem the flow, and six days later, on 24 January, von Arnim called off the attack and his men settled into their new positions, satisfied his limited objectives had been taken.

It was abundantly clear the French were simply not up to the job. They urgently needed both retraining and re-equipping, but that would mean a major shift of formations in the line. Even the French, however, could now see that their refusal to serve under the British was proving counter-productive and so finally accepted Anderson's command in First Army. This meant that, at long last, Anderson was now commander of all troops in Tunisia: British, American and French. However, although this certainly made life easier, by the end of January units had become hopelessly muddled, and while the Bowles twins, for example, could not have minded less about being attached to the British, there were differences of doctrine, culture and equipment that meant it would be far better to keep nationalities and divisions together. What's more, it was impossible for a commander to oversee the development, deployment and further training of a division if it was divided up and sent to the four winds.

Meanwhile, way to the north in Norway, SOE's Agent 24, Gunnar Sønsteby, was keenly aware that the Gestapo were now on to him and that the net was closing in around him. In the middle of January, one of his contacts, a mason named Ellingsen, had to leave his house after a couple of suspicious calls from an unknown person. To play safe, Sønsteby and his colleagues decided to stop using a flat where they had been meeting, just in case Ellingsen had been unwittingly compromised in any way. Despite this, Sønsteby decided to check the property over. It was night and snow lay thick on the ground. As he approached the building he felt certain he could see a faint glow around the blackout curtains. Cautiously, he stepped inside, climbed the stairs and rang the bell. A moment later, the door opened and he found himself looking at a pistol held by a German policeman. Behind him were two other men. Involuntarily, Sønsteby's hand moved to his coat, where he was carrying his own weapon. The policeman came right up to him and pressed the muzzle in Sønsteby's chest.

'Come inside at once!' he growled.

'Damned if I do,' Sønsteby replied, knocking the pistol aside before the man could react and scarpering down the stairs. Two shots followed him, but it was dark and they missed. Outside, a companion was waiting with a car and Sønsteby jumped in and they sped off.

Unfortunately, however, as Sønsteby had fled from the house, his briefcase had come undone and his notebook had fallen out. He was pretty sure there was nothing compromising in it, but he couldn't swear to it. Clearly, he had to get it back.

First, a change of clothes. He had a set in another house nearby but, having opened the front door, he was about to climb the stairs when he heard shots from above and the sound of running feet – clearly the Germans were there too. This was beginning to look like a comprehensive sting. Despite this, Sønsteby felt he just had to get the notebook so decided to head back to the first flat. Approaching cautiously, his hand gripping his pistol, all seemed quiet. He headed through the gate and along the side wall to the corner where he believed he had dropped it, and there it was, lying on the snow. Picking it up, he calmly walked back out of the gate once more. He had got away with it.

Not all his colleagues in the resistance were so fortunate, however. Later that night, Sønsteby managed to track down Ellingsen and speak with him. It seemed the mason had been set up too, although he had managed to shoot two Gestapo men before making good his escape. By the time Sønsteby saw him, Ellingsen was beside himself with worry – not for killing two Germans but for the reprisals that would inevitably follow. 'But this was an idea we had to banish from our consciences,' wrote Sønsteby. 'We couldn't give up the struggle because of possible innocent victims – a view which was shared by our superiors in London and Stockholm.'

Some 200 people were arrested that night in Oslo in one of the Gestapo's biggest round-up operations to date. Many were known Communists, but three of Sønsteby's network were also picked up, including his close colleagues Halvor Rivrud and T. Aarnes; both of them were beaten and tortured, although they never revealed a word.

Some days later, Sønsteby discovered what had happened. Sverre Ellingsen, the mason's wife, had been phoned a few weeks earlier by a Norwegian man telling her he had to speak urgently with her husband. Sønsteby and Ellingsen had discussed this and decided that perhaps they should call the man. When Ellingsen did, the man said his name was Monsen and he had been under arrest by the Gestapo. However, he had been released and had important messages and information for the resistance.

The more Sønsteby and Ellingsen discussed it, the more they smelled a rat, yet they decided to meet Monsen all the same; after all, if he was in the pocket of the Gestapo, he would need to gain some contacts in the resistance. To that end, it seemed unlikely the Germans would strike at Monsen's first meeting with them. None the less, they had not taken any chances: a car was left running outside and they had been armed. Sønsteby was convinced the man was a traitor the moment he saw him. 'There was something queer about his eyes,' he noted. 'After talking with him for a few minutes and arranging another meeting, neither Ellingsen nor I were in doubt: the man was an informer, a traitor.'

Needless to say, they had not attended the second meeting but, after the night of arrests, Sønsteby realized the Gestapo now knew his name. 'But what of it?' he wrote. 'I just had to adapt to the fact and carry on.' However, he recognized it might be prudent to get out of Oslo for a little while. Three days later, he took the trip to Stockholm in an Esso tanker driven by a friend, Sønsteby in disguise as the driver's mate and Ellingsen hidden in a stripped-out locker compartment. They made it without incident. For the moment, Sønsteby had eluded the Gestapo.

On 14 January, it had been Fritz Bayerlein's birthday and at Feldmarschall Rommel's HQ he was serenaded and toasted, and reminded what a good fellow he was. Later that night, however, the British had attacked with yet another blistering artillery barrage and the birthday celebrations quickly came to an end. Major Hans von Luck and his recce group had joined the 164th Light Division in an attempt to stem the flow, but by the 17th Rommel had recognized there could be no hope of holding their current position and so ordered them to fall back to the next line, which was the Homs–Tarhuna position – and the last line of defence before Tripoli. With massed British tanks advancing and enemy artillery fire pouring down upon them, Rommel became aware that Eighth Army was simultaneously about to outflank their position. 'When this news came in,' he wrote, 'I was forced to decide to give up Tarhuna immediately.' This effectively meant giving up Tripoli too, but not before most of the stores had been safely transported back across the Tunisian border and many of the port installations had been demolished.

Although it had been the right decision, abandoning Tripoli without recourse to his superiors went down very badly with Cavallero and Mussolini and they now demanded Rommel make a renewed stand. He and his staff gasped when they received this signal. 'You can either hold on to Tripoli a few more days and lose the army,' Rommel told Cavallero, 'or lose Tripoli a few days earlier and save the army for Tunisia. Make up your mind.' Of course, it was too late by then and, as if to prove the point, British motor torpedo boats also sank ten out of fourteen fuel barges just to the west of Tripoli. On 23 January, Tripoli fell and the Libyan campaign was over.

Hitler's determination to hold on to Tunisia remained undiminished, however. On 12 January, Kesselring had made a presentation at the Wolf's Lair and had spoken with his usual optimism. Hitler was still thinking it would be possible to drive the Allies all the way back to Casablanca and then finally throw them out altogether, although the next moment, when Ciano and Cavallero pleaded for more support from the Luftwaffe, Hitler turned them down for lack of resources. Now that Rommel had withdrawn into Tunisia, however, the Führer declared the moment had arrived to start offensive plans. Such were the fantastical contradictions of the Commander-in-Chief of the German Armed Forces.

And despite Hitler's offensive thinking, the knives were still out for Rommel. 'I simply can't tell you how hard it is for me to undergo this retreat and all that goes with it,' he wrote to his wife two days later. 'Day and night I'm tormented by the thought that things might go really wrong here in Africa. I'm so depressed that I can hardly do my work.' Hitler and Mussolini – and Kesselring, for that matter – had much the same concerns. Rommel had lost his lustre; he was the golden boy no more. At midday on 26 January, he received a signal from the Commando Supremo telling him that because of his ill-health he was being relieved of his command. Certainly he was not well, but Rommel was not fooled: this was a polite way of telling him he had been sacked. Generale Giovanni Messe, the Italian who had commanded the first Italian corps in the Soviet Union, was being sent to take over.

By Saturday, 13 February, Eighth Army was advancing towards the Mareth Line in south-east Tunisia, which barred their route some 80 miles to the north-west of the Libyan border. Rearguards of the

Panzerarmee Afrika were doing their best to slow the British advance, but two southern Tunisian border towns, Ben Gardane and Tataouine, had fallen and now Eighth Army was looking to swiftly capture the island of Djerba, which lay just off the Tunisian coast and which not only offered flank protection but also an airfield, an even greater asset.

The island was also home to a large and ancient community of Jews, who had survived living on the island for more than 2,000 years and who had become renowned as jewellers and goldsmiths. It was for these riches that SS troops hurried to the island that second Sabbath in February. It is often assumed that the SS never reached North Africa, but in fact an Einsatzkommando had been posted to Tunis the previous November under Obersturmbannführer Walter Rauff. His brief had been to use 'executive measures against the civil population.' This was a typical piece of Nazi vagueness, giving Rauff the authority to do pretty much whatever he wanted. Since reaching Tunis, he and his men had rounded up almost all the city's Jews, then marched them off to carry out manual labour on behalf of the Wehrmacht, building defences around Tunisian airfields and elsewhere. For the privilege of forcibly serving the Reich in such a manner, Tunis's Jews were also expected to pay all expenses out of their own pockets.

Rauff had already been part of the Einsatzkommandos operating in Poland and the Ukraine and had proved himself to be a man with no moral scruples whatsoever. A former colleague and friend of Reinhard Heydrich when they had been in the Kriegsmarine together, it had been a connection that had unquestionably helped Rauff's career. However, Heydrich had also once bailed out Rauff financially; this had placed Rauff in the former head of the RSHA's pocket. Heydrich, of course, had since been murdered in Prague, but before then Rauff had been one of his go-to men for the more unpleasant tasks of the SS. It was Rauff, for example, who had been one of the first to use mobile gas chambers in the East.

Rauff was not only very willing to both persecute and execute Jews, he was also very keen to make as much money as possible. So long as Jews carried out brutally hard labour on the part of the Reich, his orders gave him *carte blanche* to act as he saw fit, and with the Wehrmacht commanders like Rommel and von Arnim busy fighting the Allies, and with his paymasters far, far away, there were even fewer checks on his authority than there might otherwise have been.

Aware of the potential riches on Djerba, he now hurriedly packed off one of his subordinates, Obersturmführer Theodor Saevecke, to grab as much plunder as he could before Eighth Army arrived. That it was the Sabbath when Saevecke and his men arrived was an even greater offence to this particularly old order of Jews. This cut no cloth with Saevecke, however, and from the Djerban elders he demanded 50 kilograms of gold within twelve hours. If they did not produce this, he warned them, the shooting would begin. Hurriedly, the rabbis and elders went around their community collecting gold: personal trinkets, shop contents and even a large amount from the ancient Great Synagogue. Eventually, Saevecke was anxiously offered up 43 kilograms; it was, the Jewish leaders explained, all they could gather in the time. Saevecke snatched the lot, demanded the rest be produced by the following morning, then, with British guns already booming, fled back across to the mainland and made good his escape with his men, but without the final 7 kilograms. Djerba fell a few days later. Needless to say, none of the Djerban gold was ever knowingly seen again.

Back over Europe, the air war continued. In England, the RAF had become a truly polyglot force; not only were there those from the Dominions, but also those from countries crushed by Germany but which still had plenty of young men willing to continue the fight. If that meant wearing British uniforms, flying British aircraft and swearing an oath to King George VI, then so be it. The umbrella organization of the RAF provided them with a feeling of fellowship and unity with those also willing to try to defeat Nazism, but it in no way detracted from the still-powerful sense of national identity.

At Turnhouse near Edinburgh that January, 341 Squadron was forming. The RAF had decided that squadron numbers in the three hundreds should be reserved for other nationalities, and 341 was French, to be known as the 'Alsace' squadron. Among those founding pilots was a young Frenchman called Pierre Clostermann. He had been studying engineering in California when war broke out. The west coast had suited him well because his great passion was flying and had been from an early age; back in France, he had gained his pilot's licence in 1937 when still only sixteen. In the blue skies over San Diego he had been flying pretty much every day that summer, practising aerobatics and dreaming of the day, in October 1941, when he would be old enough to join the École de l'Air.

The armistice of June 1940 had rather put paid to those ambitions. His family were living in Rio de Janeiro at the time, and soon after his father wrote to him telling him he was immediately heading to London to join de Gaulle. Clostermann was to return to Rio and take his mother to Brazzaville in Free French West Africa. After that, Pierre was old enough to make up his own mind, but his father hoped he would join him in London. Sitting on the beach in Malibu, the sun beating down and peace all around him, Clostermann read and re-read the letter. The war seemed a million miles away, but he knew he had no choice but to follow his father's instructions. He had dreamed of flying a Dewoitine 520, the primary French fighter, but it was not a big leap to switch that ambition towards a Spitfire.

By Christmas 1940, he had arranged everything for his mother, helped pack up the house in Rio, and had then set off by ship for England. Now, two years later, he was finally joining his first operational squadron. The pilots arrived first – the squadron commander was René Mouchotte, a pre-war Regular who had been in Oran at the time of the armistice. Along with five others, he had taken a plane and flown to Gibraltar and then on to Britain. Another, Lieutenant Michel Boudier, was already an ace with seven victories to his name from the Battle of France. Others had flown with the RAF in Libya, while some, like Clostermann, had yet to fly in combat.

Then their aircraft arrived – Spitfires, as Clostermann had imagined during that moment of reflection on Malibu beach. British ground crew had checked them over and cleaned them up, then the Free French crosses of Lorraine had been painted on to them along with the squadron letters, N and L. Now the new squadron had its pilots and its planes. It was time to get ready for battle.

There were also now plenty of Polish squadrons serving in the RAF. During the Battle of Britain 303 had been the most successful single fighter squadron and now there were no fewer than nine such Polish squadrons operating within Fighter Command. Among them was 315 Squadron, based at Northolt, which had been joined by the American Gabby Gabreski.

They had also only recently taken delivery of the new Spitfire Mk IX, equipped with the Rolls-Royce Merlin 66 with 1,720 horsepower and a top speed of 409 mph. This was faster and more powerful than the Me109G and about on a par with the Focke-Wulf 190. It was also fitted with both machine guns and cannons and proved that, unlike the Me109 airframe, the Spitfire, in its fundamental design, still had room for further development, which, in terms of production, was good news because the fewer new machine tools – and construction skills – that were needed to develop a new aircraft, the easier mass production became. 'The plane was everything I expected and more,' noted Gabreski, 'light on the controls, fast climbing, and manoeuvrable.'

He finally flew his first combat mission in January after several weeks of hard training with the squadron. It was a circus mission over Le Havre, and Gabreski offered a short prayer before heading out into the cold morning air, wearing his sheepskin Irvin flying jacket. He noticed that his fellows were all a little on edge; the jokes were a bit coarser and the laughter a bit louder. It had been Flight Lieutenant Tadeusz Andersz who had been mentoring Gabreski, and before they headed to their waiting Spits he spoke quietly to the American, reminding him the wingman's job was to protect his leader and keep a keen watch out for the enemy. 'He reassured me that he thought I was as ready as I'd ever be, and that meant a lot coming from him,' wrote Gabreski. 'Finally, we shook hands next to my Spitfire, and it was time to go.'

As they took off and headed towards the Channel, Gabreski couldn't help thinking about what he'd got himself into. He felt the dread of the unknown, but was more worried about making a mistake, or panicking and letting the Poles down, than he was about getting hurt. Over the Channel, he spotted the formation of US bombers and they followed, high above at around 20,000 feet. He found it an eerie feeling, flying alone in that tight cockpit, knowing that all that stood between his life and death was his ability to fly the plane.

Over France, they turned north; the bombers had gone and although he scanned the sky for all he was worth, he could not see a single enemy fighter plane. Nor did anyone else; that day, they were not willing to come out and play. And so 315 Squadron flew back across the sea, over London and touched back down at Northolt, Gabreski feeling the mixed emotions of relief that he'd safely returned from his first mission and disappointment over the lack of action. His time, however, would come soon enough.

Following the Casablanca Conference, General Marshall once again sat down with Eisenhower at AFHQ in Algiers. 'There is one thing that you must understand clearly,' Marshall told him. 'Retention under your command of any American officer means to me that you are satisfied with his performance. Any man you deem unsatisfactory, you must reassign or send him home!' As it was, the culling of inadequate officers had continued. The old, pre-war US Army was rapidly changing; there was no room, as Marshall was well aware, for any dead wood.

The OKW and Commando Supremo had decided Rommel was dead wood too, but while the Feldmarschall had accepted he was leaving, he had not done so immediately. Rather, he had decided – and been sanctioned – to conduct one last action in North Africa. He had already given orders for the Mareth Line – fortifications originally built by the French between the coast and the Matmata Hills – to be strengthened. This was some 20 miles in from the Tunisian border and behind the first line of defence at Medenine. By moving most of the Panzerarmee Afrika, save some outposts at Medenine, behind the Mareth Line, Rommel reckoned he now had a bit of time on his side, because Eighth Army were unlikely to rush either position. In this, he read his opposite number correctly.

What concerned Rommel was that, if he waited with all his forces behind the Mareth Line, Eighth Army would advance from the west and the First Army from the east, and he and his men would become sandwiched in the middle, encircled and then destroyed. To ensure this didn't happen, he now planned a daring thrust into central-southern Tunisia to force the US II Corps back. Then the Panzerarmee could return to dealing with Eighth Army without constantly watching their backs.

Rommel was still worried, however, that Eighth Army might try to outflank the Mareth Line by a sweep through the desert to the south of the Matmata Hills. With this in mind, he sent Hans von Luck and his recce group to capture the old fort of Foum Tataouine, secure the area and then reconnoitre for any sign of the British. Although his column was attacked by air, they headed south and some 60 miles inland found the fort. Really, it was little more than heaped stones but, after an exchange of machine-gun fire, the French defenders soon surrendered. From the commander's rough office, von Luck signalled to General Alfred Gause, Rommel's Chief of Staff: 'Foum Tataouine occupied, garrison taken prisoner, radio destroyed, reconnaissance far to the south, no contact with enemy.' He was, he added, now returning to the Mareth Line.

Once back, he was briefed by Gause about Rommel's plan. While the Italians had been left to man the Mareth Line, the freshly re-equipped 21. Panzer had already secured the mouth of the Faïd Pass through the Eastern Dorsale – even better, they had captured more than a thousand American troops in the process. It had been an encouraging start.

What's more, the Panzerarmee Afrika was now in far better shape than it had been and the Fifth Panzerarmee was also continuing to grow in size as more transports and ships continued to make the narrow hop across the Mediterranean. Around 75 per cent of supplies were getting through, which amounted to around 40–50,000 tons per day into Bizerte and Tunis. Promised extra divisions had still not arrived, but von Arnim had around 105,000 men by the middle of February and over 200 tanks, of which eleven were Tigers. Even so, Ultra decrypts revealed that von Arnim reckoned his force was capable of only limited offensive action. On 9 February, Rommel met with both von Arnim and Kesselring. Rommel and von Arnim loathed one another, but at this meeting they managed to agree on a plan of attack – albeit a limited one. Kesselring, forever the optimist, readily concurred. In a few days' time, Rommel's Afrikakorps and von Arnim's 10. Panzer would strike at US II Corps, take the American base at Gafsa and cripple the Americans sufficiently to give Rommel's Army the breathing space to turn back and deal with Eighth Army. It was to be called Operation FRÜHLINGSWIND – 'Spring Wind'.

Meanwhile, General Walter Warlimont had been badgering Jodl to allow him to visit Rome, Tunis and the North African front. Cavallero had just been sacked and replaced by Maresciallo Vittorio Ambrosio as Chief of the Commando Supremo and Kesselring had managed to integrate some of his staff with those of the Italians in Rome, but the command structure was still a mess and, in any case, Warlimont was convinced that, for all the strategic and political reasons for holding Tunisia, the tactical necessities were now beyond their capabilities. In this he was quite correct.

Jodl eventually sanctioned the trip, which lasted ten days in the first half of February. 'Everything I saw and heard,' Warlimont wrote, 'led me to the conclusion, already reached by Field Marshal Rommel, that there could be no question of attack but that evacuation of North Africa was the order of the day.'

*

Headquarters of the 1st Armored Division was now in a large prickly-pear cactus patch just west of the small Tunisian town of Sbeitla, still dominated by the ruins of the once much larger Roman city. Recently arrived to take over as divisional G3 – operational planning – was 34-year-old Lieutenant-Colonel Hamilton Howze. Only one armoured brigade, Combat Command B, had taken part in the TORCH landings – the rest of the 'Old Ironside', as the division was known, had arrived piecemeal from England, where they had been languishing since the previous summer; despite being a staff officer, Howze had been among these later arrivals at the front. The son of a general, he was a career soldier who had passed through West Point and then joined the cavalry, and throughout the thirties had spent much of his time on horseback. Only since Pearl Harbor had he managed to transfer to an armoured unit and not until April 1942 had he joined the 1st Armored Division and soon after found himself being shipped overseas.

Howze reached the front in January and it was quickly apparent that 1st Armored was badly undertrained – a view shared by the also newly arrived division commander, Major-General Orlando 'Pinky' Ward. While Combat Command B was now tough and battle-hardened, the other three brigades had clearly largely unlearned all they had been taught back in England, and since arriving in North Africa had done no training at all.

Even worse, it was all too clear that Fredendall had taken an instant and profound dislike to Ward. The II Corps commander appeared to be increasingly unhinged. He had set up his command post at Speedy Valley, near Tébessa and 80 miles from the front, in a narrow gorge that could be accessed only by a single-lane track and was being bolstered by 200 engineers who had been brought in to create an underground bunker system. It was madness, as were Fredendall's command decisions. He ordered Ward to split up the various Combat Commands and fling them together with piecemeal artillery and infantry from 1st and 34th Divisions; units were being broken into penny packets and given point-less tasks. Ward protested but was given a swift rebuke. 'To our very great disappointment,' wrote Hamilton Howze, 'we remained split into widely separated parts.'

At the moment 21. Panzer had burst through the Faïd Pass, Fredendall had sent part of Combat Command A to help the French there, left the other half at the town of Sbeitla, and then sent Combat Command D on an offensive operation to take the Italian position at Sened Station near Maknassy, at the southern end of the Eastern Dorsale. This was an utterly pointless and half-hearted thrust in the circumstances; it proved costly and achieved little. Meanwhile, Bing Evans and the Rangers were sent to carry out a night-time raid on another Italian outpost, which was more successful, but which cost twenty Ranger casualties and, again, achieved not a lot. All this meant that 1st Armored had been dangerously split up and weakened. The French, meanwhile – and despite the urgent need to get them out of the line and re-equipped and trained – were still very thinly holding their portions of the line. Really, the southern half of the line was now a bit of a mess. II Corps was being commanded by a lunatic from a bunker far from the front, the French were incapable of offensive operations in their current state, and much of the American armour was split hither and thither. Both Anderson and Eisenhower had discussed pulling their forces back to the Grande Dorsale, where supply lines would be shorter and they could try to regroup. Neither, however, had quite managed to give the order, presumably fearing the reaction and loss of face this would cause.

As a result, when Rommel and von Arnim launched their attack on 14 February, St Valentine's Day, the Allies in their path were in absolutely no position to put up much of a fight.

From his bunker in Speedy Valley, Fredendall continued to issue crass and pointless orders. Parts of 1st Armored Division were expected to counter-attack overwhelming formations of panzers, and battalions were placed on isolated hilltops where they had no mutually supporting fire. With horrible inevitability, the American penny packets were swept aside as 10. Panzer stormed through the Faïd Pass, supported by Stukas and fighters. Fifty-one Shermans of the undercooked Combat Command A were sent in to meet this thrust, but at Sidi Bou Zid ran into 21. Panzer, who had stormed up from Maknassy and through the Maizila Pass 20 miles to the south. Dust and smoke from the Stukas and fighter-bombers added to the Americans' confusion, but the Shermans were being picked off by German anti-tank guns, one after the other.

At 1st Armored's HQ at the Cactus Patch near Sbeitla, Ward was asking Fredendall for urgent reinforcements. The II Corps commander asked General Anderson in turn. Anderson, however, was relying on out-of-date Ultra decrypts, which suggested the main thrust was coming further north, around Fondouk. Although the 70–90 enemy tanks

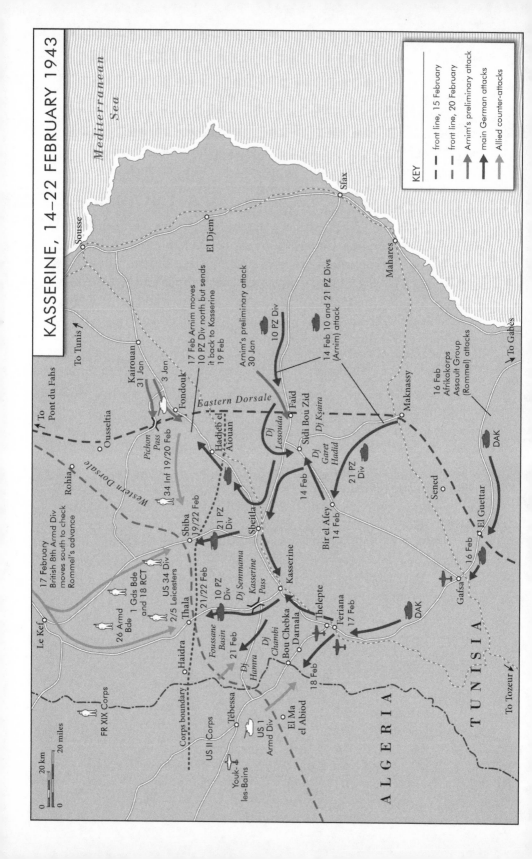

KASSERINE, 14–22 FEBRUARY 1943

Mediterranean Sea

Sousse

El Djem

Sfax

Mahares

To Tunis

Kairouan

To Pont du Fahs

Ousseltia

Rohia

Le Kef

To Gabès

KEY

- — — front line, 15 February
- ····· front line, 20 February
- ⇧ Arnim's preliminary attack
- ⬆ main German attacks
- ⬆ Allied counter-attacks

31 Jan

3 Jan

Fondouk

17 Feb Arnim moves 10 PZ Div north but sends it back to Kasserine 19 Feb

Arnim's preliminary attack 30 Jan

10 PZ Div

14 Feb 10 and 21 PZ Divs (Arnim) attack

Maknassy

16 Feb Afrikakorps Assault Group (Rommel) attacks

Eastern Dorsale

Pichon Pass

34 Inf 19/20 Feb

Hadjeb el Aïouan

Western Dorsale

Faid

Dj Lessouda

Sidi Bou Zid

Dj Ksaira

Dj Garet Hadid

14 Feb

Sened

DAK

17 February British 8th Armd Div moves south to check Rommel's advance

Sbiba 19/22 Feb

21 PZ Div

Sbeitla

21 PZ Div

Bir el Afey 14 Feb

14 Feb

El Guettar

16 Feb

26 Armd Bde 1 Gds Bde and 18 RCT

US 34 Div 2/5 Leicesters

Thala 21/22 Feb

10 PZ Div 21/22 Feb

Dj Semmama

Kasserine Pass

Kasserine

Gafsa

DAK

FR XIX Corps

Haidra

Foussane Basin 21 Feb

Dj Humra

Dj Chambi

Bou Chebka

Darnala

18 Feb

Thelepte

Feriana 17 Feb

DAK

To Tozeur

Corps boundary

Tébessa

US II Corps

El Ma el Abiod

US 1 Armd Div

Youk-les-Bains

A L G E R I A

T U N I S I A

0   20 km

0   20 miles

reported now in the Sidi Bou Zid area should have told First Army staff this had to be the main Axis effort, Anderson continued to place too much faith in Ultra and only one tank battalion from Combat Command B, still in the north with the British, was released and sent south. To make matters worse, Anderson then sent a signal to Fredendall ordering him to concentrate on 'clearing up the situation and destroying the enemy.' Anderson had fatally misread the situation, while Fredendall, still stuck in his bunker, was in no position to pass on such an order. Hamilton Howze could not believe what he was hearing. 'This was insanity,' he wrote. The best they could manage the following day was a cobbled-together force of Combat Command C and one further tank battalion. Lying in wait for them were not only over 100 panzers but also a plethora of artillery and anti-tank guns. 'General Ward didn't like it and neither did I,' added Howze.

This scratch force began riding into the Valley of Death at around midday on the 15th. Of course, it was a slaughter. By nightfall, 1st Armored had lost 98 tanks, 57 half-tracks, 29 guns and some 500 men in two days of mismatched fighting; 100 tank crews, who had been together since before America entered the war, had been blown away in this brutal baptism to combat.

Anderson, having accepted too late that the German attack was indeed the main thrust, now recommended to Eisenhower a wholesale withdrawal to the Grande Dorsale. This was rubber-stamped at 5 p.m. on the 15th. Around the same time, von Arnim told Rommel he would march towards Sbeitla and then turn north to Fondouk the following day. Rommel, meanwhile, moved forward on the 16th, heading towards Gafsa to the south-west. Seeing a road full of his own trucks, troops and tanks, he felt his confidence rising once more and, with the cheers of his troops ringing in his ears, a far more ambitious plan began to take shape in his mind. Rather than pulling back the Afrikakorps, he would reinforce it and push on towards Fériana, then either head on to Tébessa or wheel north towards Kasserine and link up with von Arnim's forces.

Rommel had begun this operation as a limited offensive only. Now, however, his blood was up once more. He was sniffing the opportunity for a major victory.

CHAPTER 41

Heavy Water

W HILE THE THUNDER of battle was raging in Tunisia, in Tripoli Montgomery had decided to hold a conference of Allied commanders at which they could discuss and share ideas and lessons learned from the recent fighting. It was not a bad idea and the turnout, all things considered, was pretty impressive. General Walter Bedell Smith, Eisenhower's Chief of Staff, made the trip to the city, as did General Patton. Tedder and Alexander also showed up, although Montgomery was disappointed there were not more divisional commanders from Tunisia. That they might have had their hands full already does not appear to have occurred to him.

While, of course, Montgomery was happy to give a talk about how he had won at Alamein, he had, to his credit, never denied the important role of air power in that victory and, despite growing personal tensions, now gave Mary Coningham the platform to speak about the development of tactical air power, from which he could properly articulate these ideas into a semi-formal creed. 'The doctrine that we have evolved by trial in war over a period of many months,' Coningham told his audience, 'could, I think, be stated in its simplest form as follows: the soldier commands the land forces, the airman commands the air forces; both commanders work together and operate their respective forces in accordance with a combined Army-Air plan, the whole operation being directed by the Army Commander.'

This was something that he and Tedder had been vociferously arguing for for the past eighteen months; it was also a view with which Larry

Kuter, Coningham's new American deputy, concurred wholeheartedly. As Coningham now pointed out, the army fought on the ground along a front that could be divided into many sectors. The air front, however, was indivisible. The army had one battle to fight: the land battle. But the air had two: first, it had to beat the enemy in the air, then it could go into battle against the enemy land forces 'with maximum possible hitting power.' They lived in a technical age, he told them, and there was much to learn about their professions. 'In plain language,' he added, 'no soldier is competent to operate the Air, just as no airman is competent to operate the Army.'

Mutual support was the key. 'Sedaka is a good example of the standard that we have reached,' he said. This was a site halfway between Benghazi and Tripoli and one that had, the previous December, been earmarked as a potential landing ground. Advance units of 7th Armoured Division had arrived there one evening and by the following morning had cleared a landing strip, equipped it with anti-aircraft guns, motor transport and fuel. Soon after, two fighter squadrons had touched down and later that day attacked targets just 40 miles east of Tripoli. By the time they had landed back down again, more fuel, ammunition and maintenance teams had also been flown in. These transport planes could then be used to fly wounded soldiers back to the rear. 'You can imagine the effect on the morale of the Army,' Coningham continued, 'when it is known that badly wounded cases, if trundled over the desert, very often die.'

He also pointed out that another reason air commanders should make the decision on what and where to bomb was that they often had a better appreciation of the targets on offer. He gave an example: an army unit at the front might report a concentration of 200 enemy vehicles and armour, but their request for an air attack is then turned down. Perhaps 15 miles away, however, an even bigger concentration of enemy armour is discovered, which, from experience, they know might well affect the whole course of the battle some time later. 'The smaller formations of the Army must understand that penny packets of air are a luxury which can only be afforded at certain times, and that judgement on the question of targets is the result of agreement between the Army and Air Commanders, and in accordance with the Army Commander's broad directive on policy.'

As Coningham was ready to point out, experience backed up the rightness of this doctrine and his speech marked a key moment in the development of Allied air power. Coningham was articulating his doctrine for tactical air power, or close air support. While the efficiency and effectiveness of this co-operation between air and army clearly had further potential for evolution, the principles were both sound and provided a blueprint for that future development. There were still plenty in the Army, however, who disagreed with Coningham's theories about the independence of what he called the 'tactical air force' – Patton, who had been listening, included. Eisenhower endorsed the policy but, Larry Kuter believed, was not convinced. Winning the hearts and minds of the Army commanders would be an enormous task as the Allies continued to develop their way of war.

Von Arnim's panzers had actually been held up by Combat Command A at Sbeitla long enough to bring a semblance of order and to enable the American forces there, the 1st Armored Headquarters included, to pull out in reasonable order on 17 February and head towards Kasserine and then on through the Kasserine Pass. Meanwhile, Anderson had ordered reinforcements southwards to block the passes through the Grande Dorsale, including the British 6th Division and also the US 18th RCT. By this time, the 18th had spent forty-eight days continually in the line in the Medjez sector and now were finally moving only to help stem another crisis. They were to take up positions across the valley next to the Sbiba–Sbeitla road. They reached their new positions on the morning of 18 February, and at Company G's line Tom Bowles began furiously digging in. His brother, Henry, was also busy. As a wireman in HQ Company, his job was to lay down the telephone lines between battalion headquarters and the various company HQs, which meant scurrying with a wire buddy across unfamiliar ground with a large spool of wire. With battalion HQ at least half a mile behind the companies, this was a tiring and time-consuming task.

Meanwhile, to the south, Rommel had surged on down the Gafsa–Fériana road and by afternoon had not only taken Fériana but was now marching on the airfield at Thelepte. While the fighters there were quick to move out, Bing Evans and the Rangers had been the last to leave, glancing back with disgust at the sight of thirty-four unserviceable fighters burning, the columns of smoke billowing into the air. With the Afrikakorps hard on their heels, they hurried off to make a stand up the Dernaia Pass on the road to Tébessa.

By the following night, 18/19 February, Major Hans von Luck had joined Rommel's advance and was ordered to try to take the Kasserine Pass in a surprise assault, then hold it open for the follow-up units, which included 15. Panzer and Adolf Lamm and his crew. Heading off at dawn with his motorcycle escorts in front, he had hoped to catch the Americans off guard. The defence was finally stiffening, however, and they soon came under heavy artillery fire directed by forward observation officers on the heights at either side. 'I couldn't get through,' wrote von Luck. 'Neither could a rifle regiment that was sent in against the pass.'

Rommel's advance was now running out of steam. Von Arnim had turned his thrust north towards Fondouk, rather than west. Rommel was furious. Once again, he felt a golden opportunity for a crushing victory had been foiled – just a bit more fuel, or another panzer division, such as 10. Panzer, and he was certain they would have done it. Just up the road at Tébessa were the main American supply dumps. Get those, and they could keep going and strike deep into the Allied rear.

This, however, was starting to sound like an all-too-familiar refrain. Rommel never seemed to have enough; that was true, but it was always someone else's fault – the Higher Command, their Italian allies, a lack of promised fuel. The biggest problem, however, was that Rommel always overreached himself. Once again, he had passed his culmination point, and the stiffer opposition his forces were now facing rather proved the point. Von Arnim understood this, which was why he had sensibly concentrated on Fondouk; this would help expand the northern bridgehead and ensure the east of the country remained clear for the inevitable link-up with the Panzerarmee Afrika when the time came. And so he refused Rommel's appeal. Rommel then turned to Kesselring, who gave him the provisional go-ahead. 'I feel like an old cavalry horse that has suddenly heard the bugles sound again,' Rommel said.

The Commando Supremo, however, were also worried about sending him deep into Algeria, so while they handed him control of both 10. and 21. Panzer, they demanded he wheel northwards towards Le Kef, not Tébessa. Like von Arnim, they had recognized that, by careering off into Algeria, Rommel would have exposed his rear and risked much more than he was likely to have gained. Needless to say, Rommel was furious. 'This,' he wrote, 'was an appalling and unbelievable piece of short-sightedness.' But for once he obeyed his orders, turned north-east and headed towards the Kasserine Pass.

On 19 February, 21. Panzer came face to face with the blocking force of the British 1st Guards Brigade, three battalions of the 34th Red Bulls and the 18th RCT of the Big Red One. The Germans made little progress, losing around twenty panzers to the Guards and then turning towards the 18th RCT. By 5 p.m., some thirty panzers were thundering down on the Americans. Company G found themselves bearing the brunt; Tom Bowles's mortar team fired shell after shell against the panzers, who were making no more progress than they had against the Guards. Henry Bowles and his wiring buddy were scuttling to and fro mending damaged telephone lines, concentrating on the job in hand and trying desperately not to think about the enemy shells pounding their lines. Behind, newly arrived British 17-pounders linked to the American positions were knocking out one tank after another. These bigger, better anti-tank guns were superb: easy to handle, quick-firing and with a velocity greater than that of the dreaded 88mm. A 17-pounder could even knock out the dreaded Tiger tank; and it could make short work of every other panzer in the Axis arsenal. Ever since the start of the desert war, the British had needed a really first-class anti-tank gun that could fire at more than 3,000 feet per second and over ranges of more than 2,000 yards. The 17-pounder was the answer.

The combination of fire-power and joint Anglo-US resilience showed just how far these troops had come since Longstop. There was now no confusion between battalion commanders. Defensive positions had been properly prepared and each man knew exactly what he had to do. Suddenly, Rommel's forces did not look quite so formidable after all. By dusk, 21. Panzer was falling back and later, under cover of darkness, men of Company G headed out on patrol and, armed with new Bazookas – hand-held anti-tank grenade launchers – finished off four panzers lying disabled in front of them.

Rommel's forces had more success the following day, with 10. Panzer pressing on towards Thala, but the opposition had been growing, the defence more dogged and, by the 22nd, Operation FRÜHLINGSWIND had finally run out of steam. That morning, Rommel drove up the road towards Thala and, after consulting with his commanders, accepted that the Allies had grown too strong. Around 1 p.m., he met up with Kesselring and together they agreed to call off the entire offensive and to withdraw in stages. Before they parted, however, Kesselring offered him the job of the new Army Group Afrika. 'Apparently,' noted Rommel, 'as a result of the Kasserine offensive, I had ceased to be *persona non grata*.' Warily, he accepted, glad to be able to have some wider influence over his men once more but less happy to play 'whipping-boy' for the Führer's HQ, the Commando Supremo and the Luftwaffe. Moreover, he still badly needed medical treatment. First, though, he had to head back to southern Tunisia. Waiting there to smash through the Mareth Line was his old enemy, British Eighth Army.

In the snowy wilderness of the Hardangervidda in central-southern Norway, Jens-Anton Poulsson and his team were still camped out waiting to complete their mission against the heavy-water plant at Vemork. After the fiasco of October, they had been told to stay put, carry out reconnaissance and research and await instructions. Still in regular radio contact with London, they were told that a new Norwegian sabotage team would be parachuted in, codenamed GUNNERSIDE. Their part of the operation was now renamed SWALLOW. A drop had been planned for December, but once again atrocious weather intervened and it had been aborted, so Poulsson and his team had to stay put for a little while longer. 'Before Christmas,' said Poulsson, 'we had a very bad time and had to eat Iceland moss, which can be used. We mixed it with some oatmeal.' Fortunately, on Christmas Eve, Poulsson had managed to shoot a reindeer and their strength had quickly returned. By the middle of February, they had shot a number – enough, at any rate, to keep them going. In between, they had kept busy: gathering wood, hunting, researching contacts and gathering the containers from the original drop back in October, which they stored in their mountain hut. The temperatures remained intensely cold; little did they realize it, but the region was in the throes of one of the worst winters on record, with temperatures rarely above 30 degrees below.

On 23 January, it had seemed that GUNNERSIDE was once again on, by which time Poulsson had an inflamed foot and Knut Haugland was sick. On this occasion it was perhaps just as well that the mission was again aborted due to bad weather. By the middle of February, however, the entire SWALLOW team was fit once more and finally, on 16 February, they received the news that their colleagues were on their way. And this time, the weather held. At two minutes past midnight on the 17th, six men and eleven containers floated downwards to the white expanse below.

Almost inevitably, however, fate intervened. Having gathered most of their supplies, more snow arrived and with it a vicious wind. Travelling across the plain with 30-kilogram packs on their backs and two toboggans with more than 50 kilograms of kit on each was simply not possible. Having found a mountain hut, the GUNNERSIDE team had no choice but to shelter there until the winds passed. That, though, was not for a further six days. When it at last died down, they set out to link up with Poulsson and his team, only to run into a reindeer hunter. Like SWALLOW, they had strict instructions to kill anyone they saw, but felt unable to do so. As it happened, the hunter proved not only a fine skier but a superb guide as well. Soon after, they met up with two of the SWALLOW team; Poulsson had not only insisted his men hunker down until the storm passed, but had correctly deduced the route the GUNNERSIDE team would take to try to rendezvous.

After an elated greeting and a first smoke for Poulsson and his companions in four months, it was time to get on with the mission. The reindeer hunter was released with five days' rations and sworn to secrecy – it was a risk they felt morally they had to take – then they sat down to discuss their plan. Poulsson's team had had more than enough time to work out a course of action. Lying halfway up a sheer mountain face, the only real option was across the lone bridge that spanned the gorge. It was guarded by just two men, armed only with pistols. In total, this remote plant, considered physically almost impregnable, was guarded by just fifteen men, working in three shifts, which meant only five were ever on duty at one time. There was also a garrison of a further forty men at the nearby dam, as well as flak and searchlights, and a garrison of around 200 troops at Rjukan. Finally, two signals-tracking stations had also been established; they had not, however, been directed on to the Hardangervidda and so neither the SWALLOW nor GUNNERSIDE parties, in regular radio contact, had been detected.

None the less, despite the small number of guards actually at the plant, the problem was that, once the shooting started, the nearby garrisons would be swiftly alerted. Even if they managed to lay the charges, the chances of them safely getting away again seemed slight. The only alternative was to try to climb the gorge and break in without alerting the guards, but that meant crossing the river at the foot of the gorge, which was now in thaw, deep and fast-flowing. Whichever way one looked at it, the chances of them both succeeding in their mission and then getting away again to safety looked slight.

Poulsson now guided both parties south to another hut closer to the plant and the following day reached it safely. They were now just 3 miles from Rjukan, and a few miles more from the Vemork heavy-water plant. At 9 a.m. on the morning of the 28th, Sergeant Claus Helberg from Poulsson's team set off in daylight to recce a possible crossing point; like Poulsson, he was from Rjukan and knew the ground well. Five hours later, he returned safely with a big smile on his face, reporting that he'd found a place where they might cross – it was still icy and, although breaking up, he reckoned they could cross it easily. Even so, both Poulsson and Joachim Rønneberg, the GUNNERSIDE leader, were still in favour of attacking across the bridge: it would be easier, they could without difficulty take out the two guards and, they reckoned, this ease of access outweighed the risks that might be caused by the sound of shooting. The others – Helberg included – favoured crossing the gorge and climbing their way. Although Poulsson and Rønneberg were the leaders, they held a vote and the gorge route won the day.

By the time they set off that evening, a wind had whipped up and the snow was melting. Reaching the bottom of the gorge undetected, they managed to get across the river despite the creaking and groaning of the ice underfoot. Although there was a full moon, it was dark in the gorge but there was just enough light to see to climb. They all managed to get up to the rock shelf on which were built huts, barracks and a small rail track. A further 100 metres above was the plant itself; they could see the guards pacing the bridge at the foot of the winding track leading to it. Fifteen minutes later, at midnight, the guards changed. The teams ate some food, made final checks, then, half an hour later, they moved out. Poulsson was in the covering party, taking up position near a wooden shed. With chloroform and Tommy guns, his group now stood guard while the demolitions team broke through a wire gate then split into pairs, each with a set of explosives.

Poulsson was only 20 yards from the guard hut. Keeping in the shadows, he and the other four men in the cover party watched and waited, the minutes passing inexorably. Twenty-five minutes had passed and they were just beginning to feel twitchy when they heard a bang – but a very small bang, all things considered. The machinery in the plant was still humming, which disguised some of the noise, but, to Poulsson's amazement, a lone guard emerged from the hut, looked around with his torch, saw nothing, then retreated inside. Little did the saboteurs know it at the time, but dull thuds and rumbles were not uncommon at the plant. There were also often rumbles and indistinct explosive sounds from falling snow and ice. What's more, the sound of the power station and the thickness of the concrete muffled the explosion enormously; and in any case, their task had been to sabotage the heavy-water plant, not blow up the entire structure.

Soon after, the saboteurs rejoined the cover guard, their mission completed successfully, and together they clambered back down the way they had come in. Inside, one civilian night foreman and a single guard had been encountered, and neither had raised the alarm; in fact, so far, the mission had gone better than they could have possibly expected.

As they were crossing back over the river, however, sirens began wailing. Hurrying back up the slope on the far side, they were about to cross the road when a car approached. Keeping hidden, they waited for it to pass, then crossed, picked up their skis and the other equipment that they had hidden earlier, and began the climb back up to the Hardangervidda, following the line of the cable car.

As they reached the plateau, the wind whipped up once more and the snow beneath them was frozen. This was good: it meant they would leave no tracks. Back down below, the plant was a flurry of lights, vehicles and men, but no Germans were following the Norwegians. Calming, and with no small amount of relief, they trekked towards a hut they had used on the approach to Rjuken. After waiting for yet another storm to pass, the two teams split up. Five of them made their way to Sweden, mostly on skis, while four remained in the area to help the local resistance, and Poulsson and Helberg managed to get to Oslo, skiing initially and then calmly catching a train. None of them was caught. 'We had the feeling,' said Poulsson, 'that we were living under a lucky star.'

More than half a ton of heavy water and much vital equipment had been destroyed – a huge setback for German atomic weapons research. As it happened, neither the Werner Heisenberg nor Kurt Diebner research teams were likely to be creating an atomic bomb any time soon, but their research efforts were progressing; the attack on Vemork was thus a big blow. The raid had also proved that no corner of occupied Europe was now safe from attack. Three thousand German troops were poured into the area, while plans were immediately put in place to rebuild and strengthen the defences of the Vemork plant – all of which was a major headache at a time when Germany could ill afford such measures.

The Allies were striking back: on land, at sea, and even with small groups of saboteurs too. Very soon they would be significantly increasing their attacks from the air as well. As Goebbels had told his audience on 18 February, the age of total war had arrived.

'You folks at home must be disappointed at what had happened to our American troops in Tunisia,' wrote Ernie Pyle in the wake of the Kasserine setback. 'So are we over here. Our predicament is damned humiliating . . . we've lost a great deal of equipment, many American lives, and valuable time and territory – to say nothing of face.' In fact, II Corps had lost 6,000 killed and wounded and 3,000 taken prisoner. German losses had been as bad, however, and were felt more keenly. But Pyle was quick to reassure his readers that Tunisia remained primarily a British show and that a bit of perspective was needed; there was still absolutely no doubt that the Allies would win in Tunisia.

All he wrote was quite true. Much has been made of this first knock-back in Tunisia, yet throughout history defeats have often actually proved rather enabling in the long term. In the big scheme of things, the bloody nose they had just received was very much a setback rather than a rout and provided an important wake-up call for the US Army. It had reminded them they were still new to war, with much to learn, and yet they had also very quickly regained their balance and contributed significantly to blocking further Axis ambitions.

The key now was to make the most of these lessons and learn from them – and swiftly. In his column, Pyle reckoned there were two key things the Allies had to grasp. 'We must spread ourselves thicker on the front lines,' he wrote, 'and we must streamline our commands for quick and positive action in emergencies.' Pyle might have been a writer rather than a soldier, but there was much in what he said. What the Allies needed was firm, decisive leadership and some clear vision. Fortunately, they were about to get it.

General Alexander had arrived in Algiers to take command of 18th Army Group on 17 February and, after a brief talk with Eisenhower, had hurried to the front, where it was raining and cold and he was forced to wear a sheepskin leather jacket over his desert uniform. Always urbane, Alexander still managed to look every inch the fighting general.

He was, by some margin, the most experienced commander in North

Africa and over the course of his long career he had witnessed war in all its many facets: success and defeat, advances and retreats, and at all levels. Now, under stormy skies and through the mud, he drove from one headquarters to another, speaking to commanders and staffs, and visiting as much of the front as he could. What he saw were units that were mixed up, a total lack of unified command and a lot of chaos and confusion. 'There is no policy and no plan,' he wrote to Brooke. 'The air is much the same. This is a result of no firm direction or centralised control from above.' He had also been horrified by Fredendall's headquarters and all he had seen there; Ward's 1st Armored HQ, on the other hand, had impressed him as being under control and working smoothly. Generally, though, he was disturbed by the lack of training amongst American troops, although he had not, for example, seen the 18th RCT in action at Sbiba. On the other hand, most of the American troops he spoke to showed admirable honesty and humility, and expressed their wish to profit from the recent fighting. 'Yes! Such a spirit is most praiseworthy,' wrote Alexander in his report to General Brooke. What's more, whatever failings they may have shown were, he accepted, entirely to be expected from inexperienced troops taking to the field for the first time. 'It is,' he added, 'up to us to help them.'

Immediately, he issued orders that there were to be no more withdrawals and that certain key positions must be held at all costs. He ordered Montgomery to bring Eighth Army up to the Mareth Line to help persuade Rommel that his forces were needed back in the southeast. He also announced that, from now on, American, British and French forces were to be organized into their own sectors and all battalions and regiments returned to the command of their parent divisions. Static troops were to hold the line, while any armoured and motorized troops were to be withdrawn and grouped into mobile reserves. There would be re-equipping and training for all, and as soon as possible. The Americans were also to be given British 6-pounders to replace their 37mms and, lastly, there was to be no more failure. Any future operations had to be offensive and guaranteed of success.

It was this final assertion that dictated his plan for the defeat of the Axis armies in North Africa. It seemed to him that there were several clear factors that should affect his decision-making. The first was that Axis troops and supplies were still being flown and shipped to Tunisia. Enemy forces would continue to rise unchecked unless the supply line between Sicily and Tunisia was cut. Admiral Cunningham's naval forces were playing their part, but really, the most urgent requirement was to gain air superiority, which they most certainly did not have at present. Air power was absolutely critical.

With this in mind, it was essential to capture airfields closer to the Tunisia–Sicily air bridge – in other words, along the coastal plain on the far side of the Eastern Dorsale, south of Enfidaville and north of the southern town of Gabès. There were only two realistic means of reaching these plains in force: through the Gabès Gap to the south, or through the Fondouk Pass in the middle. The latter Alexander discounted as too risky – and for the same reasons that Eisenhower's plan to strike through the centre had been dismissed. So, rather than take the chance of being enveloped by two panzer armies, he decided to crush the two of them together in a vice in the Tunis bridgehead. Eighth Army was the most experienced, battle-hardened and confident of his forces, so it made sense to launch the next Allied offensive with them.

The campaign would be divided into two phases. The first objective would be to get Eighth Army north of the Gabès Gap, where it would link up with First Army and then gain the freedom for manoeuvre. In the second phase, both armies would be directed towards securing airfields. Once control of the skies had been won, the Allies would be able to co-ordinate the striking power of air, land and naval forces for the final showdown. It was a sound plan of attack and provided everyone with a clear, logical and straightforward vision for victory. Order and a sense of purpose were being swiftly imposed.

CHAPTER 42

Regaining the Initiative

AT JEVER, IN northern Germany, German fighter pilots of I/JG1 were existing in much the same way as those of RAF Fighter Command had done back in 1940. On 26 February, Heinz Knoke and his fellow pilots in his *Staffel* were all sitting near their waiting Messerschmitts, ready to fly at a moment's notice and, wrapped in blankets, enjoying the warmth of the early spring sunshine. It was a fine day with a clear blue sky. Nearby, they had rigged up two speakers to a radio at the *Staffel* dispersal and were, rather illegally, listening the BBC's music programmes. Knoke was lying back idly squinting at the sky when the music stopped and the BBC announcer started speaking his usual 'drivel'.

'Shut your mouth, man,' one of the pilots said, 'and get on with the music!'

Moments later, the radio was interrupted: 'Attention, all! Attention all! Leutnant Knoke is wanted on the telephone!'

Knoke hurried off. It was the 2. Jagdfliegerdivision on the line. A large enemy formation had been picked up in the map area Dora-Dora; it was now 10.50 a.m. and Knoke's *Staffel* was put on standby. Five minutes later they were scrambled. Knoke hurried to his Messerschmitt, clambered in, fired up the plane, closed the canopy enclosing him in the cockpit and then he was off, along with eleven of his squadron, and climbing up to intercept.

'Elbe-One calling Bodo,' he said over the radio to the ground controller. 'Elbe-One calling Bodo. Report Victor.'

'Bodo calling Elbe-One,' came the swift reply. 'Bodo calling Elbe-One. Victor, Victor.'

They climbed to 25,000 feet, Knoke receiving repeated updates, then turned north, leaving vapour trails across the clear sky. Then Knoke spotted the enemy. 'It is an impressive sight,' he jotted later in his diary. 'Some three hundred heavy bombers are grouped together, like a great bunch of grapes shimmering in the sky.'

Knoke checked his guns and adjusted his reflector gun sight as they drew close towards the bombers. Now he could see them more clearly: Liberators, not Fortresses. He thought their fat bellies looked pregnant with bombs. Picking out one, Knoke muttered to himself, 'This is where I settle your hash, my friend.'

He manoeuvred for a frontal attack, the big bomber rapidly growing in size. Knoke's thumb hovered over the gun buttons as tracer began arcing towards him. He pressed the buttons, the Messerschmitt juddering with the recoil, but his aim was poor – only a few hits on the right wing – and an instant later he was whizzing past so close he thought he would almost scrape the underside of the bomber, only to be jolted violently as he was caught in the slipstream. More tracer followed him as he sped on and circled for a second attack. Head-on again, but this time from a little below. Gun buttons, and now machine guns and cannons, pumped bullets and shells towards the bomber and this time he saw he'd hit his mark. Swerving at the last moment to avoid collision, he banked and looked back to see the Liberator sheer away from the rest of the formation.

Twice more he attacked, this time diving from above the tail. Tracer continued to stab towards him but, with his fifty-five seconds of ammunition, Knoke was not spent yet and saw his cannons rake the top of the fuselage and starboard wing. Fire now erupted, spreading along the bomber's wing, which then broke off altogether, leaving the Liberator to plunge, spinning, almost vertically, a thick trail of black smoke following behind. Knoke saw one of the crew jump, but his parachute was on fire. 'Poor devil!' thought Knoke as the body somersaulted and fell earthwards.

Knoke now followed his victim down and watched it crash on farmland near the airfield of Anton-Quelle. A farmhouse was on fire too and so, on an impulse, he decided to land. Jumping out, he ran over to help with the rescue work, bringing out furniture, animals and machinery from the burning barns, and even a squealing pig. Both the house and the barn were saved. Blackened and choking from the smoke, he now wandered around the field, looking at the scattered remains of the Liberator. Bodies – and bits of bodies – of the crew lay strewn beside the still-smoking wreckage. A hundred yards from the main part of the wreck, he found a pilot's seat and a small undamaged doll, presumably a mascot.

Amazed by what he had done and seen, he then clambered back into his Me109, took off and an hour later was back at Jever. It had been his fourth victory on his 164th operational mission and 1,004th flight. Between them they had shot down five bombers for no losses of their own; a good day's work for his *Staffel*. Later, though, as he wrote up his diary, Knoke felt more reflective. 'I cannot help thinking about the bodies of the American crew,' he wrote. 'When will our turn come? Those men share in common with ourselves the great adventure of flying. Separated for the moment by the barrier of war, we shall one day be reunited by death in air.'

Brigadier-General Larry Kuter warmed to General Alexander immediately and was delighted to discover the new Army Group commander not only recognized the importance of air power but also fully supported the tactical doctrine outlined by Coningham. As if to underline the point, Alexander insisted on having his Tactical Headquarters right beside that of the newly named North African Tactical Air Force (NATAF), initially at Constantine, but soon to be relocated to an encampment among olive trees in hills 50 miles further south at Aïn Beïda. At the centre of the encampment was a large khaki marquee, which was the Operations Centre, dominated by a large map table. This marquee, noted Kuter, 'was the heart of ground-air co-operation and collaboration.' There would be no more bunkers, no more disconnect and no more doubt about the common purpose. Here, in pleasant and convivial surroundings, the new Allied leadership could get on with winning in North Africa.

Coningham arrived soon after Alexander and brought with him his old friend and sidekick Tommy Elmhirst, back from London and now NATAF's chief of administration. Coningham immediately wrote out an order insisting there were to be no more defensive umbrellas, then told his new team they were to take over command of all forward air bases, both British and American, fuse them, reorganize them and get command of the air over Tunisia. Then they would help the soldiers to run the Germans out of Africa before May. His tone was louder and more overtly bullish than that of Alexander, but had much the same effect. From the moment of his arrival, there was no more doubt, about either who was in charge or the clarity of vision. Or, for that matter, the outcome.

The two HQs began messing together. Despite the setback at Kasserine, both Alexander and Coningham exuded confidence and good cheer to all. Alexander told Tommy Elmhirst that whenever he took on a new job it was always in the middle of a retreat. 'He was quite imperturbable,' wrote Elmhirst, 'and a very pleasant and cheerful mess mate – more than I could ever say of Monty.'

There were now 'morning prayers' each day at which the senior NATAF staff would meet and talk through anything that needed discussing. In the evening, before supper with Alexander and his staff, they would all have a drink in Coningham's caravan. This way, everyone was kept up to speed and at the same time forged a strong sense of teamwork and even friendship. Kuter thought this was the perfect set-up. Meanwhile, Elmhirst got down to licking NATAF into shape with the same vigour he had devoted to the Desert Air Force. The administrative side of NATAF was in a hopeless mess. 'The only thing really first-class,' he wrote, 'was the fighting spirit of both British and American aircrews. All they needed was to be organised and directed.'

By working flat-out, within two weeks the squadrons had been moved into wings, a day-bomber group had been formed, new airfields had either been built or were under construction, ancillary units had been moved forward to where they would be of most use to the fighting units, lines of supply had been straightened, fuel and ammunition dumps had been established, and spares had been brought up from Algiers. He also discovered that American flying efficiency had been held back by a shortage of lorries, meaning that supplies were not coming forward quickly enough. Soon after, Elmhirst managed to collar General Bedell Smith about the matter. The American squadrons got their lorries within a week. On another occasion, Coningham was at Thelepte talking to one of the senior American officers there. It was cold and damp and the American apologized for not being able to offer his guests a drink. On his return, Coningham sent him a bottle of rum. 'Thereafter,' noted Elmhirst, 'our friendship and co-operation prospered exceedingly.'

*

Before Alexander had completed his reorganizations, von Arnim surprised the British in the north by launching a renewed thrust on 26 February, codenamed Operation OCHSENKOPF – a three-pronged attack that roughly followed the same axes along which the first fighting had taken place back in November. Von Arnim had been given permission for this attack from Kesselring, but had not consulted his new Army Group commander, so demonstrating the contempt in which he held Rommel. Thus, while the Allied command was beginning to gel with a shared fellowship and common purpose, the Axis command was continuing to splinter.

Along the Béja road, the newly arrived British troops, including 17-pounder-equipped artillery, held the panzers at Hunt's Gap for an entire day; by nightfall, they had been overrun with appalling losses, but three German panzer battalions had been so badly knocked, they were forced to delay their further advance by forty-eight hours, by which time First Army had been able to bring up reinforcements.

Further south, the second German thrust had been sent towards Medjez and Bou Arada, but had also been held and then forced back. Von Arnim, however, had not given up yet and on 28 February his forces again attacked towards Béja through the railway stop at Sidi Nsir. This time, the battle lasted ten days, but the Germans could still not force a way through, despite bringing to bear a number of the new and giant Tiger tanks. The British had learned that when stout-hearted infantry occupied properly dug-in positions and were supported by plenty of well-trained artillery, it was very difficult for the enemy to break them. Artillery – that is, concentrated fire-power – was becoming the key ingredient in the evolving British Army's way of war.

Meanwhile, in the Battle of the Atlantic, the Allies had had two much-improved months. The mass of U-boats had managed to sink only 44 ships and 307,196 tons in January, and 67 ships and 362,081 tons in February. That was obviously still a lot, but it wasn't the horrific levels of the previous autumn. What's more, the decisions taken at Casablanca were starting to kick in. The number of VLR Liberators in RAF Coastal Command had been doubled, and also now operating from the UK was the American 25th Anti-Submarine Wing. While the latter focused on ASW operations in the Bay of Biscay, the VLRs were now able to push all their efforts on to mid-ocean operations. Even better, the Americans came equipped with new, superb 10cm-wavelength radar, which not only offered the kind of range and clarity that had been unthinkable just a year or two earlier, but which was also undetectable by the German Metox. Admiral Max Horton now had more destroyers from the Royal Navy's Home Fleet, while the rested and retrained Canadians were ready to rejoin the mid-ocean from the middle of the month. At last, the Canadians had new destroyers, frigates and much-improved ASW equipment. What's more, Horton was now bringing in what he called 'Support Groups' – fast, well-equipped destroyers whose task was not to protect convoys but rather hunt down U-boats. 'I feel strongly,' wrote Horton, 'that the solution of the German U-boat menace will be found only by the development of highly trained Support Groups working in co-operation with an adequate number of very long-range aircraft.' The Admiralty agreed to provide five such Support Groups for the Atlantic.

That month, a joint Anglo-US-Canadian Convoy Conference was held in Washington, where it was agreed that the US Navy would from now on withdraw from escort duties in Atlantic convoys, allowing more American warships to sail for the Pacific, although they would still operate in their coastal waters. A new Canadian Northwest Atlantic Command was created under Admiral Leonard Murray in Halifax, which left Admiral Horton and his Western Approaches Command a free hand to run the mid-ocean battle on their own. There was also to be an increased cycle of convoys that would see the volume of Atlantic shipping double.

There was, however, one more downturn to overcome. For much of 1942, the code-breakers at Bletchley Park had been unable to crack German naval Enigma traffic, but then had come a break. Through January and February, they had been cracking U-boat signals within twenty-four hours, which was enough for Western Approaches Command to act upon them and steer convoys away from trouble. Unfortunately, by March the brief window had passed and once again cracking Enigma was taking too long to have a tactical effect. There were up to seventy U-boats operating mid-Atlantic, and with the help of B-Dienst they were achieving their highest interception rates of the war. Some forty U-boats were massed together to attack convoys HX229 and SC122 between 16 and 20 March. Never before had so many been brought together for the same operation. The mid-Atlantic was awash with flotsam and debris, as one merchant ship after another went down. In all, twenty-one merchantmen were sunk for the loss of just one U-boat. For both the Royal Navy and the Merchant Navy, these two convoys, combined in an effort to make themselves stronger, were amongst the most horrific and harrowing losses of the war so far, while for the whole of March, the U-boats were responsible for a further 633,731 tons of Allied shipping.

Yet, while the escorts of HX229 and SC122 had been unable to cope, the truth was that the U-boats had been corralled into the mid-Atlantic gap. They had proved lethal enough when the combination of signals intelligence and air gap worked in their favour, but the moment it did not, then they would be caught like rats in a barrel; after all, there was nowhere else where they could operate effectively. However bad March 1943 might have appeared from the outside, the Allies were now poised to deliver what they hoped would be a fatal blow.

Back in Tunisia, while von Arnim had been striking in the north, Generale Messe had been preparing a spoiling attack on Eighth Army in the south. Now commanding the renamed Italian Panzer Army, he had decided to strike at Medenine, where Montgomery, at Alexander's request, had sent forward 51st Highland and 7th Armoured Divisions. They had arrived and were in position by 5 March. Medenine lay around 25 miles south of the Mareth Line, and the movement of these two divisions forward had left Eighth Army 'off balance' and without the logistical support Montgomery would have liked. If ever there was a time to deal Eighth Army a painful blow, it was during the ten days these two divisions lay isolated at the front.

Messe's new Chief of Staff was the newly promoted Generalmajor Fritz Bayerlein, who felt very keenly the loss of German control at the top; in fact, it was the first time the divisions of the Afrikakorps had fallen under the direct command of an Italian. From the outset, it was clear Bayerlein and Messe were never going to get along. 'Generale Messe was an arrogant, stuck-up officer,' wrote Bayerlein. 'He did not know and did not understand how to lead troops.' After listening to some of Messe's lectures, which he thought revealed a complete lack of tactical nous and appreciation of how to use mobile panzer forces, Bayerlein decided the only hope for the Afrikakorps was if he ignored the proposed command structure and effectively took control of all German troops himself. 'I took everything into my own hands,' he noted. 'I did this without him. I took the responsibility at my own risk.'

As far as Bayerlein was concerned, one of Messe's biggest failings was his inability to act decisively and quickly, and this was certainly the case at Medenine. Unable to organize his forces swiftly enough, his attack did not go in until dawn on 6 March. By this time, most of XXX Corps had reached the front too, including the New Zealanders and 8th Armoured Brigade. Whatever vulnerability Eighth Army may have had had now gone.

Messe's attack got nowhere, hit by a wall of concentrated artillery fire, as Adolf Lamm discovered. He had never experienced an artillery barrage like it. In his tank, they continued to fire back, but he had a feeling they were not hitting anything very much. Then suddenly, at around 7.30 a.m., a massive blow hit them and Lamm cried out as the heavy radio fell from its mountings on to his legs and the tank turned on its side. A brief stunned silence followed, then Oberleutnant Heinrich Schellhaas shouted, 'Out!' The others leaped out of the hatches while Lamm pulled his legs from underneath the radio, took hold of the hatch and, in agony, pulled himself up and out. As he tried to stand, his knees gave way and he tumbled and fell in front of the stricken panzer. 'My fear overcame my pain,' he wrote. 'I tried to walk. The others pulled and pushed me. We had to get away from there!' They managed to hole themselves up in a dried wadi as the thunderous sound of shelling continued all around them. Shrapnel hissed and fizzed in Lamm's ears as he tried to claw away some soil and bury himself in the ground.

By nightfall, the Italian Panzer Army was in full retreat to the Mareth Line as the British pushed forward. Adolf Lamm and his fellows had managed to stagger back later, his bruised legs still painful but improving. 'All attacks easily held,' Montgomery signalled to Alexander, 'and nowhere has enemy had any success.' His own tank losses had been nil. The Battle of Medenine had been a disaster for the Axis. 'The cruellest blow,' noted Rommel, 'was the knowledge that we had been unable to interfere with Montgomery's preparations. A great gloom settled over us all.'

The Sherwood Rangers had been held in reserve throughout the day-long battle, but the following day, 7 March, they broke leaguer and Major Stanley Christopherson sent out half his squadron to mop up. 'They got one prisoner,' jotted Christopherson in his diary, 'who turned out to be a Pole but in appearance looked to be the usual blonde, well-made, thick-necked German.' When questioned later, the Pole confessed he had been forced to fight for the Germans but had given himself up on purpose so he could fight for the Allies against them instead. The recce party also came back with other prizes, including American bathing trunks, presumably only recently captured, as well as a notebook with detailed drawings of US equipment. Christopherson also put down his own opinions on the battle. The Axis, he thought, had not properly reconnoitred beforehand. 'This only goes to prove once again,' he wrote, 'that the anti-tank gun will always beat the tank.'

How right he was. Recently, the Sherwood Rangers had been out of the line, training hard with the new artillery assigned to the brigade. The previous summer, they had arrived at the front every bit as green and undertrained as the US 1st Armored had been. But battle experience, success and plenty of hard training were making them wise in the ways of modern warfare. The Sherwood Rangers, like much of the British Army in this third year of war, were evolving into a very effective force who now knew how to beat their enemy.

The bulk of the Italian Panzer Army now fell back behind the Mareth Line, where they were bombarded from the air and shelled by the British artillery. Giuseppe Santaniello was at regimental headquarters two days later, on 8 March, when another heavy bombardment was under way. The phone rang with the news that a dugout of No. 4 gun had received a direct hit, with one dead and five badly injured. A few minutes later, the updated news was three dead, then a little after five dead and one wounded. The lone survivor was brought to headquarters. 'Lying prone on the stretcher is a pulp of meat and blood,' scribbled Santaniello. 'The shrapnel has struck his head, his torso, his legs, his feet. He's moaning and his moans tear at the heart. "Leave me be, sir, let me die in peace . . . Mamma, Mamma, I shan't see you again . . . It's a horrible thing, sir, to die."' They stuffed field dressings on to him to try to staunch the flow, but it was no use. Finally, the seventh member of the crew and the only survivor was brought in with a splinter in his knee. He was crying. Another of the men hugged him. 'He's literally shell-shocked,' noted Santaniello.

With the failure at Medenine, Rommel now consulted with his Army commanders. Whatever von Arnim's and Rommel's differences, they both agreed, as did Messe, that a bridgehead in the north was now their best option. Together, the two armies had amassed more than 350,000 men, and it clearly made sense to have them fighting side by side. This would mean the Italian Panzer Army falling back to Enfidaville, which, while it would hand the Allies some airfields, would also mean a substantial shortening of their supply lines; as it stood, they were only getting around 70,000 of the 120,000 tons of supplies a month they needed. With this agreed, Rommel signalled both the OKW and Commando Supremo his intention to withdraw the Italian Panzer Army into the Tunis bridgehead and so reduce the front from 400 miles to 100. That number of troops, with their combined armour and artillery, still supported by the Luftwaffe and with shortened supply lines, would be a truly formidable nut for the Allies to crack. Kesselring was not so keen on the idea, however; nor, needless to say, was Hitler. With this news, Rommel was close to utter despair once more and so decided it was time for him to return to Germany, to see the Führer in person and then to get his much-delayed medical care.

Learning of Rommel's imminent departure, Major Hans von Luck, whose forces were now in reserve behind the Mareth Line, rang General Alfred Gause, the Chief of Staff, and asked whether he might see the Feldmarschall and say goodbye in person.

'Of course,' Gause told him, 'he will be glad to see the commander of his favourite battalion.'

Von Luck hurried to Rommel's command post and found the Feldmarschall in his caravan, surrounded by maps. He hadn't seen his chief for some weeks and was shocked at how ill and physically weak he looked. 'May I,' said von Luck, 'in the name of each individual member of my battalion, say goodbye to you, till we meet again, sometime, somewhere. We'll hold out here for as long as we can, always after the example you have given us.'

At this, Rommel looked up. There were tears in his eyes. 'Rommel's tears,' wrote von Luck, 'the tears of a great man now cast down, moved me as much as anything I saw in the war.'

On 9 March, Rommel left Africa for the last time. It would be left to von Arnim, as the new Army Group commander, to face the Allied forces. And he would be doing so with his armies still separated and with the Italians now waiting for Eighth Army behind the Mareth Line.

*

By the time Rommel left Africa, Alexander was satisfied his forces were now in much better fettle and almost ready to go back on the offensive. Anderson still commanded First Army, although he had remained in post by a hair's breadth. Certainly, General Kenneth Anderson had not had an easy situation: dashed Allied hopes that had been beyond his control, a build-up of forces slower than anyone would have liked, and appalling winter weather. None the less, Alexander had not been impressed by Anderson's handling of the situation and had realized that the First Army commander did not have the force of character to gel his troops together; he firmly believed it was vital that an Army commander created an atmosphere in which staff and subordinates all followed the chief's clear and firm leadership. The right person to replace him, however, was not available. And so Anderson remained in post.

The same could not be said for the extraordinary Fredendall, although Eisenhower had taken longer to realize what a liability he was. Having never commanded in battle himself, the Supreme Commander was still very much feeling his way and, despite the talking-to from Marshall, had needed to hear it from several others before wielding the axe. 'I'm sure you must have better men than that,' Alexander had told him with typical understatement. Others were even more damning, not least Major-General Omar Bradley, who had just arrived in theatre. An old friend and colleague of Eisenhower's, he had come at the Supreme Commander's specific request.

'What do you think of the command here?' Eisenhower asked him.

'Pretty bad,' Bradley replied.

'Thanks, Brad,' said Eisenhower. 'You've confirmed what I thought.'

On 7 March, Fredendall was sent home and General Patton took over as the new commander of US II Corps.

On 13 March, Teddy Suhren became Gruppenführer and Chief of Staff of the 27th U-boat Flotilla in Gotenhafen under his good friend Erich Topp. Their task was to prepare crews for the front by practising convoy attacks on escorts and target ships – this was their last bit of training before being sent out into the Atlantic and elsewhere. Suhren was happy that this gave him the chance to head back out to sea, but each training course was just ten days long. Both he and Topp knew this was woefully short, particularly since it was painfully clear that neither the officers nor crews arriving at the 27th Flotilla were up to the job and were altogether too green. Both men agreed the training period should be at least two months. 'It was obvious,' noted Suhren, 'how ill-prepared they were for it.' Having lots of U-boats now operating in the Atlantic was one thing, but whether the crews were both trained and skilled enough to take on the Allies' renewed effort to smash them was quite another matter.

Not so very far from Gotenhafen was the Luftwaffe air base at Jever, home to JG1. Leutnant Heinz Knoke's flight had been thinking of different ways of attacking the American daylight bombers now regularly flying over. His good friend Dieter Gerhard had suggested they try bombing them. Knoke had thought this an inspired idea and the two had talked late into one evening, discussing exactly how this might work. The Me109G was capable of carrying up to 500 lb, either as a single bomb or a rack of small anti-personnel bombs. What Gerhard had envisioned was this: they would fly over the dense American bomber formation, some 3,000 feet above them, then simply drop their pattern of bombs. Not all would hit, but they reckoned enough would and, what's more, this would put them out of range of the Americans' defensive fire, which, as they had already discovered, was not to be taken lightly.

At first Knoke's group commander thought the idea a great joke, but Knoke convinced him the plan was a serious one and within a few days practice bombs had arrived, as well as a rogue target and a Ju88 to tow it. His pilots had embraced the idea enthusiastically and they all began practising hard. Knoke was delighted; he had high hopes for this novel approach.

Now, at just a little after 2 p.m. on Thursday, 18 March, they were suddenly scrambled without time to load up their Messerschmitts. As they clambered into their aircraft, Gerhard shouted across to Knoke that he was going to bag the American formation leader. Knoke laughed and asked him whether the Americans had started painting rank badges on their planes.

Climbing high, they soon spotted the formation, then dived down and into them. Knoke hit one with his first pass and saw it explode and disintegrate. For a moment, he was in danger of colliding with a falling engine and a spinning, flaming wing section, but he managed to fly clear in the nick of time. It was his fifth victory; he was now an official ace. Climbing back up to make another pass, he saw his friend flying right in the middle of the enemy formation and, after sending one Fortress down, lining up to fire at the formation leader. Knoke was horrified – tracer was pouring towards Gerhard from the guns of the surrounding Fortresses from every conceivable angle. His friend, he thought, must have gone completely insane. Knoke now dived down to help, firing indiscriminately, but then he saw Gerhard dive away, his plane leaving a long trail of smoke. Knoke dived down after him and watched him bail out and his parachute open, but as he flew past he saw his friend's face contorted in pain. He landed in the sea and Knoke marked his location, radioed for help and circled overhead. Gerhard managed to clear himself of his parachute and get himself into his dinghy but, as far as Knoke could tell, he appeared to have been hit in the stomach and was now unconscious.

Knoke flew back to Jever, refuelled, then flew back out again but could no longer find him. The sea was a big place. Back to Jever, and the waiting game. Evening came, then night fell and finally the call came through. Dieter Gerhard had been found and picked up, but he was already dead.

The following day, Knoke went to the mortuary in Cuxhaven where Gerhard now lay, bearing a wreath. Looking down on his dead friend it seemed as though he were asleep, not gone for ever. Later, back at Jever, Knoke took out his diary. 'Good night, Dieter,' he scribbled. 'You have earned your rest, after fighting and dying for our beloved German fatherland. You were my best friend: I shall never forget you. Alone now, I shall continue fighting in this great battle for Germany.'

CHAPTER 43

Into the Gap

FRIDAY, 5 MARCH 1943 was an important day in the history of RAF Bomber Command because that night Air Marshal Harris was launching the start of his all-out strategic air offensive against Germany. After more than a year in office, he finally reckoned his command was ready. He had more than 400 heavy bombers and nearly 700 in all; his Lancasters could each deliver up to 10,000 lb of bombs – serious amounts of destructive power. He also had improved navigation devices in Oboe and a new and even more sophisticated piece of equipment, H2S, which was, in effect, the first ever ground mapping radar. Together these developments had already delivered a marked improvement in target accuracy. The Pathfinders, too, were a more proficient force than they had been when first set up. His crews were trained and ready, and a month earlier, on 4 February, he had received a new directive approved at Casablanca. 'Your prime objective,' it instructed, 'will be the progressive destruction and dislocation of the German military, industrial and economic system, and the undermining of the morale of the German people to a point where their capacity for armed resistance is fatally weakened.' In other words, he was being given *carte blanche* to area-bomb German cities. The directive wanted him to target factories and industrial plants, but other collateral damage was to be seen as part and parcel of the bombing campaign and was now woven into one of Harris's objectives.

'I was at last,' wrote Harris, 'able to undertake with real hope of success, the task which had been given me when I first took over the

Command a little more than a year before, the task of destroying the main cities of the Ruhr.'

The first night's target was Essen, the largest and most important manufacturing centre among a wide spread of industrial cities and home to Krupp, one of Germany's leading armaments manufacturers. It was no easy target, as it was packed with flak guns, searchlights and often covered with industrial haze. The main bomber force consisted of 442 aircraft, of which 261 were heavies. The Pathfinder Force (PFF) included eight Oboe-carrying Mosquitoes, and although three were forced to return with technical defects, the remainder marked their targets perfectly, despite haze over the city. Essen was bombed blind, signalling an important move forward in the sophistication of bombing.

The damage was immense: 160 acres of destruction, 53 separate buildings within the Krupp works hit, a horrific 3,018 houses destroyed and a further 2,166 seriously damaged. Nearly 500 people were killed. Harris was in no doubt that a turning point in the war had been reached. 'You have set a fire in the belly of Germany,' he wrote in a signal to all the men of Bomber Command, 'which will burn the black heart out of Nazidom and wither its grasping limbs at the very roots.'

Wing Commander Guy Gibson had not flown on the Essen raid, but he did fly on 11 March, against Stuttgart, another Ruhr city. It was to be his seventy-second and final mission with 106 Squadron. After nearly a year commanding this increasingly successful and honed bomber squadron, the exhausted young wing commander was finally going to be given a rest.

Gibson and his crew took off from Syerston at 10.20 p.m. Crossing the French coast, they ran into some flak, mostly concentrated in flashes around a straggler who had strayed off course. Otherwise, Gibson thought it a perfect night for flying. There was little cloud and a three-quarter moon, which shone so brightly his cockpit was lit up almost as though it were day. Below, he saw France spread out beneath them, milky-grey and partly shielded by a thin gauze of cloud. All around him – either side, above and below – he could see the Lancasters of the bomber stream forging ahead. He thought the big bombers looked as though their chins were somehow thrust forward with more purpose than he'd ever noticed before. All seemed calm. All seemed set.

Then suddenly his flight engineer, freshman pilot Flying Officer Walter Thompson, called out, 'Port outboard's going, sir!'

As Gibson hastily looked to his left out across the wing, he saw Thompson was right – it was packing up – and he could now feel it on the throttle. No power at all from the port outer engine. In his heavily laden Lancaster, he would have to lose height.

This was bad luck. To turn around would mean the mission would not count. He would feel obliged to do another one, and then this would not be his last op with 106 after all.

Behind him, Norman Scrivener, his navigator, was at his station, watching the air-speed needle dropping.

'What shall I do, Scriv?' Gibson asked.

'It's up to you, sir,' Scrivener replied.

'OK, Scriv, we are going on at low level. We will try to climb up to bomb when we get there.'

The Lancaster gently fell away, out of formation. They were now over the Reich and flak was pumping up towards them from Mannheim, Frankfurt and Mainz. Gibson could see it bursting all around the bomber stream above him, but fortunately they had not spotted his lone lame duck. 'Now and again,' he noted later, 'I caught sight of a Lancaster far above, four miles above, as it got into the beam of a searchlight and as a light flashed on its wings.'

As they arrived over Stuttgart, fires were already raging. Suddenly, an 8,000lb bomb hurtled past his wing-tip, and a few moments later a heavy flash erupted below and then the Lancaster bounced and jolted, 'as though it were a leaf'.

Gibson was now in an extremely precarious position, directly below the bomber stream, sandwiched between the enemy ground defences and a rain of falling heavy explosives and incendiaries, any one of which could have blown his aircraft to pieces. However, flying on, they eventually reached the target and duly dropped their load, the stricken Lancaster lurching upwards at the sudden and dramatic loss of weight. Banking around, Gibson thrust the stick forward and dived for the deck. It was now 11.20 p.m.

They were still a long way from home, however. There were night-fighters around and, for Gibson, there was the small matter of nursing a crippled Lancaster. The next few hours were going to be both testing and physically exhausting as he tried to counteract the extra torque from the starboard engines.

Flying at 4,000 feet the entire way, they managed to avoid being picked up by either German night-fighters or flak, successfully crossed the North Sea and, nearly three and a half torturous hours after leaving Stuttgart, touched back down at Syerston. He had survived.

Later that day, Gibson was recommended for a Bar to his Distinguished Service Order. The recommendation was received by AVM Ralph Cochrane, the CO of 5 Group, who responded that since Gibson's DSO had been awarded only the previous December, perhaps a second DFC, a lesser gong, would be more appropriate. When this then found its way to Harris's desk, the C-in-C scribbled in his own hand, 'Any Captain who completes 172 sorties in outstanding manner is worth two DSOs if not a VC. Bar to DSO approved.'

Gibson knew nothing of this. He woke up late that morning, feeling exhausted. 'I wanted to think,' he wrote, 'and I wanted to be alone. After a year of this sort of thing I was getting a bit weary. It seems that no matter how hard you try, the human body can take just so much and no more.'

On 14 March, having said his farewells to his squadron and expecting leave with his wife, he was summoned to 5 Group Headquarters where he was ushered into AVM Cochrane's office and was congratulated on the Bar to his DSO.

'How would you like the idea,' Cochrane then asked him, 'of doing one more trip?' Gibson thought about the flak and German night-fighters, but reluctantly agreed. Really, he had little choice in the matter. Cochrane could not tell him much more, but this was a plan, recently given the green light by Air Chief Marshall Portal, to bomb the key German dams feeding the Ruhr using a newly developed bomb that could bounce over the vertical torpedo nets strung out in front of the dam walls. On impact with the dam wall, it would sink and then explode, the pressure of the water above massively enhancing the destructive power of the explosive.

As Gibson soon learned, he was to help create and train a new squadron specifically to perform this daring operation. It would mean flying low rather than at the usual 18,000-plus feet. Because of water levels in the dams and the moon cycle, they would have to carry out the attack in the middle of May. Harris had been furious – it meant drawing off a number of his precious Lancasters for an operation that he believed had little chance of success and was therefore not worth the time, resources and effort. Frankly, he had a point. On the other hand, if it could be done then the benefits would be enormous.

*

Back in Tunisia, Lieutenant-Colonel Hamilton Howze was delighted that Patton had been given command of II Corps. 'He was profane and color-ful,' wrote Howze. 'More importantly, however, he was aggressive and bold . . . He shook up II Corps Headquarters by getting it off its behind and fining everybody for poor saluting or for appearing without a helmet; he shook up divisions by telling them that he wanted to see more dead bodies, American as well as German.' Not everyone was as enamoured with Patton as Howze, however. Bing Evans thought him a show-off. Given an order to wear neckties, the men ignored it and tied blue cotton kerchiefs around their necks instead. 'We didn't buy the necktie bullshit,' noted Ralph Schaps. Others viewed him as a dangerous glory-seeker. 'He was OK,' said Tom Bowles, although he and his brother were so laid-back they didn't really care too much who was in command. At any rate, Patton certainly created the kind of 'atmosphere' about him of which Alexander approved, and one thing was for sure: none of the American troops of II Corps could have possibly doubted who was now in charge.

By the middle of March, Alexander had given all his commanders very clear directives. Montgomery was planning to attack the Mareth Line on 20 March and he was largely left alone to make his preparations as he saw fit. Alexander decided to keep Patton on a much tighter leash, however. His reasoning was entirely sound. He knew the American commander was an indomitable fighter, but also believed that he was like a stallion that needed to be kept on a tight rein in case he galloped away. The way to turn II Corps into a really effective fighting force, Alexander felt certain, was to set them achievable goals that both gave them fighting experience and helped build up confidence. He did not want Patton to push his corps beyond their capabilities only for them to be knocked back. General Doc Ryder's 34th Red Bulls were to take the northern sector, 1st Armored to recapture Thelepte, and the Big Red One to take back Gafsa. Under no circumstances was Patton to go beyond the Eastern Dorsale.

This left Patton chomping at the bit, but Bradley felt these restrictions were justified. 'Better, I thought, that we learn to walk before we run,' he wrote, 'and I believe for all his tough talk, Patton believed that too.' Bradley was probably right. Certainly, Patton was worried about the state of the troops. He definitely thought discipline was slack. The Red Bulls were 'too defensive' in attitude, and 1st Armored was 'timid'. At least, though, he thought the battle-hardened Big Red One seemed to be in good order.

The Mareth Line ran along the northern edge of the Wadi Zagzaou, a dried and sometimes deep river bed, largely impassable to any kind of vehicle, even tanks. In places its cliffs were sheer and as much as 12 feet deep, while beyond was a long network of concrete pillboxes and bunkers, as well as wire and, by now, large numbers of mines. The line stretched for 22 miles and was bordered by the sea on one side and on the other the Matmata Hills, a long and dense range of mountains that ran roughly north–south.

Montgomery's plan of attack was to launch another two-fisted assault – head on at the Mareth Line with General Sir Oliver Leese's XXX Corps and with X Corps, now commanded by General Brian Horrocks, once more the mobile reserve ready to exploit. However, the second part of the punch was an ambitious outflanking manoeuvre into the desert to the west of the Matmata Hills and then, at their north, through the valley that lay between them and the Djebel Tebaga and led on to the coastal plains around Gabès. This was the Tebaga Gap, which had been recognized as a key pass centuries before by the Romans.

Generale Messe had also recognized there was a chance the Allies might try to outflank them in this way and so the remains of the old Roman fortified wall were now defended by mostly Italian troops. However, Montgomery hoped that the New Zealand Corps, especially created for the purpose, might be able to smash its way through and then cut in behind the retreating Italian Panzer Army as it fell back from the Mareth Line.

Meanwhile, to the north, Patton's II Corps began their march eastwards as part of the co-ordinated effort to put pressure on the enemy and draw as many troops away from the Mareth Line as possible. The intention was to stretch the Axis forces from all angles, hopefully to breaking point. Patton was still worried about the state and ability of his now 90,000 men, and so toured all the units giving pep talks. 'We must be eager to kill, to inflict on the enemy – the hated enemy – wounds, death and destruction,' he told them. 'If we die killing, well and good, but if we fight hard enough, viciously enough, we will kill and live.'

Whether this kind of rabble-rousing had much effect is unclear. Certainly neither of the Bowles twins could remember a single word he said to them. However, the American advance began well. The Big Red

One took Gafsa on 17 March and then they pushed on towards El Guettar, which was captured by the Rangers the following day. From here, Colonel Darby sent his men out to locate some of the enemy's defensive positions in the razorback pink hills on either side of the road that led to Gabès. Bing Evans, who had received a battlefield commission, was now a lieutenant and was put in charge of one of two patrols. He was leading just ten men but, moving stealthily into the hills during the night, they located much of the Italian Centauro Division.

The following night, they moved up again, this time in force. It was 6 miles of rocky, dangerous terrain, but they were used to such night-time marches by now. By dawn they were all in position, overlooking the Italians' guns, which were all facing away from them towards the main American positions. As the first rays of sunlight hit the jagged tops of the mountain behind them, Darby blew his bugle and the Rangers, yelling and shouting like banshees, charged down the slopes while others covered them with machine-gun fire. 'They didn't know what had hit them,' said Evans. Emerging from fox-holes and tents, the stunned Italians were taken completely by surprise. Incredibly, the Rangers did not lose a single man in the entire attack.

Meanwhile, the 26th Infantry pushed forward along the main valley road, the Italian guns remaining silent and some 700 men now prisoner. It was a good day for the Big Red One because the 18th RCT also captured a key hill feature a few miles further south. They were now within spitting distance of El Guettar.

Operation GALLOP was the name of Eighth Army's attack on the Mareth Line, but it was nothing of the sort. General Leese was certainly not prone to bellyaching or disagreeing with Montgomery in any way, but there was a price to pay for having yes-men as subordinates. Leese, and Horrocks too, were solid and dependable but certainly lacked much tactical flair. As a result, Leese had attacked the Mareth Line with under-gunned Valentines, mostly still armed with 2-pounders, rather than using Shermans, which had a mixture of solid shot and high explosive, or even, for that matter, the new 17-pounder anti-tank guns, which would have been ideal for bunker-busting. To make matters worse, it rained, and torrentially too, so that the dried-up Wadi Zagzaou quickly became not so dry after all. The infantry fared much better, managing to make a sizeable bridgehead, but Leese then sent yet more Valentines through the gap rather than anti-tank guns, which would have swiftly dealt with the inevitable counter-attack.

It was an extraordinarily poor decision, made worse because the air forces, so important as aerial artillery and for smashing panzer thrusts, were by then grounded by the rain. By dusk, 15. Panzer had knocked out thirty Valentines and the bridgehead had been pushed back.

While XXX Corps were attempting to smash the Mareth Line, the newly created New Zealand Corps had been making its long route march into the desert around the Matmata Hills. Although it had been mounted in secrecy, Generale Messe had soon twigged what was going on and had posted the German 164th Light Division to reinforce the Italians there; he had also sent the 21. Panzer, although they had not yet arrived by the time the leading elements of the New Zealand Corps reached the entrance to the Tebaga Gap. Among the spearheads were the Sherwood Rangers, still part of 8th Armoured Brigade and attached to the New Zealanders for the operation.

The Sherwood Rangers' tanks began firing at the enemy artillery while the New Zealanders opened up with captured German 88mms, much to the delight of everyone who saw them in action; inexplicably, they'd still not been given any of the 3.7-inch anti-aircraft guns massed back in Egypt. It was also the first time the Sherwood Rangers had been without Colonel 'Flash' Kellett as their officer commanding; he had been promoted to deputy brigade commander.

During the night, the New Zealanders forced a path through the minefields at the mouth of the Tebaga Gap, but General Bernard Freyberg, another Eighth Army commander lacking in any kind of tactical flair or imagination, had decided to halt for the night. Inevitably, by dawn the chance for a quick breakthrough had gone. German troops had arrived overnight and set up machine-gun posts, artillery and anti-tank positions on the high ground.

Monday, 22 March was a bitterly cold morning as Stanley Christopherson led his squadron through the New Zealand infantry and quickly came under fire. 'The shelling was extremely unpleasant,' he jotted in his diary. 'The enemy held wonderful observation posts.' They still managed to knock out a 50mm gun, capture some prisoners and push out of the congested area around the old Roman wall, but they were unable to get much further. RAF tank-busters roared overhead and the valley became shrouded in an array of different-coloured smoke and dust – from exploding shells, burning vehicles, yellow smoke signals put up for the RAF and pink smoke signals fired into the sky by the Axis.

During the afternoon, the RAF reported enemy tanks manoeuvring behind the high ground now in front of them. Christopherson decided to climb out of his tank and lead some of his troopers on stalk around the ridge. Unbeknown to him, a German tank crew on the other side had had the same thought. As a result, they came face to face, took one quick look at each other, then beat a hasty retreat to their respective tanks.

Then news arrived that their much-loved former CO, Flash Kellett, had been killed that morning. It was a great blow to them all.

Back in northern Germany, Leutnant Heinz Knoke finally tested Dieter Gerhard's bombing theories on 22 March, four days after his friend's death. Deciding to carry out a test sortie himself, he handed over command of the rest of the flight to one of his flight sergeants and watched them take off while he laboured with a 500lb bomb slung under his Me109G. It was so heavy it caused one of his tyres to burst before he could get airborne. This was swiftly repaired, but in getting into the air he managed to miss the top of No. 2 Hangar by only a few inches. It was not an auspicious start. Now that he was finally airborne, the Messerschmitt was so sluggish it took him twenty-five minutes to labour his way up to 30,000 feet. By that time, the smoke and fires below told him the Americans had already bombed Wilhelmshaven, but he soon caught up with them over Heligoland on their return flight. Edging forward until he was over the Fortresses, he weaved and dipped his wings in an effort to line himself up and felt a clatter of bullets hit his wings as he did so. Fusing the bomb, he took a final rough aim, then pressed the release button. As he watched it fall, he banked steeply. Suddenly it exploded right in the centre of a row of B-17s. A wing broke off one, and two others plunged away. One bomb, three hits.

Back at Jever, his *Gruppe* and *Geschwader* commanders were ecstatic.

'Good Lord, Knoke, you must do that again with your whole flight!' Oberstleutnant Erich Mix, the Geschwaderkommodore, told him. Mix had been flying at the time and had seen the bomb hit the Fortresses.

'That is my intention, sir,' Knoke replied.

'Do you believe that it will work?'

Actually, Knoke wasn't so sure. He had probably been lucky; the plane had been awful to fly and he now had eight bullet holes in his wings.

Later, he was woken by the telephone at his bedside. It was the Jever switchboard with a top-priority call from Luftwaffe headquarters. Knoke was put through to a major on the Reichsmarschall's staff who then grilled him about his action earlier that day.

'Who issued the order for this bombing operation?' he asked.

'No one, sir,' Knoke replied. 'I acted on my own initiative.'

A moment later he was being put through to Göring himself. 'I am delighted over the initiative you have displayed,' the Reichsmarschall told him. 'I want personally to express to you my particular appreciation.'

Knoke was astounded; he couldn't help laughing at the thought as he switched off the light and tried to go back to sleep.

The next day, however, came a severe reprimand from General Kammhuber, now commander of XII. Fliegerkorps. He was so incoherent with rage, Knoke had to hold the telephone at arm's length.

'Well,' said Kammhuber at length, 'do you have anything to say for yourself?'

'Yes, sir,' Knoke replied. 'Last night the Reichsmarschall telephoned me and personally expressed his appreciation of my initiative.'

That deflated Kammhuber all right, but Knoke was already rather regretting the whole affair – it was hard to imagine such a fuss had been caused by the dropping of one lousy bomb. And really, having done it once, Knoke was not at all sure any more that it was a tactic really worth pursuing.

In Tunisia, General Alexander had been pleased with the progress of the Americans, and so now changed his orders to Patton, instructing him to press on to take Maknassy and to be prepared to push on into the plain if necessary. The town was swiftly captured by 1st Armored Division, who arrived to find it already abandoned.

Back at the Mareth Line, General Tuker was massively unimpressed. He had been glad to be back at the front, but had already had to threaten to resign to avoid having his division split up by Horrocks. Then his sappers had been called in by Leese to build two crossing points across the Wadi Zagzaou – which they had managed effortlessly. Now Tuker was given another task: a smaller outflanking operation not around the Matmata Hills, but through them. His infantry were trained in mountain warfare and, as Tuker had already prepared for just such an operation, he was able to get his men cracking right away. 'But now came a sad disappointment,' he wrote. Just as his 5th Brigade were entering Medenine en route into the hills, the British 1st Armoured Division were also passing through on their way to bolster the New Zealanders. 'We had previously reconnoitred every possible way round that beastly village,' noted Tuker, 'and there was none.' And so they were stuck, as hundreds of tanks, trucks and other vehicles squeezed through and then were in turn held up by 7th Armoured Division following on the tail of the rest of the New Zealand Corps. Tuker was fuming. The delay cost him and his men twenty-four precious hours and they were unable to push into the Matmata Hills until the night of 24/25 March.

The Big Red One was now dug in along a 12-mile line in the mountains either side of the Gafsa–Gabès road to the east of El Guettar. Tom Bowles and his fellows in Company G, the 18th RCT, were on an isolated *djebel* and digging in when they heard a strange, distant rumbling coming from the east, which grew steadily. A mist had settled along the valley beneath them so that, even though the first sliver of sunlight was creeping over the valley opposite, Tom Bowles could still not see clearly what the sound was. Then suddenly tracer cut across the sky, followed by the deeper thunder of larger guns. As the sun rose and the mist cleared, there before them was a valley full of tanks, half-tracks and other vehicles: 10. Panzerdivision had arrived.

Tom's brother, Henry, also had a ringside view, as he had been busily wiring the various companies when the panzers loomed into sight. The panzers rumbled forward, overrunning the American positions in the valley in front of them, but just as it looked as though they might repeat the slaughter of Sidi Bou Zid, they came up against a wadi running across their path and beyond it a screen of anti-tank guns. The violence of the ensuing battle was ferocious. Round after round screamed across the narrow stretch of land between the panzers and the waiting Americans. Amidst the dust and smoke, eight panzers were knocked out as they struggled through the thick minefield, while a further thirty were smashed by the American high-velocity tank destroyers and artillery. By mid-morning, 10. Panzer was withdrawing.

As the panzers pulled back, so the Stukas arrived overhead, hurtling so close the Americans felt as though they could reach out and touch them, while at the same time German artillery shells screamed down, exploding relentlessly. A second aerial onslaught arrived that afternoon, by which time Bing Evans and the rest of the Rangers had been hastily brought in to bolster the defence. Then the panzers attacked again, this time with their infantry up front, but, with remarkable discipline for men so new to battle, the American infantry and anti-tank screen waited until the attackers were just 1,500 yards away and then opened up, their shells tearing into the German advance. The men of 10. Panzer fell like flies. 'My God,' muttered Patton, who was watching, 'it seems a crime to murder good infantry like that.' For a second time, the Germans were forced to withdraw.

They had only fallen back, however, not withdrawn, and now began to dig in themselves. The following night, German motorcyclists roared into the valley below Tom Bowles's positions and, dismounting, began climbing the hill towards them.

'D'you think we can hold 'em?' Sergeant de Jarlais asked Tom.

'Yeah, can hold 'em,' Bowles replied. He quickly began firing his mortar, but he only had thirty-six mortar bombs left. Enemy mortars were landing in turn all around him, exploding with an ear-splitting din, followed by the whizz and hiss of flying rock and shrapnel. The Germans were getting closer. One shell landed just 20 yards in front of him, killing Sergeant Dees and another man instantly. Then Tom's friend Patti hurried over. 'The lieutenant says we're going to surrender,' he told Bowles. 'Let's get out of here.'

Bowles and his buddy had no intention of surrendering, so they scrambled over the rocks, down a small cliff and fell into a pool of water, but then got themselves up and away to the comparative safety of battalion HQ. 'I never hated anything so much in all my life as leaving those guys up there,' Bowles admitted.

His brother, Henry, had also found himself in the firing line, caught out in cross-fire in the middle of a wiring operation. Eventually, they were rescued by their own artillery, which, through their field telephone, they were able to direct. As the shells came in, Henry and his buddy made a dash for it, bullets pinging in their wake, and thankfully managed to make it to safety. Both were awarded the Silver Star. 'For escaping, I guess,' said Bowles.

By 25 March, Tom Bowles's Company G had been all but wiped out and the other companies had suffered heavily too. What's more, the forward positions had been overrun. Further to the north, 1st Armored had been pushing forward against stiff Axis opposition and Pinky Ward, the divisional commander, was wounded in what was, frankly, a suicidal attack insisted upon by Patton.

That same day, Alexander came to see the II Corps commander. He still believed Patton needed to be closely controlled, but the developing situation required yet another change of orders. With Eighth Army about to emerge through the Tebaga Gap, Alexander now wanted II Corps to try to push on towards Gabès and, he hoped, emerge into the plain ahead of the retreating Italian Panzer Army.

Only 35 or so miles to the south, meanwhile, the New Zealanders had been reinforced by the arrival of X Corps, which included Sergeant Albert Martin and the men of the 2nd Rifle Brigade, now back with 7th Armoured Division. They had crossed into Tunisia on 13 March, having spent the first two months of the year out of the line back in Egypt. Some of Martin's old mates had been posted home, there were a number of new faces and, after this period of calm and retraining, he was gloomily aware of his imminent return to action. Now, after a long and uncomfortable journey, he felt he had got used to the idea of being at the front once more.

The plan was for the Desert Air Force to carpet-bomb the German positions first and for the armour and infantry then to burst through. The bombers would come over during the night, then more bombers and fighters would pummel the enemy positions during the day. Dale Deniston's 66th Fighter Squadron was one of sixteen in action that day, Friday, 26 March. Their task was to dive-bomb any Axis transport, troops and gun positions they saw. Leading the flight as top cover, he dropped his bomb and opened fire with his machine guns, blasting away, although he did not hang around to see the results of his efforts. He heard the clatter of small arms hitting his own plane and soon after saw that his oil was getting hot, that he was losing hydraulic fluid and that his radio was bust.

He had no choice but to turn back, make sure he was over friendly territory and then belly-land. But the ground was rough and, as he braced himself and then hit the deck, the engine was ripped off on a mound and came back over the cockpit, thankfully missing Deniston entirely. 'Shaken up a bit, but OK,' he jotted later. 'Quickly unbuckled seat and shoulder belts, jumped out in case of fire, forgot my throat mike was still strapped around my neck and nearly got hung up.' He then counted twenty holes in his plane. Fortunately, he was uninjured and, even better, an American *New York Times* correspondent had seen him come in and picked him up in a Jeep. He'd been lucky. Very lucky.

At 4 p.m. that day, with the Desert Air Force gone, the artillery opened up and the New Zealand infantry, with the 8th Armoured Brigade following, began advancing behind a creeping barrage. Ahead of them was nothing but smoke, dust and explosions, but this did not stop the Axis gunners replying with their own guns. By 7.30 p.m., however, the attackers had broken through 21. Panzer and were around 4 miles further down the valley. The Sherwood Rangers had halted as darkness fell, but could see there was still some fighting around a feature called Point 209 behind them and to their right. Stanley Christopherson felt they had done well, though, having destroyed six enemy tanks, two 88mms and two 50mm guns. But they had suffered too: Christopherson had lost his great friend Sam Garrett, who had been killed in the fighting.

They eventually leaguered for the night, although it was an uncomfortable place to be. Fires from burning tanks flickered, silhouetting them against the night. Near them was a knocked-out panzer, whose headless commander hung limply from the turret. In the darkness, they could hear the rumble of a tank engine and Christopherson expected a counter-attack at any moment. At dawn, however, they realized they'd been listening to another casualty of the battle. With its engine still running, a Mk IV was idling where it had stopped, its crew all dead. The rising sun also revealed to the astonished Sherwood Rangers the sheer levels of destruction of the previous day. All around them lay the wreckage of blackened and smashed tanks and vehicles and, among them, the bodies of the dead.

Fighting continued that day, but the Axis were pulling out, the battle over. X Corps followed through, but bad weather, dust storms plus a hastily cobbled-together anti-tank screen by the Afrikakorps prevented the British armour from surging ahead. Albert Martin and his mates faced their first serious fight since their return, unhooking their 6-pounders and firing furiously, but for another day Horrocks's men were held at bay, which was time enough for Messe to withdraw the rest of his forces from the Mareth Line. By the time X Corps was finally out into the plain, the enemy had gone.

CHAPTER 44

Closing In

IN TUNISIA, THE fighting continued, although Hans von Luck had, like Rommel before him, now left Africa for the last time. Unexpectedly summoned to see von Arnim on 27 March, the Army Group commander had outlined to him an evacuation plan. He wanted him to be his personal emissary to present this to Hitler. Von Luck pointed out that he had little chance of getting to the Führer – after all, he was a mere major. 'We've all thought of that,' von Arnim replied. Hitler, he said, was contemptuous of all his generals. He was more likely to listen to a mere major, especially one fresh from the front, than to any more senior commander. He was to fly to Rome, get the evacuation plan signed by Kesselring, then go on to Berlin and get it signed by Guderian, the new Chief of the General Staff of the OKH. From there he was to try to see Hitler at the Berghof. Then he was to fly back. Speed was of the essence, von Arnim told him.

He was, however, doomed to fail. At Berchtesgaden he was refused an audience with Hitler and also told he would not be returning to Tunisia.

In the meantime, Generale Messe's Italian Panzer Army had fallen back to a new defensive position that stretched along the Wadi Akarit between the mountains of the Eastern Dorsale and the coast to the north of Gabès. General Bayerlein was effectively now commanding the Italian Panzer Army, as Messe had set himself up in a new command post 150 miles to the north at Enfidaville.

Among the first troops of Eighth Army to arrive south of the Wadi Akarit were those of Tuker's 4th Indians. He immediately recognized that gaining control of the Fatnassa Hills and Zouai Heights at the western end of the position was key to smashing the Axis defences. The patrols he sent out confirmed what he had suspected: the heights could be infiltrated by his men. At a planning conference on 2 April, he suggested his men do just this, during the night, and from there they could direct fire, help punch a hole in the enemy line through which X Corps could pour and then pivot to the coast to encircle the Italian Panzer Army. Infiltration, followed by speed and mobility, would be key.

Montgomery, however, had already dismissed the capture of the heights as impossible; but later, talking in private with General Leese, Tuker was able to persuade the XXX Corps commander that before the main assault was due to begin in the early hours of 6 April, his men would have captured the massif and also built a crossing point over the western end of the enemy's anti-tank ditch. Leese agreed to Tuker's suggestions and set off at once to discuss it with Montgomery. 'Eighth Army conceded on all our points,' noted Tuker.

As Tuker predicted, his men secured the heights and the crossing points, and by 7.35 a.m. all the first objectives had been taken. Horrocks arrived at 4th Indian HQ soon after and, with thousands of Italians already being rounded up, Tuker told him the way was clear for X Corps and they could finish the Italian Panzer Army there and then. Unfortunately, however, and despite having immediate authority from Montgomery to send in the armour, Horrocks dithered. Not until 1 p.m., some five hours after Tuker had reported that the path was clear, did the first tanks get moving, even though Tuker had sent his own trucks over the anti-tank ditch to resupply his forward infantry at 9.20 a.m. The bulk of X Corps, meanwhile, did nothing. The Sherwood Rangers were chomping at the bit, but nothing happened. Finally, at 4 p.m., Horrocks postponed the attack until the following morning, the soonest moment a large air bombardment to support them could be arranged. Tuker was appalled. His men had done all the hard work and X Corps had been handed the chance to fold up the Italian Panzer Army on a plate. Needless to say, overnight Messe's forces pulled back. That Horrocks had squandered such a wonderful opportunity was extraordinary folly.

Air reconnaissance showed that the Axis forces were now pulling out of the El Guettar and Maknassy areas as well and heading back up through the eastern coastal plain. On 7 April, II Corps linked up with troops of Eighth Army on the Gafsa–Gabès road. Expecting such an enemy retreat, Alexander ordered an attack using both the British IX Corps to strike through the pass at Pichon and the US 34th Red Bulls through the Fondouk Pass just to the south.

In fact, the Red Bulls had already begun attacking the Fondouk Pass at the end of March. For Sergeant Ralph Schaps and his pals in the 135th Infantry, it was the first proper taste of action they had experienced – and for a number it would be their last, too, as the enemy mortars, machine guns and artillery began taking a terrible toll.

The next day, they tried again, advancing over the open ground of the pass. They made the first objective but couldn't quite take the second ridge and so withdrew a short way, set up their own guns, mortars and MGs and waited for the inevitable counter-attack. 'Living through an artillery barrage or mortar barrage,' said Schaps, 'is the most terrifying experience you can imagine. The shriek of the artillery shells, the explosions jarring the ground and the complete helplessness that envelops you, makes it difficult to keep your senses. The screams of the wounded only add to the horribleness of the scene.'

The Red Bulls held their positions and another pause in the fighting took place. During that time, Schaps was sent back to pick up some replacements and was appalled to discover the rookies now joining them were hardly trained at all. Then, on 7 April, they jumped off again, this time with the British 6th Armoured Division to the north and with a night attack, even though they had never practised a night attack or barely done any night training. Once again, they failed to break through.

The British didn't fare much better, but the British press put the blame on the inexperience of the Red Bulls, which infuriated Patton. 'God damn all British and all so-called Americans who have their legs pulled by them,' wrote Patton in his diary. This was written in private and when his blood was up, and Patton was an emotionally charged man at the best of times. Like most people, he resented criticism of his countrymen but also usually calmed down swiftly. He treated his diary as a means of letting off steam, but for all the choice one-liners there was much he wrote that was more measured and calmer. In any case, many of the concerns expressed about II Corps' inexperience reflected his own views. 'I have little confidence in Ward or in 1st Armored Division,' he noted on 28 March. 'Our people, especially the 1st Armored Division, don't want to fight – it is disgusting,' he added a few days later.

Alexander worried there was a lack of confidence in the officers, who were considered generally too inexperienced, and this was having an effect on discipline. Again, this was a concern shared by Patton. Brigadier-General Larry Kuter had met up with Patton just after the Fondouk attack. 'He said he had lost 286 junior officers because most of them had to do the work that sergeants and corporals should have been trained to do,' recorded Kuter. 'He concluded tearfully, "I still couldn't make the sons of bitches fight."'

Another growing bugbear for Patton, however, was that Eighth Army seemed to be getting the lion's share of close air support. Matters came to a head on 1 April, when some German aircraft attacked one of Patton's observation posts, killing three men, including his ADC, of whom he'd been particularly fond. That evening, through a combination of grief, anger and mounting frustration, he added to his daily situation report, 'Forward troops have been continuously bombed all morning. Total lack of air cover for our units has allowed German air forces to operate almost at will.' He then fired it off with a far wider distribution than normal.

This prompted a stinging response from Coningham, sent to everyone who had seen Patton's sitrep, pointing out that over the II Corps front just seventeen bombers and twelve fighters had appeared all day, killing only four people. In contrast, there had been 92 Allied fighters and bombers over the enemy airfields concerned, plus 90 bombers on Sfax and in total 362 fighter sorties in all that day, with 260 of those over Patton's front. '12th AIR SUPPORT COMMAND,' he added, 'have been instructed not to allow their brilliant and conscientious air support of 2 CORPS to be affected by this false cry of "Wolf".'

This spat caused no small amount of consternation among the Allied command. On 3 April, Tedder, Larry Kuter and Tooey Spaatz met at Thelepte to discuss Patton's claims. Tedder, especially, was furious with Coningham; he felt it could have led to a major crisis in Anglo-US relations, as did the ever-mindful Eisenhower. Tedder, Spaatz and Kuter then drove on to see Patton, who was still bolshy and unrepentant. Alexander, on the other hand, thought that Patton had rather deserved it. Spaatz also sided with Coningham. On Tedder's insistence, however, Coningham was forced to apologize and even visited Patton on 4 April. They shook hands, then lunched together. 'We parted friends,' recorded Patton.

A lot of nonsense has been written about American Anglophobia in the war. Too many historians have revelled in the various personality clashes, cherry-picking pithy quotations rather than attempting to contextualize those comments properly. In almost every case, those most prone to anti-British or anti-American ranting prove to be difficult characters who tended to end up having spats with large numbers of people, regardless of nationality. Furthermore, all too often, not enough consideration is given to the enormous responsibilities placed on the shoulders of these men. Most people who feel very strongly about something will fight tooth and nail for what they believe. In the war, generals and commanders had the lives of many men to consider too. It is not surprising that sometimes these people clashed, even ferociously so. Patton and Coningham were both incredibly strong and virile characters, and Patton especially hot-headed, which contributed to making them such fighting, vigorous commanders. Their spat, however, was not about nationality – Coningham was an Australian-born New Zealander in any case – but about doctrine. Furthermore, Coningham had been defending 12th Air Support Command, which was American, not British.

Another potential blow-up occurred when General Omar Bradley discovered Alexander had no plans to use II Corps in the final assault on the Tunisian bridgehead. Because the British part of First Army was already in the north, and because Eighth Army, the most experienced, was now advancing up the coastal plain towards Enfidaville, Alexander was merely thinking logically. It was, however, one instance when the Army Group Commander's usual diplomacy skills faltered. Since it had been agreed that Patton would lead US forces in Sicily, he was to hand over II Corps to Bradley so that he could concentrate on preparing for HUSKY, the invasion of Sicily. Eisenhower suggested Bradley speak to Alexander in person.

On 28 March, he did just that and, of course, Alexander disarmed him immediately. 'We were impressed with Alexander,' jotted Captain Chester Hansen, Bradley's aide. 'He was a striking and possessed individual who simply exuded an air of confidence.' He also readily agreed to use II Corps in the final push; they would operate on the northern flank of First Army, albeit without the Big Red One. Having accepted this was the most battle-hardened division, they too were now earmarked for HUSKY and so were being withdrawn for intensive amphibious training. Bradley also had his way with the Red Bulls. After Fondouk, Alexander felt they should be withdrawn and sent off to his newly established Battle School for intensive training with live ammunition and all arms. 'Give me the division,' Bradley pleaded, 'and I'll promise you they will take and hold their very first objective.' Alexander conceded that point too.

This did not mean 34th Division did not undergo intensive training, however. After being pulled back to Maktar, where they were given showers, fresh food and clean uniforms, they began licking themselves into shape, drawing on what they had learned and carrying out plenty of night training especially. They also worked on co-ordinating the heavy weapons units with the rifle platoons. 'We had never had any training in this very important segment of an attack situation,' said Ralph Schaps. 'The rifle company commanders hardly knew we existed as we had never trained with them in a simulated combat situation.' It rather proved to him how unprepared they had been for war, and it had cost them a lot of casualties. But they had learned. 'The old saying, "the quick and the dead" took on a new meaning,' he said. 'Either you learned quick or you were dead.'

Since the ramming of *U-357*, HMS *Hesperus* had been in dock having urgent repairs carried out, which meant a well-earned period of pro-tracted leave for her skipper, Commander Donald Macintyre. The timing could not have been better, as his wife had borne him a son the previous November and it had allowed him the chance to spend some time at home with his family. By April, however, *Hesperus* was finally ready and, like most Royal Navy destroyers operating in the Atlantic, was now armed and equipped with all the latest weaponry and ASW gizmos, including new 10cm radar and the twenty-four-charge Hedgehog. Macintyre also had some new crew, including officers. Bill Williams, his old First Lieutenant, had been given his own command and was replaced by Bill Ridley. In Lyulph Stanley, he had a new navigator too.

After a few days of tactical exercises for everyone to get used to each other, Macintyre once again took over command of B2 Escort Group on ONS4 – the convoy code for the new northerly route that crossed the mid-ocean gap closer to both Iceland and Nova Scotia. Horrendous weather had pummelled those crossing at the end of March and in the early part of April, and by the 17th they found themselves pitched in a gale so bad the convoy almost stopped. For the next few days, they ploughed on, grimly hoping for better times as the ship lurched forward then climbed, waves sloshing over the bow and icy spray soaking those on the bridge. Macintyre had sent *Whitehall* on ahead to Iceland to pick up ships for the mid-ocean. He had wondered whether they would ever manage to link up in such atrocious weather, but miraculously the storm subsided, the seas calmed and, to Macintyre's relief, the two convoys hove in sight of each other as planned.

Soon after, one of the VLR Liberators attached to the convoy signalled a U-boat sighting. The failure of the Liberator to give the correct position relative to the convoy, however, meant that the escorts found neither the Liberator nor the submarine and so a chance to attack and destroy had gone begging. 'How we prayed,' wrote Macintyre, 'for a little intelligent training to be given to these Coastal Command aircrews to match their enthusiasm and courage.' It was frustrating, but these were teething issues that were, thankfully for the Allies, fairly easy to resolve.

The next challenge was for the two destroyers, *Hesperus* and *Whitehall*, to refuel. Mid-ocean refuelling was just one more of the many innovations that had taken place since the start of the war. Macintyre always rather dreaded it, however. It was a very difficult operation, invariably on a swell that was stronger than either ship would have liked. Destroyer and tanker had to pull alongside one another, without crashing, bows and sterns invariably rising and pitching, while still moving forward. 'As the two ships get closer,' wrote Macintyre, 'their mastheads swinging in giddy arcs towards and away from one another, the seas heave foam and foam between them.' A line marked with bunting was then passed between the two bridges – a basic aid to help the eye judge the distance between the two. Then a derrick from the tanker would swing out with a hose. The entire procedure required immense concentration and vigilance from all involved and usually took around an hour. It was also a somewhat weather-dependent operation. *Hesperus* had managed this incredibly tricky feat in some pretty heavy weather, but there were limits. 'Day after day would go by,' noted Macintyre, 'while fuel got lower in the tanks and COs developed duodenal ulcers thinking of what would happen if the weather did not moderate.'

On this occasion, all went well, however, and by 22 April they had reached the mid-ocean gap and had been joined by one of Horton's new support groups, which included four destroyers and the escort carrier HMS *Biter*. By now, their Huff-Duff operator was picking up a stream of U-boat traffic that made it clear they were approaching a wolfpack patrol line. The following day, Good Friday 1943, Macintyre, up on the bridge, was told a U-boat had been sighted, and close too – within 10 miles. *Hesperus* hurried off and soon after, using the Zeiss binoculars he had taken from U-boat captain Otto Kretschmer a year earlier, Macintyre spotted the submarine then watched it hurriedly crash-dive. Soon they were picking it up on their ASDIC. It was time to use their new killer, Hedgehog. The conditions were good and contact remained – 'Ping, ping' could be heard on the ASDIC as they crept within range. 'Fire!' called out Bill Ridley, but nothing happened. A rapid check revealed that inexperience with their new weapon was the issue – each of the twenty-four bombs had its own safety pin and these had not been removed in time.

Now joined by *Clematis*, they made ASDIC contact with the submarine again and this time decided to loose off another new weapon – a one-ton depth charge that was fired from their torpedo tubes. They heard and felt the explosion, a vast plume of water erupted high into the sky and then they heard strange noises on the ASDIC which suggested the U-boat was rising to the surface. Excitement was mounting on the bridge as they expected to see the U-boat break the water at any moment, but there was no sign of it. Still, Macintyre was convinced it had to be fairly near the surface, and so, with the Hedgehog now primed, he ran another sweep, more slowly this time, then on the order twenty-four bombs flew through the air.

No one spoke as they hit the water and disappeared. Agonizing moments later two explosions could be heard thudding through the ship, then Bill Ridley said, 'Got him, by God!' and popped up out of the ASDIC control area. And so they had. *U-191*, a Mk IXC, had been ripped apart and sank with all hands. The crew had been led by Kapitänleutnant Helmut Fiehn on their first combat patrol. Once again, inexperience and insufficient training had done for this rookie crew.

With this further success under their belts, the convoy continued on its way. On Easter Sunday, Macintyre heard the sighting of another U-boat via Huff-Duff. This time, one of *Biter*'s escort-carrier Swordfish flew off and, soon after, spotted the submarine, which dived before it could attack. Meanwhile, one of the support group's destroyers, HMS *Pathfinder*, had hurried towards the scene, made contact and sunk *U-203*. 'This,' wrote Macintyre, 'was sea/air co-operation as it should be, and made us realize what could be done with properly trained aircraft.'

They had no more trouble that convoy. ONS4 had crossed the Atlantic safely.

Wing Commander Guy Gibson was now commanding his new squadron, named 617, up at Scampton, just to the north of Lincoln. He alone had been let in on the secret of the bouncing bomb, codenamed UPKEEP, and had had several meetings with its inventor, Barnes Wallis, the Assistant Chief Designer at Vickers-Armstrong. In reality, it was a depth charge, but weighed 4 tons and, when approaching the target, would need to rotate at 500 revolutions per minute. Trials of this new weapon were proving worryingly mixed, and a further complication was that the only aircraft capable of carrying such a thing was a Lancaster, which was made not by Vickers but by A. V. Roe and needed various modifications. Fortunately, Wallis and A. V. Roe's chief designer, Roy Chadwick, were getting on well and co-operating fully; the specially adapted Lancasters were on their way. For Gibson, however, the pressures remained immense. Flying out of formation at over 18,000 feet was one thing; operating at 100 feet off the deck in formation with a 4-ton rotating bomb strapped underneath required different skills. Intensive training was required, but because of all the various meetings and trips down south to confer with Wallis, Gibson was getting less than many of the other crews in 617 Squadron.

Meanwhile, the Alsace Squadron had flown their first combat missions. Now based at Biggin Hill and equipped with Mk IX Spitfires, they were all delighted to have been given what they considered a prestige posting at one of Fighter Command's premier airfields. Pierre Clostermann first flew on 28 March when 341 Squadron flew top cover for 611 Squadron commanded by Wing Commander Al Deere, one of Fighter Command's leading aces. The plan was for 611 Squadron to swoop in low and try to catch the FW190s of III/JG2 at Evreux-Fauville. As he clambered into his Spit, Clostermann was both nervous and excited about perhaps scoring his first victory. The idea he might be killed did not even cross his mind.

Forty minutes after taking off, they were crossing the coast between Dieppe and Saint-Valéry, at full throttle. A small amount of light flak greeted them, then they dropped their auxiliary fuel tanks.

'Brutus, there are planes taxiing on the ground at the end of the runway,' Clostermann heard the CO, Commandant René Mouchotte, tell Deere. Looking down, Clostermann now saw them too, their cockpits glinting in the sunlight. A moment later 611 Squadron appeared, but around twenty FW190s had already taken off and they quickly became all caught up in the mêlée.

Fascinated by this, the Frenchmen had failed to notice further 190s speeding towards them. Fortunately, one of their pilots spotted them in time. Someone called out, 'Break!' and a moment later Clostermann had the stick pulled in towards him as he performed a tight turn. He felt breathless, on the verge of blacking out, when a Focke-Wulf began firing at him, luminous tracers hurtling past his wing tips. Now two further FWs were on to him and he couldn't think how he was going to get away.

'Turban Yellow One, Two calling, help!' he cried out over the radio, but all he got in reply was a terse, 'Shut up.'

His pursuer, meanwhile, had caught up on him so fast, Clostermann could see the black eagle painted on the fuselage and what looked like a yellow propeller spinner. Then the Focke-Wulf suddenly rolled to port and slid underneath him, diving down out of the fray to 3,000 feet, his wingman still assiduously following him. Clostermann had barely had a chance to gather his wits when Al Deere gave the order to break and head back home.

Clambering out of his Spitfire, Clostermann saw Lieutenant Ludwig Martell walking towards him. 'So, my little Clo-Clo,' he said, 'did I detect a touch of panic?' Clostermann was mumbling a reply when Mouchotte, who had overheard, said, 'Don't worry about it, we've all been there in the early days. Sort yourself out, go and have some supper and a beer. It's over for today.'

At Debden, meanwhile, the former Eagle Squadron pilots, now part of the 4th Fighter Group, were converting on to new Republic P-47 Thunderbolts. This was a big, elliptical-winged, radial-engine, 7-ton beast of a fighter aircraft. Armed with .50-calibre machine guns, it was a heavyweight bruiser that lacked the feline grace of the Spitfire but was solid, very fast, immensely robust and certainly could pack a punch.

Among the first to fly the new fighter in the 4th FG was Jim Goodson, who then checked it out with Don Blakeslee, now CO of 335 Fighter Squadron. It was, Goodson had to admit, daunting to haul 7 tons of plane around the sky after the finger-tip touch of the Spitfire, but he also recognized its advantages. Blakeslee, however, was grumbling. He liked his Spit. 'For one thing,' Goodson told his friend, 'they'll never be able to dive away from us again.'

Blakeslee was leading the group on 15 April as they flew over Belgium. Suddenly they spotted a couple of FW190s and they attacked; as usual, the FWs dived away. The Americans followed and, although it took them a while, they managed to catch them. Blakeslee opened fire at 500 feet and literally blew his victim out of the sky.

Back at Debden, Goodson caught up with the man who had scored the group's first victory in a P-47. 'I told you the jug could out-dive them!' Goodson said.

'Well, it damn well ought to be able to dive,' muttered Blakeslee. 'It sure as hell can't climb.'

Bomber Command's assault on the Ruhr continued. Duisburg was attacked on the night of 26/27 March, Essen again on 3/4 April; 635 buildings were destroyed and 526 badly damaged. Then Duisburg twice more on 8/9 and 9/10 April, and Frankfurt on 10/11 April. Stuttgart was hit on 14/15 April. Although the Ruhr was the main focus, part of Harris's policy was to attack targets throughout the Reich. Berlin, for example, was attacked twice. During the first, on 27/28 March, a secret Luftwaffe stores depot was hit by chance, destroying a large quantity of valuable radio, radar and other equipment. All in all, the destruction caused was mixed; some raids were considerably more accurate and effective than others. But the damage and casualties were rising, adding to the misery of ordinary Germans, who were already feeling the losses of so many men on the Eastern Front, the scarcity of food and almost every conceivable consumable, and who were beginning to realize the war had turned against them.

What's more, while the RAF attacked by night, increasing numbers of American bombers were flying over by day as Eighth Air Force's strength steadily grew. On 17 April, for example, over 100 B-17s attacked Bremen. Among those taking off to intercept was Heinz Knoke and his flight from JG1 now equipped with their single 500lb bombs. Flying above the enemy, they dropped them as rehearsed, but not one hit the Fortresses. With their Me109s suddenly agile once more, they dived down and attacked in the traditional way with machine guns and cannons. Knoke made three runs at one Fortress and saw it finally catch fire. It was his seventh victory.

*

Back out in Tunisia, the Allied air forces were slowly but surely retaking the initiative. The 'New Order', as Tommy Elmhirst called it, seemed to be working. 'As our air attacks on Luftwaffe airdromes began to increase,' noted Larry Kuter, 'their attacks on our ground forces began to diminish.' There were still rumblings from certain quarters, however, although the matter was finally settled at a planning meeting at Alexander's Tac HQ at Ain Beida on 14 April. Spaatz was due to be there, but his plane had been delayed and so once again it was left to Alexander to defend Coningham's air policy, this time against a brick wall of obstinacy from Patton, Bradley and even Mark Clark. Spaatz finally arrived, which prompted another round of grousing from the Army commanders, until eventually Eisenhower cut in and told them he was getting goddamned tired of hearing the ground forces claiming they needed control of the air. 'One would believe that our case has been settled,' noted Kuter. And that was that, the matter finally put to bed. If only Eisenhower had spoken up earlier.

Meanwhile, more and more aircraft and equipment were arriving. Ken Neill and the 225 Squadron pilots were now entirely equipped with Spitfires. They were all delighted about that. New Mk IXs were also arriving and with them fresh pilots. Among the new arrivals was Flight Lieutenant Cyril 'Bam' Bamberger, who after a stint instructing was now operational once more. After a quick Spitfire refresher course, he had joined 64 Squadron only to learn they were being sent north to Scotland. Bamberger had wanted a more active posting, and so managed to get transferred overseas. By the middle of April he was on a ship to North Africa and by the 27th had reached Kalaa Djerda in Tunisia to join 93 Squadron, part of 324 Wing. 'My previous operational experience,' he noted, 'had mostly been confined to defending so to me it was very exhilarating to be on the offensive, seeking out the enemy instead of being sought.'

There were other improvements: new American radar installed at 242 Group's HQ, for example, which now gave warning of enemy attacks and which was more powerful than British versions and covered the entire northern half of Tunisia. The net was closing in, as Rommel had known it would, and as Warlimont had tried, in vain, to warn on his return to Rastenburg. Despite this, Hitler and Mussolini, with no regard at all for the tactical and operational limitations they faced, had reaffirmed that Tunisia was to be held at all costs. Supplies and reinforcements they could ill afford to spare poured in. However, with more ships being sunk and with no means of replacing them, the air bridge had become ever more important: Ju52s and huge new six-engine Messerschmitt 323s that had just come into service in very limited numbers.

When the weather allowed – and increasingly it did – these air armadas would regularly make up to two trips a day. From the many intelligence sources now available to them, NATAF began to get an increasingly clear picture of when these missions might occur and so, with Spaatz's and Coningham's approval, Kuter began preparing to intercept this air bridge using as many Allied aircraft as possible in an operation codenamed FLAX. On 5 April, long-range US P-38s shot down thirteen enemy transports north-east of Cap Bon. A further fourteen were destroyed on airfields in Sicily and eighty-five more were damaged. Also helping was the growing RAF operation from the once-beleaguered island of Malta.

Alexander had always known that the moment the Allies were able to regain the initiative in the air, the battle would be almost won. By 16 April, the 57th FG had reached El Jem, halfway up the Tunisian coastal plain and home to one of the best-preserved Roman amphitheatres in the world. Two days later, Palm Sunday, they were scrambled late in the afternoon; an intelligence warning had reached them that around 100 Ju52s were approaching Tunis. Four squadrons of P-40s and eighteen Spitfires took off, intercepted the German transports and, in what became known as the 'Palm Sunday Turkey Shoot', seventy-four enemy aircraft were shot down and destroyed. 'What a day! What a day for making history,' wrote Dale Deniston, who had flown earlier that afternoon and so had missed the slaughter. He was distraught. 'Breaks my heart.'

The change of fortunes was dramatic. Since the third week in March, 519 Axis aircraft had been shot down and nearly twice as many again destroyed or damaged on the ground. In the same period, the Allies had lost 175. The Allies were masters of the air. Victory on the ground now beckoned.

CHAPTER 45

Victory for the Allies

O N THE EASTERN Front, both sides had paused for breath once more. After the defeat at Stalingrad, German forces had fallen back on a broad front, with the Red Army in hot pursuit. By the end of February, it had been the Russians who were now over-extended and von Manstein, having given up Kharkov, counter-attacked and re-took the town once more. At that, the front at long last quietened.

Despite the enormous setbacks, Hitler, inevitably, had refused to believe the Germans were finished in the Soviet Union and began plans for his next offensive, Operation ZITADELLE, which would eradicate a huge salient that had emerged in the line around the town of Kursk.

Meanwhile, he had continued to send ever more reinforcements to the Mediterranean and North African theatres. The Eastern Front might have been a far bigger area of operations, but the Mediterranean Front was, strategically, every bit as important, if not more so as far as Hitler was concerned.

And while there were still many more troops along the Eastern Front, the Mediterranean was now the primary theatre for the Luftwaffe. Among the recent arrivals into Tunisia from the Eastern Front was Macky Steinhoff, now promoted to Oberstleutnant and sent to command JG77. He had been on leave with his wife back in Germany when he'd been called by Adolf Galland. The General of Fighters had been in a sombre mood and was worried about the American daylight raids over the Reich. He had, he told Steinhoff, asked the Reichsmarschall for a greater build-up of the fighter arm and for improved armament to the

FW190s and Me109s. When he had predicted that one day the Flying Fortresses would be able to fly to Berlin, Göring had brushed the suggestion aside and said he refused to listen to such defeatist tittle-tattle.

Then Galland had come to the point. Steinhoff was needed: there was a shortage of commanders. He had a choice: a command in France or North Africa. Having never been to North Africa before, and thinking it might be an adventure, Steinhoff chose the latter and took over from the much-loved Joachim Müncheberg, who had been killed by American Spitfire pilots on 23 March during the Mareth battle.

Steinhoff flew to North Africa via Rome, where he met with Kesselring and was allowed to attend an Air Conference, in which the various grandees prognosticated optimistically about the future course of the Tunisian campaign. Steinhoff was unimpressed – by the glitter of these peacocks and by what they were saying.

'As soon as you've familiarised yourself with the theatre,' Kesselring told him, 'it is essential that you convince the people in your group that North Africa must be held – held at all costs. We shall be reinforcing the bridgehead and narrowing the front so that the position can be held without difficulty. But we must get the very best out of the air component.'

Arriving at La Fauconnerie airfield in northern Tunisia at the end of March, Steinhoff met his pilots, many of whom had been fighting in North Africa for over a year. 'Finding a pilot over the age of twenty-one was difficult,' said Steinhoff, 'and so many of their faces reminded me of Marseille, who was now long dead. Most of the old-timers were already dead, captured, or crippled.'

He gave them a pep talk he did not believe, but which he felt was what Kesselring had wanted him to say – and felt rather ashamed for doing so. It was as though he were a stepfather and eyed with great suspicion. What's more, he also learned that RAF and USAAF pilots were usually a cut above those in the Soviet Union, as were their planes. Soon after arriving, he went on a sortie in which he came under attack and had his engine and radiator shot up by a Spitfire. He crash-landed, although fortunately for him behind friendly lines. 'We were already on our heels at that time,' he said.

By the end of April, they were even more on their heels. The end in Africa was now almost upon them, the Axis forces wilting under the Allies'

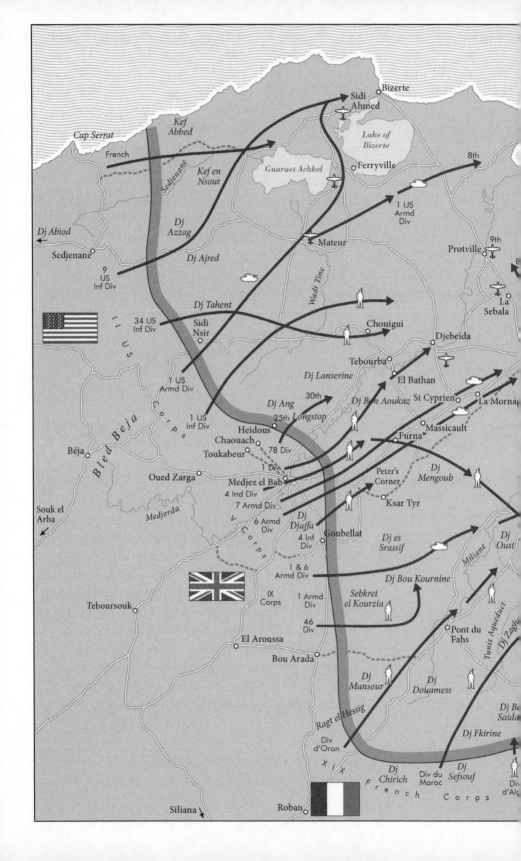

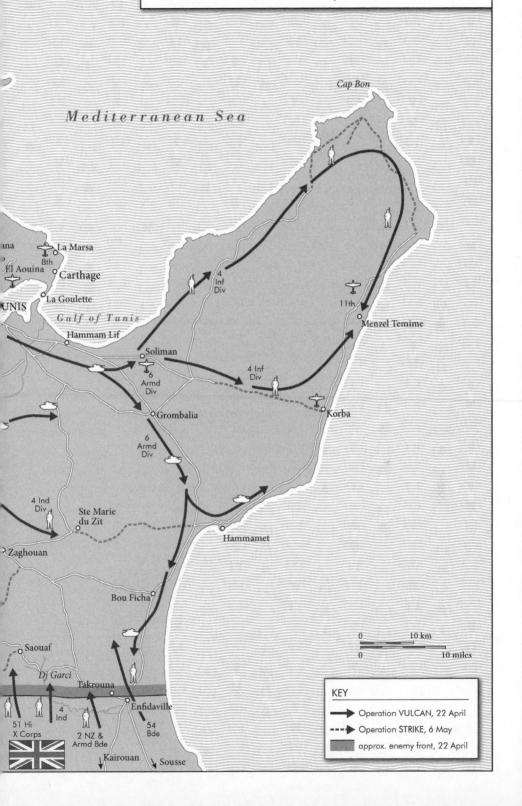

THE END IN TUNISIA, APRIL–MAY 1943

Cap Bon

Mediterranean Sea

ana
La Marsa
8th
El Aouina
Carthage
La Goulette
UNIS
Gulf of Tunis
Hammam Lif
Soliman
6
Armd
Div
Grombalia
6
Armd
Div

4
Inf
Div

4 Inf
Div

11th
Menzel Temime

Korba

4 Ind
Div

Ste Marie
du Zit

Hammamet

Zaghouan

Bou Ficha

Saouaf

Dj Garci

Takrouna

Enfidaville

51 Hi
X Corps

4
Ind

2 NZ &
Armd Bde

54
Bde

Kairouan   Sousse

KEY

Operation VULCAN, 22 April

Operation STRIKE, 6 May

approx. enemy front, 22 April

0   10 km

0   10 miles

greater industrial capacity, superior supply lines and now, in these final stages, fire-power. In terms of growing experience and combat efficiency, the Allies were pipping their opponents too.

Alexander's final plan of attack was called Operation VULCAN. Since the Enfidaville position was some 50 miles from Tunis and a natural defensive line, Eighth Army, he decided, were to take a secondary role. The main effort was to go to First Army, with the Americans in the north striking towards Bizerte and the British in the centre, with the Medjerda Valley, that place of stubborn hills and mud just a few short months ago, the primary axis of advance on Tunis.

With so many Axis troops now in the Tunis bridgehead, this was always going to be a tough fight, however, and so it proved. And despite being relegated, Montgomery still hoped to force a way through the Enfidaville position and reach Tunis first. In this he was to be disappointed. One of the most bitter and hard-fought fights of the entire campaign took place at Takrouna, where the Italians heroically defended and the Maori Battalion equally heroically threw themselves at this rocky redoubt. As elsewhere, however, the sacrifice on both sides achieved little, as the New Zealanders were unable to force a way through.

Nor were British IX Corps, which had been reinforced by 1st Armoured Division from Eighth Army. Albert Martin and his mates had been appalled at having to switch armies. Arriving into the line in their battered desert drill alongside Tommies still wearing khaki Battledress, he felt they were almost two completely different species rather than fellow Brits. Neither breed was able to force a gap, however. On 29 April, 2nd Rifle Brigade had been given the job of making a night attack on the Djebel Bou Kournine, known as the 'Two Tits'. They nearly got to the summit – but nearly was not enough. 'We were a sombre group,' noted Martin, 'as we returned empty-handed to our positions.'

Further to the north, General Bradley had realized that the Army campaign in Tunisia was all about capturing the high ground. Although II Corps was nominally under First Army and thus Anderson, in practice Alexander had given Bradley a pretty free hand and, although their mission had been planned out in fine detail, the new II Corps commander was in entire agreement and so began their operations confident both in his corps' aims and that he was likely to be left to get on with it.

First on the list for attack was a series of mutually supporting hills, so he ordered them to be attacked simultaneously. These were captured by the Big Red One, not without cost, and by 26 April they had slugged their way forward by 5 miles before they too became bogged down. The thorn in their progress was the Djebel Tahent, or, more simply, Hill 609. Not only did it dominate the valleys on either side, but the Germans had dug in and looked to be in no mood to give it up.

He gave the task of capturing it to the 34th Red Bulls. 'Get me that hill,' he told General Doc Ryder, 'and no one will ever again doubt the toughness of your division.' They began their assault on 28 April. Three times the Red Bulls stormed the peak only to be pushed back. A fourth attempt was tried with tanks on 30 April and this time, by afternoon, the summit was theirs. Counter-attacks were successfully beaten off and by 2 May all of Hill 609 and the surrounding high ground was occupied by the triumphant Red Bulls. As at Takrouna, both sides had fought with grim and bitter determination, but on this occasion, their earlier humiliations a distant memory, the men of the 34th Division prevailed.

Watching this battle of wills had been Ernie Pyle, whose missives from the front were now syndicated to more than 120 newspapers and who was now read by millions upon millions of Americans and even Londoners. 'I love the infantry because they are the underdogs,' he wrote. 'They are the guys that wars can't be won without.' He watched one column of men traipsing back down a hill looking dog-tired, unshaven and numb from battle. Exhausted though they were, Pyle had spoken to a lot of men and had noticed how much tougher they had become. 'He wants to see the Germans overrun, mangled, butchered in the Tunisian trap,' he wrote. 'Say what you will, nothing can make a complete soldier except battle experience.'

Sergeant Ralph Schaps certainly agreed. His Heavy Weapons Company had been given the neighbouring Hill 490 to attack. By this time, he'd seen enough dead, heard enough dying and had understood what it was to come under fire, to be shelled and mortared. By the time they finally took Hill 490, he had just eight men left in his section and, although now low on ammunition, had captured an MG34. Exhausted, he fell asleep but was woken by the sound of his captain hollering at him. 'In front of me I saw the biggest Kraut I had ever seen,' he said, 'and I was glad I had set up the captured gun ready for action. The Krauts were attacking in force and that Jerry MG saved me that morning.'

Schaps and his mates found more than seventy machine-gun positions on their hill alone. The battle had been a triumph for the Red Bulls and showed just how quickly the greenhorns from the United States were becoming hardened, proficient soldiers. 'We had been vindicated,' wrote Schaps, 'and shown that we were as good as any combat soldiers in the world.'

A little to the south, the British 78th Division finally cleared Longstop Hill on 27 April, but IX Corps had now run out of steam. Alexander realized some fresh impetus was needed and on 30 April visited Montgomery at Eighth Army Tac HQ south of Enfidaville. Monty was not on good form. He'd been in Cairo planning for HUSKY, had caught tonsillitis and was generally under the weather; he also had his mind more on Sicily. He was well aware that any further attempt to break the Enfidaville position was pointless, but his vanity made him unable to resist another attempt to be the first in Tunis. Both Tuker and even Freyberg had repeatedly warned both Montgomery and Horrocks, but on 28 April the new-to-battle 56th Division was launched along the coast and bloodily beaten back.

Even Montgomery now conceded Eighth Army should take a back seat. Instead, Alexander asked him to send his best troops for a renewed strike through the Medjerda Valley. Despite his antipathy to the Indian Army, Montgomery recommended his two outstanding divisions: 7th Armoured and 4th Indian, two units that, coincidentally, had formed the nucleus of the Western Desert Force that had smashed the Italians back in 1940. They would be added to IX Corps and, with General John Crocker, the corps commander, wounded, Horrocks took over temporary command.

This suited Tuker just fine; it was what he'd hoped for all along, not least because he knew Horrocks was starting to listen to him. It had been a very long time in coming, but General Tuker was about to be given the chance to plan, shape and fight the final battle according to his own tactics and principles.

On his arrival at Medjez el Bab, Tuker visited Horrocks's new Tac HQ where he heard the proposed plan of battle. In essence, it was to be a dawn attack supported by artillery. Tuker kept quiet at the time, but then carried out his own reconnaissance of the battlefield along with his divisional artillery commander. The extent of the hills in enemy hands convinced him a daylight attack would be a massive error, and at the next conference he strongly pressed an alternative view. This was to launch a night attack with an artillery barrage to cover the sound of the advance. Artillery was to be fired in massive concentrations, pinpointed on to one target after another, just as he had prescribed at Alamein. Each gun, he proposed, should be given 1,000 rounds, which he had discovered was perfectly feasible, rather than the 450 Horrocks had suggested. This was to be preceded by plenty of aerial photography to provide accurate and detailed analysis of enemy positions.

After being rebuffed by his superiors repeatedly ever since his arrival in the Middle East, he now won nearly all his points. Horrocks's chief concern had been the lack of night training, but Tuker assured him his men would do this on their own and promised that by morning he would have tanks, anti-tank guns, mortars and machine guns in among the enemy's forward positions to make sure the rest of the infantry succeeded easily in the final punch. He did, however, have to accept a 'token' barrage, although he ensured this was managed by his own artillery commander. Tuker called his plan 'the perfect infiltration battle'.

Operation STRIKE, when it was launched after dark on 5 May 1943, went almost entirely to plan, just as Tuker had predicted. Massed formations of night-bombers arrived, followed by devastating artillery fire. Some 450 guns blasted one position after another, so that instead of one gun per stretch of front, all rained down their shells on one target, pummelling it with untold ferocity then moving on to the next. Some 16,600 shells fell on the German positions that night.

In the early hours of 6 May, the 4th Indians attacked through the thick, reedy grass and, with the deafening sound of the guns and the lack of moon, gained total surprise. With bayonet and *kukri* – the Gurkha's curved sword-knife – they simply broke the enemy will. One panzer grenadier regiment was almost entirely annihilated. As dawn broke, the infantry were swarming over their objectives and new British medium Churchill tanks rumbled behind them through wheatfields prinked with red poppies.

This utterly devastating attack was not over yet, however. Assembled on nearby Grenadier Hill was an audience of commanders, journalists and even politicians. Among them was Air Vice-Marshal Coningham, and at 7 a.m. he and the others there were able to look up and see the first bomber and fighter formations roar over. Not one enemy aircraft interfered as the Germans were once again pummelled by this devastating display of tactical air power. Below, 3.7-inch anti-aircraft guns now had their barrels lowered to horizontal and were used in a role that could and should have been used years earlier.

Once again, Horrocks was slow to push through his armour but, unlike at Wadi Akarit, this time it mattered little. The Axis were beaten, crushed by the overwhelming Army and air combination and by a battle plan that was simple, devastatingly effective and proved, beyond doubt, that Tuker should have been listened to many long months earlier.

Today, the Battle of Medjerda is almost entirely forgotten, but it was fought against highly disciplined German troops and blasted a hole and a route clear through to Tunis that no other attack had managed. So perfectly was it fought, it had not developed into a long, drawn-out slogging match as at Alamein, Mareth and Tebaga; the assumption therefore has been that the opposition had already been almost broken. That is to do Tuker's plan and the massed Allied fire-power, both on the ground and from the air, a massive disservice. It was won quickly because it was very probably the best-fought British battle so far in the war. It deserves to be better remembered.

Tunis fell the next day, 7 May, as did Bizerte, to the Americans. The following day, the 8th, all available Allied shipping was sent to patrol off Cape Bon. 'Sink, burn, destroy,' signalled Admiral Cunningham with emphatic ruthlessness. 'Let nothing pass.'

As it happened, there was little in the way of shipping to sink or destroy; only around 800 men were captured at sea. The rest were rounded up in their droves and placed in hastily organized wired corrals, among them Adolf Lamm and Giuseppe Santaniello. For them and some quarter of a million other men – more than had been lost at Stalingrad – the war was over. Total Axis casualties for the entire North African campaign were double that – around half a million. It had been no side-show.

Fittingly, it was General Tuker to whom the Axis commander, von Arnim, finally surrendered, on 12 May. Tuker looked scruffy in his worn pullover and lack of medal ribbons. Von Arnim, by contrast, was dressed immaculately. Messe signed the surrender document the following day, the 13th. Perhaps equally fittingly, the Afrikakorps was the last to throw in the towel.

The Sherwood Rangers, who had lost their CO, Donny Player – one of the original horsemen from their pre-war yeomanry days – before Enfidaville, had been stuck there for several weeks but now suddenly found the front collapsed and themselves on the move once more, helping to round up prisoners. 'Somehow,' jotted Stanley Christopherson, 'it is extremely difficult to fully realise that the war out here is finished.'

At 1.16 p.m., 13 May 1943, Alexander signalled to Churchill: 'Sir, it is my duty to report that the Tunisian campaign is over. All enemy resistance has ceased. We are masters of the North African shores.'

Out in the Atlantic, the battle was also reaching its climax. On Tuesday, 11 May, as night fell, Commander Donald Macintyre was out on the bridge of his destroyer, HMS *Hesperus*. He was alert, tense and, like the rest of his crew, fully aware that they would surely be soon in action. Macintyre was out for revenge. Earlier that day a U-boat had managed to penetrate their defences and sink two ships in broad daylight; these were the first two that Macintyre's B2 Escort Group had lost in nine months and he had been furious. As darkness fell, however, so the Huff-Duff office had been ringing repeatedly with reports of U-boats signalling. Most were from bearings behind the convoy and so Macintyre had placed *Hesperus* on station astern.

'This is the likely quarter for an attack tonight, George,' he told Lieutenant Carlow, the Watch Officer, as he joined him on the bridge. 'Warn the radar operators to keep a specially keen watch astern.'

An hour passed, then another and another. The customary mugs of cocoa had been passed around and the First Watch, from 8 p.m. to midnight, was nearly over when the report they had all been waiting for finally came through. 'Very small contact just come up, sir. Bearing 230 degrees. Range 5 miles.'

By that second week in May, the wolfpacks were beginning to be crushed out in the mid-Atlantic. Following in the wake of ONS4 had been ONS5, protected by B7 Escort Group and backed up with the 3rd Support Group. These escorts, like Macintyre's *Hesperus*, were equipped with Huff-Duff as well as the new Type 271 10cm radar, so that although B-Dienst was able to plot the course of this northerly convoy, the 28-strong wolfpacks were struggling to penetrate the defensive screen. Over the course of one night, they made some twenty-six attempts to get at the convoy, but were driven off every time. By the time the mid-ocean battle was over, the mass of U-boats had managed to break through and sink twelve ships, but they had lost nine of their own.

It marked a turning point and one the Royal Navy was determined to exploit. With most of the Canadians now operating in their own command in the north-west Atlantic, responsibility for the mid-ocean rested largely with the British. More than fifty VLR Liberators were now supporting them, along with a number of American aircraft too. Many of them were now equipped with yet another ingenious new weapon: the Mk 24 Mine, which was an air-launched acoustic homing torpedo that could be dropped in the wake of a diving U-boat and would follow it, explode and destroy it. It was a lethal bit of kit. Liberators, Catalinas, escort-carrier Swordfish and new US Avengers – all were now playing their part, spotting, tracking, bombing and destroying U-boats. They no longer had anywhere to hide. The mid-ocean gap had been effectively closed.

Now, on the night of 11 May, it was *Hesperus*'s chance to play a part in that battle. Alarm gongs sounded through the ship as Macintyre swung her around and rang down to the engine room for full speed. Then, still using Otto Kretschmer's binoculars, he strained through the darkness, desperately looking for the U-boat. Suddenly, he spotted a line of white on the surface – a U-boat's wake. Altering course a few degrees to port in an effort to cut her off, he hoped they might catch the enemy by surprise before it had a chance to dive deep. They were catching it and fast, but as they neared they could see white plumes of spray as the U-boat opened vents and began to submerge. As they reached the spot, there was still the familiar, strange swirl of phosphorescence on the surface.

'Get the first pattern away by eye,' called out Macintyre. 'Shallow settings.'

Moments later, he heard Bill Ridley call out, 'Fire one! Fire two! Fire three!' over the intercom. Out shot the depth charges, followed moments later by huge geysers of water erupting high into the air. Macintyre was confident they must have shaken the enemy sub at the very least. Now, he knew, was the time to hammer her without respite. Reducing speed, the ASDIC quickly picked up a contact. It was clear the sub had gone deep, so Macintyre opted for another pattern of depth charges; it was not time for Hedgehog.

Another round exploded. Down below on *Hesperus*'s quarter-deck, the depth-charge parties reloaded once more. At dock, they could do this in just fifteen seconds, but it was a different kettle of fish out at sea manoeuvring 750lb canisters in the middle of an action in an Atlantic swell. Even so, they managed it in pretty quick time, but as the ship was

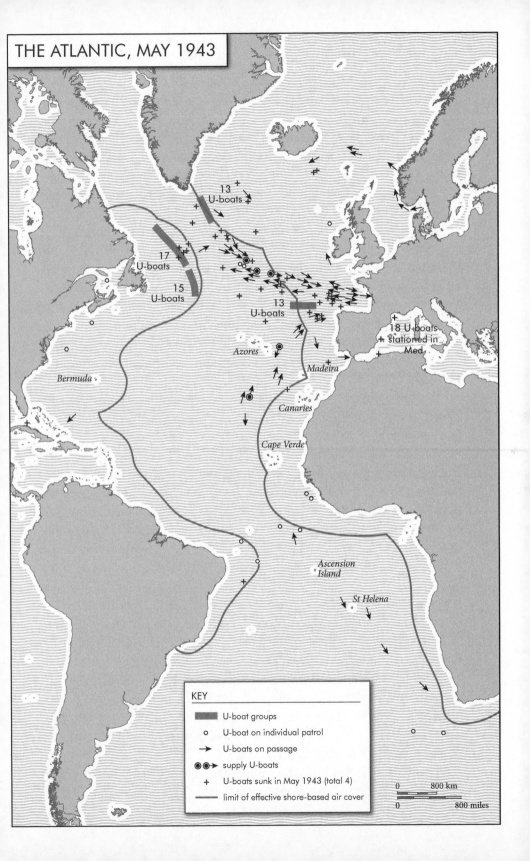

THE ATLANTIC, MAY 1943

13
U-boats

17
U-boats

15
U-boats

13
U-boats

18 U-boats
stationed in
Med

Azores

Madeira

Bermuda

Canaries

Cape Verde

*Ascension
Island*

St Helena

KEY

▰	U-boat groups
○	U-boat on individual patrol
→	U-boats on passage
◉◉→	supply U-boats
+	U-boats sunk in May 1943 (total 4)
⎯	limit of effective shore-based air cover

0   800 km

0   800 miles

preparing for another run, so the ASDIC operators picked up signs of tanks being blown and the U-boat rising. Moments later, there she was, on the surface and stopped in the water. She was too close for *Hesperus* to use her 4.7-inch guns, but the 20mm Oerlikons opened, raking several of the German crew who had been making for their own gun. Then *Hesperus* passed close by, dropped more depth charges set for the minimum depth of 50 feet, then Macintyre turned the ship again.

To his astonishment, however, the U-boat managed to get her engines started and move off. This time, *Hesperus*'s gunners could open fire with the 4.7-inch guns, but still the submarine did not sink. Rather, it stopped again, looking sinister and stubborn. For all his enormous experience, Macintyre could not think what he should do. He would have liked to have rammed her – but ramming was now officially discouraged.

'Bill,' he said to Ridley, standing beside him on the compass platform, 'do you think we could roll her over by a gentle ram so as not to damage the ship?'

'Try it, sir,' he replied. 'We are getting very short of depth-charges and we are going to need plenty before we are finished with this convoy. I don't want to have to use any more to finish off this bastard.'

So they tried it, and the U-boat rolled over on its beam ends, lay like that for a moment, but then slowly righted itself. On the other hand, it was lying low in the water and Macintyre felt the end must surely be near. With the convoy now 30 miles away, he decided it was time to get on their way. 'Precious time could not be spared to stay and deliver the *coup de grâce*,' he noted, 'and pick up the survivors, with all the delay that would entail.' And so they turned and left the sinking U-boat to its fate.

Only, it wasn't sinking just yet. The boat was *U-223*, commanded by Oberleutnant Karl-Jürg Wächter on their second patrol and, unbeknown to Macintyre and the rest of *Hesperus*'s crew, he had no intention of throwing in the towel just yet. The boat was flooded, an engine had caught fire, and there was debris and wreckage throughout. Incredibly, twelve hours later, the crew managed to get *U-223* going again and began limping back home. Twelve days later, on 24 May, they made it safely to Saint-Nazaire. *U-223* and her crew had had possibly one of the luckiest reprieves of any U-boat in the war so far.

Meanwhile, *Hesperus* managed to rejoin the convoy and the following day picked up a contact, this time giving their quarry no second chance.

After one attack, the ASDIC operators could hear the U-boat was in trouble, and a second pass finished the job – on board *Hesperus* they could feel the underwater explosion through the hull. They circled the spot for a while and eventually saw a spreading pool of oil with floating debris and smashed woodwork. Pausing to quickly pick up a few specimens for evidence, on one they found a glob of flesh. *U-186*, a Mk IXC on its second patrol, had perished with all hands.

By now they were almost out of depth charges, but they still had a role to play: even if they could not sink a U-boat, they could make it dive. Repeated contacts were made, and *Hesperus*, *Whitehall* and the other escorts all had their share of duels. In one passage, eleven U-boats in contact with the convoy were all driven off successfully. On *Hesperus*, the crew were haggard, unshaven and exhausted, yet Macintyre had found it an exhilarating experience. What's more, they suffered no more losses at all. 'By the 16 May,' wrote Macintyre, 'the convoy was safely through the danger area. The loss of two ships still rankled but we felt we had avenged them.'

News of the Allied victory in North Africa reached Churchill, Roosevelt and the Joint Chiefs of Staff during their latest conference, this time in Washington. The news was especially welcome to the British Prime Minister, who, a little under a year earlier, had suffered the ignominy of hearing about the fall of Tobruk whilst with the President. Now, in May 1943, the Mediterranean was open once more, North Africa was secured and Anglo-US forces had been tested in battle and proved they could, together, beat their enemies.

And there was better news for Churchill just a few days later. On the night of 16/17 May, against the odds, Wing Commander Guy Gibson had led his new squadron on an attack against the German dams. Germany's two largest, the Möhne and Eder, had been breached using Barnes Wallis's bouncing bomb, UPKEEP. Despite mental and physical exhaustion, Gibson had led his crews, got them to the Möhne, dropped his own bomb from the ludicrously low level of precisely 60 feet above the water, and then repeatedly flown around again in an effort to draw flak from the dam wall and its surroundings. When the Möhne had finally been breached, he then led those still carrying the UPKEEP to the mist-covered Eder Dam, Germany's largest. Somehow, he managed to get back home again, although eight of the nineteen crews on the raid were not so fortunate. By any reckoning, however, Gibson's performance that night had been leadership of the highest calibre – for which he would soon be honoured with Britain's highest award for valour, the Victoria Cross.

In Berlin, the reaction was one of shock and horror. The dams were prestige structures, proudly known to almost every German in the land. The Möhne, especially, was vital for industrial processes in the Ruhr and both were needed for drinking water in the cities near them, as well as for dousing the flames caused by Allied bombing. Villages had been swept away, twelve factories completely destroyed and a further ninety-one damaged. Twenty-five rail and road bridges had gone, while power stations even in Dortmund had been closed down due to the damage. These dams and the damaged third one, the Sorpe, would all have to be repaired, as would the factories and bridges, and every dam in the Reich given bigger, better anti-aircraft defences. The cost was going to be astronomical – and at a moment in the war when Germany could least afford such a diversion of money, resources, manpower, time and effort.

Even more sinister was the fact that the attack had been delivered by so few aircraft and using a new and unknown weapon. Maximum damage caused by few weapons delivered by a few or even a lone aircraft was what every combatant nation was striving for. The Allies had just stolen a big and worrying march.

As if to ram the point home, Air Marshal Harris then ordered his Bomber Command to continue their pounding of the Ruhr. On 23/24 May, 826 aircraft hit Dortmund, destroying 2,000 homes completely. Four nights later, over 500 aircraft hit Essen yet again.

These were dark days for the Third Reich, and there was worse to come this month of May 1943.

Out in the Atlantic during the middle part of May, ten convoys passed through the waiting wolfpacks, and of the 370 merchantmen that sailed, just six were sunk and half of those were stragglers. The wolfpacks, however, lost thirteen U-boats. At the same time, air operations over the Bay of Biscay had also been stepped up, new radar and the new homing mines all playing their part. By the time May was over, forty-one U-boats had been sunk and among the young German submariners gone for ever was Dönitz's only son. 'Wolf-pack operations against convoys in the North Atlantic, the main theatre of operations,' recorded Dönitz, 'were no longer possible.' On 24 May, he ordered them all to withdraw, and with the utmost caution. 'We had,' he added, 'lost the Battle of the Atlantic.'

With the wolfpacks beaten, the Allies could start to plan realistically for the final stage of the war. For Italy, defeat was now nearing. Mussolini's influence was waning and the Italian people, who had never wanted war in the first place, were weary of defeat, of death, of destruction and grinding hardship. For Germany, too, there could now be no way back. Despite Milch's aircraft-production revolution and the public claims of an armaments miracle by Speer, and regardless of the thin hopes laid on future wonder weapons now being developed, Germany was running out of steam. Food, fuel, manpower – those three most important requirements for sustained modern warfare: there was not enough of any, while the costs of maintaining Nazi rule in the occupied territories was becoming greater and greater as people under their yoke began to increase their resistance to that rule.

In the opening two years of the war, many Germans had still believed they truly would rise again with the Third Reich. Victories had come thick and fast then. Even in those early years, the cracks had been there, however, and the foundations decidedly fragile. These last two years had seen those hopes shattered. Instead of victories had come reverses, on land, on sea and in the air. Suddenly, in May 1943, and so soon on the back of the calamity in the East, the disasters had come thick and fast. Goebbels had promised total war and that was what the German people were getting: bombed by day and by night, their great cities beginning to crumble, their most famous edifices smashed. At sea, the U-boats had been vanquished, while on land the net was closing around them: from the south, from the east and from the west.

America and Britain, meanwhile, could enjoy this flurry of successes, but only briefly. Germany was beaten, but Hitler, who still ruled with his iron will, had always vowed that the Reich would last a thousand years or there would be Armageddon. Two years of war still lay ahead as the Allies began their long march to final victory.

Glossary

ADC	Aide de Camp
AOC	Air Officer Commanding
AI	Air Interception
ASDIC	British naval vessels' onboard sonar
Auftragstaktik	mission command
AWPD	American War Plans Division
BdU	Befehlshaber der U-Boote (C-in-C of German submarines)
BEF	British Expeditionary Force
Bewegungskrieg	Operational war of movement
'brew-up'	a tank hit and burning
C-in-C	Commander-in-Chief
CIGS	Chief of the Imperial General Staff
CO	Commanding Officer
DFC	Distinguished Flying Cross
DSO	Distinguished Service Order
Fahnenjunker	officer cadet
Fallschirmjäger	German paratroopers
Feldwebel	German NCO equivalent to sergeant
GC&CS	Government Code and Cypher School
He	Heinkel
HF/DF	high-frequency direction finding
HG	Gibraltar to UK convoy route
Huff-Duff	Slang for HF/DF
HX	North America to UK convoy route
IO	Intelligence Officer
JG	*Jagdgeschwader* – fighter group
Ju	Junkers
KG	*Kampfgeschwader* – bomber group
leaguer	night-time tank formation – a rough circle usually
Me	Messerschmitt

MG	machine gun
MOMP	Mid-Ocean Meeting Point
M/T	mechanized transport
NCO	non-commissioned officer
NCS	Naval Control of Shipping
NDAC	National Defense Advisory Committee
NEF	Newfoundland Escort Force
Oberjäger	most junior NCO in the German airborne and mountain divisions
OG	UK to Gibraltar convoy route
OKH	Oberkommando des Heeres, the German Army High Command
OKM	Oberkommando der Marine, the German Navy High Command
OKW	Oberkommando der Wehrmacht, German Combined Operations Staff
ON	UK to North America convoy route
OPM	Office of Production Management
OT	Organization Todt, a civil and military engineering organization established by Fritz Todt and using the RAB, civil labour force and later mostly enforced labour
PT	physical training
RAD	Reichsarbeitsdienst – Reich Labour Service, for teenage boys between school and joining the military
RNVR	Royal Navy Volunteer Reserve
RWM	Reichswirtschaftministerium – Reich Ministry for Economic Affairs
SASO	Senior Air Staff Officer
SC	North America to UK slow convoy route
SD	Sicherheitsdienst – Nazi security service
SIM	Servizio Informazioni Militari – Italian Military Intelligence Service
sitrep	situation report
sortie	individual operational flight by a pilot, e.g. a squadron of twelve aircraft would amount to twelve sorties
SPAB	Supply Priorities and Allocations Board
Staffel	German squadron
TA	Territorial Army
Tac R	Tactical Reconnaissance
Unteroffizier	sergeant
WPB	War Production Board
2WO	Second Watch Officer
ZG	Zerstörergeschwader – Messerschmitt 110 fighter group

Cumulative Gains and Losses of Merchant Ships Outside Enemy Control

(1,600 gross tons and over)

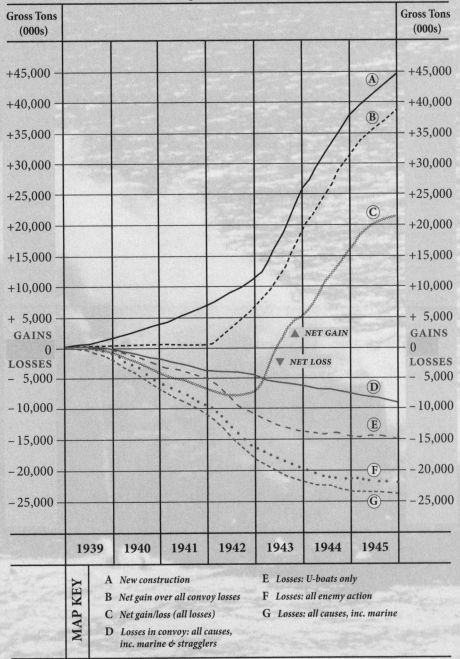

MAP KEY

A New construction
B Net gain over all convoy losses
C Net gain/loss (all losses)
D Losses in convoy: all causes, inc. marine & stragglers

E Losses: U-boats only
F Losses: all enemy action
G Losses: all causes, inc. marine

Source: Eric Grove (ed.), Defeat of the Enemy Attacks on Shipping, *Plan 15*

Allied Merchant Shipping

PERIOD	ATLANTIC						
	In convoy			Stragglers		Independent	
	Ships sunk/ convoyed	% Loss rate	% Sinkings in period	Ships sunk	% Sinkings in period	Ships sunk	% Sinkings in period
July–Dec 1941	92 / 6,000	1.5	61	20	13	39	26
Jan–31 July 1942	46 / 9,800	0.5	8	16	3	510	89
Aug 1942–May 1943	313 / 26,300	1.2	48	74	11	269	41

Source: Eric Grove (ed.), The Defeat of the Enemy Attack on Shipping, 1939–1945, Naval Staff Histo

U-boat Strength and Losses

DATE	Total U-boats at beginning of month	Boats in training and trials	Training boats	Front line boats	
1941					
July	153	58	42	53	
August	168	59	45	64	
September	186	65	48	73	
December	236	99	49	88	
1942					
January	249	100	58	91	
February	257	99	57	101	
March	272	104	57	111	
April	283	107	57	119	
May	292	114	54	124	
June	309	124	59	126	
July	329	132	59	138	
August	339	137	59	149	
September	356	122	62	172	
October	364	107	62	195	
November	372	103	62	207	
December	381	115	62	204	
1943					
January	400	125	62	213	
February	415	132	62	221	
March	417	125	63	229	
April	431	130	65	236	
May	432	124	68	240	

Figures in brackets indicate losses in Baltic and during training.

Losses from all U-boat Action

TOTAL	In convoy		Stragglers		Independent		TOTAL
	Ships sunk	% Sinkings in period	Ships sunk	% Sinkings in period	Ships sunk	% Sinkings in period	
151	95	56	20	12	54	32	**169**
572	51	8	17	3	577	9	**645**
656	348	44	75	10	359	46	**782**

U-boats in Atlantic	U-boats in Mediterranean	U-boats in Arctic	U-boats in Black Sea	New in service	Total losses
51	–	2	–	19	**1**
62	–	2	–	19	**3**
63	6	4	–	24	**3(1)**
60	23	5	–	22	**10**
65	21	4	–	15	**3**
76	21	4	–	16	**2**
80	21	10	–	18	**6**
80	20	19	–	17	**3**
85	19	20	–	20	**4**
88	17	21	–	21	**3**
99	16	23	–	21	**11(1)**
110	16	23	–	21	**10(1)**
134	15	23	–	18	**11(1)**
161	15	19	–	23	**16**
162	17	26	2	23	**13(1)**
159	20	23	2	23	**5**
166	22	21	3	22	**6**
178	22	18	3	21	**19(1)**
193	19	14	3	27	**16(2)**
195	17	21	3	18	**15**
207	18	12	3	26	**41**

Source: Germany and the Second World War, *Vol. 6, Table III.iii.I*

German, British and American Combat Aircraft Production

DATE	Single-engine Fighters			Twin-engine Aircraft			Four-engine Aircraft		
	German	British	USA	German	British	USA	German	British	USA
1941									
3rd Quarter	242	550	174	242	550	174	6	50	18
4th Quarter	221	559	320	221	559	320	3	57	64
1942									
1st Quarter	396	625	395	396	625	395	12	89	125
2nd Quarter	349	692	473	349	692	473	20	142	182
3rd Quarter	420	681	174	420	681	174	24	191	237
4th Quarter	449	659	484	449	659	484	27	232	329
1943									
1st Quarter	642	697	525	642	697	525	642	321	457
2nd Quarter	865	687	741	865	687	741	865	387	700

Source: Sir Charles Webster and Noble Frankland, The Strategic Air Offensive Against Germany, 1939–1945, *Vol. IV*

Total Production, Imports and Supply of Oil
(Figures in tons)

DATE	In Britain	In Germany
1941	13, 051, 000	4, 920, 000
1942	10, 232, 000	4, 988, 000
1943	14, 828, 000	5, 647, 000

Source: Sir Charles Webster and Noble Frankland, The Strategic Air Offensive Against Germany, 1939–1945, *Vol. IV, Appendix 49, and* Fighting With Figures, *Table 5.14*

TIMELINE
May 1941 – May 1943

--- **1941** ---

MAY

19 Fallujah in Iraq retaken.
Formal Italian surrender in East Africa.
German airborne forces land in Crete.

27 DAK with newly arrived 15. Panzerdivision retakes Halfaya Pass.

30 Revolt in Iraq collapses.

JUNE

1 Germans secure Crete.

2 Greek Government-in-Exile formed in Egypt.

3 New Iraqi Government formed.

4 Alexandria bombed by Luftwaffe.

8 British and Free French forces launch Operation EXPORTER, attacking Vichy Syria and Lebanon from Palestine.

9 British and Free French forces advance 40 miles and take Tyre.

15 Operation BATTLEAXE launched to relieve Tobruk.

16 British suffer heavy tank losses.

17 BATTLEAXE called off – 91 tanks lost.

22 Operation BARBAROSSA launched.

26 Finland declares war on Russia.

JULY

4 Tito issues national call to arms in Yugoslavia.

5 Wavell relieved and replaced by Auchinleck.

7 US Marines begin to relieve British garrison on Iceland.

12 Britain and USSR sign mutual assistance pact.

15 Convention of Acre marks end of campaign against Vichy French in Lebanon and Syria.
British forces enter Beirut.

26 Auchinleck flies to London for future strategy talks.

27 Germans enter Tallinn, Estonia.

AUGUST

5 Army Group Centre gains huge pocket at Smolensk.

9–12 Mid-Atlantic Conference, Argentia, Newfoundland.

25 British and Soviet forces invade Iran to prevent it joining Axis.

31 Persian Gulf secured by Allies.

SEPTEMBER

5 Hitler orders one more strike for Moscow.

8 Siege of Leningrad begins.

14 Rommel probes forward with 21. Panzerdivision hoping for fuel dump.

17 British and Soviet forces occupy Tehran.

19 Germans capture Kiev.

23 Army Group South takes Crimea.

24 Formation of Comité national français.

25 Rommel fails to find fuel and falls back to Libyan border.

26 Eighth Army formed, including XIII and XXX Corps. Ninth Army created in Palestine, Tenth Army in Iraq and Iran.

OCTOBER

2 General Cunningham's plan for Operation CRUSADER approved by Auchinleck.

18 Germans penetrate defence line 80 miles from Moscow.

24 Army Group South captures Kharkov.

30 Army Group Centre halted by weather.

31 RAF raids on Benghazi and Tripoli.

NOVEMBER

15 Advance on Moscow resumes.

18 Launch of Operation CRUSADER – Rommel caught off guard. XXX Corps advances 50 miles and captures airfield at Sidi Rezegh.

20 Besieged garrison at Tobruk ordered to break out and link up with XXX Corps.

23 5th SA Brigade destroyed by Axis forces.

26 General Cunningham wants to halt, but Auchinleck sacks him and replaces him with General Neil Ritchie as Eighth Army CO.

27 Tobruk garrison links up with NZ Division at El Duda.

29 Soviet counter-attack on Rostov forces German withdrawal.

DECEMBER

5 German drive on Moscow halted.

7 Axis forces pull back to Gazala. Japanese attack on Pearl Harbor.

8 Tobruk officially relieved.

11 Germany and Italy declare war on USA.

15 Eighth Army attacks at Gazala – Rommel orders retreat.

19 British forces retake Derna. Hitler appoints himself C-in-C of OKH.
   Italian human torpedo raid on Alexandria.

22 Opening of Anglo-US strategic conference Arcadia in Washington.

23 Axis forces abandon Benghazi.

27 Successful Commando raid on Vaagso, south-west Norway.

1942

January

1 Jean Moulin parachutes into unoccupied France.

4 Axis forces complete withdrawal from Cyrenaica.

21 Rommel launches fresh offensive into Cyrenaica.

26 First US forces arrive in Britain.

February

4 Rommel halts at Gazala.

8 Red Army creates big pocket at Demyansk.

19 Trial of Blum, Daladier et al. begins.

March

19 Soviets fail to relieve Leningrad.

April

Laval returns to power.

5 Hitler orders directive for Caucasus.

8 US delegation reaches Britain.

20 47 Spitfires reach Malta.

May

5 Operation IRONCLAD – British invasion of Vichy Madagascar.

10 Aerial victory for RAF over Malta.

12 Soviet offensive south of Kharkov launched.

27 Rommel launches assault on Gazala Line.

29 Soviet forces around Kharkov destroyed.

June

7 Jews in France's occupied zone required to wear yellow star.

21 Fall of Tobruk.

30 German Sixth Army opens summer offensive.
   British Eighth Army falls back to Alamein Line.

July

3 Germans take Sevastopol.

16 4,000 Parisian Jews rounded up and arrested.

24 Allies agree to launch Operation TORCH.

AUGUST

9 Maikop oilfields reached by German forces.

10 Germans reach outskirts of Stalingrad.

11 Hitler, Speer, Pleiger et al. meet to discuss coal crisis.

13 Hitler sets in motion increased building of Atlantic Wall.

15 Tanker *Ohio* reaches Malta.

19 Failed Dieppe raid.

24 Stalin orders Stalingrad to be held.

30 Rommel's last offensive at Alam Halfa.

SEPTEMBER

23 Rommel flies to see Hitler.

OCTOBER

11–17 October Blitz of Malta.

22 US Desert Air Force activated.

23 Launch of 2nd Battle of Alamein.

NOVEMBER

2 Army Group A advance into Caucasus comes to final halt.
    Final breakthrough begins at Alamein.

8 Operation TORCH: Allied invasion of Vichy north-west Africa.

11 Germans occupy Vichy France.

13 British re-enter Tobruk.

19 Russian counter-offensive at Stalingrad begins.

20 British re-enter Benghazi.

23 German forces trapped at Stalingrad.

24 Beginning of renewed Allied efforts to reach Tunis.

26 Hitler orders Paulus to hold at Stalingrad.

30 Further Russian attacks on lower Chir.

DECEMBER

12 Von Manstein launches Stalingrad relief operation.

16 Further Soviet attacks launched against Army Group B.

24 Darlan assassinated.

28 Hitler sanctions further withdrawals, putting Stalingrad 125 miles east of main front.

1943

JANUARY

3 Army Group A begins withdrawal from Caucasus.
Axis forces begin series of attacks in Tunisia.

8 Paulus rejects Soviet surrender demand.

10 Final Soviet offensive against Stalingrad begins.

12 Russian relief operation attempted at Leningrad.

13 Red Army offensive across the Don.
Führer order on complete conscription.

14–24 Casablanca conference.

23 Eighth Army enters Tripoli.

30 French Militia formed under Joseph Darnand.

FEBRUARY

2 Final German surrender at Stalingrad.

8 Red Army retakes Kursk.

13 SS gold raid on Djerba.

14 Red Army liberates Rostov.

15 *Le Service du travail obligatoire* becomes law in France.

16 Germans abandon Kharkov.

16/17 Operation GUNNERSIDE launched.

19 Rommel takes Kasserine Pass.

20 German counter-attack in the Ukraine.

MARCH

6 Eighth Army victory at Battle of Medenine.

9 Rommel leaves North Africa.

15 Germans retake Kharkov.

17 US II Corps takes Gafsa.

20–27 Eighth Army wins Battle of Mareth Line.

APRIL

6 Battle of Wadi Akarit.

19 Jewish uprising in Warsaw Ghetto.

19–21 Eighth Army repulsed at Enfidaville.

22 First Army opens final offensive in Tunisia.

MAY

5–6 Operation STRIKE – the Battle of Medjerda.

7 Fall of Tunis and Bizerte.

13 Final Axis surrender in Tunisia.

12–25 Trident Conference in Washington – agreed that Italy to be knocked out of war before opening second front.

15 Formation of Conseil National de la Résistance (CNR).

16–17 Operation CHASTISE – 617 Squadron raid on the German dams.

Notes

Abbreviations used in notes

AI   Author interview

BA-MA   Bundesarchiv-Militärarchiv, Freiburg, Germany

CCA   Churchill College Archives, Cambridge, UK

DDE   *The Papers of Dwight David Eisenhower*

DTA   Deutsches Tagebucharchiv, Emmendingen, Germany

EPL   Eisenhower Presidential Library, Abilene, Kansas, USA

FADN   Fondazione Archivio Diaristico Nazionale, Pieve Santo Stefano, Italy

GSWW   Militärgeschichtliches Forschungsamt: *Germany and the Second World War*

IWM   Imperial War Museum, London, UK

NARA   National Archives and Records Administration, Washington DC, USA

TNA   The National Archives, Kew, London, UK

USAHEC   United States Army Heritage & Education Center, Carlisle, Pennsylvania, USA

WSC   Winston Churchill, *The Second World War*

Part I: America Enters the War

1. The Largest Clash of Arms

16   'What I observed . . .': Balck, *Order in Chaos*, p. 4

20   'Then Russia will . . .': ibid, p. 217

20   'For us the only course . . .': ibid, p. 218

21   'The upcoming campaign . . .': cited in *GSWW*, Vol. IV/I, p. 482

21   'The socialist idea . . .': ibid

21   'The controlling machinery . . .': Halder, *Halder War Diary*, 17/3/1941

22   'The troops have to realize . . .': cited in *GSWW*, Vol. IV/I, p. 485

22   'At the present time . . .': Balck, p. 217

2. Manoeuvring

26   'It is thus probably . . .': Halder, *Halder War Diary*, 3/7/1941

27   'This will also reduce . . .': Trevor-Roper, *Hitler's War Directives*, 33a

28   'We very soon had to accustom . . .': von Luck, *Panzer Commander*, p. 67

29   'help and support of any kind . . .': cited in Bellamy, *Absolute War*, p. 237

30   'I did not come from America alone.': cited in Sherwood, *White House Papers of Harry L. Hopkins*, Vol. I, p. 321

30   'Tell him that Britain has . . .': cited in Roll, *The Hopkins Touch*, p. 122

31   'He is excited as a schoolboy . . .': Colville, *Fringes of Power*, Vol. II, 1/8/1941

31   'no aggrandisement, territorial or other . . .': cited in WSC, Vol. III, pp. 385–6

33   'fit and cheerful . . .': Hinchliffe, *Lent Papers*, p. 108

33   'Last night my eighth kill . . .': ibid

34   'cleared for procurement . . .': NARA RG 92/1890, Box 551

34   'In deciding upon . . .': NARA RG92/1890, Box 539

35   'Esquire may be an authority . . .': ibid

36   'Daddy died on 31 July.': AI with Henry Bowles

36   'You'd have planes flying over . . .': ibid

37   'There was a lot of griping . . .': Deane and Schaps, *500 Hundred Days of Front Line Combat*, p. 30

39   'Oh happy day!': Deniston, *Memoirs of a Combat Fighter Pilot*, p. 4

39   'I think you just need . . .': Gabreski, *Gabby: A Fighter Pilot's Life*, p. 18

40   'The training brings . . .': ibid, p. 35

40   'The sacrifices made so far . . .': cited in Suchenwirth, *Historical Turning Points in the German Air Force War Effort*, p. 74

41   'The rest of us . . .': cited in Irving, *Rise and Fall of the Luftwaffe*, p. 117

3. Summer '41

42   'If only we had a free hand . . .': Knoke, diary, 22/6/1941

43   'The gruppe had 12–15 kills . . .': Bethke, *Erinnerungen*, p. 147

44   'The wrecks inhibited . . .': Kirchner, *Erinnerungen*, p. 29

44   'Our Russian campaign . . .': Herrmann, *Eagle's Wings*, p. 130

44   'Whoever said that must be mad.': cited in Irving, *Rise and Fall of the Luftwaffe*, p. 116

47   'Never have I been so deceived . . .': ibid, p. 122

50   'amounted to the prickliness . . .': Spears, *Fulfilment of a Mission*, p. 159

50   'These Frenchmen are British officers . . .': this conversation is recounted in ibid, p. 153

51   'This persistent claim to meddle . . .': de Gaulle, *Call to Honour*, p. 204

52   'Auchinleck was not familiar with . . .': Lyttelton, *Memoirs of Lord Chandos*, p. 262

52   'Between July and October, no fewer than 300 . . .': figures from Playfair, *Mediterranean and the Middle East*, Vol. III, p. 4

53   'The colonel told me all this . . .': Christopherson, diaries, 13–19/7/1941
55   'Be it on your own head . . .': Cooper, *One of the Originals*, p. 5
56   'Descending into a patch of soft . . .': ibid, p. 20

4. The US Navy Goes to War
59   'You're all finished! . . .': cited in Fairbanks, *A Hell of a War*, p. 56
59   'Now go out and get the public . . .': cited in ibid, p. 60
60   'I damn near blubbered . . .': ibid, p. 66
60   'Do we want to beat the enemy . . .': cited in Warlimont, *Inside Hitler's Headquarters*, p. 186
61   'a tactical victory only': ibid, p. 191
62   'The problems began to increase . . .': von Schell, 'Grundlagen der Motorisierung und ihre Entwicklung im Zweiten Weltkrieg', *Wehrwissenschaftliche Rundschau*, 13
62   '1. Occupy the city . . .': cited in *GSWW*, Vol. IV/II, p. 645
63   'Nevertheless, Roosevelt should . . .': ibid
63   'Our goal, as before . . .': details and quotations from this memorandum come from Halder, *Halder War Diary*, 13/9/1941, and Warlimont, p. 192
65   'I felt there was no action . . .': AI with Eric Brown
65   'We sat speechless and aghast . . .': Brown, *Wings on My Sleeve*, p. 14
66   'After that, it was easy.': ibid, p. 17
67   'The only thing picked up . . .': ibid, p. 26
70   'We were frustrated and weary . . .': Goodson, *Tumult in the Clouds*, p. 54
70   'The fortune of a hero . . .': cited in Kershaw, *The Few*, p. 219
70   'I no longer have much enthusiasm . . .': Bethke, *Erinnerungen*, p. 153
71   'Biggin Hill is the fold . . .': Offenberg, *Lonely Warrior*, p. 183
71   'After flying for about an hour . . .': ibid, p. 200

5. The Sinking of the *Reuben James*
74   'For several hours we drove . . .': Street, *Hitler's Whistle*, 28/6/1941
74   'There is no doubt . . .': ibid, 3/9/1941
75   'Everywhere one sees . . .': ibid, 28/9/1941
75   'The Minister of Food . . .': Churchill, *War Speeches*, Vol. II, 30/9/1941
76   'Until we reached base . . .': Topp, *Odyssey of a U-Boat Commander*, p. 3
77   'It appears there were many victims . . .': Ciano, *Diary*, 31/10/1941
77   'I hope for one thing . . .': ibid, 1/7/1941
77   'Let's make it a century . . .': ibid, 25–9/10/1941
78   'They have nothing else . . .': ibid, 9/10/1941
78   'Mussolini has swallowed . . .': ibid, 5/11/1941
80   'The result was a holocaust . . .': Cunningham, *Sailor's Odyssey*, p. 420
80   'All, I mean all . . .': Ciano, 9/11/1941
81   'It puts a strain . . .': Suhren and Brustat-Naval, *Teddy Suhren*, p. 105
81   'Bosun, what speed are we doing?': ibid, pp. 107–8. This episode is

recounted in his memoirs as though it were *U-564*'s first patrol, but the course he took, the setting off Gibraltar and the descriptions given are clearly those of his third patrol, running from 16 September to 1 November 1941

82   'In fact, I was scared . . .': Fairbanks, *A Hell of a War*, p. 74
82   'Now hear this!': ibid, p. 76

6. Crusaders

85   'The Army Commander-in-Chief . . .': TNA CAB 41/25; Playfair, *Mediterranean and the Middle East*, Vol. II, p. 288
86   'During the bumpy ride . . .': Cooper, *One of the Originals*, p. 28
87   'It was clear to David Stirling . . .': ibid
87   'Not a very comradely action . . .': cited in Irving, *Rise and Fall of the Luftwaffe*, p. 135
88   'Now there is another . . .': cited in ibid, p. 137
90   'Chief problems now and in the future . . .': Baldwin, *New York Times*, 2/11/1941
91   'I am going to attack the day after tomorrow . . .': cited in Moorehead, *African Trilogy*, p. 230
92   'It was novel, reckless . . .': ibid, p. 235
92   'In all directions . . .': Martin, *Hellfire Tonight*, p. 94
93   'I've had to break off the action . . .': Liddell Hart, *Rommel Papers*, p. 174
94   'We are off again . . .': Martin, diary, 8/12/1941, BA-MA

7. Unravelling

95   'This war is going to last . . .': cited in von Luck, *Panzer Commander*, p. 76
96   'We sensed catastrophe . . .': ibid, p. 79
96   'As a result of their numerical . . .': Balck, *Order in Chaos*, p. 225
97   'Why don't you go and tell . . .': cited in ibid, p. 226
98   'Our troops were far too . . .': cited in Tooze, *Wages of Destruction*, p. 507
98   'This war can no longer . . .': ibid
100   'officially, rationing provided . . .': figures from ibid, Table II.III.33, p. 529, and Noakes, *Nazism*, Vol. 4, Doc. 1268, p. 520
100   'of a totally impoverished . . .': cited in *GSWW*, Vol. V/IIA, p. 523
101   'He refuses to believe . . .': cited in Tooze, p. 499
101   'simplification and increase in performance . . .': this entire memorandum can be found at BA-MA RW19/2178, p. 172
103   'The most frightful aspect . . .': Halder, *Halder War Diary*, 7/12/1941
103   'Hitler has overreached himself . . .': cited in von Luck, p. 80
103   'Take us with you . . .': ibid, p. 81
104   'Only the will to reach . . .': ibid, p. 82
104   'Is it important?': cited in Fairbanks, *A Hell of a War*, p. 82

8. World War

109   'I feel that this country united . . .': Stimson and Bundy, *On Active Service in Peace and War*, p. 393

109   'It's quite true . . .': cited in WSC, Vol. III, p. 538

109   'United we could subdue . . .': ibid, p. 540

109   'We can't lose the war . . .': cited in Kershaw, *Hitler, 1936–1945*, p. 442

Part II: Eastern Influences
9. Battles at Sea

114   'You have heard the news . . .': Warlimont, *Inside Hitler's Headquarters*, p. 208

118   'It was an eerie sight . . .': AI with Eric Brown

118   'And so we stood there . . .': ibid

119   'You all right, Winkle?': Brown, *Wings on My Sleeve*, p. 38

119   'We couldn't wake them up . . .': AI with Eric Brown

119   'pulped, literally . . .': cited in Blair, *Hitler's U-Boat War: The Hunters 1939–1942*, p. 416

121   'Stepping up production . . .': Beasley, *Knudsen*, p. 335

121   'Britain would produce an impressive . . .': figures from *Statistics Relating to the War Effort of the United Kingdom*, Table 10, and GSWW, Vol. V/IIB, p. 700

121   'These figures and similar figures . . .': www.presidency.ucsb.edu

122   'Let's go ahead on what the President wants . . .': Beasley, p. 337

10. Strategic Blunders

123   'As a result . . .': Warlimont, *Inside Hitler's Headquarters*, p. 216

124   'The urgent concrete questions . . .': ibid, p. 221

124   'Hours and hours . . .': ibid, pp. 221–2

124   'When I imagine these . . .': Sack, Diary, 16/11/1941, DTA

126   'Everything was drowning . . .': Balck, *Order in Chaos*, p. 227

127   'We shall master it . . .': cited in GSWW, Vol. IV/II, p. 724

127   'Can I have them in Warsaw . . .': Balck, p. 241

128   'Führer holds forth . . .': extracts from Halder, *Halder War Diary*, 20/12/1941–2/1/1942

128   '. . . as high as 244': figures from GSWW, Vol. V/IB, p. 1,011

128   'i.e., 25.96 percent . . .': Halder, 5/1/1942

130   'Instead of completing . . .': Balck, p. 235

131   'Do you know what . . .': ibid

132   'fifty-three new U-boats . . .': figures from Blair, *Hitler's U-Boat War: The Hunters 1939–1942*, Appendix I

134   'Thus, at the beginning of 1942 . . .': Dönitz, *Memoirs*, p. 197

11. Carnage Off America

136   'The usual naval woes.': Ciano, *Diary*, 13/12/1941

136   'Thus our last two remaining . . .': Cunningham, *Sailor's Odyssey*, p. 434

138   'The role of our armoured forces . . .': *Notes from the Theatres of War*, No. 2, Part 1

139   'When I reported back . . .': Suhren and Brustat-Naval, *Teddy Suhren*, p. 120

140   'It should be borne in mind . . .': Admiral King to Vice-Chief of Naval Operations, 2 April 1942, cited in Morison, *History of the United States Naval Operations in World War II*, Vol. I, p. 256

142   'The problem before us now . . .': Kennedy, *The Business of War*, p. 18

143   'From them on I went through . . .': Recollections: Lieutenant (N) Richard (Dick) Callery Pearce, www.canadasnavalmemorial.cn

145   'The conditions off Newfoundland . . .': Macintyre, *U-boat Killer*, p. 59

12. Fighters and Bombers

146   'We were at war!!!': Deane and Schaps, *500 Days of Front Line Combat*, p. 31

146   'we went nuts over these . . .': ibid, p. 34

147   'the aircraft industry had produced . . .': figures from Webster and Frankland, *Strategic Air Offensive Against Germany*, Vol. IV, Appendix XXIII

147   'I take up the youngsters . . .': Offenberg, *Lonely Warrior*, p. 202

148   'I cannot explain to you all . . .': cited in ibid, p. 205

148   'I mention this because . . .': cited in Overy, *Bombing War*, p. 259

149   'recent attacks on industrial towns . . .': cited in *Strategic Air Offensive Against Germany*, Vol. IV, p. 136

150   'The criticism cannot be countered . . .': Bufton Papers, CCA

151   'Well, they are sowing the wind.': Harris, *Bomber Offensive*, p. 52

151   'On the day that I took over . . .': ibid, p. 73

151   'best part of a thousand . . .': cited in Tedder, *With Prejudice*, p. 253

154   'Never have I felt so keenly . . .': Cunningham, *Sailor's Odyssey*, p. 452

13. Steel and Strategy

158   'Dr. Todt's plane has just crashed . . .': Speer, *Inside the Third Reich*, p. 274

159   'Herr Speer, I appoint you . . .': this and the subsequent conversations are cited in ibid, pp. 274–7

160   'Never in my life . . .': ibid, p. 280

161   'This is the most important . . .': cited in Warlimont, *Inside Hitler's Headquarters*, p. 226

161   'England remains our main . . .': cited in ibid, p. 209

166   'We have had no chance . . .': Schlange-Schöningen, *The Morning After*, p. 179

166   'We behaved like devils . . .': Wendel, *Hausfrau at War*, p. 143

168   'His decisions shall be final.': cited in Klein, *A Call to Arms*, p. 297
168   'As I understood my job . . .': Nelson, *Arsenal of Democracy*, p. 208

14. Seeds of Resistance
170   'I herewith commission you . . .': cited at www.jewishvirtuallibrary.org
171   'I saw not a single SS man . . .': Knoller, *Living with the Enemy*, p. 108
172   'Now I could obtain rations again.': ibid, p. 111
173   'At last someone was leading . . .': Mathieu Laurier (Paul Vigouroux), *Il reste le drapeau noir et les copains*, p. 16
175   'Those of you who remain . . .': www.herodote.net
175   'More and more now . . .': Jean Moulin, *Report on Activities . . .*; cited in Foot, *SOE in France* (1st edn), Appendix E
176   'The object to be achieved . . .': ibid
178   'I knew I had to give up trying . . .': Sønsteby, *Report from No. 24*, p. 26
179   'We had hoped they'd send . . .': Poulsson, IWM 27189
181   'The point was to be as unobtrusive . . .': AI with Gunnar Sønsteby

15. Heat and Dust
183   'I could have shot him.': Lyttelton, *Memoirs of Lord Chandos*, p. 282
184   'The work was killing . . .': ibid, p. 288
184   'In the middle of these . . .': ibid
185   'But that formula failed . . .': Ciano, *Diary*, 29/4–2/5/1942
186   'generous German participation . . .': *GSWW*, Vol. VI, p. 659
186   'You can imagine how the Italians . . .': cited in Suchenwirth, *Historical Turning Points*, p. 95
187   'The first grey, misty sight . . .': Fairbanks, *A Hell of a War*, p. 101
187   'They're having a helluva time . . .': ibid, p. 106
188   'We were all acutely aware . . .': cited in ibid, p. 112
188   'I blushed and stumbled . . .': ibid, p. 113
189   The supporters are . . .': Ciano, 13/5/1942
190   'I need not have worried . . .': Macintyre, *U-Boat Killer*, p. 67
192   'And they would have all made . . .': Suhren and Brustat-Naval, *Teddy Suhren*, p. 122
192   'a staggering 125 ships were sunk': figures from *DEAS*, Table 13
194   'A large and clumsy star . . .': von Luck, *Panzer Commander*, p. 3
194   'What a contrast . . .': ibid, p. 93
194   'Glad you're here . . .': ibid, p. 94
195   'I learned to travel by compass . . .': ibid, p. 97
196   'He was possibly the best . . .': Heaton and Lewis, *German Aces Speak*, p. 155
197   'We're launching a decisive . . .': Liddell Hart, *Rommel Papers*, p. 204

16. Into the Cauldron
199   'To us it was the most beautiful . . .': Deane and Schaps, *500 Days of Front Line Combat*, p. 37

200   'weakened in strength and morale': Cline, *Washington Command Post:*
      The Operations Division (US Army in World War II), p. 153
200   'I hope that at long last . . .': Eisenhower, Diary, 22/4/1942, EPL
201   'Who's smoking?': Clark, *Calculated Risk*, p. 19
202   'The first thing I saw . . .': AI with Billy Drake
207   'What difference does it make . . . ?': cited in Wilmot, *Tobruk*, p. 300
208   'He did not accept . . .': Tuker Papers, IWM 14075
209   'Cavallero is a faithful follower . . .': Ciano, *Diary*, 17/5/1942
209   'Which raises some very . . .': ibid
210   'ordinary day': Martin, diary, 26/5/1942, BA-MA
210   'Jerry was on his way . . .': ibid, 27/5/1942
210   'It was a ghostly scene . . .': von Luck, *Panzer Commander*, p. 99
212   'a whole bloody German armoured division': TNA, CAB 44/97
212   'We were in the best of spirits . . .': von Luck, p. 99
213   'You are lucky in your bad luck . . .': ibid, p. 100

17. Combined Production

214   'An interesting question . . .': Balck, *Order in Chaos*, p. 243
214   'One thing is clear . . .': ibid, p. 244
217   'I fought with France . . .': Boris, *Combattant de la France Libre*, pp. 91–2
217   'It's said we've knocked out . . .': Martin, diary, 29/6/42, BA-MA
218   'Get a move on . . .': TNA CAB 47/97
219   'The thousandth day . . .': Gwladys Cox, diary, 31/5/1942
219   'Some reports say . . .': ibid, 26/5/1942
220   'So passes in fitting manner . . .': ibid, 4/6/1942
220   'devastating repulse . . .': ibid, 7/6/1942
220   'At a stroke . . .': WSC, Vol. IV, p. 226
220   'I have a very strong feeling . . .': Lowenheim, *Roosevelt and Churchill:*
      Their Secret Wartime Correspondence, Doc. 136, 31/5/1942, p. 271
220   'We are disturbed here about . . .': Sherwood, *White House Papers of*
      Harry L. Hopkins, Vol. II, p. 585
221   'You will have no set . . .': cited in Beasley, *Knudsen*, p. 351
222   'It was never part of my job . . .': Nelson, *Arsenal of Democracy*, p. 198,
      and Klein, *A Call to Arms*, p. 307
223   'Soon there were lobster shells . . .': Lyttelton, *Memoirs of Lord Chandos*,
      p. 308

18. The Fall of Tobruk

226   'Massacres of entire . . .': Ciano, *Diary*, 27/5/1942
226   'From this he draws . . .': ibid, 31/5/1942
226   'You are brave soldiers': cited in Boris, *Combattant de la France Libre*, p. 94
227   'I hope you haven't . . .': ibid, p. 96
228   'He could have been viewed . . .': cited in Heaton and Lewis, *Star of Africa*,
      p. 107

228   'Usually we knew roughly . . .': AI with Billy Drake
229   'You'd get in as close . . .': ibid
229   'That's why the golden rule . . .': ibid
229   'Low-level machine-gunning . . .': TNA AIR 41/26
229   'I am sure everything is being done . . .': TNA AIR 23/904
230   'The defence was conducted . . .': Liddell Hart, *Rommel Papers*, p. 212
230   'If we had not taken it . . .': TNA AIR 41/26
230   'Clench your teeth, please . . .': von Luck, *Panzer Commander*, p. 101
233   'the prospects of success . . .': Alanbrooke, *War Diaries*, 16/4/1942
234   'I certainly do want to read it . . .': Eisenhower, *Crusade in Europe*, p. 58
234   'It looks as if you boys go together.': Clark, *Calculated Risk*, p. 20
235   'Which for anybody . . .': Ciano, 4/6/1942
238   'Not all bullets kill . . .': Boris, p. 103, and AI
239   'The possibility of having to relieve . . .': Kennedy, *Business of War*, p. 235
239   'I don't know what we can do . . .': cited in ibid, p. 241
240   'I doubt that Army's . . .': ibid
240   'Everything has been a jumble . . .': Martin, diary, 19/6/1942, BA-MA
241   'One of those suicide patrols . . .': ibid, 20/6/1942
241   'This is one of the heaviest . . .': WSC, Vol. IV, p. 344
241   'This was one of the worst . . .': Tuker, *Approach to Battle*, p. 85

19. Sea and Sand

242   'We had the jack hammers . . .': AI with Ted Hardy
242   'Soldiers of the Panzerarmee Afrika!': Liddell Hart, *Rommel Papers*, p. 233
243   'lie behind me like a dream.': ibid, p. 235
244   'If we had diverted . . .': Kennedy, *Business of War*, p. 247
245   'Quick-decision men . . .': Moorehead, *Daily Express*, 23/6/1942
245   'Personally, I've had enough . . .': Martin, diary, 23/6/1942, BA-MA
246   'Up and down the whole time . . .': Suhren and Brustat-Naval, *Teddy Suhren*, p. 129
246   'No more was seen or heard . . .': ibid, p. 132
247   'At the same moment . . .': ibid
248   'Mersa Matruh fell yesterday . . .': Liddell Hart, p. 241
248   'Rock, wastes, arid . . .': Spayd, *Bayerlein*, p. 79
249   'Things are not going as well . . .': Liddell Hart, p. 249
249   'Mary's handling of the air battle . . .': Elmhirst Papers, CCA
249   'bloody good commander.' AI with Billy Drake
249   'when the orders went out . . .': Elmhirst Papers, CCA
250   'The Royal Air Force had reached . . .': Spayd, p. 83
250   'three flamers and 34 severely damaged . . .': TNA, AIR 27/873
250   'I have prepared landing grounds . . .': ibid, 41/26
251   'It was then that I became . . .': ibid, 23/1397

20. Thousand Bomber Raid

253   'This is the most glorious . . .': Cox, diary, 1/6/1942
253   '1,500 PLANES IN BIGGEST RAID': *Daily Mirror*, 1/6/1942
254   'I'm always terrified . . .': AI with Eric Brown
254   'It's a horrible business . . .': Gibson, *Enemy Coast Ahead Uncensored*,
         p. 174
254   'Very dark but good . . .': TNA AIR 4/37
255   'It is out of the question . . .': cited in Irving, *Göring*, p. 357
256   'How is such an engine . . .': cited in Irving, *Rise and Fall of the Luftwaffe*,
         p. 171
256   'Comparison of German aircraft . . .': ibid, p. 163
257   'Overall, numbers of flak units . . .': figures from *GSWW*, Vol. VI,
         pp. 610–11
258   'Once again, God mercifully looked after me . . .': Hinchliffe, *Lent Papers*,
         p. 142

21. Sea and Steppe

259   'Flying debris rains down . . .': Suhren and Brustat-Naval, *Teddy Suhren*,
         p. 133
259   'PK man!': ibid, p. 134
262   'He was, he told them . . .': all quotes in this episode from ibid,
         pp. 134–43
263   'At 1900 an Admiralty message . . .': Fairbanks, *A Hell of a War*, p. 136
263   'Small black, brown, and grey . . .': ibid, p. 138
263   'Suddenly it was pierced . . .': Herrmann, *Eagle's Wings*, p. 149
264   '1829: A plane is falling in flames . . .': Fairbanks, p. 139
264   'We hate leaving PQ17 behind . . .': ibid, p. 140
266   'Mobility is considerably . . .': cited in Warlimont, *Inside Hitler's
         Headquarters*, p. 240
267   'Serious shortage . . .': ibid
267   'Soviet Air Force had 6,600 aircraft . . .': figures from *GSWW*, Vol. VI,
         Table VI.I.6, p. 894
268   'It was an intoxicating picture . . .': Balck, *Order in Chaos*, p. 249
268   'The situation is getting . . .': Halder, *Halder War Diary*, 23/7/1942
270   'Russia, if it used . . .': cited in *GSWW*, Vol. VI, p. 898

22. Gathering Strength

274   'I'd just come from the war . . .': cited in Stevenson, *A Man Called
         Intrepid*, p. 169
276   'The Eighth must do well . . .': Davis, *Carl A. Spaatz and the Air War in
         Europe*, p. 83
277   'We had a cover of Spitfires . . .': AI with Ralph Burbridge
279   'Well, I hardly know . . .': Butcher Diary, 23/7/1942, EPL

280   'At last the lads . . .': Cheall, *Fighting Through from Dunkirk to Hamburg*, p. 38

282   'I figured it was bad . . .': AI with Warren 'Bing' Evans

283   'They had their hearts . . .': ibid

283   'Sorry, we just can't . . .': cited in Mowat, *And No Birds Sang*, p. 7

284   'Thank heavens, this is it! . . .': ibid, p. 10

284   'There you are, luv . . .': ibid, p. 13

285   'Fragments fly about like flaming torches . . .': cited in Hinchliffe, *Lent Papers*, pp. 46–7

285   'best friend and bartender one could wish for.': cited in Heaton and Lewis, *German Aces Speak*, p. 160

285   'So you now have, what . . .': cited in ibid, p. 122

287   'He arrived in an Air Commodore's rig . . .': Elmhirst Papers, CCA

287   'I think what is required here . . .': cited in Connell, *Auchinleck*, p. 698

287   'A new army of the Middle East . . .': Moorehead, *African Trilogy*, p. 421

23. Last Chance in Africa

288   'General Rommel was our great hero . . .': Wendel, *Hausfrau at War*, p. 158

289   'alarming symptoms of deteriorating morale': *GSWW*, Vol. VI, p. 746

289   'Naturally, Mussolini has been absorbing . . .': Ciano, *Diary*, 20/7/1942

289   'The tone of the Duce's . . .': ibid, 24/7/1942

290   'If you compare that . . .': Kirchner, *Erinnerungen*

290   'Everyone was very worked up . . .': ibid

292   'From there we learned . . .': Luigi Marchese, FADN

292   'The absence of drinking . . .': ibid

293   'The convoy reached . . .': Walter Mazzacuto, FADN

294   'The battle is dependent . . .': cited in Spayd, *Bayerlein*, p. 89

296   'The effect was stupendous.': Cooper, *One of the Originals*, p. 53

297   'Abandon ship!': ibid, p. 61

298   'What the hell's wrong?': ibid, p. 64

298   'The scene of devastation . . .': ibid

298   'destroy at the earliest opportunity . . .': cited in Alexander, *Alexander Memoirs*, p. 16

299   'They were bewildered, frustrated and fed up . . .': ibid, p. 13

300   'He gave an excellent talk . . .': this entire account of Montgomery's briefing was recorded by Elmhirst, Elmhirst Papers, CCA

301   'The weather was not . . .': AI with Warren 'Bing' Evans

302   'This was the most depressing news of the summer.': Clark, *Calculated Risk*, p. 46

302   'entirely convinced': WSC, Vol. IV, p. 450

302   'When Stalin asked me . . .': ibid, p. 49

302   'The planners of TORCH . . .': ibid, p. 50

303   'We had a lot of losses . . .': Francesco Cavalero, IWM 12528
304   'I remained in the sky . . .': ibid
305   'Unless I get 2,000 cubic metres . . .': cited in Spooner, *Supreme Gallantry*, p. 182

24. The End of the German Dream

307   'Herr Pleiger, if, due to the shortage . . .': cited in Tooze, *Wages of Destruction*, p. 574
307   'The fuel situation does not allow . . .': BA-MA RW19/2922
308   'The greengrocers are full . . .': Cox, diary, 19/8/1942
308   'Today I've driven . . .': Street, *Hitler's Whistle*, p. 293
308   'From the reborn countryside . . .': *The Great Harvest, 1942*, IWM UKY 405
308   'Total grain harvested . . .': figures from Murray, *Agriculture*, Appendix Table VI
309   '200 million tons a month . . .': figures from Howlett, *Fighting with Figures*, Table 8.13
310   'Time and again . . .': Macintyre, *U-Boat Killer*, p. 73
310   'for the development of a powerfully armed . . .': both memos cited in Dönitz, *Memoirs*, pp. 269–70
314   'Wave after wave . . .': Spayd, *Bayerlein*, p.91
314   'Of the four generals . . .': ibid
316   'Swarms of low-flying fighter bombers . . .': Liddell Hart, *Rommel Papers*, p. 279
316   'Disappointment and dejection filled our hearts . . .': Luigi Marchese, FADN
316   'It was clear . . .': ibid
316   'With the failure . . .': Spayd, p. 95
317   'An important lesson . . .': ibid, p. 96
317   'the current priority for manpower . . .': figures from Parker, *Manpower*, Table 18, p. 179

Part III: The Allies Strike Back

25. A Brief Discourse on Tanks and Fire-power

321   'The German weapon . . .': Lyttelton Papers, CCA
321   'There has been some suggestion . . .': ibid
322   'Oh, yes, but I prefer . . .': ibid
322   'We fully realized . . .': Kennedy, *Business of War*, p. 242
324   'The consequence was . . .': Balck, *Order in Chaos*, p. 232
324   German Mk IV numbers: from BA-MA RH19/1257, and Russian T34s from *GSWW*, VI
328   'Tanks and motor vehicles . . .': von Schell, 'Grundlagen der Motorisierung und ihre Entwicklung im Zweiten Weltkrieg', *Wehrwissenschaftliche Rundschau*, 13

26. A Brief Discourse on Training and Morale

331   'The bombing had not begun . . .': Cox, diary, 3/9/1942

331   'One feels years older . . .': ibid

332   'I have carefully considered . . .': TNA CAB79/57

332   'urgent need of intensive training': Churchill Papers, 20/80, CCA

332   'a regrettable fact that our troops . . .': cited in Holland, *Together We Stand*, p. 315

334   'It was very hard . . .': AI with Franz Maassen

335   'We still thought . . .': ibid

335   'No one had taught these people . . .': Severloh, *WN 62*, p. 26

335   'Our real training . . .': ibid

336   'Better to know instinctively . . .': cited in Nicolson, *Alex*, p. 118

336   'We crawled, squirmed and wriggled . . .': Mowat, *And No Birds Sang*, p. 13

336   'Before the first week . . .': ibid, p. 14

339   'The games were over . . .': Martin, *Hellfire Tonight*, p. 27

340   'Subordinate commanders must . . .': *Army Training Memorandum No. 39*, 17 April 1941

341   'I am only one out of . . .': Knoke, *I Flew for the Führer*, p. 17

341   'I believe . . .': Günther Sack, DTA, 797, 7–13

341   'I was young and gung-ho . . .': AI with Franz Maassen

343   'They were bewildered . . .': Alexander, *Alexander Memoirs*, p. 12

27. Return of the Hero

346   'astronomical indemnities': Ciano, *Diary*, 30/8/1942

346   'One cannot fail twice . . .': ibid

346   'The sinking of our ships . . .': ibid, 3/9/1942

347   'Our hair stands on end . . .': Suhren and Brustat-Naval, *Teddy Suhren*, p. 154

347   'Consequence, nearly total . . .': ibid, p. 155

347   'We are bombing Germany . . .': cited in Harris, *Bomber Offensive*, p. 116

348   'A VERY HOT TARGET': Gibson logbook, TNA AIR 4/48

350   'We should immediately . . .': Melinsky, *Forming the Pathfinders*, p. 68

351   'Sir, you will never . . .': ibid

352   'This last letter . . .': cited in ibid, p. 75

352   'In the opinion of the Air Staff . . .': Portal Papers, Folder 9, 14/6/1942, Christ Church College, Oxford

353   'The bombs, incendiaries first . . .': Gibson, *Enemy Coast Ahead Uncensored*, p. 187

353   'In recognition of your . . .': Suhren and Brustat-Naval, p. 159

28. Getting Ready

355   'I felt this as a terrible rebuke . . .': Knoller, *Living with the Enemy*, p. 114

356   '7h30 – To the baker's . . .': cited in Cobb, *The Resistance*, p. 134

357   'Times of sacrifice . . .': Luchaire, *Ma drôle de vie*, p. 148
357   'I wish for German victory . . .': cited in Vinen, *The Unfree French*, p. 197
358   'Men are already gathering . . .': Frenay, *The Night Will End*, p. 20
358   'Every worker who remains . . .': ibid, p. 180
359   'Tell those brave people . . .': cited in Pineau, *La Simple vérité*, p. 185
360   'The resistance was not only . . .': de Gaulle, *War Memoirs: The Call to Honour*, p. 277
361   'The eyes of the Army . . .': cited in Stevens, *Fourth Indian Division*, p. 188
363   'The impact of Monty's visit . . .': Martin, *Hellfire Tonight*, p. 162
365   'Flying over the British . . .': Deniston, *Memoirs of a Combat Fighter Pilot*, p. 27
365   'I set the flaps . . .': ibid, p. 24
366   'We made one pass . . .': ibid, p. 32
367   'The basic formation was . . .': AI with Billy Drake
367   'The trick was to leave it . . .': ibid
367   'They were a great bunch . . .': ibid
370   'I am blinded . . .': Heaton and Lewis, *Star of Africa*, p. 177

29. The Vicious Circle

371   'The relations between . . .': Harry Butcher Papers, EPL
372   'Britain may look . . .': *A Short Guide to Great Britain*
372   'And we were there . . .': AI with Henry and Tom Bowles
372   'You can call a man . . .': cited in Winton, *Cunningham*, p. 278
373   'dark colours . . .': Ciano, *Diary*, 22/9/1942
373   'It is because . . .': ibid
373   'If we lose the war . . .': cited in ibid, 8/10/1942
373   'great shame': ibid, 27/9/1942
374   'My nerves are worn out . . .' : Halder, *Halder War Diary*, 24/9/1942
374   'The Führer repeatedly said . . .': cited in Tooze, *Wages of Destruction*, p. 544
376   'carapace of sand and sweat': Luigi Marchese, FADN
376   'An inventor of tortures . . .': Giuseppe Santaniello, FADN
376   'And we presumed to bring . . .': ibid
376   'The mountain people . . .': ibid
377   'I'd say that Athens . . .': ibid
377   'Morale here is very high . . .': ibid
378   'I've great admiration . . .': cited in Frenay, *The Night Will End*, p. 187
378   'Général, the Secret Army . . .' ibid
378   'I must warn you . . .': ibid
378   'With their sense of reality . . .': von Luck, *Panzer Commander*, p. 105
379   'I'm glad you're here again . . .': ibid, p. 94
379   'So, Luck, now you know . . .': ibid, pp. 106–10
380   'Inform you that only . . .': cited in Cobb, *The Resistance*, p. 125
382   'How are you, gentlemen?': Frenay, p. 195

382   'To one arriving from France . . .': ibid, p. 202
382   'I know. Try and explain . . .': cited in ibid, p. 202
383   'I had an unremarkable . . .': AI with Gunnar Sønsteby
385   'However sceptical . . .': WSC, Vol. IV, p. 341
387   'As a boy and young man . . .': Poulsson, IWM 27189

30. Lighting the Torch
388   'More men and equipment . . .': cited in Herman, *Freedom's Forge*, p. 187
388   'I wish that every man . . .': cited in ibid, p.188, and Heiner, *Henry J. Kaiser*, p. 129
389   'It is a miracle . . .': cited in Heiner, p. 129
389   'Those who delay us . . .': Clark, *Calculated Risk*, p. 52
390   'It's great not to argue . . .': cited in ibid, p. 53
390   'Hurrah!': WSC, Vol. IV, p. 487
390   'Mission planned for early take-off . . .': 97th Bombardment Group, NARA (record stack not available)
391   'There was nothing great . . .': Goodson, *Tumult in the Clouds*, p. 60
391   'Where are the others?' ibid, p. 61
392   'There was no *esprit de corps* . . .': ibid, p. 63
392   'He was a great believer . . .': ibid
392   'We'll form up this way . . .': this episode is recounted in ibid, pp. 63–5
393   'Quite impossible . . .': cited in Spayd, *Bayerlein*, p. 97
395   '82 IN FOUR DAYS': *Times of Malta*, 15/10/1942
396   'I've got a message for you . . .': Clark, p. 66
397   'Mast asserts . . .': ibid, p. 71
397   'When do I go?': ibid, p. 67
398   'I think we were all nervous . . .': cited in Mears, *Real Heroes of Telemark*, p. 49
399   'It is in this level of command . . .': *DDE*, Vol. 1, p. 627
399   'If there is anything . . .': Elmhirst Papers, CCA
400   'Let me have the word . . .': Churchill Papers, 20/81, CCA

31. Lightfoot
404   'An infinite number of flashing tongues . . .': Giuseppe Santaniello, FADN
404   'As hard as I tried . . .': ibid
404   'I felt a bit sorry . . .': AI with Ted Hardy
405   'Now there was nothing . . .': Luigi Marchese, FADN
405   'The battle started . . .': Elmhirst Papers, CCA
405   'I think we have definitely . . .': ibid
405   'ZIP 2200 hours . . .': Churchill Papers, 20/81/87, CCA
406   'The layer on the third gun . . .': Giuseppe Santaniello, FADN
407   'When the engine runs . . .': Christopherson, diaries, 23/10/1942
407   'EDWARD. I have been hit . . .': ibid

407   'It was quite one of the worst . . .': ibid
409   'The battle is filled . . .': Giuseppe Santaniello, FADN
409   'For them everything that burns . . .': ibid
409   'A tense day . . .': Elmhirst Papers, CCA
410   'We were surrounded by all the trappings . . .': Martin, *Hellfire Tonight*, p. 170
413   'Have you another piece?': cited in Harry Butcher Papers, EPL

32. Supercharge
416   'They suffered heavy losses . . .': cited in Spayd, *Bayerlein*, p. 100
417   'How much faith is there . . .': Giuseppe Santaniello Diary, FADN
417   'tragic and oppressive vigil.': ibid
418   'From the squaddies' point of view . . .': AI with Albert Martin
420   'Is it possible, I wonder . . .': Martin, *Hellfire Tonight*, p. 178
420   'Our best effort yet . . .': Elmhirst Papers, CCA
421   'I decided that I would blow . . .': Montgomery, *Memoirs*, p. 132
422   'I know all about you . . .': cited in Clark, *Calculated Risk*, p. 90
422   'We set off in an optimistic mood.': ibid, p. 93
423   'The sky was simultaneously filled . . .': Spayd, p. 102
423   'The day of death': Giuseppe Santaniello, FADN
424   'Monty now has Rommel . . .': Tuker Papers, IWM 14075
424   'Explain our situation clearly . . .': Spayd, p. 103
424   'Your sand has known . . .' Giuseppe Santaniello, FADN
424   'Dearest Lu, The battle is going . . .': Liddell Hart, *Rommel Papers*, p. 320
425   'In the situation . . .': cited in Spayd, p. 103
425   'When we read this order . . .': ibid
425   'We were completely stunned.': Liddell Hart, p. 321
426   'All is chaos and confusion . . .': Giuseppe Santaniello, FADN
426   'Bayerlein, Hitler's order . . .': Spayd, p. 104

33. Cutting Losses
429   'The best weapons bring victory . . .': cited in Tooze, *Wages of Destruction*, p. 555
430   'It is with great personal regret . . .': cited in Speer, *Debden Warbirds*, p. 9
431   'At dawn today . . .': *Stars and Stripes*, 29/10/1942
432   'I have a proper fear . . .': Bethke, diary, 9/5/1942, DTA
433   'I will call the group . . .': ibid, 6/9/1942
433   'A glance at the map . . .': Knoke, diary, 22/6/1942
434   'definitely superior': ibid, 2/10/1942
435   'I begin to look at my plane . . .': ibid
436   'so that the enemy gets . . .': cited in Irving, *Rise and Fall of the Luftwaffe*, p. 165
437   Aircraft production figures: from Webster and Frankland, *Strategic Air Offensive Against Germany*, Vol IV, Table XXIV, p. 497
438   'Ring out the bells!': Churchill Papers, 20/82, CCA

438   'We got soaked to the skin . . .': AI with Albert Martin
438   'The rain continued practically . . .': Christopherson, diaries, 6/11/1942
439   'Our group had been . . .': Luigi Marchese, FADN
439   'Then, in that sandy defile . . .': ibid
440   'It was heart-rending . . .': von Luck, *Panzer Commander*, p. 118
440   'I shall never forget . . .': ibid, p. 119
440   'Through Hitler's crazy order . . .': ibid, p. 120
440   'What had become of Rommel's . . .': ibid
441   'He's thrown his coat . . .': cited in Clark, *Calculated Risk*, p. 94
442   'Warning order . . .': cited in Harry Butcher Papers, EPL, p. 144
442   'Now let's get it clear as to my part . . .': this entire conversation is recorded in Clark, pp. 96–8
442   'He'd been very unfavourably impressed . . .': Frenay, *The Night Will End*, p. 192

34. Invasion

445   'For us, the Führer's will . . .': Warlimont, *Inside Hitler's Headquarters*, p. 269
448   'This is what we had trained for . . .': AI with Warren 'Bing' Evans
448   'That was the only . . .': ibid
449   'The eyes of the world . . .': letter to troops, early November 1942, in Blumenson, *Patton Papers*, p. 102
450   'We were getting a little uneasy . . .': Deane and Schaps, *500 Days of Front Line Combat*, p. 45
450   'The French treated us . . .': ibid, p. 46
452   'Darling B . . .': Blumenson, p. 103
453   'I saw him lying there . . .': AI with Tom Bowles
453   'Kiss Darlan's stern . . .': cited in Butcher, Diary, 8/11/1942, EPL
454   'Everywhere around us . . .': Clark, *Calculated Risk*, p. 104
454   'I'm glad you're here . . .': ibid, p. 105
454   'You will do nothing of the kind.': ibid, p. 113
455   'The only tough nut . . .': cited in Blumenson, p. 109
455   'God favors the bold . . .': ibid

Part IV: Crushing the Wolfpacks
35. The Blackest Month

458   Harvest figures: British from Murray, *Agriculture*, Table 11, p. 175; German from *GSWW*, Vol. V/IA, Table II.II.3, p. 469
458   'Barley carting . . .': cited in McCormick, *Farming, Fighting and Family*, p. 176
459   'The enemy, I am quite convinced . . .': Suhren and Brustat-Naval, *Teddy Suhren*, p. 176
461   'He found submarines a bit . . .': ibid, p. 177
462   'Boredom and monotony . . .': Macintyre, *U-Boat Killer*, p. 82
463   'A nice chap . . .': Wight-Boycott, diary, 7/11/1942, IWM 6854

464   'From now on . . .': cited in Kershaw, *Hitler: Nemesis, 1936–1945*, p. 539
464   'In a crisis like this . . .': Warlimont, *Inside Hitler's Headquarters*, p. 272
464   'I must confess . . .': Ciano, *Diary*, 8/11/1942
465   'Amé says that . . .': ibid, 8/11/1942
467   'The past four days . . .': Clark, *Calculated Risk*, p. 123
467   'Are we fighting Nazis . . .': cited in Citino, *Wehrmacht Retreats*, p. 30
469   'I wasn't one of those people . . .': AI with Ken Neill
469   'And in came these ex-Battle of Britain . . .': ibid
469   'But we were soon to discover there were . . .': ibid

36. Setbacks
474   'In my year-plus in *Arvida* . . .': Recollections: Lieutenant (N) Richard (Dick) Callery Pearce, www.canadasnavalmemorial.cn
475   'It was a tragedy . . .': ibid
476   'We must show Giraud . . .': Frenay, *The Night Will End*, p. 214
478   'The mighty national uprising . . .': cited in McFarren and Iglesias, *Devil's Agent*, p. 49
478   'I was only a lieutenant . . .': ibid
478   'In that case, we'd just have to try . . .': conversation recounted in Frenay, p. 218
480   'We knew the operation . . .': Poulsson, IWM 27189
480   'It was a sad and bitter blow . . .': ibid
480   'Keep up your hearts . . .': ibid
481   'A Panzer III needs . . .': Adolf Lamm, *Erinnerungen*, DTA
482   'The Royal Dragoons are on the radio . . .': von Luck, *Panzer Commander*, p. 125
482   'Went on a mission . . .': Deniston, *Memoirs of a Combat Fighter Pilot*, p. 57
483   'A victorious army . . .': Tuker, *Approach to Battle*, p. 265
484   'We were reflecting . . .': ibid, p. 262
484   'Mary and I had just one idea . . .': Elmhirst Papers, CCA
485   'The whole tone . . .': cited in Orange, *Coningham*, p. 123

37. Year End
487   'They started dropping . . .': AI with Ken Neill
490   'Idiots! Last year . . .': Giuseppe Santaniello, FADN
491   'The idea behind it . . .': AI with Ken Neill
491   'For Christ's sake . . .': ibid
492   'Those are your troubles . . .': cited in Harry Butcher Papers, ELP, p. 193
492   'The day's lessons . . .': Howe, *Battle History of the 1st Armored Division*, p. 97
494   'The passage of convoy . . .': Macintyre, *U-Boat Killer*, p. 84
495   'Full speed!': this account from ibid, pp. 85–90
498   'His removal from the scene . . .': Clark, *Calculated Risk*, p. 130

38. The Critical Theatre

499   'To the bad news . . .': Ciano, *Diary*, 18/12/1942

499   'I believe that at heart . . .': ibid, 19–20/12/1942

500   'But surely we have . . .': this conversation is recorded in Suhren and Brustat-Naval, *Teddy Suhren*, pp. 189–90

501   'I had repeatedly suffered . . .': Dönitz, *Memoirs*, pp. 309–10

501   'He acted like a sixteen year-old.': cited in Roll, *The Hopkins Touch*, p. 244

503   Shipping figures: from Behrens, *Merchant Shipping and the Demands of War*, Appendix XLVII, p. 293

505   Populations figures according to the 1942 edition of *Whitaker's Almanack*: USA – 131,669,275; Britain – 44,790,485

506   'The people of Britain . . .': cited in Roskill, *War at Sea*, Vol. II, p. 370

507   'The war has imposed upon us . . .': Knoke, diary, 27/1/1943

507   'Long target tabulations . . .': ibid, 27/1/1943

507   'At a time like this . . .': ibid, 27/1/1942

508   'Even in a thousand years . . .': cited in Stargardt, *The German War*, p. 329

509   'What a dull, stale, flat joke . . .': Schlange-Shöningen, *The Morning After*, p. 194

509   'He asked her to forgive . . .': Wendel, *Hausfrau at War*, p. 161

509   'A hush fell over the country . . .': ibid, p. 162

509   'I may as well say it . . .': ibid

510   'The shops are literally empty . . .': Schlange-Schöningen, p. 192

512   'The English claim . . .': cited in Kershaw, *Hitler, 1936–1945*, p. 561, and Irving, *Goebbels*, p. 754

39. Living Dangerously

514   'The sun was lazy . . .': Pyle, *Here Is Your War*, p. 124

515   'It is no exaggeration . . .': Moorehead, *African Trilogy*, p. 497

515   'This perishing cold . . .': ibid, pp. 511–12

516   'The volume was somewhat less . . .': AI with Henry Bowles

518   'There was a lot of excitement . . .': Deniston, *Memoirs of a Combat Fighter Pilot*, p. 41

518   'I had no compunction . . .': AI with Billy Drake

519   'There was one of those great . . .': Gibson, *Enemy Coast Ahead Uncensored*, p. 198

520   'But it is very important . . .': ibid, p. 199

520   'We set off . . .': ibid

521   'And where a moment before . . .': www.trove.nla.gov.au

521   'Good trip and fairly successful.': TNA AIR 4/48

522   'Please hold me . . .': cited in Morris, *Guy Gibson*, p. 132

522   'Lay off that stuff!': cited in Atkinson, *An Army at Dawn*, p. 273

524   'Fredendall had them parceled . . .': Kuter, Autobiography, USAHEC, p. 283

525   'It appeared to me . . .': ibid, p. 272

525   'It was all rather embarrassing . . .': Moorehead, p. 540
526   'The tank crews were savouring . . .': Cooper, *One of the Originals*, p. 68
527   'All we had was a . . .': ibid, p. 70
528   'No-one felt too brave . . .': AI with Ralph Burbridge
529   'Pilot from top turret!': cited in Gulley, *The Hour Has Come*, p. 80
530   'It was terrifying . . .': AI with Ralph Burbridge
530   'No business, Doc.': ibid
530   'A Fortress really can take a beating . . .': ibid
530   'UNKINDEST CUT OF ALL . . .': *Stars and Stripes*, 3/2/1943

40. Frühlingswind

531   'The Germans will not remain . . .': cited in Butcher, Diary, 18/1/1943, EPL
533   'Come inside at once!': Sønsteby, *Report from No. 24*, p. 7
533   'But this was an idea . . .': ibid, p. 75
534   'There was something queer . . .': ibid
534   'When this news came in . . .': Liddell Hart, *Rommel Papers*, p. 387
535   'You can either hold on to Tripoli . . .': ibid, p. 389
535   'I simply can't tell you . . .': ibid, p. 390
536   'executive measures against . . .': Walter Rauff dossier, BA-MA
539   'The plane was everything . . .': Gabreski, *Gabby: A Fighter Pilot's Life*, p. 62
539   'He reassured me . . .': ibid, p. 65
539   'There is one thing that you must . . .': cited in D'Este, *Eisenhower*, p. 386
540   'Foum Tataouine occupied . . .': von Luck, *Panzer Commander*, p. 140
541   'Everything I saw and heard . . .': Warlimont, *Inside Hitler's Headquarters*, p. 309
542   'To our very great disappointment . . .': Howze, 'Thirty-five Years and Then Some', Chapter V, p. 8, USAHEC
545   'clearing up the situation . . .': cited in Holland, *Together We Stand*, p. 548
545   'This was insanity': ibid
545   'General Ward didn't like it . . .': ibid

41. Heavy Water

546   'The doctrine that we have evolved . . .': this entire speech from TNA AIR 23/1709
549   'I couldn't get through . . .': von Luck, *Panzer Commander*, p. 142
549   'I feel like an old cavalry horse . . .': cited in Irving, *Trail of the Fox*, p. 246
549   'This was an appalling . . .': Liddell Hart, *Rommel Papers*, p. 402
550   'Apparently, as a result . . .': ibid, p. 407
551   'Before Christmas we had . . .': Poulsson, IWM 27189
554   'We had the feeling . . .': Jens-Anton Poulsson interview, 'Heroes? Not Us', *Guardian*, 12/5/2003
555   'You folks at home . . .': Pyle, MSS III, 23/2/1943

555   'We must spread ourselves . . .': ibid
556   'There is no policy and no plan . . .': TNA WO 214/11

42. Regaining the Initiative
558   'Shut your mouth, man . . .': this episode is recounted in Knoke, diary, 26/2/1943, USAHEC
560   'was the heart of ground-air . . .': Kuter, diary, 18/2/1943, USAHEC
561   'He was quite imperturbable . . .': Elmhirst Papers, CCA
561   'The only thing really first-class . . .': ibid
561   'Thereafter our friendship . . .': ibid
563   'I feel strongly that the solution . . .': Chalmers, *Max Horton and the Western Approaches*, p. 165
564   'Generale Messe was an arrogant . . .': Spayd, *Bayerlein*, p. 118
564   'I took everything into my own . . .': ibid, p. 118
565   'My fear overcame my pain . . .': Adolf Lamm, *Erinnerungen*, DTA
565   'All attacks easily held . . .': TNA WO 214/10286
565   'The cruellest blow . . .': Liddell Hart, *Rommel Papers*, p. 416
565   'They got one prisoner . . .': Christopherson, diaries, 7/3/1943
566   'This only goes to prove . . .': ibid
566   'Lying prone on the stretcher . . .': Santaniello, 8/3/1943, FADN
567   'Of course, he will be glad . . .': this episode recounted in von Luck, *Panzer Commander*, pp. 143–4
568   'I'm sure you must have better men . . .': Alexander interview with George F. Howe, USAHEC
568   'What do you think of the command . . .?': Bradley and Blair, *General's Life*, p. 142
569   'It was obvious how ill-prepared . . .': Suhren and Brustat-Naval, *Teddy Suhren*, p. 197
570   'Good night, Dieter . . .': Knoke, diary, 19/3/1943

43. Into the Gap
571   'Your prime objective . . .': Webster and Frankland, *Strategic Air Offensive Against Germany*, Vol. IV, p. 153
571   'I was at last . . .': Harris, *Bomber Offensive*, p. 144
572   'You have set a fire . . .': cited in Searby, *Everlasting Arms*, p. 96
572   'Port outboard's going, sir!': this incident recounted in Gibson, *Enemy Coast Ahead Uncensored*, pp. 235–7
574   'Any Captain who completes . . .': cited in Morris, *Guy Gibson*, p. 141
574   'I wanted to think . . .': Gibson, p. 214
574   'How would you like the idea . . .': ibid, p. 215
575   'He was profane and colorful . . .': Howze, 'Thirty-five Years and Then Some', USAHEC
575   'We didn't buy the necktie . . .': Deane and Schaps, *500 Days of Front Line Combat*, p. 61]

575   'Better, I thought, that we learn . . .': Bradley and Blair, *General's Life*, p. 142

575   'too defensive . . . timid . . .': Blumenson, *Patton Papers*, pp. 188–9

576   'We must be eager to kill . . .': ibid, p. 187

577   'They didn't know what had hit them.': AI with Warren 'Bing' Evans

578   'The shelling was extremely unpleasant . . .': Christopherson, diaries, 22/3/1943

579   'Good Lord, Knoke!': this episode is recounted in Knoke, diary, 22/3/1943

581   'But now came a sad disappointment.': Tuker Papers, IWM 14075

582   'My God, it seems a crime . . .': cited in Rick Atkinson, *An Army at Dawn*, p. 443

582   'D'you think we can hold 'em?': AI with Tom Bowles

582   'For escaping, I guess.': AI with Henry Bowles

583   'Shaken up a bit . . .': Deniston, *Memoirs of a Combat Fighter Pilot*, p. 88

44. Closing In

585   'We've all thought of that.': von Luck, *Panzer Commander*, p. 145

586   'Eighth Army conceded . . .': Tuker, *Approach to Battle*, p. 320

587   'Living through an artillery barrage . . .': Deane and Schaps, *500 Days of Front Line Combat*, p. 63

587   'God damn all British . . .': Blumenson, *Patton Papers*, p. 218

587   'I have little confidence . . .': ibid, pp. 199–201

588   'He said he had lost . . .': Kuter, Autobiography, USAHEC, p. 287

588   'Forward troops have been continuously . . .': cited in Bradley and Blair, *General's Life*, p. 147

588   '12th AIR SUPPORT COMMAND . . .': cited in Kuter, p. 287

588   'We parted friends': Blumenson, p. 208

589   'We were impressed with Alexander . . .': Hansen, Diary, 28/3/1943, USAHEC

590   'Give me the division . . .': Bradley and Blair, p. 150

590   'We had never had any training . . .': Deane and Schaps, p. 64

591   'How we prayed . . .': Macintyre, *U-Boat Killer*, p. 106

591   'As the two ships . . .': ibid, p. 107

591   'Day after day would go by . . .': ibid, p. 108

592   'Got him, by God!': ibid, p. 110

592   'This was sea/air co-operation . . .': ibid

593   'Brutus, there are planes . . .': this episode is recounted in Clostermann, *The Big Show*, pp. 29–30

595   'For one thing . . .': this episode is recounted in Goodson, *Tumult in the Clouds*, pp. 70–71

596   'As our air attacks . . .': Kuter, p. 288

596   'One would believe . . .': ibid

596   'My previous operational . . .': Bamberger, *Three Jumps at the Pantry Door and a Slide Down*, unpublished manuscript, Chapter 6

597   'What a day!': Deniston, *Memoirs of a Combat Fighter Pilot*, p. 95

45. Victory for the Allies

599   'As soon as you've familiarised . . .': Steinhoff, *Messerschmitts Over Sicily*, p. 49

599   'Finding a pilot over the age . . .': Heaton and Lewis, *German Aces Speak*, II, p. 166

599   'We were already on our heels . . .': ibid, p. 167

602   'We were a sombre group . . .': Martin, *Hellfire Tonight*, p. 215

603   'Get me that hill . . .': Bradley and Blair, *General's Life*, p. 156

603   'I love the infantry . . .': Ernie Pyle syndicated column, 3/5/1943

603   'In front of me . . .': Deane and Schaps, *500 Days of Front Line Combat*, p. 67

604   'We had been vindicated . . .': ibid, p. 69

605   'the perfect infiltration battle': TNA CAB 140/145

606   'Sink, burn, destroy . . .': Cunningham, *Sailor's Odyssey*, p. 529

608   'Somehow it is extremely difficult . . .': Christopherson, diaries, 13/5/1943

608   'Sir, it is my duty to report . . .': Churchill Papers, 20/111, CCA

608   'This is the likely . . .': Macintyre, *U-Boat Killer*, p. 124

608   'Very small contact just . . .': ibid, p. 125

609   'Get the first pattern away . . .': ibid, pp. 124–37

612   'Wolf-pack operations against . . .': Dönitz, *Memoirs*, p. 341

Selected Sources

PERSONAL TESTIMONIES

Author Interviews

Beamont, Roland 'Bee'
Bob, Hans-Ekkehard
Boris, Jean-Mathieu
Bowles, Henry D.
Bowles, Tom
Brothers, Peter
Brown, Eric 'Winkle'
Burbridge, Ralph
Byers, Bill
Carter, Bob
Cremonini, William
Davies, Alf
Drake, Billy
Field, Norman
Halloran, Walter
Hardy, Ted

Herrmann, Hajo
Jackson, Andrew
Klein, Josef 'Jupp'
Laity, Bill
Maassen, Franz
Martin, Albert
McInnes, Bill
Munro, Les
Neumann, Julius
Reed, James
Roberts, Eldon 'Bob'
Semken, John
Shaw, Peter
Sønsteby, Gunnar
Wellum, Geoffrey

Imperial War Museum, London

Behrendt, Hans-Otto
Cavalero, Francesco
Clark, Mark
Cormeau, Yvonne
Darley, Horace 'George'
Dönitz, Karl
Finch, Thomas
Galland, Adolf
Gilhesphy, John
Herget, Wilhelm
Hilse, Rolf

Kehrl, Hans
Kretschmer, Otto
Maloubier, Robert
Neary, Tom
O'Connor, Richard
Poulsson, Jens-Anton
Pullini, Emilio
Roberts, Gilbert
Speer, Albert
Warlimont, Walter

Rutgers, State University of New Jersey

Bruyere III, Walter
Kinaszczuk, Thomas

UNPUBLISHED MEMOIRS, DIARIES, ETC.

Churchill College Archives, Cambridge

Bufton, Air Vice-Marshal Sydney, Papers, memoir, diary
Chandos, Oliver Lyttelton, Lord, Papers
Cunningham, Admiral Viscount Hyndhope, Papers
Elmhirst, Air Marshal Sir Thomas, Papers
Lewin, Ronald, Papers

Fondazione Archivio Diaristico Nazionale, Pieve Santo Stefano

Fabbri, Sergio, Memoir
Magini, Publio, Memoir
Marchese, Luigi, Memoir
Mazzucato, Walter, Memoir
Santaniello, Giuseppe, Memoir

Imperial War Museum, London

Cox, Gwladys, Diary
Milch, Field Marshal Erhard, Diary and papers
Montgomery, Field Marshal Bernard, Papers
Tuker, General Sir Francis, Papers
Wight-Boycott, Vere, Diary and papers

Deutsches Tagebucharchiv, Emmendingen

Bethke, Siegfried, *Erinnerungen*, diary, logbook
Kirchner, Hans-Hellmuth, *Erinnerungen: Mein Lebenslauf bis zur Familiengründung*
Lamm, Adolf, *Erinnerungen*
Sack, Günther, Diary
Schild, Heinrich, Untitled memoir and diary

United States Army Heritage & Education Center, Carlisle, Pennsylvania
US Army Historical Division, Foreign Military Studies Series

Blumentritt, Günther, *Thoughts on World War II*
Göring, Hermann, *An Interview with Reichsmarschall Hermann Göring: German Military Strategy*
Hansen, Chester B., Diary
Hingel, Julius, *Capture of Crete*
Holtzendorff, Hans-Henning von, *Reasons for Rommel's Successes in Africa, 1941–42*
Howze, Hamilton, *Thirty-five Years and Then Some*
Kuter, *Autobiography*
Müller-Hillebrand, Hermann, *Germany and Her Allies in World War II: A Record of Axis Collaboration Problems*
—, *German Tank Strength and Loss Statistics*
Piske, Dr Arthur, *Logistical Problems of the German Air Force in Greece, 1941–43*
Rath, Hans-Joachim, *1st Stuka Wing*
Reinhardt, Hellmuth, *Utilization of Captured Material by Germany in World War II*
Rommel, Lucie, Interview
Warlimont, Walter, *An Interview with Gen. Art. Walter Warlimont: Norway, North Africa, French Resistance, German–American Relations, Dieppe, Sitzkrieg*

Unpublished Memoirs, Doctorates, etc.

Giffard, Hermione S., *The Development and Production of Turbojet Aero-Engines in Britain, Germany and the United States, 1936–1945*
Harper, George C., Recollections
Marsh, Robert, Notes

Others

Bamberger, Cyril 'Bam', *Three Jumps at the Pantry Door and a Slide Down*, and logbook
Christopherson, Stanley, Diaries
Ellis, Ray, *Once a Hussar*
Elmhirst, Air Marshal Sir Thomas, KBE, CB, AFC, Recollections
Fairbairn, John, The Diary of an Ordinary Fighter Pilot
Marks, John, Papers
Martin, Albert, Diary
Semken, John, Diary and album
Smyth, A. J. M., *Abrupt Sierras*

CONTEMPORARY PAMPHLETS, BOOKLETS AND TRAINING MEMORANDA

The Air Battle for Malta, HMSO, 1944

Army Life, War Department Pamphlet 21-13, US Government Printing Office, 1944

Army Training Memorandum, No. 39, April 1941, War Office

Army Training Memorandum, No. 42, January 1942, War Office

Army Training Memorandum, No. 43, May 1942, War Office

Army Training Memorandum, No. 44, October 1942, War Office

Ausbildungsvorschrift für die Infanterie, Heft 2a, 1941

The Battle of the Atlantic: The Official Account of the Fight Against the U-Boats, 1939–1945, HMSO, 1946

The Battle of Britain August–October 1940, Air Ministry, HMSO, 1941

Bomber Command, Air Ministry, HMSO, 1941

Bomber Command Continues, Air Ministry, HMSO, 1942

Brief Notes on the Italian Army, Prepared by GSI, GHQ, Middle East Forces, August 1942

Coastal Command, HMSO, 1942

Combat Instruction for the Panzer Grenadier, Helmut von Wehren, 1944, English translation by John Baum

Combined Operations 1940–1942, HMSO, 1943

Company Officer's Handbook of the German Army, Military Intelligence Division, US War Department, 1944

Der Dienst-Unterricht im Heere, Dr jur. W. Reibert, E. S. Mittler & Sohn, Berlin, 1941

The Development of Artillery Tactics and Equipment, War Office, 1951

Documents Concerning German–Polish Relations and the Outbreak of Hostilities Between Great Britain and Germany on September 3, 1939, HMSO, 1939

Documents on German Foreign Policy 1918–1945, Series D, Volume IX, HMSO, 1957

Documents on German Foreign Policy 1918–1945, Series D, Volume X, HMSO, 1957

Documents on the Origin of the War, Auswärtiges Amt, 1939, No. 2, Berlin 1939

East of Malta, West of Suez, Prepared by the Admiralty, HMSO, 1943

Field Service Pocket Book, various pamphlets, War Office, London, 1939–1945

Final Report by The Right Honourable Sir Nevile Henderson on the Circumstances Leading to the Termination of his Mission to Berlin, September 20, 1939, HMSO, 1939

The Fleet Air Arm, Prepared by the Admiralty, HMSO, 1943

France, Volume II, Naval Intelligence Division, 1942

France, Volume III, Naval Intelligence Division, 1942

Front Line 1940–1941, HMSO, 1942

German Infantry Weapons, Military Intelligence Service, US War Department, 1943

The German Squad in Combat, Military Intelligence Service, US War Department, 1944

German Tactical Doctrine, Military Intelligence Service, US War Department, 1942

German Tank Maintenance in World War II, Department of the US Army, June 1954

Germany, Volume III, Naval Intelligence Division, 1944

The Gunnery Pocket Book, 1945, Admiralty, 1945

Handbook of German Military Forces, TM-E 30-451, US War Department, 1945

Handbook on the British Army with Supplements on the Royal Air Force and Civilian Defense Organizations, TM 30-410, US War Department, September 1942

Handbook on the Italian Military Forces, Military Intelligence Service, US Army, August 1943

His Majesty's Minesweepers, HMSO, 1943

Home Guard Manual 1941, War Office, 1941

Infantry Training, Part VIII: *Fieldcraft, Battle Drill, Section and Platoon Tactics*, War Office, 1944

Infantry Training: Training and War, HMSO, London, 1937

Instruction Manual for the Infantry, Volume II: *Field Fortifications of the Infantry, 1940*, H.Dv. 130/11, English translation by John Baum

Instruction Manual for the Infantry, Volume 2a, *The Rifle Company, 1942*, H.Dv. 103/2a, English translation by John Baum

Instruction Manual for the Infantry, Volume 3a, *The Machinegun Company, 1942*, H.Dv. 130/3a, English translation by John Baum

Italy, Volume I, Naval Intelligence Division, 1944

Italy, Volume II, Naval Intelligence Division, 1944

Kampf um Norwegen, Oberkommando der Wehrmacht, 1940

Land at War, HMSO, 1945

The Mediterranean Fleet: Greece to Tripoli, HMSO, 1944

Merchantmen at War, Prepared by the Ministry of Information, London, HMSO, 1944

Notes from the Theatres of War, No. 1: *Cyrenaica, November 1941*, War Office, February 1942

Notes from the Theatres of War, No. 2: *Cyrenaica, November/December 1941*, War Office, March 1942

Notes from the Theatres of War, No. 4: *Cyrenaica, November 1941/January 1942*, War Office, May 1942

Notes from the Theatres of War, No. 6: *Cyrenaica, November 1941/January 1942*, War Office, July 1942

Notes from the Theatres of War, No. 10: *Cyrenaica and Western Desert, January/June 1942*, War Office, October 1942

Notes on the French Army, War Office, 1936

Peace and War: United States Foreign Policy 1931–1941: The Official American Document Issued by the Department of State, Washington, HMSO, 1943

Pilot's Notes General, Air Ministry, 1943

RAF Middle East: The Official Story of Air Operations, Feb 1942–Jan 1943, HMSO, 1945

The Rise and Fall of the German Air Force (1933–1945), Air Ministry, 1948

R.O.F.: The Story of the Royal Ordnance Factories, 1939–48, HMSO, 1949

Roof Over Britain: The Official Story of the A.A. Defences, 1939–1942, HMSO, 1943

Der Schütze-Hilfsbuch, 1943, Oberst Hasso von Wedel and Oberleutnant Pfafferott, Richard Schröder Verlag, Berlin, 1943

Shooting to Live, Capt. W. E. Fairbairn and Capt. E. A. Sykes, 1942

Statistics Relating to the War Effort of the United Kingdom, HMSO, November 1944

Tactics in the Context of the Reinforced Infantry Battalions, Generalmajor Greiner and Generalmajor Degener, 1941, English translation by John Baum

TEE EMM: Air Ministry Monthly Training Memoranda, Volumes I, II, III, Air Ministry, 1939–1945

The Tiger Kills: The Story of the Indian Divisions in the North Africa Campaign, HMSO, 1944

Transport Goes to War: The Official Story of British Transport, 1939–1942, HMSO, 1942

Truppenführung: On the German Art of War, Bruce Condell and David T. Zabecki (eds), Stackpole, 2009

We Speak From the Air: Broadcasts by the RAF, HMSO, 1942

What Britain Has Done 1939–1945, issued by the Ministry of Information, 1945

Whitaker's Almanack, 1940

Whitaker's Almanack, 1942

Whitaker's Almanack, 1944

OFFICIAL HISTORIES

American Battle Monuments Commission, *American Armies and Battlefields in Europe*, US Government Printing Office, 1938

Aris, George, *The Fifth British Division 1939 to 1945*, Fifth Division Benevolent Fund, 1959

Behrens, C. B. A., *Merchant Shipping and the Demands of War*, HMSO, 1955

Butler, J. R. M., *Grand Strategy*, Volume II, HMSO, 1957

Cline, Ray S., *United States Army in World War II: Washington Command Post: Operations Division*, Office of the Chief of Military History, Dept of the Army, 1951

Cody, J. F., *28 (Maori) Battalion*, War History Brand, Wellington, 1956

Court, W. H. B., *Coal*, HMSO, 1951

Craven, Wesley Frank, and James Lea Cate, *The Army Air Forces in World War II*, Volume II: *Europe: Torch to Pointblank*, University of Chicago Press, 1949

Derry, T. H., *The Campaign in Norway*, HMSO, 1952

Douglas, W. A. B., et al., *No Higher Purpose: The Official Operational History of the Royal Canadian Navy in the Second World War*, Volume II, Part I, Vanwell, 2002

Duncan Hall, H., and C. C. Wrigley, *Studies of Overseas Supply*, HMSO, 1956

Echternkamp, Jörg (ed.), *Germany and the Second World War*, Volume IX/I: *German Wartime Society 1939–1945: Politicization, Disintegration, and the Struggle for Survival*, Clarendon Press, 2008

Fairchild, Byron, and Jonathon Grossman, *United States Army in World War II: The Army and Industrial Manpower*, Office of the Chief of Military History, 1959

Foot, M. R. D., *SOE in France*, HMSO, 1966 (original first edition)

Gibbs, N. H., *Grand Strategy*, Volume I, HMSO, 1976

Greenfield, Kent Roberts, et al., *United States Army in World War II: The Organization of Ground Combat Troops*, Historical Division Department of the Army, 1947

Grove, Eric (ed.), *The Defeat of the Enemy Attack on Shipping, 1939–1945: A Revised Edition of the Naval Staff History*, Volumes 1A and 1B, Ashgate, 1997

Hancock, W. K., and M. M. Gowing, *British War Economy*, HMSO, 1949

Hastings, Major R. H. W. S., *The Rifle Brigade in the Second World War 1939–1945*, Gale & Polden, 1950

Hinsley, F. H., *British Intelligence in the Second World War*, HMSO, 1993

—, et al., *British Intelligence in the Second World War*, Volume I: *Its Influence on Strategy and Operations*, HMSO, 1979

Howard, Michael, *Grand Strategy*, Volume IV: *August 1942–September 1943*, HMSO, 1972

Howe, George F., *United States Army in World War II: Northwest Africa: Seizing the Initiative in the West*, Office of the Chief of Military History, 1957

Institution of the Royal Army Service Corps, *The Story of the Royal Army Service Corps 1939–1945*, G. Bell and Sons, 1955

Knickerbocker, H. R., et al., *United States Army in World War II: Danger Forward: The Story of the First Division in World War II*, Society of the First Division, 1947

Lee, Ulysses, *United States Army in World War II: The Employment of Negro Troops*, Office of the Chief of Military History, 1966

Lindsay, T. M., *Sherwood Rangers*, Burrup, Mathieson & Co., 1952

Matloff, Maurice, and Edwin M. Snell, *United States Army in World War II: Strategic Planning for Coalition Warfare 1941–1942*, Office of the Chief of Military History, 1953

Maughan, Barton, *Australia in the War of 1939–1945: Tobruk and Alamein*, Collins, 1987

Militärgeschichtliches Forschungsamt, *Germany and the Second World War*, Volume I: *The Build-up of German Aggression*, Clarendon Press, 2003

—, *Germany and the Second World War*, Volume II: *Germany's Initial Conquests in Europe*, Clarendon Press, 2003

—, *Germany and the Second World War*, Volume III: *The Mediterranan, South-East Europe, and North Africa, 1939–1941*, Clarendon Press, 2008

—, *Germany and the Second World War*, Volume IV: *The Attack on the Soviet Union*, Clarendon Press, 2009

—, *Germany and the Second World War*, Volume V: *Organization and Mobilization of the German Sphere of Power*, Part 1: *Wartime Administration, Economy and Manpower Resources, 1939–1941*, Clarendon Press, 2000

—, *Germany and the Second World War*, Volume V: *Organization and Mobilization of the German Sphere of Power*, Part 2B: *Wartime Administration, Economy and Manpower Resources, 1942–1944/5*, Clarendon Press, 2003

—, *Germany and the Second World War*, Volume VI: *The Global War*, Clarendon Press, 2001

—, *Germany and the Second World War*, Volume VII: *The Strategic Air War in Europe and the War in the West and East Asia, 1943–1944/5*, Clarendon Press, 2006

Morison, Samuel Eliot, *History of the United States Naval Operations in World War II*, Volume I: *The Battle of the Atlantic, September 1939–May 1943*, Naval Institute Press, 2010

—, *History of the United States Naval Operations in World War II*, Volume II: *Operations in North African Waters, October 1942–June 1943*, Little, Brown and Co., 1990

Murray, Keith A. H., *Agriculture*, HMSO, 1955

Nicholson, Lt-Col. G. W. L., *Official History of the Canadian Army in the Second World War*, Volume II: *The Canadians in Italy 1943–1945*, Department of National Defence, 1957

Orpen, Neil, *South African Forces World War II*, Volume III: *War in the Desert*, Purnell, 1971

Palmer, Robert R., et al., *United States Army in World War II: The Procurement and Training of Ground Combat Troops*, Historical Division Department of the Army, 1948

Parker, H. M. D., *Manpower: A Study of War-Time Policy and Administration*, HMSO, 1957

Playfair, Major-General I. S. O., et al., *The Mediterranean and the Middle East*, Volume I: *The Early Successes against Italy*, HMSO, 1954

—, *The Mediterranean and the Middle East*, Volume II: *The Germans Come to the Help of Their Ally 1941*, HMSO, 1956

—, *The Mediterranean and the Middle East*, Volume III: *British Fortunes Reach Their Lowest Ebb*, HMSO, 1960

Postan, M. M., *British War Production*, HMSO, 1952

—, et al., *Design and Development of Weapons*, HMSO, 1964

Richards, Denis, *Royal Air Force 1939–1945*, Volume I: *The Fight at Odds*, HMSO, 1953

—, *Royal Air Force 1939–1945*, Volume II: *The Fight Avails*, HMSO, 1954
—, *Royal Air Force 1939–1945*, Volume III: *The Fight is Won*, HMSO, 1954
Rissik, David, *The D.L.I. at War: The History of the Durham Light Infantry 1939–1945*, The Depot: Durham Light Infantry, n.d.
Roskill, Captain S. W., *The War at Sea 1939–1945*, Volume I: *The Defensive*, HMSO, 1954
—, *The War at Sea 1939–1945*, Volume II: *The Period of Balance*, HMSO, 1956
Savage, C. I., *Inland Transport*, HMSO, 1957
Scott, J. D., and Richard Hughes, *The Administration of War Production*, HMSO, 1955
Stevens, Lieut-Colonel G. R., *Fourth Indian Division*, McLaren & Son, 1949
Voss, Capt. Vivian, *The Story of No. 1 Squadron S.A.A.F.*, Mercantile Atlas, 1952
Wardlow, Chester, *United States Army in World War II: The Transportation Corps: Movements, Training, and Supply*, Office of the Chief of Military History, 1956
Webster, Sir Charles, and Noble Frankland, *The Strategic Air Offensive Against Germany, 1939–1945*, Volume I: *Preparation*, Naval & Military Press, 2006
—, *The Strategic Air Offensive Against Germany, 1939–1945*, Volume II: *Endeavour*, Naval & Military Press, 2006
—, *The Strategic Air Offensive Against Germany, 1939–1945*, Volume III: *Victory*, HMSO, 1961
— *The Strategic Air Offensive Against Germany, 1939–1945*, Volume IV: *Annexes & Appendices*, Naval & Military Press, 2006
Topography of Terror: Gestapo, SS and Reich Security Main Office on Wilhelm- and Prinz-Albrecht-Strasse: a Documentation, Stifflung Topographie des Terrors, 2010

MEMOIRS, BIOGRAPHIES, ETC.

Agius Ferrante, Anne, *No Strangers in the Silent City*, Andrew Rupert, 1992
Alanbrooke, Field Marshal Lord, *War Diaries 1939–1945*, Weidenfeld & Nicolson, 2001
Aldridge, Arthur with Mark Ryan, *The Last Torpedo Flyers*, Simon & Schuster, 2012
Alexander of Tunis, Field Marshal Earl, *The Alexander Memoirs*, Frontline, 2010
Allaway, Jim, *Hero of the Upholder*, Airlife, 1991
Ambrose, Stephen E., *The Supreme Commander: The War Years of Dwight D. Eisenhower*, University of Mississippi, 1999
Ardizzone, Edward, *Diary of a War Artist*, Bodley Head, 1974
Atkins, Peter, *Buffoon in Flight*, Ernest Stanton, 1978
Aubrac, Lucie, *Outwitting the Gestapo*, University of Nebraska Press, 1985
Avon, The Rt Hon. The Earl of, *The Eden Memoirs: Facing the Dictators*, Cassell, 1962

—, *The Eden Memoirs: The Reckoning*, Cassell, 1965

Badoglio, Marshal Pietro, *Italy in the Second World War*, Oxford University Press, 1948

Balck, Hermann, *Ordnung im Chaos*, Biblio, 1981

Ball, Edmund F., *Staff Officer with the Fifth Army*, Exposition Banner Book, 1958

Barnham, Denis, *One Man's Window*, William Kimber, 1956

Baruch, Bernard M., *Baruch: My Own Story*, Henry Holt & Co., 1957

Beamont, Roland, *My Part of the Sky*, Patrick Stephens, 1989

Beasley, Norman, *Knudsen: A Biography*, McGraw Hill, 1947

Beauvoir, Simone de, *Wartime Diary*, University of Illinois Press, 2009

Behrendt, Hans-Otto, *Rommel's Intelligence in the Desert Campaign*, William Kimber, 1985

Below, Nicolaus von, *At Hitler's Side: The Memoirs of Hitler's Luftwaffe Adjutant 1937–1945*, Greenhill, 2004

Bennett, Donald, *Pathfinder*, Goodall, 1998

Bennett, Donald V., and William R. Forstchen, *Honor Untarnished: A West Point Graduate's Memoir of World War II*, Forge, 2003

Bigland, Tom, *Bigland's War: War Letters of Tom Bigland, 1941–45*, Printfine, 1990

Binder, L. James, *Lemnitzer: A Soldier for His Time*, Brassey's, 1997

Birrell, Dave, *Big Joe McCarthy: The RCAF's American Dambuster*, Nanton Lancaster Society, 2012

Blumenson, Martin (ed.), *The Patton Papers, 1949–1945*, Da Capo, 1996

Bob, Hans-Ekkehard, *Betrayed Ideals: Memoirs of a Luftwaffe Fighter Ace*, Mönch, 2004

Boelcke, Willi A. (ed.), *The Secret Conferences of Dr Goebbels 1939–43*, Weidenfeld & Nicolson, 1970

Bolitho, Hector, *Combat Report: The Story of a Fighter Pilot*, Batsford, 1943

Booth, T. Michael, and Duncan Spencer, *Paratrooper: The Life of General James M. Gavin*, Casemate, 2013

Borghese, J. Valerio, *Sea Devils*, Andrew Melrose, 1953

Boris, Jean-Mathieu, *Combattant de la France Libre*, Tempus, 2012

Bradford White, Francelle, *Andrée's War: How One Young Woman Outwitted the Nazis*, Elliott & Thompson, 2014

Bradley, Omar N., and Clay Blair, *A General's Life*, Simon & Schuster, 1983

Brereton, Lewis H., *The Brereton Diaries*, William Morrow, 1946

Brett-James, Antony, *Conversations with Montgomery*, William Kimber, 1984

Brown, Captain Eric 'Winkle', *Wings on My Sleeve*, Phoenix, 2007

Bullitt, Orville H. (ed.), *For the President, Personal and Secret: Correspondence between Franklin D. Roosevelt and William C. Bullitt*, André Deutsch, 1973

Burns, James MacGregor, *Roosevelt: The Soldier of Freedom, 1940–1945*, Weidenfeld & Nicolson, 1971

Campbell Begg, Dr Richard, and Dr Peter Liddle, *For Five Shillings a Day:*

Personal Histories of World War II, HarperCollins, 2002

Cartwright-Hignett, Elizabeth (ed.), *Three Ladies of Siena: The Wartime Journals of the Chigi-Zondadari Family, 1943–1944*, Iford, 2011

Chambrun, René de, *I Saw France Fall*, Jarrolds, 1941

Chandler, Alfred D., Jr (ed.), *The Papers of Dwight David Eisenhower – The War Years*, Volume I, John Hopkins Press, 1970

Charlwood, Don, *No Moon Tonight*, Goodall, 1994

Cheall, Bill, *Fighting Through from Dunkirk to Hamburg: A Green Howard's Wartime Memoir*, Pen & Sword, 2011

Cheshire, Leonard, *Bomber Pilot*, Hutchinson, 1943

Churchill, Winston S., *The Second World War*, Volume I: *The Gathering Storm*, Cassell, 1948

—, *The Second World War*, Volume II: *Their Finest Hour*, Cassell, 1949

—, *The Second World War*, Volume III: *The Grand Alliance*, Cassell, 1950

— (ed. Charles Eade), *The War Speeches of the Right Hon. Winston S. Churchill*, Volume II: *The Unrelenting Struggle*, Cassell, 1942

Ciano, Count Galeazzo, *Diary, 1937–1943*, William Heinemann, 1947

Clark, Mark, *Calculated Risk*, Harper & Brothers, 1950

Clostermann, Pierre, *The Big Show: The Greatest Pilot's Story of World War II*, Cassell, 2005

Colville, Jock, *The Fringes of Power: Downing Street Diaries*, Volume 1, Sceptre, 1986

—, *The Fringes of Power: Downing Street Diaries*, Volume II, Sceptre, 1987

Connell, John, *Auchinleck: A Critical Biography*, Cassell, 1959

Cooper, Johnny, *One of the Originals*, Pan, 1991

Cowles, Virginia, *The Phantom Major*, Companion Book Club, 1958

Cox, Rachel S., *Into Dust and Fire: Five Young Americans Who Went First to Fight the Nazi Army*, NAL Caliber, 2012

Crook, David, *Spitfire Pilot*, Faber & Faber, 1942

Cunningham, Admiral of the Fleet Viscount, *A Sailor's Odyssey*, Hutchinson, 1951

Currie, Jack, *Lancaster Target*, Goodall, 1981

Dahl, Roald, *Going Solo*, Penguin, 1986

—, *Over to You*, Penguin, 2011

Davis, Richard G., *Carl A. Spaatz and the Air War in Europe*, Center for Air Force History, 1993

Deane, Theresa M., and Schaps, Joseph E. (eds), *500 Days of Front Line Combat: The WWII Memoir of Ralph B. Schaps*, iUniverse Inc., 2003

Demarne, Cyril, *The London Blitz: A Fireman's Tale*, After the Battle, 1991

Deniston, Dale R., *Memoirs of a Combat Fighter Pilot: World War II and Korea*, D. R. Deniston, 1995

D'Este, Carlo, *Eisenhower: A Soldier's Life*, Henry Holt, 2002

Doe, Bob, *Bob Doe: Fighter Pilot*, CCB Associates, 1999

Dönitz, Karl, *Memoirs: Ten Years and Twenty Days*, Cassell, 2000

Doolittle, Gen. James H., *I Could Never Be So Lucky Again*, Bantam Books, 1992

Dos, Margarete, and Kirsten Lieff, *Letters from Berlin*, Lyons Press, 2013

Drake, Billy, with Christopher Shores, *Billy Drake, Fighter Leader*, Grub Street, 2002

Dundas, Hugh, *Flying Start*, Penguin, 1990

Dutton, David, *Neville Chamberlain*, Hodder Education, 2001

Eisenhower, Dwight D., *Crusade in Europe*, William Heinemann, 1948

Embry, Basil, *Wingless Victory*, Morley Books, 1973

Engel, Major Gerhard, *At the Heart of the Reich: The Secret Diary of Hitler's Army Adjutant*, Greenhill, 2005

Fairbanks, Douglas, Jr, *A Hell of a War*, St Martin's Press, 1993

Farrell, Nicholas, *Mussolini: A New Life*, Phoenix, 2004

Franks, Norman, *Buck McNair: Canadian Spitfire Ace*, Grub Street, 2001

Freidel, Frank, *Roosevelt: A Rendezvous with Destiny*, Little, Brown & Co., 1990

Frenay, Henri, *The Night Will End: Memoirs of the Resistance*, Abelard, 1976

Gabreski, Francis, *Gabby: A Fighter Pilot's Life*, Schiffer, 2008

Gafencu, Grigore, *The Last Days of Europe: A Diplomatic Journey in 1939*, Frederick Muller, 1947

Galland, Adolf, *The First and the Last*, Fontana, 1970

Gane Pushman, Muriel, *One Family's War*, Tempus, 2000

Gaulle, General Charles de, *War Memoirs: The Call to Honour 1949–1942*, Collins, 1955

—, *War Memoirs: Unity 1942–1944*, Weidenfeld & Nicolson, 1956

Gibson, Guy, *Enemy Coast Ahead*, Michael Joseph, 1946

—, *Enemy Coast Ahead Uncensored*, Crécy, 2014

Giese, Otto, and James E. Wise, Jr, *Shooting the War: The Memoir and Photographs of a U-Boat Officer in World War II*, Naval Institute Press, 2003

Gilbert, Martin, *Finest Hour: Winston S. Churchill 1939–1941*, Minerva, 1983

Główczewski, Jerzy, *The Accidental Immigrant*, Xlibris, 2007

Gnecchi-Ruscone, Francesco, *When Being Italian Was Difficult*, Milano, 1999

Goodson, James, *Tumult in the Clouds*, Penguin, 2003

Görlitz, Walter (ed.), *The Memoirs of Field Marshal Wilhelm Keitel*, Cooper Square Press, 2000

Greene, Jack, and Alessandro Massignani, *The Black Prince and the Sea Devils: The Story of Valerio Borghese*, Da Capo, 2004

Gregg, Victor, with Rick Stroud, *Rifleman: A Front Line Life*, Bloomsbury, 2011

Grossjohann, Georg, *Five Years, Four Fronts*, Aberjona Press, 1999

Grundon, Imogen, *The Rash Adventurer*, Libri, 2007

Guderian, Heinz, *Panzer Leader*, Penguin, 2000

Guingand, Major-General Sir Francis de, *Operation Victory*, Hodder & Stoughton, 1960

Häberlen, Klaus, *A Luftwaffe Bomber Pilot Remembers: World War II from the Cockpit*, Schiffer, 2001

Hahn Beer, Edith, *The Nazi Officer's Wife*, Little, Brown & Co., 1999

Halder, Franz, *The Halder War Diary, 1939–1942*, Greenhill Books, 1988

Haney, Richard Carlton, *When Is Daddy Coming Home?: An American Family during World War II*, Wisconsin Historical Society Press, 2005

Harris, Sir Arthur, *Bomber Offensive*, Collins, 1947

Hartog, Kristen den, and Tracy Kasaboski, *The Occupied Garden: A Family Memoir of War-Torn Holland*, St Martin's Press, 2008

Hayes, Paul M., *Quisling*, David & Charles, 1971

Heaton, Colin D., and Anne-Marie Lewis, *The German Aces Speak: World War II through the Eyes of Four of the Luftwaffe's Most Important Commanders*, Zenith Press, 2011

—, *The German Aces Speak II: World War II through the Eyes of Four More of the Luftwaffe's Most Important Commanders*, Zenith Press, 2014

—, *The Star of Africa: The Story of Hans Marseille,* Zenith Press, 2012

Heiner, Albert P., *Henry J. Kaiser: Western Colossus*, Halo, 1991

Hélion, Jean, *They Shall Not Have Me*, Arcade, 2012

Henderson, Sir Nevile, *Failure of a Mission*, Hodder & Stoughton, 1940

Henrey, Mrs Robert, *A Farm in Normandy*, J. M. Dent & Sons Ltd, 1952

—, *London Under Fire 1940–45*, J. M. Dent & Sons, 1969

Herrmann, Hajo, *Eagle's Wings*, Airlife, 1991

Hill, Alan, *Hedley Verity: A Portrait of a Cricketer*, Kingswood Press, 1986

Hinchliffe, Peter, *The Lent Papers: Helmut Lent*, Cerberus, 2003

Hodgson, Godfrey, *The Colonel: The Life and Wars of Henry Stimson, 1867–1950*, Alfred A. Knopf, 1990

Hodgson, Vere, *Few Eggs and No Oranges: The Diaries of Vere Hodgson, 1940–45*, Persephone, 1999

Horrocks, Lt-Gen. Sir Brian, *A Full Life*, Collins, 1960

Humbert, Agnès, *Résistance: Memoirs of Occupied France*, Bloomsbury, 2009

Hurd, Anthony, *A Farmer in Whitehall: Britain's Farming Revolution 1939–1950*, Country Life, 1951

Irving, David, *Göring*, Macmillan, 1989

—, *The Rise and Fall of the Luftwaffe: The Life of Erhard Milch*, Weidenfeld & Nicolson, 1973

—, *The Trail of the Fox: The Life of Field Marshal Erwin Rommel*, Book Club Associates, 1977

Ismay, General Lord, *The Memoirs*, Viking Press, 1960

Johnson, Boris, *The Churchill Factor: How One Man Made History*, Hodder & Stoughton, 2014

Johnson, Johnnie, *Wing Leader*, Penguin, 1959

Kennedy, Major-General Sir John, *The Business of War*, Hutchinson, 1957

Kennedy, Ludovic, *Sub-Lieutenant: A Personal Record of the War at Sea*, Batsford, 1941

Kershaw, Alex, *The Few: The American Knights of the Air Who Risked Everything to Fight in the Battle of Britain*, Da Capo, 2006

King, Ernest J., *Fleet Admiral King: A Naval Record*, W. W. Norton & Co., 1956

Kippenberger, Major-General Sir Howard, *Infantry Brigadier*, Oxford University Press, 1949

Klemperer, Victor, *I Shall Bear Witness: The Diaries, 1933–1941*, Phoenix, 2014

—, *To The Bitter End: The Diaries of Victor Klemperer, 1942–45*, Phoenix, 2000

Knappe, Siegfried, with Ted Brusaw, *Soldat: Reflections of a German Soldier, 1936–1949*, Dell, 1992

Knoke, Heinz, *I Flew for the Führer*, Cassell, 2003

Knoller, Freddie, *Living with the Enemy: My Secret Life on the Run from the Nazis*, Metro, 2005

König, Marie-Pierre, *Bir-Hacheim, 10 Juin 1942 (Ce jour-là)*, Laffont, 1971

Kynoch, Joseph, *Norway 1940: The Forgotten Fiasco*, Airlife, 2002

Laidler, Graham, *The World of Pont*, Element Books, 1983

Laurier, Mathieu, *Il reste le drapeau noir et les copains*, Regain, 1953

Leahy, Admiral, *I Was There*, Victor Gollancz, 1950

Lee, Asher, *Goering: Air Leader*, Duckworth, 1972

Leutze, James (ed.), *The London Observer: The Journal of General Raymond E. Lee, 1940–1941*, Hutchinson, 1972

Liddell Hart, B. H. (ed.), *The Rommel Papers*, Collins, 1953

Lloyd, Air Marshal Sir Hugh, *Briefed to Attack*, Hodder & Stoughton, 1949

Lochner, Louis P. (ed.), *The Goebbels Diaries*, Hamish Hamilton, 1948

Lowenheim, Francis L., et al., *Roosevelt and Churchill: Their Secret Wartime Correspondence*, Barrie & Jenkins, 1975

Luchaire, Corinne, *Ma drôle de vie*, Deterna, 1949

Luck, Hans von, *Panzer Commander*, Cassell, 2002

Lyttelton, Oliver, *The Memoirs of Lord Chandos*, Bodley Head, 1962

MacGibbon, John, *Struan's War*, Ngaio Press, 2001

Macintyre, Captain Donald, *U-Boat Killer*, Rigel, 2004

Mack Smith, Denis, *Mussolini*, Paladin, 1983

Mahlke, Helmut, *Memoirs of a Stuka Pilot*, Frontline, 2013

Manstein, Field Marshal Erich von, *Lost Victories*, Zenith Press, 2004

Manville, Roger, and Heinrich Fraenkel, *Heinrich Himmler*, Greenhill, 2007

Martin, Albert, *Hellfire Tonight: The Diary of a Desert Rat*, Book Guild, 1996

Mazière, Christian de la, *Ashes of Honour*, Tattoo, 1976

McCormick, Miranda, *Farming, Fighting and Family: A Memoir of the Second World War*, History Press, 2015

McFarren, Peter, and Fadrique Iglesias, *The Devil's Agent: Life, Times and Crimes of Klaus Barbie*, Xlibris, 2013

McLaughlin, John J., *General Albert C. Wedemeyer: America's Unsung Strategist in World War II*, Casemate, 2012

Melinsky, Hugh, *Forming the Pathfinders: The Career of Air Vice-Marshal Sydney Bufton*, History Press, 2010

Mellenthin, F. W. von, *Panzer Battles*, Futura, 1977

Messenger, Charles, *Hitler's Gladiator: The Life and Wars of Panzer Army Commander Sepp Dietrich*, Skyhorse, 2011

Middleton, Drew, *The Sky Suspended*, Secker & Warburg, 1960

Miller, Lee G., *The Story of Ernie Pyle*, Viking Press, 1950

Millgate, Helen D. (ed.), *Mr Brown's War: A Diary of the Second World War*, Sutton, 1998

Moen, Marcia, and Margo Heinen, *Heroes Cry Too: A WWII Ranger Tells His Story of Love and War*, Meadowlark, 2002

Monsarrat, Nicholas, *Life is a Four-Letter Word*, Book One: *Breaking In*, Pan, 1966

—, *Life is a Four-Letter Word*, Book Two: *Breaking Out*, Pan, 1972

Montgomery, Field-Marshal the Viscount, *The Memoirs*, Collins, 1958

Morris, Richard, *Guy Gibson*, Penguin, 1995

Morrison, Joan Wehlen, *Home Front Girl*, Chicago Review Press, 2013

Mowat, Farley, *And No Birds Sang*, Douglas & McIntyre, 2012

Muggeridge, Malcolm (ed.), *Ciano's Diplomatic Papers*, Odhams Press Limited, 1948

Murrow, Edward R., *This Is London*, Cassell, 1941

Neil, Tom, *A Fighter In My Sights*, J&KH, 2001

—, *Onwards to Malta*, Corgi, 1994

Nelson, Donald M., *The Arsenal of Democracy: The Story of American War Production*, Harcourt, Brace and Co., 1946

Nicolson, Harold, *Diaries and Letters, 1939–1945*, Collins, 1967

Nicolson, Nigel, *Alex: The Life of Field Marshal Earl Alexander of Tunis*, Weidenfeld & Nicolson, 1973

Offenberg, Jean, *Lonely Warrior*, Granada, 1969

Ophüls, Marcel, *The Sorrow and the Pity: The Text from the Film*, Paladin, 1975

—, *Coningham: A Biography of Air Marshal Sir Arthur Coningham*, Methuen, 1990

—, *Park*, Grub Street, 2001

Orange, Vincent, *Dowding of Fighter Command*, Grub Street, 2008

Overy, Richard, *Goering*, Phoenix, 2000

Palmer, John, *Luck On My Side*, Pen & Sword, 2002

Parbery, Sergeant Alf, *Alf's War: With the Sixth Infantry Division*, Australian Military History Publications, 2005

Peyton, John, *Solly Zuckerman*, John Murray, 2001

Pickersgill, J. W., *The Mackenzie King Record*, Volume I: *1939–1944*, University of Toronto Press, 1960

Pineau, Christian, *La Simple vérité, 1940–1945*, Phalanx, 1983

Pocock, Tom, *Alan Moorehead*, Pimlico, 1990

Pogue, Forrest C., *George C. Marshall: Ordeal and Hope, 1939–1942*, MacGibbon & Kee, 1966

— (ed.), *George C. Marshall – Interviews and Reminiscences for Forrest Pogue*, Marshall Foundation, 1991

Probert, Henry, *Bomber Harris: His Life and Times*, Greenhill, 2006

Pyle, Ernie, *Ernie Pyle in England*, Robert M. McBride & Co., 1941

Reynaud, Paul, *In the Thick of the Fight*, Cassell, 1955

Richey, Paul, *Fighter Pilot*, Batsford, 1941

Rieckhoff, Generalleutnant H. J., *Trumpf oder Bluff? 12 Jahre Deutsche Luftwaffe*, Inter Avia, 1945

Riols, Noreen, *The Secret Ministry of Ag. & Fish: My Life in Churchill's School for Spies*, Macmillan, 2013

Ripley, Tim, *Wehrmacht: The German Army in World War II, 1939–1945*, Reference Group Brown, 2003

Roberts, Andrew, *The Holy Fox: The Life of Lord Halifax*, Phoenix, 1991

Rohland, Walter, *Bewegte Zeiten*, Seewald, 1978

Roll, David L., *The Hopkins Touch: Harry Hopkins and the Forging of the Alliance to Beat Hitler*, Oxford University Press, 2013

Rudel, Hans-Ulrich, *Stuka Pilot*, Barbarossa Books, 2006

Rumpf, Hans, *The Bombing of Germany*, Holt, Rinehart, and Winston, 1961

Saward, Dudley, *Bomber Harris*, Sphere, 1985

Scheffel, Charles, with Barry Basden, *Crack and Thump! With a Combat Infantry Officer in World War II*, Camroc Press, 2007

Schlange-Schöningen, Hans, *The Morning After*, Victor Gollancz, 1948

Schmidt, Dr Paul, *Hitler's Interpreter*, William Heinemann, 1951

Schroeder, Liliane, *Journal d'Occupation: Paris 1940–1944*, François-Xavier de Guibert, 2000

Schroth, Raymond A., *The American Journey of Eric Sevareid*, Steerforth Press, 1995

Searby, John, *The Everlasting Arms: The War Memoirs of Air Commodore John Searby DSO, DFC*, William Kimber, 1988

Self, Robert, *Neville Chamberlain*, Ashgate, 2006

— (ed.), *The Neville Chamberlain Diary Letters*, Volume 4: *The Downing Street Years, 1934–1940*, Ashgate, 2005

Senger und Etterlin, General Frido von, *Neither Fear Nor Hope*, Presidio, 1989

Sereny, Gitta, *Albert Speer: His Battle with Truth*, Picador, 1996

Sevareid, Eric, *Not So Wild a Dream*, Atheneum, 1976

Severloh, Hein, *WN 62: A German Soldier's Memoirs of the Defence of Omaha Beach*, Hek Creativ Verlag, 2011

Sherwood, Robert E., *The White House Papers of Harry L. Hopkins: An Intimate History*, Volume I: *September 1939–January 1942*, Eyre & Spottiswoode, 1948

Shirer, William L., *Berlin Diary*, Hamish Hamilton, 1942

Slessor, Sir John, *The Central Blue*, Cassell, 1956

Soames, Mary, *A Daughter's Tale*, Doubleday, 2011

Sønsteby, Gunnar, *Report from No. 24*, Barricade Books, 1999

Spagnuolo, Mark M., *Mustang Ace: The Story of Don S. Gentile*, Cerberus, 1986

Spayd, P. A., *Bayerlein: From Afrikakorps to Panzer Lehr*, Schiffer, 2003

Spears, Major-General Sir Edward, *Assignment to Catastrophe*, Reprint Society, 1954

—, *Fulfilment of a Mission: Syria and Lebanon, 1941–1944*, Leo Cooper, 1977

Speer, Albert, *Inside the Third Reich*, Phoenix, 1995

Sperber, A. M., *Murrow: His Life and Times*, Freundlich Books, 1986

Spooner, Tony, *Warburton's War*, Crécy, 1994

Squires, Mary, *An Army in the Fields*, Minerva Press, 2000

Stahl, Peter, *The Diving Eagle: A Ju88 Pilot's Diary*, William Kimber, 1984

Steinhilper, Ulrich, and Peter Osborne, *Spitfire on my Tail: A View from the Other Side*, Independent Books, 1989

Steinhoff, Johannes, *Messerschmitts Over Sicily*, Pen & Sword, 2004

—, et al., *Voices from the Third Reich: An Oral History*, Da Capo, 1994

Stevenson, William, *A Man Called Intrepid: The Secret War*, Skyhorse Publishing, 1976

Stimson, Henry L., *Prelude to Invasion: An Account Based upon Official Reports by Henry L. Stimson, Secretary of War*, Greenwood Press, 1974

Stimson, Henry L., and McGeorge Bundy, *On Active Service in Peace and War*, Harper & Brothers, 1948

Street, A. G., *Ditchampton Farm*, Eyre & Spottiswoode, 1946

—, *From Dusk Till Dawn*, Oxford University Press, 1989

—, *Hitler's Whistle*, Eyre & Spottiswoode, 1943

—, *Round the Year on the Farm*, Oxford University Press, 1946

Street, Pamela, *My Father, A.G. Street*, Robert Hale, 1969

Suhren, Teddy, and Fritz Brustat-Naval, *Teddy Suhren – Ace of Aces*, Frontline, 2011

Taylor, A. J. P., *Beaverbook*, Hamish Hamilton, 1972

Taylor, Fred (ed.), *The Goebbels Diaries 1939–1941*, Sphere, 1982

Tedder, Marshal of the Air Force Lord, *With Prejudice*, Cassell, 1966

Tobin, James, *Ernie Pyle's War: America's Eyewitness to World War II*, University Press of Kansas, 1997

Topp, Erich, *The Odyssey of a U-Boat Commander: Recollections of Erich Topp*, Prager, 1992

Vann, Frank, *Willy Messerschmitt*, Patrick Stephens, 1993

Vansittart, The Rt Hon. Lord, *Lessons of My Life*, Hutchinson, 1942

Verity, Hugh, *We Landed by Moonlight*, Crécy, 2000

Warlimont, Walter, *Inside Hitler's Headquarters 1939–1945*, Presidio (n.d., but originally published 1962)

Warner, Oliver, *Cunningham of Hyndehope: Admiral of the Fleet*, John Murray, 1967

Weinronk, Jack 'Cobber', *The Vaulted Sky*, Merlin Books, 1993

Wendel, Else, *Hausfrau at War*, Odhams Press, 1957

Werner, Herbert A., *Iron Coffins*, Cassell, 1999

West, Nigel (ed.), *The Guy Liddell Diaries*, Volume I: *1939–1942*, Routledge, 2009

—, *The Guy Liddell Diaries*, Volume II: *1942–1945*, Routledge, 2009

Williams, Charles, *The Last Great Frenchman: Life of General de Gaulle*, John Wiley & Sons, 1993

Wilmot, Chester, *Tobruk 1941*, Penguin, 1993

Wing, Sandra Koa (ed.), *Our Longest Days: A People's History of the Second World War*, Profile, 2007

Winterbotham, F. W., *The Ultra Spy*, Papermac, 1989
Winn, Godfrey, *Godfrey Winn's Scrapbook of the War*, Hutchinson, 1942
Winton, John, *Cunningham: The Greatest Admiral since Nelson*, John Murray, 1998
Woodhouse, C. M., *Something Ventured*, Granada, 1992
Young, Desmond, *Rommel*, Collins, 1950
Young, Edward, *One of Our Submarines*, Wordsworth, 1997
Younghusband, Eileen, *One Woman's War*, Candy Jar Books, 2013

EQUIPMENT, WEAPONS AND TECHNICAL BOOKS

Barker, A. J., *British and American Infantry Weapons of World War 2*, Arms and Armour Press, 1969
Bidwell, Shelford, and Dominick Graham, *Fire-Power: British Army Weapons and Theories of War 1904–1945*, George Allen & Unwin, 1982
Bouchery, Jean, *The British Soldier*, Volume 1: *Uniforms, Insignia, Equipment*, Histoire & Collections, n.d.
—, *The British Soldier*, Volume 2: *Organisation, Armament, Tanks and Vehicles*, Histoire & Collections, n.d.
Brayley, Martin, *The British Army 1939–45 (1): North-West Europe*, Osprey, 2001
—, *British Web Equipment of the Two World Wars*, Crowood Press, 2005
Bruce, Robert, *German Automatic Weapons of World War II*, Crowood Press, 1996
Bull, Dr Stephen, *World War II Infantry Tactics*, Osprey, 2004
—, *World War II Street-Fighting Tactics*, Osprey, 2008
Chamberlain, Peter, and Chris Ellis, *Tanks of the World*, Cassell, 2002
Chesneau, Roger (ed.), *Conway's All the World's Fighting Ships 1922–1946*, Conway Maritime Press, 1980
Clark, Jeff, *Uniforms of the NSDAP*, Schiffer, 2007
Corciani, P., and P. P. Battistelli, *Italian Army Elite Units and Special Forces 1940–43*, Osprey, 2011
Dallies-Labourdette, Jean-Philippe, *S-Boote: German E-Boats in Action 1939–1945*, Histoire and Collections, n.d.
Davies, W. J. K., *German Army Handbook 1939–1945*, Military Book Society, 1973
Davis, Brian L., *German Combat Uniforms of World War II*, Volume II, Arms & Armour Press, 1985
Dibbs, John, and Tony Holmes, *Hurricane: A Fighter Legend*, Osprey, 1995
Dunning, Chris, *Courage Alone: The Italian Air Force 1940–1943*, Hikoki, 1998
Farrar-Hockley, Anthony, *Infantry Tactics 1939–1945*, Almark, 1976
Fleischer, Wolfgang, *The Illustrated Guide to German Panzers*, Schiffer, 2002
Forty, George, and Jack Livesey, *The Complete Guide to Tanks and Armoured Fighting Vehicles*, Southwater, 2012

Gander, Terry, and Peter Chamberlain, *Small Arms, Artillery and Special Weapons of the Third Reich*, Macdonald and Jane's, 1978

Gordon, David B., *Equipment of the WWII Tommy*, Pictorial Histories, 2004

—, *Uniforms of the WWII Tommy*, Pictorial Histories, 2005

—, *Weapons of the WWII Tommy*, Pictorial Histories, 2004

Grant, Neil, *The Bren Gun*, Osprey, 2013

Griehl, Manfred, and Joachim Dressel, *Luftwaffe Combat Aircraft: Development, Production, Operations, 1935–1945*, Schiffer, 1994

Gunston, Bill, *Fighting Aircraft of World War II*, Salamander, 1988

Hart, S., et al., *The German Soldier in World War II*, Spellmount, 2000

Hogg, Ian V. (intro.), *The American Arsenal: The World War II Official Standard Ordnance Catalog of Small Arms, Tanks, Armored Cars, Artillery, Antiaircraft Guns, Ammunition, Grenades, Mines, etcetera*, Greenhill Books, 1996

—, *The Guns 1939–1945*, Macdonald, 1969

Jowett, Philip S., *The Italian Army 1940–45 (1): Europe 1940–43*, Osprey, 2000

—, *The Italian Army 1940–45 (2): Africa 1940–43*, Osprey, 2001

Kay, Antony L., and J. R. Smith, *German Aircraft of the Second World War*, Putnam, 2002

Konstam, Angus, *British Battlecruisers 1939–45*, Osprey, 2003

Lagarde, Jean de, *German Soldiers of World War II*, Histoire & Collections, n.d.

Lavery, Brian, *Churchill's Navy: The Ships, Men and Organisation 1939–1945*, Conway, 2006

Lee, Cyrus A., *Soldat*, Volume Two: *Equipping the German Army Foot Soldier in Europe 1943*, Pictorial Histories, 1988

Lepage, Jean-Denis G. G., *German Military Vehicles*, McFarland & Company, 2007

Lüdeke, Alexander, *Weapons of World War II*, Parragon, 2007

Mason, Chris, *Soldat*, Volume Eight: *Fallschirmjäger*, Pictorial Histories, 2000

McNab, Chris, *MG 34 and MG 42 Machine Guns*, Osprey, 2012

Mundt, Richard W., and Cyrus A. Lee, *Soldat*, Volume Six: *Equipping the Waffen-SS Panzer Divisions 1942–1945*, Pictorial Histories, 1997

Musgrave, Daniel D., *German Machineguns*, Greenhill Books, 1992

Myerscough, W., *Air Navigation Simply Explained*, Pitman & Sons, 1942

Saiz, Augustin, *Deutsche Soldaten*, Casemate, 2008

Stedman, Robert, *Kampfflieger: Bomber Crewman of the Luftwaffe 1939–45*, Osprey, 2005

Suermondt, Jan, *World War II Wehrmacht Vehicles*, Crowood Press, 2003

Sumner, Ian, and François Vauvillier, *The French Army 1939–1945 (1)*, Osprey, 1998

Sutherland, Jonathan, *World War II Tanks and AFVs*, Airlife, 2002

Trye, Rex, *Mussolini's Soldiers*, Airlife, 1995

Vanderveen, Bart, *Historic Military Vehicles Directory*, After the Battle, 1989

Williamson, Gordon, *Gebirgsjäger*, Osprey, 2003

—, *German Mountain and Ski Troops 1939–45*, Osprey, 1996

—, *U-Boats vs Destroyer Escorts*, Osprey, 2007
Windrow, Richard, and Tim Hawkins, *The World War II GI: US Army Uniforms 1941–45*, Crowood Press, 2003

GENERAL

Addison, Paul, and Angus Calder (eds), *Time to Kill: The Soldier's Experience of War in the West, 1939–1945*, Pimlico, 1997
Asher, Michael, *The Regiment: The Real Story of the SAS*, Viking, 2007
Bailey, Roderick, *Forgotten Voices of the Secret War*, Ebury Press, 2008
Baldoli, Claudia, Andrew Knapp and Richard Overy (eds), *Bombing, States and Peoples in Western Europe, 1940–1945*, Continuum, 2011
Barnett, Corelli, *The Audit of War: The Illusion and Reality of Britain as a Great Power*, Papermac, 1987
—, *Engage the Enemy More Closely*, Penguin, 1991
— (ed.), *Hitler's Generals*, Weidenfeld & Nicolson, 1989
Barr, Niall, *Pendulum of War: The Three Battles of Alamein*, Jonathan Cape, 2004
Bartz, Karl, *Swastika in the Air: The Struggle and Defeat of the German Air Force 1939–1945*, William Kimber, 1956
Baumbach, Werner, *Broken Swastika*, George Mann, 1974
Baumer, Robert W., and Mark J. Reardon, *American Iliad: The 18th Infantry Regiment in World War II*, Aberjona Press, 2004
Bekker, Cajus, *The Luftwaffe War Diaries*, Corgi, 1969
Bell, P. M. H., *A Certain Eventuality: Britain and the Fall of France*, Saxon House, 1974
Bellamy, Chris, *Absolute War: Soviet Russia in the Second World War*, Pan, 2007
Bidwell, Shelford, *Gunners at War*, Arrow, 1972
Bishop, Patrick, *Bomber Boys: Fighting Back, 1940–1945*, Harper Press, 2007
—, *Fighter Boys: Saving Britain 1940*, HarperCollins, 2003
Black, Jeremy, *Rethinking World War Two: The Conflict and Its Legacy*, Bloomsbury, 2015
Blackbourn, David, *History of Germany, 1780–1918: The Long Nineteenth Century*, Blackwell, 2003
Blair, Clay, *Hitler's U-Boat War: The Hunters, 1939–1942*, Cassell, 2000
—, *Hitler's U-Boat War: The Hunted, 1942–1945*, Cassell, 2000
Boberach, Heinz (ed.), *Meldungen aus dem Reich: Auswahl aus den geheimen Lagerberichten des Sicherheitsdienstes der SS 1939–1944*, Deutscher Taschenbuch Verlag, 1968
Bosworth, R. J. B., *Mussolini's Italy: Life Under the Dictatorship*, Penguin, 2006
Bowman, Martin W., *USAAF Handbook 1939–1945*, Sutton, 2003
Bowyer, Chaz, *Men of the Desert Air Force*, William Kimber, 1984
Brendon, Piers, *The Dark Valley: A Panorama of the 1930s*, Pimlico, 2001

Browning, Christopher R., *Ordinary Men: Reserve Police Battalion 101 and the Final Solution in Poland*, Penguin, 2001

Bryant, Arthur, and Edward Shanks, *The Battle of Britain/The Few*, Withy Grove Press, 1944

Buchheim, Lothar-Günther, *U-Boat War*, Collins, 1978

Budiansky, Stephen, *Battle of Wits*, Penguin, 2000

Burgwyn, H. James, *Mussolini Warlord: Failed Dreams of Empire 1940–1943*, Enigma Books, 2012

Burleigh, Michael, *Moral Combat: A History of World War II*, Harper Press, 2011

—, *The Third Reich: A New History*, Pan, 2001

Butler, Rupert, *Hitler's Death's Head Division*, Pen & Sword, 2004

Caddick-Adams, Peter, *Monty and Rommel: Parallel Lives*, Preface, 2011

—, *Snow and Steel*, Preface, 2014

Caine, Philip D., *American Pilots in the RAF: The WWII Eagle Squadrons*, Brassey's, 1998

Calder, Angus, *The Myth of the Blitz*, Pimlico, 1992

—, *The People's War: Britain 1939–1945*, Pimlico, 1992

Cardozier, V. R., *The Mobilization of the United States in World War II: How the Government, Military and Industry Prepared for War*, McFarland, 1995

Carrard, Philippe, *The French Who Fought for Hitler: Memories from the Outcasts*, Cambridge University Press, 2010

Carver, Michael, *Dilemmas of the Desert War*, Batsford, 1986

— (ed.), *The War Lords*, Little, Brown and Co., 1976

Chant, Christopher, *Handbook of British Regiments*, Routledge, 1988

Churchill, Winston S., *The Story of the Malakand Field Force*, Lightning Source UK, 2009

Citino, Robert M., *Death of the Wehrmacht: The German Campaigns of 1942*, Kansas University Press, 2007

—, *The German Way of War: From the Thirty Years' War to the Third Reich*, University Press of Kansas, 2005

—, *The Path to Blitzkrieg: Doctrine and Training in the German Army, 1920–1939*, Stackpole, 1999

—, *The Quest for Decisive Victory: From Stalemate to Blitzkrieg in Europe, 1899–1940*, University Press of Kansas, 2002

—, *The Wehrmacht Retreats: Fighting a Lost War, 1943*, Kansas University Press, 2012

Clark, Christopher, *Iron Kingdom: The Rise and Downfall of Prussia, 1600–1947*, Penguin, 2007

Clayton, Tim, and Phil Craig, *End of the Beginning*, Hodder & Stoughton, 2002

Cloutier, Patrick, *Regio Esercito: The Italian Royal Army in Mussolini's Wars 1935–1943*, Patrick Cloutier, 2013

Cobb, Matthew, *The Resistance: The French Fight Against the Nazis*, Pocket Books, 2009

Collier, Basil, *Hidden Weapons: Allied Secret or Undercover Services in World War II*, Pen & Sword, 2006

Collingham, Lizzie, *The Taste of War: World War II and the Battle for Food*, Penguin Press, 2012

Corum, James S., *The Luftwaffe: Creating the Operational Air War, 1918–1940*, University Press of Kansas, 1997

Creveld, Martin van, *Fighting Power: German and US Army Performance 1939–1945*, Greenwood Press, 1982

—, *Supplying War: Logistics from Wallenstein to Patton*, Cambridge University Press, 1977

Dallek, Robert, *Franklin D. Roosevelt and American Foreign Policy, 1932–1945*, Oxford University Press, 1995

Davidson, Basil, *Special Operations Europe*, Readers Union, 1980

Davis, Kenneth S., *The American Experience of War, 1939–1945*, Secker & Warburg, 1967

Davis Biddle, Tami, *Rhetoric and Reality in Air Warfare*, Princeton University Press, 2002

Deakin, F. W., *The Brutal Friendship: Mussolini, Hitler, and the Fall of Italian Fascism*, Pelican, 1966

Deichmann, Paul, *Spearhead for Blitzkrieg: Luftwaffe Operations in Support of the Army, 1939–1945*, Greenhill, 1996

Deighton, Len, *Blood, Tears and Folly: An Objective Look at World War II*, Pimlico, 1995

Dennis, Peter, *Decision by Default: Peacetime Conscription and British Defence, 1919–39*, Routledge and Kegan Paul, 1972

Dierich, Wolfgang, *Kampfgeschwader 'Edelweiss': The History of a German Bomber Unit 1939–1945*, Ian Allan, 1975

DiNardo, R. L., *Germany and the Axis Powers: From Coalition to Collapse*, Kansas University Press, 2005

—, *Germany's Panzer Arm in WWII*, Stackpole, 2006

—, *Mechanized Juggernaut or Military Anachronism?*, Stackpole, 2008

Dimbleby, Jonthan, *The Battle of the Atlantic: How the Allies Won the War*, Penguin Viking, 2015

Donnelly, Larry, *The Other Few*, Red Kite, 2004

Doubler, Michael D., *Closing with the Enemy: How GIs Fought the War in Europe, 1944–1945*, University Press of Kansas, 1994

Downing, David, *The Devil's Virtuoso: German Generals at War 1940–45*, New English Library, 1977

Draper, Alfred, *Operation Fish: The Race to Save Europe's Wealth, 1939–1945*, Cassell, 1979

Duggan, Christopherson, *Fascist Voices: An Intimate History of Mussolini's Italy*, Vintage, 2013

Earnshaw, James Douglas, *609 at War*, Vector, 2003

Eberle, Henrik, and Matthias Uhl (eds), *The Hitler Book*, John Murray, 2006

Edgerton, David, *Britain's War Machine: Weapons, Resources and Experts in the Second World War*, Allen Lane, 2011

—, *England and the Aeroplane*, Macmillan, 1991

—, *Warfare State: Britain, 1920–1970*, Cambridge University Press, 2006

Ellis, John, *The Sharp End: The Fighting Man in World War II*, Pimlico, 1993

—, *The World War II Databook: The Essential Facts and Figures for All the Combatants*, Aurum, 1995

Elphick, Peter, *Liberty: The Ships That Won the War*, Chatham, 2001

Estes, Kenneth, *A European Anabasis*, Helion, 2015

Evans, Richard, *The Third Reich at War*, Penguin, 2009

—, *The Third Reich in Power*, Penguin, 2006

Farquharson, J. E., *The Plough and the Swastika: The NSDAP and Agriculture in Germany, 1928–45*, Sage Publications, 1976

Fennell, Jonathan, *Combat and Morale in the North African Campaign*, Cambridge University Press, 2011

Fletcher, David, *The Great Tank Scandal: British Armour in the Second World War*, Part I, HMSO, 1989

Flower, Desmond, and James Reeves (eds), *The War 1939–1945: A Documentary History*, Da Capo, 1997

Foot, M. R. D., *Resistance: European Resistance to Nazism 1949–45*, Eyre Methuen, 1976

Forty, George, *British Army Handbook, 1939–1945*, Sutton, 1998

—, *US Army Handbook, 1939–1945*, Sutton, 1995

Fraser, David, *And We Shall Shock Them: The British Army in the Second World War*, Cassell, 1999

Frieser, Karl-Heinz, *The Blitzkrieg Legend*, Naval Institute Press, 2005

Fullilove, Michael, *Rendezvous with Destiny: How Franklin D. Roosevelt and Five Extraordinary Men Took America into the War and into the World*, Penguin Press, 2013

Gardiner, Juliet, *The Thirties: An Intimate History*, Harper Press, 2011

—, *Wartime: Britain 1939–1945*, Review, 2005

Gildea, Robert, *Marianne in Chains: In Search of the German Occupation of France 1940–45*, Pan, 2003

Gilmour, David, *The Pursuit of Italy: A History of a Land, Its Regions and Their Peoples*, Penguin, 2012

Ginn, Peter, et al., *Wartime Farm*, Mitchell Beazley, 2012

Goerlitz, Walter, *History of the German General Staff*, Praeger, 1967

Goldhagen, Daniel Jonah, *Hitler's Willing Executioners*, Abacus, 1997

Graves, Charles, *The Home Guard of Great Britain*, Hutchinson, 1943

Grigg, P. J., *Prejudice and Judgment*, Alden Press, 1948

Grunberger, Richard, *A Social History of the Third Reich*, Phoenix, 2005

Guedalla, Philip, *Middle East 1940–1942: A Study in Air Power*, Hodder & Stoughton, 1944

Guingand, Francis de, *Generals at War*, Hodder & Stoughton, 1964

Gulley, Thomas F., et al., *The Hour Has Come: The 97th Bomb Group in World War II*, Taylor Publishing, 1993

Hall, David Ian, *The Strategy for Victory: The Development of British Tactical Air Power, 1919-1943*, Praeger Security International, 2008

Handel, Michael I. (ed.), *Intelligence and Military Operations*, Frank Cass, 1990

Hansell, Haywood S., Jr, *The Air Plan That Defeated Hitler*, Arno Press, 1980

Harries, Meirion and Susie, *Soldiers of the Sun: The Rise and Fall of the Imperial Japanese Army*, Random House, 1991

Harrison, Frank, *Tobruk: The Great Siege Reassessed*, Brockhampton Press, 1996

Harrison, Mark (ed.), *The Economics of World War II*, Cambridge University Press, 2000

Harrison Place, Timothy, *Military Training in the British Army, 1940-1944: From Dunkirk to D-Day*, Frank Cass, 2000

Hay, Ian, *The Army at War: The Battle of Flanders*, HMSO, 1941

Herman, Arthur, *Freedom's Forge: How American Business Produced Victory in World War II*, Random House, 2012

Hewitt, Nick, *Coastal Convoys, 1939-1945: The Indestructible Highway*, Pen & Sword, 2008

Holland, James, *The Battle of Britain*, Bantam Press, 2010

—, *Fortress Malta*, Orion, 2003

—, *Heroes*, Harper Collins, 2007

—, *Together We Stand – North Africa 1942-1943: Turning the Tide in the West*, Harper Collins, 2005

—, *The War in the West*, Volume I, *Germany Ascendant*, Bantam Press, 2015

Holmes, Richard, *Bir Hacheim: Desert Citadel*, Ballantine, 1971

—, *Soldiers: Army Lives and Loyalties from Redcoats to Dusty Warriors*, Harper Press, 2011

—, *The World at War*, Ebury Press, 2011

House, Jonathan M., *Combined Arms Warfare in the Twentieth Century*, Kansas University Press, 2001

Howard, Michael, *The Mediterranean Strategy in the Second World War*, Greenhill Books, 1993

Howarth, Stephen, and Derek Law (eds), *The Battle of the Atlantic 1939-1945: The 50th Anniversary International Naval Conference*, Greenhill, 1994

Howlett, Peter, *Fighting with Figures: Statistical Digest of the Second World War*, Central Statistical Office, 1995

Hoyt, Edwin P., *The GI's War: American Soldiers in Europe During World War II*, Cooper Square Press, 2000

Hylton, Stuart, *Their Darkest Hour: The Hidden History of the Home Front, 1939-1945*, Sutton, 2003

Irons, Roy, *The Relentless Offensive: War and Bomber Command, 1939-1945*, Pen & Sword, 2009

Irving, David (ed.), *Breach of Security: The German Secret Intelligence File on Events Leading to the Second World War*, William Kimber, 1968

Jackson, Ashley, *The British Empire and the Second World War*, Hambledon Continuum, 2006

Jackson, W. G. F., *The North African Campaign, 1940–43*, Batsford, 1975

Jordan, Jonathan W., *Brothers, Rivals, Victors: Eisenhower, Patton, Bradley and the Partnership That Drove the Allied Conquest in Europe*, NAL Caliber, 2012

Jörgensen, Christer, *Rommel's Panzers*, Reference Group Brown, 2003

Joseph, Frank, *Mussolini's War*, Helion, 2010

Kallis, Aristotle A., *Nazi Propaganda and the Second World War*, Palgrave Macmillan, 2008

Kaplan, Philip, and Jack Currie, *Wolfpack: U-Boats at War 1939–1945*, Aurum, 1997

Keegan, John (ed.), *Churchill's Generals*, Abacus, 1991

Kemp, Anthony, *The SAS at War, 1941–1945*, Penguin, 2000

Kemp, Lt-Commander P. K., *Victory at Sea*, White Lion Publishers, 1957

Kershaw, Ian, *Fateful Choices: Ten Decisions That Changed the World, 1940–1941*, Allen Lane, 2007

—, *Hitler, 1936–1945: Nemesis*, Penguin, 2001

Kite, Ben, *Stout Hearts: The British and Canadians in Normandy 1944*, Helion, 2014

Klein, Maury, *A Call to Arms: Mobilizing America for World War II*, Bloomsbury Press, 2013

Knox, MacGregor, *Common Destiny: Dictatorship, Foreign Policy, and War in Fascist Italy and Nazi Germany*, Cambridge University Press, 2000

—, *Hitler's Italian Allies: Royal Armed Forces, Fascist Regime, and the War of 1940–1943*, Cambridge University Press, 2000

—, *Mussolini Unleashed, 1939–1941: Politics and Strategy in Fascist Italy's Last War*, Cambridge University Press, 1982

Kohn, Richard H., and Joseph P. Harahan, *Air Superiority in World War II and Korea*, Office of Air Force History, United States Air Force, 1983

Lampe, David, *The Last Ditch: Britain's Secret Resistance and the Nazi Invasion Plan*, Greenhill Books, 2007

Langhorne, Richard (ed.), *Diplomacy and Intelligence during the Second World War: Essays in Honour of F. H. Hinsley*, Cambridge University Press, 1985

Lavery, Brian, *Hostilities Only: Training the Wartime Royal Navy*, Conway, 2004

—, *In Which They Served: The Royal Navy Officer Experience in the Second World War*, Conway, 2009

Lawrence, W. J., *No. 5 Bomber Group RAF*, Faber, 1951

Le Tissier, Tony, *The Third Reich Then and Now*, After the Battle, 2005

Lewin, Ronald, *The Life and Death of the Afrika Korps*, Pen & Sword, 2003

—, *Rommel as Military Commander*, Pen & Sword, 2004

—, *Ultra Goes to War: The Secret Story*, Penguin, 2001

Liddell Hart, B. H., *The Other Side of the Hill*, Cassell, 1951

Longmate, Norman, *The Real Dad's Army: The Story of the Home Guard*, Arrow, 1974

Lucas, James, *German Army Handbook, 1939–1945*, Sutton, 1998

Lund, Paul, and Harry Ludlam, *Trawlers Go to War*, New English Library, 1973

Mackenzie, William, *The Secret History of SOE: Special Operations Executive 1940–1945*, St Ermin's Press, 2000

Macksey, Major K. J., *Afrika Korps: Rommel's Desert Soldiers*, Ballantine, 1968

Macrae, Stuart, *Winston Churchill's Toyshop: The Inside Story of Military Intelligence (Research)*, Amberley, 2010

Mak, Geert, *In Europe: Travels Through the Twentieth Century*, Vintage, 2008

Mallman Showell, Jak P., *Hitler's Navy*, Seaforth Publishing, 2009

—, *Hitler's U-Boat Bases*, Sutton, 2007

Mason, Philip, *A Matter of Honour: An Account of the Indian Army, Its Officers & Men*, Book Club Edition, 1974

Mass Observation, *War Begins at Home*, Chatto & Windus, 1940

Mazower, Mark, *Hitler's Empire: Nazi Rule in Occupied Europe*, Allen Lane, 2008

McGaw Smyth, Howard, *Secrets of the Fascist Era*, Southern Illinois University Press, 1975

McGuirk, Dal, *Rommel's Army in Africa*, Stanley Paul, 1987

McKay, Sinclair, *The Secret Life of Bletchley Park*, Aurum, 2011

—, *The Secret Listeners*, Aurum, 2013

McKee, Alexander, *The Coal-Scuttle Brigade*, New English Library, 1957

McKinstry, Leo, *Hurricane: Victor of the Battle of Britain*, John Murray, 2010

—, *Spitfire: Portrait of a Legend*, John Murray, 2008

McLaine, Ian, *Ministry of Morale*, George Allen & Unwin, 1979

McManus, John C., *Grunts: Inside the American Infantry Experience*, NAL Caliber, 2010

McNab, Chris (ed.), *German Paratroopers*, MBI, 2000

Mears, Ray, *The Real Heroes of Telemark*, Coronet, 2004

Meilinger, Colonel Phillip S., *The Paths of Heaven: The Evolution of Airpower Theory*, Air University Press, 1997

Messenger, Charles, *The Second World War in the West*, Cassell, 2001

Michel, Henri, *The Shadow War: Resistance in Europe 1939–45*, Andre Deutsch, 1972

Middlebrook, Martin, and Chris Everitt, *The Bomber Command War Diaries*, Penguin, 1990

Mierzejewski, Alfred C., *The Collapse of the German War Economy, 1944–1945: Allied Air Power and the German National Railway*, University of North Carolina Press, 1988

Milner, Marc, *The Battle of the Atlantic*, Tempus, 2005

Milward, Alan S., *War, Economy and Society, 1939–1945*, University of California Press, 1979

Mitcham, Samuel W., *Hitler's Legions: The German Army Order of Battle, World War II*, Leo Cooper, 1985

Moorehead, Alan, *African Trilogy: The Desert War, 1940–1943*, Cassell, 2000

Moorhouse, Roger, *The Devil's Alliance: Hitler's Pact With Stalin, 1939–1941*, Bodley Head, 2014

Morley-Mower, Geoffrey, *Messerschmitt Roulette*, Phalanx, 1993

Mortimer, Gavin, *The SAS in World War II: An Illustrated History*, Osprey, 2011

—, *Stirling's Men: The Inside History of the SAS in World War II*, Cassell, 2005

Morton, H. V., *Atlantic Meeting*, Methuen & Co., 1943

Murray, Williamson, *Luftwaffe: Strategy for Defeat*, Grafton, 1988

—, and Allan R. Millett, *A War to Be Won: Fighting the Second World War*, Belknap Harvard, 2000

—, *Military Innovation in the Interwar Period*, Cambridge University Press, 1996

Neitzel, Sönke, and Harald Welzer, *Soldaten: On Fighting, Killing and Dying*, Simon & Schuster, 2012

Nielsen, Generalleutnant Andreas, *The German Air Forces Staff*, USAF Historical Studies No. 173, Arno Press, 1968

Noakes, Jeremy (ed.), *Nazism 1919–1945*, Volume 4: *The German Home Front in World War II*, University of Exeter Press, 1998

Noakes, J., and G. Pridham (eds), *Nazism 1919–1945*, Volume 2: *State, Economy and Society 1933–1939*, University of Exeter Press, 1984

—, *Nazism 1919–1945*, Volume 3: *Foreign Policy, War and Racial Extermination*, University of Exeter Press, 1988

Oberkommando der Wehrmacht, *Fahrten und Flüge gegen England*, Zeitgeschichte-Verlag Berlin, 1941

Ohler, Norman, *Blitzed: Drugs in Nazi Germany*, Allen Lane, 2016

Overy, Richard, *The Bombing War: Europe 1939–1945*, Allen Lane, 2013

— (ed.), *The New York Times Complete World War II 1939–1945*, Black Dog & Levanthal, 2013

Owen, James, *Commando: Winning World War II Behind Enemy Lines*, Abacus, 2012

Owen, Roderic, *The Desert Air Force*, Arrow, 1958

Owings, Alison, *Frauen: German Women Recall the Third Reich*, Penguin, 1995

Pallud, Jean-Paul, *The Desert War Then and Now*, After the Battle, 2012

Paxton, Robert O., *French Peasant Fascism*, Oxford University Press, 1997

Peitz, Bernd, *Afrikakorps: Rommel's Tropical Army in Original Color*, Schiffer, 2005

Petrow, Richard, *The Bitter Years*, Book Club Edition, 1974

Pitt, Barrie, *The Crucible of War: Auchinleck's Command*, Phoenix, 1986

—, *The Crucible of War: Montgomery and Alamein*, Phoenix, 1986

Porten, Edward P. von der, *The German Navy in World War II*, Arthur Baker, 1970

Price, Alfred, *Instruments of Darkness: The History of Electronic Warfare*, Macdonald and Jane's, 1978

Prysor, Glyn, *Citizen Sailors: The Royal Navy in the Second World War*, Viking, 2011

Reynolds, David, *The Creation of the Anglo-American Alliance, 1937–1941*, University of North Carolina Press, 1982

Richards, Denis, *RAF Bomber Command in the Second World War: The Hardest Victory*, Penguin, 2001

Ritchie, Sebastian, *Arnhem: Myth and Reality*, Robert Hale, 2011

—, *Industry and Air Power: The Expansion of British Aircraft Production, 1935–1941*, Routledge, 1997

Roberts, Andrew, *Eminent Churchillians*, Phoenix, 1995

—, *The Storm of War*, Harper Perennial, 2011

Rosenbaum, Ron, *Explaining Hitler: The Search for the Origins of His Evil*, Papermac, 1998

Roskill, Stephen, *The Navy at War, 1939–1945*, Wordsworth Editions, 1998

Rutherford, Ward, *Kasserine: Baptism of Fire*, Ballantine, 1970

Saunders, Andy, *No. 43 'Fighting Cocks' Squadron*, Osprey, 2003

Schell, Adolf von, *Battle Leadership*, Major Edwin F. Harding, 1933

Schramm, Percy E., *Kriegstagebuch des Oberkommandos der Wehrmacht 1939–1941*, Teilband I, Bernard & Graefe Verlag, 1982

—, *Kriegstagebuch des Oberkommandos der Wermacht 1940–1941*, Teilband II, Bernard & Graefe Verlag, 1982

Seydewitz, Max, *Civil Life in Wartime Germany: The Story of the Home Front*, Viking Press, 1945

Seymour, Miranda, *Noble Endeavours: The Life of Two Countries, England and Germany, in Many Stories*, Simon & Schuster, 2014

Shores, Christopher, and Brian Cull, with Nicola Malizia, *Malta: The Spitfire Year, 1942*, Grub Street, 1991

Shores, Christopher, and Hans Ring, *Fighters Over the Desert*, Neville Spearman, 1969

Short, Brian, et al., *The Front Line of Freedom: British Farming in the Second World War*, British Agricultural History Society, 2006

Smart, Nick, *Biographical Dictionary of British Generals of the Second World War*, Pen & Sword, 2005

Speer, Frank E., *The Debden Warbirds: The Fourth Fighter Group in World War II*, Schiffer, 1999

Spick, Mike, *Aces of the Reich: The Making of a Luftwaffe Fighter-Pilot*, Greenhill, 2006

—, *Allied Fighter Aces of World War II*, Greenhill, 1997

—, *Luftwaffe Fighter Aces*, Greenhill, 1996

Spitzy, Reinhard, *How We Squandered the Reich*, Michael Russell, 1997

Spooner, Tony, *Supreme Gallantry: Malta's Role in the Allied Victory 1939–1945*, John Murray, 1996

Stargardt, Nicholas, *The German War: A Nation Under Arms, 1939–1945*, Bodley Head, 2016

Stephenson, Michael, *The Last Full Measure: How Soldiers Die in Battle*, Crown, 2012

Stevenson, David, *1914–1918: The History of the First World War*, Penguin, 2005

Suchenwirth, Richard, *Historical Turning Points in the German Air Force War Effort*, University Press of the Pacific, 2004

—, *The Development of the German Air Forces, 1919–1939*, University Press of the Pacific, 2005

—, *Command and Leadership in the German Air Force*, USAF Historical Studies No. 174, Arno Press, 1969

Sweet, John Joseph Timothy, *Iron Arm: The Mechanization of Mussolini's Army, 1920–40*, Stackpole, 2007

Terraine, John, *The Right of the Line*, Hodder & Stoughton, 1985

Thacker, Toby, *Joseph Goebbels: Life and Death*, Palgrave Macmillan, 2008

Todman, Daniel, *Britain's War: Into Battle, 1937–1941*, Allen Lane, 2016

Tooze, Adam, *The Wages of Destruction: The Making and Breaking of the Nazi Economy*, Penguin, 2007

Trevor-Roper, H. R. (ed.), *Hitler's War Directives 1939–1945*, Pan, 1966

Tuker, Sir Francis, *Approach to Battle*, Cassell, 1963

Urban, Mark, *The Tank War: The Men, The Machines, The Long Road to Victory 1939–45*, Little, Brown & Co., 2013

Various, *World War II: Day by Day*, Dorling Kindersley, 2004

Vasco, John, *Messerschmitt Bf 110: Bombsights Over England*, Schiffer, 2002

Vella, Philip, *Malta: Blitzed But Not Beaten*, Progress Press Co., 1997

Vinen, Richard, *The Unfree French: Life under the Occupation*, Penguin, 2007

Ward, Sadie, *War in the Countryside, 1939–45*, Cameron Books, 1988

Warwicker, John, *Churchill's Underground Army*, Frontline Books, 2008

Weal, John, *Jagdgeschwader 2 'Richthofen'*, Osprey, 2000

—, *Jagdgeschwader 27 'Afrika'*, Osprey, 2003

—, *Jagdgeschwader 52: The Experten*, Osprey, 2004

—, *Jagdgeschwader 53 'Pik-As'*, Osprey, 2007

Weale, Adrian, *The SS: A New History*, Abacus, 2012

Wells, Mark K., *Courage and Air Warfare: The Allied Aircrew Experience in the Second World War*, Frank Cass, 1997

Werth, Alexander, *France 1940–1955*, Robert Hale, 1956

Wheal, Elizabeth-Anne, and Stephen Pope, *The Macmillan Dictionary of the Second World War*, Macmillan, 1989

Wheeler-Bennett, Sir John (ed.), *Action This Day: Working with Churchill*, Macmillan, 1968

White, Antonia, *BBC at War*, BBC, 1946

Whiting, Charles, *Hunters from the Sky: The German Parachute Corps, 1940–1945*, Cooper Square Press, 2001

Williams, Michael, *Steaming to Victory: How Britain's Railways Won the War*, Preface, 2013

Williamson, Gordon, *Waffen-SS Handbook, 1933–1945*, Sutton, 2003

Willmott, H. P., *The Great Crusade*, Pimlico, 1992

Winder, Simon, *Germania*, Picador, 2010

Wingate, John, *The Fighting Tenth*, Leo Cooper, 1991

Winterbotham, F. W., *The Ultra Secret*, Book Club edition, 1974

Wood, Derek, and Derek Dempster, *The Narrow Margin: The Battle of Britain and the Rise of Air Power, 1930–1949*, Pen & Sword, 2003

Woodman, Richard, *Malta Convoys*, John Murray, 2000

—, *The Real Cruel Sea: The Merchant Navy in the Battle of the Atlantic, 1939–1943*, John Murray, 2005

Wynn, Humphrey, *Desert Eagles*, Airlife, 1993

Wynn, Kenneth G., *Men of the Battle of Britain*, Gliddon Books, 1989

Wynter, Brigadier H. W., *Special Forces in the Desert War, 1940–1943*, Public Record Office War Histories, 2001

Ziegler, Frank H., *The Story of 609 Squadron: Under the White Rose*, Crécy, 1993

Ziegler, Philip, *London at War, 1939–1945*, Pimlico, 2002

PAMPHLETS, JOURNALS, PERIODICALS AND MAGAZINES

Anon., 'German Army Transport', *Automobile Engineer*, October 1945

Denkhaus, Raymond A., 'Convoy PQ 17', *World War II Magazine*, February 1997

Felton, Monica, *Civilian Supplies in Wartime Britain*, Ministry of Information, 1945

Jarvis, Peter, *The Invasion of 1940*, Markham Memorial Lecture, Bletchley Park Reports, No. 18, March 2003

Peaty, John, 'Myth, Reality and Carlo D'Este', *War Studies Journal*, Volume 1, No. 2, Spring 1996

Pether, John, *Funkers and Sparkers: Origins and Formation of the Y Service*, Bletchley Park Reports, No. 17, September 2000

Schell, Adolf von, 'Grundlagen der Motorisierung und ihre Entwicklung im Zweiten Weltkrieg', *Wehrwissenschaftliche Rundschau,* 13, 1963

Topp, Erich, 'In Memoriam Engelbert Endrass: Castor Mourns Pollux', in Theodore P. Savas (ed.), *Silent Hunters: German U-Boat Commanders of World War II*, Savas Publishing, 2013

Widder, Werner, '*Auftragstaktik and Innere Führung*: Trademarks of German Leadership', *Military Review*, September–October 2002

Zabecki, David, 'Auftragstaktik'

—, 'The Greatest General No-One Ever Heard Of', *World War II Magazine*, May 2008

ONLINE

Pearce, Richard 'Dick', *Recollections*, www.canadasmemorial.ca

Interview with World War II Luftwaffe Eagle Johannes Steinhoff, www.historynet.com

White, Ian, 'A Short History of Air Intercept Radar and the British Night-Fighter, Part One, 1936–1945', www.600squadronassociation.com

Acknowledgements

Enormous thanks is owed to a number of people. First of all, I am very grateful to all the veterans who, over the past dozen years or so, have taken the trouble to talk to me at such length. I am also very grateful to the staffs of the various museums and archives, although especial thanks go to Richard Hughes at the Imperial War Museum in London, to Doug McCabe at the University of Ohio, all the staff at the Tagebuch Archiv in Emmendingen and the Bundesarchiv-Militärarchiv in Freiburg, the staff at the United States Army Heritage & Education Center at Carlisle Barracks, Pennsylvania, and Cathy Pugh of the Second World War Experience Centre in Yorkshire.

I have been fortunate enough to be able to pick the brains of a number of friends and colleagues, including Professor John Buckley and Professor David Zabecki. However, there are five people to whom I am particularly grateful and who have all become great friends, and who have freely given plenty of wise counsel and advice whenever it has been asked for. The first is Sebastian Cox, Head of the Air Historical Branch at RAF Northolt. The second is Stephen Prince, Head of the Naval Historical Branch at Portsmouth. Professor Jeremy Black has also been a much-valued friend and academic mentor. Professor Rick Hillum is my technical guru and the best advisor I could hope for on any scientific matters. My greatest thanks, however, goes to Dr Peter Caddick-Adams, whose perspectives, vast knowledge and friendship have been invaluable. Thank you.

A number of other people have helped with translations and research. In France, Elizabeth Gausseron and Alienor Youchtchenko; in Italy, James Owen. My thanks, also, to David Walsh, a great friend who accompanied me to the various Italian archives. In Germany, Michelle Miles and Ingo Maerker have carried out an impressive amount of work and have become good friends as well as colleagues. Frances Bryon also helped with some key research, for which I am very grateful. Huge thanks are due to Lalla Hitchings for transcribing so many of my interviews, and to Tom and Mark Hitchings for their help with this too, and also to Rachel Sykes, who has transcribed a number of interviews. My thanks to you all.

A number of other friends and colleagues have helped along the way: Oliver Barnham, Paul Beaver, David Christopherson, Peter Day, Clive Denney, Rebecca Dobbs, Freya Eden-Ellis, Andrew Galt, Graham Goodey, my big brother Tom Holland, Tobin Jones, Alex Langlands, Rob Owen, James Petrie, Richard Pocock, Rob Schäfer, James Shopland, Guy Walters, Rowland White, and Aaron Young. All have contributed in one way or another.

I would also like to thank all those at Bantam Press and Grove Atlantic. To Larry Finlay, Mads Toy, Steve Mulcahey, Phil Lord, Vivien Thompson, and all at Bantam – thank you so much. I am also enormously grateful to Brenda Updegraff for her truly superb copy-editing and to Darcy Nicholson for all her enormous help and support. Particular thanks, however, go to Morgan Entrekin and Jamison Stoltz in New York, and to Bill Scott-Kerr in London, who could not have been a better friend and supporter. To you three, huge thanks.

Thank you, also, to Adam Wheatley, Nick Hartwell and Kerry Ann Robinson at First Artist Mission – you've been brilliant. A very big thank you is also due to everyone at Conville and Walsh and now the PEW Agency, but especially Patrick Walsh – a great agent and even better friend.

Finally, I would like to thank my family as they put up with the second volume of this rather monster project. I know you live through it too, and I am, I promise, eternally grateful. Rachel, Ned and Daisy – thank you.

Picture Acknowledgements

All photographs have been kindly supplied by the author except those listed below. Every effort has been made to trace copyright holders; those overlooked are invited to get in touch with the publishers.

Part Opener Pages:

Pages 14 and 15
Pearl Harbor: Fox Photos/Getty.

Pages 112 and 113
Eastern front, October 1943: Atlantic-Press/Getty.

Pages 318 and 319
Oran, November 1942, Operation TORCH: Popperfoto/Getty.

Pages 456 and 457
Depth charge, North Atlantic: Corbis/Getty.

Illustration Sections:

Section 1

Page 1
British troops searching the ruins of the Temple of Ball, near Palmyra, 1941: © Imperial War Museum/E 4087.

Page 3
General Claude Auchinleck, July 1942: The Print Collector/Getty Images.

Pages 4 and 5
Truck like that used by Albert Martin: © Imperial War Museum/E 14841; Pearl Harbor attack: photo by US Navy/The LIFE Picture Collection/Getty Images.

Appendices

Page 617–19
Allied tanker sinking, North Atlantic: US Navy/Museum of Science and Industry, Chicago/Getty.

Page 620
Grumman, Long Island, New York: Bettman/Getty.

Index